KU-609-847

# SPORTS LAW
# CASES & MATERIALS

BY

RUSS VERSTEEG

# VANDEPLAS PUBLISHING
## UNITED STATES OF AMERICA

UNIVERSITY OF WINCHESTER
LIBRARY

**VerSteeg, Russ**

**Sports Law: Cases & Materials**

UNIVERSITY OF WINCHESTER

03013685 344.099
VER

Published by:

**Vandeplas Publishing - June 2007**

801 International Parkway, 5th Floor
Lake Mary, FL. 32746 - USA

www.vandeplaspublishing.com

ISBN-13: 978-1-60042-022-1
Library of Congress Control Number: 2007928687
© Russ VerSteeg 2007

Printed in the United States of America

# Contents

# Foreword

A book often reflects more about its author than about the book's content. That is probably true about this book. I have been teaching Sports Law for ten years at New England School of Law in Boston, Massachusetts. During that time, I have developed a certain perspective about what constitutes "Sports Law." In my experience, many students sign up for my class wanting to become a sports agent, and they assume that a class on Sports Law will prepare them for that. Although I always want to encourage students to dream and to pursue those dreams, in my opinion sports agency comprises only a small fraction of what Sports Law is. When all is said and done, I typically counsel students to think in very broad terms about the multiple possibilities of what a career in Sports Law could entail. To that end, I encourage students to consider the multifaceted possibilities of how they might merge their passion for sports with their interest and training in law.

Thus, this book is designed to introduce students to a variety of topics that relate to Sports Law, not just sports agency. Given that goal, the text includes cases that concern very diverse topics. The first chapter is something of an "immersion chapter," throwing students into cases intended to catch their attention and strike a nerve about a number of the most sensitive and volatile Sports Law topics today - drugs, the Olympic Games, and the relationships among individuals, the government, and various private organizations. The subsequent chapters tackle Torts, Contracts, Antitrust and Labor Law, Constitutional Law, legal aspects of the NCAA, Agency, and Intellectual Property. The principal goal is to provide a broad-brush introduction to most of the topics that are likely to confront a modern Sports Lawyer. Probably the most notable omission is Tax Law. In my opinion, the tax laws are so specialized and subject to change that even a cursory treatment would run the risk of misleading the reader.

The book is intended to be used by undergraduate, graduate, or law students. I have intentionally limited the number of cases that deal with each topic. Many law school case books today are simply too large. They contain so much material that they are impractical. For the benefit of undergraduates and graduate students, I have tried to define legal terms and explain legal doctrines in a clear, concise manner. For law students, I have tried to avoid "talking down" to them when presenting those definitions and explanations. It is a difficult balance, and I hope that the law students will consider those definitions and explanations as refreshers.

Most of the questions are meant to be either thought-provoking or are intended to encourage students to restate and clarify major points. I hope that the questions encourage students not to settle for simplistic legal thinking. I believe that in an expanding and emerging field such as Sports Law we need consistently to challenge traditional legal thinking and analysis, and constantly explore new paradigms if we are going to protect the interests of those people involved in sports and further the values that sports encourage.

I think that students may read the chapters in almost any order. So a professor should not feel "chained" to the textbook's order. This is the order that I have found works best for me, but others should feel free to arrange his or her syllabus differently, depending upon individual preference. The only glaring exception to that general statement is that Chapters 2-4 are probably best read in sequence. Also, Chapters 8 (Title IX) and 9 (NCAA) will probably make more sense to students if they have first read Chapter 7 (Constitutional Law) but I wouldn't say that that is mandatory.

I have liberally edited the cases and articles included in this text. I ordinarily use *** to indicate that I have omitted a sentence or more from the original. But in other instances, I have cut sentences, paragraphs, and/or entire sections from cases without making any notation. My goal in editing the materials has been to focus students' attention on only one, two, or occasionally three issues in each case; and to remove those issues that I considered esoteric, overly-complex, and/or tangential to the main point of the case or article. I have cut most footnotes from the cases and articles. When I have retained footnotes, I have simply renumbered them, beginning sequentially with each case or article in the text (*i.e.,* so the footnote numbers in this text do not match the footnote numbers in the original case or article).

There is a long list of people whom I would like to thank. First, I owe a debt of thanks to John O'Brien, Dean of New England School of Law, who first asked me if I'd be interested in teaching Sports Law. Similarly, I'd like to thank the Board of Trustees of New England School of Law who funded my work on this project with an Honorable James R. Lawton Summer Research Stipend in the summer of 2005. I would also like to thank the authors who have granted permission to use articles and/or portions of articles as part of the text. A number of people have also allowed me to use their photographs. I think that photographs add a special touch to a law text, and so I especially appreciate those permissions. Professors Elizabeth Spahn (second cousin, once-removed, yes indeed, of Warren Spahn... "Spahn & Sain and pray for rain") and Sonya Garza (a rabid Texas Longhorn fan/alumna) helped me with some of the finer points of Constitutional Law, and I'm indebted to them for their assistance. Professor James Bemiller at the University of Tennessee (and one of the most accomplished pole vault coaches of the modern era) contributed many thoughts and ideas in conversations about how to best teach and write about Sports Law. I've had three research assistants whose help has been invaluable. Amy Peterson (a former figure skater and lifetime Pittsburgh Steelers fan), Jayme Yarow, and Melissa Gill (a former dancer and ice hockey aficianado) are responsible for a great deal of the research, notes, and details. Melissa Gill was the driving force in the macroscopic planning and organization, obtaining permissions, keeping track of organizational details, and formatting the text. Hundreds of students who took my Sports Law classes at New England School of Law during the past 10 years have contributed by raising insightful questions, making perceptive comments, and catching mistakes in the cases, materials, and text. I take full responsibility for errors in the book. I hope that you find it useful.

Russ VerSteeg
Boston, May 2007

# Dedication

I would like to dedicate this book to my friend, Jan Johnson. Jan set the World Indoor Pole Vault Record at 17-7, and won the Bronze Medal at the 1972 Munich Olympic Games. Since then, he has devoted most of his energy and time to improving the sport of pole vaulting. He's been a tireless advocate of safety, serving as the USATF Pole Vault Safety Chairman. He's coached thousands of aspiring and accomplished vaulters at his Sky Jumpers camps and in colleges, such as Southern Illinois, LSU, Cuesta and Cal-Poly/SLO. His enthusiasm is infectious. He brings wisdom, devotion, unbridled energy, and a genuine spark to the sport that none other can. Jan and I first connected in 2002, and since then I've worked with him on a number of issues and projects. I've coached at his camps and clinics, trying to absorb as much about coaching from him as I could. I've worked with him on the ASTM pole vault subcommittees in an effort to improve safety. I've worked on his Pole Vault Safety Certification Board (www.pvscb.com), and run PVSCB clinics with him. And we've been writing about Pole Vault history together. If he had not encouraged me and given me opportunities to use my legal training to help the sport of pole vaulting, it is doubtful that I would have accomplished much in this field. Thank you, Jan. I appreciate what you've done for the sport of pole vaulting and for me, personally.

# A Note For Undergraduates & Graduate Students on the American Legal System, Courts, and Appellate Decisions

## I. Civil vs. Criminal Cases

In the American legal system today there are a number of important distinctions that are useful to understand. First, there are basically two types of cases: Criminal and Civil. For example, if a police officer stops you and gives you a ticket (requiring that you pay a fine) for speeding in your car or for drunk driving, the officer charges you with a criminal violation, because the state legislature has passed written laws (statutes) that prohibit speeding and drunk driving. If you refuse to pay your fine, the district attorney could charge you and have your case tried in state court as a criminal matter. When the state government, usually represented by the district attorney, prosecutes a defendant/accused, that case is a criminal case.

On the other hand, a civil case is a case brought not by the government but typically by one individual (for example, a private citizen) against another individual. For example, let's suppose that when you were speeding or driving drunk, you also lost control of your car and hit another car, causing property damage to the car that you hit and personal injury to the other driver. The driver of the other car may sue you in state court as a civil matter, using various legal theories – such as negligence – in an effort to recover from you the money needed to repair or replace the car and for medical expenses, or as compensation for pain, suffering, or permanent injuries/loss caused by the fact that you caused the accident.

## II. Roles of Judge & Jury

Without going into exceptional circumstances, in both criminal and civil cases, the people involved typically have an opportunity to have a jury decide the case. A judge presides, and the judge is responsible for deciding abstract legal questions and explaining the law to the jurors. The jurors are responsible for deciding questions about facts. Ordinarily, that means that the jurors get to decide which witnesses they believe are telling the truth and when and how events occurred. So the judge will explain to the jury that it is illegal to have a certain amount of blood-alcohol when driving (that's the law) but the jurors will decide whether they believe the accuracy of the breathalizer test and/or the witness's testimony regarding how many glasses of wine he or she drank.

## III. Appeals

After the jury reaches a verdict (criminal cases) or decides whether a defendant is liable (civil cases) and therefore owes the plaintiff money (and if so how much), in some circumstances the party who lost at trial has the right to appeal the decsion of the trial court. In most states, there is an intermediate appellate court (such as the Massachusetts Appeals Court) to which a person may appeal a trial court decision. As a rule, when appealing to an intermediate state appeals court, three appellate judges will read the lawyers' briefs about the case, and will listen to oral arguments and ask the lawyers questions before making an appellate decision. Ordinarily, an appeals court does not review the jury's decisions regarding the facts (there are some limited exceptions to that statement) but rather the appellate judges must decide whether the trial judge made a mistake about "the law." For example, if the trial judge mistakenly told the jurors the wrong blood-alcohol limit, or if the judge mistakenly gave an incorrect legal definition of "negligence" to the jury, those are the types of legal errors that could be grounds for reversal on appeal.

After the appellate court has rendered its written decision, in some circumstances a person may appeal *that decision* to the state's highest court (typically called the "supreme court"...except in New York where they call their trial courts supreme courts), such as the Massachusetts Supreme Judicial Court (SJC). The appeals process at the supreme court level is similar to the process at the intermediate appeals court, but ordinarily all justices (typically nine in number) read the lawyers' briefs and participate in the oral arguments with the lawyers. Again, the supreme court typically only reviews issues of law, not fact.

## IV. Federal Courts

This summary so far has focused on the state court systems. But an analogous group of courts exists to consider cases involving federal criminal and civil laws. The federal courts also consider cases involving questions of U.S. Constitutional Law as well as certain cases where the parties are from different states (diversity jurisdiction). The U.S. District Courts are the federal trial courts where there may be juries. The Federal Appellate Courts (there are many different federal courts of appeals which consider cases, depending upon which region of the country the District Court case came from) are the intermediate courts of appeal in the federal system. And the U.S. Supreme Court is the highest court in the country.

## V. Written Opinions

Most of the cases in this text are civil cases, but see if you can spot the criminal exceptions. Many of the decisions are written by appellate judges, either from intermediate appellate state or federal courts, or from state supreme courts or the U.S. Supreme Court. Thus, what you will be reading will be judges' explanations regarding questions of law. So you will have the opportunity to read what a group of judges thinks the correct ruling on the law should be. Therefore, by the time that these judges get around to writing the opinion that you will read, the people involved (typically the plaintiff and the defendant) have already presented their arguments, witnesses, and documentary and forensic evidence at trial to a judge and a jury in a courtroom. In addition, the lawyers representing the parties have then, after the trial, researched statutes, constitutions, law review articles, and other prior appellate decisions relating to the same or similar legal questions, and have written appellate briefs, explaining their legal analysis for the appeallate judges. The appellate judges, in turn, have read those briefs, and the lawyers have met with the appellate judges at oral argument, where each side has had a certain amount of time to verbally explain their analysis of the law and the judges have had an opportunity to ask the lawyers questions. After oral arguments, the judges have had an opportunity to discuss the legal questions and collaborate to write the decision/case that you read in this text. One judge usually writes the "majority opinion," usually what you read in the text, but occasionally other judges disagree with the majority and write their own "dissenting opinion" to explain why they disagree with the majority. Every now and then, a judge will also write a "concurring opinion" if he or she basically agrees with the majority's result, but wishes to add his or her own reasons or spin on why.

## VI. Summary Judgment

There is one other way that judges frequently resolve cases: summary judgment. After the plaintiff's lawyer has filed his/her complaint and after the defendant's lawyer has filed his/her answer, it is possible that both parties essentially agree on the facts that really matter to a case (*i.e.*, who did what to whom, when, how, and why). In those instances, we say that there are "no genuine issues of material fact." If there are no genuine issues of material fact, then there is no reason to have a jury, since, as you may recall, that's what the jury is for, to decide what the facts are.

If there are no genuine material facts in dispute (and therefore no need for a jury), one or both parties may then file a motion for summary judgment. If the trial judge agrees that there are no genuine questions regarding material facts, then the judge simply must decide questions about "the law." In other words, the judge is free to determine whether the plaintiff or defendant wins by applying the abstract legal rules that are applicable to the facts as agreed upon by the parties. Decisions based on summary judgment are very efficient because they save everybody the time and expense of a trial.

Decisions based on summary judgment, like a court's decision based on the outcome of a jury trial, may be appealed to higher courts. Many of the cases in this text are appeals from a trial judge's decision on a motion for summary judgment.

# Chapter 1

## Olympics, Private Associations, Performance Enhancing Drugs

---

This chapter serves as a broad introduction to a variety of sports law topics. Here you will meet a number of contemporary and emotionally-charged issues and questions regarding the different levels of power and influence that affect decisions relating to the Olympic Games, problems regarding the use of performance-enhancing substances and drugs, and issues relating to the scope of power that private associations possess to control their own members.

Every two years, for several weeks, the sports world's attention focuses on the Olympic Games (alternating Summer Games and Winter Games since 1994). The business and political concerns associated with the Games are immense. These materials present background information regarding the structure and organization of the Olympics. Pay particular attention to the roles played by the various organizations involved (*e.g.,* IOC, USOC, and NGB's). In some ways, the issues that relate to these Olympic organizations will continue to be relevant in later chapters where we meet other sports organizations such as the National Collegiate Athletic Association (NCAA) and the various professional sports organizations such as Major League Baseball (MLB), the National Football League (NFL), and the National Basketball Association (NBA). As is true with most aspects of law and society, as the financial stakes associated with the Olympics have risen, the legal issues have multiplied correspondingly. The Court of Arbitration for Sport, for example, is just one additional layer of complexity that has become part of the judging and officiating process of the Olympic Games.

During the past several years, legal issues relating to performance enhancing drugs have dominated the sports pages. The BALCO scandal, Major League Baseball, and Congress have harnessed our attention on anabolic steroids in particular. The issues surrounding steroid use and other performance-enhancing drugs provide fertile ground for thinking about and examining the values associated with the legal aspects of sports.

The first case, *Defrantz*, has a lot of information. You may wish to think about it on distinct levels. *First*, try to understand the facts and events that led up to this controversy. What are the roles of the IOC, USOC, and various government officials (including President Carter). What are the athletes asking for? *Second*, the athletes are relying on a federal statute (written law) and arguing that the USOC has violated that statute in a manner that will injure them. The court discusses at length its analysis of the statute and why it (the court) does not think that the USOC has violated it. When taking notes, isolate that discussion and see if you can explain in your own words why the court thinks that there has been no statutory violation. *Third*, the court discusses whether the USOC has violated the constitutional rights of the athletes. Pay attention to the court's discussion of "state action" and note the court's determination as to why it believes that none of the athletes' constitutional rights were violated.

# Anita DeFrantz v. United States Olympic Committee
### 492 F.Supp. 1181 (1980)
### United States District Court, District of Columbia

JOHN H. PRATT, District Judge.

## MEMORANDUM OPINION

Plaintiffs, 25 athletes and one member of the Executive Board of defendant United States Olympic Committee (USOC), have moved for an injunction barring defendant USOC from carrying out a resolution, adopted by the USOC House of Delegates on April 12, 1980, not to send an American team to participate in the Games of the XXIInd Olympiad to be held in Moscow in the summer of 1980. Plaintiffs allege that in preventing American athletes from competing in the Summer Olympics, defendant has exceeded its statutory powers and has abridged plaintiffs' constitutional rights.

For the reasons discussed below, we find that plaintiffs have failed to state a claim upon which relief can be granted. Accordingly, we deny plaintiffs' claim for injunctive and declaratory relief and dismiss the action.

## THE FACTS

In essence, the action before us involves a dispute between athletes who wish to compete in the Olympic Games to be held in Moscow this summer, and the United States Olympic Committee, which has denied them that opportunity in the wake of the invasion and continued occupation of Afghanistan by Soviet military forces. Because this dispute confronts us with questions concerning the statutory authority of the USOC, its place and appropriate role in the international Olympic movement, and its relationship to the United States Government and with certain United States officials, we begin with a brief discussion of the organizational structure of the Olympic Games and the facts which have brought this action before us. These facts are not in dispute.

According to its Rules and By-laws, the International Olympic Committee (IOC) governs the Olympic movement and owns the rights of the Olympic games. IOC Rules provide that National Olympic Committees (NOC) may be established "as the sole authorities responsible for the representation of the respective countries at the Olympic Games," so long as the NOC's rules and regulations are approved by the IOC. The USOC is one such National Olympic Committee.

The USOC is a corporation created and granted a federal charter by Congress in 1950. Pub.L. No. 81-805, 64 Stat. 899. This charter was revised by the Amateur Sports Act of 1978, Pub.L. No. 95-606, 92 Stat. 3045, 36 U.S.C. ss 371 et seq. Under this statute, defendant USOC has "exclusive jurisdiction" and authority over participation and representation of the United States in the Olympic Games.

The routine procedure initiating the participation of a national team in Olympic competition is the acceptance by the NOC of an invitation from the Olympic Organizing Committee for the particular games. In accordance with this routine procedure under IOC Rules, the Moscow Olympic Organizing Committee extended an invitation to the USOC to participate in the summer games. Recent international and domestic events, however, have made acceptance of this invitation, which must come on or before May 24, 1980, anything but routine.

On December 27, 1979, the Soviet Union launched an invasion of its neighbor, Afghanistan. That country's ruler was deposed and killed and a new government was installed. Fighting has been at times intense, casualties have been high, and hundreds of thousands of Afghan citizens have fled their homeland. At present, an estimated 100,000 Soviet troops remain in Afghanistan, and fighting continues.

President Carter termed the invasion a threat to the security of the Persian Gulf area as well as a threat to world peace and stability and he moved to take direct sanctions against the Soviet Union. These sanctions included a curtailment of agricultural and high technology exports to the Soviet Union, and restrictions on commerce with the Soviets. The Administration also turned its attention to a boycott of the summer Olympic Games as a further sanction against the Soviet Union.

As the affidavit of then Acting Secretary of State Warren Christopher makes clear, the Administration was concerned that "(t)he presence of American competitors would be taken by the Soviets as evidence that their invasion had faded from memory or was not a matter of great consequence or concern to this nation." The Administration's concern was sharpened because "(t)he Soviet Union has made clear that it intends the Games to serve important national political ends. For the U.S.S.R., international sports competition is an instrument of government policy and a means to advance foreign policy goals."

4

With these concerns in mind, the Administration strenuously urged a boycott of the Moscow games. On January 20, 1980, President Carter wrote the President of the United States Olympic Committee to urge that the USOC propose to the IOC that the 1980 summer games be transferred from Moscow, postponed, or cancelled if the Soviet forces were not withdrawn within a month. On January 23, 1980 the President delivered his State of the Union Message, in which he said that he would not support sending American athletes to Moscow while Soviet military forces remained in Afghanistan.

Following these statements, the United States House of Representatives passed, by a vote of 386 to 12, a Concurrent Resolution opposing participation by United States athletes in the Moscow Games unless Soviet troops were withdrawn from Afghanistan by February 20th. The Senate passed a similar resolution by a vote of 88 to 4.

As this was unfolding, the USOC's 86 member Executive Board held a meeting in Colorado Springs on January 26, 1980, inviting White House counsel Lloyd Cutler to address them "because no officer or any member of the Board was knowledgeable about the far-reaching implications of the Soviet invasion." According to USOC President Kane, in early January some USOC officers became concerned that sending American athletes to Moscow could expose them to danger if hostility erupted at the games, and that acceptance of the invitation could be seen as tacit approval of or at least acceptance of the Soviet invasion. Mr. Culter also met with USOC officers at least twice in February to discuss the matter further. On each occasion, according to the Kane affidavit, Mr. Cutler urged Mr. Kane to convene an emergency meeting of the USOC Executive Board to act on the Moscow problem. However, legal counsel for the USOC advised Mr. Kane that only the House of Delegates and not the USOC Executive Board could decide whether or not to send a team to Moscow.

On March 21, 1980, President Carter told members of the Athletes Advisory Council, an official body of the USOC, that American athletes will not participate in the Moscow summer games. On April 8, 1980, the President sent a telegram to the president and officers of the USOC and to its House of Delegates, urging the USOC vote against sending an American team to Moscow. In an April 10th speech, the President said that "if legal actions are necessary to enforce (my) decision not to send a team to Moscow, then I will take those legal actions." Among the legal measures the President apparently contemplated was invoking the sanctions of the International Emergency Economic Powers Act, 50 U.S.C. ss 1701 et seq. On April 10 and 11, 1980, the 13 member Administrative Committee of the USOC met in

Colorado Springs and voted to support a resolution against sending a team to Moscow. Only Anita DeFrantz, a plaintiff in this action, dissented.

At the President's request and over initial objections by the USOC, Vice President Mondale addressed the assembled House of Delegates prior to their vote on April 12, 1980. The Vice President strongly and vigorously urged the House of Delegates to support a resolution rejecting American participation in the summer games in Moscow.

After what USOC President Kane describes in his affidavit as "full, open, complete and orderly debate by advocates of each motion," the House of Delegates, on a secret ballot, passed by a vote of 1,604 to 798, a resolution which provided in pertinent part:

> RESOLVED that since the President of the United States has advised the United States Olympic Committee that in light of international events the national security of the country is threatened, the USOC has decided not send a team to the 1980 Summer Games in Moscow . . .
> FURTHER RESOLVED, that if the President of the United States advises the United States Olympic Committee, on or before May 20, 1980, that international events have become compatible with the national interest and the national security is no longer threatened, the USOC will enter its athletes in the 1980 Summer Games.

Plaintiffs describe these attempts by the Administration to persuade the USOC to vote not to send an American team to Moscow as "a campaign to coerce defendant USOC into compliance with the President's demand for a boycott of the Olympic Games." In addition, plaintiffs' complaint alleges that the President and other Executive Branch officials threatened to terminate federal funding of the USOC and that they raised the possibility of revoking the federal income tax exemption of the USOC if the USOC did not support the President's decision to boycott the 1980 Games. The complaint also alleges that these officials state that the Federal government would provide increased funding to the USOC if the USOC supported a boycott.

\*\*\*

Plaintiffs allege that ...[the inability to compete in the Games] will result in great and irreparable injury to the athletes. "Many would lose a once-in-a-lifetime opportunity to participate in the Olympic Games, and the honor and prestige that such participation affords. Most of the class members are at or near their physical peaks at the present time and will not physically be capable of reaching the same or higher levels at a later period of their lives."

In summary, plaintiffs ask this court to declare the April 12, 1980 resolution of the USOC House of Delegates null and void because it violated statutory authority and constitutional provisions and to permanently enjoin the USOC from carrying out that resolution.

\*\*\*

Because of the time constraints involved in this action, this court granted plaintiffs' motion that a trial of the action on the merits be advanced and consolidated with the hearing of the application for a preliminary and permanent injunction.

\*\*\*

ANALYSIS

This action presents us with several issues for decision, falling into two distinct categories; one is statutory and the other is constitutional. We turn first to the statutory issues.

### 1. The Amateur Sports Act of 1978

Plaintiffs allege in their complaint that by its decision not to send an American team to compete in the summer Olympic Games in Moscow, defendant USOC has violated the Amateur Sports Act of 1978, supra, (The Act).... We deal with two of the alleged violations here. Reduced to their essentials, these allegations are that the Act does not give, and that Congress intended to deny, the USOC the authority to decide not to enter an American team in the Olympics, except perhaps for sports-related reasons, and that the Act guarantees to certain athletes a right to compete in the Olympic Games which defendant denied them. We consider each allegation in turn.

### (a) The USOC's Authority Not to Send a Team to Moscow

The United States Olympic Committee was first incorporated and granted a federal charter in 1950. Pub.L. No. 81-805, supra. However, predecessors to the now federally-chartered USOC have existed since 1896, and since that time, they have exercised the authority granted by the International Olympic Committee to represent the United States as its

National Olympic Committee in matters pertaining to participation in Olympic games. It is unquestioned by plaintiffs that under the International Olympic Committees Rules and By-laws, the National Olympic Committees have the right to determine their nation's participation in the Olympics. IOC Rule 24B provides that "NOC's shall be the sole authorities responsible for the representation of the respective countries at the Olympic Games . . ." and Chapter 5, paragraph 7 of the By-laws to Rule 24 provides that "(r)epresentation covers the decision to participate . . . .". Nothing in the IOC Charter, Rules or By-laws requires a NOC, such as the USOC, to accept an invitation to participate in any particular Olympic contest and the President of the IOC has said that participation in the Olympic games is entirely voluntary. As defendant has argued, an invitation to participate is just that, an invitation which may be accepted or declined.

Because defendant USOC clearly has the power under IOC Rules to decide not to enter an American team in Olympic competition, the question then becomes whether the Amateur Sports Act of 1978, which rewrote the USOC's charter, denies the USOC that power. Plaintiffs emphatically argue that it does, and defendant and the Government just as emphatically argue that it does not.

Plaintiffs' argument is simple and straightforward: The Act by its terms does not expressly confer on the USOC the power to decline to participate in the Olympic Games, and if any such power can be inferred from the statute, the power must be exercised for sports-related reasons. Defendant and the Government respond that the Act gives the USOC broad powers, including the authority to decide not to accept an invitation to send an American team to the Olympics.

The principal substantive powers of the USOC are found in s 375(a) of the Act.[1] In determining whether the USOC's authority under the Act

---

[1] They are to: "(1) serve as the coordinating body for amateur athletic activity in the United States directly relating to international amateur athletic competition; (2) represent the United States as its national Olympic committee in relations with the International Olympic Committee . . .; (3) organize, finance, and control the representation of the United States in the competitions and events of the Olympic Games . . . and obtain, either directly or by delegation to the appropriation national governing body, amateur representation for summer games." 36 U.S.C. s 375(a)(1), (2), (3). The "objects and purposes" section of the Act includes the provision, also found in the 1950 Act, that the USOC shall "exercise exclusive jurisdiction . . . over all matters pertaining to the participation of the United States in the Olympic Games . . . including the representation of the United States in such games . . . ." Id., s 374(3).

8

encompasses the right to decide not to participate in an Olympic contest, we must read these provisions in the context in which they were written. In writing this legislation, Congress did not create a new relationship between the USOC and the IOC. Rather, it recognized an already long-existing relationship between the two and statutorily legitimized that relationship with a federal charter and federal incorporation.[2] The legislative history demonstrates Congressional awareness that the USOC and its predecessors, as the National Olympic Committee for the United States, have had a continuing relationship with the IOC since 1896. Congress was necessarily aware that a National Olympic Committee is a creation and a creature of the International Olympic Committee, to whose rules and regulations it must conform. The NOC gets its power and its authority from the IOC, the sole proprietor and owner of the Olympic Games.

In view of Congress' obvious awareness of these facts, we would expect that if Congress intended to limit or deny to the USOC powers it already enjoyed as a National Olympic Committee, such limitation or denial would be clear and explicit. No such language appears in the statute. Indeed, far from precluding this authority, the language of the statute appears to embrace it. For example, the "objects and purposes" section of the Act speaks in broad terms, stating that the USOC shall exercise "exclusive jurisdiction" over ". . . all matters pertaining to the participation of the United States in the Olympic Games . . . .". We read this broadly stated purpose in conjunction with the specific power conferred on the USOC by the Act to "represent the United States as its national Olympic committee in relations with the International Olympic Committee," and in conjunction with the IOC Rules and By-laws, which provide that "representation" includes the decision to participate. In doing so, we find a compatibility and not a conflict between the Act and the IOC Rules on the issue of the authority of the USOC to decide whether or not to accept an invitation to field an American team at the Olympics. The language of the statute is broad enough to confer this authority, and we find that Congress must have intended that the USOC exercise that authority in this area, which it already enjoyed because of its long-standing relationship with the IOC. We accordingly conclude that the USOC has the authority to decide not to send an American team to the Olympics.

---

[2] To the extent the USOC was granted extended power by the 1978 Act, the legislative history makes clear, and the plaintiffs do not dispute the fact, that these powers were primarily designed to give the USOC supervisory authority over United States amateur athletic groups in order to eliminate the numerous and frequent jurisdictional squabbles among schools, athletic groups and various national sports governing bodies.

Plaintiffs next argue that if the USOC does have the authority to decide not to accept an invitation to send an American team to the Moscow Olympics, that decision must be based on "sports-related considerations." In support of their argument, plaintiffs point to ss 392(a)(5) and (b) of the Act, which plaintiffs acknowledge "are not in terms applicable to the USOC," but rather concern situations in which national governing bodies of various sports,[3] which are subordinate to the USOC, are asked to sanction the holding of international competitions below the level of the Olympic or Pan American Games in the United States or the participation of the United States athletes in such competition abroad. These sections provide that a national governing body may withhold its sanctions only upon clear and convincing evidence that holding or participating in the competition "would be detrimental to the best interests of the sport." Plaintiffs argue by analogy that a similar "sports-related" limitation must attach to any authority the USOC might have to decide not to participate in an Olympic competition. We cannot agree.

The provision on which plaintiffs place reliance by analogy is specifically concerned with eliminating the feuding between various amateur athletic organizations and national governing bodies which for so long characterized amateur athletics. As all parties recognize, this friction, such as the well-publicized power struggles between the NCAA and the AAU, was a major reason for passage of the Act, and the provisions plaintiffs cite, among others, are aimed at eliminating this senseless strife, which the Senate and House Committee reports indicate had dramatically harmed the ability of the United States to compete effectively in international competition. In order to eliminate this internecine squabbling, the Act elevated the USOC to a supervisory role over the various amateur athletic organizations, and provided that the USOC establish procedures for the swift and equitable settlement of these disputes. *** [I]t also directed that the national governing bodies of the various sports could only withhold their approvals of international competition for sports-related reasons. Previously, many of these bodies had withheld their sanction of certain athletic competitions in order to further their own interests at the expense of other groups and to the detriment of athletes wishing to participate.

In brief, this sports-related limitation is intimately tied to the specific purpose of curbing the arbitrary and unrestrained power of various athletic organizations subordinate to the USOC not to allow athletes to compete in

---

[3] A national governing body is a non-profit amateur sports organization which acts as this country's representative in the corresponding international sports federation for that particular sport. It sets goals and directs policy in the sport it governs and has the power to sanction internal competitions held in the United States in their sport.

international competition below the level of the Olympic Games and the Pan American Games. This purpose has nothing to do with a decision by the USOC to exercise authority granted by the IOC to decide not to participate in an Olympic competition.

\*\*\*

We therefore conclude that the USOC not only had the authority to decide not to send an American team to the summer Olympics, but also that it could do so for reasons not directly related to sports considerations.

### (b) Athletes Statutory Right to Compete in the Olympics

Plaintiffs argue that the Act provides, "in express terms" an "Athlete's Bill of Rights," pointing to the following provisions in the Act's "objects and purposes" section, which directs that the USOC shall:

> provide for the swift resolution of conflicts and disputes involving amateur athletes, national governing bodies, and amateur sports organizations, and protect the opportunity of any amateur athlete, coach, trainer, manager, administrator, or official to participate in amateur athletic competition. (emphasis supplied). 36 U.S.C. s 374(8).

A similar provision is contained in s 382b, which provides that:

> The (USOC) shall establish and maintain provisions for the swift and equitable resolution of disputes involving any of its members and relating to the opportunity of an amateur athlete, coach, trainer, manager, administrator, or official to participate in the Olympic Games . . . or other such protected competition as defined in such constitution and bylaws.

Plaintiffs argue that the Report of the President's Commission on Olympic Sports, which was the starting point for the legislation proposed, and the legislative history supports their argument that the statute confers an enforceable right on plaintiffs to compete in Olympic competition. Again, we are compelled to disagree with plaintiffs.

The legislative history and the statute are clear that the "right to compete," which plaintiffs refer to, is in the context of the numerous jurisdictional disputes between various athletic bodies, such as the NCAA and the AAU, which we have just discussed, and which was a major impetus for the Amateur Sports Act of 1978. Plaintiffs recognize that a major purpose of the Act was to eliminate such disputes. However, they go on to argue that the Presidential report, which highlighted the need for strengthening the USOC in order to eliminate this feuding, made a finding that there is little difference between an athlete denied the right to compete because of a boycott and an athlete denied the right to compete because of jurisdictional bickering.

The short answer is that although the Congress may have borrowed heavily from the Report on the President's Commission, it did not enact the Report. Instead, it enacted a statute and that statute relates a "right to compete" to the elimination of jurisdictional disputes between amateur athletic groups, which for petty and groundless reasons have often deprived athletes of the opportunity to enter a particular competition. Sections 382b and 374(8) originated in Senate Bill 2727, and were adopted by the House of Representatives without change. We quote at length from the Senate Report, S.Rep. No. 770, supra, at 5-6, which clarifies beyond doubt the meaning of the language unsuccessfully relied on by plaintiffs:

Athletes' Rights

That section of S. 2727 relating to an athlete's opportunity to participate in amateur athletic competition represents a compromise reached in the amateur sports community and accepted by the Committee. Language contained in the first version of the Amateur Sports Act, S. 2036, would have included a substantive provision on athletes' rights. This provision met with strong resistance by the high school and college communities. Ultimately, the compromise reached was that certain substantive provisions on athletes' rights would be included in the USOC Constitution, and not in the bill.

As reported, S. 2727 makes clear that amateur athletes, coaches, trainers, managers, administrators, and other officials have the right, which will be guaranteed in the Olympic Committee Constitution, to take part in the Olympic Games, the Pan-American Games, world championship competition, and other competition designated by the Olympic Committee.

\*\*\*

Further, as differences between amateur sports organizations are settled, athletes will no longer be used as pawns by one organization to gain advantage over another. The Committee feels that S. 2727, by establishing guidelines for the amateur sports community, will bring about a resolution of those controversies which have so long plagued amateur sports. With the coordinating efforts of the Olympic Committee, the vertical structure which S. 2727 promotes, and a cooperative attitude on the part of amateur sports organizations, athletes should, in the future, realize more opportunities to compete than ever before.

The Senate Report makes clear that the language relied on by plaintiffs is not designed to provide any substantive guarantees, let alone a Bill of Rights. Further, to the extent that any guarantees of a right to compete are included in the USOC Constitution as a result of this provision, they do not include a right that amateur athletes may compete in the Olympic Games despite a decision by the USOC House of Delegates not to accept an invitation to enter an American team in the competition. This provision simply was not designed to extend so far. Rather, it was designed to remedy the jurisdictional disputes among amateur athletic bodies, not disputes between athletes and the USOC itself over the exercise of the USOC's discretion not to participate in the Olympics.

(c) Statutory Cause of Action

Plaintiffs argue that they have a private cause of action under the Amateur Sports Act of 1978 to maintain an action to enforce their rights under that Act. This argument assumes (1) the existence of a right and (2) the capability of enforcing that right by a private cause of action. As the foregoing discussion establishes, we have found that the statute does not guarantee plaintiffs a right to compete in the Olympics if the USOC decides not to send an American team to the Olympic Games and we have found that defendant has violated no provision of the Act. Thus, the "right" the plaintiffs seek to enforce under the Act simply does not exist. (Plaintiffs have pointed to no express private right of action in the statute, and none exists). Under these circumstances, we cannot find that plaintiffs have an implied private right of action under the Amateur Sports Act to enforce a right which does not exist.

\*\*\*

Congress never intended to give plaintiffs a right to compete in the Olympics if the USOC determines not to enter a team. It necessarily follows that Congress therefore did not intend to create an implied private cause of action under the statute allowing plaintiffs to sue to enforce a right to compete in the Olympics. To believe otherwise is to believe that by its silence Congress intended to confer a cause of action to enforce nonexistent rights. This we cannot do. Not only is the legislative history barren of any implication that Congress intended to confer an enforceable right to compete in the Olympics in the face of a decision by the USOC not to compete, but it is also barren of any implication that Congress intended to create a private cause of action in such circumstances.

As noted above, to the extent Congress provided protection for amateur athletes to compete, it did so in terms of eliminating the rivalries between sports organizations. For this reason, s 395 of the Act establishes detailed procedures for the USOC's consideration and resolution of jurisdictional and eligibility issues, subject to review by arbitration under 36 U.S.C. s 395(c) (1). Even for disputes covered by s 395, there is therefore no private cause of action.

Because we conclude that the rights plaintiffs seek to enforce do not exist in the Act, and because the legislative history of the Act nowhere allows the implication of a private right of action, we find that plaintiffs have no implied private right of action under the Amateur Sports Act of 1978 to maintain this suit.

## 2. Constitutional Claims

Plaintiffs have alleged that the decision of the USOC not to enter an American team in the summer Olympics has violated certain rights guaranteed to plaintiffs under the First, Fifth and Ninth Amendments to the United States Constitution. This presents us with two questions: (1) whether the USOC's decision was "governmental action"(state action), and, assuming state action is found, (2) whether the USOC's decision abridged any constitutionally protected rights.

### (a) State Action

Although federally chartered, defendant is a private organization. Because the Due Process Clause of the Fifth Amendment, on which plaintiffs place great reliance, applies only to actions by the federal government, plaintiffs must show that the USOC vote is a "governmental act," i. e., state action. In defining state action, the courts have fashioned two guidelines. The first involves an inquiry into whether the state:

> . . . has so far insinuated itself into a position of interdependence with (the private entity) that it must be recognized as a joint participant in the challenged activity. Burton v. Wilmington Parking Authority, 365 U.S. 715, 725, 81 S.Ct. 856, 862, 6 L.Ed.2d 45 (1961).

In *Burton*, the Supreme Court found state action, but it did so on wholly different facts than those existing here. The private entity charged with racially discriminating against plaintiff was a restaurant which was physically and financially an integral part of a public building, built and maintained with public funds, devoted to a public parking service, and owned and operated by an agency of the State of Delaware for public purposes. Noting the obvious and deep enmeshment of defendant and the state, the court found that the state was a joint participant in the operation of the restaurant, and accordingly found state action. Here, there is no such intermingling, and there is no factual justification for finding that the federal government and the USOC enjoyed the "symbiotic relationship" which courts have required to find state action. The USOC has received no federal funding and it exists and operates independently of the federal government. Its chartering statute gives it "exclusive jurisdiction" over "all matters pertaining to the participation of the United States in the Olympic Games . . .." 36 U.S.C. s 374(3). To be sure, the Act does link the USOC and the federal government to the extent it requires the USOC to submit an annual report to the President and the Congress. But this hardly converts such an independent relationship to a "joint participation."

The second guideline fashioned by the courts involves an inquiry of whether:

> . . . there is a sufficiently close nexus between the state and the challenged action of the regulated entity so that the action of the latter may be fairly treated as that of the state itself. Jackson v. Metropolitan Edison Co., 419 U.S. 345, 351, 95 S.Ct. 449, 453, 42 L.Ed.2d 477 (1974).

*Jackson* provides an indication of how close this nexus must be in order to find state action. In that case, the Supreme Court found there was no state action even though the defendant was a utility closely regulated by the state, and even though the action complained of (the procedure for termination of electrical services) had been approved by the state utility commission. In the instant case, there was no requirement that any federal government body approve actions by the USOC before they become effective.

Plaintiffs clearly recognize this, but they argue that by the actions of certain federal officials, the federal government initiated, encouraged, and approved of the result reached (i. e., the vote of the USOC not to send an American team to the summer Olympics). Plaintiffs advance a novel theory. Essentially, their argument is that the campaign of governmental persuasion, personally led by President Carter, crossed the line from "governmental recommendation," which plaintiffs find acceptable and presumably necessary to the operation of our form of government, into the area of "affirmative pressure that effectively places the government's prestige behind the challenged action," and thus, results in state action. We cannot agree.

Plaintiff can point to no case outside the area of discrimination law which in any way supports their theory, and we can find none. Furthermore, this Circuit's Court of Appeals has addressed what level of governmental involvement is necessary to find state action in cases not involving discrimination.

> Each party cites numerous cases dealing with the amount of governmental involvement which is necessary before a private entity becomes sufficiently entangled with governmental functions that federal jurisdiction attaches. If any principle emerges from these cases, it would appear to be that, at least where race is not involved, it is necessary to show that the Government exercises some form of control over the actions of the private party. Spark v. Catholic University of America, supra, at 1281-82.

Here there is no such control. The USOC is an independent body, and nothing in its chartering statute gives the federal government the right to control that body or its officers. Furthermore, the facts here do not indicate that the federal government was able to exercise any type of "de facto " control over the USOC. The USOC decided by a secret ballot of its House of Delegates. The federal government may have had the power to prevent the athletes from participating in the Olympics even if the USOC had voted to allow them to participate, but it did not have the power to make them vote in a certain way. All it had was the power of persuasion. We cannot equate this with control. To do so in cases of this type would be to open the door and usher the courts into what we believe is a largely nonjusticiable realm, where they would find themselves in the untenable position of determining whether a certain level, intensity, or type of "Presidential" or "Administration" or "political" pressure amounts to sufficient control over a private entity so as to invoke federal jurisdiction.

We accordingly find that the decision of the USOC not to send an American team to the summer Olympics was not state action, and therefore, does not give rise to an actionable claim for the infringements of the constitutional rights alleged.

### (b) Constitutionally Protected Rights

Assuming arguendo that the vote of the USOC constituted state action, we turn briefly to plaintiffs' contention that by this action they have been deprived of their constitutional rights to liberty, to self-expression, to travel, and to pursue their chosen occupation of athletic endeavor. Were we to find state action in this case, we would conclude that defendant USOC has violated no constitutionally protected right of plaintiffs.

We note that other courts have considered the right to compete in amateur athletics and have found no deprivation of constitutionally protected rights. As the Government has pointed out in Parish v. National Collegiate Athletic Association, 506 F.2d 1028 (5th Cir. 1975), basketball players sought an injunction to prevent the NCAA from enforcing its ruling declaring certain athletes ineligible to compete in tournaments and televised games. The court, quoting Mitchell v. Louisiana High School Athletics Association, 430 F.2d 1155, 1158 (5th Cir. 1970), stated that:

> . . . the privilege of participation in interscholastic activities must be deemed to fall . . . outside the protection of due process.

Plaintiffs have been unable to draw our attention to any court decision which finds that the rights allegedly violated here enjoy constitutional protection, and we can find none. Plaintiffs would expand the constitutionally-protected scope of liberty and self-expression to include the denial of an amateur athlete's right to compete in an Olympic contest when that denial was the result of a decision by a supervisory athletic organization acting well within the limits of its authority. Defendant has not denied plaintiffs the right to engage in every amateur athletic competition. Defendant has not denied plaintiffs the right to engage in their chosen occupation. Defendant has not even denied plaintiffs the right to travel, only the right to travel for one specific purpose. We can find no justification and no authority for the expansive reading of the Constitution which plaintiffs urge. To find as plaintiffs recommend would be to open the floodgates to a torrent of lawsuits. The courts have correctly recognized that many of life's disappointments, even major ones, do not enjoy constitutional protection. This is one such instance.

At this point, we find it appropriate to note that we have respect and admiration for the discipline, sacrifice, and perseverance which earns young men and women the opportunity to compete in the Olympic Games. Ordinarily, talent alone has determined whether an American would have the privilege of participating in the Olympics. This year, unexpectedly, things are different. We express no view on the merits of the decision made. We do express our understanding of the deep disappointment and frustrations felt by thousands of American athletes. In doing so, we also recognize that the responsibilities of citizenship often fall more heavily on some than on others. Some are called to military duty. Others never serve. Some return from military service unscathed. Others never return. These are the simple, although harsh, facts of life, and they are immutable.

**Notes & Questions**

1.  The United States Government seemed to be saying that there was something wrong or tainted by the Soviet Union's plans to make a political statement with the Games: "(t)he Soviet Union has made it clear that it intends the Games to serve important national political ends.  For the U.S.S.R., international sports competition is an instrument of government policy and a means to advance foreign policy goals."  Clearly this was nothing new.  Isn't this precisely what occurred at the 1936 Berlin Olympics when Aldolf Hitler used the Games as a stage to promote his ideology?  Isn't this just the sort of thing that the United States did when it hosted the Games in Los Angeles in 1984 four years after the Moscow Games, promoting U.S. democratic ideals?  Isn't the politicization of the Games something that we've simply come to expect as part of the modern Games?  Should the host country's politics be grounds for deciding whether to participate?

2. What do you think about the U.S. Government's threats to alter the USOC's tax exempt status and its funding as a means to persuade the USOC not to send a team to Moscow?

3. Explain in your own words the chain of command structure among the IOC, USOC, and the NGB's?

4. Based on the discussion in this case, can you formulate a scenario in which "state action" would be present?

5. DeFrantz became the fifth woman ever named to hold a seat on the 93-member IOC, and is both the first African-American and the first American woman to serve on the committee. She became the first female vice-president of the IOC executive committee in 1997. She was instrumental in convincing 43 African nations not to boycott the 1984 Los Angeles Games when South African runner Zola Budd was allowed to compete for Great Britain. Only Ethiopia, an ally of the boycotting Soviet Union, refused. In 1992, Defrantz became chair of the IOC's Committee on Women and Sports and played a key role in adding women's soccer and softball to the Atlanta Games as medal sports in 1996.


## Delisa Walton-Floyd v. The United States Olympic Committee
965 SW2d 35 (1998)
Court of Appeals of Texas, Houston (1st Dist.)

ANDELL, Justice.

****

### Background

The USOC coordinates the United States's participation in international amateur athletic competitions. It resolves disputes among athletes and sports organizations or between competing sports organizations, and provides uniformity in the area of amateur athletics, thereby protecting the rights of amateur athletes to compete. The USOC has the power to sue and be sued. 36 U.S.C.A. § 375(a)(1), (5), (6) (West 1988).

The USOC selects the United States's governing bodies for every sport in the Olympics and Pan-American games. 36 U.S.C.A. § 375(a)(4) (West 1988). In track and field, the USOC recognizes The Athletic Congress (TAC) as the national governing body.[1] TAC coordinates and conducts track and field competitions to ensure competitions comply with the rules and regulations of the International Amateur Athletic Federation (IAAF). The IAAF rules provide for punishment or suspension of athletes who use certain performance enhancing drugs. The IAAF publishes a list of the banned substances.

---

[1] Editor's note: Today TAC has changed its name to USA Track & Field.

The USOC issued the appellant a card listing many of the more common substances on the banned list. The card warns:

> This list is not complete. It is the athlete's responsibility to check the status of all medications. CALL THE USOC HOTLINE 1-800-233-0393.

The appellant's husband, who was also her trainer, obtained a box of Sydnocarb. He testified the box appeared to be labeled in Russian, he could not read the writing, and he did not have it translated. The box had no instructions and did not list ingredients.

The appellant's husband testified that he called the USOC hotline to inquire about Sydnocarb's status and that the USOC operator told him Sydnocarb was a carbohydrate supplement not on the banned list. He admitted, however, that the hotline operator did not specifically tell him that Sydnocarb was safe to use, nor did she give any other assurances. The appellant called the hotline, with similar results, then began using Sydnocarb. She and her husband testified they called the hotline on subsequent occasions to inquire about the status of Sydnocarb, and that each time, the USOC's operator told them it was not on the banned list.

After the appellant's semi-final heat at the IAAF World Championships, she provided meet officials with a urine sample, which they divided into two samples. The first sample tested positive for amphetamines, a prohibited substance. IAAF officials told her the test results and invited her to attend a testing of the second sample, which also tested positive for amphetamines. The IAAF relayed the results to TAC, which suspended her from further competition. The appellant eventually discovered that Sydnocarb was the apparent source of the amphetamines.

The appellant alleges the following USOC acts and omissions were negligent:

(a) providing her with erroneous and false information through the hotline;
(b) not properly informing and warning her of the possible effect of ingesting Sydnocarb;
(c) not advising her that the use of Sydnocarb would result in the failure of the IAAF drug test;
(d) providing her with information that Sydnocarb was a carbohydrate supplement and not a substance on the banned list;
(e) not informing and educating its hotline personnel concerning Sydnocarb and the risk involved in using it;

(f) not keeping its list of banned substances up to date to include Sydnocarb despite actual knowledge and industry knowledge concerning Sydnocarb and the fact that it represented an amphetamine derivative;

(g) not testing or researching Sydnocarb despite calls from athletes inquiring whether the drug could be used; and

(h) not maintaining a system that would accurately identify the composition of drugs brought to its attention by athletes inquiring through the hotline.

Furthermore, she alleges the USOC negligently breached various duties prescribed by the Amateur Sports Act of 1978 (the Act). 36 U.S.C.A. § § 371-396, 392(a)(3), (5), (6), (8), (9) (West 1988). She also alleges that the USOC owed her a duty, because the USOC represented itself as an expert in the field of illegal substances, instructed athletes to use its hotline to obtain information on those substances, provided her with inaccurate information, and intentionally or negligently misled her regarding the risk of taking Sydnocarb.

In response, the USOC moved for summary judgment based on the following grounds:

(1) the Act does not permit a private cause of action for damages, and it does not create any legal duties to prevent an athlete from experimenting with drugs; therefore, federal law precludes such actions;

(2) because there is no evidence that the USOC possessed a pecuniary interest in the hotline, the appellant's cause of action for negligent misrepresentation is barred;

(3) under Texas law, the USOC's status as a charitable organization limits damages;

(4) there is no evidence of malice supporting the appellant's claim for punitive damages.

The appellant replied that: (1) the Act creates an implied cause of action for damages, and even absent such a private right of action in the Act, one who voluntarily undertakes an affirmative course of action for the benefit of another owes a duty of reasonable care; and (2) a negligent misrepresentation claim does not require a pecuniary interest if the defendant conveys the information in the course of business. The court granted the USOC's motion.

## Standard of Review

Summary judgment is proper only when a movant establishes that there is no genuine issue of material fact and that the movant is entitled to judgment as a matter of law. *Randall's Food Mkts., Inc. v. Johnson,* 891 S.W.2d 640, 644 (Tex.1995); *Bangert v. Baylor College of Medicine,* 881 S.W.2d 564, 566 (Tex.App.--Houston [1st Dist.] 1994, writ denied). In reviewing the summary judgment, we must indulge every reasonable inference in favor of the nonmovant and resolve any doubts in its favor. *Johnson,* 891 S.W.2d at 644; *Marchal v. Webb,* 859 S.W.2d 408, 412 (Tex.App.--Houston [1st Dist.] 1993, writ denied). In reviewing a grant of summary judgment, this Court will take all evidence favorable to the nonmovant as true. *Johnson,* 891 S.W.2d at 644; *Bangert,* 881 S.W.2d at 565.

## Discussion

We are asked to determine whether the USOC owed the appellant a federal statutory or Texas common-law duty. In seven points of error, the appellant asserts: (1) the USOC owed her a federal statutory and Texas common-law duty; (2) there are fact issues whether the USOC had breached those duties; (3) fact issues exist whether damages can be limited; and (4) fact issues exist whether the USOC was grossly negligent.

### Private Right of Action Under the Amateur Sports Act

The appellant maintains the Act provides for an implied private cause of action for monetary damages when the USOC fails to comply with the duties imposed by Congress. She further maintains that Congress would not have included a specific provision allowing the USOC to be sued if it did not intend to create a private cause of action. 36 U.S.C.A. § 375(a)(6) (West 1988). The USOC argues the Act's legislative history, underlying purposes, and caselaw contravene the appellant's interpretation.

The United States Supreme Court prescribes four factors to consider in finding an implied cause of action: (1) whether the plaintiff is a member of a class for whose special benefit the statute was enacted; (2) whether there is an indication of Congressional intent to create or deny a private remedy; (3) whether a private remedy would be consistent with the statute's underlying purposes; and (4) whether the cause of action traditionally is relegated to state law. *Cort v. Ash,* 422 U.S. 66, 79, 95 S.Ct. 2080, 2088, 45 L.Ed.2d 26 (1975). The factors need not be equal in weight, and the central inquiry remains whether Congress intended to create, either expressly or by implication, a private cause of action. [citations omitted].

Because no Texas court has considered this issue, we turn to federal cases for guidance. Federal courts have interpreted the Act and its legislative history not to imply private causes of action against the USOC.[2] *Oldfield v. The Athletic Congress,* 779 F.2d 505, 506-08 (9th Cir.1985); *Michels v. United States Olympic Committee,* 741 F.2d 155, 157-58 (7th Cir.1984); *DeFrantz v. United States Olympic Committee,* 492 F.Supp. 1181, 1190-92 (D.D.C.1980); *Martinez v. United States Olympic Committee,* 802 F.2d 1275, 1281 (10th Cir.1986).

In analyzing the Act's legislative history, the courts have looked to four factors to determine Congress did not intend a private cause of action:

1) The Act strongly favors athletes resolving their disputes through the internal mechanisms provided by the USOC rather than the judicial system.
2) The Act expressly provides causes of actions for certain violations set out within the Act.
3) The USOC's Constitution, which is not part of the Act and was not approved by Congress, establishes the right to a private cause of action against the USOC.
4) The original Act was designed to settle disputes between organizations seeking recognition as national governing bodies for a particular sport and to shield amateur athletes from suffering harm because of internal conflicts. When rechartered in 1978, the Act added internal grievance procedures for athletes.

In *Oldfield,* TAC denied a shot putter's attempt to reestablish amateur status four years after he signed a professional contract. 779 F.2d at 506.

---

[2] Actions against the USOC have proven successful in two scenarios: (1) disputes between organizations and the USOC, *United States Wrestling Fed'n v. Wrestling Division of the AAU, Inc.,* 545 F.Supp. 1053, 1061 (N.D.Ohio 1982); Edward E. Hollis, III, Note, *The United States Olympic Committee and the Suspension of Athletes: Reforming Grievance Procedures Under the Amateur Sports Act of 1978,* 71 Ind.L.J. 183, 188; and (2) breach of contract allegations. *Harding v. United States Figure Skating Ass'n,* 851 F.Supp. 1476, 1480 (D.Or.1994); *Reynolds v. International Amateur Athletic Fed'n,* 841 F.Supp. 1444, 1448 (S.D.Ohio 1992). Intervention is appropriate only in the most extraordinary circumstances, where the association has clearly breached its own rules, the breach will imminently result in serious and irreparable harm to the plaintiff, and the plaintiff has exhausted all internal remedies. *Harding,* 851 F.Supp. at 1479. As a general rule, courts should not intervene in the merits of the underlying dispute, but if they do, then they should limit injunctive relief to correcting the breach of the rules. *Id.*

Because of his professional status, TAC deemed Oldfield ineligible to compete in the Olympic Trials. *Id.* Oldfield brought suit for an injunction and damages against TAC and the USOC, alleging the two organizations had arbitrarily denied him the right to compete in violation of the Act. *Id.* While the plaintiff conceded no express right existed, he contended that an inferred right allowing a private cause of action existed. *Id.* at 507.

The Ninth Circuit denied Oldfield's motion for injunctive relief, but the court did not enjoin his damages claim. *Id.* at 506. However, the district court granted summary judgment on the damages claim, and the Ninth Circuit affirmed. *Id.* at 508.

The Ninth Circuit noted that the Act, as originally proposed, contained a provision referred to as the "Amateur Athletes' Bill of Rights," which expressly granted athletes the power to contest in federal court the actions of any sports organization that threatened to deny them the opportunity to participate. *See* S. 2036, 94th Cong. § 304(a) (1977); *Oldfield,* 779 F.2d at 507. The final version of the Act excluded the provision allowing athletes to sue in federal court and inserted it in the USOC's Constitution. *Oldfield,* 779 F.2d at 507. The court in *Oldfield* explained that the USOC's Constitution is not part of the Act, and thus, the provision did not allow private individuals to litigate in federal court. *Id.*

In *Michels,* the International Weightlifting Federation (IWF) suspended a weightlifter for two years because drug test results revealed an impermissible testosterone level. 741 F.2d at 156. The plaintiff brought suit against the IWF, the U.S. Weightlifting Federation, and the USOC, contending the USOC violated the Act. The plaintiff claimed the test results were invalid and he had a right to a hearing on the matter. *Id.* Based on the Act's legislative history, the Seventh Circuit held that the Act contained no private right of action to require the USOC to hold a hearing. The court noted that Congress's refusal to insert the bill of rights provision into the final version indicates that it considered and then rejected a cause of action for athletes to enforce the Act's provisions. *Id.* at 158. In concurrence, Judge Richard Posner suggested that in light of the Act's provisions to resolve disputes internally, the USOC is better equipped to handle disputes involving athletes. *Id.* He continued, "There can be few less suitable bodies than the federal courts for determining the eligibility, or the procedures for determining eligibility, of athletes to participate in the Olympic Games." *Id.*

The court in *DeFrantz* considered the case of 25 athletes and one executive member of the USOC who sought an injunction prohibiting the USOC from implementing USOC's House of Delegates' resolution to decline an invitation to 1980 Moscow Summer Olympics. 492 F.Supp. at 1183. The Court held the Act did not confer an enforceable right to an amateur athlete to compete in Olympic competition as the Act confers the broad authority to the USOC to make all decisions regarding competitions and participation. *Id.* at 1188. Furthermore, even if such a right to compete existed, the court noted that the Act does not imply a private cause of action to enforce such a right. *Id.* at 1192. The court noted that the Act sought to protect the opportunity for athletes to compete and prevent rivalries between sports organizations. *Id.* The court looked to 36 U.S.C. § 395 (1988) and found established procedures for the internal consideration and resolution of jurisdictional and eligibility issues. *Id.* The court also cited 36 U.S.C. § 395(c)(1), which grants any aggrieved party the right to review by arbitration after exhaustion of other USOC remedies, as confirming the Act's intent to handle disputes internally. *Id.*

Finally, in *Martinez,* a personal representative of the estate of an amateur boxer, who died from injuries sustained in a boxing tournament, filed a wrongful death action against the USOC and other various organizations responsible for the event. 802 F.2d at 1275. The Tenth Circuit, relying on the analysis of the Act's legislative history in *DeFrantz,* dismissed the suit for failure to state a federal cause of action. *Id.* at 1281. The Court found no indication in the Act that Congress intended the USOC to be liable to athletes injured while competing in events not fully controlled by the USOC. *Id.*

The appellant attempts to distinguish the above cases on the basis of the remedy sought by the plaintiff and scope of USOC control of the events. First, the appellant asserts that, with the exception of *Martinez,* all the cases cited by the USOC stand only for the proposition that Congress did not intend to create an implied right of action in favor of an athlete *to enjoin* the USOC or one of the National governing bodies from restricting that athlete's right to participate in amateur sporting events. The appellant argues that she seeks damages, not participation. The appellant does not present any cases in support of her position; instead, she directs the Court's attention to certain alleged duties conferred upon the USOC by the Act and to the fact that the USOC may be sued.

To permit the appellant to bring forth a private claim for damages would directly contravene *Oldfield,* wherein the Ninth Circuit expressly denied the plaintiff a cause of action for his damages claim. The legislative history of the Act indicates that Congress did not intend to provide individual athletes a private cause of action. If Congress had so intended, then it would not have removed the bill of rights from the original version of the Act.

Moreover, if Congress desired to differentiate between monetary claims and injunctions, then it could have so provided in the Act.***

*Voluntary Assumption of a Duty Under State Law*

The appellant argues the Act imposes a duty upon the USOC or a duty exists through voluntary assumption of the hotline service. Since we have held there is no private cause of action under the Act, we must determine whether the USOC assumed a duty under state tort law. The appellant maintains that even absent a statutory duty under the Act, the USOC voluntarily undertook an affirmative course of action for her benefit. She asserts the USOC assumed the obligation to exercise reasonable care. The USOC claims it does not owe the appellant any duty under Texas tort law, because: (1) statutory goals and objectives cannot form the basis of a common law negligence action; (2) the USOC did not voluntarily assume a duty to the appellant; and (3) the Act pre-empts any common-law negligence action.

In determining whether a private cause of action existed under state tort law, the Appellate Division of the New Jersey Superior Court felt bound to follow federal case law. *Dolan v. U.S. Equestrian Team, Inc.,* 257 N.J.Super. 314, 608 A.2d 434, 437 (App.Div.1992). The court noted:

> [W]e believe the Act should be uniformly interpreted; that it would be inappropriate to attribute different or unique meanings to its provisions in New Jersey and thus create a jurisdictional sanctuary from the Congressional determination that these types of disputes should be resolved outside the judicial process. *Id.* 608 A.2d at 437.

We agree with *Dolan.* The interest of maintaining consistent interpretations among jurisdictions requires the Act to pre-empt claims asserted under state tort law. To hold a common law duty exists outside the scope of the Act, thereby enabling an individual athlete to bring suit, threatens to override legislative intent and opens the door to inconsistent interpretations of the Act.

We hold that the USOC did not owe the appellant a duty under any of the theories pleaded. ****

We affirm.

**Notes & Questions**

1. Exactly why is it that the courts conclude that athletes do not have a private cause of action under the Amateur Sports Act?

2. When law students learn about contracts, one doctrine that they study is promissory estoppel. Fundamentally, promissory estoppel allows parties to recover contract-like damages in circumstances where they have reasonably relied on another's promise. This doctrine is found in the Restatement of Contracts (Second) Section 90. Should promissory estoppel operate to provide a cause of action when the telephone hot-line operators give out advice upon which they must know that athletes place reasonable reliance? Explain why or why not.

3. Explain whether you think that this result is "fair." Why or why not?

4. Is there a clear cause and effect relationship between Walton-Floyd's taking Sydnocarb and failing the drug test? In civil law cases, we typically require that proof be shown by "a preponderance of the evidence." In other words, the trier of fact (typically the jury) must be convinced that the evidence relating to a given fact tips the scale at least 51% in order for that fact to be considered "proven." This is very different from the standard required in criminal law cases where proof of facts is required to be "beyond a reasonable doubt." There are also some types of civil law cases where proof must be greater than "by a preponderance of the evidence," and that standard is usually referred to as "by clear and convincing evidence." The "clear and convincing evidence" standard is not as high a burden as "beyond a reasonable doubt" but it is appreciably higher than "by a preponderance of the evidence." In cases involving athletes and drugs use, do you think that there should be a requirement of proof by a preponderance of evidence, clear and convincing evidence, or beyond a reasonable doubt? Explain your reasoning. Is the burden even relevant? Why or why not?

## Mary Decker Slaney v.
## The International Amatuer Athletic Federation and the United States
## Olympic Committee
244 F 3d 580 (2001)
United States Court of Appeals, Seventh Circuit

FLAUM, Chief Judge.

Former Olympic runner Mary Decker Slaney ("Slaney") brought suit against the International Amateur Athletic Federation ("IAAF") and the United States Olympic Committee ("USOC") shortly after an IAAF arbitration panel determined that Slaney had committed a doping offense. *** Slaney now appeals the district court's decision, arguing that: (1) the New York Convention does not bar adjudication of her claims against the IAAF [and] (2) the Amateur Sports Act does not preempt all state-law claims by a participating athlete against the USOC... *** For the reasons stated herein, we affirm the decision of the district court.

BACKGROUND

In the course of her storied career, middle-distance runner Mary Decker Slaney has captured a multitude of United States and world records. She is considered by many to be one of the most celebrated female athletes of the past century, as well as one of the greatest runners of all-time. While Slaney began running in 1969, it was not until fifteen years later that she received international attention. At the 1984 Los Angeles Games, Slaney was considered a favorite to medal in the 3000 meters competition. While the world watched on, half-way through the race, Slaney began jostling for position with Zola Budd, a South African born, barefooted runner. When the pair became entangled, Slaney was tripped up by Budd. Slaney tumbled onto the infield, injuring her hip. As she crashed to the infield, any chance for an Olympic medal came crashing down with her. To this day, an indelible picture of Slaney, fallen on the side of the track and writhing in pain, remains in the minds of many who witnessed the event.

Slaney rebounded from her Olympic defeat and continued to compete, overcoming countless injuries. In June of 1996, she competed in the 5000 and 1500 meter races in the national trials for the Atlanta Olympics. Following her 5000 meter race, Slaney provided the USOC with a urine sample which was tested for prohibited substances including exogenous testosterone.

Because current technology cannot detect the presence of prohibited testosterone in the body, testing programs measure the ratio of testosterone to epitestosterone ("T/E") in the body. This test, referred to as the T/E test, assumes that an ordinary T/E ratio in humans is one to one, and thus any ratio of above six to one is consistent with "blood doping." The ratio was established at six to one in order to account for non-doping factors that might cause elevated ratios in female athletes. Factors which may influence T/E ratio include an individual changing birth control pills, age, menstrual cycle, bacterial contamination of the urine sample, and alcohol use.

Slaney's test was conducted at the University of California at Los Angeles ("UCLA") Laboratory. The test revealed that Slaney's T/E ratio was elevated significantly beyond the permitted six to one ratio.[1] The laboratory notified both the USOC and the IAAF[2] of its findings. According to Slaney, the USOC informed United States of America Track and Field, Inc. ("USATF")[3] of its mandatory duty to investigate whether Slaney's specimen should be declared positive for testosterone. However, it appears that the USATF played no such role, as the actual investigation was conducted by the IAAF. The IAAF's investigating doctor analyzed Slaney's samples, her past test results, and two additional samples. Slaney claimed that her elevated level was the result of (1) her menstrual cycle, and (2) her changing of birth control pills. Furthermore, Slaney posited that there was no scientific validity to the hypothesis that a T/E ratio above six to one was not normal for female athletes. Nonetheless, on February 5, 1997, the IAAF adopted the investigating doctor's recommendation and found Slaney's specimen positive for the prohibited substance testosterone.

---

[1] Specifically, Slaney's samples tested at ratios of 9.5:1 to 11.6:1.

[2] The IAAF is an unincorporated organization based out of Monaco, which was founded to coordinate and control track and field activities around the world. The IAAF, which has a membership of federations representing over 200 nations and territories, establishes worldwide rules for track and field competitions which are embodied in the IAAF Constitution and other regulations. Each federation governs track and field competitions within its own territory and has agreed with all other federations to follow IAAF rules in doing so.

[3] In addition to its Olympic duties, the USOC has been designated as the coordinating body for all amateur sports in this nation by the Ted Stevens Olympic and Amateur Sports Act ("Amateur Sports Act"), 36 U.S.C. § 220501 et seq. Under the Amateur Sports Act, the USOC is required to select a national governing body for each amateur sport. For track and field, the USATF, an Indianapolis corporation, has been designated as the governing body. As the national governing body, the USATF is subject to the Amateur Sports Act. Furthermore, the USATF is also a member of the IAAF, and is responsible for enforcing the IAAF's rules and regulations.

As a result of the IAAF's decision, IAAF and USOC rules required the USATF to hold a hearing to determine whether Slaney had committed a doping offense. Slaney asked the USATF Custodial Board to dismiss her case, and also filed a complaint with the USOC under its rules. The USOC complaint alleged that the USATF proceedings against her violated the Amateur Sports Act as well as the USOC Constitution and By-Laws. Specifically, the complaint alleged that the use of the T/E test on female athletes had not been scientifically validated, that the test discriminated against women by shifting the burden to an athlete to prove by clear and convincing evidence that she was innocent, and that the IAAF had failed to conduct a proper investigation.

Concerned with the dilatory nature of the USOC and the USATF proceedings, on June 10, 1997, the IAAF suspended Slaney on an interim basis. The suspension occurred just prior to the National Track and Field Championships in Indianapolis. Furthermore, the IAAF ensured compliance with the suspension by invoking its contamination rule, whereby anyone who competed with a suspended athlete (in this instance Slaney) would themselves be suspended. The IAAF's actions prompted the USATF Custodial Board to suspend Slaney pending a hearing before the USATF Doping Hearing Board, effectively mooting her motion to dismiss the case against her.

Slaney received her hearing before the USATF Doping Hearing Board on September 14, 1997. The Hearing Board, unpersuaded by the testimony of the IAAF's investigating doctor, unanimously determined that no doping violation had occurred. Satisfied with the USATF Hearing Board's finding that the IAAF's rules regarding the use of the T/E ratio test were vague and inconsistent and the six to one ratio was not scientifically proven to be inconsistent with the normal ratio in humans, Slaney withdrew her complaint with the USOC.

The IAAF was unsatisfied with the USATF Hearing Board's findings, and invoked arbitration of the USATF's decision.[4] Slaney and the USATF opposed arbitration, but both were represented before the IAAF Arbitral Panel ("the Tribunal"). In late January 1999, the Tribunal issued an interlocutory decision upholding the IAAF's interpretation of how to adjudicate a testosterone doping offense, and found that the rules were neither vague nor inconsistent. Thus, once the IAAF showed that Slaney

---

[4] Because of indications, during the late 1970's, that some national track and field federations were turning blind eyes to their athletes' drug abuse, the IAAF established worldwide testing procedures and eligibility rules. Rules 21-23 require all disputes between the IAAF and members to be submitted to an arbitration panel.

30

had a T/E ratio greater than six to one, Slaney had to come forth and show by clear and convincing evidence that the elevated ratio was attributable to a pathological or physiological condition. Believing that it was scientifically impossible to prove by clear and convincing evidence that her high T/E ratio was due to pathological or physiological factors, Slaney withdrew from the arbitration, followed by the USATF. Ultimately, the Tribunal ruled that Slaney had committed a doping offense.

Slaney filed suit in the District Court for the Southern District of Indiana raising numerous state-law contract and tort claims against both the IAAF and the USOC. *** On November 5, 1999, the district court entered a judgment and order dismissing Slaney's state-law claims against the IAAF and USOC pursuant to Fed.R.Civ.P. 12(b)(1), and dismissing Slaney's 18 U.S.C. § § 1962(c) and (d) claims pursuant to Fed.R.Civ.P. 12(b)(6). Specifically, the district court held that the United Nations Convention on the Recognition and Enforcement of Foreign Arbitral Awards, 9 U.S.C. § 201 ("New York Convention"), barred Slaney's claims against the IAAF, as those claims had been the subject of a valid arbitration decision. With regard to Slaney's claims against the USOC, the court held that the Amateur Sports Act, 36 U.S.C. § 220501 *et seq.*, gives the USOC the exclusive right to determine disputes over eligibility and does not create a private right of action.***

Slaney now appeals the decision of the district court. She contends that (1) the New York Convention does not bar her claims against the IAAF [and] (2) the Amateur Sports Act does not preempt all state-law claims made by an athlete against the USOC.***

NEW YORK CONVENTION DEFENSES

Slaney ...suggests that even if we are to determine that she is bound by the arbitration panel's decision, the New York Convention provides exceptions in which a court need not enforce a foreign arbitral decision, and that those defenses to enforcement are applicable to the Tribunal's decision.

The first such defense raised by Slaney is that the Tribunal's decision should not be enforced because she was denied the opportunity to present her case. Slaney contends that under the IAAF rules, the IAAF has the burden of proving beyond a reasonable doubt that a doping offense has occurred. Her defense, she puts forth, was that the IAAF could not scientifically prove beyond a reasonable doubt that any prohibited substance was in her urine. Thus, when the Tribunal concluded it was bound by the IAAF's position--that upon a showing that an athlete had a T/E ratio greater than 6:1 the burden shifted to the athlete to show by clear and convincing evidence that the elevated ratio was due to a pathological or physiological condition--the Tribunal in effect denied Slaney a meaningful opportunity to present her case.

Article V(1)(b) of the New York Convention states that recognition and enforcement of an award may be refused if the party against whom it is invoked furnishes proof that it "was not given proper notice of the appointment of the arbitrator or of the arbitration proceedings or *was otherwise unable to present his case.*" (emphasis added). A court of appeals reviews a district court's decision confirming an arbitration award under ordinary standards: accepting findings of fact that are not clearly erroneous and deciding questions of law *de novo.* [Case citations omitted] As we have noted, in order to comport with the requirement that a party to a foreign arbitration be able to present her case, we require that the arbitrator provide a fundamentally fair hearing. A fundamentally fair hearing is one that "meets the minimal requirements of fairness--adequate notice, a hearing on the evidence, and an impartial decision by the arbitrator." Nevertheless, parties that have chosen to remedy their disputes through arbitration rather than litigation should not expect the same procedures they would find in the judicial arena. Specifically, concerning evidentiary matters, the Supreme Court has noted that "[a]rbitrators are not bound by the rules of evidence." *Bernhardt v. Polygraphic Co.,* 350 U.S. 198, 203-04 n. 4, 76 S.Ct. 273, 100 L.Ed. 199 (1956). The extent of an arbitrator's latitude is such that an "arbitrator is not bound to hear all of the evidence tendered by the parties.... [H]e must [merely] give each of the parties to the dispute an adequate opportunity to present its evidence and arguments." It is when the exclusion of relevant evidence actually deprived a party of a fair hearing that it is appropriate to vacate an arbitral award. *See id.*

In *Generica,* we surveyed several cases in which an arbitrator's award was not enforced by the courts on the grounds raised now by Slaney. For example, in *Tempo Shain Corp. v. Bertek, Inc.,* 120 F.3d 16, 21 (2d Cir.1997), the court held that, under the FAA § 10(a), an arbitration panel's refusal to continue hearings to allow a witness to testify, the only witness with evidence of fraud not found from other sources, was fundamental unfairness and misconduct sufficient to vacate the award. In *Iran Aircraft Indus. v. Avco Corp.,* 980 F.2d 141, 146 (2d Cir.1992), a court also vacated an arbitration award, in that instance because the tribunal changed evidentiary rules during the hearing and thus prevented a party from presenting its documentary evidence. [Case citations omitted] Our examination of these cases leads us to conclude that Slaney's allegation has no merit. This defense to enforcement of a foreign arbitration need not apply when a panel employs a burden-shifting test in a fair manner. Slaney was not denied an opportunity to present her evidence. Rather, the arbitrator's decision merely maintained the same standard of proof the IAAF had always been guided by. As such, Slaney's complaint does not truly attack the procedure implemented by the arbitration panel, but rather an underlying evidentiary decision of the panel. Unfortunately for Slaney, as the Supreme Court has noted, arbitrators are not bound by the rules of evidence. *Bernhardt,* 350 U.S. at 203-04 n. 4, 76 S.Ct. 273. Thus, this attempted defense must fail.

Slaney's final submission on this issue is that "presuming she had committed a doping offense based on a test that is scientifically invalid and discriminatory towards female athletes violated the 'most basic notions of morality and justice.' " Slaney further postulates that "eliminating the presumption of [her] innocence based upon her elevated T/E ratio also violates ... explicit public policy that is well defined and dominant and is ascertained by reference to the laws and legal precedents and not from general considerations of supposed public interests."

According to Article V(2)(b) of the New York Convention, "[r]ecognition and enforcement of an arbitral award may also be refused if the competent authority in the country where recognition and enforcement is sought finds that: ... [t]he recognition or enforcement of the award would be contrary to the public policy of that country."***

Reduced to its essence, Slaney contends that the burden-shifting approach adopted by the IAAF violates United States public policy. We disagree. According to the parties, proving the presence of exogenous testosterone in the body by scientific tests is not possible at the present time. Therefore, the IAAF has adopted the rebuttable presumption of ingestion from a high T/E ratio in an athlete's urine, as detailed throughout this opinion. Were the IAAF not to make use of the rebuttable presumption, it would be nearly impossible, absent eyewitness proof, to ever find that an athlete had ingested testosterone. As the IAAF notes, criminal defendants are frequently required to come forward with proof establishing a basis for asserting affirmative defenses. [citations omitted]. We hope that at some juncture, science will develop a means for detecting exogenous testosterone in athletes, such that an athlete's T/E ratio of 11.6:1 can be discounted if it is based on innocent factors. However, until that point in time, we are confident that requiring an athlete to prove by clear and convincing evidence that her elevated ratio was due to pathological or physiological factors does not invoke a violation of United States public policy as federal case law has required in order for a court to refuse to enforce a foreign arbitral award.

Thus, having found that (1) Slaney participated in the IAAF arbitration, (2) her present state-law complaint seeks to relitigate issues decided by the IAAF Tribunal, (3) the New York Convention mandates enforcement of the arbitrator's decision, and (4) there is no defense that should bar enforcement of the arbitration decision, we find that the district court did not err in dismissing Slaney's state-law claims against the IAAF pursuant to Fed.R.Civ.P. 12(b)(1).

STATE-LAW CLAIMS AGAINST THE USOC

Much as it does against the IAAF, Slaney's complaint alleges state-law violations against the USOC. And, much like it did with regard to the state-law claims against the IAAF, the district court dismissed Slaney's state-law claims against the USOC, pursuant to Rule 12(b)(1). The district court granted USOC's motion to dismiss after determining that the Amateur Sports Act preempted Slaney's state-law claims against the Committee, and that the Act did not provide for a private right of action under which Slaney could seek to have those claims addressed by the district court. Slaney challenges the decision of the district court, arguing that the preemption doctrine does not apply in this arena, such that the Amateur Sports Act poses no jurisdictional barrier to the adjudication of Slaney's state-law claims against the USOC. Once again, we review a district court's dismissal of a complaint pursuant to Fed.R.Civ.P. 12(b)(1) *de novo*.

We begin by noting that Slaney does not challenge the district court's statement that the Amateur Sports Act creates no private right of action. In fact, Slaney seeks to distance her case from those in which plaintiffs have attempted to bring suit under the Act. As stated in her appellate brief, "[n]or is Mrs. Slaney seeking to pursue a claim under the Amateur Sports Act. In many of the cases cited by the District Court, the plaintiffs asserted an implied right in the Amateur Sports Act to bring an action [to] enforce the USOC's obligations under the Act. *Martinez v. USOC*, 802 F.2d 1275, 1280 (10th Cir.1986); *Michels v. United States Olympic Committee*, 741 F.2d 155, 156 (7th Cir.1984); *Oldfield v. Athletic Congress*, 779 F.2d 505, 507 (9th Cir.1985); *DeFrantz v. United States Olympic Committee*, 492 F.Supp. 1181, 1191 (D.D.C.1980). Mrs. Slaney does not dispute the results in those cases; they are simply irrelevant." Thus, we concentrate our inquiry on the issue of whether the Amateur Sports Act precludes the court from examining Slaney's state-law claims.

According to the Amateur Sports Act, one of the purposes of the USOC is to exercise exclusive jurisdiction over all matters pertaining to

34

United States participation in the Olympic Games. *See* 36 U.S.C. § 220503(3). The Act also states that the USOC is designed "to provide swift resolution of conflicts and disputes involving amateur athletes, national governing bodies, and amateur sports organizations," and "to encourage and provide assistance to amateur athletic activities for women." *Id.* at § § 220503(8), 220503(12).

Beginning with the often quoted language from the concurrence in *Michels v. United States Olympic Committee,* the district court reiterated that "there can be few less suitable bodies than the federal courts for determining the eligibility, or procedures for determining the eligibility, of athletes to participate in the Olympic Games." 741 F.2d 155, 159 (7th Cir.1984) (Posner, J., concurring). From there, the court cited numerous cases which have adopted the principle that eligibility decisions fall within the USOC's exclusive jurisdiction over all matters pertaining to United States participation in the Olympic Games. For example, in *Dolan v. United States Equestrian Team, Inc.,* 257 N.J.Super. 314, 608 A.2d 434, 437 (App.Div.1992), the court focused on the need for uniformity in determining questions of eligibility, and held "that it would be inappropriate to attribute different or unique meanings to [the Amateur Sports Act's] provisions in New Jersey and thus create a jurisdictional sanctuary from the Congressional determination that these types of disputes should be resolved outside the judicial processes." Similarly, in *Walton-Floyd v. United States Olympic Committee,* 965 S.W.2d 35, 40 (Tex.Ct.App.1998), the court noted that "[t]he interest of maintaining consistent interpretations among jurisdictions requires the Act to pre-empt claims asserted under state tort law. To hold a common law duty exists outside the scope of the Act, thereby enabling an individual athlete to bring suit, threatens to override legislative intent and opens the door to inconsistent interpretations of the Act." We agree with the district court and the courts in *Dolan* and *Walton-Floyd* that strict questions of athletes' eligibility are preempted by the Amateur Sports Act's grant of exclusive jurisdiction to the USOC over all matters pertaining to United States participation in the Olympic Games. However, that conclusion does not end our analysis.

In *Foschi v. United States Swimming Inc.,* 916 F.Supp. 232 (E.D.N.Y.1996)--a case relied upon by Slaney for the proposition that the Amateur Sports Act does not create complete preemption--the court addressed issues of federal jurisdiction in the context of state-law claims against the USOC, and other amateur athletic organizations. While the district court did not dismiss those claims as being preempted by the Amateur Sports Act, that decision can be understood by examining the claims alleged. There, the plaintiff alleged that her contractual due process right was violated when United States Swimming, among other things, contravened its own rules. While there is no dispute that the USOC has exclusive jurisdiction when it comes to eligibility determinations, the courts can still play a role in ensuring that the organization follows its rules for determining eligibility. The extent of the courts' powers in this area was previously examined by way of a suit brought by an athlete who captured the world's attention for reasons other than her competitive achievements. In *Harding v. United States Figure Skating Ass'n,* 851 F.Supp. 1476, 1479 (D.Or.1994) *vacated on other grounds,* 879 F.Supp. 1053 (D.Or.1995), the court defined (we believe correctly) the limited role that federal courts should play in eligibility determinations. There, the court cautioned that "courts should rightly hesitate before intervening in disciplinary hearings held by private associations.... Intervention is appropriate only in the most extraordinary circumstances, where the association has clearly breached its own rules, that breach will imminently result in *serious* and irreparable harm to the plaintiff, and the plaintiff has exhausted all internal remedies." Yet, while carving out this limited exception to the preemption created by the Amateur Sports Act, the opinion forewarned that while examining whether internal rules had been complied with, the courts "should not intervene in the merits of the underlying dispute." *Id.*

With this understanding of the limits of preemption, we turn to Slaney's claims against the USOC. Slaney suggests that nothing in the Act precludes her from bringing her state-law claims regarding the USOC's administration of its drug testing program, and specifically "the unlawful manner in which the USOC conducts its doping program." Based on our analysis above, we disagree. An inspection of the state-law claims that Slaney brings against the USOC reveals that, despite her best efforts to suggest to the contrary, Slaney is challenging the method by which the USOC determines eligibility of its athletes. Slaney's first state-law cause of action against the USOC is a breach of contract claim. Slaney suggests that the USOC violated its contractual obligations to Slaney by which she suffered damages. While Slaney attempts to skirt the issue, what she is actually alleging is that she was injured by the USOC's determination that she was ineligible to compete. Similarly, Slaney's negligence claim against the USOC posits that the USOC breached a duty to Slaney by using the T/E ratio as a proxy for doping, and that as a result Slaney was damaged. Slaney's other state-law claims are no different.

We note that throughout her complaint Slaney attempts to avoid any mention of the fact that her damages arise from the USOC's determination regarding her eligibility. We assume that such a tactic is a recognition of what we have already stated: the USOC has exclusive jurisdiction, under the

Amateur Sports Act, to determine all matters pertaining to eligibility of athletes. Yet, Slaney cannot escape the fact that her state-law claims, whether framed as breach of contract, negligence, breach of fiduciary duty, fraud, constructive fraud, or negligent misrepresentation, are actually challenges to the method by which the USOC determines eligibility of athletes. Slaney does not suggest that the organization contravened its own guidelines, and as Slaney freely admits, the Amateur Sports Act creates no private cause of action. Thus, the district court was correct in determining that it lacked subject matter jurisdiction over Slaney's state-law claims against the USOC and thus in dismissing those causes of action pursuant to Fed.R.Civ.P. 12(b)(1).

CONCLUSION

Slaney participated in a valid arbitration with the IAAF which, under the New York Convention, we are obligated to recognize. Thus, the issue decided in that arbitration cannot be relitigated. Because adjudication of the state-law claims alleged against the IAAF in Slaney's complaint would necessitate relitigation of the issue decided in the arbitration, the district court correctly determined that it lacked subject-matter jurisdiction over those claims. Likewise, the district court correctly determined that it lacked jurisdiction to adjudicate Slaney's state-law claims against the USOC, finding that those claims were preempted by Congress's grant of exclusive authority to the USOC to determine the eligibility of American athletes. \*\*\*

For the foregoing reasons, we AFFIRM the decision of the district court.

**Notes & Questions**

1. Jurisdiction is the power (or authority) to decide any given issue. Certain courts have jurisdiction to decide certain types of cases. State courts, for example, typically have jurisdiction to decide contract and tort disputes. Federal courts have jurisdiction over matters of Federal Constitutional law. Is one aspect of this case simply a question about what entity has jurisdiction to decide factual issues? What entity has the authority to determine whether there has been a doping violation? Is the final arbiter USATF, the USOC, or the IAAF?

2. To what extent or degree should the courts be involved in reviewing the determinations of independent bodies such as USATF, the USOC, IAAF, or decisions made by arbitrators? Explain your answer.

3. Today many sports contracts as well as the constitutions and/or bylaws of many sports organizations and professional leagues stipulate that controversies will be decided by private arbitration (*e.g.*, American Arbitration Association/AAA) rather than litigated by the courts. As this case explains, arbitration panels typically need not follow the rules of evidence that apply in the regular state and federal court systems. As a rule, arbitration decisions are quicker and less expensive than litigation in the courts. The *Slaney* case illustrates a bedrock principle of our public policy regarding arbitration. As a rule, courts refuse to review the validity of arbitration decisions unless exceptional or egregious unfairness will result.

4. What should the relationship be between science (*i.e.*, the technology available to test for the presence of banned substances) and sports?

5. What level of scientific reliability should be required to render an athlete ineligible? Explain your answer.

6. The March 1982 issue of *Track & Field News* reported the following at page 54:

> Getting around the IAAF's ban on anabolic steroids hasn't been too tough, as most users simply switch to testosterone, which has been legal. The "legality," however, has arisen only because there was no reliable test to prove whether or not the testosterone, which aids in building muscle mass, was the body's own or had been induced.
>
> That fly has been removed from the ointment, the IOC announced in early February, as Medical Commission Chairman Prince Alexandre de Merode revealed that West German Researcher Dr. Manfred Donicke had established a reliable testing procedure.
>
> The method involves calculating the ratio between two naturally occurring substances – epitestosterone and testosterone. Apparently only certain ratios can occur naturally, and any administration of foreign testosterone will upset the balance.

7. Mary Decker Slaney was the only American runner, man or woman to hold all American records from 800 to 10,000-meters at the same time, and was inducted into the National Distance Running Hall of Fame in 2003.

Mary Decker Slaney, photo reprinted with permission of the National Distance Running Hall of Fame

## Sports Court Rules American Gymnast Paul Hamm Can Keep His Disputed Olympic Gold

*By Nancy Armour, AP Sports Writer  Oct 21, 2004*

Paul Hamm can keep his Olympic gold medal.

Sports' highest court rejected a South Korean appeal Thursday, ruling that Hamm is the rightful champion in the men's all-around gymnastics competition at the Athens Games.

"The decision from CAS confirms what I've always felt in my heart, which is that I was champion that night and Olympic gold medalist," Hamm said. "I was just pleased it's all over with."

The decision by a three-judge panel from the Court of Arbitration for Sport ends a saga that began more than two months ago, when South Korea's Yang Tae-young claimed a scoring error cost him the title. Yang finished with the bronze medal.

Yang asked the court to order international gymnastics officials to change the results, and adjust the medal rankings so he would get the gold and Hamm the silver. But the judges dismissed the appeal, leaving Hamm with the gold and Yang with his bronze. Kim Dae-eun of South Korea was the silver medalist.

The verdict is final and cannot be appealed.

"An error identified with the benefit of hindsight, whether admitted or not, cannot be a ground for reversing a result of a competition," the judges said.

Hamm won the gold Aug. 18, rallying from 12th place with only two events left to become the first American man to win gymnastics' biggest prize.

But two days later, gymnastics officials discovered that Yang had been wrongly docked a tenth of a point on his second-to-last routine, the parallel bars. Yang ended up with the bronze, 0.049 points behind Hamm. Add that extra 0.100, though, and Yang would have finished on top, 0.051 points ahead of the American.

That, however, assumes everything in the final rotation played out the same way - a big if.

40

The International Gymnastics Federation (FIG) acknowledged the error and suspended three judges. But it said repeatedly it would not change the results because the South Koreans didn't protest until after the meet.

In their ruling, the judges said the Korean protest was submitted too late - and added that the court was not in a position to correct results even if a mistake were admitted.

"The solution for error, either way, lies within the framework of the sport's own rules," the panel said.

In Athens, the South Koreans appealed to the U.S. Olympic Committee and the International Olympic Committee. It brought back memories of the figure skating scandal at the Salt Lake City Games in 2002, when Canadians Jamie Sale and David Pelletier were given duplicate gold medals after a French judge said she had been "pressured" to put a Russian couple ahead of them.

But there were no such signs of impropriety in this case, and IOC president Jacques Rogge flatly refused to even consider the idea of giving Yang a gold medal.

Then FIG president Bruno Grandi confused the issue, writing a letter to Hamm and asking him to surrender the gold medal. In the letter, Grandi wrote, "The true winner of the all-around competition is Yang Tae-young."

Buoyed by that statement, Yang filed an appeal on the final day of the games with CAS.

The panel praised both gymnasts, saying they "have comported themselves with dignity, despite the controversy."

"They were the victims of this unusual case because a shadow of doubts has been cast over Hamm's achievement in winning the sport's most prestigious prize and because Yang may have been deprived of an opportunity of winning it," CAS said.

The tug-of-war over the medal has overshadowed Hamm's performance, one of the greatest comebacks in gymnastics history.

The defending world champion appeared to lose a chance at any medal, let alone the gold, when he botched the landing of his vault and stumbled backward, plopping down on a judges' table. His score of 9.137 dropped him to 12th place with only two events left.

But one by one, the gymnasts above him faltered. And Hamm was spectacular, closing with a pair of 9.837s on the parallel bars and high bar to win the gold.

"I feel like I had to win my medal in three ways, really," Hamm said last month in an interview with The Associated Press. "Obviously, in competition. Then with the media. Then in court. It really feels like I've been battling this whole time."

**Notes & Questions**

1. Presumably, there will always be judging and umpiring errors that occur in sport. In addition to the simple subjective nature of judging some sports (*e.g.*, equestrian, diving, figure skating, gymnastics), some officiating will inevitably result in errors of judgment (*e.g.*, a replay reveals that a runner at first base is safe not out, a line call in tennis, and the like). Some sports such as fencing use sophisticated electronic equipment to assist judges. The same is true when football referees consult an instant replay or when basketball officials review a replay in order to determine whether a shot was released before or after time had expired. But as the Hamm situation demonstrates, occasionally officials will make quantitative, mathematical errors that can seriously alter the outcome of a contest. Should courts be involved in reviewing any of these types of officiating errors? Appellate judges are accustomed to review the decisions of trial court judges for error. Why should courts not be permitted to review the decisions of sports judges as well?

2. If courts were to get into the business of reviewing sports officials, can you suggest what sort of standard of review ought be be applied? Are there certain types of determinations (mistakes about rules...like mistakes about law, mistakes about facts, mistakes about interpretations?) which lend themselves to judicial review better than others? Explain your answer.

3. In response to the growing number of sports-related disputes, the Court of Arbitration for Sport (the CAS – the entity that decided the Paul Hamm case) was created in 1984. The idea for such an arbitral body is credited to the president of the International Olympic Committee (IOC) H.E. Juan Antonio Samaranch who yearned to create a sports-specific jurisdiction. The CAS is

located in Lusanne, Switzerland with additional courts in New York and Sydney as well as ad-hoc courts in Olympic host cities as necessary. The CAS has jurisdiction over two types of disputes: those that are commercial in nature, and those that are disciplinary in nature. Commercial disputes may include contractual disputes as well as those disputes that would result in civil liability. A large number of disciplinary disputes are doping-related. A dispute may be submitted to the CAS only if there is an arbitration agreement between the parties that specifies recourse to the CAS. "An international court like the CAS, which can offer specialist knowledge, low cost and rapid action, provides a means of resolving sports disputes adapted to the specific needs of the international sporting community."

# MISSING THE TARGET: HOW PERFORMANCE-ENHANCING DRUGS GO UNNOTICED AND ENDANGER THE LIVES OF ATHLETES

E. Tim Walker
10 VILLANOVA SPORTS & ENTERTAINMENT L.J. 181 (2003)

## I. Introduction

Sports are a partial reflection of societal norms and values. In that regard, culture and sports have their shortcomings as well as their successes. Although both areas have fallen to the epidemic of drug addiction, the drug problem in the sports community still remains somewhat of a mystery. Amateur and professional athletic organizations implemented drug testing policies to determine which players use illegal drugs and to deter others from trying them. These "doping" policies require taking urine samples throughout the year. Vials of urine are then analyzed for street drugs, and in specific instances, for performance-enhancing drugs.

Drug testing policies, especially those in high schools and in professional sports, are criticized for lenient policy administration and testing too few substances. At the crux of the debate are performance-enhancing drugs that are left completely off the list of tested substances in high school anti-doping schemes. Professional sports organizations like the National Football League ("NFL") and Major League Baseball ("MLB") include performance-enhancing drugs on their lists of banned substances, yet it is debatable whether athletes are tested for these substances and whether athletes' use of them is disclosed adequately to the media. The bottom line is, a doping problem exists in all levels of all sports. The remedy to this problem must extend beyond mandatory drug testing.

This Comment focuses on the anti-doping policies of different athletic organizations and groups within both the amateur and professional ranks. Section II examines the drug testing policies of assorted athletic settings, using high school athletics, the National Collegiate Athletic Association ("NCAA"), and the World Anti-Doping Agency ("WADA") as examples of amateur sports, as well as the NFL and MLB to contrast the anti-doping policies that exist within the professional sports arena. Section III discusses the frustrations encountered by these policies, using the field of available performance-enhancing drugs as a gauge for the policies' successes and failures. Section IV briefly summarizes the shortcomings of contemporary anti-doping policies, and suggests ways organizations can improve their efforts to eradicate the use of performance-enhancing drugs.

## II. Background

The problem of doping in sports pervades both amateur and professional athletic organizations. The differences in their approaches have been drastic, with professional sports' emphasis on counseling and amateur sports' focus on testing. The regulation of substance policies in professional sports has been limited because the Supreme Court has only evaluated the constitutionality of drug policies under the Fourth Amendment as applied to high school drug testing. Anti-doping measures of other sports levels remain untouched by the courts, and have been amended only through administrative processes and collective bargaining agreements.

Because most athletic institutions have been deemed private actors by the courts, they administer their drug testing mechanisms with more freedom than high school athletic programs. Therefore, many experts have concluded that professional sports and some amateur athletic organizations manipulate the amount of exposure that doping problems receive. Furthermore, some drug tests have failed to identify correctly past drug use by an athlete. In response to these criticisms, athletic organizations have attempted to enact anti-doping programs that address these concerns.

A. Amateur Athletics

1. Drug Testing Policies at the High School Level

Educational institutions have become a focal point for American culture and public growth. In *Elkins v. United States*, the Court held that the

44

Search and Seizure Clause of the Fourth Amendment applied to states through the Fourteenth Amendment. In *T.L.O. v. New Jersey*, the Court held that the Fourth Amendment applied to school officials because they "act as representatives of the State, not merely as surrogates for parents . . . ." No matter how important the societal function, the Court has always sought to balance the students' interests against the state's goals under the Fourth Amendment. For students to receive protection, there must be an intrusion on an expectation of privacy "society is 'prepared to recognize as legitimate.'" This interest is weighed against the government's interest in educating children.

According to the Supreme Court, drug testing through urine is a search and seizure because it "intrudes upon expectations of privacy that society has long recognized as reasonable . . . ." Normally, the Fourth Amendment requires that officials obtain a warrant through probable cause before conducting any kind of search, but the Court applied the less exacting "special needs" doctrine in the public school setting because the probable cause requirement would hinder educational needs. In *Vernonia School District v. Acton*, the Court alleviated the need for the school to obtain a warrant before testing student-athletes for drugs because athletes have a diminished expectation of privacy.

After the ruling in *Acton*, school boards acted quickly to implement similar drug testing programs. Drug testing and policies prohibiting the consumption of alcohol were deemed to protect adequately the health and safety of the student-athlete. The Supreme Court in *Vernonia* ruled that considerations such as the health and safety of the students were valid and "perhaps compelling" government concerns.

The Court further elaborated its desire for eradicating drug problems in *Board of Education v. Earls*. The Court's ruling in *Earls* extended the principles of *Vernonia* to include students who participate in non-athletic extracurricular activities. The policy instituted by the school district tested for illegal street drugs, but not for performance-enhancing drugs. Consequently, the decision allowed school districts to update their policies to combat the developing drug situation among students.

Only one case has involved a challenge to a drug testing policy that detected the presence of both performance-enhancing drugs and street drugs. This is because most school districts limit their anti-doping policies to street drugs to adhere to the Fourth and Fourteenth Amendment standards.

## 2. NCAA's Anti-Doping Policy

The NCAA has been an innovator in the fight against drug use by athletes in detecting the intake of both street drugs and performance-enhancing substances. The organization has dealt only with state constitutional and First Amendment challenges to the policy, and not with opposition based on the Search and Seizure Clause of the Fourth Amendment. If the actions of the state and private party are so intertwined and indistinguishable that they become joint participants, the private party is considered a state actor. The NCAA has not been deemed a state actor for purposes of imposing its policies on member colleges and universities, and therefore has evaded Fourth Amendment constraint.

The NCAA refined its anti-doping procedure, making athletes consent to the policy by signing a release allowing random testing. Testing is implemented according to strict procedures. Drug-testing crews pass the specimens of urine to the representatives of the National Center for Drug-Free Sports at the championship site. The collected urine samples are checked for an extensive list of banned substances such as anabolic steroids and diuretics.

A positive test result for any of the substances renders the athlete ineligible for any further contests until he or she obtains a negative test. If there is a second positive finding, the student is allowed an institutional appeal, which must be submitted in writing within forty-eight hours of notification. If the athlete's request for eligibility is denied, he or she may be reinstated only after producing a negative test sample.

The main purpose of the NCAA anti-doping policy has been to "protect[ ] the health and safety of intercollegiate athletes." Many of the tested drugs have serious side effects known to the medical community. The public has become aware of the possible pernicious effects of anabolic agents, such as serious contribution to liver damage in steroid users. Therefore, the NCAA has kept drug testing in its athletic program to ensure that intercollegiate athletics remain steroid-free.

## 3. The Olympic Movement and Anti-Doping

Performance-enhancing drugs have plagued the Olympics since their inception in ancient Greece. The extent of the doping problem in the Olympics, however, was not actually realized until the 1950s and 1960s. Because "the side effects of the substances used were unclear," the International Olympic Committee ("IOC") created a Medical Commission, which developed the initial list of banned substances. To fully prohibit the use of banned substances, the IOC asked international federations such as the United States Olympic Committee ("USOC") to test for performance-enhancing drugs during non-competition.

The Olympic movement has been eager to coordinate a coherent drug testing structure for its athletes. In 1999, the IOC called a conference, now known as the Lausanne Declaration, to draw support for one body of code overseeing all of the anti-doping movement for Olympic athletes. This conference created the Olympic Movement Anti-Doping Code, enforced by the newly formed World Anti-Doping Agency ("WADA"), which "applie [d] to all athletes, coaches, instructors, officials, and to all medical and . . . [other] staff working with athletes . . . ." The WADA has taken an independent observer role at the Olympic Games, seeking to ensure that testing is implemented in a correct and impartial manner.

The WADA and the Olympic Movement Anti-Doping Code have created a vast list of banned substances for which athletes are tested at various times throughout their careers. An athlete can be tested at any time regardless of whether the games are in session. If asked to produce a sample, the athlete is accompanied by a monitor of the same sex. The anti-doping effort was not unified until the emergence of WADA, so it may take time before all the organizations have the identical policy. The WADA, therefore, must wait before all the WADA doping policies are encoded and are uniformly enforced at every single event.

B. Professional Sports

1. The National Football League's Drug Policy

The NFL has been touted for its steroid testing policy, but criticized for the policy's results. The NFL drug testing policy was established through collective bargaining with the NFL Players Association ("NFLPA"). The NFL is not subject to constitutional restraints applied to entities such as public school districts because the court has not declared the NFL to be a state actor. The NFL sought tougher principles through year-long random drug testing, but was unable to overcome NFLPA's pressure for less frequent testing.

The current collective bargaining agreement between the NFL and the NFLPA was struck in 1998, and has been extended through 2007. The NFL's banned substances list is one of the most comprehensive of the professional sports associations, including almost as many substances as

WADA's list. The testing, however, is not as frequent as the NCAA's or WADA's testing because most players are only tested once during the NFL pre-season. Also, the testing for more serious substances is not consistent until the player enters an "intervention stage." Finally, though the NFL's drug policy appears to be tough on performance-enhancing drugs, actual positive tests are not made public because the collective bargaining agreement mandates confidentiality of the results. Thus, the successes and failures of the drug policy are therefore subject to serious speculation.

## 2. Major League Baseball's View on Doping in Sport

MLB and the MLB Players Association, one of the most powerful professional players' unions, failed in their attempt to institute a drug policy in June of 1984. The program began as a war "almost exclusively against cocaine [abuse], . . . the most serious drug problem." MLB's 1997 drug program expanded the published list of tested substances to include marijuana, opiates, and PCP, but not for performance-enhancing drugs. The Medical Advisor for the MLB administered testing four times throughout the year, under the supervision of a trained collector.

MLB also initiated an educational program termed the Employee Assistance Program or "EAP," which provided information to the players about drug use and confidential counseling for those with drug problems. This program, which was primarily voluntary, went beyond testing to ensure that players understand the dangers associated with drugs. In the NFL, the Commissioner ensures confidentiality of both test results and counseling. Unlike the NFL, however, MLB formerly tested only for street drugs and not for performance-enhancing drugs. Therefore, it was difficult to determine how many of the MLB players used performance-enhancing drugs on a consistent basis.

MLB's new policy, enacted as part of the 2002 collective bargaining agreement, is the first measure towards banning the use of performance-enhancing drugs in baseball. MLB players will be tested for steroids beginning in 2003, followed by more testing after a determination that the use is widespread. The agreement declared that MLB would not mark steroids as prohibited substances. The testing in 2003 will be administered through two announced tests during the season. The program levies fines or suspensions for players who use performance-enhancing substances or illegal street drugs. Although MLB's new program is a small stride to reducing drug use in baseball, it is at least progress.

## III. Analysis

The testing procedures implemented by professional and amateur sports were designed to reduce existing drug use among participants and to deter others from beginning use. It appears, however, that the testing mechanisms in place for many sports today are more of a pretense than an actual force against drugs. The anti-doping policies of athletics, especially professional athletics, resemble a public policy ploy to boost community perception that drugs are not tolerated and that the integrity of play in sports is sound. The policies presented by amateur and professional sports have several loopholes, however, enabling athletes to cheat testing procedures and excel at the sport using state-of-the-art performance-enhancing drugs. Serious shortcomings in testing indicate that it should not be relied on so heavily for adequate drug deterrence. Indeed, many problems exist in testing mechanisms, especially in what the tests probe for, who is tested, and when the testing takes place.

### A. Most Testing Does Not Include Performance-Enhancing Drugs

Drug testing of athletes is most crucial in high school and professional sports, yet neither seems to test for performance-enhancing drugs. High school, where adolescents learn educational disciplines and grow into adults, should be the first place for administrators to ensure that students do not use stimulants or anabolic agents. The Supreme Court has declared the safety of students to be a valid government interest that outweighs the students' constitutional protection from unreasonable searches and seizures. It would be logical, therefore, for the Supreme Court to authorize testing in high schools for performance-enhancing drugs, as long as the privacy and safety of the students are considered.

Televised sports like the Olympics and MLB, are also to blame for the rise in students' use of performance-enhancing drugs. Because neither of the organizations has regulated performance-enhancing drugs successfully, fans have taken these supplements, desiring to appear and perform like professional athletes. The WADA, for example, prohibits the use of human growth hormone, but at the 2000 Olympic Games in Sydney, it had no way of testing the substance's presence in athletes' bodies. With this knowledge, athletes can use performance-enhancing drugs to help them succeed without detection through anti-doping tests. The testing does not detect all banned substances, and therefore, athletes constantly gain an unfair advantage over other participants because it is clear that "the candy store remains open."

MLB also has serious hurdles to overcome regarding testing for performance-enhancing substances. In reality, because of the strength of the players' union, baseball players are never subject to random testing outside the four announced tests throughout the year. MLB's new testing program does not ban performance-enhancing drugs. Players in professional baseball, therefore, have virtually no deterrent from abstaining from the use of performance-enhancing drugs. MLB players may use such substances more openly than in other sports, although their effects may be questionable. Whether it helps or hurts a baseball player's performance, the mere use of such substances conveys a message to younger players across the nation that cheating to win is acceptable as long as the player is not caught. For this reason alone, anti-doping policies need to be strengthened to test every substance known to enhance performance, and educational programs need to be implemented to uncover the dangers associated with the use of such substances.

B. Athletes Are Not Tested Often Enough to Fully Detect Drug Use

Most professional and amateur sports subject their players to random testing throughout the season, and sometimes in the off-season. This testing scheme, however, does not ensure that players will be deterred from using stimulants or anabolic agents during the season or off-season. The NFL, for example, always tests during the pre-season and then randomly through the regular and post-season. The problem with this scheme is that players have an extremely low probability of being tested after the initial instance in the pre-season. The NFL does not test for performance-enhancing drugs often enough to dissuade drug use throughout the season. Therefore, players in the NFL could start taking performance-enhancing drugs after their first test in the pre-season because of the low probability that they will be tested again. The testing procedures offered by the NFL could be deemed a façade because the NFL would never unveil a huge doping scandal in its sport. A public view that NFL players abuse substances regularly would harm the players directly, and subsequently, the NFL would lose television ratings and profits.

Poor testing schemes also affect the NCAA, where non-football players are tested at an even lower frequency, making it possible to never be tested during the athlete's four years at college. Professional sports, like MLB, have inferior policies because MLB tells its players ahead of time when they will be tested. Therefore, MLB players can abstain from using performance-enhancing substances after the announcement with hopes that the remnants of the drugs will have left the body.

The testing method at the Olympic level is also an example of how anti-doping schemes are attractive on their face, yet only meant to prevent public perception of cheating in sports. The IOC, under direction of the WADA, tests only the top three finishers and one randomly chosen athlete during the Olympic Games. This anti-doping policy is effective in ensuring that athletes who win are not cheating, but does little to protect the health of every athlete because it fails to prevent all athletes from using performance-enhancing drugs. Accordingly, the testing only tests as many athletes as necessary to dissuade media criticism of doping in the games.

If athletes play sports as a "consensual activity, entered into by individuals of their own free will," then the IOC and other Olympic organizations should make participation contingent upon mandatory, random testing of every athlete on a frequent basis. Although some may argue this is an invasion of the athlete's privacy, voluntary consent by the athlete and the significant countervailing interest of protecting the health and safety of all participants should be sufficient to pass any federal or state privacy law. Consequently, the IOC and the WADA would be able to administer an anti-doping policy which would eradicate completely testable drugs, and fulfill its goal of protecting the health and safety of the athlete.

The pursuit of glory and money should never prevail over the health and safety of an athlete. The NFL and USOC should expose fully all scandals they are accused of concealing and prevent them from reoccurring. The life of any athlete, whether he or she is a high school student or a multi-million dollar professional star, is not worth the price that the media and the public put on the individual's performance on the field. Amateur and professional sports have made strides in anti-doping efforts; however, both need to improve their testing methods to deter athletes fully from using performance-enhancing drugs.

C. Accompanying Drug Testing with Additional Mandatory Procedures May Be Best Tactic to Ensure Drug-Free Sports

Anti-doping policies of professional and amateur sports have relied heavily on drug testing as the major deterrent against using performance-enhancing drugs. When considering the inaccuracy of urine testing, it seems logical to devote more energy to deterring drug use before it begins by informing athletes of the dangers associated with drugs that enhance performance and appearance. Educational programs, which teach the hazards and evils associated with all types of drugs, should be integrated with anti-doping policies. Most professional and collegiate sports only offer optional counseling or educational procedures for the athletes. Because the pressures of professional and amateur sports are immense, counseling and educational programs should be mandatory. Students and professional athletes will then learn about the serious risks that result from using performance-enhancing drugs.

Most sports organizations do not make educational programs mandatory for participation in the sport. By requiring educational programs as part of the anti-doping program, athletes can achieve an understanding of the serious problems of performance-enhancing drug use before they use. An additional benefit of drug education would be the deterrent effect for those athletes who formerly used performance-enhancing drugs. Drug education could "be a great improvement to the current program which tempts athletes to merely avoid detection of drug use." Thus, recognizing that drug education programs enhance drug use prevention, heads of anti-doping agencies have contemplated education as a deterrent for drug use in youth sports.

The best option for athletic organizations would be to combine the current drug testing policies with mandatory educational programs, while still striving for better and swifter methods of detecting drug use. Because many sports organizations have created drug testing policies already, it would be foolish to extinguish them. Without education, however, many athletes at younger ages will begin to experiment with performance-enhancing drugs that can be purchased easily at stores across the country.

The current anti-doping policies of amateur and professional sports have substantially evolved since their inceptions, but still must advance considerably before all athletes are drug-free. If the sports world is serious about banishing drug use, steps must be taken to ensure that drug-testing programs are adequate enough to deter athletes from using drugs to enhance performance. First, anti-doping policies must include performance-enhancing drugs in the list of substances that in fact are tested. Second, all athletes must be tested consistently. Finally, anti-doping policies must expand to include drug education and other preventative methods to deter drug use by athletes fully at multiple levels. For anti-doping efforts to succeed, sports organizations must hold their own players publicly accountable and not conceal their drug use. Until all these problems are solved, drug use will remain an enormous dilemma within competitive sports.

# IV. Conclusion

Unfortunately, illegal drug use has plagued athletes just as it has the rest of society. Athletic organizations have made it their goal to combat this problem through anti-doping policies. These policies focus on drug testing "to deter and detect drug use." With the exception of high school athletic drug testing programs, sports organizations have been immune from Fourth Amendment principles. Therefore, many of the anti-doping programs are subject merely to privacy issues and bargaining power.

Drug testing programs have progressed substantially since their inceptions, yet they still receive heavy criticism for various reasons. The latest battles focus on whether drug testing policies actually test the appropriate drugs to protect athletes fully and prevent drug abuse. Consequently, sports organizations such as the WADA and NCAA have enlarged their banned substances lists to include almost every conceivable performance-enhancing drug. The surge to ban every substance, however, does not mean that every prohibited substance is tested. Furthermore, even if the substance is banned and tested, it does not follow that every player will be tested for the substance during competition or during the off-season.

It is necessary to substantially amend the anti-doping policies of many sports organizations. Too many athletes are taking substances to assist their performance, which is affecting sports of all types. This produces problems in youth athletic programs because young adults tend to emulate their favorite player to gain a competitive edge. Performance-enhancing drugs have become the new battleground in sports, as organizations seek "to redirect sport back to its competitive roots without the influence of unfair advantages and victory without honor." Furthermore, because performance-enhancing drugs are not subject to the policies of the Food and Drug Administration ("FDA"), conducting more studies is crucial to assess fully the true problems associated with such substances. Congress and the FDA must corral this problem through new, coherent legislation.

The current drug testing scheme is inadequate to fight this war, and much more needs to be done. Mandatory education, especially for youth sports, must become a cornerstone for drug deterrence. Until athletic organizations' anti-doping policies involve more education and truly efficient testing, athletes of all levels will continue to use performance-enhancing drugs.

UNIVERSITY OF WINCHESTER

**Notes & Questions**

1. Obviously, the place of performance-enhancing drugs (such as anabolic steroids) in sports has been a major topic of discussion in the national and international media during the past several years since Walker's Comment was first published in 2003. Major League Baseball and the National Football League have been nearly turned upside-down examining the issue. Presumably, rule makers have decided to ban such substances on two grounds. First they provide users an "unfair advantage." Second, they pose serious health risks to their users. Therefore, in order to preserve the integrity of sport and to provide a level playing field among participants, and in order to prevent undue health risks to participants, such substances are prohibited.

2. What criteria should rule makers use to determine what substances are prohibited and what substances are permitted? Where do we draw the line between advanced nutrition versus "illegal" substances? Should there be a uniform standard among all major sports? Why or why not?

3. As is true with computer hackers, are not the cheaters always going to be just one step ahead of the enforcement officials?

4. Isn't this the type of problem that simply will never go away? Is the use of technology to enhance performance any different from the use of technology to enhance athletic equipment. Rule makers regulate the designs and materials of golf clubs, golf balls, baseball bats, football helmets, tennis racquets, and countless other types of sports equipment. Presumably, rule makers must constantly monitor technological progress to prohibit unfair advantage and to prevent safety hazards related to technological improvements in equipment also.

5. MLB's regulation of performance-enhancing drugs has come a long way since 1998 when news and rumors swirled around Mark McGuire. In January 2005, a new steroid-testing policy was announced by MLB commissioner Bud Selig and the union's executive director Donald Fehr. Featured in the new agreement is a 10-day penalty without pay for first-time offenders. Previously, when testing began in 2003 a first positive test led a player to be put on a clinical track, and nothing further. As a result of the new agreement, the list of banned substances has been expanded to include substances classified as prohormones or precursors. These include but are not limited to androstenedione (Andro, for short), norandrostenediol, Ephedra, human growth hormone, THG, designer steroids, diuretics, and masking agents which all will be banned. On December 8, 2005 the players union

unofficially approved the agreement by a unanimous vote. See Snow, Chris, *MLB Steroid Policy Outlined: First Time Offenders Will Be Penalized*, The Boston Globe, Jan. 14, 2005, http://www.boston.com/sports/baseball/articles/2005/01/14/mlb_steroid_poli cy_outlined/?page=1.

6. Barry Bonds, who has been implicated in the BALCO scandal, filed for free agency in the fall of 2006 after his 5 year, $90 million contract with the San Francisco Giants expired. Talks of a new contract were circulating throughout the baseball community. At the time Bonds was only 22 home runs away from breaking Hank Aaron's longstanding record. See **www.espn.com,** *New Contract Talks Are in Place between Bonds, Giants,* http://sports.espn.go.com/mlb/news/story?id=2648951, (last visited November 7, 2006).

7. The NFL places recreational drugs such as marijuana in a category separate from steroids and other performance-enhancing drugs. While the policy on performance enhancing drugs is one of zero tolerance, for recreational drugs there are graduated steps of punishment. After an athlete tests positive for recreational drugs, he is given a second test before suspension ensues. Fines and suspension are the result of a third violation. The NFL treats recreational drugs as more of a medical problem and attempts to get the player professional help to deal with his addiction. See Collinsworth, Cris, *The Best Policy: NFL'S Drug Testing*, http://www.nfl.com/news/story/6744864 (last updated October 23, 2003) and O'Hara, Mike, *Rogers Leaves Big Void: Defensive Line is Forced to Scramble in Wake of Tackle's Suspension for Using Banned Substance*, The Detroit News http://detnews.com/apps/pbcs.dll/article?AID=/20061019/SPORTS0101/610 190347/1004/SPORTS (last updated October 19, 2006).

8. Ricky Williams, the notorious Miami Dolphins running back, was suspended for the 2006 season. As a result of being caught in possession of marijuana, his fourth offense, Williams was placed on the CFL negotiation list for the 2006 season. Williams now plays for the Toronto Argonauts, but under contract, he will return to play for the Miami Dolphins for the 2007 season. See Battista, Judy, *Fourth Drug Violation Bars Dolphins' Williams for 2006,* http://select.nytimes.com/gst/abstract.html?res=FA0D17FE385B0C758EDD AD0894DE404482&n=Top%2fReference%2fTimes%20Topics%2fPeople% 2fW%2fWilliams%2c%20Ricky.

9. On August 21, 1991, the IAAF put into effect a stringent policy on performance-enhancing drugs. The policy establishes a minimum suspension of four years (an increase of two years from the previous term). "The suspension would be extended to include the same event from which the athlete was disqualified, which means if a violation occurred in the Olympics and the succeeding Games were scheduled more than four years later, the suspension would remain in effect until the subsequent Olympics ended." Many critics of the new policy claim that such a suspension could potentially end an athlete's career. See Janofsky, Michael, *TRACK AND FIELD; I.A.A.F Cracks Down on Use of Steroids*, www.newyorktimes.com, August 22, 1991. The IAAF policy is updated each year, presumably to stay current on new drugs and new regulations. The current policy mandates both in competition and out of competition testing and includes exemptions for therapeutic use. There is no advanced notice afforded to the athletes for out of competition testing with the exception of extenuating circumstances. The list of prohibited substances for out of competition testing ranges from anabolic substances to hormones and diuretics. In terms of in competition testing, the banned list includes stimulants, narcotics, recreational drugs, and glucocorticosteroids. The penalty incurred as a result of a positive test can be anywhere from two months to two years of ineligibility. The new banned substances list has been approved and will go into effect in September, 2007. The current policy can be found at http://www.iaaf.org/newsfiles/33046.pdf.


## RESOLUTION OF DOPING DISPUTES IN OLYMPIC SPORT: CHALLENGES PRESENTED BY "NON-ANALYTICAL" CASES

Cameron A. Myler
40 NEW ENGLAND LAW REVIEW 747 (2006)


I did compete as an Olympic athlete. I never used any performance enhancing substances, and although I represent athletes now who have been charged with the use of substances, I certainly do not endorse it and I see the need for a strong anti-doping program both in Olympic and professional sports. I competed when there were still two Germanies and the women on the East German team seemed to grow by exponential factors every year. When I was sixteen or seventeen and competing, I did not quite understand what that was all about, but I definitely do now.

Most recently, an athlete whom I represented, Christy Gains, was charged with a number of anti-doping rule violations in connection with the Bay Area Laboratory Co-Operative ("BALCO"), and I am sure we have heard more about that than we might want to. For purposes of this discussion, I think BALCO is instructive on a number of issues that have arisen in Olympic sport anti-doping programs.

First, I will give you a little bit of an overview of the process in Olympic sport and how disputes are adjudicated and then I will talk about a couple of particular cases that deal with this notion of a non-analytical positive, *i.e.*, the charging of an athlete with a doping offense when the U.S. Anti-Doping Agency ("USADA") or other doping agency has no positive test.[1]

First, the World Anti-Doping Agency ("WADA") is basically the umbrella under which all anti-doping efforts in the Olympic sphere occur. It was formed in 1999,[2] basically at the behest of the International Olympic Committee and it since has become a more independent entity so it has more perceived fairness and independence. WADA's stated purposes are to protect the fundamental rights of athletes to participate in doping-free sport and thus promote health, fairness, and equality for athletes worldwide,[3] and secondly to ensure harmonized, coordinated, and effective anti-doping programs at the international and national level with regard to the protection, deterrence, and prevention of doping.[4] WADA was really a very big step forward in anti-doping efforts because...there are...more than 200 countries that are members of the International Olympic Committee. Before WADA was created,the countries all had different programs, each of the sports had different programs, and there was not a whole lot of coordination between them. WADA has as its primary document the World Anti-Doping Code (hereinafter "WADA Code"), and all of the stakeholders in the Olympic movement, including the International Olympic Committee, each of the National Olympic Committees, and all of the international federations for sport had to adopt and implement the WADA Code prior to the opening ceremonies of the Olympic Games last year in Athens.[5] Included in the

---

[1] Sally Jenkins, This Agency Lacks the Inside Dope, WASH. POST, May 17, 2004, at D01, available at http://washingtonpost.com/wp-dyn/articles/A31738-2004 May16.html.
[2] World Anti-Doping Agency, WADA History, http://www.wada-ama.org (follow "About WADA – History" hyperlink) (last visited Apr. 6, 2006).
[3] World Anti-Doping Agency, Mission, http://www.wada-ama.org (follow "About WADA – Mission" hyperlink) (last visited Apr. 6, 2006).
[4] See id.
[5] Copenhagen Declaration on Anti-Doping in Sport, Mar. 2003, available at http://www.wada-ama.org/rtecontent/document/copenhagen_en.pdf; WORLD ANTI-DOPING AGENCY, WORLD ANTI-DOPING CODE 6 (2003), available at http://www.wada-ama.org/rtecontent/document/code_v3.pdf.

WADA Code…is the definition of doping that has become standard throughout, and the burdens and standard of proof that are required in the adjudication of disputes as well as the types of evidence that can be used to prosecute athletes.

In this country, the U.S. Olympic Committee basically has contracted with the USADA (United States Anti-Doping Agency) which again like WADA is an independent agency. It was formed in 2000[6] to remove the function of drug testing from each of the different sports because of conflicts of interest. Unlike WADA, USADA conducts all of the testing and adjudicates disputes in Olympic sport.

There are a couple of different general types of doping offenses in Olympic sport. In all of the professional sports we are really dealing with just positive tests. In Olympic sport, in addition to the positive tests of a urine or blood sample for a variety of different substances, there is also the notion of a "non-analytical positive."[7] The "non-analytic positive" allows USADA to charge athletes with having violated a rule even if they do not have a positive test. It is not really a new concept, but BALCO has since raised some new issues. For example, included within these non-analytical positive cases, could be refusing to submit to drug testing, admitting to the use of a substance, tampering with any part of the drug testing process, missing three tests within an eighteen month period (this actually constitutes a positive test and an athlete would be banned for two years in Olympic sport for having missed three tests), possessing substances, trafficking, administering substances to other athletes (this is really more directed at coaches), encouraging, aiding, abetting, covering up, or any other type of complicity involving an anti-doping rule violation. So, the scope is really quite broad.

Prior to BALCO, some charges were brought based on the forgoing violations, but during the BALCO scandal, a number of Olympic athletes were charged with violations. USADA basically was trying to prove that the Olympic athletes had used substances based on documents that were seized by the federal government in BALCO.

The following are a few comments about the adjudication process itself. If an athlete's sample tests positive or if he or she is charged with some

---

[6] U.S. Anti-Doping Agency, What We Do, http://www.usantidoping.org/what/ (last visited Apr. 6, 2006).
[7] Dave Kindred, Smoke, Fire and Tainted Olympic Dreams, SPORTING NEWS, May 31, 2004, at 64, available at http://findarticles.com/p/articles/mi_m1208/is_22_228/ai_ n6126783.

other offense, USADA will submit his or her information to the appropriate review board.[8] The review board decides on the papers alone with no oral argument whether there is evidence to proceed. Not surprisingly there is almost always enough evidence to proceed. At that point, the athlete is formally charged with an offense and a sanction is recommended. The athlete can accept the sanction or he or she can challenge it. Prior to the adoption of the WADA Code, an athlete had the choice of having a case heard under the modified American Arbitration Association (AAA) commercial rules[9] before a panel of one or three arbitrators who are members of the Court of Arbitration for Sport (CAS) in North America.[10] Alternatively, an athlete could go straight to the Court of Arbitration for Sport and pick from about 250 arbitrators worldwide.[11] However, now he or she must go to the AAA first.

It is clear that the anti-doping organization has the burden of proof to establish charges against the athlete. It used to be that many sports required the doping agency to prove its charges beyond a reasonable doubt, but now under the WADA Code the new standard to prove an allegation is "to the comfortable satisfaction of the hearing body bearing in mind the seriousness of the allegation which is made."[12] It is a relatively ambiguous standard, which is not something that a lot of American lawyers are necessarily familiar with, although we are certainly becoming more so. The WADA Code enumerates the standard as between a balance of the probabilities but less than a reasonable doubt, which is basically a "clear and convincing standard."

In the case of a positive test, it is assumed that the laboratory has conducted its testing properly. In those circumstances, the USADA only needs to show that, according to the lab documents, there has been a positive test. Then the burden shifts to the athlete to show that there has been some error in the testing process. Then, if the athlete can do that, the burden shifts back to the doping agency. But in a non-analytical case, the doping agency bears the burden of proof the entire time; it has to prove its entire case.

---

[8] See U.S. ANTI-DOPING AGENCY, PROTOCOL FOR OLYMPIC MOVEMENT TESTING 5
(2004), available at http://www.usantidoping.org/files/active/what/protocol.pdf.
[9] Am. Arbitration Ass'n, Sports Arbitration Including Olympic Athlete Disputes Introduction, http://www.adr.org/SportsOlympic (last visited Apr. 6, 2006).
[10] Id.
[11] Id.
[12] WORLD ANTI-DOPING AGENCY, supra note 5, at 12, art. 3.1.

As to the type of evidence that can be used in a positive test case, it is clear that all sorts of documents from the laboratory will be available. In a non-analytical case, the nature and scope of evidence are pretty vague. The WADA Code states that "[f]acts related to anti-doping rule violations may be established by any reliable means, including admissions."[13] That, however, is all the WADA Code says. There is really not a lot of guidance there and only a couple of cases have been decided so far. For example, consider the case of Michelle Collins.[14] She was an Olympic track athlete who broke a number of world and American records a couple of summers ago and who was then charged by the USADA with having violated basically everything. They essentially named every single rule that they could, and said she had violated them and [that she had] taken all sorts of different steroids and other prohibited substances. Michelle was prosecuted with no positive test, but USADA had emails between Michelle and Victor Conte. Michelle apparently admitted in some of those emails that she used substances. USADA also relied on a number of blood and urine tests from BALCO but none of those were positive. They tried to infer from the results that she had used steroids. What is new, a little disturbing, and something athletes should be concerned about, is that USADA tried to conclude that because her endogenous steroid profiles (the steroids that your own body makes including testosterone and epitestosterone) were suppressed, the only explanation could be that she was taking some external source of steroid. The WADA Code, and none of the rules currently in place in the Olympic movement, really contemplated such a use of a longitudinal study. They were looking at the results of Michelle's tests over a pretty long period of time. The panel found her guilty. They found that USADA had proved its case beyond a reasonable doubt, which they could have done based on the admissions alone. But what was a little more troubling was that they found the blood and urine tests did show that she had used prohibited substances. Unfortunately, her lawyer actually stipulated that all of the test results were correct, which was something that was highly contested in Christy Gaines's case and in another one similar to Christy's case.

These non-analytical positive cases really raise some issues that are a concern to Olympic athletes. If Congress decides to subject professional athletes to the same sorts of testing and anti-doping programs, then other athletes will also have this concern. The cost for the athlete could be enormous. Usually, the adjudication of a positive test case takes at most a

---

[13] Id. at 12, art. 3.2.

[14] See, e.g., Michelle Collins Suspended for Doping, USATODAY.COM, Dec. 10, 2004, available at http://www.usatoday.com/sports/olympics/summer/track/2004-12-10-col
lins-suspended_x.htm.

couple of months, partly because athletes are competing and want a quick resolution of their cases. Christy's case went on for a year and a half and the legal fees were nearly $400,000. USADA spent 2.5 million dollars to prosecute her case and some other BALCO cases. Most athletes cannot afford this.

A second issue is the mere inference of wrongdoing. Marion Jones was a great example of this. Marion was never charged with any kind of doping offense, but USADA inferred that she may have used some substances based on documents they saw from BALCO. Marion's career and her reputation were tarnished, even though she was never charged. A third issue is the doping agency's authority in these cases. USADA often seems like a quasi-criminal-kind of investigatory body and I am not certain their powers go quite as far as they think they should.

The fourth and final issue relates to the costs. The time involved in resolving disputes is a big issue for athletes since Olympic and professional athletes have a limited time window in which they can compete. In protracted cases, the athlete is unofficially sanctioned from competing while the case is being heard. In the sport of track and field, and other sports, however, athletes can compete in meets only if the race director invites them.

There already have been a number of issues relating to these non-analytical positive cases that have arisen, and I think they will only continue to be more prevalent going forward.


**Notes & Questions**

1. The following story regarding sprint coach, Trevor Graham, comes from Cherry, Gene, *Crawford Leaves Coach Graham*;
**http://abcnews.go.com/Sports/wireStory?id=2636561**
(last updated November 7, 2006):

> Graham, who has coached some of the world's top sprinters, was indicted last week by a U.S. grand jury on three counts of making false statements related to steroid distribution. Graham helped unmask the BALCO doping scandal in 2003 by sending the U.S. Anti-Doping Agency (USADA) a used syringe with small amounts of the previously undetectable steroid THG. He is charged with lying to federal agents investigating the scandal. Graham is due to be arraigned in

San Francisco on Nov. 16 and could face as much a five years in prison for each count if found guilty. His attorney has said Graham is not guilty. Graham also is under investigation by the International Association of Athletics Federations (IAAF) and USADA, and the U.S. Olympic Committee (USOC) has banned him from using its facilities. More than six athletes Graham has coached have been suspended for doping or tested positive for performance-enhancing drugs.

2. And then there is this story about 2006 Tour De France winner, Floyd Landis:

> After testing positive for high and synthetic testosterone, Floyd Landis still maintains his innocence. Landis is scheduled to go before an arbitration panel in January or February and will formally appeal doping violations that could cost him his Tour de France and a two-year ban. *Landis' Online Defense Argues Lab Made Mistakes* http://sports.espn.go.com/oly/cycling/news/story?id=262244 5 (Last updated October 12, 2006).

***For Further Reading on Olympic Sports, Private Associations, Drug Testing see:***

Ian S. Blackshaw, *Have the Wheels Already Been Invented: The Court for Arbitration in Sport,* TMC Asser Press 2002.

Laurence M. Rose, *Drug Testing in Professional and College Sports*, 36 U.KAN.L.REV. 787 (1988).

John A. Scanlan, Jr., *Playing the Drug Testing Game: College Athletes, Regulatory Institutions and the Structures of Constitutional Argument*; 62 IND. L.J. 863 (1987).

John C. Weistart & Cym H. Lowell, Law of Sports, §1.03 Status of the Amateur Athlete (Bobbs-Merrill Company, Inc., 1979).

John C. Weistart & Cym H. Lowell, Law of Sports, §§ 1.25, 2.07 Drugs (Bobbs-Merrill Company, Inc., 1979).

# Chapter 2

## Torts I: Athlete-To-Athlete injuries; Facilities Operators

Lawyers and law students are familiar with the law of Torts. First year students spend many hours learning about intentional torts, such as assault and battery, and various aspects of negligence, and perhaps product liability as well. For example, law students learn that in order to prove negligence, a plaintiff must prove, by a preponderance of the evidence, that the defendant: 1) owed a duty of reasonable care to the plaintiff; 2) breached that duty by failing to act as a reasonable person would have acted under those or similar circumstances; 3) proximately caused harm to the plaintiff (*i.e.*, the plaintiff's harm was a foreseeable consequence of the defendant's conduct); and, 4) the plaintiff suffered an injury as a result of the defendant's breach of duty.

The first two cases, *Jaworski* and *McKichan*, explore athlete-to-athlete injuries. Pay particular attention to how and why the courts treat these injuries differently from non-sports injuries. The next two cases, *Benejam* and *Strickland*, look at the liability of owners of facilities. Law students often read cases that deal with the liability of property owners. Many courts have said, for example, that property owners owe a "higher duty of care" to persons who have been invited onto their property (*e.g.*, guests such as spectators) than persons who are trespassers. You may wish to ask yourself how the courts' reasoning in *Benejam* and *Strickland* compares with the standard "invitor/invitee" analysis, and whether the fact that sports are involved makes any difference in the courts' decisions.

# Cynthia A. Jaworksi v. Harry Kiernan
241 Conn. 399 (1997)
Supreme Court of Connecticut

CALLAHAN, Chief Justice.

The sole issue in this appeal is what duty of care the defendant, Harry Kiernan, owed the plaintiff, Cynthia A. Jaworski, while both were participating on opposing teams in an adult coed soccer game sponsored by the recreation department of the town of South Windsor. We conclude that the defendant owed the plaintiff a duty of care to refrain from reckless or intentional conduct. Because the jury determined that the defendant's conduct, which caused the plaintiff's injuries, was negligent only, and not reckless or intentional, we reverse the judgment of the trial court.

The jury reasonably could have found the following facts. The South Windsor recreation department sponsors an outdoor adult coed soccer league. On May 16, 1993, during a game, the defendant made contact with the plaintiff while she was shielding the soccer ball from the opposition so that the goalie on her team could retrieve the ball. As a result of this incident, the plaintiff suffered an injury to her left anterior cruciate ligament, which caused a 15 percent permanent partial disability of her left knee.

The plaintiff brought this action against the defendant in two counts. In the first count, she alleged that the defendant failed to exercise due care and that his conduct was negligent and careless in that he "hit" and "tripped" her from behind and that he challenged a female player, both in violation of league rules.[1] The plaintiff further alleged that the defendant's negligent conduct caused her injury. In the second count, the plaintiff alleged that the defendant's conduct was wanton and reckless, citing the same violations of league rules, and claiming that his conduct caused identical harm. The defendant moved to strike the plaintiff's negligence count, claiming that a participant in an athletic contest is, as a matter of law, not liable to a coparticipant for injuries sustained as a result of simple negligence during the playing of the game. The defendant's motion was denied. The defendant

---

[1] One rule in effect for league games was the "challenge rule," which provides: "No male player may challenge a female player, however, he may 'post up' if more than six feet away at the time of possession. In the event of an infraction, the female player will be awarded a direct free kick (the exception is [the] goalie in the penalty area). "Any male player who is called for challenging a female player twice during the course of a game may be charged with unsportsmanlike conduct (at discretion of referee) and awarded a yellow card." South Windsor Recreation Dept., Adult Coed Soccer Program Rules and Regs. (1992).

then filed a special defense to the plaintiff's action, alleging that the plaintiff's own conduct was negligent, and that the plaintiff's negligence exceeded his alleged negligence. The jury returned a verdict for the plaintiff on the first count of her complaint, the negligence count, and found no comparative negligence attributable to the plaintiff. The jury found for the defendant on the second count of the plaintiff's complaint wherein she had alleged reckless conduct. The jury awarded the plaintiff damages in the amount of $20,910.33, the exact amount of her medical bills.

Because we conclude that participants in a team athletic contest owe a duty to refrain only from reckless or intentional conduct toward other participants, we reverse in part the judgment and remand the case with direction to strike the first count of the plaintiff's complaint.

The plaintiff, in support of the trial court's conclusion that negligence is the proper standard of care to apply to team athletic competition, argues that the theory of negligence is flexible enough to fix a person's standard of care for any set of circumstances.[2] In addition, the plaintiff cites *Walsh v. Machlin,* 128 Conn. 412, 23 A.2d 156 (1941), wherein the plaintiff was injured when struck by a golf ball, for the proposition that we have already determined that negligence is the appropriate standard to apply to conduct that occurs during an athletic contest. In particular, the plaintiff points to our statement in *Walsh* that "[i]t is undisputed that the duty to the plaintiff which rested upon the defendant while playing this game was the usual one of reasonable care under the circumstances." *Id.,* at 414, 23 A.2d 156. The plaintiff also argues that the assumption of risk principles upon which a reckless conduct standard of care is based--*i.e.,* that plaintiffs have assumed

---

[2] The jury was instructed that it could consider the following factors when assessing the defendant's alleged negligence: "In the present context you may wish to consider the following circumstances, along with any other you deem relevant in determining whether the defendant breached his duty to act as a reasonable person under all of the circumstances of a sports event. What type of sport and game were involved, which in this case was an amateur coed recreational soccer game. The generally accepted customs and practices of amateur coed recreational soccer including the types of contact and the level of violence generally accepted in such games; whether the game was conducted pursuant to a recognized set of rules, and, if so, what those rules were; whether the conduct as you find it to be violated a rule of the game, and, if so, whether the rule was designed for the safety of participants; what risks were and were not inherent in the coed recreational soccer game as was expected to be played in this setting; the presence or absence of protective equipment; the ages, physical characteristics and skills of the participants; what degree of competitiveness was involved; what knowledge of the rules and customs of the game the participants possessed; what relationship the conduct of the participants bore to the ultimate purpose of the contest."

the risk of negligent conduct, but not of reckless or intentional conduct, by their participation in the athletic contest--(1) are incompatible with Connecticut law, and 2) have been replaced by General Statutes § 52-572h, and therefore, the reckless conduct standard is inappropriate. Last, the plaintiff makes a public policy argument, stating that "society has an obligation not to tolerate behavior which is unreasonable, especially when it involves the violation of [athletic] safety rules."

The defendant, on the other hand, summarizes cases from foreign jurisdictions, the vast majority of which has adopted an intentional or reckless conduct standard of care for athletic contests. He also presents two public policy arguments, which he contends support that conclusion: (1) promoting vigorous competition and participation; and (2) avoiding a flood of litigation. ***

We first note that the determination of whether a duty exists between individuals is a question of law. Only if a duty is found to exist does the trier of fact go on to determine whether the defendant has violated that duty.

"Duty is a 'legal conclusion about relationships between individuals, made after the fact, and imperative to a negligence cause of action. The nature of the duty, and the specific persons to whom it is owed, are determined by the circumstances surrounding the conduct of the individual.' 2 D. Pope, Connecticut Actions and Remedies, Tort Law (1993) § 25:05, p. 25-7. Although it has been said that 'no universal test for [duty] ever has been formulated'; W. Prosser & W. Keeton, [Torts (5th Ed.1984)] § 53, p. 358; our threshold inquiry has always been whether the specific harm alleged by the plaintiff was foreseeable to the defendant. 'The ultimate test of the existence of the duty to use care is found in the foreseeability that harm may result if it is not exercised.... By that is not meant that one charged with negligence must be found actually to have foreseen the probability of harm or that the particular injury which resulted was foreseeable, but the test is, would the ordinary [person] in the defendant's position, knowing what he knew or should have known, anticipate that harm of the general nature of that suffered was likely to result?'

"A simple conclusion that the harm to the plaintiff was foreseeable, however cannot by itself mandate a determination that a legal duty exists. Many harms are quite literally 'foreseeable,' yet for pragmatic reasons, no recovery is allowed. *** A further inquiry must be made, for we recognize 'that "duty" is not sacrosanct in itself, but is only an expression of the sum total of those considerations of policy which lead the law to say that the plaintiff is entitled to protection.' W. Prosser & W. Keeton, supra, § 53, p.

358. "While it may seem that there should be a remedy for every wrong, this is an ideal limited perforce by the realities of this world. Every injury has ramifying consequences, like the ripplings of the waters, without end. The problem for the law is to limit the legal consequences of wrongs to a controllable degree."... *Maloney v. Conroy,* supra, at 401- 402, 545 A.2d 1059. The final step in the duty inquiry, then, is to make a determination of 'the fundamental policy of the law, as to whether the defendant's responsibility should extend to such results.' W. Prosser & W. Keeton, supra, § 43, p. 281."

Our first step in an analysis of whether a duty exists and the extent of the defendant's duty, therefore, is to determine the foreseeability of the plaintiff' injury, *i.e.,* whether a reasonable person in the defendant's position, knowing what he knew or should have known, would have anticipated the harm that resulted from his actions. Soccer, while not as violent a sport as football, is nevertheless replete with occasions when the participants make contact with one another during the normal course of the game. When two soccer players vie for control of the ball, the lower limbs are especially vulnerable to injury.[3] If a player seeks to challenge another player who has possession of the ball or seeks to prevent another player from gaining possession of the ball,[4] the resulting contact could reasonably be foreseen to result in injury to either player. We conclude, therefore, that the plaintiff's injury was foreseeable.

Having concluded that the plaintiff's injury was a foreseeable consequence of the defendant's actions, we need to determine as a matter of policy the extent of the legal duty to be imposed upon the defendant. In order to determine the extent of the defendant's responsibility, we consider: (1) the normal expectations of participants in the sport in which the plaintiff and the defendant were engaged; (2) the public policy of encouraging continued vigorous participation in recreational sporting activities while weighing the safety of the participants; (3) the avoidance of increased litigation; and (4) the decisions of other jurisdictions.

In athletic competitions, the object obviously is to win. In games, particularly those played by teams and involving some degree of physical

---

[3] Indeed, the league in which the parties participated, cognizant of probably leg injuries, required participants to wear shin guards and prohibited the use of metal spikes on participants' shoes.

[4] The jury returned to a general verdict for the plaintiff on the negligence count, and therefore, made no finding regarding whether the plaintiff had possession of the ball when the injury occurred and whether the challenge rule; see footnote 1, had been violated.

contact, it is reasonable to assume that the competitive spirit of the participants will result in some rules violations and injuries. That is why there are penalty boxes, foul shots, free kicks, and yellow cards. Indeed, the specific rules applicable to *this game* demonstrate that rules violations were expected in the normal course of the game... Some injuries may result from such violations, but such violations are nonetheless an accepted part of any competition. Simply put, when competitive sports are played, we expect that a participant's main objective is to be a winner, and we expect that the players will pursue that objective enthusiastically. We also anticipate that players in their enthusiasm will commit inadvertent rules violations from which injuries may result. The normal expectations of participants in contact team sports include the potential for injuries resulting from conduct that violates the rules of the sport. These expectations, in turn, inform the question of the extent of the duty owed by one participant to another. We conclude that the normal expectations of participants in contact team sports counsel the adoption of a reckless or intentional conduct duty of care standard for those participants.

A proper balance of the relevant public policy considerations surrounding sports injuries arising from team contact sports also supports limiting the defendant's responsibility for injuries to other participants to injuries resulting from reckless or intentional conduct. The Appellate Court of Illinois, in *Nabozny v. Barnhill,* 31 Ill.App.3d 212, 334 N.E.2d 258 (1975), was the first appellate court, of which we are aware, to address the issue that is before us today. In *Nabozny,* the court described the tension between two relevant public policy considerations as follows: "This court believes that the law should not place unreasonable burdens on the free and vigorous participation in sports by our youth. However, we also believe that organized, athletic competition does not exist in a vacuum. Rather, some of the restraints of civilization must accompany every athlete on to the playing field." *Id.,* at 215, 334 N.E.2d 258. The court thereafter concluded that a player was liable only for deliberate, wilful or reckless conduct. *Id.*

We too appreciate the tension between promoting vigorous athletic competition on the one hand and protecting those who participate on the other. As have most jurisdictions, we conclude that this balance is best achieved by allowing a participant in an athletic contest to maintain an action against a coparticipant only for reckless or intentional conduct and not for merely negligent conduct. We believe that participants in recreational sports will not alter their enthusiasm for competition or their participation in recreational activities for fear of liability for injuring someone because of their reckless or intentional conduct. We are convinced, however, that liability for simple negligence would have an opposite effect. We also are convinced that a recklessness standard will sufficiently protect participants in athletic contests by affording them a right of action against those who cause injuries not inherent in the particular game in which the participants are engaged. In other words, we believe that the reckless or intentional conduct standard of care will maintain civility and relative safety in team sports without dampening the competitive spirit of the participants.

A final public policy concern that influences our decision is our desire to stem the possible flood of litigation that might result from adopting simple negligence as the standard of care to be utilized in athletic contests. If simple negligence were adopted as the standard of care, every punter with whom contact is made, every midfielder high sticked, every basketball player fouled, every batter struck by a pitch, and every hockey player tripped would have the ingredients for a lawsuit if injury resulted. When the number of athletic events taking place in Connecticut over the course of a year is considered, there exists the potential for a surfeit of lawsuits when it becomes known that simple negligence, based on an inadvertent violation of a contest rule, will suffice as a ground for recovery for an athletic injury. This should not be encouraged.

The majority of jurisdictions addressing this issue has chosen to adopt either a reckless or an intentional conduct standard of care when determining liability for injuries that occur during an athletic contest. *Nabozny v. Barnhill,* supra, 31 Ill.App.3d 212, 334 N.E.2d 258, also involved an injury received during a soccer game. The plaintiff was a goalie on one team and had fielded the ball within the penalty area surrounding his goal. The ball had been passed to the plaintiff by a teammate who was closely pursued by the defendant, an opponent. The defendant did not turn away after the plaintiff had fielded the ball, but continued to run toward him and subsequently kicked the plaintiff, causing injury. The court concluded that "a player is liable for injury in a tort action if his conduct is such that it is either deliberate, wilful or with a reckless disregard for the safety of the other player so as to cause injury to that player, the same being a question of fact to be decided by a jury." *Id.*, at 215, 334 N.E.2d 258.

\*\*\*

In *Crawn v. Campo,* 136 N.J. 494, 496, 643 A.2d 600 (1994), the "[p]laintiff was playing catcher in a pickup softball game and was injured when [the] defendant, attempting to score from second base, either slid or ran into him at home plate." In rejecting the negligence standard, the court concluded: "One might well conclude that something is terribly wrong with a society in which the most commonly-accepted aspects of play--a traditional source of a community's conviviality and cohesion--spurs litigation. The heightened recklessness standard recognizes a commonsense distinction between excessively harmful conduct and the more routine rough-and-tumble of sports that should occur freely on the playing fields and should not be second-guessed in courtrooms." *Id.,* at 508, 643 A.2d 600.

Finally, we address the plaintiff's contention that in *Walsh v. Machlin,* supra, 128 Conn. 412, 23 A.2d 156, we imposed the negligence standard as the appropriate standard to be used for injuries occurring during athletic contests. *Walsh* is, however, distinguishable.

In *Walsh,* both the plaintiff's and the defendant's golf balls were roughly one hundred feet from the green. "Standing by the defendant's ball, the plaintiff and [the] defendant discussed the club the defendant should use and the defendant selected his mashie niblick.[5] The plaintiff, seeing the defendant about to prepare to take his shot, said, 'Now put it on the green,' and walked away at almost right angles to the direct and intended line of flight from the ball to the green. Without calling 'Fore,' the defendant swung at his ball, shanked it so that it was deflected at almost a ninety degree angle to the right and hit the plaintiff in the eye as he turned to look back over his left shoulder just as he had reached his ball, causing him serious injury." *Id.,* at 413, 23 A.2d 156.

Our conclusion herein does not conflict with *Walsh* because, initially, we decide the standard to be applied to only those injuries occurring during team athletic contests involving contact as part of the game. Golf, generally, is neither a team sport in the true sense nor a sport where contact with other participants is a part of the game. Further, the normal expectations of participants in a golf match are far different from those inherent in soccer, and therefore a different standard of care may be appropriate. We, therefore, leave the question of what standard of care might be applicable in other factual circumstances for another day.

Applying the foregoing considerations to the facts before us, we conclude that, as a matter of policy, it is appropriate to adopt a standard of care imposing on the defendant, a participant in a team contact sport, a legal duty to refrain from reckless or intentional conduct. Proof of mere negligence is insufficient to create liability.

---

[5] Mashie niblick: "[A]n iron golf club with a loft between those of a mashie and a niblick--called also number six iron." Webster's Third New International Dictionary.

70

The judgment is reversed in part and the case is remanded with direction to strike the first count of the plaintiff's complaint.

In this opinion the other justices concurred.

## Notes & Questions

1. Why should the rules of tort liability in an athletic context be any different from ordinary rules of tort liability?

2. First year law students learn the principle of "negligence per se." As was noted in the introduction to this chapter, the general rule regarding proof of negligence requires that a plaintiff prove four elements: duty, breach, proximate cause, and injury. However, when an action is characterized as negligence *per se*, a court waives the necessity for a plaintiff to produce certain types of evidence. The court simply demands less proof from the plaintiff.

For example, most jurisdictions agree that if a defendant violates a written law (statute), and if the plaintiff is injured as a result of the defendant's violation of that statute, and if the plaintiff is a member of the class of persons whom the statute was designed to protect, then the doctrine of negligence *per se* is applicable. Fundamentally, in such circumstances, a plaintiff does not need to prove the standard negligence elements of duty and breach (elements that are often very difficult to prove). Rather, the doctrine of negligence *per* se allows a court to substitute proof that the defendant violated a statute and that the plaintiff was in the class of persons whom the statute was designed to protect in place of the ordinary requirements that the plaintiff must prove duty and breach. The theory is simple. Proof that a defendant violated a statute and that the plaintiff belongs to the protected class take the place of - or substitute for - proof that the defendant owed a duty to the plaintiff and that the defendant breached that duty. The violation of the statute *by itself* (*per se*) proves that the defendant breached a duty owed to the plaintiff.

Would a similar analysis be useful for sports? In other words, should courts consider that a rule violation (*e.g.*, in football pulling an opponent's facemask or running into a kicker or punter) is similar to violation of a statute for purposes of a negligence *per se* analysis? What would be the advantages of such an analysis? Disadvantages?

3. Explain the role of comparative negligence with respect to athlete-to-athlete injuries during competition. Can you articulate the relationship between the doctrine of assumption of risk, consent, and contributory or comparative negligence in such cases? What are the doctrinal choices that courts are faced with in these circumstances? The next case explains more about what these legal terms mean and how courts may consider them in the context of athletic competition.

4. At the close of this decision, the court notes that soccer is a sport that involves a significant amount of physical contact (unlike golf); and suggests that the "contact" factor is relevant. Sports such as skydiving, gymnastics, ski jumping, and pole vaulting, technically speaking, are not contact sports in the traditional sense (like soccer and football). Do you think that the liability rules for injuries caused by participation in those sports should be any different from the rule articulated in this case? Why or why not?

### Stephen McKichan v. St. Louis Hockey Club
967 SW 2d 209 (1998)
Missouri Court of Appeals, Eastern District, Division One.

GRIMM, Presiding Judge.

In this personal injury case, plaintiff, a professional hockey goaltender, was injured during a game. He sued the opposing player (defendant player) who charged into him. In addition, he sued the defendant player's "owner," defendant herein.

Defendant player filed a counterclaim. About three weeks before trial, plaintiff and defendant player dismissed their claims against each other with prejudice. The case proceeded against defendant under a vicarious liability theory and a jury awarded plaintiff $175,000.

Both parties appeal. Defendant raises six points; its second point controls. In that point, defendant alleges the trial court erred in finding it vicariously liable for defendant player's acts because the conduct at issue was a risk inherent in professional hockey and one assumed by plaintiff. We agree and reverse. Plaintiff's cross-appeal claiming the trial court erred in granting defendant's motion for directed verdict on his punitive damages claim is denied as moot.

# I. Background

In 1988, plaintiff signed a contract with the Vancouver Canucks, a professional National Hockey League team. The team assigned him to its professional "minor league" International Hockey League (IHL) team, the Milwaukee Admirals.

On December 15, 1990, the Milwaukee Admirals played the Peoria Rivermen in a regulation IHL game in Peoria, Illinois. The Peoria Rivermen is an IHL team affiliated with defendant.

IHL hockey is played on an ice rink measuring at least 200 feet by 85 feet with goals on opposing ends of the ice. The rink is surrounded by a wall made partially of clear plexiglass, customarily referred to as the "boards." The rink is divided in two by a center line. On each side of the center line is a line called the "blue line." The blue lines are parallel to the center line and have to be at least 60 feet from the boards behind the goals. A game consists of three twenty-minute periods.

In the second period, an incident took place between plaintiff and defendant player. Plaintiff was penalized as a result of that incident.

During the third period, plaintiff and defendant player were both playing and "on the ice." A videotape of the incident discloses that defendant player was skating near center ice and plaintiff was positioned in front of his goal. The hockey puck was shot in the general direction of plaintiff's goal by defendant player's teammate. However, it traveled over the goal and the boards and out of play. As the puck was traveling, plaintiff skated several yards to the side of the goal. A linesman blew his whistle stopping play. About this time, plaintiff began turning his body toward the boards and moved closer to them. As plaintiff was moving away from the goal, defendant player was skating from the near blue line toward plaintiff.

Defendant player continued skating toward plaintiff after a second whistle. Holding his stick, defendant player partially extended both arms and hit plaintiff with his body and the stick, knocking plaintiff into the boards. Plaintiff fell to the ice and was knocked unconscious. Defendant player received a "match penalty" from the referee and was suspended for a period of games by the IHL.

## II. Discussion

Defendant's second point alleges the trial court erred in denying its motion for judgment notwithstanding the verdict. It contends that the "contact at issue, a check between opposing players, is a risk inherent in professional hockey and one assumed by professional hockey players."

The case was tried under Illinois contact sports law as it has been applied to amateur sports. To the extent that this law is relevant, the practical significance of which forum's law applies is minimal if any because Missouri has essentially adopted the Illinois standard.

In amateur contact sports, both Illinois and Missouri courts have held that ordinary negligence is insufficient to state a claim for an injury caused by a co-participant. *See, e.g. Pfister v. Shusta,* 167 Ill.2d 417, 212 Ill.Dec. 668, 669, 657 N.E.2d 1013, 1014 (1995); *Ross v. Clouser,* 637 S.W.2d 11, 14 (Mo.banc 1982). Rather, in amateur contact sports, liability must be predicated on "willful and wanton or intentional misconduct." *Pfister,* 212 Ill.Dec. at 669, 657 N.E.2d at 1014.

In *Pfister,* the plaintiff and the defendant were engaged in a spontaneous can kicking game in the hall of a college dormitory. During the game, the plaintiff allegedly pushed the defendant and the defendant responded by pushing the plaintiff. As a result, the plaintiff was injured when his left hand and forearm went through a glass door of a fire extinguisher case. The Ilinois Supreme Court adopted the "willful and wanton" requirement first created by an Illinois appellate court in *Nabozny v. Barnhill,* 31 Ill.App.3d 212, 334 N.E.2d 258 (1975).

*Nabozny* involved a high school soccer game. The plaintiff, a goalie, went down on his left knee, received a pass, and pulled the ball to his chest. The defendant, an opposing player, was running toward the ball and continued to run toward the plaintiff after he gained possession of the ball. The defendant kicked the plaintiff's head causing injuries. The *Nabozny* court held that the ordinary care standard did not apply in this amateur contact sport. Instead, it adopted a new rule "in order to control a new field of personal injury litigation." *Id.* at 261. It held that a participant would be liable for injuries if the participant's conduct was either "deliberate, wilful or with a reckless disregard for the safety of the other player." *Id.* at 261

Missouri essentially adopted the *Nabozny* rule in *Ross. Ross,* 637 S.W.2d at 13-14. *Ross* involved a slow pitch church league softball game. There, the defendant base runner was injured after colliding with the plaintiff, an opposing third baseman. The trial court submitted the case to the jury on a negligence theory. In reversing and remanding, the supreme court stated "a cause of action for personal injuries incurred during athletic competition must be predicated on recklessness, not mere negligence...." This heightened standard has been accepted by many jurisdictions and applied to both formal and informal amateur contact sports. Under these decisions involving amateur contact sports, ordinary negligence principles are inapplicable. Thus, these courts have implicitly found that conduct which might be "unreasonable" in everyday society is not actionable because it occurs on the athletic field. In contact sports, physical contact and injuries among participants is inherent and unwarranted judicial intervention might inhibit the game's vigor.

All of the above cases discuss the contact sports law in the context of amateur sports. Neither parties' briefs, nor our own research, disclose any Illinois or Missouri case applying the contact sports law to professional sports. In fact, the parties have referred us to only two cases discussing participant liability in professional athletics, *Averill v. Luttrell,* 44 Tenn.App. 56, 311 S.W.2d 812 (1957) and *Hackbart v. Cincinnati Bengals, Inc.,* 601 F.2d 516 (10th Cir.1979).

*Averill* involves minor league professional baseball players. There, the plaintiff was at bat when the pitcher threw three inside pitches and a fourth pitch which hit the plaintiff. The plaintiff threw his bat in the direction of the pitcher's mound. As that happened, the catcher, "without any warning whatsoever, stepped up behind [the plaintiff] and struck him a hard blow on the side or back of the head with his fist." The plaintiff sued both the catcher and his baseball club and obtained a judgment against both defendants.

Only the baseball club appealed. The *Averill* court reversed the judgment. The opinion does not discuss the standard of care owed by one professional player to another. Rather, it held that the club was not liable for the wilful acts of the catcher when he stepped outside of the club's business and committed an act wholly independent and foreign to the scope of his employment. *Id.*

The other case is *Hackbart.* In that case, the plaintiff, a professional football player, placed one knee on the ground after his team intercepted a pass and watched the play. An opposing player hit the back of the plaintiff's head with his right forearm, causing both players to fall to the ground. Later, the plaintiff sued the opposing player and his team for a neck injury. The trial court entered judgment for the defendants and the plaintiff appealed.

On appeal, the *Hackbart* court reversed and remanded. It held that "recklessness is the appropriate standard." In addition to considering whether the contact sports exception is applicable to the facts before us, the doctrines of assumption of risk and consent also must be considered. In general, a voluntary participant in any lawful sport assumes all risks that reasonably inhere to the sport insofar as they are obvious and usually incident to the game. Under contact sports analysis as applied to amateur sports, participants in team sports assume greater risks of injury than nonparticipants or participants in non-contact sports.

In practice, the concepts of duty, assumption of risk, and consent must be analyzed on a case-by-case basis. Whether one player's conduct causing injury to another is actionable hinges upon the facts of an individual case. Relevant factors include the specific game involved, the ages and physical attributes of the participants, their respective skills at the game and their knowledge of its rules and customs, their status as amateurs or professionals, the type of risks which inhere to the game and those which are outside the realm of reasonable anticipation, the presence or absence of protective uniforms or equipment, the degree of zest with which the game is being played, and other factors.

We apply these concepts and factors to the case before us. The specific game was a professional hockey game, not an amateur game. It was not a pickup, school, or college game.

Rough play is commonplace in professional hockey. Anyone who has attended a professional hockey game or seen one on television recognizes the violent nature of the sport. In order to gain possession of the puck or to slow down the progress of opponents, players frequently hit each other with body checks. They trip opposing players, slash at them with their hockey sticks, and fight on a regular basis, often long after the referee blows the whistle. Players regularly commit contact beyond that which is permitted by the rules, and, we are confident, do it intentionally. They wear pads, helmets and other protective equipment because of the rough nature of the sport.

Professional hockey is played at a high skill level with well conditioned athletes, who are financially compensated for their participation. They are professional players with knowledge of its rules and customs, including the violence of the sport. In part, the game is played with great intensity because its players can reap substantial financial rewards. We also recognize that the professional leagues have internal mechanisms for penalizing players and teams for violating league rules and for compensating persons who are injured.

In summary, we find that the specific conduct at issue in this case, a severe body check, is a part of professional hockey. This body check, even several seconds after the whistle and in violation of several rules of the game, was not outside the realm of reasonable anticipation. For better or for worse, it is "part of the game" of professional hockey. As such, we hold as a matter of law that the specific conduct which occurred here is not actionable.

The trial court's judgment is reversed.

Stephen McKichan , photo published courtesy of Stephen McKichan

## Notes & Questions

1. What difference does it make that this injury occurs in a professional game rather than an amateur game?

2. At what point does a hockey player's conduct go beyond that which is reasonably anticipated? Does the nature of the sport matter? For example,

would this type of violence be considered within the bounds of reasonable anticipation in baseball or basketball? How about tennis, golf, track and field, equestrian, ice dancing? How does the court's statement that "a voluntary participant in any lawful sport assumes all risks that reasonably inhere to the sport insofar as they are obvious and usually incident to the game" help answer this question? Or if it doesn't answer the question, how does this statement help to provide guidelines for answering the question on an ad hoc, case by case, or sport by sport, basis?

3. Also relevant is the principle of vicarious liability, or *respondeat superior.* Fundamentally, the doctrine of *respondeat superior* ("let the one above reply") imposes tort liability on employers for the torts of their employees. This doctrine only applies when an employee is acting within the scope of his or her employment. For example, when a pizza shop delivery driver, while in the process of making a pizza delivery, negligently causes an auto accident, the persons injured by the pizza shop driver's negligence will be successful in their lawsuit against the pizza shop (*i.e.,* the owners or the corporation). We say that the pizza shop is vicariously liable for the negligence of its employee while the employee was acting within the scope of his or her employment. On the other hand, courts might reach a different legal result if the delivery driver had not been in the process of delivering pizzas when the accident occurred. For example, if the delivery driver instead had decided to drive to the next county to engage in a drug deal on his way back from a pizza delivery, a court may decide that the act of driving to the next county to engage in a drug deal was so far removed from his employer's purpose, that such conduct should no longer be considered "within the scope of employment." In such circumstances, courts frequently state that the employee was on his own "frolic or detour" and therefore the employer cannot be held vicariously liable under the doctrine of *respondeat superior.* This is what the *Averill* court held when it found that the catcher who hit the batter on the head had " stepped oputside the club's business and committed an act wholly independent and foreign to the scope of his employment."

How might a court determine when an athlete's conduct constitutes a "frolic or detour," relieving the team, club, or organization of liability? When Pedro Martinez tossed Don Zimmer to the ground - when Zimmer was charging Martinez - was Martinez's conduct a "frolic and detour?"

4. Tennessee Titans defensive lineman Albert Haynesworth made history for the NFL's longest suspension for on-field action. Haynesworth was suspended for five games as a result of a head stomp on a helmet-less Dallas Cowboys center Andre Gurode. The action began early in the third quarter

in the Titans vs. Cowboys game on October 1, 2006, after a 5-yard touchdown run by the Cowboys' Julius Jones. Following the run Gurode's helmet came off and he was on his back. Haynesworth was standing over him and proceeded to first kick Gurode's unprotected head and then scraped his cleats across Gurode's face and forehead. Officials threw a penalty flag and in protest Haynesworth removed his helmet and tossed it, earning Haynesworth a second personal foul and ejection. The suspension began immediately and was without pay costing Haynesworth an estimated $190,000 of his $646,251.00 salary. See Weir, Tom, Titans' Haynesworth Suspended Five Games For Stomping Incident; http://www.usatoday.com/sports/football/nfl/titans/2006-10-02-haynesworth-suspension_x.htm, Oct. 2, 2006.

Analyze Haynesworth's conduct using the legal rules articulated in *McKichan*. Explain whether you think that either Haynesworth or the Tennessee Titans ought to be liable to Gurode for his injuries.

5. Stephen McKichan currently runs a school for goalies in Ontario Canada.

## Benejam v. Detroit Tigers
### 635 NW 2d 219 (2001)
#### Court of Appeals of Michigan

BANDSTRA, C.J.

In this case, we are asked to determine whether we should adopt, as a matter of Michigan law, the "limited duty" rule that other jurisdictions have applied with respect to spectator injuries at baseball games. Under that rule, a baseball stadium owner is not liable for injuries to spectators that result from projectiles leaving the field during play if safety screening has been provided behind home plate and there are a sufficient number of protected seats to meet ordinary demand. We conclude that the limited duty doctrine should be adopted as a matter of Michigan law and that there was no evidence presented at trial that defendants failed to meet that duty. Further, we conclude that there is no duty to warn spectators at a baseball game of the well-known possibility that a bat or ball might leave the field. We therefore conclude that there is no evidence to support the verdict rendered on behalf of plaintiffs against defendant and we reverse and remand.

## FACTS

Plaintiff Alyssia M. Benejam, a young girl, attended a Tigers game with a friend and members of the friend's family and was seated quite close to the playing field along the third base line. The stadium was equipped with a net behind home plate, and the net extended part of the way down the first and third base lines. Although Alyssia was behind the net, she was injured when a player's bat broke and a fragment of it curved around the net.[1] There was no evidence, and plaintiffs do not contend, that the fragment of the bat went through the net, that there was a hole in the net, or that the net was otherwise defective.

Plaintiffs sued the Tigers, claiming primarily [2] that the net was insufficiently long and that warnings about the possibility of projectiles leaving the field were inadequate.[3] The Tigers responded with motions before, during, and after trial arguing that, as a matter of law, plaintiffs could not or did not present any viable legal claim. Those motions were all denied by the trial court. Alyssia suffered crushed fingers as a result of the accident and the jury awarded plaintiffs noneconomic damages (past and future) totaling $917,000, lost earning capacity of $56,700 and $35,000 for past and future medical expenses. Damages are not at issue on appeal.

## STANDARD OF CARE/PROTECTIVE SCREENING

Defendant argues that although there is no Michigan law directly on point, other jurisdictions have balanced the safety benefits of providing a protective screen against the fact that such screening detracts from the allure of attending a live baseball game by placing an obstacle or insulation between fans and the playing field. The rule that emerges in these cases is that a stadium proprietor cannot be liable for spectator injuries if it has satisfied a "limited duty"--to erect a screen that will protect the most

---

[1] Most of the evidence at trial suggested that the bat fragment curved around the net, although it may have traveled in a straight line and bounced off a nearby seat before striking Alyssia.

[2] In addition, plaintiffs elicited evidence at trial that the Tigers' home plate was too close to the spectator stands (about sixteen inches less than the sixty feet required by a league rule). However, there was no evidence that the league rule was for safety purposes (rather than to define the playing field), nor to suggest how this discrepancy materially increased the risk of injury to Alyssia. Nonetheless, plaintiffs did not include the issue in their "theory of the case" presentation to the jury and do not argue this matter on appeal.

[3] Plaintiffs also sued the maker of the bat, Hillerich and Bradsby, but settled that claim before trial.

dangerous area of the spectator stands, behind home plate, and to provide a number of seats in this area sufficient to meet the ordinary demand for protected seats. In this case, there is no dispute that the Tigers constructed a protective screen behind home plate, and there was no evidence that the screen was insufficient to meet the ordinary demand for protected seating. Defendant argues the circuit court erred in failing to recognize the limited duty doctrine....

Plaintiffs argue against application of the limited duty doctrine and contend that, under usual principles of premises liability, the circuit court correctly concluded that a jury question was presented. Defendant (an invitor) had a duty to exercise ordinary care and prudence and maintain premises reasonably safe for invitees like Alyssia. Plaintiffs argue that the jury verdict was supported by sufficient evidence that the defendant failed to fulfill this duty because it did not provide a screen extending long enough along the third (and first) base lines.

There is no Michigan case law directly on point. Our review of precedents from other jurisdictions finds overwhelming, if not universal, support for the limited duty rule that defendant advocates.

The logic of these precedents is that there is an inherent risk of objects leaving the playing field that people know about when they attend baseball games. See, *e.g.*, *Swagger, supra* at 185 ("[n]o one of ordinary intelligence could see many innings of the ordinary league [baseball] game without coming to a full realization that batters cannot and do not control the direction of the ball"), quoting *Brisson v. Minneapolis Baseball & Athletic Ass'n*, 185 Minn. 507, 509-510, 240 N.W. 903 (1932).[4] Also, there is inherent value in having most seats unprotected by a screen because baseball patrons generally want to be involved with the game in an intimate way and are even hoping that they will come in contact with some projectile from the field (in the form of a souvenir baseball). See, *e.g.*, *Rudnick, supra* at 802, 202 Cal.Rptr. 900 ("the chance to apprehend a misdirected baseball is as much a part of the game as the seventh inning stretch or peanuts and Cracker Jack"). In other words, spectators know about the risk of being in the stands and, in fact, welcome that risk to a certain extent. On the other hand, the area behind home plate is especially dangerous and spectators who want protected seats should be able to find them in this area. Balancing all of these concerns, courts generally have adopted the limited duty doctrine that prevents liability if there are a sufficient number of protected seats behind

---

[4] Although many of the cases relied on considered baseballs and other objects that left the field of play and caused injury, we see no difference analytically between those situations and the bat fragment at issue here.

home plate to meet the ordinary demand for that kind of seating. If that seating is provided, the baseball stadium owner has fulfilled its duty and there can be no liability for spectators who are injured by a projectile from the field.

An oft-cited precedent, *Akins v. Glens Falls City School Dist.,* 53 N.Y.2d 325, 441 N.Y.S.2d 644, 424 N.E.2d 531 (1981), provides a good illustration of the reasoning employed. There, a spectator at a baseball game was permanently and seriously injured when a sharply hit foul ball struck her in the eye. As is the case in Michigan, New York has disavowed the "assumption of risk" doctrine and thus the *Akins* court analyzed the situation anew, without reliance on that doctrine. In doing so, the court reasoned that an owner of a baseball field is not an insurer of the safety of its spectators. Rather, like any other owner or occupier of land, it is only under a duty to exercise 'reasonable care under the circumstances' to prevent injury to those who come to watch the games played on its field. [*Id.* (citations omitted).]

The court noted that "many spectators prefer to sit where their view of the game is unobstructed by fences or protective netting and the proprietor of a ball park has a legitimate interest in catering to these desires." Balancing the interests involved, the court adopted what it considered to be the "majority rule"--"the owner must screen the most dangerous section of the field--the area behind home plate--and the screening that is provided must be sufficient for those spectators who may be reasonably anticipated to desire protected seats on an ordinary occasion." *Id.* The *Akins* court reasoned that this rule appropriately recognizes the "practical realities of this sporting event."

We find *Akins* and similar precedents to be well-reasoned and persuasive. It seems axiomatic that baseball fans attend games knowing that, as a natural result of play, objects may leave the field with the potential of causing injury in the stands. It is equally clear that most spectators, nonetheless, prefer to be as "close to the play" as possible, without an insulating and obstructive screen between them and the action. In contrast, a smaller number of spectators prefer the protection offered by screening. The most dangerous part of the spectator stands is the area in the lower deck behind home plate and along each of the baselines. Certainly home plate is the center of the most activity on the field. Most notably, it is there that pitched balls, traveling at great speeds in a line that would extend into the stands, are often deflected or squarely hit into those stands. Quite logically, the limited duty rule protects a stadium owner that provides screening for this most dangerous area and, in so doing, accommodates baseball patrons who seek protected seating. Because the limited duty rule is based on the desires of spectators, it further makes sense to define the extent of screening that should be provided behind home plate on the basis of consumer demand.

Plaintiffs do nothing to argue substantively against the limited duty rule, but merely argue that baseball stadium cases should be governed by usual invitor-invitee principles, not any special "baseball rule." Thus, plaintiffs argue that the jury properly determined that defendant failed to exercise "ordinary care" and failed to provide "reasonably safe" premises. However, the limited duty rule does not ignore or abrogate usual premises liability principles. Instead, it identifies the duty of baseball stadium proprietors with greater specificity than the usual "ordinary care/reasonably safe" standard provides. The limited duty precedents "do not eliminate the stadium owner's duty to exercise reasonable care under the circumstances to protect patrons against injury." *Friedman, supra* at 574, quoting *McNiel v. Ft. Worth Baseball Club,* 268 S.W.2d 244, 246 (Tex.Civ.App. 1954). Rather, these precedents "define that duty so that once the stadium owner has provided 'adequately screened seats' for *all* those desiring them, the stadium owner has fulfilled its duty of care as a matter of law." *Id.* The limited duty doctrine establishes the "outer limits" of liability and " thereby prevent[s] a jury from requiring [a stadium owner] to take precautions that are clearly unreasonable." *Bellezzo, supra* at 554, 851 P.2d 847. By providing greater specificity with regard to the duty imposed on stadium owners, the rule prevents burgeoning litigation that might signal the demise or substantial alteration of the game of baseball as a spectator sport.

We also note that the precedents applying the limited duty rule are consistent with the reasoning of the closest Michigan case available, *Ritchie-Gamester v. City of Berkley,* 461 Mich. 73, 597 N.W.2d 517 (1999). *Ritchie* is not directly on point because it did not involve a spectator at a sporting event but, instead, considered a person injured while participating in recreational ice skating. ****

The Court's reasoning in *Ritchie* is similar to that employed by the limited duty precedents described above. For most fans, the everyday reality of attending a baseball game includes voluntarily subjecting oneself to the risk that a ball or bat might leave the field and cause injury. The limited duty rule comports more nearly with that everyday reality than would usual invitor-invitee principles of liability. While requiring that protected seats be provided for those who want them, the limited duty rule leaves the baseball stadium owner free, without fear of liability, to accommodate the majority of fans who prefer unobstructed and uninsulated contact with the game. Under usual invitor-invitee principles of liability, fear of litigation would likely require screening far in excess of that required to meet the desires of baseball fans.

This case, tried under usual invitor-invitee principles of liability, provides a good example. Plaintiff's expert testified that, on the basis of his review of accidents occurring over time in the spectator stands between first base and third base, reasonable safety precautions would include screening in that entire area. In another case, where an injury occurred farther down the baseline, testimony and argument would likely be adduced to support a further extension as "reasonably necessary" to protect fans. The logical result of having these cases governed by usual invitor-invitee principles of liability would be that warned against in *Akins,* "[E]very spectator injured by a foul ball, no matter where he is seated or standing in the ball park, would have an absolute right to go to the jury on every claim of negligence."

Both because the limited duty doctrine represents a good accommodation of the interests that must be balanced in this case and because it is consistent with the reasoning employed in *Ritchie,* we adopt that doctrine as a matter of Michigan law. Specifically, we hold that a baseball stadium owner that provides screening behind home plate sufficient to meet ordinary demand for protected seating has fulfilled its duty with respect to screening and cannot be subjected to liability for injuries resulting to a spectator by an object leaving the playing field.[5] We do not today hold that a baseball stadium operator that does not provide this level of protection can be held liable. For reasons previously noted, there may be an argument that would prevent the imposition of liability in that situation as well. In any event, that is not the situation presented on this appeal and we express no opinion regarding the merits of any such argument.

Applying the limited duty rule here, we conclude that plaintiffs have failed to provide any proof sufficient to find that liability could be imposed. Clearly, there was a screen behind home plate and there was no proof whatsoever that persons wanting seats protected by the screen could not be accommodated. To the contrary, uncontested testimony by Tigers ticket personnel established that protected seating is generally open and available to fans who want it. Accordingly, we conclude that the screening provided by defendant was sufficient under the limited duty doctrine applicable in this case.

---

[5] This assumes, of course, that the screening provided is not in a state of disrepair or otherwise in a condition whereby projectiles can permeate it and allow injuries to occur in the protected area of the stands.

Plaintiffs also argue that defendant failed to provide an adequate warning regarding the possibility that some object might come flying off the field and cause injury in the stands. However, we conclude that defendant did not have any duty to warn regarding this well-known risk.

Plaintiffs rely primarily on *Falkner v. John E. Fetzer, Inc.,* 113 Mich.App. 500, 317 N.W.2d 337 (1982). While acknowledging the "generally accepted proposition that there is no duty to warn of the risk of being hit by batted balls when attending a baseball game, because the risk is obvious," the *Falkner* panel nonetheless reasoned that "plaintiffs presented an apparently unique record in an attempt to demonstrate that the magnitude of the risk involved is much greater than commonly believed" and, therefore, reasoned that it was "proper to submit to the jury the question whether it would be reasonable to require defendant to warn spectators of the unexpectedly high degree of risk." The opinion does not indicate why the record before the panel was "unique." In any event, we conclude that *Falkner* cannot reasonably be understood as suggesting that, in all cases, baseball stadiums have a duty to warn spectators of the risk that objects from the field might cause injury.

As discussed above, one of the premises of the universally adopted limited duty rule for protective screening is the fact that baseball spectators generally know that attending a game involves risks from off-field projectiles. Accordingly, precedents from other jurisdictions conclude that there is no duty to warn regarding this risk. [case citations omitted] As noted by one court, "[i]t would have been absurd, and no doubt would have been resented by many patrons, if the ticket seller, or other employees, had warned each person entering the park that he or she would be imperiled by vagrant baseballs...." *Keys v. Alamo City Baseball Co.,* 150 S.W.2d 368, 371 (Tex.Civ.App.1941).

We find these precedents to be compelling and persuasive. Further, having concluded that the limited duty rule should be adopted in Michigan partly on the premise that spectators know about the dangers of objects leaving the field, it would be inconsistent to impose a duty to warn of those dangers.

\*\*\*

We conclude that defendant had no duty to warn plaintiffs regarding the well-known risk that some object might leave the playing field and cause injury.[6]

Having concluded that, under the facts of this case, defendant did not breach any duty to provide screening and was under no duty to provide a warning to plaintiffs regarding the risk of injury from objects leaving the field, we reverse the jury verdict and remand this matter for entry of an order finding no cause of action against defendant.

We reverse and remand.

---

[6] We further note that plaintiffs presented little if any evidence regarding how the language of the warnings actually given (a general announcement over the loudspeaker, a notice on the center field video board, and small print language on the back of the ticket) were inadequate. Nor was there any evidence concerning the warning systems used at other ball parks or whether some more effective warning would have made any difference in this case (Alyssia's friend's mother, who chose the seating behind the protective netting, testified that she knew of the risks of balls and bats entering the stands). Accordingly, even if we were to recognize a duty to warn in this context we would conclude that plaintiffs did not present sufficient evidence to support a finding of liability on this basis.***

Tiger Stadium, Detroit, Michigan, Photo courtesy of Andrew Clem

**Notes & Questions**

1. Articulate the so-called "limited duty" rule in your own words? Does it apply only to baseball stadium owners? Or is it applicable to owners of other sporting venues?

2. Assuming that the limited duty rule is applicable in some fashion to other sporting venues, how might it be modified to apply to other types of sporting venues? Can you think of specific types of sporting venues that might pose particular difficulties in applying the limited duty rule?

3. Explain the relationship between the limited duty rule and the doctrine of assumption of risk.

4. Is there a fundamental difference between the duty owed by a venue owner to spectators versus the duty owed to participants? If so, explain the nature of that difference. If not, explain why not.

5. Explain the relationship between the rule articulated in *Benejam* and the rule articulated in *Jaworski*.

# Frances C. Williams v. Rudolph S. Strickland
## 251 NC 767 (1960)
### Supreme Court of North Carolina

PARKER, J.

In 1957 two men and their wives[,] the…defendants[,] purchased a tract of land, which was conveyed to them in fee simple, and began the construction thereon of a stock car race track. On 14 August 1957, the… defendants organized Strickland Enterprises, Inc. to engage in the amusement business, including the operation of a stock car race track. The four individual defendants are the sole stockholders and officers of this corporation. ***

On 24 August 1957, the…defendants began holding stock car races on the premises and charging admission thereto under the name of Edgecombe Speedway. Edgecombe Speedway was and is open to the public as a place of amusement, and the operators of it invited the public to attend the stock car races. Large numbers of people attended the races.

On 22 September 1957, plaintiff, with numerous other persons, purchased from the operators of Edgecombe Speedway admission tickets. There were no grandstand or bleacher seats provided, and plaintiff, with a crowd of other spectators, stood up beyond one end of the race track to watch the races. During the races, and while a number of racing cars were going around the race track at high speeds, a wheel came off one of the racing cars making a turn at the end of the race track near which plaintiff and a crowd of spectators were standing, and 'flew' toward plaintiff at a high speed, striking her and causing her serious injuries.

Defendants were negligent, which negligence was the proximate cause of her injuries, in that: One. They provided no seats of any kind for paid spectators, who were required to stand near the race track to see the races. Two. They failed to provide a fence, wall, or barricade of sufficient height and strength to protect plaintiff and other paid spectators from wheels that at times come off speeding stock car racers and fly through the air at high speeds, though defendants knew, or, in the exercise of due care, should have known, that it is not uncommon for wheels to come off such racing cars during a race, and might likely injure a spectator. In spite of this foreseeable danger, defendants only strung one cable about 18 inches high above the ground, separating the race track proper from the area in which plaintiff, and other paid spectators were standing watching the races. Three. They failed to inspect the racing cars prior to the race during which plaintiff was injured to see if the wheels of the racing cars were in safe condition for racing. Four. Defendants failed to warn plaintiff of the increased danger of standing near the end of the race track, and failed to fence off or rope off such area, though defendants knew, or should have known, such area was relatively more dangerous for spectators during a race than the area surrounding other parts of the race track.

\*\*\*

Plaintiff prays that she have judgment against the...defendants...for $15,500....

Since plaintiff purchased an admission ticket, and entered on the race track premises, a business conducted for profit, in the character of a patron, he occupied the status of an invitee. *Hahn v. Perkins*, 228 N.C. 727, 46 S.E.2d 854.

"One who invites the public to attend a race between motor vehicles and charges an admission fee is bound to exercise reasonable care to make the place provided for spectators reasonably safe, but, although a spectator is injured, no liability may be imposed on the persons conducting the races, in the absence of a showing of negligence on their part." 61 C.J.S. Motor Vehicles s 577, p. 682.

The general rule is that the owner or operator of an automobile race track is charged with the duty of exercising reasonable care, under the circumstances present, for the safety of patrons, that is a care commensurate with the known or reasonably foreseeable danger. Annotation, 37 A.L.R.2d 393, where many cases are cited.

*Smith v. Cumberland County Agricultural Society*, 163 N.C. 346, 79 S.E. 632, 633, Ann.Cas.1915B, 544, was an action for injuries sustained by plaintiff, who was caught by his foot in the trail rope of a balloon which ascended from the fair grounds of defendant, and was carried in the air for some distance. Plaintiff paid his fare for entrance to the fair. The Court said: "The owner of a place of entertainment is charged with an affirmative positive obligation to know that the premises are safe for the public use and to furnish adequate appliances for the prevention of injuries which might be anticipated from the nature of the performance, and he impliedly warrants the premises to be reasonably safe for the purpose for which they are designed.' He is not an insurer of the safety of those attending the exhibition, but he must use care and diligence to prevent injury, and by policemen or other guards warn the public against dangers that can reasonably be foreseen.'

In *Hallyburton v. Burke County Fair Association*, 119 N.C. 526, 26 S.E. 114, 38 L.R.A. 156, it was held that defendant, under whose auspices and on whose grounds a horse race took place, is not negligent, and therefore responsible for an injury caused to a spectator, who had paid his entrance fee and was standing where spectators usually stand when watching a race, by a horse which bolted the track, when defendant had provided a building from which the race could be safely viewed, and had enclosed the race track on both sides by a substantial railing.

This is said in Annotation, 37 A.L.R.2d 394: "If the need is obvious or experience shows that an automobile race of the character and in the place proposed requires, in order to afford reasonable protection to spectators, the erection of fences or similar barriers between the track and the places assigned to them, it becomes a part of the duty in exercising reasonable care for their safety to provide fences or barriers, the adequacy of which is dependent on the circumstances present, principally the custom of the business." In this same annotation…will be found a number of cases in respect to the absence or inadequacy of fences, barricades, or other protective devices, where under the circumstances of individual cases, a recovery has been upheld and denied.

In *Atlantic Rural Exposition, Inc. v. Fagan*, 1953, 195 Va. 13, 77 S.E.2d 368, 37 A.L.R.2d 378, the court affirmed a judgment on a verdict of a jury against both the lessor and the lessee, the sponsors, promoters, and supervisors of an automobile racing exposition, upon evidence sufficient to pose a question of fact as to whether the defendants had exercised that care to protect the plaintiff, as a spectator, which might, under the circumstances shown, be expected of reasonably prudent persons acting under the same or similar circumstances, commensurate with the known and reasonably foreseeable dangers, particularly in the matter of providing an adequate fence which would be reasonably calculated to safeguard spectators at a stock car race in the event of detachment of a wheel of a racing car at a point at or near the bleachers.

\*\*\*

We think that the complaint with its amendments contains a sufficient statement of a cause of action against the…defendants predicating their liability, at least, on their failure to exercise care commensurate with the known or reasonably foreseeable dangers incident to motor vehicles racing at high speeds for the reasonable protection and safety of plaintiff, a patron, and its other patrons, watching the race, in that no seats of any kind were provided for plaintiff and there was an absence or inadequacy of fences, barricades, or other protective devices around the race track for plaintiff's safety, while he was watching the racing automobiles.

**Notes & Questions**

1. How can a race track owner balance the spectators' desire to be right on top of the action with the need for safety? At what point does law impinge upon the rights of venue owners and spectators by taking a role that is overly-paternalistic? How is this issue related to our ordinary safety rules of the road, such as laws requiring drivers and occupants of automobiles to wear seat belts or laws requiring motorcyclists to wear helmets?

2. What could the race track owners have done in this case to have avoided liability?

3. If you were giving advice to an entrepreneur who wanted to open a dirt motocross track for teenagers, how would you begin to determine what sorts of safety precautions would be necessary for spectators?

4. What is the relationship between industry standards for safety in these types of venues and legal liability?

For exceptionally dangerous activities such as equestrian sports and skiing, a number of state legislatures have passed special statutes providing immunity for the venue operators who provide venues for these types of recreactional activities. See generally, Terrence J. Centner, *Tort Liability for Sports and Recreational Activities: Expanding Statutory Immunity for Protected Classes and Activities*, 26 J. Legis. 1 (2000).

### *Further Reading on Athlete-to-Athlete Injuries and Facilities Operators Liability*:

Roger I. Abrams, *Two Sports Torts: The Historical Development of the Legal Rights of Baseball Spectators*, 38 TULSA L. REV. 433 (2003).

Walter T. Champion, *At the Old Ball Game and Beyond: Spectators and The Potential for Liability*, 14 AM. J. TRIAL ADVOC. 495 (1991).

Peter C. Gopleurd, *Allocation of Risk Between Hockey Fans and Facilities: Tort Liability After the Puck Drops*, III, 38 TULSA L. REV. 445 (2003).

Gordon J. Hylton, *A Foul Ball in the Courtroom:The Baseball Spectator Injury as a Case of First Impression*, 38 TULSA L. REV. 485 (2003).

Daniel E. Lazaroff, *Torts and Sports: Participant Liability to Co-Participants for Injuries Sustained During Competition*, 7 U. Miami Ent. & Sports L. Rev. 191 (1990).

John C. Weistart & Cym H. Lowell, Law of Sports, §8.02 Liability for Injury to Participants (Bobbs-Merrill Company, Inc., 1979).

John C. Weistart & Cym H. Lowell, Law of Sports, §8.03 Liability for Injury to Spectators  (Bobbs-Merrill Company, Inc., 1979)

Ray Yasser, *In the Heat of Competition:Tort Liability of One Participant to Another*, 5 SETON HALL J. SPORT L. 253 (1995).

# Chapter 3

## Torts II: Coach Liability; Equipment

---

The Torts cases that you have read thus far have required you to think about injuries caused by co-participants and injuries caused by those responsible for providing a sports venue for athletes and spectators. *Moose v. MIT* introduces the topic of coach liability. This case also provides a platform for considering assumption of risk and contributory negligence. Here we consider the extent to which a coach or athlete him/herself should be considered legally responsible for injury. As we know, injuries are an ordinary part of athletics because all games involve varying degrees of risk. The fundamental question here is whether or under what circumstances a coach should be held liable. A related question is whether and to what degree an athlete should be deemed to have consented to the risks involved in his/her sport, or to what degree an athlete can be considered responsible for his/her own injuries through contributory or comparative fault.

*McCormick* and *Pell* explore the extent to which equipment manufacturers and sellers can be held responsible for sports injuries. These cases give us the opportunity to delve into the world of products liability. As such, they also require us to think about the roles played by sports equipment manufacturers and the potential effects that legal decisions may have on the sports equipment industry as a whole. The tension is easy to understand. If litigation and insurance costs are too high, manufacturers will be likely to quit. Obviously there are a number of exceptionally negative consequences that could flow from manufacturers fleeing the marketplace due to fears of litigation and rising insurance costs. As you read these cases, think about what steps courts might take in order to balance the consumers' needs for safety with the needs of the manufacturers to stay in business so that various sports (*i.e.,* sports that rely on specialized equipment) can continue to thrive. Consider also the special problems confronted by manufacturers of safety equipment such as football, baseball, bicycle, and hockey helmets. *Pell* provides an excellent example of the kinds of obstacles that exist for suppliers of gymnastic equipment. The note that concludes this chapter summarizes and explains the legal theories (both tort and commercial law) that relate to sports equipment.

## Moose v. Massachusetts Institute of Technology
43 Mass.App.Ct. 420 (1997)
Appeals Court of Massachusetts,Middlesex

SMITH, Justice.

The plaintiff, Garret Moose, filed a negligence action against the Massachusetts Institute of Technology (MIT) and two of its track and field coaches, Paul Slovenski and Halston Taylor, seeking damages for injuries sustained while Moose was practicing pole vaulting at the institution. The plaintiff alleged that the defendants were negligent with respect to their coaching techniques and the equipment they furnished to him at the time he was injured. In response to special questions a jury found that each defendant, as well as the plaintiff, was negligent and that the defendants' negligence was the proximate cause of the plaintiff's injuries. The jury assessed damages at $615,000. The percentages of negligence were attributed as follows: plaintiff--fifteen percent, MIT--forty-five percent, Taylor--twenty-five percent, Slovenski--fifteen percent. The court entered judgment in the sum of $522,750 after deducting fifteen percent from the award for the plaintiff's negligence. The judgment provided that MIT's liability was $20,000 plus interest and costs because it was a charitable organization.

****

Pole vaulting is a sport in which the object is to obtain the maximum vertical lift in order to clear a horizontal bar set at some height above the ground. In competition, after vaulters have cleared the bar, it is then adjusted upwards until a winner emerges.

To be able to go over the bar, a vaulter takes an approach run towards the bar carrying a long pole. When the vaulter gets near to the bar, he places one end of the pole into the vaulting box--an indentation in the ground almost directly beneath the bar. The box slants downward at the bottom and has metal sides. Once the pole is planted in the box, the vaulter uses the momentum from his approach run to bend the pole. When the pole bends back, the vaulter is lifted upwards and hopefully over the bar. Once over the bar, the vaulter lands on a foam mattress called the landing pit which cushions the vaulter's fall.

The defendant Slovenski, who had been the pole vaulting coach since November, 1990, was coaching Moose at the time of the accident. The defendant Taylor was head track and field coach and responsible for supervising Slovenski's activities as pole vaulting coach. Taylor's functions as head track and field coach included supervising the sports equipment in order to make sure it was safe, recommending the purchase of new equipment, and providing a safe environment for MIT track athletes.

In January of 1991, the plaintiff was a senior at MIT, majoring in aeronautical engineering. He was also a member of MIT's men's track and field team and had been involved in pole vaulting since the spring of his freshman year. On January 21, 1991, the day of the accident, the plaintiff was practicing pole vaulting under Slovenski's direct supervision at MIT's indoor track and field facility. The plaintiff was injured when after executing a pole vault, his heels hooked on the back edge of the landing pit and he fell backward, striking his head on the hard track surface. The back of the pit abutted the indoor track; the back left corner of the pit was two to three inches from the inside lane of the indoor track and the right rear corner was about two feet from the running surface. The track was made of concrete, covered with a thin layer of rubber.

The pit was purchased in 1980 and was thirteen feet in length; the minimum length required by NCAA rules was twelve feet with a recommended length of sixteen feet. Pits with more length were available since at least 1981 but a budgeting crisis at MIT affected the track team and the coaches' ability to purchase new equipment. About a year and one-half after the accident, Taylor had the pit replaced with one that was seventeen feet long.

Both Slovenski and Taylor had witnessed, or at least were aware of, vaulters bouncing off the pit mattress and landing over the sides and front of the pit resulting in the vaulter sustaining second impact injuries. The day of the accident there were no pads at the back or sides of the pit, although in the past, the coaches had placed pads on the sides and sometimes at the back of the pit. Slovenski was aware that some colleges used supplemental padding at the back of the pit. Prior to the accident, Taylor never discussed the padding issue with Slovenski. At the time of the accident, supplemental padding was available and Taylor could have ordered that pads be placed in the area at the back of the pit.[1]

On January 21, 1991, pursuant to Slovenski's instructions, the plaintiff was using a training pole to practice pole vaulting drills. There was evidence that the training pole that was being used by the plaintiff was too light for the plaintiff's weight.[2] The selection of a soft training pole for a heavy, fast athlete places the athlete at serious risk of a "blow through."[3]

After performing a number of drill techniques, Slovenski instructed the plaintiff to combine two of the vaulting techniques and go through the full vaulting motions. The approach run for these vaults was fifty feet and the plaintiff was to make his approach at about one-half his normal speed. Slovenski told the plaintiff to use the same training pole for the full vaults.

The plaintiff performed the first two of the full vaults. After he performed each vault, Slovenski gave him pointers on his performance. Before each vault, except the last one, Slovenski told the plaintiff to keep his speed down. However, after at least one of these vaults, he landed on the center of the pit, beyond where he should have landed. That landing indicated that he needed either to use a heavier pole, raise his grip, or shorten his approach run. Although proper coaching technique requires that these adjustments be made, Slovenski did not order any of these adjustments nor did he warn the plaintiff that he was overpenetrating.

A coach who is teaching proper pole vaulting techniques should have a vaulter under observation during the vaulter's entire approach run. Once a

---

[1] The plaintiff's expert, Earl Bell, testified that supplemental padding should always be used around the pit's entire perimeter, especially around the back of the pit where the most serious injuries occur. Bell also testified that in his opinion, it was an unsound practice to locate the pit so that it abutted the hard track surface and it was unreasonable to fail to pad the hard surfaces abutting the pit. Bell also criticized the instructions and supervision given to the plaintiff before the accident.

[2] A training pole is a more flexible pole than a competition pole. Because it is more flexible, it is easier to bend; therefore, vaults may be practiced at slower speeds. Although there was a factual dispute as to the exact characteristics of the pole that the plaintiff was using when he was injured, the jury were free to accept the plaintiff's testimony that he was using a thirteen foot pole which was intended for persons weighing from 120-150 pounds. At the time of the accident, the plaintiff weighed 175 pounds.

[3] A "blow through" is a term used in track and field circles to describe over penetration of the pole vault landing pit. It occurs when a vaulter uses a pole too soft and small for his weight, speed, and abilities. As the vaulter jumps, the pole overbends sending the vaulter to the back of the pit instead of upward to the bar.

98

coach notices that a vaulter is running too fast, the coach should order the vaulter to abort the vault. In the past, other coaches had interrupted the plaintiff's vaults at various stages due to safety concerns, including when he was twenty-five feet into the vault approach run.

Slovenski did not observe the plaintiff's final approach run until the plaintiff had completed twenty-five feet of that run. When Slovenski first observed the plaintiff, he thought the plaintiff was running too fast, and he knew the plaintiff was going to make a bad vault. Slovenski did not instruct the plaintiff to slow down or to abort his vault.

When the plaintiff made the vault, he went up about thirteen feet; when he landed, his heels hooked on the back edge of the pit and he fell backward, striking his head on the hard track surface. Immediately after the accident, Taylor found the plaintiff lying on the track unconscious and convulsing.

The plaintiff was taken to Massachusetts General Hospital where he was diagnosed as having sustained a skull fracture with associated contusions to the brain. While the plaintiff was hospitalized, Slovenski visited him and told him that he was having nightmares and he felt that the accident was his fault. Slovenski also told the plaintiff that when he saw him on his final approach it occurred to him that he had not reminded him to keep his speed down, but he did not say anything to the plaintiff because he did not want to break the plaintiff's concentration.

On appeal, the defendants claim that they are entitled to judgments notwithstanding the verdicts, because there was no evidence to support a finding that they should have reasonably foreseen that the plaintiff would land beyond the back of the pit and hit his head on the track surface.

The defendants appear to have misinterpreted the law pertaining to reasonable foreseeability. It is only the risk which results in the harm that must be reasonably foreseeable, not the precise manner of the accident or the extent of the harm. *Luz v. Stop & Shop, Inc., of Peabody,* 348 Mass. 198, 204, 202 N.E.2d 771 (1964) ("To be held liable the defendant need not have foreseen the precise manner in which the injuries occurred."). See Restatement (Second) of Torts § 435(1) (1965): ("If the actor's conduct is a substantial factor in bringing about harm to another, the fact that the actor neither foresaw nor should have foreseen the extent of the harm or the manner in which it occurred does not prevent him from being liable").

The question whether the risk of injury was foreseeable is almost always one of fact. *Simmons v. Monarch Mach. Tool Co.,* 413 Mass. 205, 211, 596 N.E.2d 318 (1992). From the evidence before the jury, the plaintiff's accident was reasonably foreseeable by the defendants. The length of the landing pit and its location very close to a hard surface did not provide a safe environment for pole vaulters. It was also reasonably foreseeable that a vaulter using a training pole too light for his weight and running too fast on his approach run, would be carried across the pit and upon landing, end up beyond the back of the pit thereby incurring injury. \*\*\*\*

The following facts were adduced at trial on the issue of damages. The plaintiff sustained a fractured skull and contusions to the brain as a result of the accident. He spent two weeks at Massachusetts General Hospital and five days at Spaulding Rehabilitation Hospital. His treating physician testified that while the plaintiff was hospitalized, he experienced hypersensitivity to sound, sensitivity to light, difficulty with logic and word finding, as well as difficulty organizing information, solving problems, and switching from one idea to another.

The plaintiff was discharged from the hospital on February 8, 1991. Upon his release from the hospital, the plaintiff returned to MIT and continued to actively pole vault for the men's track and field team. The plaintiff, however, lacked the motor coordination to do complex physical activity. The plaintiff continued to experience hypersensitivity to sound and difficulty with word choices. He also experienced loss of his sense of smell and taste and had a reduced ability to scan near material with his right eye.

In regard to his school work, the plaintiff found that he was so exhausted that sitting through classes and trying to do homework was beyond his stamina; he was also having trouble absorbing the material and making the deductions that were needed in order to be successful. Further, the plaintiff experienced episodes of double vision and blurry vision, especially while trying to read at length.

At the plaintiff's May 14, 1991, physical examination, his doctor noted that the plaintiff continued to have problems with visual accommodation, hypersensitivity to sound, concentration, and word-finding. He was also experiencing changes in his personality function manifesting itself in the form of increased irritability, difficulty inhibiting anger, and rage attacks. All of the symptoms were consistent with his head injury.

There was evidence that as a result of the accident, the plaintiff had a lost earning capacity of $25,000 per year and based on that figure, there was testimony from the plaintiff's expert that the plaintiff's lifetime lost earning capacity, discounted to present value, was $1,309,835. Thus, in light of these facts, we hold that the judge did not abuse his discretion by refusing to grant a new trial on the issue of damages because the jury's award of $615,000 was neither greatly disproportionate to the injury proven nor do we think it represents a miscarriage of justice.

Judgments affirmed.

## Notes & Questions

1. Why doesn't the court merely conclude that Moose assumed the risk of pole vaulting? After all, he was a college senior majoring in aeronautical engineering at one of the most prestigious technical universities in the world (*i.e.*, he was a rocket scientist "in training"). If anyone can be assumed to have completely understood the physics and attendant risks of the sport of pole vaulting, wouldn't he have been the poster child? Isn't pole vaulting an obviously and inherently dangerous sport?

2. To what standard of conduct does the court hold coach Slovenski? Is he judged under ordinary negligence principles? A professional standard (coaches malpractice?)?

3. Is coach Slovenski held responsible for negligence? If so, why isn't he judged using the intentional or willful misconduct standard that the court applied in the athlete-to-athlete injury cases (*i.e., Jaworski* and *McKichan*)?

4. In a sport such as track and field, is it reasonable to expect a head coach constantly to supervise the practices for each event? Is it reasonable to hold a track and field coach liable for negligence if s/he fails to prevent an injury? How is that humanly possible, given the multiple events in track and field and limited resources at most high schools and colleges?

5. How important do you think the testimony of the plaintiff's expert witness, Earl Bell, was? Explain your answer.

6. If coach Slovenski had screamed at Moose, and told him to "abort!" just before he planted his pole, would he have been liable for Moose's injuries if Moose had been injured as a result of being abruptly distracted by the coach's scream at the most critical and intense moment of the vault? If so, then is the

court right saying that Slovenski should have yelled and told him to abort? Isn't this just an impossible "Catch 22"?

7. For an analysis of the issues raised in this case and others related to pole vault safety, *see* Russ VerSteeg, *Negligence in the Air: Safety, Legal Liability and the Pole Vault*, 4 TEXAS REV. ENT. & SPORTS L. 109 (2003).

Today women and girls also compete in the pole vault, an exciting and dangerous sport. Jessica Sullivan, Connecticut Record Holder: 11 feet 6 inches, courtesy The New London Day.

## McCormick v. Lowe & Campbell Athletic Goods Co.
144 SW 2d 866 (1940)
Kansas City Court of Appeals, Missouri

CAMPBELL, Commissioner.

The defendant, Lowe & Campbell Athletic Goods Company, furnished a vaulting pole which broke while plaintiff was using it in vaulting, and thus caused him to fall and be injured. He brought this suit to recover for his injuries, had a verdict and judgment in the amount of $7,500. The defendant has appealed.

\*\*\*\*

The facts are: Plaintiff, in March and April, 1937, was a high school student in the Deuel County High School at Chappell, Nebraska. He was a skilled high school pole vaulter. The defendant at that time and continuously for a long time prior thereto was engaged in manufacturing and selling various kinds of athletic goods, among which were vaulting poles. The Deuel County High School, on March 4, 1937, sent to the defendant an order as follows: "1-T14-vaulting pole (hand picked) vaulter only weighs 120 lb."

This order was made from defendant's catalogue, reading in part as follows:

No Guarantee on Vaulting Poles or Javelins Bamboo vaulting poles being a product of nature and subjected to various kinds of treatment cannot be guaranteed against splitting or breaking. Keep in a cool, dry place laid flat on a level floor. Avoid Heated basements and sudden change of temperature. \*\*\*

'Extra Select' Bamboo Vaulting Poles

We import our bamboo poles direct from Japan in large quantities and are thus assured of the best selection in all lengths. Special tape of extra strength is used in wrapping and they are wood plugged. The 'select' poles are 'Red-Head' marked.

No. T10-10-foot Bamboo Pole, wrapped and plugged ..
$4.00 $2.75
No. T14-14-foot Bamboo Pole, wrapped and plugged ..
$7.00 $4.90
No. T16-16-foot Bamboo Pole, wrapped and plugged ..
$7.75 $5.45

After sorting out the 'extra select' poles there are many left
that are perfectly usable and thoroughly satisfactory for the
average high school vaulter. These are good, strong,
serviceable poles. ***

No. T6J-8-foot Bamboo Pole, without tape or plug .. $.60
$.40.

The defendant, acting on that order, sent to the school a bamboo
vaulting pole which was too short, crooked, and not properly balanced. In a
few days thereafter the school's athletic coach, Miller, advised defendant's
traveling salesman, Hal Bowers, of the condition of the pole, and Bowers
promised to make an adjustment on account of the defect, and to supply
another pole. The promise was kept and the second pole was delivered by
the defendant to the school on April 22. Plaintiff on the day the pole arrived
took it to the athletic field, vaulted twice with it, and each time his handhold
was about 8 feet, 2 inches from the lower end of the pole. He then made a
third vault in the usual manner, and while his body was crossing the crossbar
the pole "just snapped off"; "just cracked off", in consequence of which
plaintiff fell and was seriously injured. The break was underneath the tape
which defendant had put on the pole.

The superintendent of the high school, for the plaintiff, testified he
saw the second pole when it was delivered at the school, but could not
remember whether or not he "lifted it".

George Miller, an experienced pole vaulter and coach of athletics
and science teacher of the school, testified that the pole which was ordered
on March 4 was not satisfactory, was poorly balanced and not straight; that
he informed Bowers of the condition of the pole, and that he thought plaintiff
had a chance to break the state record in vaulting; that they wanted to get a
16-foot pole, "straight pole and better balanced pole", and that Bowers said
he would "order it himself"; that he received the second pole, took it in his
hands "to determine how much spring and elasticity it had, put some weight
on it, it seemed to have quite a bit of elasticity. Then I turned it over to"

104

plaintiff. This witness was not present at the time of the accident. However, he examined the pole, evidently in a few minutes thereafter, and found the pole did not bend or buckle; that it was "broken clear in two and that the break was almost smooth", no splitting or splintering.

In the cross-examination of the witness he testified that he saw nothing indicating the pole was dangerous.

"Q. And you thought it (pole) was all right? A. I had never gotten a pole that I was able to break before; there was no reason why I should suspicion it being a defective pole."

Mr. Miller further testified that he recalled seeing two instances in which a vaulter broke a bamboo pole; that in those instances the pole "did not break clear in two, the vaulter hanging on to the pole with one hand has pushed away from the vaulting pole and on top of that he supports his arms and head so that the feet come down first"; that the poles buckled, "they never break entirely in two", and that the pole here involved was the only pole which broke "completely."

Plaintiff's witness, G. Harry Clay, testified he had had experience in testing materials for strength and defects, was a graduate of Rose Polytechnic Institute with the degree of B. S.; that he took an engineering course in an engineering school, was a member of the American Chemical Society, and that he was local counselor of that society, had been a member of American Society for Testing Materials; that for 10 years he was connected with the Kansas City Testing Laboratory which specialized in the testing of engineering materials, construction materials, road materials, "and all that sort of thing"; that bamboo is used as a structural material in the Orient and in South America; that he had made a study of bamboo by searching literature and experimenting on his own account; that the literature he had read was the Encyclopedia Brittanica, the year books and bulletins of the Agricultural Department of the United States; that from his study and experiments he was familiar with the physical characteristics and properties of bamboo poles; that the principles of testing bamboo were the same as the principles used in testing other structural materials. He further testified he examined the pole, the breaking of which caused plaintiff to be injured, and found a defect therein; that his conclusion there was a defect was based on his examination of the break itself; "it (pole) was broken short off just as a piece of brittle oak breaks off", "from the fact that bamboo breaks in an entirely different way"; and that bamboo breaks by long splits and cracks from the distortion of the cross section.

"Q. Now, if a bamboo pole is not defective, tell the jury how the pole will break or buckle or bend if it is subjected to more stress and strain than it can stand? A. Well, I can probably illustrate that with a fishing pole or with any of these pieces if I had the strength, but it breaks first by being distorted. As the pole is bent that circle becomes an ellipse. That flattening of the section of the pole results in cracking, probably through one or two of the knobs. That weakens the whole pole and it breaks, but not in two. It will bend clear double before it will break in two.

"Q. That is when it is not defective. A. That is when it is not defective."

Plaintiff testified he had been pole vaulting for 10 years prior to the accident; that during that time he had not seen or heard of a pole breaking during a vault, but had heard of one splitting; that he took the pole in question from the school building to the athletic field and vaulted twice "successfully"; that at each of said times his hold was 8 feet, 2 inches from the butt of the pole; that he then placed his hold 11 feet, 3 inches from the butt of the pole, and proceeded to vault in the usual manner and that in the vault the pole broke "completely apart."

The defendant's witness, Charles Regelbrugge, testified he had been in charge of the vaulting pole department of the defendant for eight years; that defendant each year obtains 4000 to 6000 bamboo poles "in the raw" which were harvested in Japan; that the poles when received were each 18 to 20 feet in length and that 15 to 50 per cent of them were defective; that the defective ones could in some instances be discovered by "merely looking" at them, other defective poles could be discovered only by testing them; that when the defendant received an order for a vaulting pole it sent to him a work ticket on which was stated the length and type of pole ordered and in some instances the weight of the person who would use the pole in vaulting; that in filling the order he selected a pole, cut it to the length stated on the work ticket, then tested it by throwing his weight upon it "in four different positions"; he then caused a maple-wood plug to be inserted in the butt of the pole; the pole was then painted and wrapped in numerous places with adhesive tape. In his cross-examination this witness said he had no recollection of testing any pole that was sent to Chappell, Nebraska.

****

He further testified he tested a pole for the purpose of making sure it would hold the person for whom it was intended and for the purpose of discovering defects.

106

"Q. And would the test that you customarily made before you sent these poles out to customers disclose defects? A. Yes, sir, we could sure find that."

Further pertinent facts will be referred to in ruling the questions involved in this appeal.

In contending the plaintiff failed to make a submissible case, the defendant says it gave notice to the Deuel County High School that "bamboo vaulting poles will break and split." Defendant's catalogue said it did not guarantee bamboo poles against splitting or breaking; that it bought bamboo poles in large quantities and was thus assured of the best selection; that special tape of extra strength was used in wrapping the poles. These statements cannot be construed as notice to either the school or plaintiff that the pole was or might be a defective one. On the contrary, the statements are sufficient to induce belief in the mind of a reasonably prudent person that defendant had made the "best selection" and had exercised due care in preparing the pole for the use for which it was intended. However, apart from the statements in the catalogue, we conclude the evidence...shows that it was the practice and custom of defendant to inspect and test each bamboo vaulting pole before sending it to the purchaser. In other words, defendant recognized it was under duty to inspect and test a vaulting pole before releasing it to be used in vaulting. The purpose of such test...was to "make sure" the pole would hold the weight stated in the work ticket (in the instant case 120 pounds) to discover defects; and that such testing as defendant customarily made would "sure" disclose any existing defect. It follows, of course, if the pole were defective, and that a reasonably careful test would have disclosed the defect, then the jury could find defendant failed to make such test.

The defendant argues that the pole was a product of nature; that it was a seller, not the manufacturer of the pole. The bamboo, when received by defendant, was a product of nature. When defendant, by the several acts hereinbefore stated, made the product of nature into a vaulting pole, it manufactured the pole. *H. H. Kohlsaat & Co. v. O'Connell*, 255 Ill. 271, 90 N.E. 689.

From an examination of the numerous cases cited in the briefs relating to the so-called modern rule governing liability of a manufacturer in cases such as the present one, we conclude that a manufacturer of a product is under duty to exercise ordinary care to test the product to determine whether or not it has a defect which would render it unsafe when applied to its intended use; that a failure to perform such duty renders the manufacturer liable to a person injured in consequence of such failure while using such article in the ordinary and usual manner. [case citations omitted]

Defendant at the time it sent the second pole to the school knew plaintiff intended to use that pole in vaulting. It was therefore its duty to exercise reasonable care in testing the pole to ascertain whether or not it was free of defects which would endanger plaintiff when he put the pole to the intended use.

The defendant insists there was no evidence showing that the pole was defective; that its evidence "demonstrates" the pole was inspected and tested. Neither of these contentions can be sustained. There was evidence to the effect the pole "snapped off". This was sufficient, when taken in connection with the evidence of Clay, to enable the jury to find the pole was brittle. The only evidence which it can be said tended to show the pole which broke was tested, was that of Regelbrugge who stated the manner in which he customarily tested bamboo vaulting poles. *** He was the only witness who knew whether the pole was or was not tested, and his evidence on that subject was not sufficient to conclusively show he tested the pole in question. The jury could very well find that if he had thrown his weight upon the pole in four different positions as he stated he customarily did, the pole would have "snapped off" because it was brittle. Regelbrugge further testified that in "some years" he broke one-half of the poles in testing them; that he tested the poles to make sure "they would hold the man they were ordered for."

"Q. If that man was a 150-pound man, you wouldn't give it any more of a test, would you? A. No, sir.

"Q. And if he was a 200-pound man you wouldn't give it any more of a test, would you? A. No, sir.

***

"Q. And you would give it the same kind of a test without regard to what size person it was being ordered for? A. Yes, sir."

Plainly, the court cannot say such a method of testing was a reasonably careful method. The question was one for the trier of the fact.

Defendant, in contending no case was made for the jury, says that plaintiff failed to prove any act or omission on its part was the proximate cause of his injuries; that plaintiff was guilty of contributory negligence "and had assumed the risk incident" to engaging in pole vaulting.

The facts stated above were sufficient to warrant the jury in finding the pole was defective and unsafe for its intended use; that if defendant had tested it in a reasonably careful manner the defect would have been discovered and the injury averted. Thus the failure of the defendant to properly test the pole was the direct cause of the accident.

Plaintiff assumed the ordinary risk of pole vaulting but he did not assume risks due to the negligence of the defendant. He did not, prior to the accident, know or have cause to believe the pole was not a safe one to use in vaulting. He vaulted three times in the usual and skillful manner. This was not negligence as a matter of law. In this connection it must be remembered Miller, an experienced pole vaulter, testified he had never had a pole which he could break, and that he had no cause to "suspicion" the pole in question was a defective pole. It may be the defendant's opinion evidence was sufficient to allow the jury to find plaintiff was guilty of contributory negligence, but the court could not tell the jury it must believe that evidence.

****

Defendant offered in evidence three photographs of the vaulting box used by plaintiff at the time of accident. The photographs were, on plaintiff's objection, excluded from the evidence. At the time plaintiff was injured the vaulting box was buried level with ground. About May 15 the box was taken from the ground and placed near the school house where it remained exposed to the elements until the photographs were taken on August 31. As shown in one of the photographs there was a crack in the bottom of the vaulting box which, according to defendant's opinion evidence, rendered it unsafe for use. The only evidence touching the condition of the vaulting box on April 22 was to the effect it was in good condition; and that there was no crack in it which "would have caused any difficulty in making a successful pole vault." Nor was there evidence showing the photographs were correct representation[s] of the vaulting box. In such circumstances we cannot convict the trial court of error in excluding the photographs. [case citations omitted]

The record is free of error prejudicial to the defendant. The judgment should be and it is affirmed

**Notes & Questions**

1. This case was decided using ordinary negligence principles. It pre-dates the advent of modern strict products liability. After you have read the note at the end of this chapter about tort and commercial law theories relating to sports equipment, and after you have taken the time to digest and absorb the modern rubric of products liability, look back at the facts of this case and test yourself to see whether you are able to articulate a rule of the case more satisfactory than the one that this court in 1940 enunciated.

2. The defendant offered to place into evidence pictures of the vault box (the metal trough into which a pole vaulter plants the pole). The trial court excluded the photographs. Explain for what purpose the defendant was trying to introduce those photographs into evidence?

3. What sort of testing protocol do you think would be appropriate for a manufacturer of modern fiberglass vaulting poles? If you were asked to advise a pole manufacturer about testing procedures, what would you suggest in order to avoid liability? Currently the manufacturers test poles at the factory using sophisticated equipment in order to assign a weight-rating to them (*i.e.,* what the maximum body weight of the vaulter using the pole should be), and the manufacturers also use machines to test the poles by bending them in excess of 90 degrees (a stress test) to be certain that the pole is unlikely to break due to some structural defect.

4. What warning labels, if any, would you advise a pole manufacturer to place on the poles that it sells? (an issue taken to interesting heights/lengths in the next case).

5. *See* Russ VerSteeg, *Pole Vault Injuries: Product Liability and Commercial Law Theories*, 5 TEXAS REV. ENT. & SPORTS L. 237 (2004); Russ VerSteeg, *Arresting Vaulting Pole Technology*, 9 VANDERBILT J. ENT. & TECH. L. 93 (2005).


### Lauren M. Pell v. Victor J. Andrew High School and AMF
#### 462 NE 2d 858 (1984)
Appellate Court of Illinois, First District, Fifth Division

WILSON, Justice:

This is an appeal by defendant AMF, Inc. ("AMF")...on a jury verdict for plaintiff Lauren M. Pell for permanent injuries plaintiff sustained during gym class while performing a somersault off a trampoline manufactured by AMF. Prior to trial, plaintiff and defendants School District 230 and Victor J. Andrew High School entered into a settlement agreement for $1.6 million. Thereafter, the jury awarded plaintiff $5 million against AMF on the theory of strict liability, which amount was set off by the $1.6 million settlement figure and resulted in a final judgment against AMF for $3.4 million.

On appeal, AMF contends that...(1) AMF cannot be held liable for failure to provide warnings and instructional materials to either of the other defendants; (2) because the proximate cause of plaintiff's injury was the school district's wilful and wanton misconduct in failing to properly instruct and supervise plaintiff in the use of the trampoline; and (3) because plaintiff's knee condition was the proximate cause of her injury. AMF contends further that the trial court erred (4) in refusing to allow AMF to present evidence on the issue of plaintiff's comparative negligence; (5) in admitting exhibits that dealt with full size trampolines; (6) in refusing to admit two of AMF's exhibits, and (7) in finding that plaintiff's settlement with the school district was made in good faith. For the reasons hereinafter set forth, we affirm.

On December 29, 1980, plaintiff, a 16-year-old sophomore and beginner gymnast at Victor J. Andrew High School, was injured as the result of a somersault she performed on a product manufactured by AMF, called a mini-trampoline or trampolette ("mini-tramp"). This equipment consists of a 37-inch, square-shaped metal frame holding a "bed" of polypropylene fabric with rubber cables which lace the "bed" to the frame. Two adjustable metal leg sections can be used to set the frame at any angle or to fold the equipment flat.

The mini-tramp was sold to School District 230 with a heat-laminated caution label affixed to the bed which stated:

> Caution. Misuse and abuse of this trampoline is dangerous and can cause serious injuries. Read instructions before using this trampoline. Inspect before using and replace any worn, defective, or missing parts. Any activity involving motion or height creates the possibility of accidental injuries. This unit is intended for use only by properly trained and qualified participants under supervised conditions. Use without proper supervision can be dangerous and should not be undertaken or permitted.

When the mini-tramp was assembled by a faculty member at the high school, the bed was placed so that the caution label was on the bottom, facing the floor, as opposed to the top where it would be visible to a performer. There were printed warnings also on the frame of the mini-tramp, however they were covered by frame pads on each of the four sides.

On the day of the injury, plaintiff had first performed two somersaults off the mini-tramp. Both of the school's coaches, Charlene Nutter, the varsity gymnastics coach, and Cathi Miles, were present in the gymnasium. Miles, who worked primarily with the freshmen and sophomore students, witnessed plaintiff's third somersault from a distance of approximately 10 feet. Plaintiff testified that she took a few running steps up to the mini-tramp and jumped onto the bed. When she went into the air, at the point when her feet were straight up and down above her, plaintiff said she felt a sharp pain in her knee and was unable to properly complete her somersault. She collapsed onto a nearby mat, severing her spine.

Plaintiff then filed a cause of action against Victor J. Andrew High School, School District 230, Crown Mats, Inc. And AMF. As previously explained, a pre-trial settlement between the high school and school district resulted in their dismissal and rendered moot portions of Counts I and II of plaintiff's complaint; plaintiff also dismissed Crown Mats, Inc. because of insufficient evidence.

Counts III, IV, VII, and VIII of plaintiff's complaint alleged that AMF's mini-tramp was not reasonably safe for its intended use; that AMF failed to adequately warn or advise plaintiff that use without a harness, safety belt and supervision by a trained instructor would result in severe injury and that AMF carelessly and negligently failed to provide a support harness or restraining device to prevent improper landing. Plaintiff further alleged that as a direct and proximate result of the defect in the mini-tramp, plaintiff landed on her neck, severed her spine and was permanently paralyzed.

In reply, AMF filed affirmative defenses asserting that (1) plaintiff had assumed the risk of injury because she knew of the condition of the mini-tramp and the dangers involved in using it, and (2) that any verdict against AMF must be reduced by the percentage of plaintiff's contributory negligence.

\*\*\*

At the close of all the evidence, the question of comparative negligence was...addressed during a post-trial discussion on jury instructions, where the court determined that " \* \* \* this case really turns on proximate cause. \* \* \* I am taking the view [that] this is not an appropriate case for application of the principles of comparative negligence." The court once again reiterated its reasons for not instructing the jury on comparative negligence, stating that there had been absolutely no evidence of assumption of the risk as well. The jury was thereafter given an instruction on strict liability. It returned a verdict against AMF and assessed plaintiff's damages at $5 million. Following the entry of judgment on this verdict, AMF appealed.

OPINION

Initially, AMF maintains that...it cannot be held liable, as a matter of law, for failing to provide warnings and instructional materials for using the mini-tramp since the school district as well as the high school had all of the appropriate instructional materials. We find this reasoning unpersuasive, however, because it misstates the central issue presented to the trier of fact, which was the unreasonably dangerous condition of the mini-tramp which, plaintiff alleged, existed because AMF failed to *adequately* warn of the equipment's propensity to cause severe spinal cord injuries if used for somersaulting without a safety device operated by a trained instructor.

Warnings must be adequate to perform their intended function of risk reduction. Warnings may be inadequate, however, if they: (1) do not specify the risk presented by the product; (2) are inconsistent with how a product would be used; (3) if they do not provide the reason for the warnings; or (4) if they do not reach foreseeable users. [case citations omitted]

Considering these principles, in our opinion there was sufficient evidence in the instant case from which the jury could conclude that AMF's warnings were ineffective. First, the warnings did not specify the risk of severe spinal cord injury which would result in permanent paralysis during somersaulting off the mini-tramp if performed without a spotter or safety harness. Charlene Nutter, head coach at the high school, testified that she did not know that the mini-tramp had any more risk involved in it than did any other gymnastic equipment and had she known, she would have taken precautions.

Coach Cathi Miles was also unaware of any rule that somersaults should not be performed on a mini-tramp without a spotter or overhead mechanical safety belt, although she had used the safety harness with a larger (full size) trampoline as well as the mini-tramp.

In addition, the jury could have reasonably determined that the warnings were inadequate because their location was inconsistent with the equipment's use. Plaintiff presented evidence that the assembly instructions failed to specify that the warning label should be placed in such a manner that it would be clearly visible to a gymnast. As a result, the warning label on the "bed" was placed underneath, facing the floor. The warnings on the sides of the metal frame were also ineffective because they were covered by frame pads.

In addition, because there was evidence that AMF had regularly participated in the United States Gymnastic Safety Association ("USGSA"), the jury could have easily concluded that AMF was familiar with the warnings that that association recommended which were that the labels should explain the reason for a warning and should be clearly visible to a mini-tramp user. **** Thus, the jury in this case, which examined the mini-tramp from a distance of a few feet, was able to determine whether AMF's warnings were adequate. We are convinced that this determination was correct.

AMF next contends that the…the proximate cause of plaintiff's injury was the school district's failure to provide plaintiff with proper gymnastic instructions in the safe use of the mini-tramp. We cannot agree.

In a strict liability action, a manufacturer may remain a contributing cause of an injury if the intervening acts or omissions of others were foreseeable. Foreseeability means that which is objectively reasonable to expect, not what might conceivably occur. This is ordinarily a question of fact for the jury. Liability will also attach if the defendant's conduct contributed in whole or in part to the injury, so long as it was *one* of the proximate causes.

In the case before us, there was sufficient evidence to support a finding that it was objectively foreseeable that mini-tramp users such as plaintiff would not always be under the direct supervision of a coach and that neither a gymnast nor a coach would have sufficient knowledge of the dangers of the mini-tramp because the warnings were inadequate. As we have previously explained, plaintiff submitted ample evidence which strongly suggested that AMF's warnings were inadequate. Additionally, the record shows that... coaches were not "told to put the kids in harnesses if they're using a mini-tramp to avoid crippling injuries from doing a somersault." In our judgment, therefore...the evidence...demonstrated that (1) the absence of direct supervision was reasonably foreseeable, and (2) that AMF's failure to adequately warn of the risk of serious injury was a proximate cause of plaintiff's injury. ***

Next, as an alternative to the preceding argument, AMF maintains that plaintiff's "idiosyncratic" knee condition was the proximate cause of her injury and that because this condition was unforeseeable, AMF did not have a duty to warn or to protect plaintiff against the danger of performing on the mini-tramp with such a condition. AMF relies on our recent decision in *Presbrey v. The Gillette Co.* (1982), 105 Ill.App.3d 1082, 61 Ill.Dec. 816, 435 N.E.2d 513, where we reversed the trial court's decision in favor of the plaintiff after determining that plaintiff's evidence failed to show that the defendant's product (deodorant) contained an ingredient to which a substantial number of the population was allergic. We found instead that the proximate cause of the plaintiff's injury was due to the *plaintiff's* idiosyncratic reaction or allergy to the product and not to the company's failure to warn of a defect.

In the case at bar, however, plaintiff testified that her knee had never been such a problem for her that she could not practice gymnastics, although it had been "locking up" on her during her diving (swimming) practice in her freshman year. Unlike the plaintiff in *Presbrey*, therefore, whose unusual susceptibility was a successful defense to liability because the manufacturer did not know and had no reason to know that a small minority of the users of its product was allergic to an ingredient in the product, the jury in the instant matter could reasonably determine that plaintiff's injury was not caused by any unusual propensity on her part.  Thus, even if AMF had known of plaintiff's "knee condition," it would not be absolved of the duty to adequately warn users of the high risk of injury associated with the mini-tramp.

AMF next contends that the trial court's refusal to give several of its jury instructions improperly precluded the jury from considering the percentage of contributory negligence attributed to plaintiff. ****

In *Coney v. J.L.G. Industries, Inc.* (1983), 97 Ill.2d 104, 73 Ill.Dec. 337, 454 N.E.2d 197, our supreme court upheld the principle that contributory negligence is *not* a defense in a strict product liability tort action.  Comparative fault *is* applicable to strict liability cases, the court determined, but only insofar as the defenses of misuse and assumption of the risk are concerned.  Moreover, these defenses no longer preclude recovery in such actions.  Thus, once a defendant's liability is established, and where both the defective product *and* the plaintiff's misconduct contribute to cause the damages, the comparative fault principle will operate to reduce the plaintiff's recovery by that amount which the trier of fact finds him at fault.

In the case at bar, AMF failed to establish that plaintiff's alleged negligence rose to the level of misuse of the mini-tramp or that she assumed the risk of injury.  Rather, we are of the opinion that the evidence showed that because the warnings as well as any other information AMF provided about the mini-tramp were ineffective and failed to warn that use of the equipment without a safety device and proper supervision could result in permanent injury, plaintiff was unaware that somersaulting off of this product could result in serious injury.  Furthermore, because there was no evidence that plaintiff had used the mini-tramp for a purpose that was neither intended nor reasonably foreseeable, AMF's allegation of misuse of the product will be rejected.

We further note that the *Coney* decision mentioned above was recently applied by this court in a strict liability action where the defendant alleged, like AMF in the case at bar, that the comparative fault principle should apply to all aspects of plaintiff's culpability, including the plaintiff's alleged contributory negligence.  *** We reject this contention since permitting the ordinary contributory negligence of a plaintiff to reduce damages in strict liability actions would frustrate the policy considerations underlying this tort theory.  In such actions, the focus is on the design and performance of the product and the plaintiff is relieved of the burden of proving negligence.  Moreover, a consumer's unobservant or inattentive failure to discover or guard against a defect is not a damage reducing factor. The trial court's ruling, which denied AMF's request for a contributory negligence instruction, will therefore prevail.

\*\*\*

Accordingly, for all of the foregoing reasons, the judgment of the circuit court of Cook County will be affirmed.

AFFIRMED.

## Notes & Questions

1. Must a manufacturer warn of obvious dangers? Why or why not? For example, must the manufacturer of carving knives warn users that the blades are sharp and might cut them?

2. Manufacturers now place multiple warning labels on products. Do consumers actually take them seriously? Or have we become so desensitized to them that we simply ignore them as if they were saying "blah, blah, blah"? One might well ask whether frequent flyers pay any attention to the airline crew's safety instructions regarding seatbelts, oxygen masks, and seat cushions as flotation devices as they taxi toward the runway?

3. Given the context of this injury (occurring in a high school gym class), is the plaintiff's claim - that she would not have attempted the somersault if there had been a visible warning label on the mini-tramp -credible? Isn't it more likely that she simply would have complied with the instructions of her gym teacher, no matter what type of warning label was on the apparatus? If true, what bearing should that fact have on the outcome of this decision?

4. Does this case teach manufacturers that they must specify: "Be certain to affix this warning label in a location where its user will be able to read it."? Isn't this a bit ridiculous? In terms of proximate cause, isn't it more reasonable to believe that the person who assembled the mini-tramp with the warning label on the wrong side (*i.e.,* facing downwards) was really the proximate cause of the plaintiff's injury, not AMF?

5. In light of this case, how would you advise a manufacturer of sporting goods equipment to deal with warning labels?

6. Explain the court's ruling regarding the defendant's claim that the plaintiff was contributorily negligent. What is the relationship between the doctrine of strict products liability, comparative negligence, misuse, and assumption of risk?

# Notes on Product Liability and Warranty/Commercial Law Theories for Sports Equipment Cases [1]

Generally, a person injured by an arguably defective, commercially supplied product has available at least three separate and distinct causes of action: negligence, breach of implied warranty, and strict liability in tort. In some cases, a fourth cause of action, breach of an express warranty, is available.[2]

## I. Product Liability

### A. General

The size of jury awards in sports-related product liability lawsuits can be substantial. Twenty years ago in a case involving a high school student who was injured on a mini-trampoline "the jury awarded plaintiff $5 million against AMF on the theory of strict liability...." The classic Sports Law treatise - The Law of Sports by Weistart and Lowell - articulates the general rule regarding sports equipment and product liability succinctly: "The suppliers of athletic equipment have a duty to exercise care for the protection of those who use their equipment or who may be endangered by its use." Another popular Sports Law treatise acknowledges: "In any sports-related accident, a products liability suit that puts the sports equipment

---

[1] Adapted from Russ VerSteeg, *Pole Vault Injuries: Product Liability and Commercial Law Theories*, 5 TEXAS REV. ENT. & SPORTS L. 237 (2004). I have edited out nearly all footnotes to make the note easier to read.

[2] Gary Uberstine, Editor; Joel Corry, Jeffrey Pressman, Assistant Editors, LAW OF PROFESSIONAL AND AMATEUR SPORTS (VOL. 3 2002) § 15:14 at 15-23 (hereinafter "GARY UBERSTINE, EDITOR; JOEL CORRY, JEFFREY PRESSMAN, ASSISTANT EDITORS"). *See also* Douglas Houser, John Ashworth, Ronald Clark, *Product Liability in the Sports Industry* 23 TORT & INSURANCE LAW JOURNAL 44, 47 (1987)("Today a person injured by a defective product has a choice of distinct, yet related, theories of recovery upon which to base his action, e.g., strict liability, negligence, or breach of warranty.").

under scrutiny should at least be considered." That same treatise explains further:

> Under a theory of strict liability in tort, a commercial supplier who sells a product 'in defective condition unreasonably dangerous to the user or consumer' is subject to liability for harm caused. Liability attaches even if the seller has exercised all possible care and even though the user or consumer has no contractual relation with the seller. The determination of whether a product is defective is made with reference to a reasonable consumer's expectations. Assumption of risk and misuse of the product are defenses.

The doctrine of product liability serves broad economic and social purposes. Because fault (*i.e.*, the failure to act like a reasonable person under similar circumstances) is not a criterion for a finding of liability in this context, product liability saddles manufacturers/sellers with the costs of injuries caused by their products. In one sense, manufacturers/seller are in a better position to guard against injury than are the individuals who wind up being hurt by their products. Hence, product liability imposes accident costs on the superior risk bearer. As Thomas Van Flein has stated:

> The touchstone of products liability is risk allocation. Liability imposed against the product manufacturer for economic and non-economic harm caused to consumers transfers the real costs of defective products to the manufacturers and retailers (who profit from the products) rather than the injured consumers or society as a whole.

Most American jurisdictions have adopted section 402A of the Restatement, Second, of Torts for their general definitions and general rules regarding products liability. Section 402A provides:

> (1) One who sells any product in a defective condition unreasonably dangerous to the user or consumer or to his property is subject to liabilityor physical harm thereby caused to the ultimate user or consumer, or to his property, if the seller is engaged in the business of selling such a product, and

(a) it is expected to and does reach the user or consumer without substantial change in the condition in which it is sold.

(2) The rule stated in Subsection (1) applies although
(a) the seller has exercised all possible care in the preparation and sale of his product, and
(b) the user or consumer has not bought the product from or entered into any contractual relation with the seller.

According to one commentator, "Section 402A imposes strict liability upon one who sells a product in a defective condition which is unreasonably dangerous to the user or consumer. The liability is in tort rather than warranty and therefore the various contract rules, such as notice of breach, do not apply."

It is common to define a product "defect" by actually recognizing three distinct types of product defects: 1) manufacturing defects; 2) design defects; and, 3) failures to warn adequately. Weistart & Lowell also identify and focus on these separate defects:

> [A] manufacturer must exercise reasonable care in the manufacture of a product which it should know would involve an unreasonable risk of physical harm, if not carefully made. The manufacturer also has the duty to exercise reasonable care in the adoption of a safe design for its products and may be liable for injuries to foreseeable users caused by a design which makes the product dangerous for the uses for which it was manufactured. In addition, the producer has a duty to test for and warn against any hidden dangers.

In a similar fashion, Uberstein explains:

> A review of case law reveals that there are three basic types of defects: manufacturing flaws, design flaws, and marketing flaws. Manufacturing flaws can be described as individual product imperfections, such as a coffee roll with a pebble in it. Design flaws impugn the entire product line. In litigation concerning the Ford Pinto, it was contended that all the Pintos of a given year were defective because Ford placed the gas tank in a dangerously vulnerable position behind the rear axle. This would be an example of

an alleged design defect. Finally, marketing flaws arise when the seller fails to provide needed instructions regarding proper use, or to provide adequate warnings concerning less obvious dangers.

Another key component of this definition of a defective product is the issue of what renders a product "unreasonably dangerous." In their article "Product Liability in the Sports Industry," Houser, Ashworth, and Clark posit:

> A defective product is "unreasonably dangerous" when the product is "dangerous to an extent beyond that which would be contemplated by the ordinary consumer who purchases it, with the ordinary knowledge common to the community as to its characteristics." It can be argued that an allegedly defective product used for an extended period of time without injury is prima facie not "unreasonably dangerous."

Similarly, Uberstein writes:

> The determination of whether a product is in a defective condition unreasonably dangerous depends on whether a reasonably prudent consumer would expect the defect to be present. By way of illustration, a cherry pie with a cherry pit in it would not be regarded as in a defective condition unreasonably dangerous. The reasonable consumer would expect to find a pit in a cherry pie every now and then.

Another important aspect of the law of product liability to bear in mind is that courts have gradually expanded the scope of potential plaintiffs. As Houser, Ashworth, and Clark note:

> Around 1965, the definitions of "user" and "consumer'"began to broaden gradually so that today an injured plaintiff may bring an action in strict liability even though he was not literally 'using' the product. Examples of the relaxation of this requirement include a bystander who was injured by the explosion of a shotgun, the driver of a car struck by another car, and a bystander injured by the explosion of a beer keg.

## B. Design Defects Introduction

According to Uberstein,

> The modern products liability case often revolves around a claim that the product is defectively designed. In such a case, the plaintiff impugns the conscious design choice of the manufacturer and attempts to show a safer, economically feasible design. In determining whether the manufacturer's choice of design renders the product in a "defective condition unreasonably dangerous," courts have been unable to agree on a single standard.

Houser, Ashworth, and Clark note:

> The nature of sports, however, is such that a great many of the products used serve the sole purpose of protecting the user. Face masks, batting helmets, releasable ski bindings, knee pads and braces, football helmets, goggles, railings, floor pads, mouthpieces, roll bars and shoulder pads are a few examples of such protective products. *A defect in a piece of protective sports equipment is more apt to make that product 'unreasonably dangerous' because its sole purpose is to protect the user.*

One court succinctly summarized the applicable legal doctrine as follows:

> it is well established that a product, although virtually faultless in design, material, and workmanship, may nevertheless be deemed defective so as to impose liability upon the manufacturer for physical harm resulting from its use, where the manufacturer fails to discharge a duty to warn or instruct with respect to potential dangers in the use of the product. Generally, the duty to warn arises where the supplier knows or should have known of the danger involved in the use of its product, or where it is unreasonably dangerous to place the product in the hands of a user without a suitable warning. However, where the danger or potentiality of danger is known or should be known to the user, the duty does not attach.

The court explained its reasoning further, stating,

> the law should supply the presumption that an adequate
> warning would have been read and heeded, thereby
> minimizing the obvious problems of proof of causation.
> We find such an approach to be meritorious, workable, and
> desirable. Comment j of Restatement (2d) Torts, § 402A
> (1965), provides a presumption protecting the
> manufacturer where a warning is given: "Where warning
> is given, the seller may reasonably assume that it will be
> read and heeded; ..." However, where there is no warning,
> as in the case at bar, the presumption of comment j that the
> user would have read and heeded an adequate warning
> works in favor of the plaintiff user. In other words, the
> presumption of causation herein is that [the plaintiff]
> would have read an adequate warning concerning the
> danger of a user's foot slipping between the elastic cables
> of Aqua Diver and heeded it, resulting in his not using the
> Aqua Diver.

Houser, Ashworth, and Clark emphasize two important points regarding the adequacy of product warnings. First, "There is, of course, no duty to warn of dangers that could have been readily recognized by the ordinary user." Furthermore, the appropriate standard for determining sufficiency of a warning would seem to be whether an ordinary consumer could read and understand the warnings so as to be able to take the necessary precautions. "Whether or not a given warning is adequate depends upon the language used and the impression that it is calculated to make upon the mind of an average user of the product."

## C. Defenses

As is true in all litigation, it is generally useful to distinguish between direct defenses and affirmative defenses. A direct defense relies on an argument that directly refutes an element of a plaintiff's prima facie case. For example, in a product liability suit, one element that a plaintiff must prove by a preponderance of the evidence is that the product in question was "defective unreasonably dangerous." Therefore, one direct defense in a product liability suit would be for a defendant to marshal facts and reasoning that tend to show that the product was not more dangerous than a reasonable consumer would have expected (*i.e.*, and therefore not defective unreasonably dangerous). An affirmative defense, on the other

123

hand, is an argument that does not attempt to refute an element of the plaintiff's prima facie case, but instead, seeks to show an alternative explanation for the plaintiff's injury or justification for the defendant's conduct.

In a product liability lawsuit, defendants commonly raise five different (but in some cases related) affirmative defenses: 1) Plaintiff misused the product or used the product in a manner that the manufacturer/seller did not intend (but the plaintiffs misuse must not have been reasonably foreseeable); 2) Manufacturer/seller provided proper instructions and/or warnings regarding the product's use which the plaintiff failed to heed (and if plaintiff had heeded those warnings the product would have been safe); 3) Use or normal wear and tear over time have significantly changed the product from the condition that it was in when it left the manufacturer's/seller's control; 4) Plaintiff assumed the risk of injury; 5) Unforeseeable superseding conduct by a third party (*e.g.*, a coach's negligence) was the proximate cause of the plaintiffs injury, not the defendant's product.

**1) Plaintiff misused the product or used the product in a manner that the manufacturer/seller did not intend (but the plaintiff's misuse must not have been reasonably foreseeable)**

**2) Manufacturer/seller provided proper instructions and/or warnings regarding the product's use which the plaintiff failed to heed (and if plaintiff had heeded those instructions/warnings the product would have been safe).**

Weistart and Lowell articulate this rule as follows: "The seller may avoid liability by giving proper instructions and warnings which, if followed, will make the product safe. The seller may also reasonably assume that such directives will be read and followed."

**3) Use and/or normal wear and tear over time have significantly changed the product from the condition that it was in when it left the manufacturer's/seller's control.**

**4) Plaintiff assumed the risk of injury (but was not contributorily negligent).**

But assumption of risk as that concept relates to the legal theory of negligence is distinctly different from assumption of risk as that concept relates to strict product liability. In order to assume risk for product liability, a plaintiff must know of a product's defect and must use it voluntarily, in the face of that knowledge. *Moore v. Sitzmark Corp.* provides an apt illustration of assumption of risk in the context of sports equipment product liability. In *Moore,* the plaintiff broke her leg when her ski binding failed to release during a fall. Although the plaintiff had signed a waiver of liability and although she was aware that skiing was a dangerous activity, in order to determine whether she had assumed the risk of a defective design, the court quoted the applicable statute for the proposition that she would have to have actually known of the defect in the ski bindings and yet persisted in skiing on them, notwithstanding that knowledge: "It is a defense that the user or consumer bringing the action knew of the *defect* and was aware of the danger and nevertheless proceeded unreasonably to make use of the product and was injured by it." The court explained further:

> [Defendants] merely argue Moore knew her bindings would not release under all circumstances. Absent the threshold showing that Moore knew of a defect in the bindings, neither Salomon nor Sitzmark is entitled to summary judgment on the grounds of incurred risk. The trial court's grant of summary judgment on Moore's strict liability theory was improper.

In footnote 4 of the opinion, the court drew the analogy to the kinds of risks assumed by pole vaulters: "In a similar case, the Missouri Court of Appeals held a high school pole vaulter assumed the inherent risks of pole vaulting, but not the risks of the manufacturer's negligence."

**5) Unforeseeable superseding conduct by a third party (*e.g.*, a coach's gross negligence) was the proximate cause of the plaintiff's injury, not the defendant's product.**

Theoretically, if a third party's conduct intervenes in an unforeseeable manner, that third party's unforeseeable act may relieve an equipment manufacturer/seller/defendant of liability for injury caused by a defective product.

We label such acts by a third party which are unforeseeable as "superseding" acts. Acts by a third party which are unforeseeable and therefore "superseding" are said to "break the chain of causation" and thereby would legally supersede the equipment manufacturer's/seller's liability (*i.e.*, a superseding act relieves the manufacturer/seller of liability).

## II. Commercial Law Theories

### A. General

In addition to strict product liability, an injured athlete may also (or in the alternative) look to commercial law; specifically the Uniform Commercial Code ("UCC") for legal theories of recovery against manufacturers/sellers. Under the UCC, one theory of legal liability available to plaintiffs is warranty law. Nearly all jurisdictions in the United States have adopted Article Two of the UCC. Article Two provides at least three different warranties that are likely to apply in the sale of most sporting goods equipment. Specifically, the most obvious warranty theories are breach of: 1) express warranty (§ 2-313); 2) implied warranty of merchantability (§ 2-314); and, 3) implied warranty of fitness for a particular purpose (§ 2-315). In addition to these, another commercial law theory that an injured plaintiff should keep in mind arises under the warranties created pursuant to the Magnuson Moss Warranty Act. The UCC warranties may apply to the various types of sports equipment and apparatus which constitute "goods" as that term is defined in the UCC.

### B. Express Warranty

### General

According to § 2-313 of the UCC, a seller may create an express warranty in a number of ways.

> **§ 2-313 Express Warranties by Affirmation, Promise, Description, Sample.**
>
> (1) Express warranties by the seller are created as follows:
>
> (a) Any affirmation of fact or promise made by the seller to the buyer which relates to the goods and becomes part of the basis of the bargain creates an express warranty that the goods shall conform to the affirmation or promise.
> (b) Any description of the goods which is made part of the basis of the bargain creates an express warranty that the goods shall conform to the description.
> (c) Any sample or model which is made part of the basis of the bargain creates an express warranty that the whole of the goods shall conform to the sample or model.

(2) It is not necessary to the creation of an express warranty that the seller use formal words such as "warrant" or "guarantee" or that he have a specific intention to make a warranty, but an affirmation merely of the value of the goods or a statement purporting to be merely the seller's opinion or commendation of the goods does not create a warranty.

## C. Implied Warranty of Merchantability

Section 2-314 of the UCC contains the general rules regarding the implied warranty of merchantability.

### § 2-314. Implied Warranty: Merchantability; Usage of Trade.

(1) Unless excluded or modified (Section 2-316), a warranty that the goods shall be merchantable is implied in a contract for their sale if the seller is a merchant with respect to goods of that kind....

(2) Goods to be merchantable must be at least such as

(a) pass without objection in the trade under the contract description; and

(b) in the case of fungible goods, are of fair average quality within the description; and

(c) are fit for the ordinary purposes for which such goods are used; and

(d) run, within the variations permitted by the agreement, of even kind, quality, and quantity within each unit and among all units involved; and

(e) are adequately contained, packaged, and labeled as the agreement may require; and

(f) conform to the promise or affirmations of fact made on the container or label if any.

(3) Unless excluded or modified (Section 2-316) other implied warranties may arise from course of dealing or usage of trade.

To begin with, in order for this warranty to apply, the seller must be a "merchant" as that term is defined as a term of art in the UCC. Suffice it to say that a sporting goods store, a sporting goods supply catalogue company, and manufacturing companies themselves will generally be considered "merchants" for purposes of this rule. In order to be considered a "merchant," triggering § 2-314, a seller must regularly deal in goods of the kind. A coach, a school, another athlete, or an occasional eBay seller will ordinarily not come within the scope of the "merchant" rule for purposes of section 2-314.

## D. Implied Warranty of Fitness for a Particular Purpose

UCC § 2-315 ("Implied Warranty: Fitness for a Particular Purpose") states: "Where the seller at the time of contracting has reason to know any particular purpose for which the goods are required and that the buyer is relying on the seller's skill or judgment to select or furnish suitable goods, there is...an implied warranty that the goods shall be fit for such purpose.

## E. Liability for Personal Injury

A manufacturer's/seller's breach of any warranty - express § 2-313), implied merchantability § 2-314), or implied fitness for a particular purpose (§ 2-315) - could easily subject him/her to liability for injuries to a vaulter pursuant to §§ 2-715(2)(b) and 2-719(3).

### § 2-715 Buyer's Incidental and Consequential Damages

(2) Consequential damages resulting from the seller's breach include...

(b) injury to person or property proximately resulting from any breach of warranty.

### § 2-719 Contractual Modification or Limitation of Remedy

(4) Consequential damages may be limited or excluded unless the limitation or exclusion is unconscionable. Limitation of consequential damages for injury to the person in the case of consumer goods is prima facie unconscionable but limitation of damages where the loss is commercial is not.

## F. Defenses to Warranty Actions

## 1. Lack of Privity

A lack of privity may be one legal obstacle that could prove difficult for some plaintiffs. Traditionally, at common law, a person who was injured by a product was barred from bringing a contract action against a seller unless s/he (*i.e.*, the plaintiff) was in privity of contract with the seller. Although the common law has relaxed this privity rule somewhat, and although the UCC has a specific provision, § 2-318, designed to address the issue, the rule may present special problems in the context of sports equipment liability. Section 2-318 defines the scope of both plaintiffs and defendants contemplated by Article 2 for personal injury.

### § 2-318 Third Party Beneficiaries of Warranties Express or Implied

**Note:** *If this Act is introduced in the Congress of the United States this section should be omitted. (States to select one alternative)*

#### Alternative A

A seller's warranty whether express or implied extends to any natural person who is in the family or household of his buyer or who is a guest in his home if it is reasonable to expect that such person may use, consume or be affected by the goods and who is injured in person by breach of the warranty. A seller may not exclude or limit the operation of this section.

#### Alternative B

A seller's warranty whether express or implied extends to any natural person who may reasonably be expected to use, consume or be affected by the goods and who is injured in person by breach of the warranty. A seller may not exclude or limit the operation of this section.

**Alternative C**

A seller's warranty whether express or implied extends to any person who may reasonably be expected to use, consume or be affected by the goods and who is injured by breach of the warranty. A seller may not exclude or limit the operation of this section with respect to injury to the person of an individual to whom the warranty extends.

On the issue of potential plaintiffs, § 2-318 offers three different alternatives, gradually progressing from very restrictive to very expansive. Alternative A provides, in part, that a seller's warranty "extends to any natural person who is in the family or household of his buyer or who is a guest in his home if it is reasonable to expect that such person may use...or be affected by the goods and who is injured in person by breach of the warranty."

Comment Three to § 2-318 addresses the issue of "vertical privity." Comment Three provides, in part: "this section...is neutral and is not intended to enlarge or restrict the developing case law on whether the seller's warranties, given to his buyer who resells, extend to other persons in the distributive chain." Hence, § 2-318 makes it a matter of state law, for example, whether a plaintiff-buyer may sue a wholesaler and/or a manufacturer - in addition to a direct retailer from whom s/he bought the product. As a rule, the majority of American jurisdictions permit a plaintiff to sue a wholesaler and/or manufacturer, despite a technical lack of vertical privity between those entities and the typical buyer.

## 2. Limitation or Exclusion of Liability

To be sure, sellers may exclude or modify express and implied warranties by employing the mechanics of § 2-316.

If a manufacturer wishes to minimize its exposure to liability for breach of warranty, I suggest that manufacturers insist on language such as the following:

> **WARRANTY DISCLAIMER: THE**
> **MANUFACTURER EXPRESSLY DISCLAIMS ANY**
> **EXPRESS OR IMPLIED WARRANTIES,**
> **INCLUDING THE WARRANTY OF**
> **MERCHANTABILITY AND/OR THE WARRANTY**

**OF FITNESS FOR A PARTICULAR PURPOSE. SALESPERSONS MAY HAVE MADE ORAL OR WRITTEN STATEMENTS ABOUT THE MERCHANDISE WHICH IS THE SUBJECT OF THIS SALE. THE MANUFACTURER HAS NOT AUTHORIZED SUCH STATEMENTS AND SUCH STATEMENTS DO NOT CONSTITUTE WARRANTIES, SHALL NOT BE RELIED ON BY THE BUYER, AND ARE NO PART OF THE CONTRACT FOR SALE.**

This disclaimer must be clearly labeled as a "Warranty Disclaimer" (so that a reasonable consumer should recognize that it is not "hidden" within a purported warranty). Also, in order to be valid, it must be "conspicuous," which the UCC defines as:

> so written, displayed, or presented that a reasonable person against which it is to operate ought to have noticed it. Whether a term is "conspicuous" or not is a decision for the court.[3] Conspicuous terms include the following:

(A) a heading in capitals equal to or greater in size than the surrounding text, or in contrasting type, font, or color to the surrounding text of the same or lesser size; and

(B) language in the body of a record or display in larger type than the surrounding text, or in contrasting type, font, or color to the surrounding text of the same size, or set off from the surrounding text of the same size by symbols or other marks that call attention to the languages.

Thus, it should be written prominently in some fashion which calls attention to it; such as a contrasting color or typeface (ALL CAPS and/or **BOLDFACE** should suffice). Note that although the disclaimer/exclusionary language purports to disclaim any express warranty, § 2-316 (1) of the Code creates a rule which, as a matter of fact, makes it virtually impossible to disclaim express warranties. That section provides:

---

[3] *I.e.,* It is a question of law that the judge will decide, not a question of fact for a jury to decide.

## § 2-316 Exclusion or Modification of Warranties

(1) Words or conduct relevant to the creation of an express warranty and words or conduct tending to negate or limit warranty shall be construed wherever reasonable as consistent with each other...negation or limitation is inoperative to the extent that such construction is unreasonable.

According to the rule of § 2-316(1), when faced with this issue, courts will compare the language which the plaintiff argues creates an express warranty with the language which the defendant claims to exclude an express warranty. Then, to the extent that the court considers the two to be inconsistent, the court construes that inconsistency as rendering the purported exclusion void. The standard treatise on commercial law takes the position that courts should enforce language in a warranty disclaimer which nullifies unauthorized verbal or written statements made by salespeople such as that suggested (*i.e.*, Sales persons may have.... ").

But even if courts are unwilling to enforce a warranty disclaimer of this type, occasionally language such as this will deter a lawsuit because a consumer will read the warranty disclaimer and assume that it is valid and binding. If a disclaimer prevents even one lawsuit against a manufacturer or seller, it will be cost effective.

Section 2-715 of the UCC provides that a seller may limit or exclude liability for consequential damages. Many sellers in today's marketplace commonly do just this sort of thing by stating, for example, "In no event shall seller be liable for incidental or consequential damages. Seller's liability is limited to refund, repair, or replacement of defective goods."

However, when the consequential loss complained of is personal injury, sellers have a much more difficult task in making such an exclusion or limitation stand up in court. Subsection (3) of § 2-719 states: "Consequential damages may be limited or excluded unless the limitation or exclusion is unconscionable. Limitation of consequential damages for injury to the person in the case of *consumer goods* is prima facie unconscionable...."

The unresolved question, then, is whether sports equipment is considered "consumer goods." The general definitions section of the UCC (§ 1-201) does not define "consumer goods" but it defines "consumer" as "an individual who enters into a transaction primarily for personal, family, or household purposes."[4] Although Article 2 does not define "consumer goods," Article 9 defines "consumer goods" as "goods that are used or bought for use primarily for personal, family, or household purposes." It strikes me as strange to think that whether this type of exclusionary language is considered "prima facie unconscionable" may depend on the specific facts of each case (*i.e.*, whether the actual buyer purchases the goods on an individual basis or for an institution, such as a school or club). For example, if a school were to purchase sports equipment for its athletes, arguably that equipment would *not* come within the definition of "consumer goods," whereas if an individual athlete or a athlete's parent were to purchase the same equipment, it *would* be considered "consumer goods." It simply seems strange to think that the burden of proving unconscionability would depend on the status of who happens to purchase any given piece of equipment.

In addition, it will be useful for product manufacturers to recognize that even effective/valid warranty disclaimers might not be sufficient to insulate them from all forms of liability. As the court in *McCormick* noted: "The statements in the catalogue to the effect that defendant did not guarantee the pole against splitting or breaking did not relieve it from the consequence of its negligence."

*Further Reading on Coach's Liability and Equipment:*

Thomas R. Hurst, *Coach's Liability for Athlete's Injuries and Deaths*, 13 SETON HALL J. SPORTS L. 27 (2003).

The Law of Sports, Weistart and Lowell, §§8.06, 8.09-11.

---

[4] UCC §1-201

# Chapter 4

# Torts III: Institutions, Officials, & Waivers

---

In this chaptert we look at the liability of institutions. The principal issue is whether and/or to what extent a school, club, school board, etc. can be held responsible for injuries to athletes or spectators. What steps must an institution take to balance the need for safety and the risks that go hand-in-hand with vigorous competition? As was the case with liability for equipment manufacturers, again we must balance the need for safety with the risks that are inherent in participation in certain sports. *Kleinknecht* asks us to think about the provision of medical and emergency personnel. Costs and risks are again fundamental considerations.

*Hammond* integrates questions about assumption of risk and obvious dangers. What is the scope of a school's duty to warn athletes and their parents about the dangers associated with various sports?

*Santopietro* raises another serious issue - the responsibility of officials for the safety of participants and spectators. As any casual sports fan is well aware, officials, referees, and umpires cannot see everything. But when rule violations occur and an injury results, it is only natural that some may point an accusatory finger at the officials who, perhaps, could have prevented the rule violation in the first place.

*Hiett* and *Lund* examine another important aspect of liability for sports injuries - the enforceability of liability waivers. These cases ask what role public policy should play in using contracts and express assumption of risk to allocate risks in athletic competition. These cases, because they involve the use of contracts to allocate risk of loss, also serve as a bridge to the next chapter, Contracts.

# Kleinknecht v. Gettysburg College
989 F 2d 1360 (1993)
United States Court of Appeals, Third Circuit

HUTCHINSON, Circuit Judge.

Suzanne W. Kleinknecht and Richard P. Kleinknecht (collectively "the Kleinknechts") appeal an order of the United States District Court for the Middle District of Pennsylvania granting summary judgment to appellee Gettysburg College ("the College"). We will reverse the district court's order granting summary judgment to the College for the following reasons.

## I. *Procedural History*

Drew Kleinknecht died of cardiac arrest on September 16, 1988, while a student at the College and during a practice session of its intercollegiate lacrosse team. His parents filed this wrongful death and survival action against the College on August 15, 1990. The College filed an answer on September 11, 1990, and a motion for summary judgment on August 31, 1991. The district court initially denied the motion on November 1, 1991, but then granted the College's motion for reconsideration on January 9, 1992.

Following oral argument on January 30, 1992, the district court reversed its earlier decision and entered summary judgment in favor of the College on March 12, 1992. *Kleinknecht v. Gettysburg College,* 786 F.Supp. 449 (M.D.Pa.1992). In its opinion, the court first held that the College had no duty to anticipate and guard against the chance of a fatal arrhythmia in a young and healthy athlete. *Id.* at 454. The court also held that the actions taken by school employees following Drew's collapse were reasonable, and thus the College did not negligently breach any duty that might exist. *Id.* at 456.

\*\*\*\*

The Kleinknechts filed a timely appeal on March 25, 1992.

## II. *Factual History*

In September 1988, Drew Kleinknecht was a twenty-year old sophomore student at the College, which had recruited him for its Division III intercollegiate lacrosse team. The College is a private, four-year liberal arts school. In 1988, it had an enrollment of about two thousand students and supported twenty-one intercollegiate sports teams involving approximately 525 male and female athletes.

Lacrosse is a contact sport. In terms of sports-related injuries at the College, it ranked at least fourth behind football, basketball, and wrestling, respectively. Lacrosse players can typically suffer a variety of injuries, including unconsciousness, wooziness, concussions, being knocked to the ground, and having the wind knocked out of them. Before Drew died, however, no athlete at the College had experienced cardiac arrest while playing lacrosse or any other sport.

In September 1988, the College employed two full-time athletic trainers, Joseph Donolli and Gareth Biser. Both men were certified by the National Athletic Trainers Association, which requires, *inter alia,* current certification in both cardio-pulmonary resuscitation ("CPR") and standard first aid. In addition, twelve student trainers participated in the College's sports program. The trainers were stationed in the College's two training room facilities at Musselman Stadium and Plank Gymnasium.

Because lacrosse is a spring sport, daily practices were held during the spring semester in order to prepare for competition. Student trainers were assigned to cover both spring practices and games. Fall practice was held only for the players to learn "skills and drills," and to become acquainted with the other team members. No student trainers were assigned to the fall practices.

Drew participated in a fall lacrosse practice on the afternoon of September 16, 1988. Coaches Janczyk and Anderson attended and supervised this practice. It was held on the softball fields outside Musselman Stadium. No trainers or student trainers were present. Neither coach had certification in CPR. Neither coach had a radio on the practice field. The nearest telephone was inside the training room at Musselman Stadium, roughly 200-250 yards away. The shortest route to this telephone required scaling an eight-foot high cyclone fence surrounding the stadium. According to Coach Janczyk, he and Coach Anderson had never discussed how they would handle an emergency during fall lacrosse practice.

The September 16, 1988 practice began at about 3:15 p.m. with jogging and stretching, some drills, and finally a "six on six" drill in which the team split into two groups at opposite ends of the field. Drew was a defenseman and was participating in one of the drills when he suffered a cardiac arrest. According to a teammate observing from the sidelines, Drew simply stepped away from the play and dropped to the ground. Another

137

UNIVERSITY OF WINCHESTER
LIBRARY

teammate on the sidelines stated that no person or object struck Drew prior to his collapse.

After Drew fell, his teammates and Coach Janczyk ran to his side. Coach Janczyk and some of the players noticed that Drew was lying so that his head appeared to be in an awkward position. No one knew precisely what had happened at that time, and at least some of those present suspected a spinal injury. Team captain Daniel Polizzotti testified that he heard a continuous "funny" "gurgling" noise coming from Drew, and knew from what he observed that something "major" was wrong. Other teammates testified that Drew's skin began quickly to change colors. One team member testified that by the time the coaches had arrived, "[Drew] was really blue."

According to the College, Coach Janczyk acted in accordance with the school's emergency plan by first assessing Drew's condition, then dispatching players to get a trainer and call for an ambulance. Coach Janczyk himself then began to run toward Musselman Stadium to summon help.

The Kleinknechts dispute the College's version of the facts. They note that although Coach Janczyk claims to have told two players to run to Apple Hall, a nearby dormitory, for help, Coach Anderson did not recall Coach Janczyk's sending anyone for help. Even if Coach Janczyk did send the two players to Apple Hall, the Kleinknechts maintain, his action was inappropriate because Apple Hall was not the location of the nearest telephone. It is undisputed that two other team members ran for help, but the Kleinknechts contend that the team members did this on their own accord, without instruction from either coach.

The parties do not dispute that Polizzotti, the team captain, ran toward the stadium, where he knew a training room was located and a student trainer could be found. In doing so, Polizzotti scaled a chain link fence that surrounded the stadium and ran across the field, encountering student trainer Traci Moore outside the door to the training room. He told her that a lacrosse player was down and needed help. She ran toward the football stadium's main gate, managed to squeeze through a gap between one side of the locked gate and the brick pillar forming its support, and continued on to the practice field by foot until flagging a ride from a passing car. In the meantime, Polizzotti continued into the training room where he told the student trainers there what had happened. One of them phoned Plank Gymnasium and told Head Trainer Donolli about the emergency.

Contemporaneously with Polizzotti's dash to the stadium, Dave Kerney, another team member, ran toward the stadium for assistance. Upon seeing that Polizzotti was going to beat him there, Kerney concluded that it was pointless for both of them to arrive at the same destination and changed his course toward the College Union Building. He told the student at the front desk of the emergency on the practice field. The student called his supervisor on duty in the building, and she immediately telephoned for an ambulance.

Student trainer Moore was first to reach Drew. She saw Drew's breathing was labored, and the color of his complexion changed as she watched. Because Drew was breathing, she did not attempt CPR or any other first aid technique, but only monitored his condition, observing no visible bruises or lacerations.

By this time, Coach Janczyk had entered the stadium training room and learned that Donolli had been notified and an ambulance called. Coach Janczyk returned to the practice field at the same time Donolli arrived in a golf cart. Donolli saw that Drew was not breathing, and turned him on his back to begin CPR with the help of a student band member who was certified as an emergency medical technician and had by chance arrived on the scene. The two of them performed CPR until two ambulances arrived at approximately 4:15 p.m. Drew was defibrillated and drugs were administered to strengthen his heart. He was placed in an ambulance and taken to the hospital, but despite repeated resuscitation efforts, Drew could not be revived. He was pronounced dead at 4:58 p.m.

As the district court observed, the parties vigorously dispute the amount of time that elapsed in connection with the events following Drew's collapse. The College maintains that "Coach Janczyk immediately ran to Drew's side, followed closely by assistant coach, Anderson." Team captain Polizzotti estimated that it took him no more than thirty seconds to get from the practice field to the training room. The College contends that it took Moore no more than two minutes to get from the training room to Drew's side. In fact, the College maintains, the lacrosse team was practicing on this particular field because of its close proximity to the training room and the student trainers. The College estimates that an ambulance was present within eight to ten minutes after Drew's collapse.

The Kleinknechts, on the other hand, assert that as much as a minute to a minute and a half passed before Coach Janczyk arrived at Drew's side. With the aid of an engineering firm, the Kleinknechts constructed a map for the district court showing the paths taken by Polizzotti and Kerney, including estimates of how long it took them to arrive at their respective destinations and relay their messages to those who could be of assistance. They estimate that it took Polizzotti a minute and a half to arrive at the stadium training room from the practice field, advise someone on duty, and have that person notify Donolli. The Kleinknechts also estimate that it took Kerney two minutes and thirteen seconds to arrive at the College Union Building, speak to the student at the desk, and then have the secretary telephone for an ambulance. They point to Donolli's deposition testimony indicating that it took him approximately three minutes and fifteen seconds to arrive at the scene. The Kleinknechts further maintain, and the College does not dispute, that at least five minutes elapsed from the time that Drew was first observed on the ground until Head Trainer Donolli began administering CPR. Thus, the Kleinknechts contend that evidence exists from which a jury could infer that as long as twelve minutes elapsed before CPR was administered. They also estimate that roughly ten more minutes passed before the first ambulance arrived on the scene.

Prior to his collapse on September 16, 1988, Drew had no medical history of heart problems. The Kleinknechts themselves describe him as "a healthy, physically active and vigorous young man" with no unusual medical history until his death. In January 1988, a College physician had examined Drew to determine his fitness to participate in sports and found him to be in excellent health. The Kleinknecht's family physician had also examined Drew in August 1987 and found him healthy and able to participate in physical activity.

Medical evidence indicated Drew died of cardiac arrest after a fatal attack of cardiac arrhythmia. Post-mortem examination could not detect the cause of Drew's fatal cardiac arrhythmia. An autopsy conducted the day after his death revealed no bruises or contusions on his body. This corroborated the statements by Drew's teammates that he was not in play when he suffered his cardiac arrest and dispelled the idea that contact with a ball or stick during the practice might have caused the arrhythmia. The National Institutes of Health examined Drew's heart as part of the autopsy but found no pathology. A later examination of the autopsy records by a different pathologist, and still further study by yet another physician after Drew's body was exhumed, also failed to reveal any heart abnormality which could have explained Drew's fatal heart attack.

III. *Issues on Appeal*

The Kleinknechts...first argue that the district court erred in determining that the College had no legal duty to implement preventive

140

measures assuring prompt assistance and treatment in the event one of its student athletes suffered cardiac arrest while engaged in school-supervised intercollegiate athletic activity.   Second, the Kleinknechts maintain that the district court erred in determining that the actions of school employees following Drew's collapse were reasonable and that the College therefore did not breach any duty of care. ****

A federal court exercising diversity jurisdiction must "apply the substantive law of the state whose laws govern the action." *Robertson v. Allied Signal, Inc.,* 914 F.2d 360, 378 (3d Cir.1990) (citing *Erie R.R. v. Tompkins,* 304 U.S. 64, 58 S.Ct. 817, 82 L.Ed. 1188 (1938)).   The parties agree that Pennsylvania law applies to the present dispute.   "In cases where the state's highest court has not considered the precise question to be answered, the federal court is called upon to predict how the state court would resolve the issue should it be called upon to do so." *Id.* (citations omitted).   Because the Supreme Court of Pennsylvania has not addressed the precise issues raised by the Kleinknechts, we must attempt to predict how that Court would rule in this case.

IV. *Analysis*

1. *The Duty of Care Issue*

[2][3] Whether a defendant owes a duty of care to a plaintiff is a question of law.   *See* Restatement (Second) of Torts § 328(B) (1965) (court determines whether facts give rise to any legal duty on part of defendant) [case citations omitted]   In order to prevail on a cause of action in negligence under Pennsylvania law, a plaintiff must establish:  (1) a duty or obligation recognized by the law, requiring the actor to conform to a certain standard of conduct;  (2) a failure to conform to the standard required;  (3) a causal connection between the conduct and the resulting injury;  and (4) actual loss or damage resulting to the interests of another. *Morena,* 462 A.2d at 684 n. 5 (citing Prosser, Law of Torts § 30, at 143 (4th ed. 1971)).

The Kleinknechts assert…different theories upon which they predicate the College's duty to establish preventive measures capable of providing treatment to student athletes in the event of a medical emergency such as Drew's cardiac arrest: (1) existence of a special relationship between the College and its student athletes; [and] (2) foreseeability that a student athlete may suffer cardiac arrest while engaged in athletic activity….

a. *Special Relationship*

[4] The Kleinknechts argue that the College had a duty of care to Drew by virtue of his status as a member of an intercollegiate athletic team. The Supreme Court of Pennsylvania has stated that "[d]uty, in any given situation, is predicated on the relationship existing between the parties at the relevant time...." *Morena,* 462 A.2d at 684. The Kleinknechts argue that... a college or university owes a duty to its intercollegiate athletes to provide preventive measures in the event of a medical emergency.

In support of their argument, the Kleinknechts cite the case of *Hanson v. Kynast,* No. CA-828 (Ohio Ct.App. June 3, 1985), *rev'd on other grounds,* 24 Ohio St.3d 171, 494 N.E.2d. 1091 (1986). In *Hanson* an intercollegiate, recruited lacrosse player was seriously injured while playing in a lacrosse game against another college. The plaintiff alleged that his university breached its legal duty to have an ambulance present during the lacrosse game. The trial court granted the defendant's motion for summary judgment based on its holding, *inter alia,* that

> There is no duty as a matter of law for the Defendant College or other sponsor of athletic events to have ambulances, emergency vehicles, trained help or doctors present during the playing of a lacrosse game or other athletic events, and the failure to do so does not constitute negligence as a matter of law. *Id.* at 10.

The court of appeals reversed, concluding, "[I]t is a question of fact for the jury to determine whether or not appellee University acted reasonably in failing to have an ambulance present at the field or to provide quick access to the field in the event of an emergency." *Id.* at 6. By directing the trial court to submit the case to a jury, the court of appeals implicitly held that the university owed a duty of care to the plaintiff.

****

Like the lacrosse student in *Hanson,* Drew chose to attend Gettysburg College because he was persuaded it had a good lacrosse program, a sport in which he wanted to participate at the intercollegiate level. Head Trainer Donolli actively recruited Drew to play lacrosse at the College. At the time he was stricken, Drew was not engaged in his own private affairs as a student at Gettysburg College. Instead, he was participating in a scheduled athletic practice for an intercollegiate team sponsored by the College under the supervision of College employees. On these facts we

142

believe that the Supreme Court of Pennsylvania would hold that a special relationship existed between the College and Drew that was sufficient to impose a duty of reasonable care on the College. Other states have similarly concluded that a duty exists based on such a relationship (multiple citations).[1]

\*\*\*\*

Drew was not acting in his capacity as a private student when he collapsed. Indeed, the Kleinknechts concede that if he had been, they would have no recourse against the College. There is a distinction between a student injured while participating as an intercollegiate athlete in a sport for which he was recruited and a student injured at a college while pursuing his private interests, scholastic or otherwise. This distinction serves to limit the class of students to whom a college owes the duty of care that arises here. Had Drew been participating in a fraternity football game, for example, the College might not have owed him the same duty or perhaps any duty at all. There is, however, no need for us to reach or decide the duty question either in that context or in the context of whether a college would owe a duty towards students participating in intramural sports. On the other hand, the fact that Drew's cardiac arrest occurred during an athletic event involving an intercollegiate team of which he was a member does impose a duty of due care on a college that actively sought his participation in that sport. We cannot help but think that the College recruited Drew for its own benefit, probably thinking that his skill at lacrosse would bring favorable attention and so aid the College in attracting other students.

\*\*\*\*

In conclusion, we predict that the Supreme Court of Pennsylvania would hold that the College owed Drew a duty of care in his capacity as an intercollegiate athlete engaged in school-sponsored intercollegiate athletic activity for which he had been recruited.

---

[1] We recognize that most of these cases involve participation on sports sponsored by a public school system at the pre-college level. Arguably, the relationship between the injured participant and the sponsor is closer, and the need to import a duty based on the special nature of the relationship between a public school and its interscholastic athletes is therefore more compelling than the case of a private college and its students participating in an intercollegiate athletic program. Here, however, we think that that distinction is balanced out by Gettysburg's active recruitment of Drew to participate in its intercollegiate lacrosse program.

b. *Foreseeability*

This does not end our inquiry, however. The determination that the College owes a duty of care to its intercollegiate athletes could merely define the class of persons to whom the duty extends, without determining the nature of the duty or demands it makes on the College. Because it is foreseeable that student athletes may sustain severe and even life-threatening injuries while engaged in athletic activity, the Kleinknechts argue that the College's duty of care required it to be ready to respond swiftly and adequately to a medical emergency. *See Blake v. Fried,* 173 Pa.Super. 27, 95 A.2d 360, 364 (1953) (requiring risk "reasonably to be perceived" in order to impose duty).

Foreseeability is a legal requirement before recovery can be had. *See Griggs v. BIC Corp.,* 981 F.2d 1429, 1435 (3d Cir.1992) (foreseeability is integral part of determination that duty exists under Pennsylvania negligence law) (citing *Carson v. City of Philadelphia,* 133 Pa.Cmwlth. 74, 574 A.2d 1184, 1187 (1990)). "'The test of negligence is whether the wrongdoer could have anticipated and foreseen the likelihood of harm to the injured person, resulting from his act.'" *Id.* (quoting *Dahlstrom v. Shrum,* 368 Pa. 423, 84 A.2d 289, 290-91 (1951)).

\*\*\*\*

[I]n the context of duty, "[t]he concept of foreseeability means the likelihood of the occurrence of a general type of risk rather than the likelihood of the occurrence of the precise chain of events leading to the injury." *Suchomajcz v. Hummel Chem. Co.,* 524 F.2d 19, 28 n. 8 (3d Cir.1975) (citing Harper & James, The Law of Torts § 18.2, at 1026, § 20.5, at 1147-49 (1956)).\*\*\*

Even this determination that the harm suffered was foreseeable fails to end our analysis. If a duty is to be imposed, the foreseeable risk of harm must be unreasonable. *Griggs,* 981 F.2d at 1435. The classic risk-utility analysis used to determine whether a risk is unreasonable "balances 'the risk, in light of the social value of the interest threatened, and the probability and extent of the harm, against the value of the interest which the actor is seeking to protect, and the expedience of the course pursued.' " *Id.* at 1435-36 (quoting W. Page Keeton et al., Prosser and Keeton on the Law of Torts § 31, at 173 (5th ed. 1984) (footnotes omitted)).

No person can be expected to guard against harm from events which are not reasonably to be anticipated at all, or are so unlikely to occur that the risk, although recognizable, would commonly be disregarded.... On the other hand, if the risk is an appreciable one, and the possible consequences are serious, the question is not one of mathematical probability alone.... As the gravity of the possible harm increases, the apparent likelihood of its occurrence need be correspondingly less to generate a duty of precaution. *Id.* (quoting Prosser and Keeton, *supra* § 31, at 170-71 (footnotes omitted)).

Although the district court correctly determined that the Kleinknechts had presented evidence establishing that the occurrence of severe and life-threatening injuries is not out of the ordinary during contact sports, it held that the College had no duty because the cardiac arrest suffered by Drew, a twenty-year old athlete with no history of any severe medical problems, was not reasonably foreseeable. Its definition of foreseeability is too narrow. Although it is true that a defendant is not required to guard against every possible risk, he must take reasonable steps to guard against hazards which are generally foreseeable. *Kimble v. Mackintosh Hemphill Co.,* 359 Pa. 461, 59 A.2d 68, 71 (1948). Though the specific risk that a person like Drew would suffer a cardiac arrest may be unforeseeable, the Kleinknechts produced ample evidence that a life-threatening injury occurring during participation in an athletic event like lacrosse was reasonably foreseeable. In addition to the testimony of numerous medical and athletic experts, Coach Janczyk, Head Trainer Donolli, and student trainer Moore all testified that they were aware of instances in which athletes had died during athletic competitions. The foreseeability of a life-threatening injury to Drew was not hidden from the College's view. Therefore, the College did owe Drew a duty to take reasonable precautions against the risk of death while Drew was taking part in the College's intercollegiate lacrosse program.

Having determined that it is foreseeable that a member of the College's interscholastic lacrosse team could suffer a serious injury during an athletic event, it becomes evident that the College's failure to protect against such a risk is not reasonable. The magnitude of the foreseeable harm-- irreparable injury or death to one of its student athletes as a result of inadequate preventive emergency measures--is indisputable. With regard to the offsetting cost of protecting against such risk, the College prophesied that if this Court accepts that the College owed the asserted duty, then it will be required "to have a CPR certified trainer on site at each and every athletic practice whether in-season or off-season, formal or informal, strenuous or light," and to provide similar cardiac protection to "intramural, club sports and gym class." This "slippery slope" prediction reflects an unwarranted extension of the holding in this case. First, the recognition of a duty here is limited to intercollegiate athletes. No other scenario is presented, so the question whether any of the other broad classes of events and students posited by the College merit similar protection is not subject to resolution. Second, the determination whether the College has breached this duty at all is a question of fact for the jury. *See Suchomajcz,* 524 F.2d at 27; *see also Dougherty v. Boyertown Times,* 377 Pa.Super. 462, 547 A.2d 778, 787 (1988). This Court recognizes only that under the facts of this case, the College owed a duty to Drew to have measures in place at the lacrosse team's practice on the afternoon of September 16, 1988 in order to provide prompt treatment in the event that he or any other member of the lacrosse team suffered a life-threatening injury.

\*\*\*

The *Leahy* court described the duty a school owes its athletes as "[T]ak[ing] the form of giving adequate instruction in the activity, supplying proper equipment, making a reasonable selection or matching of participants, providing non-negligent supervision of the particular contest, and taking proper post-injury procedures to protect against aggravation of the injury." *Leahy,* 450 So.2d at 885 (quoting Annot., 35 A.L.R.3d 725, 734 (1971) (footnotes omitted)). In reversing the district court's grant of summary judgment to the College, we predict that the Supreme Court of Pennsylvania would hold that a college also has a duty to be reasonably prepared for handling medical emergencies that foreseeably arise during a student's participation in an intercollegiate contact sport for which a college recruited him. It is clearly foreseeable that a person participating in such an activity will sustain serious injury requiring immediate medical attention.

It may be that the emergency medical measures the College had in place were sufficient to fulfill this duty. It is also possible that the College could not foresee that its failure to provide emergency medical services other than those which it already had in place would substantially contribute to the death of an apparently healthy student. Nevertheless,

> [W]hether in a particular case the plaintiff has demonstrated, by a preponderance of the evidence, that the defendant's negligent conduct was a substantial factor in bringing about the plaintiff's harm, is normally a question of fact reserved for the jury, and should only be removed from the jury's consideration where it is clear, as a matter of law, that reasonable minds could not differ on the issue. *Sullivan,* 535

A.2d at 1098 (citing *Little v. York County Earned Income Tax Bureau,* 333 Pa.Super. 8, 481 A.2d 1194, 1198 (1984)).

Our holding is narrow. It predicts only that a court applying Pennsylvania law would conclude that the College had a duty to provide prompt and adequate emergency medical services to Drew, one of its intercollegiate athletes, while he was engaged in a school-sponsored athletic activity for which he had been recruited. Whether the College breached that duty is a question of fact. *See Suchomajcz,* 524 F.2d at 27; *see also Dougherty,* 547 A.2d at 787. If the factfinder concludes that such a breach occurred, we think that the question whether that breach was the proximate or legal cause of Drew's death would likewise be a question of fact.***

****

[T]wo distinct theories establish that the College owed a duty of care to Drew as an intercollegiate athlete. A special relationship existed between the College and Drew in his capacity as a school athlete. His medical emergency was within a reasonably foreseeable class of unfortunate events that could arise from participation in an intercollegiate contact sport. If, as the Supreme Court of Pennsylvania has stated, the concept of duty "amounts to no more than 'the sum total of those considerations of policy which led the law to say that the particular plaintiff is entitled to protection,' " then it strengthens our belief that that Court would hold that the policies supporting these two theories are themselves sufficient to require the College to adopt preventive measures reasonably designed to avoid possible death from a life-threatening injury a recruited athlete suffers during an intercollegiate athletic activity.

Under the facts of this case, the College owed a duty to Drew to have reasonable measures in place at the practice on the afternoon of September 16, 1988 to provide prompt treatment in the event that he or any other member of the lacrosse team suffered a life-threatening injury. The determination whether the College in fact breached this duty is a question of fact for the jury.

2. *The Reasonableness of the College's Actions*

On the duty question, it remains only for us to address the district court's second holding that the conduct of the College's agents in providing Drew with medical assistance and treatment following his cardiac arrest was reasonable.[2] The court based this determination in part, if not in whole, on its conclusion that the College had no duty to consider what emergency assistance measures would be necessary were one of its student athletes to suffer a cardiac arrest during athletic activity:

> The plaintiffs' argument was stronger when they could still assert that there was a duty of care to protect Drew from the risk of cardiac arrest but, since we have decided that it had no such duty, the actions of its agents and students subsequent to Drew's collapse were reasonable. *Kleinknecht,* 786 F.Supp. at 456.

Thus, its holding that the College did not breach any duty was dependent, at least in part, on its holding that the College had no duty to Drew to guard against emergencies occasioned by injuries the kind students participating in lacrosse might be expected to suffer. The question of breach must be reconsidered on remand in light of this Court's holding that the College did owe Drew a duty of care to provide prompt and adequate emergency medical assistance to Drew while participating as one of its intercollegiate athletes in a school-sponsored athletic activity.

V. *Conclusion*

The district court's holding that the College's duty of care to Drew as an intercollegiate athlete did not include, prior to his collapse, a duty to provide prompt emergency medical service while he was engaged in school-sponsored athletic activity will be reversed. The district court's holding that the College acted reasonably and therefore did not breach any duty owed to Drew following his collapse will likewise be reversed. We will remand this matter to the district court for further proceedings consistent with this opinion. ****

**Notes & Questions**

1. Lawyers have adopted an economic mode of analysis to evaluate safety precautions and the advisability of safety rules. A famous judge, Learned Hand, put it this way. Before adopting a safety rule, we should determine

---

[2] This is a separate and distinct duty from that which the College had in terms of maintaining prompt and adequate emergency medical attention prior to Drew's collapse. The College does not dispute that a duty of care was imposed on it at the time of Drew's collapse.

whether the costs of adopting the rule outweigh the benefits of adopting that rule (or vice versa). In short, Judge Hand said that we should compare two costs. First we should try to determine the likelihood of the injury (*i.e.,* probability or the "risk" that a given type of injury might occur) that we are trying to prevent and also try to assess the magnitude of that potential injury. According to Judge Hand, the likelihood of the injury multiplied by the magnitude of the injury equals the "cost" of that injury. That is one "cost." Second, on the other side of the equation, we should determine the costs associated with preventing that potential harm. In short, if the costs of trying to prevent the harm are greater than the costs of the harm itself, then it would *not* make sense to adopt a rule requiring the preventative measures. On the other hand if the costs of trying to prevent the harm are less than the costs of the injury, then it *would* make sense to adopt a rule requiring safety measures. The preventative measures are said to be cost-effective.

Using Judge Hand's rule – which lawyers refer to as the "Hand Formula" – we typically analyze any given proposed safety rule as follows. First, in order to evaluate the "costs" associated with an injury (*i.e.,* the injury that we are trying to prevent) we first must assess the likelihood (*i.e.,* probability) of the harm. How does one go about doing that? Well this is where empirical research from the insurance industry or other statistical studies can help. For example, in the automobile industry, empirical research can give us a good idea of the probability of certain types of car crashes. What percentage of car crashes involve what types of injuries? And what percentage of drivers are involved in those types of accidents? Secondly, we must try to assess the "magnitude of the harm." With automobile crashes, for example, the "magnitude" of injury involves at least two factors: 1) the severity of the injury (*i.e.,* grave bodily harm or death); and, 2) the costs associated with that injury (*e.g.,* the insurance costs, medical costs, pain and suffering, loss of consortium, etc. associated with grave bodily harm or death). According to the Hand Formula (the way that lawyers evaluate the advisability of safety rules), this is how we arrive at the "costs" of the injury: we multiply the probability of the injury occurring by the magnitude of the injury. So, using our empirical research we must arrive at some number to express probability (*i.e.,* a number between .000 and 1.000). Secondly, we must arrive at some number to express the "magnitude of harm" (*e.g.,* the costs associated with the grave bodily injury or death caused by certain types of automobile accidents). The next step in this Hand Formula analysis is to determine, as nearly as possible, the costs of preventing the harm. For example, in order to try to prevent grave bodily harm and death in automobile accidents, the auto industry has spent millions of dollars doing research and development for safety belts and air bags, and continues to study the effects of their use. In addition, the auto industry has spent millions of dollars manufacturing and installing safety belts and air bags in all motor vehicles. Prior to making safety belts and air bags mandatory in newly manufactured vehicles, legislators had to satisfy themselves that the costs associated with preventing grave bodily harm and death in certain types of crashes (the R & D, manufacturing and installation costs) were less than the costs of the harm (*i.e.,* "cost of the harm" defined as the probability multiplied by the costs incurred by the harm [insurance, medical, legal, etc.]). In short, legislators had to decide that it was going to cost less to prevent the injuries than the aggregate costs of the injuries themselves.

Articulate how the Hand Formula might apply to the *Gettysburg College* case.

2. Is the court saying, if Drew had been a "walk-on" athlete rather than a "recruited athlete," that the college would not have owed him a duty of care? If so, is there any rational basis for such a rule? Shouldn't the school owe the same safety/medical obligations to all of a team's members regardless of whether they are walk-ons or recruited athletes? College football teams, for example, typically have large practice squads comprised of walk-on players who rarely, if ever, even get to suit up for games. When they are injured, as they frequently are, do schools owe them a lesser duty of care than scholarship starters?

3. In light of this case, how would you advise a college athletic department regarding emergency personnel, equipment, and procedures? Should trainers be available at all team practices? Nurses? Doctors? EMT's? What equipment should be required?

4. At what point would you say that the costs of providing emergency personnel and equipment for collegiate athletic practices and competitions become too burdensome? At what point do costs become prohibitive?

5. At age 23, Hank "The Bank" Gathers lost his life to a heart condition during the West Coast Conference tournament in on March 4, 1990. Gathers had previously been diagnosed with a heart condition in December of 1989 when he fainted after missing a free throw during a conference game. Gathers was put on medication to regulate his heart beat and missed only two games. *Gathers   Dies   After   Collapse   on   the   Court* www.sportingnews.com/archives/sports2000/moments/145134.html (last updated March 12, 1990).

Three years later, the basketball community was in for another huge blow. Reggie Lewis of the Boston Celtics suffered a heart attack while shooting baskets at Brandeis University. Four months prior to his death, Lewis was disoriented and dizzy during a regular-season game. Only 4 weeks later Lewis collapsed during a playoff game. The doctors' reports were inconclusive as to whether the condition was serious, thus allowing Lewis to play. Reggie Lewis was 27 years old at the time of his death. Heller, Dick, *Celtics Fans Mourned Reggie Lewis' Death in '93* www.washtimes.com/sports/20040726-124206-5316r.htm.

6. "Affecting approximately 5,000-7,000 young people each year, sudden cardiac arrest in college athletes is sometimes caused by congenital cardiovascular conditions, such as Long QT Syndrome or Hypertrophic Cardiomyopathy (HCM). According to the Cleveland Clinic, HCM, a condition that causes excessive thickening of the heart muscle, affects as many as 1.5 million Americans, making it the most common cause of sudden cardiac arrest in people under age 30. Preventative measures such as cardiac screenings are needed to detect an individual's risk to these types of conditions. In fact, an ECG exam can help detect heart conditions that account for nearly 60 percent of sudden cardiac arrests in young athletes." *Philips join forces with A Heart For Sports to 'Save an Athlete,' furthering its commitment to help prevent sudden cardiac arrest in college athletes* www.medical.philips.com/us/news/content/file_1267.html (Last updated September 26, 2006).

## Tawana Hammond v. Board of Education of Carroll County
### 639 A 2d 223 (1994)
#### Court of Special Appeals of Maryland

MOTZ, Judge.

On August 25, 1989, appellant, Tawana Hammond, the first female high school football player in Carroll County history, was injured in her team's initial scrimmage. Three years later, Tawana and her mother, appellant Peggy Hammond, (collectively, the Hammonds) filed suit in the Circuit Court for Carroll County against appellee, the Board of Education of Carroll County (the Board), seeking $1.25 million in compensatory damages. The Hammonds asserted (1) that the high school authorities negligently failed to warn them of the potential risk of injury inherent in playing football and (2) that if they had been so warned Tawana would not have chosen to play football and her mother would not have permitted her to do so. After the parties conducted discovery, the Board moved for summary judgment, which the circuit court (Beck, J.) granted.

The record reveals that the underlying material facts are not disputed. Sixteen-year-old Tawana tried out for the Francis Scott Key High School varsity football team in the summer of 1989, prior to the beginning of her junior year in high school. Although Tawana had previously participated in a number of track events and played softball and soccer, she had never engaged in any contact sports. Tawana had watched football on television since she was six years old but did not become interested in football until her freshman year in high school; she had never observed any "really serious" injuries in these televised games, only a "twisted ankle or something." She saw a half dozen high school games during her freshman and sophomore years and saw no players hurt at those games. Tawana knew football was a "physical contact sport" and determined she wanted to play it because "[i]t was different."

In order for a student to play sports at Francis Scott Key High School, the student and the student's parent must sign a document entitled "Francis Scott Key High School Athletic Regulations and Permission Form." Both Tawana and her father, John Hammond (not a party herein), signed this form on June 18, 1989. The permission form states that the student has read the school handbook and regulations and agrees to abide by them and that the parent has read them and "consents" to the child's participation in the sport. One sentence in the permission form specifically states that "[w]e do our very best to avoid accidents, but we realize that in the normal course of events, some occur." In deposition, Tawana testified that she read the permission form and, in particular, this sentence before she started playing football and understood that she "could get a broken leg, [or] broken arm" as a result of playing varsity, tackle football.

The permission form also requires that "[e]ach participating athlete must have a special examination" by the family physician and "must be found physically fit" and "must also have parent/guardian permission to participate." Tawana submitted the required "Carroll County Public Schools Athletic Participation Health Examination Form" signed by her doctor on July 31, 1989; in it her doctor certified that she was "physically able" to compete in a list of sports, including football. Moreover, on that same date Tawana's mother, a certified nurse's aide, whose older son played football at Francis Scott Key High School until "he sprained his leg," signed the participation form. On that form, Ms. Hammond gave her "consent" for Tawana to play the several sports listed, including football. Ms. Hammond acknowledged in deposition that "injury was [her] biggest fear" for Tawana, *i.e.,* "like [a] broken leg, [or] broken arms," but that she never communicated her fears to Tawana and believed Tawana "should be allowed to do whatever it was she wanted to do."

Throughout the summer of 1989, Tawana participated in the team's weight lifting program along with the other varsity football players. She was happy with the progress that she was making in her strength training and had no concerns or fears that she would not be physically strong enough to compete on the playing field. Practice began in August. On the first day of practice, which involved some contact drills, Tawana, along with the rest of the team, was instructed by the head coach, not to tackle, block or "do anything" with the neck because "you could get a neck injury." After the first practice, a meeting was conducted for the parents of the players. Tawana and both of her parents attended that meeting, at which an official gave a presentation discussing the possibility of serious injury to the neck if the head were used for blocking or tackling.

As practices continued, Tawana had no difficulty in keeping up physically with the other players on the team. On August 25, 1989, Tawana, along with the rest of the Francis Scott Key High School varsity football team, travelled to Anne Arundel County for the team's first practice scrimmage. Prior to the scrimmage, Tawana was interviewed by a television reporter and stated that "[p]laying football is a tough sport. I do have to admit that." During the scrimmage, while carrying the ball, Tawana was tackled by a rival player and sustained multiple internal injuries including a ruptured spleen. Her spleen and part of her pancreas were removed, and she was hospitalized for some time.

On August 13, 1992, Tawana and her mother filed this suit. The circuit court granted summary judgment to the Board, concluding that (a) it had no duty to warn "of the risk of serious, disabling and catastrophic injury associated with playing on a high-school-varsity, tackle, football team;"(b) if there was a duty to warn the Hammonds it was satisfied; and (c) Tawana and her mother assumed the risk of injury as a matter of law.

On appeal, Tawana and her mother raise three questions:

1. Did the lower court err when it held, as a matter of law, that based on the appellants' training, intelligence, and experience the appellee owed no duty to warn the appellants of the risks of serious, disabling, and catastrophic injuries involved in participating in interscholastic high school football?

2. Did the lower court err when it held, as a matter of law, that the appellee fulfilled its duty to warn the appellants of the nature and extent of serious injury involved in participating in interscholastic high school football?

3. Did the lower court err in ruling, as a matter of law, that the appellants had assumed the risk of the appellant Tawana Hammond's injuries when there was sufficient other evidence presented which created an issue of triable fact as to each appellant?

The central theory espoused by the Hammonds, that the school board had a duty to warn them of the severe injuries that might result from voluntarily[1] participating on a varsity high school tackle football team, is one that, as far as we can determine, has never been adopted by any court in this country.

There are, to be sure, numerous cases in which minors injured while playing in school sporting events have sued school officials (or others similarly situated) asserting that the officials' negligence caused the participant's injuries. [case citations omitted]  In none of these cases, however, have the plaintiffs successfully asserted that the school officials were negligent because of some failure to warn the plaintiffs of the possible dangers involved in voluntarily participating in the contact sport.  In the past, plaintiffs have made claims of negligence because of asserted inadequate or improper supervision, and inadequate equipment, but the parties have not cited and we have not uncovered any case in which a plaintiff, in circumstances similar to the Hammonds, has successfully made a negligence claim based on a failure to warn of possible physical injury.

Perhaps this is because permeating the sports injury cases is the recognition that "[p]hysical contact in ... an athletic contest is foreseeable and expected." *Albers,* 487 P.2d at 939.  The "general rule is that participants in an athletic contest accept the normal physical contact of the particular sport." *Id.*  Absent evidence of "mental deficiency," and there is no claim that Tawana is not at least of average intelligence, minors are held to "sufficiently appreciate[ ] the dangers inherent in the game of football," *Whipple,* 495 P.2d at 743, to know that "football is a rough and hazardous game and that anyone playing or practicing such a game may be injured," *Hale,* 70 S.E.2d at 925,

---

[1] We note that different considerations may apply when an injury occurs during compulsory physical education classes rather than during voluntary participation in school athletic contests because, while a student usually is required to attend physical education classes and drills, a participant chooses to participate in voluntary games, and so can avoid them if he or she is weak, slow, disabled, etc. [case citations omitted]

154

and that "[f]atigue, and unfortunately, injury are inherent in team competitive sports, especially football." *Benitez,* 543 N.Y.S.2d at 34, 541 N.E.2d at 34. Thus, it is "common knowledge that children participating in games ... may injure themselves and ... no amount of supervision ... will avoid some such injuries, and the law does not make a school the insurer of the safety of pupils at play." *Brackman,* 472 S.W.2d at 739. As the Supreme Court of Oregon explained in rejecting a similar claim by a fifteen-year-old injured in a football game,

> The playing of football is a body-contact sport. The game demands that the players come into physical contact with each other constantly, frequently with great force ... the ball-carrier ... must be prepared to strike the ground violently. Body contacts, bruises, and clashes are inherent in the game. There is no other way to play it. No prospective player need be told that a participant in the game of football may sustain injury. That fact is self-evident. *Vendrell,* 376 P.2d at 412-13.

For these reasons, courts have been extremely inhospitable to claims that properly equipped, injured high school players should be able to recover from school officials for injuries sustained during an ordinary, voluntary contact sport game.[2] Thus, in the vast majority of such cases, it has been held that those asserting such claims cannot recover as a matter of law. *See Albers,* 487 P.2d at 937 (summary judgment for school district affirmed in suit brought by fifteen year old "seriously injured" during a school basketball game); *Hale,* 70 S.E.2d at 926 (holding that trial court properly sustained demurrer to claim by sixteen-year-old injured in football practice); *Kluka,* 433 So.2d at 304-05 (reversing judgment for high school student whose ankle was broken in a wrestling match); *Benitez,* 543 N.Y.S.2d at 30, 541 N.E.2d at 30 (reversing a jury verdict in excess of $800,000 for a 19 year old who suffered a broken neck in a varsity football game); *Barrett,* 223 S.E.2d at 919 (affirming grant of summary judgment to defendants in suit brought by estate of high school football player who died from injuries inflicted by a twenty-year-old rival player who was incorrectly listed as eligible to play); *Whipple,* 495 P.2d at 743-44 (directed verdict for defendant affirmed in case brought by fifteen-year-old who injured a knee in youth program football

---

[2] The exceptions involve claims not made here and facts not remotely similar to those in the case at hand. *See e.g., Tepper,* 531 N.Y.S.2d at 368 (summary judgment for defendants reversed when it was asserted that a coach was negligent in permitting a lacrosse player "of slight build and very limited experience, to go head-to-head [during a practice drill] with the 260-pound senior varsity team member, a player possessing substantially greater experience").

game); *Vendrell,* 376 P.2d at 412-14 (reversing a verdict for fifteen-year-old who fractured his neck in high school football game); *Brackman,* 472 S.W.2d at 741 (reversing jury verdict for fourteen-year-old girl injured in a softball game).

[4] ****

Here...the hazard alleged--the possibility of injury to a voluntary participant in a varsity high school tackle, football game--was "the normal, obvious and usual incident[ ]" of the activity. Accordingly...there was no duty on the part of the defendant to warn of this possibility.

In light of our conclusion that the Board had no duty to warn the Hammonds, we need not reach the question of whether Tawana assumed the risk as a matter of law. We do note, however, that there is case law supporting the circuit court's conclusion that she did. *See e.g., Whipple,* 495 P.2d at 743; *Vendrell,* 376 P.2d at 414; *Kluka,* 433 So.2d at 304; *Hale,* 70 S.E.2d at 925. *See also Nesbitt v. Bethesda Country Club, Inc.,* 20 Md.App. 226, 232, 314 A.2d 738 (1974) (quoting 4 Am.Jur.2d, *Amusements & Exhibitions* § 98 ("[a] voluntary participant in any lawful game, sport or contest, in legal contemplation by the fact of his participation, assumes all risks incidental to the game, sport or contest which are obvious and foreseeable.").[3]

Although she has not stated a cause of action against the Board, Tawana's injuries were serious, painful, and permanent. We regret them and sympathize with her. Our holding here, that school officials have no duty to warn a student or the student's parents that serious injury might result from the student's voluntary participation on a high school varsity tackle football team, does not mean that such a warning would not be a sound idea as a matter of public policy. Young men--and women--of the same age, who wish to participate in the same team contact sports, vary considerably in weight and size; unfortunately, the sport may occasionally pit the brawniest against the most slender.[4] In view of the very serious injuries suffered by Tawana, school officials may well want to consider issuing a warning of the possibility of such injuries--even though there is no legal obligation to do so.

---

[3] Again, this situation is to be contrasted with a student's arguable lack of assumption of risk in compulsory physical education classes. *See Benitez,* 543 N.Y.S.2d at 33, 541 N.E.2d at 33; *Passantino,* 383 N.Y.S.2d at 641.

[4] The Hammonds have not asserted that they were entitled to any additional warning or consideration because Tawana is a young woman and we do not suggest that there is any basis for such an argument. Moreover, there is nothing in this record to suggest that Tawana's injuries were different or more severe because of her sex.

JUDGMENT AFFIRMED.


## Notes & Questions

1. How are the plaintiff's allegations in this case regarding the school's failure to warn any different from the allegations of failure to warn in *Pell*? In both cases the plaintiffs allege that if they had received proper warnings they would not have participated in the dangerous activity.

2. The court notes that Tawana's mother was "a certified nurse's aid, whose older son played football at Francis Scott Key High School until he 'sprained his leg....'" How important do you think that those facts are to the decision? If you think that they are important, why? If not, why not?

3. The court makes it clear that there is no duty to warn of the obvious dangers of contact sports and that voluntary participants are deemed to have assumed the normal risks inherent in such sports. If those are the normal legal rules applicable to sports injuries, why were similar arguments in *Pell* unavailing?

4. Does it matter that the plaintiff in *Hammond* was injured while playing an extracurricular, voluntary sport (football) while the plaintiff in *Pell* was injured while participating in a mandatory physical education class? Does it matter that product liability was the legal theory in *Pell* whereas the *Hammond* case was tried on a theory of negligence? Should those sorts of differences matter legally?


### Raymond Santopietro, Jr. v. City of New Haven
239 Conn. 207 (1996)
Supreme Court of Connecticut

BORDEN, Associate Justice.

This appeal arises out of injuries incurred by a spectator at a softball game.

Certain facts are not in dispute. On October 16, 1988, the plaintiffs attended a softball game played at East Shore Park in New Haven by teams belonging to an organized league. The defendants David Brennan and Bruce Shepard served as the umpires for that game. ****

The plaintiff Raymond Santopietro, Jr., observed the softball game from a position behind the backstop and was not on the field of play. ****

In the sixth inning, [Mark] Piombino came to bat in the game that Santopietro, Jr., was watching and hit a fly ball. In frustration, he intentionally flung his bat toward the backstop. Somehow the bat passed through the backstop and struck Santopietro, Jr., in the head. As a result, Santopietro, Jr., suffered a fractured skull and other serious injuries.

****

A review of the evidence in the light most favorable to the plaintiffs indicates that the jury might reasonably have found the following facts. During the course of the game that Santopietro, Jr., was watching when he was injured, there occurred several incidents of unruly behavior by players who were on the same team as Piombino. Some players used vulgar language in a loud and angry manner. Players taunted members of the other team in an attempt to intimidate them. Players threw their gloves and kicked the dirt, and one player kicked a garbage can, upsetting its contents and creating a loud noise. After his turn at bat resulted in an out, another player angrily threw a bat along the ground in the direction of the bats not in use. Another player threw his glove from the pitcher's mound into the dugout. A player inside the dugout repeatedly banged a bat against the dugout, producing a loud noise. Furthermore, the jury could have inferred from the evidence presented that Brennan and Shepard were aware or reasonably should have been aware of these incidents.

After passing a written examination, Brennan and Shepard were both trained and approved to be softball umpires by the Amateur Softball Association (Association), a national organization that regulates the conduct of organized amateur softball in the United States. Both Brennan and Shepard possessed years of experience and had umpired hundreds of games. Shepard had received an award honoring him for being the best umpire in New Haven. Brennan testified that, as an umpire, he possesses specialized knowledge about softball and softball rules that is greater than the average person's knowledge. Both Brennan and Shepard were familiar with the Association's rules governing the conduct of umpires.

Brennan and Shepard testified that when they observed unsportsmanlike conduct, they would issue a warning and, if the warning was disregarded, they would eject the player from the game. Specifically, they testified that they would have taken such action if they had observed the disruptive behavior described by several witnesses, including taunting, loud swearing, kicking a garbage can, hitting the inside of the dugout with a bat, or throwing a glove from the pitcher's mound into the dugout.

Brennan and Shepard further testified that when they give a warning, it usually has the effect of stopping the disruptive behavior and preventing future improper acts. They testified that any player who tosses a bat should be ejected immediately, and Brennan testified that if he had seen a player toss a bat as described by the witnesses, he would have ejected that player without warning. They testified that such disciplinary action is an effective means by which to control the actions of players.

Shepard testified that, as an umpire, he had the duty to maintain control of the game to prevent harm to spectators, and that warnings constitute the primary means by which to maintain that control. Moreover, Brennan testified that umpires have the authority to suspend the game if necessary to keep order or to prevent harm to spectators.

Brennan and Shepard also testified that the decision of whether to impose discipline in any given instance of unruly behavior is a discretionary matter for the umpire. Brennan testified that the rule against unsportsmanlike conduct gives the umpire authority "at his discretion, to disqualify any player who exhibits unsportsmanlike conduct in the judgment of the umpire." He further testified that decisions whether to take disciplinary action in response to loud swearing, throwing a glove or kicking dirt "are umpire judgment or umpire discretion calls." Shepard testified that the question of whether unruly behavior, such as using loud and abusive language, throwing a glove or kicking a garbage can, constitutes unsportsmanlike conduct will depend on the particular situation. **** Brennan further testified concerning the subjective nature of the decision whether to discipline a player for unsportsmanlike conduct. Specifically, he stated that "the majority of the time you'll find that umpires are former players, and umpires will use the term unsportsmanlike conduct as some type of action which, had I been a player, I wouldn't like done to me, I wouldn't let another group do it to another player."

We note that this testimony confirms what is the common understanding of the umpire's task. In the absence of exceptional circumstances, a softball umpire, when confronted with unruly behavior by a player that arguably constitutes unsportsmanlike conduct, faces a spectrum of discretionary options. At one end of the spectrum is taking no action; at the other end is ejection of the player or suspension of the game. In between are warnings and other appropriate disciplinary action. The umpire has discretion, within the spectrum, to respond to the offensive behavior in the manner that the umpire finds to be most appropriate in the given circumstances.

****

We conclude that the plaintiffs were required to establish by expert testimony that the failure of Brennan and Shepard to act in the present case constituted a breach of duty, and that the plaintiffs' evidence did not satisfy that burden.

"A breach of duty by the defendant and a causal connection between the defendant's breach of duty and the resulting harm to the plaintiff are essential elements of a cause of action in negligence." *Catz v. Rubenstein,* 201 Conn. 39, 44, 513 A.2d 98 (1986); see *RK Constructors, Inc. v. Fusco Corp.,* 231 Conn. 381, 384, 650 A.2d 153 (1994) ("essential elements of a cause of action in negligence are well established: duty; breach of that duty; causation; and actual injury"). ****

"The existence of a duty is a question of law and [o]nly if such a duty is found to exist does the trier of fact then determine whether the defendant violated that duty in the particular situation at hand. *Petriello v. Kalman,* 215 Conn. 377, 382-83, 576 A.2d 474 (1990). If a court determines, as a matter of law, that a defendant owes no duty to a plaintiff, the plaintiff cannot recover in negligence from the defendant." (Internal quotation marks omitted.) *RK Constructors, Inc. v. Fusco Corp.,* supra, 231 Conn. at 384-85, 650 A.2d 153.

If the determination of the standard of care requires knowledge that is beyond the experience of an ordinary fact finder, expert testimony will be required. *Jaffe v. State Dept. of Health,* 135 Conn. 339, 349, 64 A.2d 330 (1949).

[12] We note that the plaintiffs' claims in the present case are akin to allegations of professional negligence or malpractice, which we have previously defined as "the failure of one rendering professional services to exercise that degree of skill and learning commonly applied under all the circumstances in the community by the average prudent reputable member of the profession with the result of injury, loss, or damage to the recipient of those services." (Internal quotation marks omitted.) *Davis v. Margolis,* 215 Conn. 408, 415, 576 A.2d 489 (1990). As Brennan testified, he possesses

specialized knowledge as an umpire that is greater than the average person's knowledge. An umpire obtains, through formal training and experience, a familiarity with the rules of the sport, a technical expertise in their application, and an understanding of the likely consequences of officiating decisions. As a result, the umpire possesses knowledge of the standard of care to which an umpire reasonably may be held, and of what constitutes a violation of that standard, that is beyond the experience and ken of the ordinary fact finder. Moreover, the fact finder's lack of expertise is exacerbated by the highly discretionary nature of the umpire's task. Thus, the fact finder must determine, not just whether in hindsight the umpire erred, but also whether the umpire's error constituted an abuse of his broad discretion. In such cases in which the fact finder's decision requires specialized knowledge, expert testimony is necessary "to assist lay people, such as members of the jury and the presiding judge, to understand the applicable standard of care and to evaluate the defendant's actions in light of that standard." *Id.,* at 416, 576 A.2d 489; see, *e.g.*, *Barrett v. Danbury Hospital,* 232 Conn. 242, 252, 654 A.2d 748 (1995) (medical malpractice); *Davis v. Margolis,* supra, at 416, 576 A.2d 489 (legal malpractice); *Matyas v. Minck,* supra, 37 Conn.App. at 327, 655 A.2d 1155 (negligence of engineer).

In the present case, the plaintiffs do not articulate clearly the umpire's duty upon which they base their claim. The plaintiffs principally rely upon the testimony of Shepard that an umpire's duty is "to maintain control on the field so it does not spill over to spectators."[1] Thus, the plaintiffs appear to postulate a duty owed by the umpires to maintain control of the game in such a way as to prevent harm to others. On appeal, Brennan and Shepard do not concede that such a duty exists, but argue that even if we were to assume its existence, the plaintiffs failed to define the duty. Our

---

[1] The plaintiffs also rely upon the answer by Brennan and Shepard to the complaint in which they admitted that their "duties at the game at which the plaintiff was injured included *preventing disruptive and dangerous behavior,* such as throwing of baseball bats." (Emphasis added.) We are not bound, however, by this pleading admission or their testimony concerning their duty to maintain control of the game for two reasons. First, the determination of whether a duty exists to support tort liability is a question of law to be decided by the court. *RK Constructors, Inc. v. Fusco Corp.,* supra, 231 Conn. at 384-85, 650 A.2d 153. Second, umpires cannot, as a matter of law, possibly bear such a duty, taken literally, as this concession suggests, namely, to *prevent altogether* the occurrence of disruptive and dangerous behavior. The umpires' duty, if it exists, cannot exceed the requirement to take reasonable measures to deter the occurrence of such behavior.

research indicates that no other jurisdiction has explicitly considered whether to impose or how to define such a legal duty.[2]

Therefore, for the purposes of this appeal, we assume, without deciding, that umpires such as Brennan and Shepard[3] have a duty, essentially as postulated by the plaintiffs, to exercise reasonable judgment as umpires in order to maintain control of a game so as to prevent an unreasonable risk of injury to others. The breach of this duty, however, must be proved, in the absence of exceptional circumstances, by expert testimony establishing that the allegedly negligent action or failure to act by the umpire constituted an abuse of the umpire's discretion to evaluate the particular circumstances and to take only such disciplinary action as the umpire deems appropriate. Moreover, the expert testimony must establish an abuse of that discretion sufficient to permit a jury to infer that the umpire's action or failure to act constituted such a loss of control of the game as to give rise to an unreasonable risk of injury to the plaintiff.

In fact, in the present case, the plaintiffs concede that expert testimony was required to establish whether the applicable standard of care was breached by Brennan and Shepard. The plaintiffs argue that, through

---

[2] See *Bain v. Gillispie,* 357 N.W.2d 47, 49 (Iowa App.1984) (holding that no tort exists for "referee malpractice" where sports merchandisers sued basketball referee for negligent officiating that resulted in harm to their business interests); cf. *LeNoble v. Fort Lauderdale,* 663 So.2d 1351, 1352 (Fla.App.1995) (in negligence action by fast pitch softball pitcher struck by batted ball, summary judgment improper because evidence that umpires were responsible for enforcing rules and ensuring that distance from pitching rubber to home plate complied with association's rules, and that umpire was informed that pitching rubber was improperly placed, gave rise to issues of fact to be resolved before legal question of duty could be determined). In one sports law treatise, the authors assert that such a duty does exist. "Sports officials have a duty to see that the rules for participant and spectator safety are obeyed. To the extent that the duty is not performed, they and their employers may be negligent. See, e.g., *Carabba v. Anacortes School District No. 103,* 72 Wash.2d 939, 435 P.2d 936 (1967) (liability may be imposed upon school district for referee's negligence in failing to detect an illegal wrestling hold that left a high school athlete permanently paralyzed).... An official's responsibility goes much further than enforcement of rules. Officials control the competition, and in this capacity are saddled with a general duty of care." G. Schubert, R. Smith & J. Trentadue, Sports Law (1986) § 7.5.

[3] We note that Brennan and Shepard had been formally trained and were paid to officiate the game at which Santopietro, Jr., was injured. Although this information does not affect the resolution of the present case, we acknowledge that it may be relevant if, in the future, we are required to decide whether such a duty exists. The existence or extent of a duty might be affected by whether the umpire is a paid professional or an unpaid volunteer without formal training.

162

the testimony of Brennan and Shepard, they presented sufficient positive evidence of an expert nature from which the jury could have reasonably concluded that Brennan and Shepard were negligent.

We have previously held that the plaintiff in a medical malpractice action may prove the proper standard of care and its breach through the testimony of the defendant. *Console v. Nickou,* 156 Conn. 268, 273-74, 240 A.2d 895 (1968); *Snyder v. Pantaleo,* 143 Conn. 290, 294-95, 122 A.2d 21 (1956). Similarly, in the present case, the record reveals that the testimony of Brennan and Shepard constituted expert testimony through which the plaintiffs might have established negligence. **** [T]he plaintiffs need only have produced sufficient expert testimony to permit the jury reasonably to infer, on the basis of its findings of fact, that Brennan and Shepard breached the standard of care. ****

We conclude, in the present case, that the plaintiffs failed to produce sufficient evidence that Brennan and Shepard had breached the applicable standard of care. Brennan and Shepard testified that unsportsmanlike conduct is prohibited and that it is appropriate for an umpire to take action to prevent or stop such conduct. They further testified that the umpire possesses the authority to warn players, eject them or suspend the game if necessary to deter unsportsmanlike conduct or to maintain control of a game. Moreover, when questioned about specific incidents that allegedly had occurred during the game at which Santopietro, Jr., was injured, Brennan and Shepard testified that if they had seen the incidents described by the witnesses, they would have taken some disciplinary action. They also testified, however, that the umpire possesses discretion in the application of the rule prohibiting unsportsmanlike conduct and that the decision whether to take some action against a player is made according to the judgment of the umpire based on the specific circumstances. Neither Brennan nor Shepard testified that, in the specific circumstances of that game, a reasonable umpire would have been required to take action in response to those incidents, or that it would have been unreasonable for an umpire not to have taken such action. In other words, their testimony that, in the exercise of their discretion, they would have taken action does not establish that a failure to act constituted a breach of the standard of care.

The plaintiffs did present evidence that, arguably, would support the conclusion that Brennan and Shepard improperly failed to act in response to two incidents. First, witnesses testified that a player tossed a bat toward other bats after an unsuccessful plate appearance. Brennan and Shepard testified that the local rule required them to eject immediately any player who throws a bat. Brennan further testified that the incident described by the witnesses would "merit an ejection." If we were to interpret this testimony to constitute an expert opinion that a reasonable umpire must have ejected the player in those circumstances, then this evidence would support the conclusion that Brennan and Shepard improperly failed to act with respect to that particular incident. Second, a witness testified that some players taunted members of the other team. Shepard testified that an umpire should take immediate action in response to taunting. Brennan and Shepard do not dispute the plaintiffs' evidence that they did not take any disciplinary action during the game.

The testimony of Brennan and Shepard concerning these two incidents supports a possible conclusion that they failed to exercise their discretion in a reasonable manner on two occasions during the game. The plaintiffs do not contend, however, that these two incidents suffice to establish that Brennan and Shepard breached a duty, which we assume exists, to maintain control of the game in order to prevent unreasonable risk of harm to others. The plaintiffs do not argue, and we do not assume, that Brennan and Shepard possess a duty to make every discretionary call that arises during the course of the game error free. Umpire liability, if it were to exist, must be predicated on facts sufficient to support the conclusion that their unreasonable actions or failure to act led to such a loss of control of the game as to imperil unreasonably the safety of others. We conclude, as a matter of law, that these two incidents of arguably negligent behavior are not sufficient to support such a conclusion.

We conclude, therefore, that the plaintiffs have failed to prove by expert testimony that Brennan and Shepard breached a duty of care to prevent an unreasonable risk of the injuries suffered by Santopietro, Jr. ****

The judgment is affirmed.

## Notes & Questions

1. What standard of care should apply to sports officials? Should ordinary principles of negligence apply? Or should there be a professional standard commensurate with their training? For example, would there be a different standard for a Little League umpire versus a Major League umpire?

2. Given the extreme instances of fan violence that have occurred in the past several years at youth games, is there an argument to be made that a higher level of precautions should be taken at youth sporting events?

3. How much practical control do officials actually have? Wouldn't it make more sense to require venue owners or league officials to provide security or police protection rather than putting that burden on the shoulders of game officials?

4. The court requires expert testimony to establish the standard of care applicable to the softball umpires who are defendants in this case. Why is expert testimony necessary?

5. Explain what the court means when it refers to the "discretion" of umpires? What is the relevance of "discretion" to the legal principles established in this case?

## Hiett v. Lake Barcroft Community Association, Inc.
418 SE 2d 894 (1992)
Supreme Court of Virginia

KEENAN, Justice.

The primary issue in this appeal is whether a pre-injury release from liability for negligence is void as being against public policy.

Robert D. Hiett sustained an injury which rendered him a quadriplegic while participating in the "Teflon Man Triathlon" (the triathlon) sponsored by the Lake Barcroft Community Association, Inc. (LABARCA). The injury occurred at the start of the swimming event when Hiett waded into Lake Barcroft to a point where the water reached his thighs, dove into the water, and struck his head on either the lake bottom or an object beneath the water surface.

Thomas M. Penland, Jr., a resident of Lake Barcroft, organized and directed the triathlon. He drafted the entry form which all participants were required to sign. The first sentence of the form provided:

> In consideration of this entry being accept[ed] to participate in the Lake Barcroft Teflon Man Triathlon I hereby, for myself, my heirs, and executors waive, release and forever discharge any and all rights and claims for damages which I may have or m[a]y hereafter accrue to me against the

organizers and sponsors and their representatives, successors, and assigns, for any and all injuries suffered by me in said event.

\*\*\*

Hiett alleged in his third amended motion for judgment that LABARCA...had failed to ensure that the lake was reasonably safe, properly supervise the swimming event, advise the participants of the risk of injury, and train them how to avoid such injuries. \*\*\*

In a preliminary ruling, the trial court held that, absent fraud, misrepresentation, duress, illiteracy, or the denial of an opportunity to read the form, the entry form was a valid contract and that the pre-injury release language in the contract released the defendants from liability for negligence. The trial court also ruled that such a release was prohibited as a matter of public policy only when it was included: (1) in a common carrier's contract of carriage; (2) in the contract of a public utility under a duty to furnish telephone service; or (3) as a condition of employment set forth in an employment contract.

\*\*\*\*

Hiett first argues that the trial court erred in ruling that the pre-injury release provision in the entry form did not violate public policy. He contends that since the decision of this Court in *Johnson's Adm'x v. Richmond and Danville R.R. Co.,* 86 Va. 975, 11 S.E. 829 (1890), the law in Virginia has been settled that an agreement entered into prior to any injury, releasing a tortfeasor from liability for negligence resulting in personal injury, is void because it violates public policy. \*\*\*\* In response, LABARCA...argue[s] that the decisions of this Court since *Johnson* have established that pre-injury release agreements such as the one before us do not violate public policy. We disagree with LABARCA....

The case law in this Commonwealth over the past one hundred years has not altered the holding in *Johnson*. In *Johnson,* this Court addressed the validity of a pre-injury release of liability for future negligent acts. There, the decedent was a member of a firm of quarry workers which had entered into an agreement with a railroad company to remove a granite bluff located on the company's right of way. The agreement specified that the railroad would not be liable for any injuries or death sustained by any members of the firm, or its employees, occurring from any cause whatsoever.

The decedent was killed while attempting to warn one of his employees of a fast-approaching train. The evidence showed that the train was moving at a speed of not less than 25 miles per hour, notwithstanding the railroad company's agreement that all trains would pass by the work site at speeds not exceeding six miles per hour.

In holding that the release language was invalid because it violated public policy, this Court stated:

> [T]o hold that it was competent for one party to put the other parties to the contract at the mercy of its own misconduct ... can never be lawfully done where an enlightened system of jurisprudence prevails. Public policy forbids it, and contracts against public policy are void.

This Court emphasized that its holding was not based on the fact that the railroad company was a common carrier. Rather, this Court found that such provisions for release from liability for personal injury which may be caused by future acts of negligence are prohibited "universally." 86 Va. at 978, 11 S.E. at 830.

As noted by Hiett, the cases following *Johnson* have not eroded this principle. \*\*\*\*

[C]ases decided by this Court since *Johnson* have upheld provisions for indemnification against future property damage claims. In none of these cases, however, did the Court address the issue whether an indemnification provision would be valid against a claim for personal injury.

\*\*\*\*

We agree with Hiett that the...cases have not modified or altered the holding in *Johnson*. Therefore, we conclude here, based on *Johnson,* that the pre-injury release provision signed by Hiett is prohibited by public policy and, thus, it is void. *Johnson,* 86 Va. at 978, 11 S.E. at 829.

\*\*\*

*Affirmed in part, reversed in part, and remanded.*

# Lund v. Bally's Aerobic Plus

78 Cal.App. 4th 733 (2000)

Court of Appeal, Second District, California

.

YEGAN, J.

The modern health or fitness club is a place where a person can attain physical health and fitness. It is also a place where a person can get hurt. For this reason, most, if not all, health clubs require patrons to assume the risk of physical injury associated with body building and aerobic conditioning. As we shall explain, here the waiver and release of liability operates as an effective written assumption of the risk which bars recovery.

Ellen Lund appeals from the judgment of nonsuit granted to respondents Bally's Aerobic Plus, Inc., and Bally's Total Fitness (collectively, Bally's) after the presentation of her evidence at the trial of this personal injury case. Lund unsuccessfully contends the trial court erred when it concluded her claims were barred by a waiver and release form she signed when she became a member of a Bally's gym.

### Facts and Procedural History

In late 1989 or early 1990, Lund injured her cervical spine and had surgery to fuse two vertebrae in her neck. In February 1994, she joined a Bally's health club in Simi Valley. In December of 1994, she paid Bally's $375 in addition to the cost of her membership for 20 sessions with a personal trainer, Ron Ladd. Lund told Ladd that she previously had neck surgery and that her doctor told her not to lift weight over her head. Ladd assured her that he could show her how to use the weight machines without injuring her neck. Lund followed his advice. Admittedly, with the benefit of hindsight, Ladd's assurances and Lund's acceptance of his representations were foolish.

During their first session, Ladd showed Lund how to use an incline bench press machine with a 10-pound weight. Lund lifted the weight 15 times before she felt pressure in her neck. After she lifted it three more times, Lund felt a pain, " like the top of my head broke off." She had reinjured her cervical spine, requiring another surgery. Lund sued Bally's for personal injury, contending Ladd was negligent when he instructed her on how to use the incline bench press.

The trial court granted Bally's motion for nonsuit following the presentation of her evidence at trial. It concluded that a waiver and release included in Lund's membership contract barred her claim. The waiver and release is part of the form retail installment contract prepared by Bally's that Lund signed when she joined the club in February 1994. Lund testified that, although she reviewed the financial terms of the contract, she did not read its other provisions.

Near the signature line, the contract states: "Notice to Buyer: 1. Do Not Sign This Agreement Before You Read It or if It Contains Any Blank Spaces to Be Filled in...." Lund testified she did not read this portion of the contract. A few lines later, the contract states: "Waiver and Release: This contract contains a Waiver and Release in Paragraph 10 to which you will be bound." Lund did not read this sentence. Lund also acknowledged that she did not read the waiver and release paragraph itself.

The waiver and release paragraph, printed on a following page of the contract, provides,

> 10. Waiver and Release. You (Buyer, each Member and all guests) agree that if you engage in any physical exercise or activity or use any club facility on the premises, you do so at your own risk. This includes, without limitation, your use of the locker room, pool, whirlpool, sauna, steamroom, parking area, sidewalk or any equipment in the health club and your participation in any activity, class, program or instruction. You agree that you are voluntarily participating in these activities and using these facilities and premises and assume all risk of injury, illness, damage or loss to you or your property that might result, including, without limitation, any loss or theft of any personal property. You agree on behalf of yourself (and your personal representatives, heirs, executors, administrators, agents and assigns) to release and discharge us (and our affiliates, employees, agents, representatives, successors and assigns) from any and all claims or causes of action (known or unknown) arising out of our negligence. This Waiver and Release of liability includes, without limitation, injuries which may occur as a result of (a) your use of any exercise equipment or facilities which may malfunction or break; (b) our improper maintenance of any exercise equipment or facilities, (c) our negligent instruction or supervision, and (d) you slipping and falling while in the health club or on the premises. You acknowledge that you have carefully read this Waiver and Release and fully understand that it is a release of liability. You are waiving

any right that you may have to bring a legal action to assert a claim against us for our negligence.

When she first approached Ladd about using his services, Lund knew that she would have to pay Bally's an additional fee because the services of a personal trainer were not included in the price of her membership. She also knew that Ladd was an employee of Bally's. Lund received a receipt from Ladd. The receipt acknowledges that she paid for 20 sessions but contains no substantive terms. Ladd did not require Lund to execute a personal trainer waiver and release which, according to Lund's expert, is standard in the industry.

\*\*\*\*

## Waiver and Release

Lund contends the February 1994 waiver and release does not bar her claim. First, she argues this waiver and release does not apply because she made a separate contract with Bally's to obtain the services of a personal trainer. That contract (the receipt she received from Ladd) does not contain a waiver and release. Second, Lund argues that because the February 1994 waiver and release does not specifically mention personal trainer services, injuries suffered while being personally trained are outside its scope. Finally, Lund contends the waiver and release is invalid because it violates Civil Code section 1668. We reject each of these arguments.

The dispositive question is whether the February 1994 waiver and release applies to Lund's use of Bally's weight lifting equipment under the supervision of a personal trainer employed by Bally's. (*Paralift, Inc. v. Superior Court* (1993) 23 Cal.App.4th 748, 754 [29 Cal.Rptr.2d 177].) (3) To achieve that result, the release must " 'be clear, unambiguous and explicit in expressing the intent of the parties.' " (*Id.*, at p. 755, quoting *Madison v. Superior Court* (1988) 203 Cal.App.3d 589, 597-598 [250 Cal.Rptr. 299].) Waiver and release forms are to be strictly construed against the defendant. Such a form is simply a written assumption of a known risk, *i.e.*, a risk reasonably anticipated by the plaintiff. (*Leon v. Family Fitness Center (#107), Inc.* (1998) 61 Cal.App.4th 1227, 1234 [71 Cal.Rptr.2d 923].) To be operative, the defendant's negligence which results in the plaintiff's injury must be reasonably related to the object or purpose for which the release is given. (*Id.*, at p. 1235; *Paralift, Inc. v. Superior Court, supra*, 23 Cal.App.4th at p. 757; *Madison v. Superior Court, supra*, 203 Cal.App.3d at p. 601.) (2b) Here, the trial court correctly concluded that the waiver and release clearly and unambiguously applied to bar Lund's claims.

Lund was injured while exercising with equipment provided by Bally's. Her membership contract expressly states that she engaged in these activities at her own risk, and "assume[s] all risk of injury ... that might result" from them. Moreover, the contract released Bally's from all claims arising out of its negligence, including, "injuries which may occur as a result of (a) [Lund's] use of any exercise equipment or facilities, ... [and] (c) our negligent instruction or supervision ...." The undisputed evidence demonstrates that Lund was injured while using Bally's equipment under the "instruction or supervision" of a Bally's employee. The waiver and release clearly, unambiguously and explicitly bars this claim. (*Leon v. Family Fitness Center (#107), Inc., supra*, 61 Cal.App.4th 1227, 1233; *Allabach v. Santa Clara County Fair Assn.* (1996) 46 Cal.App.4th 1007, 1015-1016 [54 Cal.Rptr.2d 330].)

That Lund was required to pay an extra fee for Ladd's services without executing a new waiver and release specifically addressing personal trainer negligence does not render the 1994 membership contract inapplicable. The release is not limited to activities included in the standard membership. Instead, it expressly applies to any exercise activity and any such activity while being instructed or supervised. Because Lund was injured while exercising and while being instructed or supervised, the release bars her claim. (*Paralift, Inc. v. Superior Court, supra,* 23 Cal.App.4th at p. 756.) We emphasize that Ladd's negligence was "... reasonably related to the object or purpose for which the release [was] given." (*Id.,* at p. 757.)[1]

Finally the waiver and release does not violate Civil Code section 1668. This statute provides: "All contracts which have for their object, directly or indirectly, to exempt anyone from responsibility for his own fraud, or willful injury to the person or property of another, or violation of law, whether willful or negligent, are against the policy of the law." (Civ. Code, § 1668.) This statute is here irrelevant. There is no allegation of fraud, willful injury or any violation of law. (4) Moreover, California courts have

---

[1] The instant waiver and release form, when measured against the rules articulated in *Leon v. Family Fitness Center (#107), Inc., supra*, 61 Cal.App.4th at pages 1234-1235, obviously does not exculpate defendant from all negligence as intended by the drafter. While it may have a chilling effect on the filing of a lawsuit, the drafter's choice of all-encompassing language may not be determinative. For example, in the health or fitness club context, the *Leon* court held that the plaintiff did not assume the risk that he would be injured by a collapsing sauna bench even though he 1. assumed the risk of injury while exercising (*id.,* at p. 1235) and 2. waived claims "... of any kind whatsoever ... resulting from or related to Member's use of the facilities ...." (*Id.,* at p. 1231; cf. *YMCA of Metropolitan Los Angeles v. Superior Court* (1997) 55 Cal.App.4th 22 [63 Cal.Rptr.2d 612].)

consistently held that, "although exculpatory clauses affecting the public interest are invalid (citation omitted), exculpatory agreements in the recreational sports context do not implicate the public interest." (*Allan v. Snow Summit, Inc.* (1996) 51 Cal.App.4th 1358, 1373 [59 Cal.Rptr.2d 813]; see also *Randas v. YMCA of Metropolitan Los Angeles* (1993) 17 Cal.App.4th 158, 161- 162 [21 Cal.Rptr.2d 245].)

The judgment is affirmed. Costs to respondent.


**Notes & Questions**

1. Describe facts that a Virginia court (*i.e., Heitt*) would consider not violative of public policy in a case involving a sports injury waiver?

2. Does the Virginia court's decision make it more likely or less likely that organizations will be willing to sponsor athletic contests such as road races? Explain your answer.

3. Is there any way to rectify the apparent contradiction regarding the validity of liability waivers between these two cases? If so, explain how. If not, explain why not. Do you think that the nature of the risks involved has any bearing on the outcomes? For example, in *Hiett*, there are countless unknown and unforeseeable risks lurking in the waters of a lake, on roads where cyclists will ride and where runners will run. But in a gym, there are a limited number of risks over which the owners presumably have a fair degree of control.

4. If you were advising a non-profit youth baseball league in Virginia, what advice would you give the board of Directors concerning a waiver of liability on their registration form? How about in California?

5. Two other troubling questions are whether a minor can validly waive liability and also whether a parent or guardian can effectively waive liability for a minor? *See Shaner v. State Sys. of Higher Educ.*, 40 Pa. D. & C.4th 308 (1998). The *Shaner* Court considered the enforceability of a waiver of liability signed by the parent of a 14-year old girl participating in a softball camp. The girl, Susan Shaner, suffered a broken leg during a softball game at Bloomsburg University summer softball camp. In order to participate in the camp the signature of her parent was required on a waiver that contained the following terms:

I desire to enroll in the 1985 Bloomsburg University softball camp. Bloomsburg University, the director, and anyone connected with the clinic do not assume liability for any injuries incurred while at camp or on the way to and from camp. Parents should contact their own insurance company to get additional insurance for their daughter if necessary.

Campers will be required to attend all sessions and must comply to all camp rules. Failure to do so may result in dismissal from camp. After an application is accepted there will be no refund of the $ 50 deposit.

Parent's signature /s/Mahlon R. Shaner

Shaner brought suit against the Pennsylvania State System of Higher Education alleging negligence. The lower court ruled that the waiver barred her claim. On appeal Shaner argued that "her father cannot legally bind her to the clause and she did not understand or agree to it. . . ." The appeals court held for Shaner, explaining that except for contracts of necessity, a minor is not competent to enter into a valid contract. The court reasoned that the release could not be enforced against the plaintiff on the grounds that (1) at 14-year old plaintiff was a minor and therefore incompetent to enter a contractual agreement; and (2) her father lacked the requisite authority to release the claim against defendant. Courts routinely hold that a minor lacks the capacity to waive liability.

*Further Reading on Institutions, Officials and Waivers*;

John C. Weistart & Cym H. Lowell, Law of Sports, §8.04 Waiver and Release of Liability (Bobbs-Merrill Company, Inc., 1979).

John C. Weistart & Cym H. Lowell, Law of Sports, §8.05 Liability for Injuries in Educational Programs (Bobbs-Merrill Company, Inc., 1979).

*Further Reading on Torts and Sports in General:*

Roger I. Abrams, *Torts and Sports: Legal Liability in Professional and Amateur Athletics*, 54 U. CIN. L. REV. 1237 (1986).

Lawrence Bershad, *Boxing in the United States: Reform, Abolition or Federal Control*, 19 SETON HALL L. REV. 865 (1989).

Walter T. Champion, *Nonprofessional Sport-Related Injuries and Assumption of Risk in Pennsylvania*, 54 PA. B.A. Q.43 (1983).

Walter T. Champion, *The Ball Bounces Back: Rutter Reverses Risk*, 82 PA. L.J. REP. 3 (March 7, 1982).

Phyllis G. Coleman, *Scuba Diving Injuries: Causes, Remedies, and Defenses*, 29 J. MAR. L. & COM. 519 (1998).

Daniel E. Lazaroff, *Golfer's Tort Lliability- A Critique of Emerging Standard*, 24 HASTINGS COMM. & ENT. L.J. 317 (2002).

Matthew J. Mitten, *AIDS and Athletics*, 3 SETON HALL J. SPORT L. 5 (1993).

Matthew J. Mitten, *Emerging Legal Issues in Sports Medicine*, 52 DEF. L.J. 265 (2003).

Matthew J. Mitten, *Enhanced Risk of Harm to One's Self as a Justification for Exclusion From Athletics*, 8 MARQ. SPORTS L. REV. 189 (1998).

Matthew J. Mitten, *Team Physicians and Competitive Athletes: Allocating Legal Responsibility for Athletic Injuries*, 55 U. PITT. L. REV. 129 (1993).

Russ VerSteeg, *Negligence in the Air: Safety, Legal Liability, and the Pole Vault*, 4 TEX. REV. ENT. & SPORTS L. 109 (2003).

Russ VerSteeg, *Running Scared: Negligence and the Running Boom*, 4 SETON HALL J. SPORT L. 447 (1994).

# Chapter 5

## Contracts

---

### A. Introductory Concepts

In many respects, contract law dominates much of Sports Law. Athletes and organizations structure a great many of their affairs by means of contracts, some simple and some complex. In youth sports, parents typically sign some type of contract and pay a fee as a registration for their children to participate. High school athletes may sign letters of intent to attend certain colleges. In collegiate athletics, student athletes receive grants in aid (scholarships) that take the form of contracts. And of course in professional sports there are individual player contracts, collective bargaining agreements forged by management and player unions, endorsement contracts, and agency contracts, just to name a few.

This chapter introduces several issues that frequently arise in sports contracts. The *Cannon* case poses a number of questions regarding the formation of contracts (*i.e.,* What constitutes an offer? What constitutes an acceptance?), as well as giving us an opportunity to consider the relative bargaining power ordinarily exercised by a professional sports franchise as compared to a college student. Typically, in order to have a valid contract, an offeree must accept an offeror's offer; and there must be some *quid pro quo* (*i.e.,* something that each is agreeing to exchange). Lawyers call that *quid pro quo* "consideration." Of course in an ordinary player contract the player's "consideration" is her promise to play for the team, while the team's "consideration" is its promise to pay money to the player. Each exchanges his/her promise in return for the other's reciprocal promise. That's consideration. *Cannon* also provides a glimpse of a fairly sophisticated topic in Contract Law, the distinction between conditions precedent and conditions subsequent.

The *Barnett* case raises the issue of contract remedies. In the majority of typical contracts cases, an aggrieved party asks the court for money damages. Courts also frequently call money damages a "legal remedy." The most common money damages that a court grants in a breach of contract case are "expectation damages." Expectation damages are the amount of money that a non-breaching party would have received if the breaching party had not breached (also referred to as the "benefit of the bargain"). The goal of expectation damages is to put the non-breaching party in the economic position that she would have been in had the other party not breached. But in *Barnett*, the plaintiff doesn't ask for money (*i.e.*, a "legal" remedy) but rather asks for the "equitable remedy" of negative injunction. In other words, the club asks for a court order that will prohibit the player from playing for any other basketball team. When a court grants an "equitable remedy," it orders a party either to do something (*i.e.*, to take some action) or to refrain from doing something. Pay particular attention to why negative injunctions are so important for some sports law contracts.

*DiNardo* presents a case involving both contract formation issues as well as the construction (*i.e.*, interpretation) of liquidated damages. Liquidated damages, unlike expectation damages or injunctions represent a sum of money to which the parties actually agreed in their contract (just in case either party later breached).

All three cases illustrate contract principles applied in a unique Sports Law setting.

## Los Angeles Rams Football Club v. Billy Cannon
### 185 F.Supp. 717 (1960)
United States District Court S.D. California, Central Division

LINDBERG, District Judge.

Plaintiff, Los Angeles Rams Football Club, a member of the National Football League, has brought this action seeking injunctive relief and a declaration of right against the defendant, Billy Cannon, a citizen and resident of the State of Louisiana. The matter in controversy exceeds the

176

value of $10,000, exclusive of interests and costs, and is within the diversity jurisdiction of this court.

Specifically, plaintiff prays for an injunction to restrain defendant from playing football or engaging in related activities for anyone other than plaintiff without the plaintiff's consent during the term of a contract or contracts allegedly entered into by the parties on November 30, 1959, and an order declaring the existence of a valid written contract or contracts.

Defendant denies he ever entered into a contract or contracts as alleged....

\*\*\*\*

The defendant, Billy Cannon, is a remarkable football player who has just finished his collegiate career with Louisiana State University. The last intercollegiate game he participated in was the Sugar Bowl game on January 1, 1960. Prior to that time, however, on November 28, 1959, or early in the morning of the 29th, he was contacted by telephone by Pete Rozelle, now Commissioner of the National Football League, but who was then and at all times material to the dispute here involved General Manager for the Los Angeles Rams. Mr. Rozelle was in Baltimore, Maryland and Billy Cannon was then in New York.

There is no question about the call being made but there is serious dispute as to the conversation had. However, we can safely assume that it had to do with football. (At this time I do not attempt to resolve the factual disputes but leave that for later consideration as I reach the issues.)

The telephone call mentioned occurred less than thirty-six hours before the annual selection meeting of the National Football League which was held in Philadelphia, Pennsylvania.

The Rams, after sifting an astonishing amount of information through a complex scouting system, concluded that Billy Cannon was the player of the current graduating crop they would most like to see on their team. The Rams, by virtue of ten losses and only two wins last season were tied for last place in the League, but as every cloud has its silver lining this fact also tied them for first draft choice at the above-mentioned selection meeting. The tie was to be broken by the flip of a coin. Thus it was that the Rams stood a fifty-fifty chance of having the first draft choice.

It has been the Rams' contention throughout that this position on the draft is so valuable that careful steps are undertaken to assure the team having the choice that it is not wasted on a player not willing to play for that team. The telephone call referred to was for the purpose of exploring that question.

On the 29th there was another telephone conversation between Mr. Rozelle and the defendant and on this occasion Mr. Rozelle was in Philadelphia. That night Billy Cannon took a train from New York to Philadelphia and registered at the Sheraton Hotel under the name of Billy Gunn at the suggestion and arrangement of Mr. Rozelle.

On the following day the selection meeting was held. The Rams won the toss of the coin and selected Billy Cannon as its first draft choice.

Immediately following the meeting defendant and Mr. Rozelle got together, met with members of the press, and discussed for the benefit of the press the fact that the Rams had received the first draft choice and had selected Billy Cannon.

Following the press interview Cannon and Rozelle went to Rozelle's hotel room where Cannon signed three sets of National Football Player Contract forms covering the years 1960, 1961 and 1962, and took possession of two checks, one for $10,000 and the other for $500.

Mr. Rozelle, on or about December 1st, left one set of said forms as filled out-- that set embracing the 1960 season-- with the then acting Commissioner, Mr. Gunsel.

Some two weeks later Billy Cannon was contacted on behalf of a Mr. K. S. Adams, Jr., who is the owner or part owner of the Houston Oilers, a football club in the recently-formed American Football League. On or about December 22nd Cannon met with Mr. Adams and others in Baton Rouge and negotiations were had with respect to a so-called personal service contract including the playing of football.

On December 30, 1959, Billy Cannon sent to the Rams a letter wherein he announced that he no longer desired to play for the Rams, purportedly revoked any offer he may have made to play for the Rams, and returned therewith the two checks above mentioned uncashed and unendorsed.

178

Prior thereto, however, it is contended that Mr. Gunsel approved the contract for the 1960 season, and the exhibit as admitted, Exhibit A, bears the signature of Mr. Gunsel alongside of which the date December 1, 1959 was written in.

At this point I propose to treat the question of whether or not a contract or contracts ever came into existence, dealing first with the instruments themselves before getting into the difficult matter of what transpired prior to and at the time of signing. The question, then, is, What is the nature of the several documents signed by Billy Cannon November 30, 1959? Disregarding for the moment the interpretations of the parties, the court must look to the instruments themselves.

We have three sets of instruments, in triplicate, each denominated National Football League Standard Players Contract, admitted in evidence as plaintiff's Exhibits A, B, C and H; H being a photo copy of the League copy of the first set. The printed form is identical in each case with the exception that there are three riders attached to each copy of the first set. The first set has the year 1960 typed in the appropriate blank; the second, 1961; and the third, 1962.

Each form states that it is a contract between Los Angeles Rams Football Club, thereinafter called the Club, and Billy Cannon, thereafter called the player. It states that in consideration of the respective promises contained therein the parties agree to the following terms:

Paragraph 1 thereunder reads as follows:

'1. The term of this contract shall be from the date of execution hereof until the first day of May following the close of the football season commencing in ------ (blank for the insertion of a given year) subject, however, to rights of prior termination as specified herein.'

Paragraph 2 obligates the player to play football for the club and the club, subject to the provisions of the contract, to hire the player as a skilled football player during the term of the contract.

Paragraph 3 contains the club's promise 'to pay the player each football season during the term of this contract the sum of $------' payable according to a given schedule.

Paragraph 4 contains the player's promise to comply with the constitution, by-laws, rules and regulations of the League and of the Club, which are made a part of the contract; the right of termination for failure to so comply; the player's agreement to submit himself to the discipline of the League and Club; the handling of disputes by the Commissioner; and other details unimportant to this litigation.

Paragraph 5 is the negative covenant whereby the player promises not to play football or engage in related activities during the term of the contract for anyone else without the permission of the Club and Commissioner.

Paragraph 6 contains the player's warranty that he is and will continue to be sufficiently highly skilled in all types of football teamplay to play professional football of the caliber required by the Club and League and that he will perform to the complete satisfaction of the Club and its Head Coach. The provision then provides the right of termination should the player fail to achieve this satisfaction.

Paragraph 7 relates to the schedule of settlement in the event of such termination.

In Paragraph 8 the player represents that he has exceptional skill as a football player and that money damages would not compensate the loss thereof and he therefore agrees that the Club may enjoin him by appropriate injunction in the event of breach.

Paragraph 9 provides for sale or assignment of the contract.

Paragraph 10 provides for renewal for a further term subject to certain conditions.

Paragraph 11 contains the player's acknowledgement of the right and power of the Commissioner to execute certain disciplinary measures in relation to bribes, attempted bribes and game throwing.

Paragraph 12 provides for reimbursement to the Club of any Workmen's Compensation Benefits.

Paragraph 13 reads, in full:

'13. This agreement contains the entire agreement between the parties and there are no oral or written inducements, promises or agreements except as contained herein. This agreement shall become valid and binding upon each party hereto only when, as and if it shall be approved by the Commissioner.'

Paragraph 14 provides that California law shall control. Paragraph 14 is the last paragraph of the form, following which there is space for the name of the Club, the signature of the Club's agent, the signature of the player, the signatures of two witnesses and space for the Commissioner's signature following the printed word "Approved." There are three date blanks, one next to the blank for the Club agent's signature, one next to the blank for the player's signature, and one next to the Commissioner's approval.

I have tried to cover as fully as necessary, but as briefly as that would permit, the form used by the Rams in their negotiations with Billy Cannon.

As heretofore indicated three sets of these forms were used. In the appropriate blank in Paragraph 1 the years 1960, 1961 and 1962, respectively, were inserted in the three sets. Each set contains the signature of Pete Rozelle for the Rams, Billy Cannon and the two witnesses. (I might state at this point, parenthetically, that no law this court is aware of requires this type of contract to be witnessed, nor does the contract itself set up such a requirement.)

Only one of the sets bears the signature of the Commissioner with respect to approval, and the evidence is to the effect that until late in December, 1959 the Commissioner was unaware of the other two sets.

The question germane at this point is just how important to these contracts is the Commissioner's approval. On this point, of course, the parties to the action are at opposite poles, plaintiff taking the position that it is an unimportant ministerial act concerning only the League and the Club, while the defendant takes the position that it is an act absolutely essential to the formation of a contract.

[1] It is the opinion of this court that on this issue the defendant must prevail. Approval by the Commissioner is essential to the formation of a contract here and this is so because the terms of the document make it so.

Keeping in mind that these forms were furnished by the Rams and not Billy Cannon, the court calls particular attention to the words regarding approval:

181

"This agreement shall become valid and binding upon each party hereto only when, as and if it shall be approved by the Commissioner."

Paraphrasing: "Shall become valid…only when…and if…it shall be approved…"

The words "shall become valid" clearly compels the conclusion that-- in the absence of approval-- it is not yet a valid agreement.

The use of the word "if" clearly suggests that approval might not happen at all.

This clause is too definite to be ignored. It jumps out at you. The words employed are too strong to permit of ambiguity. Their selection was obviously made with great care so that there would be no dispute about their meaning, and this court attaches to them the only meaning it can-- that is, that the agreement shall only become valid and binding if, as and when approved by the Commissioner.

If there were not reason enough for so holding there are further reasons inherent in the instruments themselves which makes this conclusion inescapable.

We have earlier noted that paragraph 1 describes the term of the agreement 'from the date of execution hereof until the first day of May following the close of the football season commencing in ' (whatever year is placed in the blank provided). This paragraph defines the term and it clearly allows for more than one year. If such a contract were executed today and the year 1970 were placed in the blank it would be, to my way of thinking, a contract for a term in excess of ten years.

Paragraph 3 obligates the Club 'to pay the player each football season during the term of this contract' a stated sum. This again is persuasive that this form permits a term in excess of one year unless there is more than one football season in one year.

Paragraph 1 tells us when a term ends but it does not tell us when it begins. If, as contended by plaintiff, the date of execution is the date it is signed by the Club and player, we would have in the case at bar three contracts, all commencing on November 30, 1959, one running to May of 1961, the second to May of 1962, and the third to May of 1963. And as each contract calls for payment for each season within the term Billy Cannon might have a contract calling for a grand total of $95,000, including the bonus.

This, of course, is so absurd that no one would suggest that that is what either side intended to do here.

This absurdity does not exist if it is determined that approval is essential to execution, as I find it is. When approval is essential to execution and that act fixes the beginning of the term, the Club, so long as it sits on the instrument, controls the beginning of the term thereunder and at the same time the number of seasons it shall cover. This, perhaps, may well be one of the reasons these instruments are not submitted for approval until just before the year typed in the blank.

Section 7 of Article XII of the Constitution and By-Laws of the National Football League, which, of course, is a part of the forms by reference, provides that the only instrument which will bind a player to any club is the form used here when executed and filed in the office of the Commissioner. It provides that the club first filing such a contract shall be awarded the player and that the time of filing shall be the time of filing it in the Commissioner's office. If two teams within the League signed the same player and the last team to sign the player were the first to file the contract with the Commissioner there can be no question under this provision who would be awarded the player.

For League purposes it may be very essential to provide this sort of arrangement in order to avoid disputes between teams within the League. But the only way this can be accomplished within the framework of law is to make the Commissioner's approval an essential part of execution, otherwise the Commissioner would be destroying the legal efficacy of binding contracts, a thing the courts would be powerless to do. This provision, which is within the four corners of the contract, is one more persuasive indication that approval is essential to execution.

****

It is my conclusion…that until approved, these instruments are, at most, only offers.

****

[T]he requirement for approval in these instruments…could be characterized a condition precedent to execution but it is more properly to be

183

denominated a part of execution, so made by the people who drew up the form.

If we are to adhere to the doctrine of freedom of contract we must allow parties to specify any degree of formality to the act of execution they wish so long as it doesn't violate public policy or some rule of law.

We may conclude, therefore, that what we have been loosely referring to as the 1961 and 1962 contracts were, at most, only offers and are now unquestionably revoked. That leaves the question of whether the 1960 instrument became a contract.

Having concluded as a matter of law that the alleged contracts-- Exhibits A, B and C-- under the provisions contained therein when signed by the defendant on November 30, 1959, constituted no more than an offer by Cannon to play football for the Rams until accepted by them and approved by the Commissioner. I next consider what the terms of the offer were.

It has been plaintiff's contention that they made the offer to Cannon and that he accepted that offer. That, as I have already stated, was not the result as a matter of law under paragraph 13 of the alleged contracts. Further, it must be borne in mind that plaintiff was not in a position to make a firm offer to Cannon under the Constitution and By-laws of the League until after the 'flip of the coin' which occurred on Monday, November 30, 1959, some two hours or thereabouts before Cannon signed the documents.

The terms of the offer cannot be ascertained from the several documents alone, presenting as they do, if the interpretation urged by plaintiff is followed, an ambiguity as to the term of service covered under paragraph one of the documents and the compensation to be paid under paragraph three, as I have earlier pointed out.

It becomes necessary, therefore, for the purpose of determining whether there was a manifestation of mutual assent, to consider the conversations and circumstances preceding and occurring at the time of the signing of the contract forms.

The testimony of Cannon and Rozelle as to many of the facts is directly contradictory and I shall attempt to resolve their disagreement only as to the more pertinent facts and statements such as appear essential in deciding what the understanding between them was. In so doing I have weighed the conflicting testimony with particular care, trying alternately to sustain the testimony of each within the framework of the surrounding circumstances and admitted facts as developed by the evidence.

First, with respect to the proposal submitted by Rozelle to Cannon in the course of the telephone conversations of November 28th and 29th, it should be kept in mind that Rozelle had talked with Coach Dietzel on several occasions prior to his initial conversation with Cannon. On one such occasion Rozelle agrees that he told Dietzel, in substance, that, 'We will give Billy Cannon a three-year contract starting in 1960 for fifteen thousand a year, and a $5,000 bonus for signing the contract, but again we would like to have assurance that he would be willing to sign such a contract.'

[2] Rozelle also testified that when he talked with Cannon first on Saturday evening, November 28th, he repeated the identical terms to Cannon. (Tr. 81-82). While Rozelle also testified that his subsequent proposal was 'a $10,000 bonus for signing, rather than five and for 1960 a $10,000 contract, rather than a $15,000 contract. And a $15,000 for '61 and a $15,000 for '62' it is clear that he was talking at all times about a three-year proposal. Furthermore, following the first telephone conversation with Rozelle, Dietzel called Cannon and told him that the offer Rozelle had made to him was the best he (Dietzel) had heard of a rookie getting. Whether or not Rozelle referred to his proposal as a 'package' or not it is my conclusion that Rozelle conveyed and Cannon obtained the impression that the proposal to be submitted by the Rams in the event they won the toss of the coin was to cover a three year period with total compensation, including a bonus, of $50,000. On the other hand, it likewise seems clear that Rozelle had in mind at the time he presented the Standard Players Contract forms to Cannon for signing, judging from the fact that he submitted the bonus, injury and armed services riders as to one and left but one form, namely, Exhibit A, with Acting Commissioner Gunsel and never submitted Exhibits B and C, that the transaction would result in three separate and distinct contracts-- one for each season-- to be submitted to the Commissioner for approval if the Rams so desired, as each succeeding year approached. It thus appears that there was never a meeting of the minds as between the parties with respect to the offer. Construing the Contract forms as I do, *i.e.* requiring not only the signing by the parties but also the approval of the Commissioner, the forms as signed by Cannon-- even though signed by the Rams-- must be construed as an offer by him to play for the Rams for a period of three years. This offer was never accepted by the Rams inasmuch as they requested and received the approval of the Commissioner as to the first year, 1960, only.

[3] It is true, however, that even though the signing of the Contract forms by Cannon, because of lack of approval by the Commissioner,

constituted no more than an offer, Cannon did at least take possession of the $10,000 bonus check, which, under the understanding of both parties, was payable in advance of the 1960 football season and conditioned upon the player reporting to the Rams for the 1960 training camp period. Can this be construed as an acceptance of an assumed counter-offer of the Rams for the 1960 season subject to a later approval of the Commissioner as to the proposed contract, Exhibit A? This would depend, in part at least, upon the understanding between the parties as to whether Cannon accepted the check as payment. It is undisputed that he did not endorse the check, that he left it with his banker for safekeeping, and that he returned it before the player's copy of the proposed contract, Exhibit A, approved by the Commissioner was sent to him.

Bearing on this issue Rozelle testified:

'I told Billy Cannon this would be kept in confidence, the signing would not be announced until after the Sugar Bowl and told him to take good care of the money.'

Of course, the great difficulty in resolving the factual issues involved in this case results from the fact that the signing of the alleged contracts-- Exhibits A, B and C-- was shrouded in secrecy due to the manner in which Rozelle handled the transaction. He knew from Cannon's coach, Dietzel, that he, Dietzel, was opposed to the signing of any contract. Rozelle nevertheless intended to get Cannon's signature to a contract when, as he testified, he carefully phrased his answer to Dietzel that "The Rams will do nothing to impair Cannon's eligibility for the Sugar Bowl." Cannon, on the other hand, unwittingly, I am convinced, expressed his desire to apportion his anticipated 1960 income so as to make some of it taxable for the year 1959. This, of course, might well be construed as a compelling motive for accepting the check as payment. At this juncture, however, it should be noted, that Cannon, granting his outstanding ability and prowess on the gridiron, is anything but an astute business man. His whole life and interest has been directed toward athletics and particularly football; and while he impressed me as being somewhat naive for a college senior I feel certain that he knew he couldn't accept as payment the $10,000 check that was tendered him and remain eligible to play for his school in the Sugar Bowl, nor do I believe he would intentionally disqualify himself. He didn't need to. With respect to Cannon this wasn't a chance in a lifetime to turn professional which he might lose forever if he didn't grab it immediately. By this time he must have appreciated the fact that his services were in great demand by professional football. I, therefore, am led to make the finding that Cannon did not accept the check in payment. Rather, he accepted it, believing it was not his and that he had no claim upon it until after the Sugar Bowl game.

While some, particularly those schooled-- to use the vernacular-- in the 'game for dough' may view my interpretation of the transaction as a 'Pollyanna' approach and entirely unrealistic it should be borne in mind that Cannon, while having been a highly publicized college ball player, was, in fact, and still is, it would appear, a provincial lad of 21 or 22, untutored and unwise, I am convinced, in the way of the business world. While he had entertained ambitions for years to get into professional football the proposition submitted to him by the Rams came by telephone apparently without prior notice while he was away from home and in New York for the purpose of receiving one of many rapidly accumulating honors that were being bestowed upon him. He was without counsel or advice and the whole transaction, including the signing of the alleged contracts, was completed in less than 48 hours. When Cannon arrived at the Warwick Hotel on Monday morning he did not know whether the Rams had acquired the right to draft him. He was immediately brought before the press and, as Rozelle testified, he Rozelle, heard Cannon make the statement to the effect that he would sign a contract with the Rams following the L.S.U. and Mississippi game in the Sugar Bowl on New Year's Day.

At that time it is reasonable to assume that Cannon had no idea that Rozelle would expect him to sign a written contract. Thereafter, Rozelle took Cannon and no one else with him to Rozelle's room where Rozelle had waiting for signature the partially-completed forms which he presented to Cannon for signature. Just what language Rozelle used in persuading Cannon to sign the documents I do not know and I doubt if either Cannon or Rozelle have a completely accurate recollection of what was said. I am persuaded, however, that during the 30 to 45 minutes spent in the room Rozelle conveyed the impression to Cannon that the documents would not become effective or binding upon him until after the Sugar Bowl game on New Year's Day. The admitted fact that Rozelle sought to keep their existence confidential and secret as well as the fact that Rozelle did not become concerned as to the Acting Commissioner's approval of Exhibit A until after he had learned on December 22, 1959 of the possibility that Cannon might go with the Houston Oilers lends support to the belief that Rozelle had so assured Cannon.

In view of the foregoing it is my conclusion that the accepting of possession of the check for $10,000 by Cannon was not an acceptance of payment under the alleged contract, Exhibit A.

187

\*\*\*\*

I have [reached] the conclusion that there did not come into existence a valid written contract or contracts binding upon plaintiff and defendant....
\*\*\*\*

It probably should be observed, however, that while I have already indicated that Cannon did not intentionally or knowingly make himself ineligible to play in the Sugar Bowl game because of his dealings with the Rams on November 30th, I did not reach the issue of what in fact would have made him ineligible to play under the rules of the N.C.A.A. \*\*\*\*

Judgment will be for defendant, with costs.

## Notes & Questions

1. In terms of "offer & acceptance," identify what facts the *Cannon* court considered an "offer." According to this court, what facts could have constituted an "acceptance" of that offer? By definition an offeree's counteroffer constitutes a rejection of the offeror's original offer. At one point the court suggests that there might have been a counteroffer, and possibly, an acceptance of that counteroffer. Explain.

2. The court refers to a lack of "meeting of the minds" ("It thus appears that there was never a meeting of the minds as between the parties with respect to the offer."). The phrase "meeting of the minds" is a standard part of the Contract law lexicon. But the problem is that it is really not descriptive of the concept for which it stands. As a result, many law students (and lawyers I fear!) are under the mistaken impression that both parties must somehow participate in something of a Vulcan "Mind-Meld" in order for a contract to be valid. The requirement that there be a "meeting of the minds" does not actually mean that both parties must be "thinking the same thing." Rather in modern Contract jurisprudence, we have come to accept an "objective theory" of contract formation. In order for there to be a "meeting of the minds" using the objective theory, we must ask the following questions. Would a reasonable person in the position of the offeree think that the offeror, based on the outward manifestations of the offeror's conduct, was intending to be bound by his offer? In order to answer this question, you must take into account the words (if any) used by the offeror as well as all of the surrounding circumstances (*e.g.*, tone of voice, hand gestures, facial expression, etc.). If the answer is "yes" then at least we know that,

objectively speaking, the offeror intended to make a contract. Then we must ask one more question. Would a reasonable person in the position of the offeror think that the offeree, based on the outward manifestations of the offeree's conduct, was intending to be bound by his acceptance. As was the case with objectively interpreting the offeror's offer, in order to answer this question, you must take into account the words (if any) used by the offeree as well all of the surrounding circumstances (*e.g.,* the offeree's tone of voice, hand gestures, facial expression, etc.). So in essence, the objective theory of contract relies upon the external indicia (outward manifestations of the parties' conduct) to determine whether a reasonable person standing in the other person's shoes would have perceived that the other intended to be bound by their offer and acceptance.

In sum, then, the so-called "objective theory of contracts" (*i.e.,* using the objective manifestations of the intent of the parties as a basis for determining the parties' intent to enter into a contract) has actually made the archaic and outmoded concept of "meeting of the minds" virtually obsolete. Using the objective theory of contract formation, explain the *Cannon* court's decision.

3. First year Contracts students usually learn about "conditions precedent" and "conditions subsequent." Essentially, a condition precedent is an event which acts as an "on switch" or a triggering mechanism. When two people make a bet on the outcome of a basketball game, for example, the result (*i.e.,* the winning by one team) triggers an obligation for one party to owe money to the other. The fact that one team wins and the other loses, then, is a condition precedent to an obligation for payment. The obligation of payment does not arise until one team wins and the other loses. A condition subsequent, on the other hand, acts as an "off switch". A condition subsequent ordinarily (but not always) is worded in such a way that the parties create an obligation which may be "turned off" or extinguished if a certain event later occurs. You can usually recognize a condition subsequent by words such as "unless" or "if not." For example, I could agree to pay you $100 unless the Boston Red Sox win the World Series in 2012. The way that that agreement is worded, our agreement creates an obligation on my part to pay you $100. But if the Red Sox win the World Series in 2012, that occurrence will "turn off" or "extinguish" my obligation. But we have to wait until the conclusion of the 2012 World Series in order to determine whether I'll owe you the $100.

In this case, the court suggests that the Commissioner's signature is required in order for the contract even to come into existence. Explain the applicability of terms "condition precedent" and "condition subsequent" to the approval and signature of the NFL Commissioner on the *Cannon* contracts.

Indeed, in order to be considered valid, most professional player contracts need a league commissioner's approval. Write a sentence that would make a commissioner's approval a condition precedent. Then see if you can write a sentence that would make the commissioner's approval a condition subsequent.

4. According to the court, the so-called 1961 and 1962 "contract" offers were revoked ("We may conclude, therefore, that what we have been loosely referring to as the 1961 and 1962 contracts were, at most, only offers and are now unquestionably revoked."). Exactly what facts constituted the revocation of those offers?

5. To what extent do you think that the court was simply being paternalistic and protecting Cannon, a wet-behind-the-ears kid from Louisiana, from the big-time, professional football franchise?

6. Billy Cannon is one of twenty players who played the entire ten years of the American Football League, and he is a member of the American Football League Hall of Fame. He later became a dentist and subsequently served federal prison time for counterfeiting.

Printed with permission by Topps

### Central New York Basketball, Inc. v. Richard Barnett and Cleveland Basketball Club, Inc.
181 NE 2d 506 (1961)
Court of Common Pleas of Ohio, Cuyahoga County

DANACEAU, Judge.

This is an action for injunctive relief brought by the plaintiff, Central New York Basketball, Inc., a New York corporation, against Richard Barnett and Cleveland Basketball Club, Inc., a corporation. Plaintiff owns and operates a professional basketball team under the name of Syracuse Nationals, having a franchise of the National Basketball Association, now in its 16th season.

The defendant, Richard Barnett, a professional basketball player, the No. 1 draft choice in 1959 of the plaintiff and who played for the plaintiff during the ensuing 1959 basketball season, played for the Syracuse club throughout the 1960 basketball season under a signed and executed Uniform

Player Contract of the National Basketball Association under date of March 16, 1960 by and between the plaintiff and said defendant, a copy of said agreement is attached to the petition, and was received in evidence as plaintiff's Exhibit B.

The defendant, Cleveland Basketball Club, Inc., is a member of the American Basketball League, recently organized, and owns and operates a professional basketball team.

In July of 1961, the defendants, Barnett and Cleveland Basketball Club, Inc., made and entered into an American Basketball League Player Contract in which the club engaged the player to render his services as a basketball player for a term beginning on September 15, 1961 and ending on September 14, 1962, a copy of said contract having been received in evidence as plaintiff's Exhibit A.

The National Basketball Association has professional basketball clubs in the cities of New York, Philadelphia, Syracuse, Boston, Detroit, Cincinnati, Chicago, St. Louis and Los Angeles. The American Basketball League has professional clubs in the cities of Washington, Pittsburgh, Cleveland, Chicago, Kansas City, San Francisco and Los Angeles and the State of Hawaii.

Plaintiff claims that the defendant, Barnett, is a professional player of great skill and whose talents and abilities as a basketball player are of special, unique, unusual and extraordinary character; that the defendant, Cleveland Basketball Club, Inc., knew that he was under contract with the plaintiff; that in accordance with the terms and conditions of said contract the plaintiff exercised a right to renew said contract for an additional year as provided therein and so notified the defendant Barnett, that the defendant Barnett breached the said contract by failing and refusing to play with and for the said plaintiff during the 1961-1962 playing season, and that said breach of contract was committed with the knowledge and participation of the defendant, Cleveland Basketball Club, Inc. Plaintiff claims that it cannot reasonably or adequately be compensated for damages in an action at law for the loss of defendant Barnett's services as required by said contract and on oral agreement between plaintiff and Barnett made in May of 1961, and that plaintiff will suffer immediate and irreparable damages. Plaintiff, therefore, prays:

1. that defendant Richard Barnett be restrained and enjoined, during the pendency of this action and permanently, from playing basketball or engaging in any activities relating to basketball for The Cleveland Basketball

Club, Inc., or any person, firm, club or corporation other than the plaintiff, during the 1961-1962 basketball season.

2. That defendant Cleveland Basketball Club, Inc. be restrained and enjoined, during the pendency of this action and permanently, from any interference or attempted interference with the performance by the said Richard Barnett of his contract with plaintiff.

****

The written agreement under date of March 16, 1960 and signed by the plaintiff and the defendant Barnett provides in part as follows:

5. The Player promises and agrees (a) to report at the time and place fixed by the Club in good physical condition; and (b) to keep himself throughout the entire season in good physical condition; and (c) to give his best services, as well as his loyalty, to the Club, and to play basketball only for the Club unless released, sold or exchanged by the Club; and (d) to be neatly and fully attired in public and always to conduct himself on and off the court according to the highest standards of honesty, morality, fair play and sportsmanship, and (e) not to do anything which is detrimental to the best interests of the Club or of the National Basketball Association or of professional sports.

9. The Player represents and agrees that he has exceptional and unique skill and ability as a basketball player; that his services to be rendered hereunder are of a special, unusual and extraordinary character which gives them peculiar value which cannot be reasonably or adequately compensated for in damages at law, and that the Player's breach of this contract will cause the Club great and irreparable injury and damage. The Player agrees that, in addition to other remedies, the Club shall be entitled to injunctive and other equitable relief to prevent a breach of this contract by the Player, including, among others, the right to enjoin the Player from playing basketball for any other person or organization during the term of this contract.

22. (a) On or before September 1st (or if a Sunday, then the next preceding business day) next following the last playing season covered by this contract, the Club may tender to the

Player a contract for the term of that season by mailing the same to the Player at his address following his signature hereto, or if none be given, then at his last address of record with the Club. If prior to the November 1 next succeeding said September 1, the player and the Club have not agreed upon the terms of such contract, then on or before 10 days after said November 1, the Club shall have the right by written notice to the Player at said address to renew this contract for the period of one year on the same terms, except that the amount payable to the Player shall be such as the Club shall fix in said notice; provided, however, that said amount shall be an amount payable at a rate not less than 75% of the rate stipulated for the preceding year.

(b) The Club's right to renew this contract, as provided in subparagraph (a) of this paragraph 22, and the promise of the Player not to play otherwise than with the Club have been taken into consideration in determining the amount payable under paragraph 2 hereof.

Plaintiff contends that the foregoing provisions provide for two alternatives: 1) that the parties may agree upon a signed new contract for the next succeeding playing season and 2) in the event a signed agreement is not made, the club has the right to renew the contract for a period of one year on the same terms, except that the salary shall be fixed by the club and shall be payable at a rate not less than the stipulated minimum.

The plaintiff contends that under the second alternative, the terms are the same as in the preceding year except for the amount of salary and that at the close of the renewal year, the contract has been completed and is at an end.

The construction of the contract urged by plaintiff, to which it is committed in open court, is reasonable, rational, practical, just and in accordance with the foregoing principles, and is adopted by this Court.

The defendant Barnett had previously played for the Syracuse team during the greater part of the 1959-1960 season under a signed contract.

Daniel Biasone, the President and General Manager of the Syracuse club, testified that near the close of the 1960-1961 season in March of 1961, he told the defendant Barnett that Barnett was one of seven players he would keep exempt from the forthcoming draft of players from all National

Basketball Association clubs to stock the new Chicago club and that Barnett was one of the seven players he was 'protecting.'

In the latter part of May, 1961, Mr. Biasone reached the defendant Barnett by telephone, and they discussed salary for the next season and agreed upon an increase of $3,000 which would bring the salary of Barnett to $11,500. He further testified that Barnett said, 'You mail them (contracts) down and I will sign them and return them.' On cross-examination Biasone said that he was not sure and did not know whether Barnett said 'I will sign.'

The defendant Barnett testified:

'Q  What did he say?
'A  Well, he called me up and said that he wanted to discuss contracts for the coming year.
'Q  What did you say?
'A  I said that I thought I was worth $3000 more.
'Q  And he said?
'A  He agreed. He said, 'I think you are worth $3000 more myself.'
'I said, 'Send the contracts and I will look them over."

New contracts with the signature of plaintiff thereon were mailed to the defendant Barnett on May 26, 1961; and they remained with Barnett unsigned ever since.

In June of 1961, there was a telephone conversation between Jerry Walser, the Business Manager of the Syracuse club, and the defendant Barnett in which Barnett asked for an advance. Barnett:

'Q  What else was said in this conversation?
'A  Well, I asked for an advance on my--I asked for an advance of $300.
'Q  $300?
'A  That's right.
'Q  Did he say he would send you $300?
'A  He said as soon as Mr. Biasone returned--that he was away and that as soon as he could get his signature that they would advance the $300.'

On July 10, 1961, the plaintiff, through Jerry Walser, mailed to Barnett a letter enclosing a check for $3,000. Mr. Biasone testified:

'Q * * * Was money sent to Barnett for the 61-62 season, the current season?
'A Yes.
'Q When was that sent?
'A The early part of July.
'Q Of this year?
'A This year.
'Q And why was it sent?
'A It was asked for.
'Q By whom?
'A By Dick.
'Q How much money was sent to Mr. Barnett?
'A $3000.'

The letter and check were received by Barnett and remained in the sealed envelope until produced in court during a hearing on an application for a preliminary injunction on October 9, 1961.

Finding that the contracts mailed to Barnett were not returned and not hearing from Barnett, Mr. Biasone made repeated attempts to contact or reach the defendant Barnett in July and August of 1961 by telephone, telegram and letter, to all of which there was no response. On November 6, 1961, a letter from the plaintiff to the defendant was written and mailed and received by Barnett which reads as follows:

It is our position that your 1960-61 contract with us was renewed when we came to terms and we sent you an advance. However, to abide by the letter of the contract and to make the position of the Syracuse Nationals absolutely clear, we hereby notify you that pursuant to Paragraph 22(a) of said contract, we hereby renew the same for the period of one year ending October 1, 1962. The amount payable to you under such renewed contract is hereby fixed at $11,500.

Meanwhile, during the months of June and July of 1961, Barnett met and talked to his former coach and advisor, John B. McLendon, who was the Coach of the Cleveland Pipers Basketball team of the defendant Cleveland Basketball Club, Inc. Both Barnett and McLendon stated that Barnett did not want to play for Syracuse but did want to play for the Cleveland Pipers. However, they were both concerned about the "Kenny Sears" case, then pending in the California court. It appears that Sears was trying to "jump leagues" (R. 211) to play for San Francisco and both wanted to see the outcome of the case. Undoubtedly, this explains the lack of communication from Barnett to the Syracuse club during June and July of 1961, his failure to return the contracts and his failure to open the envelope containing the letter and check enclosed therein.

Relying upon a newspaper story and their interpretation thereof to the effect that Sears "would not be penalized for going to this new League," Barnett and McLendon proceeded to take the necessary steps culminating in a signed contract between Barnett and the Cleveland Pipers with McLendon signing the contract on behalf of the Cleveland club.

The request of Barnett for an advance, whether it was $300 or $3,000, renders strong support to the claim of plaintiff that an oral agreement on a salary had been reached and that Barnett would play for Syracuse during the 1961-1962 season. Manifestly, unless there was such an understanding, there could be no salary upon which such an advance could be made. The evidence is overwhelming, and this Court finds that the plaintiff and the defendant Barnett reached an understanding that Barnett would play for Syracuse during the 1961- 1962 season at a salary of $11,500. It is also quite clear that Barnett and McLendon of the Cleveland Pipers were acting in concert in awaiting the ruling in the Sears case; and after reading the newspaper report, decided that Barnett could "jump" without penalty and sign up with the Cleveland Pipers. Barnett and McLendon decided that they had the green light and the 'jump' was made.

The defendants challenge the validity and enforceability of the renewal provisions of the contract on the ground that they lack mutuality. The renewal clauses are an integral part of the contract, and there is sufficient consideration for the obligations and duties arising thereunder.

In the celebrated case of *Philadelphia Ball Club v. Lajoie*, 202 Pa. 210, 51 A. 973, 975, 58 L.R.A. 227, 229, the opinion of the court reads:

> We are not persuaded that the terms of this contract manifest any lack of mutuality in remedy. Each party has the possibility of enforcing all the rights stipulated for in the agreement. It is true that the terms make it possible for the plaintiff to put an end to the contract in a space of time much less than the period during which the defendant has agreed to supply his personal services; but mere difference in the rights stipulated for does not destroy mutuality of remedy. Freedom of contract covers a wide range of obligation and duty as between the parties, and it may not be impaired, so

197

long as the bounds of reasonableness and fairness are not transgressed.

and at page 230, 51 A. at page 975:

> **** The court cannot compel the defendant to play for the plaintiff, but it can restrain him from playing for another club in violation of his agreement. No reason is given why this should not be done, except that presented by the argument, that the right given to the plaintiff to terminate the contract upon 10 days' notice destroys the mutuality of the remedy. But to this it may be answered that, as already stated, the defendant has the possibility of enforcing all the rights for which he stipulated in the agreement, which is all that he can reasonably ask. Furthermore, owing to the peculiar nature and circumstances of the business, the reservation upon the part of the plaintiff to terminate upon short notice does not make the whole contract inequitable.

This Court holds that the renewal provisions of the contract involved herein are valid and enforceable.

Plaintiff claims that defendant Barnett is a professional basketball player of great skill and whose talents and abilities as a basketball player are of special, unique, unusual and extraordinary character.

There is some disagreement in the testimony as to the ability and standing of Barnett as a basketball player. Daniel Biasone, the General Manager of the Syracuse club for the past 16 years, testified that: "As of now I think Richard Barnett is one of the greatest basketball players playing the game." "he is an exceptionally good shooter." "He is above average * * * with other foul shooters in the National Basketball Association and that he ranked 19th in the whole league (approximately 100 players) scoring, playing as a guard." He further testified:

> 'Q What is your opinion as to his ability, this is, as a guard, now, at driving?
> 'A Terrific.
> 'Q What is your opinion as to his ability as play making as a guard?
> 'A Good. He has all the abilities a good basketball player should have. He has all the talent of a great basketball player. He is terrific all the way around.'

Mr. Biasone also testified on cross-examination that he would place Barnett in the group of some specifically-named nine or ten unusual and extra-ordinary players in the National Basketball Association.

Mr. Biasone also testified that Barnett was a box office attraction and was asked on cross examination: 'on what basis do you say he was a great box office attraction?' He answered:

A Because he, in my opinion, he is such a tremendous ball handler and he does things that have crowd appeal, he is noticeable. He appeals to the crowd because he does things extraordinary.

Coach McLendon of the Cleveland Pipers is not so generous in his appraisal. Barnett, in his opinion, is not in the class of the specifically named outstanding basketball players. McLendon concedes that both Barnett and Neuman, now playing for Syracuse in his first year as a professional, are both "pretty good."

The defendant Barnett was asked by his counsel:

'Q Do you represent to this Court that you have exceptional and unique skill and ability as a basketball player?
'A No.
'Q Do you represent to this Court that your services are of a special, unusual and extraordinary character?
'A No.
'Q You do represent to the Court that you are a professional basketball player; is that correct?
'A Yes.
'Q Do you think you are as good as Oscar Robertson?
'A No.'

\*\*\*\*

That the defendant Barnett was 19th among the top 25 scorers in the National Basketball Association in the 1960-61 season is confirmed in the statistics published on page 113 of the official Guide (plaintiff's Exhibit 4). On page 190 of the Guide is the record of Richard Barnett which indicates that he played in 78 games (out of 79) in the 60-61 season for a total of 1,970 minutes; that his F.G.M. percentage was .452; that his F.T.M. percentage was .712 and that he scored 1,320 points for an average of 16.9. The Guide also indicates that Barnett was not among the players in the East-West All Star

Game on January 17, 1961 (Guide 144), nor was he among the players named in the U. S. Basketball Writers' All-NBA Team for 1961 (Guide 184).

The defendant Barnett may not be in the same class with the top ten basketball players. The Syracuse manager is not a disinterested witness, and he may have given an immoderate appraisal of the playing abilities of Barnett. On the other hand, neither are McLendon nor Barnett disinterested witnesses. McLendon's eagerness to secure the services of Barnett at a high salary ($13,000) indicates a higher opinion of Barnett's playing abilities than he was willing to concede at the trial of this case. Barnett was understandably under embarrassment when asked to give opinion of his own abilities and to make comparisons with another named player.

The increase of salary from $8,500 to $11,500 agreed to by plaintiff, the Cleveland Basketball Club's willingness to pay $13,000, and the latter's eagerness to secure his services, all point to a high regard for his playing abilities. Whether Barnett ranks with the top basketball players or not, the evidence shows that he is an outstanding professional basketball player of unusual attainments and exceptional skill and ability, and that he is of peculiar and particular value to plaintiff.

His signed contract with Syracuse provides:

> 9. The Player represents and agrees that he has exceptional and unique skill and ability as a basketball player; that his services to be rendered hereunder are of a special, unusual and extraordinary character which gives them peculiar value which cannot be reasonably or adequately compensated for in damages at law, and that the Player's breach of this contract will cause the Club great and irreparable injury and damage. The player agrees that, in addition to other remedies, the Club shall be entitled to injunctive and other equitable relief to prevent a breach of this contract by the Player, including, among others, the right to enjoin the Player from playing basketball for any other person or organization during the term of this contract.

The Cleveland contract contains a similar provision…

\*\*\*\*

200

The aforesaid provisions are contained in uniform players' contracts and it would seem that mere engagement as a basketball player in the N.B.A., or A.B.L., carries with it recognition of his excellence and extraordinary abilities.

An important growth in the field of equity has been the use of injunctions against the breach of negative agreements, both express and implied. Pomeroy's Specific Performance of Contract, Third Ed. at page 75 reads:

> Another class of contracts stipulating for personal acts are now enforced in England by means of an injunction. Where one person agrees to render personal services to another, which require and presuppose a special knowledge, skill, and ability in the employe, so that, in case of a default, the same services could not easily be obtained from others, although the affirmative specific performance of the contract is beyond the power of the court, its performance will be negatively enforced by enjoining its breach. This doctrine applies especially to contracts made by actors, public singers, artists and others possessing a special skill and ability. It is plain that the principle on which it rests is the same with that which applies to agreements for the purchase of land or of chattels having a unique character and value. The damages for the breach of such contracts cannot be estimated with any certainty, and the employer cannot, by means of any damages, purchase the same services in the labor market.

Pomeroy continues:

> The more recent American cases are in accord with the English rule stated in the text, and where one person agrees to render personal services to another which require and presuppose a special knowledge, skill and ability in the employee, so that in case of default, the same services could not be easily obtained from others, equity will negatively enforce the contract by enjoining its breach.

The opinion of the Court in *Philadelphia Ball Club v. Lajoie, supra,* is summarized in 58 L.R.A., 227 in the head notes a follows:

****

2. Injunction will issue to prevent a baseball player from violating his contract to serve a certain organization for a stipulated time, during which he is not to play for any other club, where he is an expert player, has been with the organization sufficiently long to have become thoroughly familiar with the team work, and is a most attractive drawing card for the public because of his great reputation for ability in the position which he fills.

3. Lack of mutuality of remedy will not prevent an injunction against breach of a contract to render exclusive services as a ball player because the options of renewal and of terminating the contract on ten days' notice rest only with the employer, where such options expressly form part of the consideration for which the compensation is paid--at least, after the contract has been partly performed.

****

[4] Professional players in the major baseball, football, and basketball leagues have unusual talents and skills or they would not be so employed. Such players, the defendant Barnett included, are not easily replaced.

The right of the plaintiff is plain and the wrong done by the defendants is equally plain, and there is no reason why the Court should be sparing in the application of its remedies.

Damages at law would be speculative and uncertain and are practically impossible of ascertainment in terms of money. There is no plain, adequate and complete remedy at law and the injury to the plaintiff is irreparable.

Professional baseball, football, and basketball require regulations for the protection of the business, the public and the players, and so long as they are fair and reasonable there is no violation of the laws on restraint of trade. The evidence before this Court does not show any unfair or unreasonable act on the part of the plaintiff and the Court concludes that the claim of the defendant that the contract is in restraint of trade is without merit.

The Court finds in favor of the plaintiff on all issues joined and permanent injunctions as requested for the 1961-1962 basketball playing season are decreed. Thereafter the said injunctions shall be dissolved.

## Notes & Questions

1. Why can't the court simply force Barnett to play for the Syracuse Nationals? Would that really be so bad?

2. On what facts does the court rely to determine that Barnett had entered into a contract with Syracuse? Where is the offer? Where is the acceptance?

3. Explain the significance of whether a player is deemed to have exceptional skills. Isn't it true that all professional basketball players, by definition, could be considered to possess exceptional skills?

4. Explain why the court says that there is no adequate remedy "at law." Hint: look back at the introduction to this chapter where the distinction between "legal remedies" and "equitable remedies" is discussed.

### Vanderbilt University v. Gerry DiNardo
174 F. 3d 751 (1999)
United States Court of Appeals, Sixth Circuit

GIBSON, Circuit Judge.

Gerry DiNardo resigned as Vanderbilt's head football coach to become the head football coach for Louisiana State University. As a result, Vanderbilt University brought this breach of contract action. The district court entered summary judgment for Vanderbilt, awarding $281,886.43 pursuant to a damage provision in DiNardo's employment contract with Vanderbilt. DiNardo appeals, arguing that the district court erred in concluding: (1) that the contract provision was an enforceable liquidated damage provision and not an unlawful penalty under Tennessee law; [and,] (2) that Vanderbilt did not waive its right to liquidated damages.... We affirm the district court's ruling that the employment contract contained an enforceable liquidated damage provision and the award of liquidated damages under the original contract.***

On December 3, 1990, Vanderbilt and DiNardo executed an employment contract hiring DiNardo to be Vanderbilt's head football coach. Section one of the contract provided:

> The University hereby agrees to hire Mr. DiNardo for a period of five (5) years from the date hereof with Mr. DiNardo's assurance that he will serve the entire term of this Contract, a long-term commitment by Mr. DiNardo being important to the University's desire for a stable intercollegiate football program....

The contract also contained reciprocal liquidated damage provisions. Vanderbilt agreed to pay DiNardo his remaining salary should Vanderbilt replace him as football coach, and DiNardo agreed to reimburse Vanderbilt should he leave before his contract expired. Section eight of the contract stated:

> Mr. DiNardo recognizes that his promise to work for the University for the entire term of this 5-year Contract is of the essence of this Contract to the University. Mr. DiNardo also recognizes that the University is making a highly valuable investment in his continued employment by entering into this Contract and its investment would be lost were he to resign or otherwise terminate his employment as Head Football Coach with the University prior to the expiration of this Contract. Accordingly, Mr. DiNardo agrees that in the event he resigns or otherwise terminates his employment as Head Football Coach (as opposed to his resignation or termination from another position at the University to which he may have been reassigned), prior to the expiration of this Contract, and is employed or performing services for a person or institution other than the University, he will pay to the University as liquidated damages an amount equal to his Base Salary, less amounts that would otherwise be deducted or withheld from his Base Salary for income and social security tax purposes, multiplied by the number of years (or portion(s) thereof) remaining on the Contract.

During contract negotiations, section eight was modified at DiNardo's request so that damages would be calculated based on net, rather than gross, salary.

Vanderbilt initially set DiNardo's salary at $100,000 per year. DiNardo received salary increases in 1992, 1993, and 1994.

In November 1994, Louisiana State University contacted Vanderbilt in hopes of speaking with DiNardo about becoming the head football coach for L.S.U. Hoolahan [Vanderbilt's Athletic Director] gave DiNardo permission to speak to L.S.U. about the position. On December 12, 1994, DiNardo announced that he was accepting the L.S.U. position.

Vanderbilt sent a demand letter to DiNardo seeking payment of liquidated damages under section eight of the contract. Vanderbilt believed that DiNardo was liable for three years of his net salary: one year under the original contract and two years under the Addendum. DiNardo did not respond to Vanderbilt's demand for payment.

Vanderbilt brought this action against DiNardo for breach of contract. DiNardo removed the action to federal court, and both parties filed motions for summary judgment. The district court held that section eight was an enforceable liquidated damages provision, not an unlawful penalty, and that the damages provided under section eight were reasonable. *Vanderbilt University v. DiNardo,* 974 F.Supp. 638, 643 (M.D.Tenn.1997). The court held that Vanderbilt did not waive its contractual rights under section eight when it granted DiNardo permission to talk to L.S.U. and that the Addendum was enforceable and extended the contract for two years. *Id.* at 643-45. The court entered judgment against DiNardo for $281,886.43. *Id.* at 645. DiNardo appeals.

I.

DiNardo first claims that section eight of the contract is an unenforceable penalty under Tennessee law. DiNardo argues that the provision is not a liquidated damage provision but a "thinly disguised, overly broad non-compete provision," unenforceable under Tennessee law.

We review the district court's summary judgment de novo, using the same standard as used by the district court. *See Birgel v. Bd. of Comm'rs.,* 125 F.3d 948, 950 (6th Cir.1997), *cert. denied,* 522 U.S. 1109, 118 S.Ct. 1038, 140 L.Ed.2d 104 (1998). We view the evidence in the light most favorable to the non-moving party to determine whether there is a genuine issue as to any material fact. *See id.* Summary judgment is proper if the record shows that "there is no genuine issue as to any material fact and that the moving party is entitled to judgment as a matter of law." Fed.R.Civ.P. 56(c).

Contracting parties may agree to the payment of liquidated damages in the event of a breach. *See Beasley v. Horrell,* 864 S.W.2d 45, 48 (Tenn.Ct.App.1993). The term "liquidated damages" refers to an amount determined by the parties to be just compensation for damages should a breach occur. *See id.* Courts will not enforce such a provision, however, if the stipulated amount constitutes a penalty. *See id.* A penalty is designed to coerce performance by punishing default. *See id.* In Tennessee, a provision will be considered one for liquidated damages, rather than a penalty, if it is reasonable in relation to the anticipated damages for breach, measured prospectively at the time the contract was entered into, and not grossly disproportionate to the actual damages. *See Beasley,* 864 S.W.2d at 48; *Kimbrough & Co. v. Schmitt,* 939 S.W.2d 105, 108 (Tenn.Ct.App.1996). When these conditions are met, particularly the first, the parties probably intended the provision to be for liquidated damages. However, any doubt as to the character of the contract provision will be resolved in favor of finding it a penalty. *See Beasley,* 864 S.W.2d at 48.

The district court held that the use of a formula based on DiNardo's salary to calculate liquidated damages was reasonable "given the nature of the unquantifiable damages in the case." 974 F.Supp. at 642. The court held that parties to a contract may include consequential damages and even damages not usually awarded by law in a liquidated damage provision provided that they were contemplated by the parties. *Id.* at 643. The court explained:

> The potential damage to [Vanderbilt] extends far beyond the cost of merely hiring a new head football coach. It is this uncertain potentiality that the parties sought to address by providing for a sum certain to apply towards anticipated expenses and losses. It is impossible to estimate how the loss of a head football coach will affect alumni relations, public support, football ticket sales, contributions, etc.... As such, to require a precise formula for calculating damages resulting from the breach of contract by a college head football coach would be tantamount to barring the parties from stipulating to liquidated damages evidence in advance. *Id.* at 642.

DiNardo contends that there is no evidence that the parties contemplated that the potential damage from DiNardo's resignation would go beyond the cost of hiring a replacement coach. He argues that his salary has no relationship to Vanderbilt's damages and that the liquidated damage amount is unreasonable and shows that the parties did not intend the provision to be for liquidated damages.

DiNardo's theory of the parties' intent, however, does not square with the record. The contract language establishes that Vanderbilt wanted the five-year contract because "a long-term commitment" by DiNardo was "important to the University's desire for a stable intercollegiate football program," and that this commitment was of "essence" to the contract. Vanderbilt offered the two-year contract extension to DiNardo well over a year before his original contract expired. Both parties understood that the extension was to provide stability to the program, which helped in recruiting players and retaining assistant coaches. Thus, undisputed evidence, and reasonable inferences therefrom, establish that both parties understood and agreed that DiNardo's resignation would result in Vanderbilt suffering damage beyond the cost of hiring a replacement coach.

\*\*\*\*

The stipulated damage amount is reasonable in relation to the amount of damages that could be expected to result from the breach. As we stated, the parties understood that Vanderbilt would suffer damage should DiNardo prematurely terminate his contract, and that these actual damages would be difficult to measure. *See Kimbrough & Co.,* 939 S.W.2d at 108.

\*\*\*\*

Vanderbilt hired DiNardo for a unique and specialized position, and the parties understood that the amount of damages could not be easily ascertained should a breach occur. Contrary to DiNardo's suggestion, Vanderbilt did not need to undertake an analysis to determine actual damages, and using the number of years left on the contract multiplied by the salary per year was a reasonable way to calculate damages considering the difficulty of ascertaining damages with certainty. *See Kimbrough & Co.,* 939 S.W.2d at 108. The fact that liquidated damages declined each year DiNardo remained under contract, is directly tied to the parties' express understanding of the importance of a long-term commitment from DiNardo. Furthermore, the liquidated damages provision was reciprocal and the result of negotiations between two parties, each of whom was represented by counsel.

We also reject DiNardo's argument that a question of fact remains as to whether the parties intended section eight to be a "reasonable estimate" of damages. The liquidated damages are in line with Vanderbilt's estimate of its actual damages. *See Kimbrough & Co.,* 939 S.W.2d at 108-09. Vanderbilt presented evidence that it incurred expenses associated with recruiting a new head coach of $27,000.00; moving expenses for the new coaching staff of $86,840; and a compensation difference between the coaching staffs of $184,311. The stipulated damages clause is reasonable under the circumstances, and we affirm the district court's conclusion that the liquidated damages clause is enforceable under Tennessee law.

## II.

DiNardo next argues that Vanderbilt waived its right to liquidated damages when it granted DiNardo permission to discuss the coaching position with L.S.U. Under Tennessee law, a party may not recover liquidated damages when it is responsible for or has contributed to the delay or nonperformance alleged as the breach. *See V.L. Nicholson Co. v. Transcon Inv. and Fin. Ltd., Inc.,* 595 S.W.2d 474, 484 (Tenn.1980).

Vanderbilt did not waive its rights under section eight of the contract by giving DiNardo permission to pursue the L.S.U. position. *See Chattem, Inc. v. Provident Life & Accident Ins. Co.,* 676 S.W.2d 953, 955 (Tenn.1984) (waiver is the intentional, voluntary relinquishment of a known right). First, Hoolahan's permission was quite circumscribed. Hoolahan gave DiNardo permission to talk to L.S.U. about their coaching position; he did not authorize DiNardo to terminate his contract with Vanderbilt. Second, the employment contract required DiNardo to ask Vanderbilt's athletic director for permission to speak with another school about a coaching position,[1] and Hoolahan testified that granting a coach permission to talk to another school about a position was a "professional courtesy." Thus, the parties certainly contemplated that DiNardo could explore other coaching positions, and indeed even leave Vanderbilt, subject to the terms of the liquidated damage provision. *See Park Place Ctr. Enterprises, Inc. v. Park Place Mall Assoc.,* 836 S.W.2d 113, 116 (Tenn.Ct.App.1992) ("All provisions of a contract should be construed as in harmony with each other, if such construction can

---

[1] Section nine provided:

> The parties agree that should another coaching opportunity be presented to Mr. DiNardo or should Mr. DiNardo be interested in another coaching position during the term of this Contract, he must notify the University's Director of Athletics of such opportunity or interest and written permission must be given to Mr. DiNardo by the Director of Athletics before any discussions can be held by Mr. DiNardo with the anticipated coaching-position principal.

be reasonably made ...".) Allowing DiNardo to talk to another school did not relinquish Vanderbilt's right to liquidated damages.

Accordingly, we affirm the district court's judgment that the contract contained an enforceable liquidated damage provision, and we affirm the portion of the judgment reflecting damages calculated under the original five-year contract.

## Notes & Questions

1. When the court says that "The liquidated damages are in line with Vanderbilt's estimate of its actual damages," is the court referring to an estimate at the time of the making of the contract? Or is the court referring to an estimate of the actual damages that Vanderbilt incurred after DiNardo's breach? Does it matter? If so, why? If not, why not?

2. The court articulates the state's rule regarding liquidated damages as follows: "In Tennessee, a provision will be considered one for liquidated damages, rather than a penalty, if it is reasonable in relation to the anticipated damages for breach, measured prospectively at the time the contract was entered into, and not grossly disproportionate to the actual damages." How does this rule compare and contrast with the Uniform Commercial Code (UCC) rule (which governs the sale of goods) in UCC 2-718(1)? UCC 2-718 (1) reads:

> Damages for breach by either party may be liquidated in the agreement but only at an amount which is reasonable in the light of the anticipated or actual harm caused by caused by the breach, the difficulties of proof of loss, and the inconvenience or nonfeasibility of otherwise obtaining an adequate remedy. A term fixing unreasonably large liquidated damages is void as a penalty.

## B. Sample Contracts

The three sample contracts in the following section allow you an opportunity to scrutinize actual contracts used in the industry. As such, they offer tremendous opportunities to learn a great deal that is practical. The Babe Ruth contract from 1930 gives us a chance to peek into the past. Pay particular attention to the language as well as the types of provisions in the Ruth contract that have survived into the modern era, still present either in general or verbatim in the contemporary MLB or NBA contracts.

Also remember that the MLB and NBA contracts are products of collective bargaining and, by their very nature, incorporate their respective league constitutions and bylaws. Hence, these documents not only introduce you to the basic *content* of a professional athlete's employment agreement, but they also indirectly teach you a great deal about the *structure and governance* of professional sports teams and leagues (*e.g.,* the powers of a commissioner and the relationships among member teams). You should read these documents carefully and critically. Use them to learn what you can about professional sports contracts, the business and corporate aspects of teams and leagues, and elements of labor law associated with collective bargaining. Some of the relationships between antitrust and labor law will be addressed in the next chapter.

(Form 1930)

# AMERICAN LEAGUE
# PLAYER'S CONTRACT

The

American League Base Ball Club
of New York
55 West 42nd Street

Of

WITH

George H. Ruth

(Player)

Of      New York, N. Y.

Approved:

*E S Barnard*

*President, American League of Professional Baseball Clubs*

**APR 1 - 1930**

, 193

163

211

# REGULATIONS

1. The Club's playing season for each year covered by this contract and all renewals hereof shall be as fixed by the American League of Professional Baseball Clubs, or, if this contract shall be assigned to a Club in another league, then by the league of which such assignee is a member.

2. The Player must keep himself in first-class physical condition and must at all times conform his personal conduct to standards of good citizenship and good sportsmanship.

3. The Player, when requested by the Club, must submit to medical examination at the expense of the Club and, if necessary, to treatment by a regular physician in good standing at the Player's expense. Disability directly resulting from injury sustained in playing baseball for the Club while rendering service under this contract shall not impair the right of the Player to receive his full salary for the season in which the injury was sustained, but only upon the express, prerequisite condition that written notice of such injury, including the time, place, cause and nature of the injury, is served upon and received by the Club within twenty days of the sustaining of said injury. Any other disability may be ground for suspending or terminating this contract at the discretion of the Club.

4. The Club will furnish the Player with two complete uniforms, exclusive of shoes, the Player making a deposit of $30.00 therefor, which deposit will be returned to him at the end of the season or upon the termination of this contract, upon the surrender of the uniforms by him to the Club. And the Club will provide and furnish the Player while "abroad" or traveling with the Club in other cities with proper board, lodging, and pay all proper and necessary traveling expenses, including Pullman accommodations and meals en route.

5. The Player, while under contract or reservation, shall not engage, without the consent of his Club, in any game or exhibition of baseball (except for the Club or for an assignee of this contract), football, basketball, or other athletic sport.

6. For violation by the Player of any regulation the Club may impose a reasonable fine and deduct the amount thereof from the Player's salary or may suspend the Player without salary for a period not exceeding thirty days, or both, at the discretion of the Club. Written notice of the fine or suspension or both and of the reasons therefor shall in every case be given to the Player.

7. In order to enable the Player to fit himself for his duties under this contract, the Club may require the Player to report for practice at such places as the Club may designate and to participate in such exhibition contests as may be arranged by the Club for a period of ..................*Forty-five*.................. days prior to the playing season without any other compensation than that herein elsewhere provided, the Club, however, to pay the traveling expenses, including Pullman accommodations, and meals en route, of the Player from his home city to the training place of the Club, whether he be ordered to go there direct or by way of the home city of the Club. In the event of the failure of the Player to report for practice or to participate in the exhibition games, as provided for, he shall be required to get in playing condition to the satisfaction of the Club's team manager, and at the Player's own expense, before his salary shall commence.

# IMPORTANT NOTICE

The attention of both Club and Player is specifically directed to the following excerpt from Article II, Section 1, of the Major League Rules:

"No Club shall make a contract different from the uniform contract or a contract containing a non-reserve clause, except with the written approval of the Advisory Council. All contracts shall be in duplicate and the Player shall retain a counterpart original. The making of any agreement between a Club and Player not embodied in the contract shall subject both parties to discipline by the Commissioner."

# American League of Professional Baseball Clubs
## UNIFORM PLAYER'S CONTRACT

**Parties**     The ....*American League Base Ball Club of New York*............................

herein called the Club, and.....GEORGE. HERMAN. RUTH................................

of .....New York,. N.. Y. ..................................... herein called the Player.

**Recital**     The club is a member of the American League of Professional Baseball Clubs. As such, and jointly with the other members of the League, it is a party to agreements and rules with the National League of Professional Baseball Clubs and its constituent clubs, and with the National Association of Professional Baseball Leagues. The purpose of these agreements and rules is to insure to the public wholesome and high-class professional baseball by defining the relations between Club and Player, between Player and club, between league and league, and by vesting in a designated Commissioner broad powers of control and discipline, and of decision in case of disputes.

**Agreement**     In view of the facts above recited the parties agree as follows:

**Employment**    1. The Club hereby employs the Player to render skilled service as a baseball player in connection

with all games of the Club during the years 1930. and. 1931...........................
including the Club's training season, the Club's exhibition games, the Club's playing season, and the World Series (or any other official series in which the Club may participate and in any receipts of which the Club may be entitled to share); and the player covenants that he will perform with diligence and fidelity the service stated and such duties as may be required of him in such employment.

**Salary**     2. For the service aforesaid the Club will pay the Player an aggregate salary of $80,000.00 ....for. each. of. said. years......., as follows:

*In semi-monthly installments after the commencement of the playing season covered by this contract, unless the Player is "abroad" with the Club for the purpose of playing games, in which event the amount then due shall be paid on the first week-day after the return "home" of the Club, the terms "home" and "abroad" meaning, respectively, at and away from the city in which the Club has its baseball field.*

If a monthly salary is stipulated above, it shall begin with the commencement of the Club's playing season (or such subsequent date as the Player's services may commence) and end with the termination of the Club's scheduled playing season, and shall be payable in semi-monthly installments as above provided.

If the Player is in the service of the Club for part of the playing season only, he shall receive such proportion of the salary above mentioned, as the number of days of his actual employment bears to the number of days in the Club's playing season.

**Loyalty**     3. (a) The Player will faithfully serve the Club or any other Club to which, in conformity with the agreements above recited, this contract may be assigned, and pledges himself to the American public to conform to high standards of personal conduct, of fair play and good sportsmanship.

(b) The Player represents that he does not, directly or indirectly, own stock or have any financial interest in the ownership or earnings of any Major League club, except as hereinafter expressly set forth, and covenants that he will not hereafter, while connected with any Major League club, acquire or hold any such stock or interest except in accordance with Section 23 (c), Article II, Major League Rules.

**Service**     4. The Player will not play during the period of this contract otherwise than for the Club or such other Clubs as may become assignees of this contract in conformity with said agreements; nor will he play any exhibition games after October 31st any year until the training season the following year, nor in any post-season exhibition game in which more than two other players of the Club participate.

**Assignment**    5. (a) In case of assignment of this contract to another Club, the Player shall promptly report to the assignee club within 72 hours from the date he receives written notice from the Club of such assignment, if not more than 1600 miles by most-direct available railroad route, plus an additional 24 hours for each additional 800 miles; accrued salary shall be payable when he so reports; and each successive assignee shall become liable to the Player for his salary during his term of service with such assignee, and the Club shall not be liable therefor. If the Player fails to report as above specified, he shall not be entitled to salary after the date he receives written notice of assignment. If the assignee is a member either of the National or American League, the salary shall be as above (paragraph 2) specified. If the assignee is any other Club the Player's salary shall be the same as that usually paid by said Club to other players of like ability.

**Termination**    (b) This contract may be terminated at any time by the Club or by any assignee upon ten days' written notice to the Player.

213

Regulations     6. The Player accepts as part of this contract the Regulations printed on the third page hereof, and also such reasonable modifications of them and such other reasonable regulations as the Club may announce from time to time.

Agreements and Rules     7. (a) The Major and Major-Minor League Agreements and Rules, and all amendments thereto hereafter adopted, are hereby made a part of this contract, and the Club and Player agree to accept, abide by and comply with the same and all decisions of the Commissioner pursuant thereto.

Publication     (b) It is further expressly agreed that, in consideration of the rights and interest of the public, the Club, the League President, and/or the Commissioner may make public the record of any inquiry, investigation or hearing held or conducted, including in such record all evidence or information given, received or obtained in connection therewith, and including further the findings and decisions therein and the reasons therefor.

Renewal     8. (a) On or before February 15th (or if Sunday, then the succeeding business day) of the year next following the last playing season covered by this contract, by written notice to the Player at his address following his signature hereto (or if none be given, then at his last address of record with the Club), the Club or any assignee hereof may renew this contract for the term of that year except that the salary shall be such as the parties may then agree upon, or in default of agreement the Player will accept such salary rate as the Club may fix, or else will not play baseball otherwise than for the Club or for an assignee hereof.

    (b) The Club's right of reservation of the Player, and of renewal of this contract as aforesaid, and the promise of the Player not to play otherwise than with the Club or an assignee hereof, have been taken into consideration in determining the salary specified herein and the undertaking by the Club to pay said salary is the consideration for both said reservation, renewal option and promise, and the Player's service.

Disputes     9. In case of dispute between the Player and the Club or any Major League Club assignee hereof, the same shall be referred to the Commissioner as an umpire, and his decision shall be accepted by all parties as final; and the Club and the Player agree that any such dispute, or any claim or complaint by either party against the other, shall be presented to the Commissioner within one year from the date it arose.

Supplemental Agreements     10. The Club and Player covenant that this contract fully sets forth all understandings and agreements between them, and agree that no other understandings or agreements, whether heretofore or hereafter made, shall be valid, recognizable, or of any effect whatsoever, unless expressly set forth in a new or supplemental contract executed by the Player and the Club (acting by its president, or such other officer as shall have been thereunto duly authorized by the president or Board of Directors, in writing filed of record with the League President and Commissioner—and that no other Club officer or employee shall have any authority to represent or act for the Club in that respect), and complying with all agreements and rules to which this contract is subject.

Special Covenants
*See "Important Notice" above.*

This contract shall not be valid or effective unless and until approved by the League President or Advisory Council, as the case may be.

Signed in duplicate this ..........10th.......... day of .......march....... A. D. 193.0.

[SEAL]

                                      American League Base Ball Club of New York
                                                           (Club)

Witness:                       By *Jacob Ruppert*
                                                           (President)

........*B. Crowdus Jr.*........       ........*George Herman Ruth*........
                                                           (Player)

........................................     ........................................
                                                      (Home address of Player)

168

214

**Notes & Questions**

1. In the "Regulations," What do you think was meant by "first-class physical condition" and "good citizenship"? These same general tenets are addressed again in paragraph 3(a) of the contract, itself, where the player "pledges himself to the American public to conform to high standards of personal conduct, of fair play and good sportsmanship." Don't these phrases strike you as somewhat trite and archaic today? How did the Babe perform on those matters?

2. Why do you think that the club was willing to pay a player his full salary for the entire season if he was injured while playing?

3. What do you think is the purpose of paragraph 5 in the "Regulations"? Does this mean that the player cannot play basketball in the driveway at his house with his teenage son or daughter? What do you think is included within the scope of "other athletic sport"? Where should the line be drawn when an athlete is cross-training to get in shape for baseball?

On February 27, 2004, the New York Yankees cut third baseman Aaron Boone from the roster after he tore a ligament in his knee during a pickup basketball game. Although seemingly innocent, Boone's participation in the basketball game was in violation of his contract with the Yankees which expressly prohibited participation in such activities. The Yankees were faced with three options: take no action and pay Boone his $5.75 million salary; void the contract thereby releasing him; or amend the contract and keep Boone on the roster. The Yankees ended up voiding the contract and Boone signed with the Cleveland Indians. "There is precedent for voiding a contract because of a player's off-field activity. In 1994, Atlanta saved about $4.6 million by releasing outfielder Ron Gant in spring training after he broke his leg in a dirt-bike accident." The Yankees, for their part, wound up signing superstar Alex Rodriguez to replace Boone. *See* Kepner, Tyler, *BASEBALL; Boone's Injury Could Cost Him His Contract*, www.select.nytimes.com, January 27, 2004.

4. Why do you think that the parties felt it necessary to include a statement in the "Recital" regarding the Commissioner's "broad powers of control and discipline, and of decision in case of disputes"?

5. Explain what you think the purposes were for the requirements in paragraph 5(a) of the contract? In sports what do we typically call "assignment" of a club's rights to another team?

6. Paragraph 8 of the contract came to be called the "reserve clause." Explain how the reserve clause operated in practical terms.

**Photo printed with permission from Topps**

## MAJOR LEAGUE

## UNIFORM PLAYER'S CONTRACT

**Parties**

Between _____, herein called the
Club, and _____of ,
_____herein called the
Player.

**Recital**

The Club is, along with other Major League Clubs, signatory to the Major League Constitution and has subscribed to the Major League Rules.

**Agreement**

In consideration of the facts above recited and of the promises of each to the other, the parties agree as follows:

**Employment**

1. The Club hereby employs the Player to render, and the Player agrees to render, skilled services as a baseball player during the year(s)_____ including the Club's training season, the Club's exhibition games, the Club's playing season, the Division Series, the League Championship Series and the World Series (or any other official series in which the Club may participate and in any receipts of which the Player may be entitled to share).

**Payment**

2. For performance of the Player's services and promises hereunder the Club will pay the Player the sum of $ _____in semi-monthly installments after the commencement of the championship season(s) covered by this contract except as the schedule of payments may be modified by a special covenant. Payment shall be made on the day the amount becomes due, regardless of whether the Club is "home" or "abroad." If a monthly rate of payment is stipulated above, it shall begin with the commencement of the championship season (or such subsequent date as the Player's services may

commence) and end with the termination of the championship season and shall be payable in semi-monthly installments as above provided.

Nothing herein shall interfere with the right of the Club and the Player by special covenant herein to mutually agree upon a method of payment whereby part of the Player's salary for the above year can be deferred to subsequent years.

If the Player is in the service of the Club for part of the championship season only, he shall receive such proportion of the sum above mentioned, as the number of days of his actual employment in the championship season bears to the number of days in the championship season.

Notwithstanding the rate of payment stipulated above, the minimum rate of payment to the Player for each day of service on a Major League Club shall be at the applicable rate set forth in Article VI(B)(1) of the Basic Agreement between the Thirty Major League Clubs and the Major League Baseball Players Association, effective September 30, 2002 ("Basic Agreement"). The minimum rate of payment for Minor League service for all Players (a) signing a second Major League contract (not covering the same season as any such Player's initial Major League contract) or a subsequent Major League contract, or (b) having at least one day of Major League service, shall be at the applicable rate set forth in Article VI(B)(2) of the Basic Agreement.

Payment to the Player at the rate stipulated above shall be continued throughout any period in which a Player is required to attend a regularly scheduled military encampment of the Reserve of the Armed Forces or of the National Guard during the championship season.

## Loyalty

3.(a) The Player agrees to perform his services hereunder diligently and faithfully, to keep himself in first-class physical condition and to obey the Club's training rules, and pledges himself to the American public and to the Club to conform to high standards of personal conduct, fair play and good sportsmanship.

## Baseball Promotion

3.(b) In addition to his services in connection with the actual playing of baseball, the Player agrees to cooperate with the Club and participate in any and all reasonable promotional activities of the Club and Major League Baseball, which, in the opinion of the Club, will promote the welfare of the Club or professional baseball, and to observe and comply with all reasonable requirements of the Club respecting conduct and service of its team and its players, at all times whether on or off the field.

**Pictures and Public Appearances**

3.(c) The Player agrees that his picture may be taken for still photographs, motion pictures or television at such times as the Club may designate and agrees that all rights in such pictures shall belong to the Club and may be used by the Club for publicity purposes in any manner it desires. The Player further agrees that during the playing season he will not make public appearances, participate in radio or television programs or permit his picture to be taken or write or sponsor newspaper or magazine articles or sponsor commercial products without the written consent of the Club, which shall not be withheld except in the reasonable interests of the Club or professional baseball.

## PLAYER REPRESENTATIONS

**Ability**

4.(a) The Player represents and agrees that he has exceptional and unique skill and ability as a baseball player; that his services to be rendered hereunder are of a special, unusual and extraordinary character which gives them peculiar value which cannot be reasonably or adequately compensated for in damages at law, and that the Player's breach of this contract will cause the Club great and irreparable injury and damage. The Player agrees that, in addition to other remedies, the Club shall be entitled to injunctive and other equitable relief to prevent a breach of this contract by the Player, including, among others, the right to enjoin the Player from playing baseball for any other person or organization during the term of his contract.

**Condition**

4.(b) The Player represents that he has no physical or mental defects known to him and unknown to the appropriate representative of the Club which would prevent or impair performance of his services.

**Interest in Club**

4.(c) The Player represents that he does not, directly or indirectly, own stock or have any financial interest in the ownership or earnings of any Major League Club, except as hereinafter expressly set forth, and covenants that he will not hereafter, while connected with any Major League Club, acquire or hold any such stock or interest except in accordance with Major League Rule 20(e).

## Service

5.(a) The Player agrees that, while under contract, and prior to expiration of the Club's right to renew this contract, he will not play baseball otherwise than for the Club, except that the Player may participate in post-season games under the conditions prescribed in the Major League Rules. Major League Rule 18(b) is set forth herein.

## Other Sports

5.(b) The Player and the Club recognize and agree that the Player's participation in certain other sports may impair or destroy his ability and skill as a baseball player. Accordingly, the Player agrees that he will not engage in professional boxing or wrestling; and that, except with the written consent of the Club, he will not engage in skiing, auto racing, motorcycle racing, sky diving, or in any game or exhibition of football, soccer, professional league basketball, ice hockey or other sport involving a substantial risk of personal injury.

## Assignment

6.(a) The Player agrees that his contract may be assigned by the Club (and reassigned by any assignee Club) to any other Club in accordance with the Major League Rules. The Club and the Player may, without obtaining special approval, agree by special covenant to limit or eliminate the right of the Club to assign this contract.

## Medical Information

6.(b) The Player agrees:

(1) that the Club's physician and any other physician consulted by the Player pursuant to Regulation 2 of this contract or Article XIII(D) of the Basic Agreement may furnish to the Club all relevant medical information relating to the Player; and

(2) that, should the Club contemplate an assignment of this contract to another Club or Clubs, the Club's physician may furnish to the physicians and officials of such other Club or Clubs all relevant medical information relating to the Player.

## No Salary Reduction

6.(c) The amount stated in paragraph 2 and in special covenants hereof which is payable to the Player for the period stated in paragraph 1 hereof shall not be diminished by any such assignment, except for failure to report as provided in the next subparagraph (d).

## Reporting

6.(d) The Player shall report to the assignee Club promptly (as provided in the Regulations) upon receipt of written notice from the Club of the assignment of this contract. If the Player fails to so report, he shall not be entitled to any payment for the period from the date he receives written notice of assignment until he reports to the assignee Club.

## Obligations of Assignor and Assignee Clubs

6.(e) Upon and after such assignment, all rights and obligations of the assignor Club hereunder shall become the rights and obligations of the assignee Club; provided, however, that

(1) The assignee Club shall be liable to the Player for payments accruing only from the date of assignment and shall not be liable (but the assignor Club shall remain liable) for payments accrued prior to that date.

(2) If at any time the assignee is a Major League Club, it shall be liable to pay the Player at the full rate stipulated in paragraph 2 hereof for the remainder of the period stated in paragraph 1 hereof and all prior assignors and assignees shall be relieved of liability for any payment for such period.

(3) Unless the assignor and assignee Clubs agree otherwise, if the assignee Club is a Minor League Baseball Club, the assignee Club shall be liable only to pay the Player at the rate usually paid by said assignee Club to other Players of similar skill and ability in its classification and the assignor Club shall be liable to pay the difference for the remainder of the period stated in paragraph 1 hereof between an amount computed at the rate stipulated in paragraph 2 hereof and the amount so payable by the assignee Club.

## Moving Allowances

6.(f) The Player shall be entitled to moving allowances under the circumstances and in the amounts set forth in Articles VII(F) and VIII of the Basic Agreement.

**"Club"**

6.(g) All references in other paragraphs of this contract to "the Club" shall be deemed to mean and include any assignee of this contract.

## TERMINATION

### By Player

7.(a) The Player may terminate this contract, upon written notice to the Club, if the Club shall default in the payments to the Player provided for in paragraph 2 hereof or shall fail to perform any other obligation agreed to be performed by the Club hereunder and if the Club shall fail to remedy such default within ten (10) days after the receipt by the Club of written notice of such default. The Player may also terminate this contract as provided in subparagraph (d)(4) of this paragraph 7. (See Article XV(I) of the Basic Agreement.)

### By Club

7.(b) The Club may terminate this contract upon written notice to the Player (but only after requesting and obtaining waivers of this contract from all other Major League Clubs) if the Player shall at any time:

(1) fail, refuse or neglect to conform his personal conduct to the standards of good citizenship and good sportsmanship or to keep himself in first-class physical condition or to obey the Club's training rules; or

(2) fail, in the opinion of the Club's management, to exhibit sufficient skill or competitive ability to qualify or continue as a member of the Club's team; or

(3) fail, refuse or neglect to render his services hereunder or in any other manner materially breach this contract.

7.(c) If this contract is terminated by the Club, the Player shall be entitled to termination pay under the circumstances and in the amounts set forth in Article IX of the Basic Agreement. In addition, the Player shall be entitled to receive an amount equal to the reasonable traveling expenses of the Player, including first-class jet air fare and meals en route, to his home city.

### Procedure

7.(d) If the Club proposes to terminate this contract in accordance with subparagraph (b) of this paragraph 7, the procedure shall be as follows:

222

(1) The Club shall request waivers from all other Major League Clubs. Such waivers shall be good for two (2) business days only. Such waiver request must state that it is for the purpose of terminating this contract and it may not be withdrawn.

(2) Upon receipt of waiver request, any other Major League Club may claim assignment of this contract at a waiver price of $1.00, the priority of claims to be determined in accordance with the Major League Rules.

(3) If this contract is so claimed, the Club shall, promptly and before any assignment, notify the Player that it had requested waivers for the purpose of terminating this contract and that the contract had been claimed.

(4) Within five (5) days after receipt of notice of such claim, the Player shall be entitled, by written notice to the Club, to terminate this contract on the date of his notice of termination. If the Player fails to so notify the Club, this contract shall be assigned to the claiming Club.

(5) If the contract is not claimed, the Club shall promptly deliver written notice of termination to the Player at the expiration of the waiver period.

7.(e) Upon any termination of this contract by the Player, all obligations of both Parties hereunder shall cease on the date of termination, except the obligation of the Club to pay the Player's compensation to said date.

**Regulations**

8. The Player accepts as part of this contract the Regulations set forth herein.

**Rules**

9.(a) The Club and the Player agree to accept, abide by and comply with all provisions of the Major League Constitution, and the Major League Rules, or other rules or regulations in effect on the date of this Uniform Player's Contract, which are not inconsistent with the provisions of this contract or the provisions of any agreement between the Major League Clubs and the Major League Baseball Players Association, provided that the Club, together with the other Major League Clubs and Minor League Baseball, reserves the right to modify, supplement or repeal any provision of said Constitution, Major League Rules or other rules and regulations in a manner not inconsistent with this contract or the provisions of any then existing agreement between the Major League Clubs and the Major League Baseball Players Association.

UNIVERSITY OF WINCHESTER LIBRARY

## Disputes

9.(b) All disputes between the Player and the Club which are covered by the Grievance Procedure as set forth in the Basic Agreement shall be resolved in accordance with such Grievance Procedure.

## Publication

9.(c) The Club, the Vice President, On-Field Operations and the Commissioner, or any of them, may make public the findings, decision and record of any inquiry, investigation or hearing held or conducted, including in such record all evidence or information given, received, or obtained in connection therewith.

## Renewal

10.(a) Unless the Player has exercised his right to become a free agent as set forth in the Basic Agreement, the Club may retain reservation rights over the Player by instructing the Office of the Commissioner to tender to the Player a contract for the term of the next year by including the Player on the Central Tender Letter that the Office of the Commissioner submits to the Players Association on or before December 20 (or if a Sunday, then on or before December 18) in the year of the last playing season covered by this contract. (See Article XX(A) of and Attachment 12 to the Basic Agreement.) If prior to the March 1 next succeeding said December 20, the Player and the Club have not agreed upon the terms of such contract, then on or before ten (10) days after said March 1, the Club shall have the right by written notice to the Player at his address following his signature hereto, or if none be given, then at his last address of record with the Club, to renew this contract for the period of one year on the same terms, except that the amount payable to the Player shall be such as the Club shall fix in said notice; provided, however, that said amount, if fixed by a Major League Club, shall be in an amount payable at a rate not less than as specified in Article VI, Section D, of the Basic Agreement. Subject to the Player's rights as set forth in the Basic Agreement, the Club may renew this contract from year to year.

10.(b) The Club's right to renew this contract, as provided in subparagraph (a) of this paragraph 10, and the promise of the Player not to play otherwise than with the Club have been taken into consideration in determining the amount payable under paragraph 2 hereof.

## Governmental Regulation-National Emergency

11. This contract is subject to federal or state legislation, regulations, executive or other official orders or other governmental action, now or hereafter in effect respecting military, naval, air or other governmental service, which may directly or indirectly affect the Player, Club or the League and subject also to the right of the Commissioner to suspend the operation of this contract during any national emergency during which Major League Baseball is not played.

## Commissioner

12. The term "Commissioner" wherever used in this contract shall be deemed to mean the Commissioner designated under the Major League Constitution, or in the case of a vacancy in the office of Commissioner, the Executive Council or such other body or person or persons as shall be designated in the Major League Constitution to exercise the powers and duties of the Commissioner during such vacancy.

## Supplemental Agreements

The Club and the Player covenant that this contract, the Basic Agreement and the Agreement Re Major League Baseball Players Benefit Plan effective April 1, 2003 and applicable supplements thereto fully set forth all understandings and agreements between them, and agree that no other understandings or agreements, whether heretofore or hereafter made, shall be valid, recognizable, or of any effect whatsoever, unless expressly set forth in a new or supplemental contract executed by the Player and the Club (acting by its President or such other officer as shall have been thereunto duly authorized by the President or Board of Directors as evidenced by a certificate filed of record with the Commissioner) and complying with the Major League Rules.

Special Covenant

_____

_____

_____

_____

_____

**Approval**

This contract or any supplement hereto shall not be valid or effective unless and until approved by the Commissioner.

Signed in duplicate this _____ day of _____ ,
A.D._____

_____
(Player)
         (Club)

By_____
(Home address of Player)            (Authorized Signature)

Social Security No._____

Approved , _____, _____
_____
Commissioner

**REGULATIONS**

1. The Club's playing season for each year covered by this contract and all renewals hereof shall be as fixed by the Office of the Commissioner.

2. The Player, when requested by the Club, must submit to a complete physical examination at the expense of the Club, and if necessary to treatment by a regular physician or dentist in good standing. Upon refusal of the Player to submit to a complete medical or dental examination, the Club may consider such refusal a violation of this regulation and may take such action as it deems advisable under Regulation 5 of this contract. Disability directly resulting from injury sustained in the course and within the scope of his employment under this contract shall not impair the right of the Player to receive his full salary for the period of such disability or for the season in which the injury was sustained (whichever period is shorter), together with the reasonable medical and hospital expenses incurred by reason of the injury and during the term of this contract or for a period of up to two years from the date of initial treatment for such injury, whichever period is longer, but only upon the express prerequisite conditions that (a) written notice of such injury, including the time, place, cause and nature of the injury, is served upon and received by the Club within twenty days of the sustaining of said

226

injury and (b) the Club shall have the right to designate the doctors and hospitals furnishing such medical and hospital services.

Failure to give such notice shall not impair the rights of the Player, as herein set forth, if the Club has actual knowledge of such injury. All workmen's compensation payments received by the Player as compensation for loss of income for a specific period during which the Club is paying him in full, shall be paid over by the Player to the Club. Any other disability may be ground for suspending or terminating this contract.

3. The Club will furnish the Player with two complete uniforms, exclusive of shoes, unless the Club requires the Player to wear nonstandard shoes in which case the Club will furnish the shoes. The uniforms will be surrendered by the Player to the Club at the end of the season or upon termination of this contract.

4. The Player shall be entitled to expense allowances under the circumstances and in the amounts set forth in Article VII of the Basic Agreement.

5. For violation by the Player of any regulation or other provision of this contract, the Club may impose a reasonable fine and deduct the amount thereof from the Player's salary or may suspend the Player without salary for a period not exceeding thirty days or both. Written notice of the fine or suspension or both and the reason therefor shall in every case be given to the Player and the Players Association. (See Article XII of the Basic Agreement.)

6. In order to enable the Player to fit himself for his duties under this contract, the Club may require the Player to report for practice at such places as the Club may designate and to participate in such exhibition contests as may be arranged by the Club, without any other compensation than that herein elsewhere provided, for a period beginning not earlier than thirty-three (33) days prior to the start of the championship season, provided, however, that the Club may invite players to report at an earlier date on a voluntary basis in accordance with Article XIV of the Basic Agreement. The Club will pay the necessary traveling expenses, including the first-class jet air fare and meals en route of the

Player from his home city to the training place of the Club, whether he be ordered to go there directly or by way of the home city of the Club. In the event of the failure of the Player to report for practice or to participate in the exhibition games, as required and provided for, he shall be required to get into playing condition to the satisfaction of the Club's team manager, and at the Player's own expense, before his salary shall commence.

7. In case of assignment of this contract, the Player shall report promptly to the assignee Club within 72 hours from the date he receives written notice from the Club of such assignment, if the Player is then not more than 1,600 miles by most direct available railroad route from the assignee Club, plus an additional 24 hours for each additional 800 miles.

Post-Season Exhibition Games. Major League Rule 18(b) provides:

(b) EXHIBITION GAMES. No player shall participate in any exhibition game during the period between the close of the Major League championship season and the following training season, except that, with the consent of the player's Club and permission of the Commissioner, a player may participate in exhibition games for a period of not less than 30 days, such period to be designated annually by the Commissioner. Players who participate in barnstorming during this period cannot engage in any Winter League activities.

Player conduct, on and off the field, in connection with such postseason exhibition games shall be subject to the discipline of the Commissioner. The Commissioner shall not approve of more than three players of any one Club on the same team. The Commissioner shall not approve of more than three players from the joint membership of the World Series participants playing in the same game.

No player shall participate in any exhibition game with or against any team which, during the current season or within one year, has had any ineligible player or which is or has been during the current season or within one year, managed and controlled by an ineligible player or by any person who has listed an ineligible player under an assumed name or who otherwise has violated, or attempted to violate, any exhibition game contract; or with or against any team which, during said season or within one year, has played against teams containing such ineligible players, or so managed or controlled. Any player who participates in such a game in violation of this Rule 18 shall be fined not less than $50 nor more than $500, except that in no event shall such fine be less than the consideration received by such player for participating in such game.

PRINTED IN U.S.A.                                    REVISED AS OF
OCTOBER 2002

228

## Major League Baseball Contract Notes & Questions

1. In paragraph 2., there is mention of the possibility of deferred payments. Why would a player wish to have deferred payments? (Ooops, I said in the Introduction that I wouldn't discuss tax law).

2. Are you surprised at the language of paragraph 3.(a)? Trite and archaic you say?

3. Explain why you think that the language in paragraph 5 (b) is different from the analogous provision in paragraph 5 of the Regulations that governed the Babe Ruth Contract.

4. In light of paragraph 6.(a), how is it that some players are able to have a "no trade" clause?

5. Look closely at paragraph 7.(b). Give concrete examples of the types of conduct that you think could trigger the "failures" in (1-3).

6. How is the procedure contemplated by paragraph 10.(a) different from the analogous provision (paragraph 8) of Babe Ruth's contract?

7. In the section entitled "Special Covenants" a player may, for example, wish to ask for bonuses as a reward for making the All Star Team, Rookie of the Year, MVP, etc. Can you think of other examples of such covenants? Think of some types of rewards that ought not be permitted? Why not?

8. In the Regulations, look at paragraph 7. Why do you think that the language regarding railroad routes (the precise wording that appeared in Babe Ruth's agreement!) has not been amended over the past 75 + years?

This sample contract is for educational purposes only and is not meant for unauthorized use in any manner. All sample documents are expressly intended for educational purposes. All player agent contracts must be obtained from the NBPA or WNBPA.

**EXHIBIT A**

### NATIONAL BASKETBALL ASSOCIATION
### UNIFORM PLAYER CONTRACT

THIS AGREEMENT made this _____ day of _____,
is by and between _____ (hereinafter called the "Team"), a member of
the National Basketball Association (hereinafter called the "NBA" or "League") and
_____ an individual whose address is shown below (hereinafter
called the "Player"). In consideration of the mutual promises hereinafter contained, the parties
hereto promise and agree as follows:

1. **TERM.**

The Team hereby employs the Player as a skilled basketball player for a term of _____ year(s)
from the 1st day of September

2. **SERVICES.**

(a) The services to be rendered by the Player pursuant to this Contract shall include: (i)
training camp, (ii) practices, meetings, and conditioning sessions conducted by the
Team during the Season, (iii) games scheduled for the Team during any Regular
Season, (iv) Exhibition games scheduled by the Team or the League during and prior
to any Regular Season, (v) the NBA's All-Star Game (including the Rookie Game)
and every event conducted in association with such All-Star Game (including, but not
limited to, a reasonable number of media sessions and any event that is part of an All-
Star Skills Competition if the Player had previously agreed to participate in that
Competition), if the Player is invited to participate therein, (vi) Playoff games
scheduled by the League subsequent to any Regular Season, and (vii) promotional
activities of the Team and the League as set forth in paragraph 13 herein.

(b) If the Player is a Veteran, the Player will not be required to attend training camp
earlier than 2 p.m. (local time) on the twenty-ninth (29th) day prior to the first game
of any Regular Season. Notwithstanding the foregoing, if the Team is scheduled
during a particular NBA Season to participate outside of North America in an

Exhibition game or a Regular Season game during the first week of the Regular Season, such Veteran Player may be required to attend the training camp conducted in advance of that Regular Season by 2 p.m. (local time) on the thirty-second (32nd) day prior to the first game of the Regular Season. Rookies may be required to attend training camp at an earlier date, but no earlier than ten (10) days prior to the date that Veterans are required to attend.

(c) Exhibition games shall not be played on the three (3) days prior to the opening of the Team's Regular Season schedule, nor on the day prior to a Regular Season game, nor on the day prior to and the day following the All-Star Game. Exhibition games prior to any Regular Season shall not exceed eight (including intra-squad games for which admission is charged), and Exhibition games during any Regular Season shall not exceed three.

**COMPENSATION.**

(a) Subject to paragraph 3(b) below, the Team agrees to pay the Player for rendering the services described herein the Compensation described in Exhibit I or Exhibit IA hereto (less all amounts required to be withheld by federal, state, and local authorities, and exclusive of any amount(s) which the Player shall be entitled to receive from the Player Playoff Pool). Unless otherwise provided in Exhibit 1, such Compensation shall be paid in twelve (12) equal semi-monthly payments beginning with the first of said payments on November 15th of each year covered by the Contract and continuing with such payments on the first and fifteenth of each month until said Compensation is paid in full.

(b) The Team agrees to pay the Player $1,500 per week, pro rata, less all amounts required to be withheld by federal, state, and local authorities, for each week (up to a maximum of four (4) weeks for veterans and up to a maximum of five (5) weeks for Rookies) prior to the Team's first Regular Season game that the Player is in attendance at training camp or Exhibition games; provided, however, that no such payments shall be made if, prior to the date on which he is required to attend training camp, the Player has been paid $10,000 or more in compensation with respect to the NBA Season scheduled to commence immediately following such training camp. Any Compensation paid by the Team pursuant to this subparagraph shall be considered an advance against any Compensation owed to the Player pursuant to paragraph 3(a) above, and the first scheduled payment of such Compensation (or such subsequent payments, if the first scheduled payment is not sufficient) shall be reduced by the amount of such advance.

(c) The Team will not pay and the Player will not accept any bonus or anything of value on account of the Team's winning any particular NBA game or series of games or attaining a certain position in the standings of the League as of a certain date, other than the final standing of the Team.

4.  **EXPENSES.**

The Team agrees to pay all proper and necessary expenses of the Player, including the reasonable lodging expenses of the Player while playing for the Team "on the road" and during the training camp period (defined for this paragraph only to mean the period from the first day of training camp through the day of the Team's first Exhibition game) for as long as the Player is not then living at home. The Player, while "on the road" (and during the training camp period, only if the player is not then living at home and the Team does not pay for meals directly), shall be paid a meal expense allowance as set forth in the Collective Bargaining Agreement currently in effect between the NBA and the National Basketball Players Association (hereinafter "the NBA/NBPA Collective Bargaining Agreement"). No deductions from such meal expense allowance shall be made for meals served on an airplane. During the training camp period (and only if the player is not then living at home and the Team does not pay for meals directly), the meal expense allowance shall be paid in weekly installments commencing with the first week of training camp. For the purposes of this paragraph, the Player shall be considered to be "on the road" from the time the Team leaves its home city until the time the Team arrives back at its home city.

5.  **CONDUCT.**

(a) The Player agrees to observe and comply with all Team rules, as maintained or promulgated in accordance with the NBA/NBPA Collective Bargaining Agreement, at all times whether on or off the playing floor. Subject to the provisions of the NBA/NBPA Collective Bargaining Agreement, such rules shall be part of this Contract as fully as if herein written and shall be binding upon the Player.

(b) The Player agrees (i) to give his best services, as well as his loyalty, to the Team, and to play basketball only for the Team and its assignees; (ii) to be neatly and fully attired in public; (iii) to conduct himself on and off the court according to the highest standards of honesty, citizenship, and sportsmanship; and (iv) not to do anything that

232

is materially detrimental or materially prejudicial to the best interests of the Team or the League.

(c) For any violation of Team rules, any breach of any provision of this Contract, or for any conduct impairing the faithful and thorough discharge of the duties incumbent upon the Player, the Team may reasonably impose fines and/or suspensions on the Player in accordance with the terms of the NBAINBPA Collective Bargaining Agreement.

(d) The Player agrees to be bound by Article 35 of the NBA Constitution, a copy of which, as in effect on the date of this Contract, is attached hereto. The Player acknowledges that the Commissioner is empowered to impose fines upon and/or suspend the Player for causes and in the manner provided in such Article, provided that such fines and/or suspensions are consistent with the terms of the NBAINBPA Collective Bargaining Agreement.

(e) The Player agrees that if the Commissioner, in his sole judgment, shall find that the Player has bet, or has offered or attempted to bet, money or anything of value on the outcome of any game participated in by any team which is a member of the NBA, the Commissioner shall have the power in his sole discretion to suspend the Player indefinitely or to expel him as a player for any member of the NBA, and the Commissioner's finding and decision shall be final, binding, conclusive, and unappealable.

(f) The Player agrees that he will not, during the term of this Contract, directly or indirectly, entice, induce, or persuade, or attempt to entice, induce, or persuade, any player or coach who is under contract to any NBA team to enter into negotiations for or relating to his services as a basketball player or coach, nor shall he negotiate for or contract for such services, except with the prior written consent of such team. Breach of this subparagraph, in addition to the remedies available to the Team, shall be punishable by fine and/or suspension to be imposed by the Commissioner.

(g) When the Player is fined and/or suspended by the Team or the NBA, he shall be given notice in writing (with a copy to the Players Association), stating the amount of the fine or the duration of the suspension and the reasons therefor.

6. **WITHHOLDING.**

(a) In the event the Player is fined and/or suspended by the Team or the NBA, the Team shall withhold the amount of the fine or, in the case of a suspension, the amount provided in Article VI of the NBA/NBPA Collective Bargaining Agreement from any Current Cash Compensation due or to become due to the Player with respect to the contract year in which the conduct resulting in the fine and/or the suspension occurred (or a subsequent contract year if the Player has received all Current Cash Compensation due to him for the then current contract year). If, at the time the Player is fined and/or suspended, the Current Cash Compensation remaining to be paid to the Player under this Contract is not sufficient to cover such fine and/or suspension, then the Player agrees promptly to pay the amount directly to the Team. In no case shall the Player permit any such fine and/or suspension to be paid on his behalf by anyone other than himself.

(b) Any Current Cash Compensation withheld from or paid by the Player pursuant to this paragraph 6 shall be retained by the Team or the League, as the case may be, unless the Player contests the fine and/or suspension by initiating a timely Grievance in accordance with the provisions of the NBA/NBPA Collective Bargaining Agreement. If such Grievance is initiated and it satisfies Article XXXI, Section 13 of the NBA/NBPA Collective Bargaining Agreement, the amount withheld from the Player shall be placed in an interest-bearing account, pursuant to Article XXXI, Section 9 of such Agreement, pending the resolution of the Grievance.

7. **PHYSICAL CONDITION.**

(a) The Player agrees to report at the time and place fixed by the Team in good physical condition and to keep himself throughout each NBA Season in good physical condition.

(b) If the Player, in the judgment of the Team's physician, is not in good physical condition at the date of his first scheduled game for the Team, or if, at the beginning of or during any Season, he fails to remain in good physical condition (unless such condition results directly from an injury sustained by the Player as a direct result of participating in any basketball practice or game played for the Team during such Season), so as to render the Player, in the judgment of the Team's physician, unfit to play skilled basketball, the Team shall have the right to suspend such Player until such time as, in the judgment of the Team's physician, the Player is in sufficiently good physical condition to play skilled basketball. In the event of such suspension, the Compensation (excluding any signing bonus or Incentive Compensation) payable to the Player for any Season during such suspension shall be reduced in the same proportion as the length of the period during which, in the judgment of the Team's physician, the Player is unfit to play skilled basketball, bears to the length of such Season.

(c) If, during the term of this Contract, the Player is injured as a direct result of participating in any basketball practice or game played for the Team, the Team will pay the Player's reasonable hospitalization and medical expenses (including doctor's bills), provided that the hospital and doctor are selected by the Team, and provided further that the Team shall be obligated to pay only those expenses incurred as a direct result of medical treatment caused solely by and relating directly to the injury sustained by the Player. Subject to the provisions set forth in Exhibit 3, if in the judgment of the Team's physician, the Player's injuries resulted directly from playing for the Team and render him unfit to play skilled basketball, then, so long as such unfitness continues, but in no event after the Player has received his full Compensation for the Season in which the injury was sustained, the Team shall pay to the Player the Compensation prescribed in Exhibit 1 to this Contract for such Season. The Team's obligations hereunder shall be reduced by (i) any workers' compensation benefits, which, to the extent permitted by law, the Player hereby assigns to the Team, and (ii) any insurance provided for by the Team whether paid or payable to the Player.

(d) The Player agrees to provide to the Team's coach, trainer, or physician prompt notice of any injury, illness, or medical condition suffered by him that is likely to affect adversely the Player's ability to render the services required under this Contract, including the time, place, cause, and nature of such injury, illness, or condition.

(e) Should the Player suffer an injury, illness, or medical condition as provided in this paragraph 7, he will submit himself to a medical examination and appropriate medical treatment by a physician designated by the Team. Such examination when made at the request of the Team shall be at its expense, unless made necessary by some act or conduct of the Player contrary to the terms of this Contract.

8.  **PROHIBITED SUBSTANCES.**

The Player acknowledges that this Contract may be terminated in accordance with the express provisions of Article XXXIII (Anti-Drug Program) of the NBA/NBPA Collective Bargaining Agreement, and that any such termination will result in the Player's immediate dismissal and disqualification from any employment by the NBA and any of its teams. Notwithstanding any terms or provisions of this Contract (including any amendments hereto), in the event of such termination, all obligations of the Team, including obligations to pay Compensation, shall cease, except the obligation of the Team to pay the Player's earned Compensation (whether Current or Deferred) to the date of termination.

9.  **UNIQUE SKILLS.**

The Player represents and agrees that he has extraordinary and unique skill and ability as a basketball player, that the services to be rendered by him hereunder cannot be replaced or the loss thereof adequately compensated for in money damages, and that any breach by the Player of this Contract will cause irreparable injury to the Team, and to its assignees. Therefore, it is agreed that in the event it is alleged by the Team that the Player is playing, attempting or threatening to play, or negotiating for the purpose of playing, during the term of this Contract, for any other person, firm, corporation, or organization, the Team and its assignees (in addition to any other remedies that may be available to them judicially or by way of arbitration) shall have the right to obtain from any court or arbitrator having jurisdiction such equitable relief as may be appropriate, including a decree enjoining the Player from any further such breach of this Contract, and enjoining the Player from playing basketball for any other person, firm, corporation, or organization during the term of this Contract. The Player agrees that the Team may at any time assign such right to the NBA for the enforcement thereof. In any suit, action, or arbitration proceeding brought to obtain such equitable relief, the Player does hereby waive his right, if any, to trial by jury, and does hereby waive his right, if any, to interpose any counterclaim or set-off for any cause whatever.

10. **ASSIGNMENT.**

(a) The Team shall have the right to assign this Contract to any other NBA team and the Player agrees to accept such assignment and to faithfully perform and carry out this contract with the same force and effect as if it had been entered into by the Player with the assignee team instead of with the Team. The Player further agrees that, should the Team contemplate the assignment of this Contract to one or more NBA teams, the Team's physician may furnish to the physicians and officials of such other team or teams all relevant medical information relating to the Player.

(b) In the event that this Contract is assigned to any other NBA team, all reasonable

236

expenses incurred by the Player in moving himself and his family to the home territory of the team to which such assignment is made, as a result thereof, shall be paid by the assignee team. Such assignee team hereby agrees that its acceptance of the assignment of this Contract constitutes agreement on its part to make such payment.

(c) In the event that this Contract is assigned to another NBA team, the Player shall forthwith be provided notice orally or in writing, delivered to the Player personally or delivered or mailed to his last known address, and the Player shall report to the assignee team within forty-eight (48) hours after said notice has been received (if the assignment is made during a Season), within one (1) week after said notice has been received (if the assignment is made between Seasons), or within such longer time for reporting as may be specified in said notice. The NBA shall also promptly notify the Players Association of any such assignment. The Player further agrees that, immediately upon reporting to the assignee team, he will submit upon request to a physical examination conducted by a physician designated by the assignee team.

(d) If the Player, without a reasonable excuse, does not report to the team to which this Contract has been assigned within the time provided in subsection (c) above, then, upon consummation of the assignment, the player may be suspended by the assignee team or, if the assignment is not consummated or is voided as a result of the Player's failure to so report, by the assignor Team. In either case, the Player's Compensation may be reduced by the NBA by the imposition of a fine in an amount equal to the lesser of (i) ten (10) percent of the Player's full Compensation for the then-current Season, or (ii) $50,000.

11. **VALIDITY AND FILING.**

(a) This Contract shall be valid and binding upon the Team and the Player immediately upon its execution.

(b) The Team agrees to file a copy of this Contract, and/or any amendment(s) thereto, with the Commissioner of the NBA as soon as practicable by facsimile and overnight mail, but in no event may such filing be made more than forty-eight (48) hours after the execution of this Contract and/or amendment(s).

(c) If pursuant to the NBA Constitution and By-Laws or the NBA/NBPA Collective

237

Bargaining Agreement, the Commissioner disapproves this Contract (or amendment) within ten (10) days after the receipt thereof in his office by overnight mail, this Contract (or amendment) shall thereupon terminate and be of no further force or effect and the Team and the Player shall thereupon be relieved of their respective rights and liabilities thereunder. If the Commissioner's disapproval is subsequently overturned in any proceeding brought under the arbitration provisions of the NBAINBPA Collective Bargaining Agreement (including any appeals), the Contract shall again be valid and binding upon the Team and the Player, and the Commissioner shall be afforded another ten-day period to disapprove the Contract (based on the Team's Room at the time the Commissioner's disapproval is overturned) as set forth in the foregoing sentence. The NBA will promptly inform the Players Association if the Commissioner disapproves this Contract.

12. **OTHER ATHLETIC ACTIVITIES.**

The Player and the Team acknowledge and agree that (i) the Player's participation in other sports may impair or destroy his ability and skill as a basketball player, and (ii) the Player's participation in basketball out of season may result in injury to him. Accordingly, the Player agrees that he will not, without the written consent of the Team, engage in (x) sports endangering his health or safety (including, but not limited to, professional boxing or wrestling, motorcycling, moped-riding, auto racing, sky-diving, and hang gliding), or (y) any game or exhibition of basketball, football, baseball, hockey, lacrosse, or other athletic sport, under penalty of such fine and/or suspension as may be imposed by the Team and/or the Commissioner of the NBA. Nothing contained herein shall be intended to require the Player to obtain the written consent of the Team in order to enable the Player to participate in, as an amateur, the sport of golf, tennis, handball, swimming, hiking, soft ball, or volleyball.

13. **PROMOTIONAL ACTIVITIES.**

(a) The Player agrees to allow the Team or the League to take pictures of the Player, alone or together with others, for still photographs, motion pictures, or television, at such times as the Team or the League may designate. No matter by whom taken, such pictures may be used in any manner desired by either the Team or the League for publicity or promotional purposes. The rights in any such pictures taken by the Team or by the League shall belong to the Team or to the League, as their interests may appear.

(b) The Player agrees that, during any year of this Contract, he will not make public appearances, participate in radio or television programs, permit his picture to be taken, write or sponsor newspaper or magazine articles, or sponsor commercial products without the written consent of the Team, which shall not be withheld except in the reasonable interests of the Team or the NBA.

(c) Upon request, the Player shall consent to and make himself available for interviews by representatives of the media conducted at reasonable times.

(d) In addition to the foregoing, and subject to the conditions and limitations set forth in Article II, Section 8 of the NBA/NBPA Collective Bargaining Agreement, the Player agrees to participate, upon request, in all other reasonable promotional activities of the Team and the NBA. For each such promotional appearance made on behalf of a commercial sponsor of the Team, the Team agrees to pay the Player $1,000 or, if the Team agrees, such higher amount that is consistent with the Team's past practice and not otherwise unreasonable.

14. **GROUP LICENSE.**

(a) The Player hereby grants to NBA Properties, Inc. the exclusive rights to use the Player's Player Attributes as such term is defined and for such group licensing purposes as are set forth in the Agreement between NBA Properties, Inc. and the National Basketball Players Association, made as of September 18, 1995 and amended January 20, 1999 (the "Group License"), a copy of which will, upon his request, be furnished the Player; and the Player agrees to make the appearances called for by such Agreement.

(b) Notwithstanding anything to the contrary contained in the Group License or this Contract, NBA Properties may use, in connection with League Promotions, the Player's (i) name or nickname and/or (ii) the Player's Player Attributes (as defined in the Group License) as such Player Attributes may be captured in game action footage or photographs. NBA Properties shall be entitled to use the Player's Player Attributes individually pursuant to the preceding sentence and shall not be required to use the Player's Player Attributes in a group or as one of multiple players. As used herein, League Promotion shall mean any advertising, marketing, or collateral materials or marketing programs conducted by the NBA, NBA Properties (or any subsidiary of NBA Properties) or any NBA team that is intended to promote (x) any game in which

239

an NBA team participates or game telecast or broadcast (including Pre-Season, Exhibition, Regular Season, and Playoff games), (y) the NBA, its teams, or its players, or (z) the sport of basketball.

15. **TEAM DEFAULT.**

In the event of an alleged default by the Team in the payments to the Player provided for by this Contract, or in the event of an alleged failure by the Team to perform any other material obligation that it has agreed to perform hereunder, the Player shall notify both the Team and the League in writing of the facts constituting such alleged default or alleged failure. If neither the Team nor the League shall cause such alleged default or alleged failure to be remedied within five *(5)* days after receipt of such written notice, the National Basketball Players Association shall, on behalf of the Player, have the right to request that the dispute concerning such alleged default or alleged failure be referred immediately to the Grievance Arbitrator in accordance with the provisions of the NBAINBPA Collective Bargaining Agreement. If, as a result of such arbitration, an award issues in favor of the Player, and if neither the Team nor the League complies with such award within ten (10) days after the service thereof, the Player shall have the right, by a further written notice to the Team and the League, to terminate this Contract.

16. **TERMINATION.**

(a) The Team may terminate this Contract upon written notice to the Player if the Player shall:

(i) at any time, fail, refuse, or neglect to conform his personal conduct to standards of good citizenship, good moral character (defined here to mean not engaging in acts of moral turpitude, whether or not such acts would constitute a crime), and good sportsmanship, to keep himself in first class physical condition, or to obey the Team's training rules; or

(ii) at any time commit a significant and inexcusable physical attack against any official or employee of the Team or the NBA (other than another player), or any person in attendance at any NBA game or event, considering the totality of the circumstances, including (but not limited to) the degree of provocation (if any) that may have led to the attack, the nature and scope of the attack, the player's state of mind at the time of the attack, and the extent of any injury resulting from the attack; or

240

(iii) at any time, fail, in the sole opinion of the Team's management, to exhibit sufficient skill or competitive ability to qualify to continue as a member of the Team; provided, however, (x) that if this Contract is terminated by the Team, in accordance with the provisions of this subparagraph, prior to January 10 of any Regular Season, and the Player, at the time of such termination, is unfit to play skilled basketball as the result of an injury resulting directly from his playing for the Team, the Player shall (subject to the provisions set forth in Exhibit 3) continue to receive his full Compensation, less all workers' compensation benefits (which, to the extent permitted by law, and if not deducted from the Player's Compensation by the Team, the Player hereby assigns to the Team) and any insurance provided for by the Team paid or payable to the Player by reason of said injury, until such time as the Player is fit to play skilled basketball, but not beyond the Season during which such termination occurred; and provided, further, (y) that if this Contract is terminated by the Team, in accordance with the provisions of this subparagraph, during the period from the January 10 of any Regular Season through the end of such Regular Season, the Player shall be entitled to receive his full Compensation for said Season; or

(iv) at any time, fail, refuse, or neglect to render his services hereunder or in any other manner materially breach this Contract.

(b) If this Contract is terminated by the Team by reason of the Player's failure to render his services hereunder due to disability caused by an injury to the Player resulting directly from his playing for the Team and rendering him unfit to play skilled basketball, and notice of such injury is given by the Player as provided herein, the Player shall (subject to the provisions set forth in Exhibit 3) be entitled to receive his full Compensation for the Season in which the injury was sustained, less all workers' compensation benefits (which, to the extent permitted by law, and if not deducted from the Player's Compensation by the Team, the Player hereby assigns to the Team) and any insurance provided for by the Team paid or payable to the Player by reason of said injury.

(c) Notwithstanding the provisions of subparagraph 16(b) above, if this Contract is terminated by the Team prior to the first game of a Regular Season by reason of the Player's failure to render his services hereunder due to an injury or condition sustained or suffered during a preceding Season, or after such Season but prior to the Player's participation in any basketball practice or game played for the Team, payment by the Team of any Compensation earned through the date of termination under paragraph 3(b) above, payment of the Player's board, lodging, and expense allowance during the training camp period, payment of the reasonable traveling expenses of the Player to his home city, and the expert training and coaching provided by the Team to the Player during the training season shall be full payment to the Player.

(d) If this Contract is terminated by the Team during the period designated by the Team for attendance at training camp, payment by the Team of any Compensation earned through the date of termination under paragraph 3(b) above, payment of the Player's board,

lodging, and expense allowance during such period to the date of termination, payment of the reasonable traveling expenses of the Player to his home city, and the expert training and coaching provided by the Team to the Player during the training season shall be full payment to the Player.

(e) If this Contract is terminated by the Team after the first game of a Regular Season, except in the case provided for in sub-paragraphs (a)(iii) and (b) of this paragraph 16, the Player shall be entitled to receive as full payment hereunder a sum of money which, when added to the salary which he has already received during such Season, will represent the same proportionate amount of the annual sum set forth in Exhibit 1 hereto as the number of days of such Regular Season then past bears to the total number of days of such Regular Season, plus the reasonable traveling expenses of the Player to his home.

(f) If the Team proposes to terminate this Contract in accordance with subparagraph (a) of this paragraph 16, it must first comply with the following waiver procedure:

   (i) The Team shall request the NBA Commissioner to request waivers from all other clubs. Such waiver request may not be withdrawn.

   (ii) Upon receipt of the waiver request, any other team may claim assignment of this Contract at such waiver price as may be fixed by the League, the priority of claims to be determined in accordance with the NBA Constitution and By-Laws.

   (iii) If this Contract is so claimed, the Team agrees that it shall, upon the assignment of this Contract to the claiming team, notify the Player of such assignment as

242

provided in paragraph 10(c) hereof, and the Player agrees he shall report to the assignee team as provided in said paragraph 10(c).

(iv) If the Contract is not claimed, the Team shall promptly deliver written notice of termination to the Player at the expiration of the waiver period.

(v) The NBA shall promptly notify the Players Association of the disposition of any waiver request.

(vi) To the extent not inconsistent with the foregoing provisions of this subparagraph (f), the waiver procedures set forth in the NBA Constitution and By-Laws, a copy of which, as in effect on the date of this Contract, is attached hereto, shall govern.

(g) Upon any termination of this Contract by the Player, all obligations of the Team to pay Compensation shall cease on the date of termination, except the obligation of the Team to pay the Player's Compensation to said date.

17. DISPUTES.

In the event of any dispute arising between the Player and the Team relating to any matter arising under this Contract, or concerning the performance or interpretation thereof (except for a dispute arising under paragraph 9 hereof), such dispute shall be resolved in accordance with the Grievance and Arbitration Procedure set forth in the NBA/NBPA Collective Bargaining Agreement.

18. PLAYER NOT A MEMBER.

Nothing contained in this Contract or in any provision of the NBA Constitution and By-Laws shall be construed to constitute the Player a member of the NBA or to confer upon him any of the rights or privileges of a member thereof.

19. RELEASE.

The Player hereby releases and waives every claim he may have against the NBA and its related entities and every member of the NBA, and against every director, officer, owner, stockholder, trustee, partner, and employee of the NBA and its related entities and/or any member of the NBA and their related entities (excluding persons employed as players by any such member), and against any person retained by the NBA and/or the Players Association in connection with the NBAINBPA Anti-Drug Program, the Grievance Arbitrator, the System Arbitrator, and any other arbitrator or expert retained by the NBA and/or the Players Association under the terms of the NBA/NBPA Collective Bargaining Agreement, arising out of or in connection with (i) any injury that is subject to the provisions of paragraph 7, (ii) any fighting or other form of violent and/or unsportsmanlike conduct occurring during the course of any practice and/or any Exhibition, Regular Season, and/or Playoff game (on or adjacent to the playing floor or in or adjacent to any facility used for practices or games), (iii) the testing procedures or the imposition of any penalties set forth in paragraph 8 hereof and in the NBA/NBPA Anti-Drug Program, or (iv) any injury suffered in the course of his employment as to which he has or would have a claim for workers~ compensation benefits. The foregoing shall not apply to any claim of medical malpractice against a Team-affiliated physician or other medical personnel.

20. **ENTIRE AGREEMENT.**

This Contract (including any Exhibits hereto) contains the entire agreement between the parties and sets forth all components of the Player's Compensation from the Team or any Team Affiliate, and there are no undisclosed agreements of any kind, express or implied, oral or written, promises, undertakings, representations, commitments, inducements, assurances of intent, or understandings of any kind that have not been disclosed to the NBA (a) involving consideration of any kind to be paid, furnished, or made available to the Player, or any person or entity controlled by or related to the Player, by the Team or any Team Affiliate, either during the term of this Contract or thereafter, or (b) concerning any future Renegotiation, Extension, or other amendment of this Contract or the entry into any new Player Contract.

## EXAMINE THIS CONTRACT CAREFULLY
## BEFORE SIGNING IT.

THIS CONTRACT INCLUDES EXHIBITS _____, WHICH ARE
ATTACHED HERETO AND MADE A PART HEREOF.

IN WITNESS WHEREOF the Player has hereunto signed his name and the Team has caused this
Contract to be executed by its duly authorized officer.

Dated: _____

By: _____

Title: _____

Team: _____

Dated: _____

Player _____

Player's Address: _____

# NBA Contract Notes & Questions

1. In paragraph 1., why do you suppose that the term "skilled basketball player" is used? Is this any different from what is expressed in paragraph 9 ("Unique Skills")? Explain.

2. In paragraph 5.(a), why should the players be asked to agree to certain parameters of conduct "at all times whether on or off the playing floor"?

3. Similarly, what types of conduct do you suppose would be considered a breach of paragraph 5.(b)(iii -iv) ("to conduct himself on and off the court according to the highest standards of honesty, citizenship, and sportsmanship; and not to do anything that is materially detrimental or materially prejudicial to the best interests of the Team or the League?" Given the track record of NBA players with domestic violence, drugs, and other types of criminal conduct over the past several years, how important is the interpretation of this language? What is the relationship between this provision and paragraph 16 ("Termination")?

4. Workers' compensation insurance provides an economically attractive alternative for employers. By providing workers' compensation benefits, employers are able to avoid costly lawsuits brought by injured employees. So if a worker in a lumber yard cuts his hand on a saw, the company's workers' compensation insurance policy pays the injured worker for his injury, based on factors such as the worker's age, experience, and the percentage of loss of function in the injured hand (*e.g.,* a 15% disability). Pursuant to paragraph 7.(c), explain how workers' compensation benefits are relevant to a professional basketball player's injury.

5. Paragraph 11.(c) addresses the possibility of the Commissioner's disapproval. Explain the Commissioner's disapproval in terms of either a condition precedent or a condition subsequent. Which term best describes the legal effect of the Commissioner's disapproval? Why?

### Further Reading on Contracts:

Roger I. Abrams, *Baseball Salary Arbitration From the Inside*, 1998 N.J.J. 24.

Bruce Burton, *New Remedies for Breach of Sports Facility Use Agreements*, 88 IOWA L. REV. 809 (2003).

Timothy Davis, *Balancing Freedom of Contract and Competing Values in Sports*, 38 S. TEX. L. REV. 1115 (1997).

Gordon J. Hylton, *The Historical Origins of Professional Baseball Grievance Arbitration*, 11 MARQ. SPORTS L. REV. 175 (2001).

Robert A. McCormick, *Baseball's Third Strike: The Triumph of Collective Bargaining in Professional Baseball*, 35 Vand. L. Rev. 1131 (1982).

Richard M. Perlmuetter, *Boston, From Blueprints to Bricks: A Survey of Current Baseball Stadium Financing Projects*, 34 URB. LAW 335 (2002).

Gary R. Roberts, *Interpreting the NFL Player Contract*, 3 MARQ. SPORTS L.J. 29 (1992).

Jan Stiglitz, *Player Discipline in Team Sports*, 5 MARQ. SPORTS L.J. 167 (1995).

John C. Weistart, *Judicial Review of Labor Agreements: Lessons From the Sports Industry*, 44 LAW & CONTEMP. PROBS. 109 (1981).

John C. Weistart & Cym H. Lowell, Law of Sports, §3.02-3.14 Legal Relationships in Professional Sports (Bobbs-Merrill Company, Inc., 1979).

# Chapter 6

## Antitrust (And Some Aspects of Labor Law)

### A. Basic Principles

I always tell my students that you can't, with a straight face, tell practicing attorneys that you've taken a Sports Law class unless you first understand the basics of Antitrust Law, and how those basics relate to Sports. The principles apply to both professional and amateur sports, and therefore this book does not artificially separate them. Remember that the Sherman Antitrust Act was a product of an era in United States history (late 19th century) when large companies, typically oil and steel, were conspiring with one another in an effort to control markets and to stifle competition. As a result, large businesses were able to put smaller ones out of business and consumers were deprived of choices. Agreements to fix prices and salaries, and conspiracies to boycott certain suppliers were the kinds of agreements which impeded free trade.

Eliminating competition is a goal of many businesses. If the Coca-Cola Company did not exist, Pepsico would probably be delighted. But sports are unique among businesses. For example, if the Red Sox did not exist, the Yankees would no longer have an important source of revenue. Red Sox fans are valuable to the Yankees because Red Sox fans pay to watch the Yankees play against the Red Sox. This is important both in terms of ticket sales and television revenues. This simple example illustrates one reason why sports are unique in business. Although teams fiercely compete on the field of play, they must cooperate in order to establish schedules, rules of play, and myriad other details that allow the teams to compete. The competition is controlled though cooperation. This principle, however, does not necessarily apply in all sports law contexts. Adidas and Nike, like Pepsico and Coca-Cola, would probably be delighted if the other were not around to compete.

Hence, due to the unique nature of sports and the admixture of cooperation that is necessary to compete, courts have had to take a flexible approach to the application of the Sherman Antitrust Act § 1, which prohibits contracts, combinations, or conspiracies that unreasonably restrain trade.

*Mackey* is an excellent case for illustrating the rudiments of the Sherman Antitrust Act § 1, and the way that it can apply to sports. This case does a nice job of presenting the law and applying it to specific facts. In so doing, it blends in the relationship to labor law and collective bargaining. Thus, it is a useful case to read first when beginning your study of antitrust and sports. *Law v. NCAA* is similar to *Mackey* in several respects. It provides an example of how Sherman § 1 may apply to the NCAA, not only to professional sports leagues. It extends some of the reasoning that you first encounter in *Mackey*; especially the court's consideration of whether to apply the per se rule or the rule of reason (rules that you will learn about in these cases).

*Wood* takes you a couple of more steps forward into the Sherman § 1 analysis and its relationship to Labor Law and collective bargaining. In *Wood* we see clearly that many aspects of the way that sports leagues operate (*e.g.,* the amateur draft) would, in fact, constitute Sherman § 1 violations but for the fact that they result from collective bargaining and are permissible under the non-statutory labor exemption. The *Clarett* case offers a more recent interpretation of antitrust rules in the context of the NFL, and suggests that the *Mackey* court may not have gotten it all completely right.

John Wolohan's article summarizes the long history of Major League Baseball's storied, if not infamous, antitrust exemption. In addition to thoroughly explaining the relevant case law, Professor Wolohan also offers an innovative perspective on the potential ramifications of the Curt Flood Act.

Section 2 of the Sherman Act was designed to prohibit illegal monopolies. Perhaps the best known sports cases that have pursued this legal theory have been the American Football League's suit against the National Football League and the United States Football League's lawsuit against the National Football League.

# 15 United States Code § 1 (Sherman Antitrust Act § 1)

## § 1. Trusts, etc., in restraint of trade illegal; penalty

Every contract, combination in the form of trust or otherwise, or conspiracy, in restraint of trade or commerce among the several States, or with foreign nations, is declared to be illegal. Every person who shall make any contract or engage in any combination or conspiracy hereby declared to be illegal shall be deemed guilty of a felony, and, on conviction thereof, shall be punished by fine not exceeding $100,000,000 if a corporation, or, if any other person, $1,000,000, or by imprisonment not exceeding 10 years, or by both said punishments, in the discretion of the court.

## John Mackey v. National Football League
543 F 2d 606 (1976)
United States Court of Appeals, Eighth Circuit

LAY, Circuit Judge.

This is an appeal by the National Football League (NFL), twenty-six of its member clubs, and its Commissioner, Alvin Ray "Pete" Rozelle, from a district court judgment holding the "Rozelle Rule"[1] to be violative of s 1 of the Sherman Act, and enjoining its enforcement.

This action was initiated by a group of present and former NFL players, appellees herein, pursuant to ss 4 and 16 of the Clayton Act, 15 U.S.C. ss 15 and 26, and s 1 of the Sherman Act, 15 U.S.C. s 1. Their complaint alleged that the defendants' enforcement of the Rozelle Rule constituted an illegal combination and conspiracy in restraint of trade denying professional football players the right to freely contract for their services. Plaintiffs sought injunctive relief and treble damages.

The district court, the Honorable Earl R. Larson presiding, conducted a plenary trial which consumed 55 days and produced a transcript in excess

---

[1] The Rozelle Rule essentially provides that when a player's contractual obligation to a team expires and he signs with a different club, the signing club must provide compensation to the player's former team. If the two clubs are unable to conclude mutually satisfactory arrangements, the Commissioner may award compensation in the form of one or more players and/or draft choices as he deems fair and equitable.

251

of 11,000 pages. At the conclusion of trial, the court entered extensive findings of fact and conclusions of law. The court granted the injunctive relief sought by the players and entered judgment in their favor on the issue of liability. This appeal followed.

The district court held that the defendants' enforcement of the Rozelle Rule constituted a concerted refusal to deal and a group boycott, and was therefore a per se violation of the Sherman Act. Alternatively, finding that the evidence offered in support of the clubs' contention that the Rozelle Rule is necessary to the successful operation of the NFL insufficient to justify the restrictive effects of the Rule, the court concluded that the Rozelle Rule was invalid under the Rule of Reason standard. Finally, the court rejected the clubs' argument that the Rozelle Rule was immune from attack under the Sherman Act because it had been the subject of a collective bargaining agreement between the club owners and the National Football League Players Association (NFLPA).

The defendants raise two basic issues on this appeal: (1) whether the so-called labor exemption to the antitrust laws immunizes the NFL's enforcement of the Rozelle Rule from antitrust liability; and (2) if not, whether the Rozelle Rule and the manner in which it has been enforced violate the antitrust laws. ****

HISTORY

We first turn to a brief examination of the pertinent history and operating principles of the National Football League.

The NFL, which began operating in 1920, is an unincorporated association comprised of member clubs which own and operate professional football teams. It presently enjoys a monopoly over major league professional football in the United States. The League performs various administrative functions, including organizing and scheduling games, and promulgating rules. A constitution and bylaws govern its activities and those of its members. Pete Rozelle, Commissioner of the NFL since 1960, is an employee of the League and its chief executive officer. His powers and duties are defined by the NFL Constitution and Bylaws.

Throughout most of its history, the NFL's operations have been unilaterally controlled by the club owners. In 1968, however, the NLRB recognized the NFLPA as a labor organization, within the meaning of 29 U.S.C. s 152(5), and as the exclusive bargaining representative of all NFL players, within the meaning of 29 U.S.C. s 159(a). Since that time, the

NFLPA and the clubs have engaged in collective bargaining over various terms and conditions of employment. Two formal agreements have resulted. The first, concluded in 1968, was in effect from July 15, 1968 to February 1, 1970. The second, entered into on June 17, 1971, was made retroactive to February 1, 1970, and expired on January 30, 1974. Since 1974, the parties have been negotiating; however, they have not concluded a new agreement.

For a number of years, the NFL has operated under a reserve system whereby every player who signs a contract with an NFL club is bound to play for that club, and no other, for the term of the contract plus one additional year at the option of the club. The cornerstones of this system are s 15.1 of the NFL Constitution and Bylaws, which requires that all club-player contracts be as prescribed in the Standard Player Contract adopted by the League, and the option clause embodied in the Standard Player Contract.[2] Once a player signs a Standard Player Contract, he is bound to his team for at least two years. He may, however, become a free agent at the end of the option year by playing that season under a renewed contract rather than signing a new one. A player "playing out his option" is subject to a 10% salary cut during the option year.

Prior to 1963, a team which signed a free agent who had previously been under contract to another club was not obligated to compensate the player's former club. In 1963, after R. C. Owens played out his option with the San Francisco 49ers and signed a contract with the Baltimore Colts, the member clubs of the NFL unilaterally adopted the following provision, now known as the Rozelle Rule, as an amendment to the League's Constitution and Bylaws:

> Any player, whose contract with a League club has expired, shall thereupon become a free agent and shall no longer be considered a member of the team of that club following the

---

[2] Paragraph 10 of the Standard Player Contract contains the following option clause: The Club may, by sending notice in writing to the Player, on or before the first day of May following the football season referred to in P 1 hereof, renew this contract for a further term of one (1) year on the same terms as are provided by this contract, except that (1) the Club may fix the rate of compensation to be paid by the Club to the Player during said further term, which rate of compensation shall not be less than ninety percent (90%) of the sum set forth in P 3 hereof and shall be payable in installments during the football season in such further term as provided in P 3; and (2) after such renewal this contract shall not include a further option to the Club to renew the contract. The phrase "rate of compensation" as above used shall not include bonus payments or payments of any nature whatsoever and shall be limited to the precise sum set forth in P 3 hereof.

expiration date of such contract. Whenever a player, becoming a free agent in such manner, thereafter signed a contract with a different club in the League, then, unless mutually satisfactory arrangements have been concluded between the two League clubs, the Commissioner may name and then award to the former club one or more players, from the Active, Reserve, or Selection List (including future selection choices) of the acquiring club as the Commissioner in his sole discretion deems fair and equitable; any such decision by the Commissioner shall be final and conclusive.

This provision, unchanged in form, is currently embodied in s 12.1(H) of the NFL Constitution. The ostensible purposes of the rule are to maintain competitive balance among the NFL teams and protect the clubs' investment in scouting, selecting and developing players.

During the period from 1963 through 1974, 176 players played out their options. Of that number, 34 signed with other teams. In three of those cases, the former club waived compensation. In 27 cases, the clubs involved mutually agreed upon compensation. Commissioner Rozelle awarded compensation in the four remaining cases.

We turn now to the contentions of the parties.

THE LABOR EXEMPTION ISSUE

We review first the claim that the labor exemption immunizes the Commissioner and the clubs from liability under the antitrust laws. Analysis of this contention requires a basic understanding of the legal principles surrounding the labor exemption and consideration of the factual record developed at trial.

History

The concept of a labor exemption from the antitrust laws finds its basic source in ss 6 and 20 of the Clayton Act, 15 U.S.C. s 17 and 29 U.S.C. s 52, and the Norris-LaGuardia Act, 29 U.S.C. ss 104, 105 and 113. Those provisions declare that labor unions are not combinations or conspiracies in restraint of trade, and specifically exempt certain union activities such as secondary picketing and group boycotts from the coverage of the antitrust laws. *See Connell Co. v. Plumbers & Steamfitters*, 421 U.S. 616, 621-22, 95 S.Ct. 1830, 44 L.Ed.2d 418 (1975). The *statutory* exemption was created to insulate legitimate collective activity by employees, which is inherently anticompetitive but is favored by federal labor policy, from the proscriptions of the antitrust laws. (emphasis added) See *Apex Hosiery Co. v. Leader,* 310 U.S. 469, 60 S.Ct. 982, 84 L.Ed. 1311 (1940).

The *statutory* exemption extends to legitimate labor activities unilaterally undertaken by a union in furtherance of its own interests. (emphasis added) *See United States v. Hutcheson,* 312 U.S. 219, 61 S.Ct. 463, 85 L.Ed. 788 (1941). It does not extend to concerted action or agreements between unions and non-labor groups. The Supreme Court has held, however, that in order to properly accommodate the congressional policy favoring free competition in business markets with the congressional policy favoring collective bargaining under the National Labor Relations Act, 29 U.S.C. s 151 et seq., certain union-employer agreements must be accorded a limited *nonstatutory* exemption from antitrust sanctions. (emphasis added) *See Connell Co. v. Plumbers & Steamfitters, supra; Meat Cutters v. Jewel Tea,* 381 U.S. 676, 85 S.Ct. 1596, 14 L.Ed.2d 640 (1965). See generally Morris, The Developing Labor Law 807-16 (1971).[3]

The players assert that only employee groups are entitled to the labor exemption and that it cannot be asserted by the defendants, an employer group. We must disagree. Since the basis of the *nonstatutory* exemption is the national policy favoring collective bargaining, and since the exemption extends to agreements, the benefits of the exemption logically extend to both parties to the agreement. (emphasis added) Accordingly, under appropriate circumstances, we find that a non-labor group may avail itself of the labor exemption. See *Meat Cutters v. Jewel Tea, supra,* 381 U.S. at 729-30, 85 S.Ct. 1596 (opinion of Justice Goldberg) [case citations omitted].

The clubs and the Commissioner claim the benefit of the *nonstatutory* labor exemption here, arguing that the Rozelle Rule was the subject of an agreement with the players union and that the proper accommodation of federal labor and antitrust policies requires that the agreement be deemed immune from antitrust liability. (emphasis added) The plaintiffs assert that the Rozelle Rule was the product of unilateral action by the clubs and that the defendants cannot assert a colorable claim of exemption.

---

[3] As the Supreme Court stated in Connell Co. v. Plumbers & Steamfitters, 421 U.S. 616, at 622, 95 S.Ct. 1830, at 1835, 44 L.Ed.2d 418 (1975): "(t)he nonstatutory exemption has its source in the strong labor policy favoring the association of employees to eliminate competition over wages and working conditions."

To determine the applicability of the nonstatutory exemption we must first decide whether there has been any agreement between the parties concerning the Rozelle Rule.

## The Collective Bargaining Agreements

The district court found that neither the 1968 nor the 1970 collective bargaining agreement embodied an agreement on the Rozelle Rule, and that the union has never otherwise agreed to the Rule. ****

## The 1968 Agreement

At the outset of the negotiations preceding the 1968 agreement, the players did not seek elimination of the Rozelle Rule but felt that it should be modified. During the course of the negotiations, however, the players apparently presented no concrete proposals in that regard and there was little discussion concerning the Rozelle Rule. At trial, Daniel Shulman, a bargaining representative of the players, attributed their failure to pursue any modifications to the fact that the negotiations had bogged down on other issues and the union was not strong enough to persist.

The 1968 agreement incorporated by reference the NFL Constitution and Bylaws, of which the Rozelle Rule is a part. Furthermore, it expressly provided that free agent rules shall not be amended during the life of the agreement.

## The 1970 Agreement

At the start of the negotiations leading up to the 1970 agreement, it appears that the players again decided not to make an issue of the Rozelle Rule. The only reference to the Rule in the union's formal proposals presented at the outset of the negotiations was the following:

> The NFLPA is disturbed over reports from players who, after playing out their options, are unable to deal with other clubs because of the Rozelle Rule. A method should be found whereby a free agent is assured the opportunity to discuss contract with all NFL teams.

There was little discussion of the Rozelle Rule during the 1970 negotiations.

Although the 1970 agreement failed to make any express reference to the Rozelle Rule, it did contain a "zipper clause":

(T)his Agreement represents a complete and final understanding on all bargainable subjects of negotiation among the parties during the term of this Agreement * * * .

While the agreement did not expressly incorporate by reference the terms of the NFL Constitution and Bylaws, it did require all players to sign the Standard Player Contract, and provided that the Standard Contract shall govern the relationship between the clubs and the players. The Standard Player Contract, in turn, provided that the player agreed at all times to comply with and be bound by the NFL Constitution and Bylaws. At trial, Tex Schramm, a bargaining representative of the club owners, and Alan Miller, a bargaining representative of the players, testified that it was their understanding that the Rozelle Rule would remain in effect during the term of the 1970 agreement.

Since the beginning of the 1974 negotiations, the players have consistently sought the elimination of the Rozelle Rule. The NFLPA and the clubs have engaged in substantial bargaining over that issue but have not reached an accord. Nor have they concluded a collective bargaining agreement to replace the 1970 agreement which expired in 1974.

Based on the fact that the 1968 agreement incorporated by reference the Rozelle Rule and provided that free agent rules would not be changed, we conclude that the 1968 agreement required that the Rozelle Rule govern when a player played out his option and signed with another team. Assuming, without deciding, that the 1970 agreement embodied a similar understanding, we proceed to a consideration of whether the agreements fall within the scope of the nonstatutory labor exemption.

Governing Principles

Under the general principles surrounding the labor exemption, the availability of the nonstatutory exemption for a particular agreement turns upon whether the relevant federal labor policy is deserving of pre-eminence over federal antitrust policy under the circumstances of the particular case. See Connell Co. v. Plumbers & Steamfitters, supra; Meat Cutters v. Jewel Tea, supra; Mine Workers v. Pennington, 381 U.S. 657, 85 S.Ct. 1585, 14 L.Ed.2d 626 (1965).

Although the cases giving rise to the nonstatutory exemption are factually dissimilar from the present case, certain principles can be deduced from those decisions governing the proper accommodation of the competing labor and antitrust interests involved here.

We find the proper accommodation to be: First, the labor policy favoring collective bargaining may potentially be given pre-eminence over the antitrust laws where the restraint on trade primarily affects only the parties to the collective bargaining relationship. [case citations omitted]. Second, federal labor policy is implicated sufficiently to prevail only where the agreement sought to be exempted concerns a mandatory subject of collective bargaining. [case citations omitted]. Finally, the policy favoring collective bargaining is furthered to the degree necessary to override the antitrust laws only where the agreement sought to be exempted is the product of bona fide arm's-length bargaining. [case citations omitted]

## Application

Applying these principles to the facts presented here, we think it clear that the alleged restraint on trade effected by the Rozelle Rule affects only the parties to the agreements sought to be exempted. Accordingly, we must inquire as to the other two principles: whether the Rozelle Rule is a mandatory subject of collective bargaining, and whether the agreements thereon were the product of bona fide arm's-length negotiation

## Mandatory Subject of Bargaining

Under s 8(d) of the National Labor Relations Act, 29 U.S.C. s 158(d), mandatory subjects of bargaining pertain to "wages, hours, and other terms and conditions of employment. . . . " *See NLRB v. Borg-Warner Corp.*, 356 U.S. 342, 78 S.Ct. 718, 2 L.Ed.2d 823 (1958). Whether an agreement concerns a mandatory subject depends not on its form but on its practical effect. *See Federation of Musicians v. Carroll*, 391 U.S. 99, 88 S.Ct. 1562, 20 L.Ed.2d 460 (1968). Thus, in *Meat Cutters v. Jewel Tea, supra*, the Court held that an agreement limiting retail marketing hours concerned a mandatory subject because it affected the particular hours of the day which the employees would be required to work. In *Teamsters Union v. Oliver*, 358 U.S. 283, 79 S.Ct. 297, 3 L.Ed.2d 312 (1959), an agreement fixing minimum equipment rental rates paid to truck owner-drivers was held to concern a mandatory bargaining subject because it directly affected the driver wage scale.

****

On its face, the Rozelle Rule does not deal with "wages, hours and other terms or conditions of employment" but with inter-team compensation when a player's contractual obligation to one team expires and he is signed by another. Viewed as such, it would not constitute a mandatory subject of collective bargaining. The district court found, however, that the Rule operates to restrict a player's ability to move from one team to another and depresses player salaries. There is substantial evidence in the record to support these findings. Accordingly, we hold that the Rozelle Rule constitutes a mandatory bargaining subject within the meaning of the National Labor Relations Act.

## Bona Fide Bargaining

The district court found that the parties' collective bargaining history reflected nothing which could be legitimately characterized as bargaining over the Rozelle Rule; that, in part due to its recent formation and inadequate finances, the NFLPA, at least prior to 1974, stood in a relatively weak bargaining position vis-a-vis the clubs; and that "the Rozelle Rule was unilaterally imposed by the NFL and member club defendants upon the players in 1963 and has been imposed on the players from 1963 through the present date."

On the basis of our independent review of the record, including the parties' bargaining history as set forth above, we find substantial evidence to support the finding that there was no bona fide arm's-length bargaining over the Rozelle Rule preceding the execution of the 1968 and 1970 agreements. The Rule imposes significant restrictions on players, and its form has remained unchanged since it was unilaterally promulgated by the clubs in 1963. ****

In view of the foregoing, we hold that the agreements between the clubs and the players embodying the Rozelle Rule do not qualify for the labor exemption. The union's acceptance of the status quo by the continuance of the Rozelle Rule in the initial collective bargaining agreements under the circumstances of this case cannot serve to immunize the Rozelle Rule from the scrutiny of the Sherman Act.

## ANTITRUST ISSUES

We turn, then, to the question of whether the Rozelle Rule, as implemented, violates s 1 of the Sherman Act, which declares illegal "every contract, combination * * * or conspiracy, in restraint of trade or commerce among the several States." 15 U.S.C. s 1. The district court found the

Rozelle Rule to be a per se violation of the Act. Alternatively, the court held the Rule to be violative of the Rule of Reason standard.[4]

****

Per Se Violation

****

The express language of the Sherman Act is broad enough to render illegal nearly every type of agreement between businessmen. The Supreme Court has held, however, that only those agreements which "unreasonably" restrain trade come within the proscription of the Act. *See Northern Pac. R. Co. v. United States*, 356 U.S. 1, 78 S.Ct. 514, 2 L.Ed.2d 545 (1958); *Chicago Board of Trade v. United States*, 246 U.S. 231, 38 S.Ct. 242, 62 L.Ed. 683 (1918); *Standard Oil Co. v. United States*, 221 U.S. 1, 31 S.Ct. 502, 55 L.Ed. 619 (1911). The "Rule of Reason" emerged from these cases.

As the courts gained experience with antitrust problems arising under the Sherman Act, they identified certain types of agreements as being so consistently unreasonable that they may be deemed to be illegal per se, without inquiry into their purported justifications. As the Supreme Court stated in *Northern Pac. R. Co. v. United States, supra,* 356 U.S. at 5, 78 S.Ct. at 518:

> (T)here are certain agreements or practices which because of their pernicious effect on competition and lack of any redeeming virtue are conclusively presumed to be unreasonable and therefore illegal without elaborate inquiry as to the precise harm they have caused or the business excuse for their use.

Among the practices which have been deemed to be so pernicious as to be illegal per se are group boycotts and concerted refusals to deal. [case citations omitted]. The term "concerted refusal to deal" has been defined as "an agreement by two or more persons not to do business with other individuals, or to do business with them only on specified terms." Note, Concerted Refusals to Deal Under the Antitrust Laws, 71 Harv.L.Rev. 1531

---

[4] It is undisputed that the NFL operates in interstate commerce. It is also recognized that the business of professional football enjoys no special exemption from the antitrust laws. See Radovich v. National Football League, 352 U.S. 445, 77 S.Ct. 390, 1 L.Ed.2d 456 (1957).

(1958). The term "group boycott" generally connotes "a refusal to deal or an inducement of others not to deal or to have business relations with tradesmen." Kalinowski, supra, 11 U.C.L.A.L.Rev. at 580 n. 49. *See also Worthen Bank & Trust Co. v. National BankAmericard Inc., supra,* 485 F.2d at 124-25.

The district court found that the Rozelle Rule operates to significantly deter clubs from negotiating with and signing free agents. By virtue of the Rozelle Rule, a club will sign a free agent only where it is able to reach an agreement with the player's former team as to compensation, or where it is willing to risk the awarding of unknown compensation by the Commissioner. The court concluded that the Rozelle Rule, as enforced, thus constituted a group boycott and a concerted refusal to deal, and was a per se violation of the Sherman Act.

There is substantial evidence in the record to support the district court's findings as to the effects of the Rozelle Rule. We think, however, that this case presents unusual circumstances rendering it inappropriate to declare the Rozelle Rule illegal per se without undertaking an inquiry into the purported justifications for the Rule.

[T]he line of cases which has given rise to per se illegality for the type of agreements involved here generally concerned agreements between business competitors in the traditional sense. *See generally Worthen Bank & Trust Co. v. National BankAmericard Inc., supra.* Here, however, as the owners and Commissioner urge, the NFL assumes some of the characteristics of a joint venture in that each member club has a stake in the success of the other teams. No one club is interested in driving another team out of business, since if the League fails, no one team can survive. See *United States v. National Football League,* 116 F.Supp. 319, 323 (E.D.Pa.1953). Although businessmen cannot wholly evade the antitrust laws by characterizing their operation as a joint venture, we conclude that the unique nature of the business of professional football renders it inappropriate to mechanically apply per se illegality rules here, fashioned in a different context. This is particularly true where, as here, the alleged restraint does not completely eliminate competition for players' services. ****

In view of the foregoing, we think it more appropriate to test the validity of the Rozelle Rule under the Rule of Reason.

Rule of Reason

The focus of an inquiry under the Rule of Reason is whether the restraint imposed is justified by legitimate business purposes, and is no more restrictive than necessary. *See Chicago Board of Trade v. United States, supra; Worthen Bank & Trust Co. v. National BankAmericard Inc., supra.*

In defining the restraint on competition for players' services, the district court found that the Rozelle Rule significantly deters clubs from negotiating with and signing free agents; that it acts as a substantial deterrent to players playing out their options and becoming free agents; that it significantly decreases players' bargaining power in contract negotiations; that players are thus denied the right to sell their services in a free and open market; that as a result, the salaries paid by each club are lower than if competitive bidding were allowed to prevail; and that absent the Rozelle Rule, there would be increased movement in interstate commerce of players from one club to another.

We find substantial evidence in the record to support these findings. Witnesses for both sides testified that there would be increased player movement absent the Rozelle Rule. Two economists testified that elimination of the Rozelle Rule would lead to a substantial increase in player salaries. Carroll Rosenbloom, owner of the Los Angeles Rams, indicated that the Rams would have signed quite a few of the star players from other teams who had played out their options, absent the Rozelle Rule. Charles De Keado, an agent who represented Dick Gordon after he played out his option with the Chicago Bears, testified that the New Orleans Saints were interested in signing Gordon but did not do so because the Bears were demanding unreasonable compensation and the Saints were unwilling to risk an unknown award of compensation by the Commissioner. Jim McFarland, an end who played out his option with the St. Louis Cardinals, testified that he had endeavored to join the Kansas City Chiefs but was unable to do so because of the compensation asked by the Cardinals. Hank Stram, then coach and general manager of the Chiefs, stated that he probably would have given McFarland an opportunity to make his squad had he not been required to give St. Louis anything in return.[5]

---

[5] Among other examples which support Judge Larson's findings are:
Marlin Briscoe indicated that he had to sign a three-year contract with Miami even though he would have preferred a single-year contract. He stated that "they would not accept anything less than a three-year contract because of what they would have to give up. . . ." Alan Page testified that the Rozelle Rule was a hindrance to free player movement, but that the principal effect is on players' salaries. Steven Falk, an attorney for Bob Hayes, testified that Dallas told the Redskins that "they (Dallas)
262

In support of their contention that the restraints effected by the Rozelle Rule are not unreasonable, the defendants asserted a number of justifications. First, they argued that without the Rozelle Rule, star players would flock to cities having natural advantages such as larger economic bases, winning teams, warmer climates, and greater media opportunities; that competitive balance throughout the League would thus be destroyed; and that the destruction of competitive balance would ultimately lead to diminished spectator interest, franchise failures, and perhaps the demise of the NFL, at least as it operates today. Second, the defendants contended that the Rozelle Rule is necessary to protect the clubs' investment in scouting expenses and player developments costs. Third, they asserted that players must work together for a substantial period of time in order to function effectively as a team; that elimination of the Rozelle Rule would lead to increased player movement and a concomitant reduction in player continuity; and that the quality of play in the NFL would thus suffer, leading to reduced spectator interest, and financial detriment both to the clubs and the players. Conflicting evidence was adduced at trial by both sides with respect to the validity of these asserted justifications.

The district court held the defendants' asserted justifications unavailing. As to the clubs' investment in player development costs, Judge Larson found that these expenses are similar to those incurred by other businesses, and that there is no right to compensation for this type of investment. With respect to player continuity, the court found that elimination of the Rozelle Rule would affect all teams equally in that regard; that it would not lead to a reduction in the quality of play; and that even assuming that it would, that fact would not justify the Rozelle Rule's anticompetitive effects. As to competitive balance and the consequences which would flow from abolition of the Rozelle Rule, Judge Larson found that the existence of the Rozelle Rule has had no material effect on competitive balance in the NFL. **** In conclusion the court held that the Rozelle Rule was unreasonable in that it was overly broad, unlimited in duration, unaccompanied by procedural safeguards, and employed in conjunction with other anticompetitive practices such as the draft, Standard Player Contract, option clause, and the no-tampering rules.

We agree that the asserted need to recoup player development costs cannot justify the restraints of the Rozelle Rule. That expense is an ordinary cost of doing business and is not peculiar to professional football. Moreover,

---

were not trading Hayes to anybody within their own division. . . ." William Sullivan president of the Patriots, said he didn't want to sign Joe Kapp, Minnesota's quarterback, and then take a chance on what Minnesota would demand.

because of its unlimited duration, the Rozelle Rule is far more restrictive than necessary to fulfill that need.

We agree, in view of the evidence adduced at trial with respect to existing players turnover by way of trades, retirements and new players entering the League, that the club owners' arguments respecting player continuity cannot justify the Rozelle Rule. We concur in the district court's conclusion that the possibility of resulting decline in the quality of play would not justify the Rozelle Rule. We do recognize, as did the district court, that the NFL has a strong and unique interest in maintaining competitive balance among its teams. The key issue is thus whether the Rozelle Rule is essential to the maintenance of competitive balance, and is no more restrictive than necessary. The district court answered both of these questions in the negative.

We need not decide whether a system of inter-team compensation for free agents moving to other teams is essential to the maintenance of competitive balance in the NFL. Even if it is, we agree with the district court's conclusion that the Rozelle Rule is significantly more restrictive than necessary to serve any legitimate purposes it might have in this regard. First, little concern was manifested at trial over the free movement of average or below average players. Only the movement of the better players was urged as being detrimental to football. Yet the Rozelle Rule applies to every NFL player regardless of his status or ability. Second, the Rozelle Rule is unlimited in duration. It operates as a perpetual restriction on a player's ability to sell his services in an open market throughout his career. Third, the enforcement of the Rozelle Rule is unaccompanied by procedural safeguards. A player has no input into the process by which fair compensation is determined. Moreover, the player may be unaware of the precise compensation demanded by his former team, and that other teams might be interested in him but for the degree of compensation sought.[6]

---

[6] The conclusion that the Rozelle Rule constitutes an unreasonable restraint of trade was reached in Kapp v. National Football League, supra, even without the prolonged inquiry which has been undertaken in this case. The court stated:

> We conclude that such a rule imposing restraint virtually unlimited in time and extent, goes far beyond any possible need for fair protection of the interests of the club-employers or the purposes of the NFL and that it imposes upon the player-employees such undue hardship as to be an unreasonable restraint and such a rule is not susceptible of different inferences concerning its reasonableness; it is unreasonable under any legal test and there is no genuine issue about it to require or justify trial. 390 F.Supp. at 82.

264

Judge Frank emphasized the harshness of a rule in the field of professional baseball similar to the Rozelle Rule:

> As one court, perhaps a bit exaggeratedly, has put it, "While the services of these baseball players are ostensibly secured by voluntary contracts a study of the system as * * * practiced under the plan of the National Agreement, reveals the involuntary character of the servitude which is imposed upon players by the strength of the combination controlling the labor of practically all of the players in the country. * * * " (I)f the players be regarded as quasi-peons, it is of no moment that they are well paid; only the totalitarian-minded will believe that high pay excuses virtual slavery. Gardella v. Chandler, 172 F.2d 402, 410 (2nd Cir. 1949).

In sum, we hold that the Rozelle Rule, as enforced, unreasonably restrains trade in violation of s 1 of the Sherman Act.

\*\*\*

CONCLUSION

In conclusion, although we find that non-labor parties may potentially avail themselves of the nonstatutory labor exemption where they are parties to collective bargaining agreements pertaining to mandatory subjects of bargaining, the exemption cannot be invoked where, as here, the agreement was not the product of bona fide arm's-length negotiations. Thus, the defendants' enforcement of the Rozelle Rule is not exempt from the coverage of the antitrust laws. Although we disagree with the district court's determination that the Rozelle Rule is a per se violation of the antitrust laws, we do find that the Rule, as implemented, contravenes the Rule of Reason and thus constitutes an unreasonable restraint of trade in violation of s 1 of the Sherman Act.

\*\*\*\*

With the exception of the district court's finding that implementation of the Rozelle Rule constitutes a per se violation of s 1 of the Sherman Act and except as it is otherwise modified herein, the judgment of the district court is AFFIRMED. The cause is remanded to the district court for further proceedings consistent with this opinion.

Photo reprinted with permission by Topps

**Notes & Questions**

1. What is the significance of the fact that the court finds "substantial evidence to support the finding that there was no bona fide arm's-length bargaining over the Rozelle Rule"?

2. A five-time Pro Bowl choice and member of two Super Bowl teams (one winner), Mackey was voted the Tight End on the NFL's 50th Anniversary Team in 1969. In Super Bowl V on January 17, 1971, he caught a pass from Johnny Unitas and scored on (at the time) a controversial 75-yard touchdown pass. The Colts won that game 16-13. In 1992, Mackey became the first pure tight end to be inducted into the Pro Football Hall of Fame.

# Norman Law v. National Collegiate Athletic Association
## 134 F 3d 1010 (1998)
### United States Court of Appeals, Tenth Circuit.

EBEL, Circuit Judge.

Defendant-Appellant the National Collegiate Athletic Association ("NCAA") promulgated a rule limiting annual compensation of certain Division I entry-level coaches to $16,000. Basketball coaches affected by the rule filed a class action challenging the restriction under Section 1 of the Sherman Antitrust Act. The district court granted summary judgment on the issue of liability to the coaches and issued a permanent injunction restraining the NCAA from promulgating this or any other rules embodying similar compensation restrictions. The NCAA now appeals, and we affirm.

## I. Background

The NCAA is a voluntary unincorporated association of approximately 1,100 educational institutions.[1] The association coordinates the intercollegiate athletic programs of its members by adopting and promulgating playing rules, standards of amateurism, standards for academic eligibility, regulations concerning recruitment of student athletes, rules governing the size of athletic squads and coaching staffs, and the like. The NCAA aims to "promote opportunity for equity in competition to assure that individual student-athletes and institutions will not be prevented unfairly from achieving the benefits inherent in participation in intercollegiate athletics."

The NCAA classifies sports programs into separate divisions to reflect differences in program size and scope. NCAA Division I basketball programs are generally of a higher stature and have more visibility than Division II and III basketball programs. Over 300 schools play in Division I, and each Division I member hires and employs its own basketball coaches.

During the 1980s, the NCAA became concerned over the steadily rising costs of maintaining competitive athletic programs, especially in light of the requirements imposed by Title IX of the 1972 Education Amendments Act to increase support for women's athletic programs. The NCAA observed that some college presidents had to close academic departments,

---

[1] Because this appeal stems from the grant of a motion for summary judgment, we review the facts taken in the light most favorable to the NCAA, the non-moving party. *See Kaul v. Stephan,* 83 F.3d 1208, 1212 (10th Cir.1996).

fire tenured faculty, and reduce the number of sports offered to students due to economic constraints. At the same time, many institutions felt pressure to "keep up with the Joneses" by increasing spending on recruiting talented players and coaches and on other aspects of their sports programs in order to remain competitive with rival schools. In addition, a report commissioned by the NCAA known as the "Raiborn Report" found that in 1985 42% of NCAA Division I schools reported deficits in their overall athletic program budgets, with the deficit averaging $824,000 per school. The Raiborn Report noted that athletic expenses at all Division I institutions rose more than 100% over the eight-year period from 1978 to 1985. Finally, the Report stated that 51% of Division I schools responding to NCAA inquiries on the subject suffered a net loss in their basketball programs alone that averaged $145,000 per school.

Part of the problem identified by the NCAA involved the costs associated with part-time assistant coaches. The NCAA allowed Division I basketball teams to employ three full-time coaches, including one head coach and two assistant coaches, and two part-time coaches. The part-time positions could be filled by part-time assistants, graduate assistants, or volunteer coaches. The NCAA imposed salary restrictions on all of the part-time positions. A volunteer coach could not receive any compensation from a member institution's athletic department. A graduate assistant coach was required to be enrolled in a graduate studies program of a member institution and could only receive compensation equal to the value of the cost of the educational experience (grant-in-aid) depending on the coach's residential status (*i.e.* a non-resident graduate assistant coach could receive greater compensation to reflect the higher cost of out-state tuition than could an in-state student). The NCAA limited compensation to part-time assistants to the value of full grant-in-aid compensation based on the value of out-of-state graduate studies.

Despite the salary caps, many of these part-time coaches earned $60,000 or $70,000 per year. Athletic departments circumvented the compensation limits by employing these part-time coaches in lucrative summer jobs at profitable sports camps run by the school or by hiring them for part-time jobs in the physical education department in addition to the coaching position. Further, many of these positions were filled with seasoned and experienced coaches, not the type of student assistant envisioned by the rule.

In January of 1989, the NCAA established a Cost Reduction Committee (the "Committee") to consider means and strategies for reducing the costs of intercollegiate athletics "without disturbing the competitive balance" among NCAA member institutions. The Committee included financial aid personnel, inter-collegiate athletic administrators, college presidents, university faculty members, and a university chancellor. In his initial letter to Committee members, the Chairman of the Committee thanked participants for joining "this gigantic attempt to save intercollegiate athletics from itself." It was felt that only a collaborative effort could reduce costs effectively while maintaining a level playing field because individual schools could not afford to make unilateral spending cuts in sports programs for fear that doing so would unduly hamstring that school's ability to compete against other institutions that spent more money on athletics. In January of 1990, the Chairman told NCAA members that the goal of the Committee was to "cut costs and save money." It became the consensus of the Committee that reducing the total number of coaching positions would reduce the cost of intercollegiate athletic programs.

The Committee proposed an array of recommendations to amend the NCAA's bylaws, including proposed Bylaw 11.6.4 that would limit Division I basketball coaching staffs to four members--one head coach, two assistant coaches, and one entry-level coach called a "restricted-earnings coach". The restricted-earnings coach category was created to replace the positions of part-time assistant, graduate assistant, and volunteer coach. The Committee believed that doing so would resolve the inequity that existed between those schools with graduate programs that could hire graduate assistant coaches and those who could not while reducing the overall amount spent on coaching salaries.

A second proposed rule, Bylaw 11.02.3, restricted compensation of restricted-earnings coaches in all Division I sports other than football to a total of $12,000 for the academic year and $4,000 for the summer months (the "REC Rule" for restricted-earnings coaches). The Committee determined that the $16,000 per year total figure approximated the cost of out-of-state tuition for graduate schools at public institutions and the average graduate school tuition at private institutions, and was thus roughly equivalent to the salaries previously paid to part-time graduate assistant coaches. The REC Rule did allow restricted-earnings coaches to receive additional compensation for performing duties for another department of the institution provided that (1) such compensation is commensurate with that received by others performing the same or similar assignments, (2) the ratio of compensation received for coaching duties and any other duties is directly proportional to the amount of time devoted to the two areas of assignment, and (3) the individual is qualified for and actually performs the duties outside the athletic department for which the individual is compensated. The REC Rule did not prevent member institutions from using savings gained by reducing the number and salary of basketball coaches to increase expenditures on other aspects of their athletic programs.

\*\*\*\*

The NCAA adopted the proposed rules, including the REC Rule, by majority vote in January of 1991, and the rules became effective on August 1, 1992.[2] The rules bind all Division I members of the NCAA that employ basketball coaches. The schools normally compete with each other in the labor market for coaching services.

In this case, plaintiffs-appellees were restricted-earnings men's basketball coaches at NCAA Division I institutions in the academic year 1992-93. They challenged the REC Rule's limitation on compensation under section 1 of the Sherman Antitrust Act, 15 U.S.C. § 1 (1990), as an unlawful "contract, combination ... or conspiracy, in restraint of trade."

The district court addressed the issue of liability before addressing issues of class certification and damages. [T]he court found the NCAA liable for violating section 1. \*\*\*\* On January 5, 1996, the district court, pursuant to 15 U.S.C. § 26, permanently enjoined the NCAA from enforcing or attempting to enforce any restricted-earnings coach salary limitations against the named plaintiffs, and it further enjoined the NCAA from "reenacting the compensation limitations embodied in [the REC Rule]." The NCAA appeals the permanent injunction.

### III. Rule of Reason Analysis

Section 1 of the Sherman Act provides, "Every contract, combination in the form of trust or otherwise, or conspiracy, in restraint of trade or commerce among the several States, or with foreign nations, is hereby declared to be illegal." 15 U.S.C. § 1. Because nearly every contract that binds the parties to an agreed course of conduct "is a restraint of trade" of some sort, the Supreme Court has limited the restrictions contained in section

---

[2] Other cost-saving measures were adopted that, *inter alia,* limited:
* the number of coaches who could recruit off campus.
* off-campus contacts with prospective student-athletes.
* visits by prospective student-athletes.
* printed recruiting materials.
* the number of practices before the first scheduled game.
* the number of games and duration of seasons.
* team travel and training table meals.
* financial aid grants to student-athletes.

270

1 to bar only "unreasonable restraints of trade." *NCAA v. Board of Regents,* 468 U.S. 85, 98, 104 S.Ct. 2948, 2959, 82 L.Ed.2d 70 (1984); *see also Standard Oil Co. v. United States,* 221 U.S. 1, 52-60, 31 S.Ct. 502, 512-16, 55 L.Ed. 619 (1911). To prevail on a section 1 claim under the Sherman Act, the coaches needed to prove that the NCAA (1) participated in an agreement that (2) unreasonably restrained trade in the relevant market. *See Reazin v. Blue Cross & Blue Shield of Kan., Inc.,* 899 F.2d 951, 959 (10th Cir.1990). The NCAA does not dispute that the REC Rule resulted from an agreement among its members. However, the NCAA does contest the district court's finding...that the REC Rule is an unreasonable restraint of trade.

Two analytical approaches are used to determine whether a defendant's conduct unreasonably restrains trade: the *per se* rule and the rule of reason. *See SCFC ILC, Inc. v. Visa USA, Inc.,* 36 F.3d 958, 963 (10th Cir.1994). The *per se* rule condemns practices that "are entirely void of redeeming competitive rationales." *Id.* Once a practice is identified as illegal *per se,* a court need not examine the practice's impact on the market or the procompetitive justifications for the practice advanced by a defendant before finding a violation of antitrust law. Rule of reason analysis, on the other hand, requires an analysis of the restraint's effect on competition. *See National Soc'y of Prof'l Engineers v. United States,* 435 U.S. 679, 695, 98 S.Ct. 1355, 1367, 55 L.Ed.2d 637 (1978). A rule of reason analysis first requires a determination of whether the challenged restraint has a substantially adverse effect on competition. *See SCFC,* 36 F.3d at 965; *United States v. Brown Univ.,* 5 F.3d 658, 668 (3d Cir.1993). The inquiry then shifts to an evaluation of whether the procompetitive virtues of the alleged wrongful conduct justifies the otherwise anticompetitive impacts. *See Brown Univ.,* 5 F.3d at 669. The district court applied the rule of reason standard to its analysis of the REC Rule.

Horizontal price-fixing is normally a practice condemned as illegal *per se. See FTC v. Superior Court Trial Lawyers Ass'n,* 493 U.S. 411, 436 n. 19, 110 S.Ct. 768, 782 n. 19, 107 L.Ed.2d 851 (1990) ("horizontal price-fixing ... has been consistently analyzed as a *per se* violation for many decades"); *United States v. Socony-Vacuum Oil Co.,* 310 U.S. 150, 223, 60 S.Ct. 811, 844, 84 L.Ed. 1129 (1940). By agreeing to limit the price which NCAA members may pay for the services of restricted-earnings coaches, the REC Rule fixes the cost of one of the component items used by NCAA members to produce the product of Division I basketball. As a result, the REC Rule constitutes the type of naked horizontal agreement among competitive purchasers to fix prices usually found to be illegal *per se.* ****

However, the Supreme Court recognized in *Broadcast Music, Inc. v. Columbia Broadcasting Sys., Inc.,* 441 U.S. 1, 23, 99 S.Ct. 1551, 1564, 60 L.Ed.2d 1 (1979), that certain products require horizontal restraints, including horizontal price-fixing, in order to exist at all. Faced with such a product--the ASCAP blanket music license which could not exist absent an agreement among artists to sell their rights at uniform prices--the Court held that a rule of reason analysis should be applied to the restraint. *Id.* at 24, 99 S.Ct. at 1564-65.

Subsequently, the Supreme Court in *NCAA v. Board of Regents* departed from the general treatment given to horizontal price-fixing agreements by refusing to apply a *per se* rule and instead adopting a rule of reason approach in reviewing an NCAA plan for televising college football that involved both limits on output and price-fixing. *See* 468 U.S. at 99-103, 104 S.Ct. at 2959-61. The Court explained:

> Horizontal price fixing and output limitation are ordinarily condemned as a matter of law under an "illegal *per se* " approach because the probability that these practices are anticompetitive is so high; a *per se* rule is applied "when the practice facially appears to be one that would always or almost always tend to restrict competition and decrease output." In such circumstances a restraint is presumed unreasonable without inquiry into the particular market context in which it is found. Nevertheless, we have decided that it would be inappropriate to apply a *per se* rule to this case. This decision is not based on a lack of judicial experience with this type of arrangement, on the fact that the NCAA is organized as a nonprofit entity, or on our respect for the NCAA's historic role in the preservation and encouragement of intercollegiate amateur athletics. *Rather, what is critical is that this case involves an industry in which horizontal restraints on competition are essential if the product is to be available at all.* 468 U.S. at 100-101, 104 S.Ct. at 2959-60 (quoting *Broadcast Music,* 441 U.S. at 19-20, 99 S.Ct. at 1562-63) (footnotes omitted and emphasis added).

The "product" made available by the NCAA in this case is college basketball; the horizontal restraints necessary for the product to exist include rules such as those forbidding payments to athletes and those requiring that athletes attend class, etc. *See id.* at 101-02, 104 S.Ct. at 2960- 61 (what a sports league and its members "market ... is competition itself.... Of course, this would be completely ineffective if there were no rules ... to create and define the competition to be marketed."). Because some horizontal restraints serve the procompetitive purpose of making college sports available, the Supreme Court subjected even the price and output restrictions at issue in *Board of Regents* to a rule of reason analysis. *See id.* at 103, 104 S.Ct. at 2961; *see also Hairston v. Pacific 10 Conference,* 101 F.3d 1315, 1318-19 (9th Cir.1996) (employing rule of reason analysis and finding that imposing sanctions for violations of NCAA rules did not violate section 1 of the Sherman Act); *Banks v. NCAA,* 977 F.2d 1081, 1088-94 (7th Cir.1992) (upholding no-draft and no-agent eligibility rules for student athletes under rule of reason analysis); *Justice v. NCAA,* 577 F.Supp. 356, 379-82 (D.Ariz.1983) (NCAA sanctions against member institution imposed for violations of NCAA rule barring compensation of student athletes did not violate antitrust laws under rule of reason analysis).

Other courts also have applied a rule of reason analysis to sports league rules, *see* I ABA Section of Antitrust Law, *Antitrust Law Developments* 115-16 (4th ed.1997) (citing cases), including restraints otherwise given *per se* treatment, *see, e.g., M & H Tire Co., Inc. v. Hoosier Racing Tire Corp.,* 733 F.2d 973, 980 (1st Cir.1984) (applying rule of reason standard to a rule requiring all auto racing competitors to use the same tire and stating that "in the sports area various agreed-upon procedures may be essential to survival"). *See also* Phillip E. Areeda, *Antitrust Law* ¶ 1478d, at 359 (1986) (noting that courts "have not woodenly applied the *per se* prohibitions developed for ordinary business situations" to sports leagues).

[In addition], the Supreme Court has made it clear that the *per se* rule is a "demanding" standard that should be applied only in clear cut cases. *See Continental T.V., Inc. v. GTE Sylvania Inc.,* 433 U.S. 36, 50, 97 S.Ct. 2549, 2557-58, 53 L.Ed.2d 568 (1977). As a result, courts consistently have analyzed challenged conduct under the rule of reason when dealing with an industry in which some horizontal restraints are necessary for the availability of a product, even if such restraints involve horizontal price-fixing agreements. *See* I ABA Section of Antitrust Law, *supra,* at 49 (citing cases). Thus, we apply the rule of reason approach in this case.

[9] Courts have imposed a consistent structure on rule of reason analysis by casting it in terms of shifting burdens of proof. *See* I ABA Section of Antitrust Law, *supra,* at 53 (citing cases). Under this approach, the plaintiff bears the initial burden of showing that an agreement had a substantially adverse effect on competition. [citations omitted]. If the plaintiff meets this burden, the burden shifts to the defendant to come forward with evidence of the procompetitive virtues of the alleged wrongful

conduct. [citations omitted]. If the defendant is able to demonstrate procompetitive effects, the plaintiff then must prove that the challenged conduct is not reasonably necessary to achieve the legitimate objectives or that those objectives can be achieved in a substantially less restrictive manner. [citations omitted]. Ultimately, if these steps are met, the harms and benefits must be weighed against each other in order to judge whether the challenged behavior is, on balance, reasonable.

[The court determined that there was a substantially adverse effect on competition and then turns to consider the pro-competitive aspects of the NCAA rule]

## B. Procompetitive Rationales

[15] Under a rule of reason analysis, an agreement to restrain trade may still survive scrutiny under section 1 if the procompetitive benefits of the restraint justify the anticompetitive effects. *See Clorox,* 117 F.3d at 56; *Hairston,* 101 F.3d at 1319; *Orson,* 79 F.3d at 1368; *Brown Univ.,* 5 F.3d at 669; *see also* I ABA Section of Antitrust Law, *supra,* at 53, 66. Justifications offered under the rule of reason may be considered only to the extent that they tend to show that, on balance, "the challenged restraint enhances competition." *Board of Regents,* 468 U.S. at 104, 104 S.Ct. at 2961.

In *Board of Regents* the Supreme Court recognized that certain horizontal restraints, such as the conditions of the contest and the eligibility of participants, are justifiable under the antitrust laws because they are necessary to create the product of competitive college sports. *Id.* at 117, 104 S.Ct. at 2968-69. Thus, the only legitimate rationales that we will recognize in support of the REC Rule are those necessary to produce competitive intercollegiate sports. The NCAA advanced three justifications for the salary limits: retaining entry-level coaching positions; reducing costs; and maintaining competitive equity. We address each of them in turn.

### 1. Retention of Entry-Level Positions

The NCAA argues that the plan serves the procompetitive goal of retaining an entry-level coaching position. The NCAA asserts that the plan will allow younger, less experienced coaches entry into Division I coaching positions. While opening up coaching positions for younger people may have social value apart from its affect on competition, we may not consider such values unless they impact upon competition. [citations omitted].

274

The NCAA also contends that limiting one of the four available coaching positions on a Division I basketball team to an entry level position will create more balanced competition by barring some teams from hiring four experienced coaches instead of three. However, the REC Rule contained no restrictions other than salary designed to insure that the position would be filled by entry-level applicants; it could be filled with experienced applicants. In addition, under the REC Rule, schools can still pay restricted-earnings coaches more than $16,000 per year by hiring them for physical education or other teaching positions. In fact, the evidence in the record tends to demonstrate that at least some schools designated persons with many years of experience as the restricted-earnings coach. The NCAA did not present any evidence showing that restricted-earnings positions have been filled by entry-level applicants or that the rules will be effective over time in accomplishing this goal. Nothing in the record suggests that the salary limits for restricted-earnings coaches will be effective at creating entry-level positions. Thus, the NCAA failed to present a triable issue of fact as to whether preserving entry-level positions served a legitimate procompetitive end of balancing competition.

## 2. Cost Reduction

The NCAA next advances the justification that the plan will cut costs. However, cost-cutting by itself is not a valid procompetitive justification. If it were, any group of competing buyers could agree on maximum prices. Lower prices cannot justify a cartel's control of prices charged by suppliers, because the cartel ultimately robs the suppliers of the normal fruits of their enterprises. Further, setting maximum prices reduces the incentive among suppliers to improve their products. Likewise, in our case, coaches have less incentive to improve their performance if their salaries are capped. As the Supreme Court reiterated in *Superior Court Trial Lawyers,* 493 U.S. at 423, 110 S.Ct. at 775, "the Sherman Act reflects a legislative judgment that ultimately competition will produce not only lower prices, but also better goods and services ... This judgment recognizes that all elements of a bargain--quality, service, safety, and durability--and not just the immediate cost, are favorably affected by the free opportunity to select among alternative offers." (internal quotations omitted).

The NCAA adopted the REC Rule because without it competition would lead to higher prices. The REC Rule was proposed as a way to prevent Division I schools from engaging in behavior the association termed "keeping up with the Joneses," *i.e.*, competing. However, the NCAA cannot argue that competition for coaches is an evil because the Sherman Act "precludes inquiry into the question whether competition is good or bad." *National Soc'y of Prof'l Engineers,* 435 U.S. at 695, 98 S.Ct. at 1367.

While increasing output, creating operating efficiencies, making a new product available, enhancing product or service quality, and widening consumer choice have been accepted by courts as justifications for otherwise anticompetitive agreements, mere profitability or cost savings have not qualified as a defense under the antitrust laws. The NCAA's cost containment justification is illegitimate because the NCAA:

> [I]mproperly assumes that antitrust law should not apply to condemn the creation of market power in an input market. The exercise of market power by a group of buyers virtually always results in lower costs to the buyers--a consequence which arguably is beneficial to the members of the industry and ultimately their consumers. If holding down costs by the exercise of market power over suppliers, rather than just by increased efficiency, is a procompetitive effect justifying joint conduct, then section 1 can never apply to input markets or buyer cartels. That is not and cannot be the law. Roberts, *supra,* at 2643.

Reducing costs for member institutions, without more, does not justify the anticompetitive effects of the REC Rule.

\*\*\*\*

### 3. Maintaining Competitiveness

We note that the NCAA must be able to ensure some competitive equity between member institutions in order to produce a marketable product: a "team must try to establish itself as a winner, but it must not win so often and so convincingly that the outcome will never be in doubt, or else there will be no marketable 'competition.' " Michael Jay Kaplan, Annotation, *Application of Federal Antitrust Laws to Professional Sports,* 18 A.L.R. Fed. 489 § 2(a) (1974). The NCAA asserts that the REC Rule will help to maintain competitive equity by preventing wealthier schools from placing a more experienced, higher-priced coach in the position of restricted-earnings coach. \*\*\*

While the REC Rule will equalize the salaries paid to entry-level coaches in Division I schools, it is not clear that the REC Rule will equalize

276

the experience level of such coaches.[3] Nowhere does the NCAA prove that the salary restrictions enhance competition, level an uneven playing field, or reduce coaching inequities. Rather, the NCAA only presented evidence that the cost reductions would be achieved in such a way so as to maintain without "significantly altering," "adversely affecting," or "disturbing" the existing competitive balance. The undisputed record reveals that the REC Rule is nothing more than a cost-cutting measure and shows that the only consideration the NCAA gave to competitive balance was simply to structure the rule so as not to exacerbate competitive imbalance. Thus, on its face, the REC Rule is not directed towards competitive balance nor is the nexus between the rule and a compelling need to maintain competitive balance sufficiently clear on this record to withstand a motion for summary judgment.[4]

## IV. Conclusion

For the reasons discussed above, we AFFIRM the district court's order granting a permanent injunction barring the NCAA from reenacting compensation limits such as those contained in the REC Rule based on its order granting summary judgment to the plaintiffs on the issue of antitrust liability.

---

[3] For example, some more-experienced coaches may take restricted-earnings coach positions with programs such as those at Duke or North Carolina, despite the lower salary, because of the national prominence of those programs. In fact, absent the REC Rule, the market might produce greater equity in coaching talent, because a school with a less-prominent basketball program might be able to entice a more-experienced coach away from a prominent program by offering a higher salary.

[4] Because we hold that the NCAA did not establish evidence of sufficient procompetitive benefits, we need not address question of whether the plaintiffs were able to show that comparable procompetitive benefits could be achieved through viable, less anticompetitive means. See I ABA Section of Antitrust Law, *supra,* at 66 (collecting cases); Areeda, *supra,* ¶ 1502, at 372 (if the defendant proves procompetitive justifications, the plaintiff must demonstrate that less restrictive means could have been used to achieve the same results to prevail under the rule of reason analysis).

277

**Notes & Questions**

1. Explain the difference between the "per se rule" and the "rule of reason."

2. Explain the difference between the "statutory labor exemption" and the "nonstatutory labor exemption."

3. Explain the significance of collective bargaining agreements and "wages, hours, and other terms and conditions of employment" to the nonstatutory labor exemption.

4. In terms of legal principles, describe the similarities and differences between *Mackey* and *Law v. NCAA*.

5. As a result of the legal rules articulated in Sherman § 1, some emerging sports businesses such as the WNBA and MLS have adopted a "single entity" corporate structure, on the theory that, if all of the league's teams are part of the same corporate entity, then, by definition, there can be no contract, combination, or conspiracy since only one corporate entity is involved.

6. In the case *NHLPA v Plymouth Whalers Hockey Club*, 419 F.3d 462 (6th Cir. 2005) the Sixth Circuit addressed a unique antitrust issue, the little known Van Ryn rule. The OHL, or Ontario Hockey League, consists of 20 teams with players aged 16 to 20. The league is a major source of players for the NHL entry draft. OHL eligibility permits each team to carry only three 20 year olds. Also, no player can be signed by an OHL team unless he was previously on a CHA, Canadian Hockey Association or USA Hockey Player's Registration the previous season. However, the NCAA does not permit players holding either registration to play for an NCAA team. Combining these rules prevents the OHL from signing any 20 year old NCAA players. This rule is often referred to as the Van Ryn rule. Mike Van Ryn was a University of Michigan hockey player, and was drafted by the New Jersey Devils NHL Team in 1998. In doing this, the Devils obtained the rights to him for one year, and at that point, if the Devils failed to sign him, he would become an unrestricted free agent. Under the terms of the Collective Bargaining Agreement, those rights could be extended only if Van Ryn remained in NCAA competition or went to play for a non-affiliated hockey league. Van Ryn did remain in NCAA competition for one year following the draft, which extended the Devil's rights to him. He then signed with an OHL club, and because the OHL is affiliated with the NHL, the Devil's rights to him were not extended. He then became a free agent and

signed with the NHL's St. Louis Blues in 2000. Had he not played for the OHL team, his only route to free agency would have been to sit the season out. Thus, the Van Ryn rule was adopted by the OHL. The OHL argues the rule gives those who have been playing for their league the advantage, while opponents argue it is to prevent NCAA players from becoming free agents. The Plaintiffs claim that this rule is anti-competitive, in violation of the Sherman Antitrust rule. However, the court determined that their argument fails. The Court explained factors to consider when weighing circumstantial evidence of a conspiracy claim: 1) whether the defendant's actions, if taken independently, would be contrary to their economic self interest; 2) whether the defendants have been uniform in their actions; 3) whether the defendants have exchanged or had the opportunity to exchange information relative to the alleged conspiracy; and, 4) whether defendants have a common motive to conspire. The court found that under this standard, there was no conspiracy. It should also be kept in mind that, as the court acknowledged, the circumstances may change with the new collective bargaining agreement.

## B. Further Considerations

### O. Leon Wood v. National Basketball Association
809 F. 2d 954 (1987)
United States Court of Appeals, Second Circuit

WINTER, Circuit Judge:

O. Leon Wood, an accomplished point-guard from California State University at Fullerton and a member of the gold medal-winning 1984 United States Olympic basketball team, appeals from Judge Carter's dismissal of his antitrust action challenging certain provisions of a collective bargaining agreement between the National Basketball Association ("NBA"), its member-teams, and the National Basketball Players Association ("NBPA"). Wood contends that the "salary cap," [and]...college draft...violate Section 1 of the Sherman Act, 15 U.S.C. § 1 (1982), and are not exempt from the Sherman Act by reason of the non-statutory "labor exemption." We disagree and affirm.

The challenged provisions are in part the result of the settlement of an earlier antitrust action brought by players against the NBA. *Robertson v. National Basketball Ass'n,* 72 F.R.D. 64 (S.D.N.Y.1976), *aff'd,* 556 F.2d 682 (2d Cir.1977). In that case, a class consisting of all NBA players challenged both the merger of the NBA with the now-defunct American Basketball Association and certain NBA employment practices, including the college draft system by which teams obtain the exclusive right to negotiate with particular college players. Following extensive pre-trial proceedings, *see Robertson v. National Basketball Ass'n,* 413 F.Supp. 88 (S.D.N.Y.1976); 67 F.R.D. 691 (S.D.N.Y.1975); 389 F.Supp. 867 (S.D.N.Y.1975), the parties settled the case on April 29, 1976. The Settlement Agreement provided for the payment of $4.3 million to the class and for substantial modification of the practices attacked by the plaintiffs.

The Settlement Agreement is effective through the 1986-87 season. It modified the college draft system by limiting to one year the period during which a team has exclusive rights to negotiate with and sign its draftees. If a draftee remains unsigned at the time of the next year's draft, he may re-enter the draft. Most important, the Settlement Agreement instituted a system of free agency allowing veteran players to sell their services to the highest bidder subject only to their current team's right of first refusal that allows it to match the best offer.

On October 10, 1980, the NBA and NBPA signed a collective bargaining agreement that incorporated the provisions of the Settlement Agreement pertinent to this action. The 1980 collective agreement expired on June 1, 1982, however, and the 1982-83 season began before a new agreement had been reached. Negotiations between the NBA and the NBPA continued and centered on the league's insistence upon controls on the growth in players' salaries. The NBA claimed that increases in players' salaries resulting from free agency were in part responsible for mounting losses and that a number of its teams might face bankruptcy absent some stabilization of expenses. The NBPA, after reviewing the teams' financial data, reached an agreement in principle with the NBA on March 31, 1983, some 48 hours before a strike deadline set by the players. This agreement was memorialized in writing on April 18, 1983, in a Memorandum of Understanding (the "Memorandum").

The Memorandum continued the college draft and free agency/first refusal provisions of the earlier agreements and, like those agreements, included provisions for fringe benefits such as pensions and medical and life insurance. However, the Memorandum also established a minimum for individual salaries and a minimum and maximum for aggregate team salaries. The latter are styled the salary cap provisions, even though they establish a floor as well as a ceiling. Under the salary cap, a team that has reached its maximum allowable team salary may sign a first-round draft choice like Wood only to a one-year contract for $75,000. An integral part of the method by which the floor and ceiling on aggregate team salaries were to be determined was a guarantee that the players would receive 53 percent of the NBA's gross revenues, including new revenues, in salaries and benefits. This combination of fringe benefits, draft, free agency, a floor and a ceiling on aggregate team salaries, and guaranteed revenue sharing was unique in professional sports negotiations.

\*\*\*\*

The Philadelphia 76ers drafted Wood in the first round of the 1984 college draft. At the time of the draft, the 76ers' team payroll exceeded the amount permitted under the salary cap. The 76ers therefore tendered to Wood a one-year $75,000 contract, the amount stipulated under the salary cap. This offer was a formality, however, necessary to preserve its exclusive rights to sign him. In fact, the team informed Wood's agent of its intention to adjust its roster so as to enable it to negotiate a long-term contract with Wood for substantially more money. Wood understandably did not sign the proffered contract.

On September 13, 1984, he turned from the basketball court to the district court and sought a preliminary injunction restraining enforcement of the agreement between the NBA and NBPA and compelling teams other than the 76ers to cease their refusal to deal with him except on the terms set out in the collective bargaining agreement and Memorandum.

Judge Carter denied Wood's motion. *Wood v. National Basketball Ass'n,* 602 F.Supp. 525 (S.D.N.Y.1984). He found that both the salary cap and college draft provisions

> affect only the parties to the collective bargaining agreement--the NBA and the players--involve mandatory subjects of bargaining as defined by federal labor laws, and are the result of bona fide arms-length negotiations. Both are proper subjects of concern by the Players Association. As such these provisions come under the protective shield of our national labor policy and are exempt from the reach of the Sherman Act. *Id.* at 528.

\*\*\*\*

Meanwhile, Wood signed a contract with the 76ers that provided for $1.02 million in total compensation over a four-year period, including a $135,000 signing bonus. Wood has since been traded.

In January 1986, the parties made an evidentiary submission to Judge Carter for a decision on the merits. This consisted of papers submitted with the motion for a preliminary injunction and a stipulation of additional facts. On February 5, 1986, Judge Carter granted judgment to the defendants. This appeal followed.

## DISCUSSION

Plaintiff views the salary cap…[and] college draft…as an agreement among horizontal competitors, the NBA teams, to eliminate competition for the services of college basketball players. As such, he claims, they constitute *per se* violations of Section 1 of the Sherman Act.

**** We may assume for purposes of this decision that the individual NBA teams and not the league are the relevant employers and that Wood would obtain considerably more favorable employment terms were the draft and salary cap eliminated so as to allow him to offer his services to the highest bidder among NBA teams. We may further assume that were these arrangements agreed upon by the NBA teams in the absence of a collective bargaining relationship with a union representing the players, they would be illegal and plaintiff would be entitled to relief.

The draft and salary cap are not, however, the product solely of an agreement among horizontal competitors but are embodied in a collective agreement between an employer or employers and a labor organization reached through procedures mandated by federal labor legislation. ****

Although the combination of the college draft and salary cap may seem unique in collective bargaining (as are the team salary floor and 53 percent revenue sharing agreement), the uniqueness is strictly a matter of appearance. The nature of professional sports as a business and professional sports teams as employers calls for contractual arrangements suited to that unusual commercial context. However, these arrangements result from the same federally mandated processes as do collective agreements in the more familiar industrial context. Moreover, examination of the particular arrangements arrived at by the NBA and NBPA discloses that they have functionally identical, and identically anticompetitive, counterparts that are routinely included in industrial collective agreements.

Among the fundamental principles of federal labor policy is the legal rule that employees may eliminate competition among themselves through a governmentally supervised majority vote selecting an exclusive bargaining representative. Section 9(a) of the National Labor Relations Act explicitly provides that "[r]epresentatives ... selected ... by the majority of the employees in a unit ... shall be the exclusive representatives of all the employees in such unit for the purposes of collective bargaining." 29 U.S.C. § 159(a). Federal labor policy thus allows employees to seek the best deal for the greatest number by the exercise of collective rather than individual bargaining power. Once an exclusive representative has been selected, the individual employee is forbidden by federal law from negotiating directly with the employer absent the representative's consent, *NLRB v. Allis-Chalmers Mfg. Co.*, 388 U.S. 175, 180, 87 S.Ct. 2001, 2006, 18 L.Ed.2d 1123 (1967), even though that employee may actually receive less compensation under the collective bargain than he or she would through individual negotiations. *J.I. Case Co. v. NLRB,* 321 U.S. 332, 338-39, 64 S.Ct. 576, 580-81, 88 L.Ed. 762 (1944).

The gravamen of Wood's complaint, namely that the NBA-NBPA collective agreement is illegal because it prevents him from achieving his full free market value, is therefore at odds with, and destructive of, federal labor policy. It is true that the diversity of talent and specialization among professional athletes and the widespread exposure and discussions of their "work" in the media make the differences in value among them as "workers" more visible than the differences in efficiency and in value among industrial workers. High public visibility, however, is no reason to ignore federal legislation that explicitly prevents employees, whether in or out of a bargaining unit, from seeking a better deal where that deal is inconsistent with the terms of a collective agreement.

****

Wood further attacks the draft and salary cap as disadvantaging new employees. However, newcomers in the industrial context routinely find themselves disadvantaged vis-a-vis those already hired. A collective agreement may thus provide that salaries, layoffs, and promotions be governed by seniority, *Ford Motor Co. v. Huffman,* 345 U.S. at 337-39, 73 S.Ct. at 685-87, even though some individuals with less seniority would fare better if allowed to negotiate individually.

Finally, Wood argues that the draft and salary cap are illegal because they affect employees outside the bargaining unit. However, that is also a commonplace consequence of collective agreements. Seniority clauses may thus prevent outsiders from bidding for particular jobs, and other provisions may regulate the allocation or subcontracting of work to other groups of workers. *See Fibreboard Paper Products Corp. v. NLRB,* 379 U.S. 203, 210-

15, 85 S.Ct. 398, 402-05, 13 L.Ed.2d 233 (1964). Indeed, the National Labor Relations Act explicitly defines "employee" in a way that includes workers outside the bargaining unit. 29 U.S.C. § 152(3).[1]

If Wood's antitrust claim were to succeed, all of these commonplace arrangements would be subject to similar challenges, and federal labor policy would essentially collapse unless a wholly unprincipled, judge-made exception were created for professional athletes. Employers would have no assurance that they could enter into any collective agreement without exposing themselves to an action for treble damages. ****

Freedom of contract is particularly important in the context of collective bargaining between professional athletes and their leagues. Such bargaining relationships raise numerous problems with little or no precedent in standard industrial relations. As a result, leagues and player unions may reach seemingly unfamiliar or strange agreements. If courts were to intrude and to outlaw such solutions, leagues and their player unions would have to arrange their affairs in a less efficient way. It would also increase the chances of strikes by reducing the number and quality of possible compromises.

The issues of free agency and entry draft are at the center of collective bargaining in much of the professional sports industry. It is to be expected that the parties will arrive at unique solutions to these problems in the different sports both because sports generally differ from the industrial model and because each sport has its own peculiar economic imperatives. The NBA/NBPA agreement is just such a unique bundle of compromises. The draft and the salary cap reflect the interests of the employers in stabilizing salary costs and spreading talent among the various teams. Minimum individual salaries, fringe benefits, minimum aggregate team salaries, and guaranteed revenue sharing reflect the interests of the union in enhancing standard benefits applicable to all players.

We also agree with the district court that all of the above matters are mandatory subjects of bargaining under 29 U.S.C. § 158(d). Each of them clearly is intimately related to "wages, hours, and other terms and conditions

---

[1] The definition provides, in pertinent part, that "[t]he term 'employee' shall include any employee, *and shall not be limited to the employees of a particular employer,* unless this subchapter explicitly states otherwise." 29 U.S.C. § 152(3) (emphasis added). *See also Reliance Ins. Cos. v. NLRB,* 415 F.2d 1, 6 (8th Cir.1969) (job applicants are "employees" within meaning of 29 U.S.C. § 152(3)); *Time-O-Matic, Inc. v. NLRB,* 264 F.2d 96, 99 (7th Cir.1959) (same); *John Hancock Mut. Life Ins. Co. v. NLRB,* 191 F.2d 483, 485 (D.C.Cir.1951).

of employment." Indeed, it is precisely because of their direct relationship to wages and conditions of employment that such matters are so controversial and so much the focus of bargaining in professional sports. Wood's claim for damages, for example, is based on an allegation of lost wages. ****

It is true that the combination of the draft and salary cap places new players coming out of college ranks at a disadvantage. However, as noted earlier, that is hardly an unusual feature of collective agreements. In the industrial context salaries, promotions, and layoffs are routinely governed by seniority, with the benefits going to the older employees, the burdens to the newer. Wood has offered us no reason whatsoever to fashion a rule based *on antitrust grounds* prohibiting agreements between employers and players that use seniority as a criterion for certain employment decisions. Even if some such arrangements might be illegal because of discrimination against new employees (players), the proper action would be one for breach of the duty of fair representation. [citations omitted].

Affirmed.

### Notes & Questions

1. What is the significance of the fact that the NBA salary cap and college draft were all arrived at through the process of collective bargaining?

2. Wood's argument "that the draft and salary cap...affect[ed] employees outside of the bargaining unit" was correct was it not? It did, after all, affect rookies, who, by definition, could not have been involved in the bargaining unit. How, then, does the court explain away the principle articulated in *Mackey* that, in order to be enforceable, this type of horizontal agreement must affect only the parties who were involved in an arm's-length bargaining process?

3. The court discussed "freedom of contract." What is the point that it is trying to make about freedom of contract in this context?

## Maurice Clarett v. National Football League
369 F.3d 124 (2004)
United States Court of Appeals, Second Circuit

SOTOMAYOR, Circuit Judge.

Defendant-appellant National Football League ("NFL" or "the League") appeals from a judgment of the United States District Court for the Southern District of New York (Scheindlin, J.) ordering plaintiff-appellee Maurice Clarett ("Clarett") eligible to enter this year's NFL draft on the ground that the NFL's eligibility rules requiring Clarett to wait at least three full football seasons after his high school graduation before entering the draft violate antitrust laws. In reaching its conclusion, the district court held, *inter alia,* that the eligibility rules are not immune from antitrust scrutiny under the non-statutory labor exemption.

We disagree and reverse.

## BACKGROUND

Clarett, former running back for Ohio State University ("OSU") and Big Ten Freshman of the Year, is an accomplished and talented amateur football player. After gaining national attention as a high school player, Clarett became the first college freshman since 1943 to open as a starter at the position of running back for OSU. He led that team through an undefeated season, even scoring the winning touchdown in a double-overtime victory in the 2003 Fiesta Bowl to claim the national championship. Prior to the start of his second college season, however, Clarett was suspended from college play by OSU for reasons widely reported but not relevant here. Forced to sit out his entire sophomore season, Clarett is now interested in turning professional by entering the NFL draft. Clarett is precluded from so doing, however, under the NFL's current rules governing draft eligibility.

Founded in 1920, the NFL today is comprised of 32 member clubs and is by far the most successful professional football league in North America. Because of the League's fiscal success and tremendous public following, a career as an NFL player "represents an unparalleled opportunity for an aspiring football player in terms of salary, publicity, endorsement opportunities, and level of competition." *Clarett,* 306 F.Supp.2d at 384. But since 1925, when Harold "Red" Grange provoked controversy by leaving college to join the Chicago Bears, the NFL has required aspiring professional football players to wait a sufficient period of time after graduating high

286

school to accommodate and encourage college attendance before entering the NFL draft. For much of the League's history, therefore, a player, irrespective of whether he actually attended college or not, was barred from entering the draft until he was at least four football seasons removed from high school. The eligibility rules were relaxed in 1990, however, to permit a player to enter the draft three full seasons after that player's high school graduation.

Clarett "graduated high school on December 11, 2001, two-thirds of the way through the 2001 NFL season" and is a season shy of the three necessary to qualify under the draft's eligibility rules. Unwilling to forego the prospect of a year of lucrative professional play or run the risk of a career-compromising injury were his entry into the draft delayed until next year, Clarett filed this suit alleging that the NFL's draft eligibility rules are an unreasonable restraint of trade in violation of Section 1 of the Sherman Act, 15 U.S.C. § 1***.

Because the major source of the parties' factual disputes is the relationship between the challenged eligibility rules and the current collective bargaining agreement governing the terms and conditions of employment for NFL players, some elaboration on both the collective bargaining agreement and the eligibility rules is warranted. The current collective bargaining agreement between the NFL and its players union was negotiated between the NFL Management Council ("NFLMC"), which is the NFL member clubs' multi-employer bargaining unit, and the NFL Players Association ("NFLPA"), the NFL players' exclusive bargaining representative. This agreement became effective in 1993 and governs through 2007. Despite the collective bargaining agreement's comprehensiveness with respect to, *inter alia,* the manner in which the NFL clubs select rookies through the draft and the scheme by which rookie compensation is determined, the eligibility rules for the draft do not appear in the agreement.

At the time the collective bargaining agreement became effective, the eligibility rules appeared in the NFL Constitution and Bylaws, which had last been amended in 1992. Specifically, Article XII of the Bylaws ("Article XII"), entitled "Eligibility of Players," prohibited member clubs from selecting any college football player through the draft process who had not first exhausted all college football eligibility, graduated from college, or been out of high school for five football seasons. Clubs were further barred from drafting any person who either did not attend college, or attended college but did not play football, unless that person had been out of high school for four football seasons. Article XII, however, also included an exception that permitted clubs to draft players who had received "Special Eligibility" from the NFL Commissioner. In order to qualify for such special eligibility, a player was required to submit an application before January 6 of the year that he wished to enter the draft and "at least three NFL seasons must have elapsed since the player was graduated from high school." The Commissioner's practice apparently was, and still is, to grant such an application so long as three full football seasons have passed since a player's high school graduation.

> Although the eligibility rules do not appear in the text of the collective bargaining agreement [itself], the NFL Constitution and Bylaws that - at the time of the agreement's adoption contained the eligibility rules - are mentioned in three separate provisions [of that collective bargaining agreement].... ****

Before the collective bargaining agreement became effective, a copy of the Constitution and Bylaws, as amended in 1992, was provided by the NFL to the NFLPA along with a letter, dated May 6, 1993, that "confirm[ed] that the attached documents are the presently existing provisions of the Constitution and Bylaws of the NFL referenced in Article IV, Section 2, of the Collective Bargaining Agreement." The May 6 letter was signed by representatives of the NFL and the NFLPA. The only other evidence presented to the district court by the NFL concerning the negotiation of the collective bargaining agreement were the two declarations of Peter Ruocco, Senior Vice President of Labor Relations at the NFLMC. In the second declaration, Ruocco attests that "[d]uring the course of collective bargaining that led to the [collective bargaining agreement], the [challenged] eligibility rule itself was the subject of collective bargaining."

****

> After Clarett filed this suit in September 2003, the parties conducted limited discovery and thereafter moved for summary judgment. Clarett sought summary judgment on the merits of his antitrust claim. The NFL asserted that ***as a matter of law, the eligibility rules were immune from antitrust attack by virtue of the non-statutory labor exemption. On February 5, 2004, the district court granted summary judgment in favor of Clarett and ordered him eligible to enter this year's draft. *Clarett,* 306 F.Supp.2d at 410-11. First, relying on the test articulated by the Eighth Circuit in *Mackey v. National Football League,* 543 F.2d 606 (8th Cir.1976), the district court rejected the NFL's argument that the antitrust laws are inapplicable to the eligibility rules because they fall within the non-statutory labor exemption to the antitrust laws. *Clarett,* 306 F.Supp.2d at 397. Specifically, the district

court held that the exemption does not apply because the eligibility rules: 1) are not mandatory subjects of collective bargaining, 2) affect only "complete strangers to the bargaining relationship," and 3) were not shown to be the product of arm's-length negotiations between the NFL and its players union. *Id.* at 393-97.\*\*\*

[O]n the merits of Clarett's antitrust claim, the district court found that the eligibility rules were so "blatantly anticompetitive" that only a "quick look" at the NFL's procompetitive justifications was necessary to reach the conclusion that the eligibility rules were unlawful under the antitrust laws. *Id.* at 408. The NFL had argued that because the eligibility rules prevent less physically and emotionally mature players from entering the league, they justify any incidental anticompetitive effect on the market for NFL players. *Id.* In so doing, according to the NFL, the eligibility rules guard against less-prepared and younger players entering the League and risking injury to themselves, prevent the sport from being devalued by the higher number of injuries to those young players, protect its member clubs from having to bear the costs of such injuries, and discourage aspiring amateur football players from enhancing their physical condition through unhealthy methods. *Id.* at 408-09. The district court held that all of these justifications were inadequate as a matter of law, concluding that the NFL's purported concerns could be addressed through less restrictive but equally effective means. *Id.* at 410. Finding that the eligibility rules violated the antitrust laws, the district court entered judgment in favor of Clarett, and, recognizing that this year's draft was then just over two months away, issued an order deeming Clarett eligible
to participate in the draft.

The NFL subsequently moved for a stay pending appeal, which the district court denied. *Clarett v. Nat'l Football League,* 306 F.Supp.2d 411 (S.D.N.Y.2004). After filing a notice of appeal, the NFL petitioned to have the appeal heard on an expedited basis and again moved to stay the district court's order pending appeal. On March 30, 2004, we agreed to hear the appeal on an expedited basis and set a substantially compressed briefing schedule. Following oral argument on April 19, we granted the NFL's motion to stay the district court's order, citing the NFL's "likelihood of success on the merits" and noting that the resulting harm to Clarett was mitigated by the NFL's promise to "hold a supplemental draft for [Clarett] and all others similarly situated" were the district court's judgment affirmed. Order of April 19, 2004. Clarett thereafter made successive applications to two Justices of the Supreme Court to lift this Court's stay order. Both applications were denied. Clarett did not participate in the NFL draft held on April 24 and 25, 2004.

## DISCUSSION

Clarett argues that the NFL clubs are horizontal competitors for the labor of professional football players and thus may not agree that a player will be hired only after three full football seasons have elapsed following that player's high school graduation. That characterization, however, neglects that the labor market for NFL players is organized around a collective bargaining relationship that is provided for and promoted by federal labor law, and that the NFL clubs, as a multi-employer bargaining unit, can act jointly in setting the terms and conditions of players' employment and the rules of the sport without risking antitrust liability. For those reasons, the NFL argues that federal labor law favoring and governing the collective bargaining process precludes the application of the antitrust laws to its eligibility rules. We agree.

[The court summarizes the Supreme Court's case law history of the non-statutory labor exemption.]

Clarett *** maintains that the boundaries of the exemption were properly identified in, and thus we should follow, the Eighth Circuit's decision in *Mackey v. National Football League,* 543 F.2d 606 (8th Cir.1976). *Mackey* involved a challenge brought by NFL players to the League's so-called "Rozelle Rule," which required NFL clubs to compensate any club from which they hired away a player whose contract had expired. Presenting arguments not dissimilar from those made in the present case, the players in *Mackey* alleged that the Rozelle Rule constituted an unlawful conspiracy amongst the NFL clubs to restrain players' abilities freely to contract their services. The NFL, for its part, asserted that the Rozelle Rule was exempt from the antitrust laws by virtue of its inclusion in the League's collective bargaining agreement with the players union. Noting that the Supreme Court had to that point applied the non-statutory exemption only in *Jewel Tea,* the Eighth Circuit gleaned from the Court's decisions, and Justice White's opinion in *Jewel Tea* in particular, that in order to fall within the non-statutory exemption, a restraint must: 1) primarily affect only the parties to the collective bargaining relationship, 2) concern a mandatory subject of collective bargaining, and 3) be the product of bona fide arm's-length bargaining. *Id.* at 614. Although the Eighth Circuit found that the Rozelle Rule satisfied the first two prongs, it nonetheless refused to apply the exemption after finding that the Rozelle Rule was not the product of arm's-length negotiations. *Id.* at 615-16. Noting that the Rozelle Rule predated the advent of the collective bargaining relationship between the NFL and its players union, the Eighth Circuit found that the record lacked sufficient evidence to conclude that the players union had received some *quid pro quo* in exchange for including the Rule in the collective bargaining agreement. *Id.* at 616. For that reason, the Eighth Circuit held that the Rozelle Rule did not fall within the non-statutory exemption, and the Rule was invalidated on antitrust grounds. *Id.* at 621-22.

Relying on *Mackey,* the district court below held that the non-statutory exemption provides no protection to the NFL's draft eligibility rules, because the eligibility rules fail to satisfy any of the three *Mackey* factors. *Clarett,* 306 F.Supp.2d at 397. Specifically, the district court found that the rules exclude strangers to the bargaining relationship from entering the draft, do not concern wages, hours or working conditions of current NFL players, and were not the product of bona fide arm's-length negotiations during the process that culminated in the current collective bargaining agreement. *Id.* at 395-97.

We, however, have never regarded the Eighth Circuit's test in *Mackey* as defining the appropriate limits of the non-statutory exemption. [The court explains some of its differences with the *Mackey* decision.]

[A]s the discussion below makes clear, the suggestion that the *Mackey* factors provide the proper guideposts in this case simply does not comport with the Supreme Court's most recent treatment of the non-statutory labor exemption in *Brown v. Pro Football, Inc.,* 518 U.S. 231, 116 S.Ct. 2116, 135 L.Ed.2d 521 (1996).

II.

Our decisions in *Caldwell (Caldwell v. Am. Basketball Ass'n,* 66 F.3d 523 (2d Cir.1995)) , *Williams (Nat'l Basketball Ass'n v. Williams,* 45 F.3d 684 (2d Cir.1995)) and *Wood (Wood v. Nat'l Basketball Ass'n,* 809 F.2d 954 (2d Cir.1987) all involved players' claims that the concerted action of a professional sports league imposed a restraint upon the labor market for players' services and thus violated the antitrust laws. In each case, however, we held that the non-statutory labor exemption defeated the players' claims. Our analysis in each case was rooted in the observation that the relationships among the defendant sports leagues and their players were governed by collective bargaining agreements and thus were subject to the carefully structured regime established by federal labor laws. We reasoned that to permit antitrust suits against sports leagues on the ground that their concerted action imposed a restraint upon the labor market would seriously undermine many of the policies embodied by these labor laws, including the congressional policy favoring collective bargaining, the bargaining parties' freedom of contract, and the widespread use of multi-employer bargaining units. Subsequent to our decisions in this area, similar reasoning led the Supreme Court in *Brown v. Pro Football, Inc.*, 518 U.S. 231, 116 S.Ct. 2116, 135 L.Ed.2d 521 (1996), to hold that the non-statutory exemption protected the NFL's unilateral implementation of new salary caps for developmental squad players after its collective bargaining agreement with the NFL players union had expired and negotiations with the union over that proposal reached an impasse. We need only retrace the path laid down by these prior cases to reach the conclusion that Clarett's antitrust claims must fail.

## A.

The plaintiff in *Wood*, O. Leon Wood, was a star college basketball player who, after being drafted by the Philadelphia 76ers, sued the NBA alleging that its policies regarding, *inter alia*, the entry draft process and team salary caps constituted unlawful agreements among horizontal competitors to eliminate competition for college players. *Wood*, 809 F.2d at 956-58. All of the challenged policies, however, were included in a collective bargaining agreement and memorandum of understanding between the NBA and its players union. Because these agreements were the result of the federally mandated bargaining process through which the union and the NBA, in light of the unique economic imperatives of professional basketball, negotiated a host of creative solutions to settle their differences, we held that to permit Wood to challenge particular aspects of their agreement on antitrust grounds would "subvert fundamental principles of our federal labor policy."

Specifically, we found that Wood's claim that the NBA's agreements prevented him from becoming a free agent and negotiating directly with the teams for the best salary contravened the principle of federal labor law that once a majority of employees votes to unionize and elects a representative, individual employees--whether in the bargaining unit or not--no longer possess the right to negotiate with the employer for the best deal possible. *Id.* at 959-60 (citing 29 U.S.C. § 159(a)). Rather, the union representative is charged with the responsibility of seeking the best overall deal for employees, which often means that some employees or prospective employees may fare worse than they would in a competitive market free from restraints. *Id.* We further rejected Wood's contention that the non-statutory exemption did not preclude his challenge because he was not a member of the union when the collective bargaining agreement became effective, observing that new union members often find themselves disadvantaged vis-a-vis more senior union members and that collective bargaining units commonly disadvantage employees outside of, or about to enter, the union. *Id.* at 960.

Eight years later, in *Williams,* a class of professional basketball players again brought an antitrust suit challenging, *inter alia,* the NBA's draft process and salary caps. *Williams,* 45 F.3d at 685-86. This time, however, the restraints challenged by the players were not encompassed in any effective agreement between the NBA and its players union, because the collective bargaining agreement had expired. *Id.* at 686. The challenged policies were implemented unilaterally by the NBA after negotiations with the players union on these subjects reached an impasse. *Id.* We nevertheless held that the NBA's conduct fell within the non-statutory exemption. *Id.* at 693. Foremost, we found that the players' antitrust claims were inconsistent with federal labor law because they imperiled the legitimacy of multi-employer bargaining, "a process by which employers band together to act as a single entity in bargaining with a common union." *Id.* at 688. From the standpoint of our labor and antitrust laws, we explained that such multi-employer bargaining units are a long-accepted and commonplace means of giving employers the tactical and practical advantages of collective action. *Id.* at 688-93. Moreover, in the context of sports leagues, we observed that multi-employer bargaining units serve the additional, important purpose of allowing the teams to establish and demand uniformity in the rules necessary for the proper functioning of the sport. *Id.* at 689. Second, we found that legality of conduct undertaken in the course of negotiations over a collective bargaining agreement is an issue committed to the specialized knowledge of the National Labor Relations Board, for which federal labor law provides a "soup-to-nuts array of rules and remedies." *Id.* at 693. Because permitting courts to police that same conduct under the auspices of the antitrust laws would disrupt that remedial scheme, we held that the non-statutory exemption was applicable. *Id.* at 693.

****[The court's discussion of *Caldwell* has been omitted]

The following year, in *Brown,* the Supreme Court was presented with facts similar to *Williams,* and eight Justices agreed that the non-statutory exemption precludes antitrust claims against a professional sports league for unilaterally setting policy with respect to mandatory bargaining subjects after negotiations with the players union over those subjects reach impasse. *Brown,* 518 U.S. at 240-42, 116 S.Ct. 2116. There, a class of professional football players challenged the NFL's unilateral institution of a policy that permitted each team to establish a new squad of developmental players and capped those players' weekly salaries after negotiations with the players union over that proposal became deadlocked. *Id.* at 234-35, 116 S.Ct. 2116. Approaching the issue largely as a "matter of logic," *id.* at 237, 116 S.Ct. 2116, the Court found that to permit antitrust liability in such a case would call into question a great deal of conduct, such as multi-employer bargaining, that federal labor policy promotes and for which labor law provides an array of rules and remedies, *id.* at 237-42, 116 S.Ct. 2116. The Court held that the non-statutory labor exemption necessarily applied not only to protect such labor policies but also to prevent "antitrust courts" from usurping the NLRB's responsibility for policing the collective bargaining process. *Id.* at 240- 42, 116 S.Ct. 2116.

The Court also rejected a number of potential limits on the exemption that were raised by the players and their supporters. First, the Court held that the exemption was not so narrow as to protect only agreements between the parties that are embodied in an existing collective bargaining agreement. *Id.* at 243-44, 116 S.Ct. 2116. Second, in finding that the League's post-impasse action was protected by the exemption, the Court dismissed the suggestion that the exemption should insulate the concerted action of employers only up to the point at which negotiations reach impasse or a "reasonable time" thereafter. *Id.* at 244-47, 116 S.Ct. 2116. **** Finally, the Court refused the players' contention that the labor of professional sports players was unique and that the market for players' services therefore should be treated differently than other organized labor markets for purposes of the non-statutory exemption. *Id.* at 248-49, 116 S.Ct. 2116.

****

Clarett argues that his case differs in material respects from *Brown,* but he does not argue, nor do we find, that the Supreme Court's treatment of the non-statutory exemption in that case gives reason to doubt the authority of our prior decisions in *Caldwell, Williams,* and *Wood.* Because we find that our prior decisions in this area fully comport--in approach and result--with the Supreme Court's decision in *Brown,* we regard them as controlling authority. In light of the foregoing jurisprudence, we therefore proceed to the merits of this appeal.

B.

Clarett argues that he is physically qualified to play professional football and that the antitrust laws preclude the NFL teams from agreeing amongst themselves that they will refuse to deal with him simply because he is less than three full football seasons out of high school. Such an arbitrary condition, he argues, imposes an unreasonable restraint upon the competitive market for professional football players' services, and, because it excludes him from entering that market altogether, constitutes a *per se* antitrust violation. The issue we must decide is whether subjecting the NFL's eligibility rules to antitrust scrutiny would "subvert fundamental principles of our federal labor policy." *Wood,* 809 F.2d at 959. For the reasons that follow, we hold that it would and that the non-statutory exemption therefore applies.

Although the NFL has maintained draft eligibility rules in one form or another for much of its history, the "inception of a collective bargaining relationship" between the NFL and its players union some thirty years ago "irrevocably alter[ed] the governing legal regime." *Caldwell,* 66 F.3d at 527. Our prior cases highlight a number of consequences resulting from the advent of this collective bargaining relationship that are relevant to Clarett's litigation. For one, prospective players no longer have the right to negotiate directly with the NFL teams over the terms and conditions of their employment. That responsibility is instead committed to the NFL and the players union to accomplish through the collective bargaining process, and throughout that process the NFL and the players union are to have the freedom to craft creative solutions to their differences in light of the economic imperatives of their industry. Furthermore, the NFL teams are permitted to engage in joint conduct with respect to the terms and conditions of players' employment as a multi-employer bargaining unit without risking antitrust liability. The arguments Clarett advances in support of his antitrust claim, however, run counter to each of these basic principles of federal labor law.

Because the NFL players have unionized and have selected the NFLPA as its exclusive bargaining representative, labor law prohibits Clarett from negotiating directly the terms and conditions of his employment with any NFL club, *see NLRB v. Allis-Chalmers Mfg. Co.,* 388 U.S. 175, 180, 87 S.Ct. 2001, 18 L.Ed.2d 1123 (1967), and an NFL club would commit an unfair labor practice were it to bargain with Clarett individually without the union's consent, *see Medo Photo Supply Corp. v. NLRB,* 321 U.S. 678, 683, 64 S.Ct. 830, 88 L.Ed. 1007 (1944).[1] The terms and conditions of Clarett's employment are instead committed to the collective bargaining table and are reserved to the NFL and the players union's selected representative to negotiate. *Allis-Chalmers Mfg. Co.,* 388 U.S. at 180, 87 S.Ct. 2001.

**** In seeking the best deal for NFL players overall, the representative has the ability to advantage certain categories of players over others, subject of course to the representative's duty of fair representation. *See Vaca v. Sipes,* 386 U.S. 171, 177, 87 S.Ct. 903, 17 L.Ed.2d 842 (1967).

---

[1] "To be sure, in sports leagues, unionized players generally engage in individual bargaining with teams. However, it must be emphasized that such individual bargaining is not an exercise of a right to free competition under the antitrust laws; rather, it is an exercise of a right derived from collective bargaining itself." *Caldwell,* 66 F.3d at 528.

The union representative may, for example, favor veteran players over rookies, *see Ford Motor Co. v. Huffman,* 345 U.S. 330, 338-39, 73 S.Ct. 681, 97 L.Ed. 1048 (1953), and can seek to preserve jobs for current players to the detriment of new employees and the exclusion of outsiders, *see Fibreboard Paper Prods. Corp v. NLRB,* 379 U.S. 203, 210-15, 85 S.Ct. 398, 13 L.Ed.2d 233 (1964); *Wood,* 809 F.2d at 960 & n. 3. \*\*\*\*

Clarett's argument that antitrust law should permit him to circumvent this scheme established by federal labor law starts with the contention that the eligibility rules do not constitute a mandatory subject of collective bargaining and thus cannot fall within the protection of the non-statutory exemption. Contrary to the district court, however, we find that the eligibility rules are mandatory bargaining subjects. Though tailored to the unique circumstance of a professional sports league, the eligibility rules for the draft represent a quite literal condition for initial employment and for that reason alone might constitute a mandatory bargaining subject. \*\*\* R. Gorman, *Labor Law* at 504 ("In accordance with the literal language of the Labor Act, the parties must bargain about the requirements or 'conditions' of initial employment."). But moreover, the eligibility rules constitute a mandatory bargaining subject because they have tangible effects on the wages and working conditions of current NFL players. Because the unusual economic imperatives of professional sports raise "numerous problems with little or no precedent in standard industrial relations," *Wood,* 809 F.2d at 961, we have recognized that many of the arrangements in professional sports that, at first glance, might not appear to deal with wages or working conditions are indeed mandatory bargaining subjects, *see Silverman v. Major League Baseball Player Relations Comm., Inc.,* 67 F.3d 1054, 1061 (2d Cir.1995). In *Silverman,* for example, we recognized that "[a] mix of free_agency and reserve clauses combined with other provisions [such as a rookie draft and salary caps] is the universal method by which leagues and players unions set individual salaries in professional sports." *Id.* We therefore held that the issues of free agency, an anti-collusion provision in players' contracts, and major league baseball's reserve system are mandatory bargaining subjects in the context of professional baseball. *Id.* Similarly, the complex scheme by which individual salaries in the NFL are set, which involves, *inter alia,* the NFL draft, league-wide salary pools for rookies, team salary caps, and free agency, was built around the longstanding restraint on the market for entering players imposed by the eligibility rules and the related expectations about the average career length of NFL players. The eligibility rules in other words cannot be viewed in isolation, because their elimination might well alter certain assumptions underlying the collective bargaining agreement between the NFL and its players union.

Furthermore, by reducing competition in the market for entering players, the eligibility rules also affect the job security of veteran players. *** Because the size of NFL teams is capped, the eligibility rules diminish a veteran player's risk of being replaced by either a drafted rookie or a player who enters the draft and, though not drafted, is then hired as a rookie free agent. *See* Michael S. Jacobs & Ralph K. Winter, Jr., *Antitrust Principles and Collective Bargaining by Athletes: Of Superstars in Peonage,* 81 Yale L.J. 1, 16 (1971) (recognizing that entry of new players through draft "has an enormous effect on those already in the unit and the collective agreement which governs them"). Consequently, as was true in *Silverman,* we find that to regard the NFL's eligibility rules as merely permissive bargaining subjects "would ignore the reality of collective bargaining in sports." *Silverman,* 67 F.3d at 1061-62.

Clarett, however, argues that the eligibility rules are an impermissible bargaining subject because they affect players outside of the union. But simply because the eligibility rules work a hardship on prospective rather than current employees does not render them impermissible. *See Wood,* 809 F.2d at 960. *** Nevertheless, such an arrangement constitutes a permissible, mandatory subject of bargaining despite the fact that it concerns prospective rather than current employees. *Wood,* 809 F.2d at 960.

****

*** Clarett [also contends] that the rules were not bargained over during the negotiations that preceded the current collective bargaining agreement. The eligibility rules, along with the host of other NFL rules and policies affecting the terms and conditions of NFL players included in the NFL's Constitution and Bylaws, were well known to the union, and a copy of the Constitution and Bylaws was presented to the union during negotiations. Given that the eligibility rules are a mandatory bargaining subject for the reasons set out above, the union or the NFL could have forced the other to the bargaining table if either felt that a change was warranted. *See NLRB v. Katz,* 369 U.S. 736, 743, 82 S.Ct. 1107, 8 L.Ed.2d 230 (1962). ****

[T]he collective bargaining agreement itself makes clear that the union and the NFL reached an agreement with respect to how the eligibility rules would be handled. In the collective bargaining agreement, the union agreed to waive any challenge to the Constitution and Bylaws and thereby acquiesced in the continuing operation of the eligibility rules contained therein--at least for the duration of the agreement. The terms of that waiver not only keep the eligibility rules in effect for the length of the agreement but also leave the NFL in control of any changes to the eligibility rules on the condition that any significant change potentially affecting the terms and conditions of players' employment would be preceded by notice to the union and an opportunity to bargain. \*\*\*\*

Clarett would have us hold that by reaching this arrangement rather than fixing the eligibility rules in the text of the collective bargaining agreement or in failing to wrangle over the eligibility rules at the bargaining table, the NFL left itself open to antitrust liability. Such a holding, however, would completely contradict prior decisions recognizing that the labor law policies that warrant withholding antitrust scrutiny are not limited to protecting only terms contained in collective bargaining agreements. *See Brown,* 518 U.S. at 243-44, 116 S.Ct. 2116; *Caldwell,* 66 F.3d at 528-29 & n. 1. \*\*\*\*

This lawsuit reflects simply a prospective employee's disagreement with the criteria, established by the employer and the labor union, that he must meet in order to be considered for employment. Any remedies for such a claim are the province of labor law. Allowing Clarett to proceed with his antitrust suit would subvert "principles that have been familiar to, and accepted by, the nation's workers for all of the NLRA's [sixty years] in every industry except professional sports." *Caldwell,* 66 F.3d at 530. We, however, follow the Supreme Court's lead in declining to "fashion an antitrust exemption [so as to give] additional advantages to professional football players ... that transport workers, coal miners, or meat packers would not enjoy." *Brown,* 518 U.S. at 249, 116 S.Ct. 2116.

## CONCLUSION

For the foregoing reasons, the judgment of the district court is REVERSED and the case REMANDED with instructions to enter judgment in favor of the NFL. The order of the district court designating Clarett eligible to enter this year's NFL draft is VACATED.

### Notes & Questions

1. Explain what this case adds to the antitrust analysis and how this court differs from the *Mackey* court.

2. Explain in your own words the legal consequences of the *Brown* case in *Clarett.*

# THE CURT FLOOD ACT OF 1998 AND MAJOR LEAGUE BASEBALL'S FEDERAL ANTITRUST EXEMPTION

John T. Wolohan
9 MARQ. SPORTS L.J. 347 (1999)

## Introduction

In 1922, Justice Oliver Wendell Holmes writing for the United States Supreme Court held that organized baseball was "purely a state affair" and while money was involved, baseball "would not be called trade or commerce in the commonly accepted use of those words." Since Justice Holmes' decision in *Federal Baseball Club of Baltimore v. National League of Professional Baseball Clubs*, organized baseball has cherished its antitrust exemption and rigorously protected and fought over it in the courts. One of the individuals who challenged baseball's unique legal position was Curt Flood, in *Flood v. Kuhn*. In 1969, Curt Flood was traded from the St. Louis Cardinals to the Philadelphia Phillies, without his knowledge or consent. When informed of the trade, Flood petitioned Bowie Kuhn, the Commissioner of Baseball at the time, requesting that he be declared a free agent. When his request was denied and with help from the Major League Baseball Players Association (MLBPA), Flood filed a federal antitrust lawsuit against Major League Baseball (MLB) claiming that baseball's reserve rule violated federal antitrust law. In 1972, the Supreme Court, for the third time in 50 years, upheld baseball's antitrust exemption even though it acknowledged that "professional baseball is a business and it is engaged in interstate commerce." In holding organized baseball exempt from federal antitrust law, the Supreme Court blindly followed Justice Holmes' decision and held that if there were "any inconsistency or illogic" in the decision it was up to Congress to remedy it, not the Court.

It took twenty-six years, but Congress has finally acted to remedy the inconsistency or illogic in baseball's antitrust exemption. Although too late to help his playing career, Flood may have finally won his victory against MLB when on October 27, 1998, President Bill Clinton signed into law the Curt Flood Act of 1998. The Curt Flood Act, which overturns part of baseball's 76-year-old antitrust exemption, grants to major league baseball players, for the first time, the same rights under antitrust law as other professional

299

UNIVERSITY OF WINCHESTER

athletes. Congress also hopes that by passing the Curt Flood Act and making the playing field between the owners and players more equal, it will bring some stability to baseball's labor relations.

Although baseball has traditionally fought hard to keep its antitrust exemption, the Curt Flood Act would never have unanimously passed in Congress if it were not for the support and urging it received from both MLB and the Players' Association. In the last Collective Bargaining Agreement (CBA), both MLB and the Players' Association agreed to "jointly request and cooperate in lobbying the Congress to pass a law that will clarify that Major League Baseball Players are covered under the antitrust laws."

To answer why MLB was willing to give up part of its cherished antitrust exemption, this paper examines both the Curt Flood Act of 1998 and the impact it will have on baseball. The paper begins with a historic review of baseball's antitrust exemption. The review is broken into three sections: pre-*Federal Baseball*, Baseball's Supreme Court trilogy and post *Flood v. Kuhn*. Next, the paper examines the Curt Flood Act of 1998; its origins, purpose and the potential impact it may have on future labor negations and disputes. Finally, the article concludes by looking at what is left of Major League Baseball's antitrust exemption after passage of Curt Flood Act of 1998 and the impact the Act will have on future antitrust lawsuits against Major League Baseball.

## History of Baseball and Federal Antitrust Law

Although the National League began playing professional baseball before Congress passed the Sherman Antitrust Act in 1890, baseball more than any other sport has had to continuously defend itself against antitrust allegations. This section of the paper examines how the courts have historically treated organized baseball under Federal antitrust laws. The review is divided into three sections: pre-*Federal Baseball*, Baseball's Supreme Court trilogy, and post *Flood v. Kuhn* to show how the courts have relied on stare decisis to let stand baseball's antitrust exemption even though the legal theory upon which the original decision was based is no longer valid.

## A. Pre-*Federal Baseball*

The first court to examine whether the rules and regulations governing professional baseball players were covered under federal antitrust laws was *American League Baseball Club of Chicago v. Chase*. In March of 1914, Harold H. (Hal) Chase signed a contract to play first base for the

Chicago White Sox. On June 15, in the middle of the season, Chase informed Chicago that he intended to back out of his contract. On June 20, Chase entered into a second contract to play with the Buffalo Club of the new Federal Baseball League. In an attempt to keep Chase in Chicago and away from the Federal League, the White Sox sought a court injunction.

Refusing to grant Chicago an injunction, the court held that although Chase had "special, unique and extraordinary characteristics as a baseball player," there was an "absolute lack of mutuality, both of obligation and remedy" in Chase's contract, that made the contract unenforceable for want of mutuality. As evidence, the court noted that the standard player contract was terminable by the employing club on only 10 days' notice, but that due to the scheme of the National Agreement, the club and organized baseball had an absolute option on the player's services for the succeeding year.

After rejecting Chicago's argument on contract grounds, the court went on to examine whether the "National Agreement and the rules and regulations adopted pursuant thereto, violated the Sherman Act." The court, while finding organized baseball had "ingeniously devised and created" a monopoly to control the business of baseball played in the United States, also found that baseball was not interstate trade or commerce within the meaning of Sherman Antitrust Act. In finding organized baseball outside the coverage of the Sherman Act, the court held that baseball "is an amusement, a sport, a game ... it is not a commodity or an article of merchandise subject to the regulation of Congress" and the Sherman Act.

The court also examined whether "organized baseball, operating under the provisions of the National Agreement and the Rules and Contracts subsidiary thereto, is an illegal combination or monopoly in contravention of the common law." After reviewing the National Agreement, which controlled the services of every professional baseball player and provided "for their purchase, sale, exchange, draft, reduction, discharge, and blacklisting," the court found that organized baseball, excluding the newly organized Federal League "is now as complete a monopoly of the baseball business for profit as any monopoly can be made and is in contravention of the common law."

The court found that:

> [W]hile the services of these baseball players are ostensibly secured by voluntary contracts, a study of the system,...as practiced under the plan of the National Agreement, reveals the involuntary character of the servitude

which is imposed upon players by the strength of the combination controlling the labor of practically all of the players in the country. This is so great as to make it necessary for the player either to take the contract prescribed by the commission or abandon baseball as a profession and seek some other mode of earning a livelihood. There is no difference in principle between the system of servitude built up by the operation of this National Agreement, which as has been shown, provides for the purchase, sale, barter, and exchange of the services of baseball players--skilled laborers--without their consent, and the system of peonage brought into the United States from Mexico and thereafter existing for a time within the territory of New Mexico. The quasi peonage of baseball players under the operations of this plan and agreement is contrary to the spirit of American institutions, and is contrary to the spirit of the Constitution of the United States.[1]

B. Baseball Supreme Court Trilogy

The most famous antitrust challenge concerning baseball, and the case that provides it with an antitrust exemption, is the first case in baseball's Supreme Court trilogy, *Federal Baseball*. The Federal League declared its intention to establish itself as a third major league in 1913 and began play in 1914. After two years of direct competition for players and fans, both the Federal League and Major League Baseball were ready to reach some form of settlement. In December of 1915, the leagues entered into a "Peace Agreement" which resulted in the dissolution of the Federal League and all of its constituent clubs. As part of the settlement, the Federal League received $600,000.00, two of its owners were allowed to buy existing major league teams, and the contracts of some Federal League players were sold to the highest bidders among the major league teams.

However, the settlement made no provisions for the Federal League team in Baltimore. With no league to play in and no where to go after the Federal League dissolved, the Baltimore team folded and its owners filed an antitrust suit alleging that organized baseball conspired to monopolize the baseball business in violation of the Sherman Act. The Baltimore franchise claimed that MLB "destroyed the Federal League by buying up some of the constituent clubs and in one way or another inducing all those clubs except the plaintiff to leave their League." A federal district court agreed with

---

[1] American League Baseball Club of Chicago, 149 N.Y.S. at 19.

Baltimore's argument and awarded them $240,000.00 in treble damages, costs, and attorney fees.

Baltimore's victory was short lived. The District Court's decision was overturned by the Court of Appeals. In reaching its decision, the Court of Appeals, citing *Chase*, held that baseball was a game and "did not constitute trade or commerce." The Court of Appeals also noted that the giving of exhibitions of baseball "is local in its beginning and in its end" and therefore not interstate.

Disappointed with the Court of Appeals' decision, Baltimore appealed to the United States Supreme Court. The Supreme Court, in upholding the Court of Appeals' decision, also held that the business of baseball was purely a state affair and did not involve interstate commerce within the meaning of the Sherman Antitrust Act. In delivering the Supreme Court's decision, Justice Holmes stated that although "competitions must be arranged between clubs from different cities and States ... the transport is a mere incident, not the essential thing."[2] Justice Holmes also found that "a baseball exhibition, although made for money, is not trade or commerce in the commonly accepted use of those words, since personal effort not related to production is not a subject of commerce."[3]

This decision to exempt baseball from federal antitrust law, would survive repeated challenges for the next seventy-six years until Congress passed the Curt Flood Act. Although not part of baseball's Supreme Court trilogy, the first case after *Federal Baseball* to challenge baseball's antitrust immunity and the one that came closest to overturning it was *Gardella v. Chandler*.[4]

Daniel Gardella was a journeyman baseball player who played baseball for the New York Giants during the 1944 and 45 seasons and was under contract with them for the 1946 season. During the 1946 spring training, with the World War II veterans having returned to the States, Gardella signed a contract to play professional baseball in Mexico. Gardella, a minor league player before the war, did not believe that he had a chance to make the Giants. Upon returning to the United States, Gardella, who only played one year in Mexico, was blacklisted from organized baseball.

---

[2] Federal Baseball, 259 U.S. at 208.
[3] Id.
[4] Gardella v. Chandler, 172 F.2d 402 (2d Cir. 1949), rev'g 79 F. Supp. 260 (S.D.N.Y. 1948).

The Commissioner of Baseball, Albert B. "Happy" Chandler, in an attempt to avert another war over players' salaries, declared that any player who jumped to the Mexican League would be barred from organized baseball. No longer able to make a living by playing organized baseball professionally, Gardella filed a lawsuit challenging baseball's reserve clause and the Supreme Court's decision in *Federal Baseball*.

The Federal District Court in New York, citing *Federal Baseball*, dismissed the case for failure to state a cause of action and Gardella appealed to the Second Circuit Court. In a 2-1 decision, the Second Circuit ruled that due to the use of radio and television the game of baseball is now interstate commerce. The Second Circuit, noted that the game of baseball and the Supreme Court's expending definition of interstate commerce had changed so much since *Federal Baseball*, decided that there was enough merit in the case to warrant a trial.

In rejecting organized baseball's argument that it was exempt from federal antitrust law under *Federal Baseball*, Judge Frank stated that "the Supreme Court's recent decisions have completely destroyed the vitality of *Federal Baseball* ... and have left that case but an impotent zombi."[5] In distinguishing *Gardella* from *Federal Baseball*, the Second Circuit found baseball's reserve clause "shockingly repugnant to moral principles"[6] which "results in something resembling peonage of the baseball player."[7] The Second Circuit also noted that unlike the situation in the *Federal Baseball* case, organized baseball now had "lucratively contracted for the interstate communication, by radio and television, of the playing of the games."[8] Finally, while acknowledging that it could not overturn a Supreme Court decision, the court stated that it was not required to "wait for a formal retraction in the face of changes plainly foreshadowed."[9]

Although remanded back to the district court for trial, the case never made it back to court. A week before the case was scheduled to be heard,

---

[5] Gardella, 172 F.2d at 403, 408-9.

[6] Id. at 409.

[7] Id.

[8] In Federal Baseball, the Supreme Court held that the traveling across state lines was but an incidental means of enabling games to be played locally and therefore insufficient to constitute interstate commerce. The Second Circuit, however, found that the interstate communication by radio and television is in no way a means, incidental or otherwise, of performing the intra-state activities and thus constituted inter state commerce. See id. at 410.

[9] "This Court's duty is to divine as best it can, what would be the event of the appeal in the case before it." Id. at 409, n. 1.

organized baseball settled with Gardella for $60,000.00. Although organized baseball received a scare in *Gardella*, the next case, the second in baseball's Supreme Court trilogy, is more indicative of how the courts have treated organized baseball's antitrust immunity. The case, *Toolson v. New York Yankees*,[10] which is actually three cases, reaffirmed that Congress had no intention of including baseball within the scope of federal antitrust law.

In *Toolson*, George Toolson, a minor league player within the Yankee farm system refused to report to the team's Eastern League affiliate after he had been demoted from the Yankees' International League team. In an attempt to free himself from his contract, Toolson filed an antitrust lawsuit against organized baseball arguing that its reserve clause and farm system denied him the opportunity to improve his livelihood.

Having lost in both the District Court and the Ninth Circuit Court of Appeal, Toolson appealed to the United States Supreme Court. *Toolson*, therefore, was the Supreme Court's first opportunity to correct *Federal Baseball* by including baseball within the scope of federal antitrust law. The Supreme Court, however, in a one page decision, upheld its decision in *Federal Baseball* ruling that Congress had no intention of including the business of baseball within the scope of the federal antitrust laws. In support of this decision, the Supreme Court noted that Congress had thirty years since *Federal Baseball* to bring the business of baseball under the scope of federal antitrust law and that during that time baseball had been allowed to develop with the belief that it was not subject to antitrust law. The Supreme Court concluded that it was the obligation of Congress to bring baseball within the scope of federal antitrust law, not the courts.

Unlike *Federal Baseball*, the Supreme Court's decision in *Toolson* was not unanimous. In his dissent, Justice Burton stated that it was impossible to believe that "organized baseball, in 1953, still is not engaged in interstate trade or commerce." In support of his conclusion, Justice Burton observed that the Supreme Court in *Federal Baseball* only held that the activities of organized baseball did not amount to interstate commerce, not that those activities were exempt from the Sherman Act. Only Congress has the power to exempt organized baseball from the antitrust laws noted Justice Burton. Justice Burton also noted that while there might be "possible justification of special treatment for organized sports" Congress had failed to pass four bills which would have granted baseball and all other professional sports a complete and unlimited immunity from the antitrust laws.

---

[10] Toolson, 346 U.S. 356.

The last case in baseball's Supreme Court trilogy was *Flood v. Kuhn*.[11] Curt Flood, an all-star outfielder with the St. Louis Cardinals, was traded to the Philadelphia Phillies in 1969, without Flood's knowledge or consent. When informed of the trade, Flood complained to Commissioner Bowie Kuhn and requested that Kuhn declare him a free agent, thereby allowing him to negotiate with any major league team he wished. When Kuhn denied his request, Flood filed a lawsuit claiming that organized baseball's reserve rule violated federal antitrust law.

In rejecting Flood's lawsuit, the District Court and the Second Circuit Court of Appeals found that *Federal Baseball* and *Toolson* were controlling and felt compelled to uphold them. Flood appealed, and "for the third time in 50 years," the Supreme Court agreed to examine whether organized baseball was within the reach of federal antitrust law.

After an extensive history of the game and some of its players, the Supreme Court held that the "longstanding exemption of professional baseball's reserve system from federal antitrust laws is an established aberration in which Congress has acquiesced, is entitled to [the] benefit of stare decisis, and any inconsistency or illogic is to be remedied by the Congress and not by the Supreme Court." Therefore, the Court held that although baseball enjoyed an exemption from the federal antitrust laws, it was an "aberration" confined to baseball.

The Supreme Court did acknowledge in *Flood* that baseball was a trade or commerce engaged in interstate commerce, but it still refused to overturn baseball's antitrust exemption. In support of its decision, the Supreme Court noted that "baseball with full and continuing congressional awareness, has been allowed to develop and to expand unhindered by federal legislative action." The Court reasoned that since Congress had failed to revoke baseball's antitrust exemption, Congress must have intended for baseball to be outside the reach of the antitrust laws.

Just as in *Toolson*, the Supreme Court's decision was not unanimous. In his dissent, Justice Douglas held that if the Supreme Court were to consider the question of baseball for the first time upon a clean slate, there would be no doubt that the Court would hold baseball subject to federal antitrust regulation.[12] As for the failure of Congress to pass legislation overruling *Federal Baseball* and subjecting baseball to federal antitrust laws, Justice Douglas argued that "the unbroken silence of Congress should not

---

[11] Flood, 407 U.S. 258.
[12] Flood, 407 U.S. at 289.

prevent us from correcting our own mistakes." If in making its decision the Court was to rely upon congressional inaction, Justice Douglas noted that Congress also failed to pass any legislation exempting professional sports from antitrust regulation.

## C. Baseball's Antitrust Exemption after *Flood*

Based upon baseball's Supreme Court trilogy, it is clear that baseball enjoys some form of exemption from antitrust laws. Therefore, the only question is the scope of that exemption. For example, is the entire business of baseball exempt or is it just baseball's reserve rule and other player controls. As the following cases demonstrate, the courts are mixed on the scope of the exemption.

### 1. A Broad View of Baseball Antitrust Exemption

The first case after *Flood* to challenge the scope of baseball's antitrust exemption was *Charles O. Finley & Co. v. Kuhn.*[13] Charles Finley, the owner of the Oakland Athletics, sued the Commissioner of Baseball Bowie Kuhn over Kuhn's decision to void the sale of three Oakland players. When Kuhn rejected the sales, Finley filed a lawsuit principally challenging the scope of the Commissioner's authority to void the sales. The complaint also argued "that the Commissioner, acting in concert with others, conspired to eliminate Oakland from baseball in violation of federal antitrust laws."

In rejecting Finley's antitrust argument, the district court held that "baseball ... is not subject to the provisions of the [Sherman Antitrust] Act." On appeal, Finley argued that any antitrust exemption professional baseball might enjoy applies only to the reserve system, and not to the entire business of baseball. In affirming the district court's decision, the Seventh Circuit Court of Appeals held that regardless of any mention of the reserve system in the *Flood* case, the Supreme Court intended to exempt the whole business of baseball, and not just the reserve system or any other particular facet of that business from the federal antitrust laws.

Another case that interpreted baseball's Supreme Court trilogy as granting MLB blanket immunity is *Professional Baseball Schools & Clubs, Inc. v. Kuhn.*[14] The plaintiff, the owner of a baseball franchise in the Carolina League, filed a lawsuit challenging baseball's "player assignment system and the franchise location system; the monopolization of the business

---

[13] Charles O. Finley & Co. v. Kuhn, 569 F.2d 527, 541 (7th Cir. 1978), cert. denied, 439 U.S. 876 (1978).
[14] 693 F.2d 1085 (11th Cir.1982).

of professional baseball, and the Carolina League's rule requiring member teams to only play games with other teams." The district court dismissed the antitrust claim for want of subject matter jurisdiction, and the plaintiff appealed. The Eleventh Circuit Court, just as the Seventh Circuit had done in Finley, rejected the antitrust argument. The Eleventh Circuit, citing baseball's Supreme Court trilogy, found that "[a]lthough it may be anomalous, the exclusion of the business of baseball from the antitrust laws is well established." Therefore, since each of the activities in the complaint concerned matters that are an integral part of the business of baseball, they fell within baseball's antitrust exemption.

### 2. A Narrow View of Baseball Antitrust Exemption

Within the last few years, there has been a willingness by some courts to chip away at baseball's federal antitrust exemption. The first case to take a more narrow view of organized baseball's antitrust exemption was *Piazza v. Major League Baseball*.[15] In *Piazza*, Vincent Piazza[16] and Vincent Tirendi reached an agreement with Robert Lurie, the owner of the San Francisco Giants, to purchase the Giants and move the team to Tampa Bay, Florida. The National League President, Bill White, and the Ownership Committee of MLB, however wanted to keep the franchise in San Francisco and rejected the proposal to relocate the Giants and began to look for local buyers. After a frantic search, local investors were finally found and Lurie sold the Giants to the local group for $100 million, $15 million less than the Piazza and Tirendi partnership had offered.

After MLB rejected their offer to purchase the team and move it to Florida, Piazza and Tirendi filed an antitrust lawsuit. In their lawsuit, the plaintiffs "claim[ed] that Baseball ha[d] monopolized the market for Major League Baseball teams and that Baseball ha[d] placed direct and indirect restraints on the purchase, sale, transfer, relocation of, and competition for such teams." Faced with another antitrust lawsuit, but relying on the baseball Supreme Court trilogy, MLB moved to dismiss the case for failure to state a cause of action as a result of baseball's antitrust exemption.

The district court refused to extend baseball's antitrust exemption to the entire "business of baseball." In refusing, the court ruled that "the exemption created by *Federal Baseball* is inapplicable ... because it is limited to baseball's reserve system."[17] In support of this conclusion, the district

---

[15] Piazza v. Major League Baseball, 831 F.Supp. 420 (1993).

[16] Vincent Piazza is the father of New York Mets catcher Mike Piazza.

[17] The court also examined the markets in which the anticompetitive activity took place. In Federal Baseball the anticompetitive activity was in the market for the

court interpreted the Supreme Court decision in *Flood* as "stripping from *Federal Baseball* and *Toolson* any precedential value those cases may have had beyond the particular facts there involved, *i.e.*, the reserve clause." There can be no doubt, the court held, that after *Flood*, "[p]rofessional baseball is a business . . . engaged in interstate commerce" and that baseball's exemption from the federal antitrust laws created by *Federal Baseball* was limited to the reserve clause. Therefore, the court concluded, since the case did not involve the reserve system, baseball's conduct could be subject to federal antitrust laws.

After the district court rejected MLB's motion to dismiss the antitrust claims based on baseball's antitrust exemption, MLB moved for an immediate appeal on the issue to the Third Circuit Court of Appeals. Judge Padova of the district court refused baseball's motion, ruling that such an action would unnecessarily delay the proceedings in the district court.

As in *Gardella*, this case also never made it to trial. A day before jury selection MLB settled the case with Piazza and Tirendi for a reported $6 million. \*\*\*

Another case that rejected baseball's claim of blanket antitrust immunity was *Postema v. National League of Professional Baseball Clubs.*[18] The plaintiff, a female umpire alleged that baseball discriminated against her in her job. Postema claimed that Baseball's conduct violated antitrust laws. Although not decided on antitrust grounds, the District Court rejected baseball's claim of blanket antitrust immunity. The court found that while "the baseball exemption to the antitrust law immunizes baseball from antitrust challenges to its league structure and its reserve system, the exemption does not provide baseball with blanket immunity ... in every context in which it operates." The court reached this decision after holding that the Supreme Court decision in *Flood* was an "endorsement of a limited view of the exemption."

The willingness of the courts in *Piazza*...and *Postema* to limit baseball's antitrust exemption has not become the rule. In *McCoy v. Major League Baseball*,[19] a federal District Court in the state of Washington

---

exhibition of baseball games. In Piazza, the anticompetitive activity is in the market for the "sale of ownership interests in  baseball teams--a market seemingly as distinguishable from the game exhibition  market as the player transportation market." 831 F. Supp. at 440.

[18] 799 F. Supp. 1475 (S.D.N.Y. 1992), rev'd on other grounds,  998 F.2d 60 (2d Cir.1993).

[19] 911 F. Supp. 454 (W.D.Wash. 1995).

interpreted baseball's Supreme Court trilogy as extending the antitrust exemption to the entire business of baseball. In *McCoy*, a group of fans and business owners brought an antitrust action against MLB steaming from the owners' alleged unfair labor practice during the 1994 strike.

In granting baseball's motion to dismiss, the District Court rejected the reasoning behind the *Piazza* courts' interpretation of baseball's antitrust exemption as only applying to baseball reserve system. After examining baseball's Supreme Court trilogy, the *McCoy* court found that baseball's antitrust exemption encompassed the entire business of baseball. The "great weight of authority," the court noted, recognizes that baseball's antitrust exemption covers the business of baseball, and until Congress or the Supreme Court sees fit to alter the rule, the exemption covers the business of baseball.

### The Curt Flood Act of 1998

As mentioned in the introduction, as part of the 1997 Basic Agreement between MLB and the MLBPA both sides agreed that they would jointly request and lobby for the passage of a law clarifying that professional baseball players are covered under antitrust law. The result of this joint effort is the Curt Flood Act.

An important aspect of the Curt Flood Act, which amends the Clayton Act by adding a new section at the end, is that it only applies to Major League Baseball players. Therefore any antitrust issues covering minor league baseball, the amateur draft, the relationship between the major leagues and the minors, franchise relocation, intellectual property, the Sports Broadcasting Act, and umpires are specifically excluded from coverage under the Curt Flood Act.

This section of the paper analyzes some of the key sections and provisions of the Curt Flood Act and their possible impact on future antitrust litigation involving MLB.

The first section to review is Section 3.

Sec. 3. Application of the Antitrust Laws to Professional Major League Baseball.

The Clayton Act (15 U.S.C. Sec.12 et seq.) is amended by adding at the end the following new section:

Sec. 27 (a) Subject to subsection (b) through (d), the conduct, acts, practices, or agreements of persons in the business of organized professional major league baseball directly relating to or affecting employment of major league baseball players to play baseball at the major league level are subject to the antitrust laws to the same extent such conduct, acts, practices, or agreements would be subject to the antitrust laws if engaged in by persons in any other professional sports business affecting interstate commerce.

In an attempt to accommodate the concerns of the minor leagues, The Senate Judiciary Committee amended the original proposal of the Curt Flood Act to include the word "directly" immediately before the phrase "relating to or affecting employment" and the phrase "major league players" before the phrase "to play baseball." The Senate Judiciary Committee included these two phrases "at the behest of the minor leagues ... to ensure that minor league players, particularly those who had spent some time in the major leagues, did not use new subsection (a) as a bootstrap by which to attack conduct, acts, practices or agreements designed to apply to minor league employment." The Act, therefore, only applies to the conduct, acts, practices, or agreements of Major League Baseball that affect the employment of Major League Baseball players. In making the changes, Senator Orrin Hatch of Utah, Chair of the Senate Judiciary Committee and the principle sponsor of the Curt Flood Act stated that the changes were "in keeping with the neutrality sought by the Committee with respect to parties and circumstances not between major league owners and major league players."

The next paragraph of the Act, § 27 (b), begins to outline the Act's restrictions.

§ 27 (b) No court shall rely on the enactment of this section as a basis for changing the application of the antitrust laws to any conduct, acts, practices, or agreements other than those set forth in subsection (a). This section does not create, permit or imply a cause of action by which to challenge under the antitrust laws, or otherwise apply the antitrust laws to, any conduct, acts, practices, or agreements that do not directly relate to or affect employment of major league baseball players to play baseball at the major league level, including but not limited to. . .

"While providing major league players with the antitrust protections of their colleagues in the other professional sports," the legislative history of the Act makes it clear that the Act "is absolutely neutral with respect to the state of the antitrust laws between all entities and in all circumstances other than in the area of employment as between major league owners and players." Senator Hatch also emphasized that the Act "affects no pending or decided cases except to the extent a court would consider exempting major league clubs from antitrust laws in their dealing with major league players." The Senate Judiciary Committee inserted the language limiting the court's ability to rely on the Flood Act in changing or supporting how the antitrust laws are applied to baseball because it felt that the language was crucial in getting the Flood Act passed.

Congress, therefore, presented with the perfect opportunity to clarify the judicial debate over the application of federal antitrust law to baseball, failed to take advantage of this opportunity. In fact, the language of the Act does not even attempt to overturn or clarify Major League Baseball's antitrust exemption in any other area except in the area of employment between major league owners and players.

The next six sections of the Act specifically identify areas excluded from coverage under the Act. The first two sections, §§ 27 (b)(1) and (2), are designed to protect the relationship between Major League Baseball and the minor leagues.

> § 27(b)(1) any conduct, acts, practices, or agreements of persons engaging in, conducting or participating in the business of organized professional baseball relating to or affecting employment to play at the minor league level, any organized professional baseball amateur or first-year player draft, or any reserve clause as applied to minor league players;

> § 27(b)(2) the agreement between organized professional major league baseball teams and the teams of the National Association of Professional Baseball Leagues, commonly known at the "Professional Baseball Agreement," the relationship between organized professional major league baseball and organized professional minor league baseball, or any other matter relating to organized professional baseball's minor leagues.

As mentioned above it was important for the Senate Judiciary Committee to accommodate the concerns of the minor leagues, and these sections accomplish this goal by "direct[ing] a court's attention to only those practices, or aspects of practices, that affect major league players." Senator Hatch included these sections at the urging of several members of the Senate Judiciary Committee because of the complex relationship between the major leagues and their affiliated minor leagues. Due to this relationship, the Senate Judiciary Committee was concerned "that the bill might inadvertently have a negative impact on the minor leagues."[20] Therefore, as long as a player is in the minor leagues, the Curt Flood Act will not apply to them or their relationship with their minor league team and league.

After addressing the minor league issue, the next area excluded from coverage is franchise expansion, relocation, or ownership issues. Section 27 (b)(3) states that:

> § 27(b)(3) any conduct, acts, practices, or agreements of persons engaging in, conducting or participating in the business of organized professional baseball relating to or affecting franchise expansion, location or relocation, franchise ownership issues, including ownership transfers, the relationship between the Office of the Commissioner and franchise owners, the marketing or sales of the entertainment product or organized professional baseball and the licensing of intellectual property rights owned or held by organized professional baseball teams individually or collectively…

The only real area MLB's antitrust exemption has not worked is in the area franchise relocation and ownership. Section 27 (b)(3), makes it clear that the conduct, acts, practices, or agreements relating to or affecting franchise expansion, location or relocation, franchise ownership issues, including ownership transfers are specifically excluded from coverage under the Act. In light of the recent litigation concerning this issue, there are two ways Congress' inaction can be interpreted.

---

[20] Cong. Rec. S 9495. Stanley Brand, vice president of the National Association of Professional Baseball Leagues expressed his concern to the Judiciary Committee that the Act did not adequately protect the minor leagues. Due to the reservations by Brand, Bud Selig, then chairman of the Major League Executive Council, wrote the Committee a letter stating that although he supported the Curt Flood Act, his support was tempered because of the concerns of the minor leagues. See S. Rep. No. 118, 105th Cong., 1st Sess. 4 (1997).

First, it could be argued that Congress, at the urging of baseball, inserted this clause for the specific purpose of challenging the decision in *Piazza*...thereby protecting MLB from future antitrust lawsuits over "affecting franchise expansion, location or relocation, franchise ownership issues." Support for this argument can also be found in a letter by the Congressional Budget Office concerning the cost of the Curt Flood Act. In the cost estimate of the Act, June O'Neill, Director of the Congressional Budget Office states that the Act "would remove baseball's current exemption from antitrust laws, except that it would retain the antitrust exemption for minor league baseball and for decisions regarding league expansion, franchise location, the amateur draft and broadcast rights, and employment relations with nonplayers, such as umpires."

The second argument is that Congress, by failing to clarify or specifically overturn *Piazza*, wanted to include this type of conduct under federal antitrust law. This argument is supported by the language at the beginning of § 27 (b) stating that "[n]o court shall rely on the enactment of this section as a basis for changing the application of the antitrust laws to any conduct, acts, practices, or agreements other than those set forth in subsection (a)."

The fourth area excluded from coverage under the Curt Flood Act is the Sports Broadcasting Act of 1961. The Sports Broadcasting Act of 1961 exempts professional football, baseball, basketball, and hockey leagues from antitrust laws in the area of network TV contracts.[21] The Act was enacted

---

[21] Before the passage of the Sports Broadcast Act of 1961, professional sports teams sold the television rights of their games individually. In 1960, the American Football League (AFL) negotiated a four-year television contract for the rights to the entire league with ABC for $1.7 million per year. The AFL's deal was unique in that for the first time an entire professional sports league pooled its television rights and sold them to a single network. The NFL fearing that the deal would provide the AFL with a competitive advantage also sought to pool its television rights. The NFL however was barred from pooling its television rights by the court in United States v. National Football League, 196 F. Supp. 445 (E.D. Pa. 1961). Believing that the NFL was at a competitive disadvantage, Pete Rozelle, the NFL Commissioner, approached Congress seeking special legislation, which would allow the league to pool its members' television rights. After hearing from Rozelle and the heads of the other professional sports leagues, Congress passed the Sports Broadcast Act of 1961. The Act exempts professional sports leagues from antitrust litigation in the limited area of pooling and selling the league's television rights as a package. The Act also restricts the ability of the leagues to define the geographical area into which the pooled telecasts may be broadcast. For more information on the Sports Broadcasting Act of 1961 See David S. Neft & Richard M. Cohen, The Football Encyclopedia: The Complete History of Professional NFL Football from 1892 to the Present 314

after the American Football League (AFL) pooled the entire league's television rights and negotiated a four-year television contract with ABC for $1.7 million per year. ABC's contract with the AFL was the first instance wherein a league sold the television rights of the entire league, up to this point teams sold their rights individually. The National Football League (NFL), worried about the competitive balance between its large and small market teams, and the impact the AFL's contract would have on the competitive balance between the leagues, entered into a league wide contract with CBS. The NFL's new contract would also pool league members' television rights and equally divide all television revenue. However, the NFL was barred from pooling its television rights by the court. With no other alternative, the NFL petitioned Congress for a limited antitrust exemption. After hearing from each of the professional sports leagues, Congress passed the Sports Broadcast Act, thereby allowing professional sports leagues to pool and sell television rights as a package.

The fifth area excluded from coverage under the Act is the relationship between organized baseball and umpires. Although Major League Umpires have their own union and their relationship with baseball has been almost as combative as that of the players, umpires are excluded from coverage under the Curt Flood Act. Also, just like in the case of franchise relocation, there is some disagreement between the courts whether umpires should be covered under baseball's antitrust immunity. In *Postema*[22] the District Court rejected Baseball's claim of blanket antitrust immunity. In fact, the court found that baseball antitrust exemption only immunized baseball from challenges to its league structure and its reserve system. The alternative view can be seen in *Salerno*. In *Salerno*, the Second Circuit Court of Appeals, after freely acknowledging its "belief that *Federal Baseball* was not one of Mr. Justice Holmes' happiest days, [and] that the rationale of *Toolson* is extremely dubious" held that overruling the Supreme Court is the exclusive privilege of the Supreme Court.[23]

Once again, Congress had the perfect opportunity to clarify this judicial debate and failed to take advantage of the opportunity. Therefore,

---

(1991); Gary R. Roberts, Pirating Satellite Signals of Blacked-Out Sports Events: A Historical and Policy Perspective, 11 Columbia--VLA Journal of Law & the Arts, 363-386 (1987); Robert A. Garrett & Philip R. Hochberg, Sports Broadcasting and the Law, 59 Indiana Law Journal, 155-192 (1984); and John T. Wolohan, NFL Broadcasts and the Home System Defense of the Federal Copyright Act, 5, Journal of Legal Aspects of Sport 35 (1995).

[22] 799 F. Supp. at 1488.

[23] Salerno, 429 F.2d at 1005.

depending on the interpretation of Congress's action or inaction, baseball's antitrust exemption may or may not include umpires.

The last area specifically excluded from coverage under the Curt Flood Act is all persons not in the business of organized professional major league baseball. Under this section, Vincent Piazza and Vincent Tirendi would be excluded from using the Curt Flood Act because they were not in the business of organized professional major league baseball at any time. Once again Congress failed to include an important group under coverage of the Curt Flood Act--individual, partnerships, corporations, trusts, or unincorporated associations who are attempting to purchase Major League Baseball teams.

After identifying what type of conduct, acts and practices are specifically excluded from coverage under the Curt Flood Act, Section 27 (c) states that only major league baseball players have standing to sue Major League Baseball under the Act. This limitation of standing seems to be directed at depriving the Justice Department, which opposed the Curt Flood Act, and the Federal Trade Commission the ability to sue Major League Baseball over player restraints.

Besides those individuals who are currently under contract, or playing baseball at the major league level, there are three other groups of individuals who qualify as major league players with standing under the Flood Act. The first group includes anyone who is under contract or playing baseball at the major league level at the time of an injury that is the subject of an antitrust complaint. The second group includes any individual who has played in the majors, and claims he has been injured in his efforts to secure a subsequent major league player's contract by an alleged violation of the antitrust laws. The final group includes anyone who was under contract or playing in the majors "at the conclusion of the last full championship season immediately preceding the expiration of the last collective bargaining agreement."

The final section of note is § 27 (d)(4), which states that:

Nothing in this section shall be construed to affect
the application to organized professional baseball of the
nonstatutory labor exemption from antitrust laws.

Due to the United States Supreme Court's decision in *Brown vs. Pro Football Inc.*,[24] the impact the Curt Flood Act will have on collective bargaining between MLB and the MLBPA is probably very little. In *Brown*, a group of professional football players challenged the right of the NFL to unilaterally, once an impasse was reached in collective bargaining process, fix the salary of all players assigned to a team's developmental squad. In upholding the NFL's right, as the employer, the Supreme Court ruled that the league's conduct fell within scope of nonstatutory labor exemption from antitrust liability. The nonstatutory labor exemption allows parties involved in collective bargaining to engage in conduct that is authorized by labor law without the fear of being sued under antitrust law by the other party. As long as there is a union, the nonstatutory labor exemption will bar the players from filing any antitrust claims. Therefore, the only way baseball players could use the Curt Flood Act would be to decertify their union.

---

[24] 518 U.S. 231 (1996). After the collective-bargaining agreement between the NFL and the NFL Players Association expired, the two sides began to negotiate a new collective-bargaining agreement. The NFL presented a plan that would permit each club to establish a "developmental squad" of substitute players, each of whom would be paid the same $1,000.00 weekly salary. The union rejected this proposal and insisted that individual squad members should be free to negotiate their own salaries. When negotiations reached an impasse, the NFL unilaterally implemented the plan.

A group of developmental squad players, unhappy over the single salary structure, filed an antitrust suit against the NFL, claiming that the NFL's agreement to pay them $1,000.00 per week was a restraint of trade in violation of the Sherman Act. The Court of Appeals for the District of Columbia, in reversing the District Court decision in favor of the players, held that the owners were immune from antitrust liability under the federal labor laws. Brown v. Pro Football 50 F.3d 1041 (D.C. DC 1995).

The Supreme Court, in upholding the Court of Appeals, held that federal labor laws shields from antitrust attack an agreement to unilaterally implement the terms of their last best good-faith wage offer when the sides have been bargaining in good faith and an impasse has been reach. Subjecting such agreements to antitrust law would cause "instability and uncertainty into the collective-bargaining process," since antitrust laws forbid or discourages organizations from the types of collective actions that are required under collective bargaining. Brown, 518 U.S. 231.

The Supreme Court also noted that it had previously found in the labor laws an implicit, "nonstatutory" antitrust exemption that applies where needed to make the collective-bargaining process work. See, e.g., Connell Construction Co. v. Plumbers, 421 U.S. 616, 622 (1975).

# Conclusion

To determine the importance of the Curt Flood Act, we must first determine what the current status of organized baseball's antitrust exemption is after the passage of the Act. Odd as it may sound, by passing the Curt Flood Act, Congress may have actually saved baseball's antitrust exemption. After the Supreme Court's decision in *Flood*, there was a trend among some courts to limit baseball's antitrust exemption to the reserve system only. Examples of baseball's shrinking antitrust exemption can be seen in *Piazza*...and *Postema*. In...these cases, the courts interpreted the Supreme Court's decision in *Flood* as placing limits on baseball's antitrust exemption, narrowly applying the exemption only to baseball's player reserve system.

Still, not every court interpreted *Flood* as placing limits on baseball's antitrust exemption. The *Finley* and *McCoy* courts, for example, upheld an industry wide antitrust exemption when they held that until Congress acted to limit baseball's antitrust exemption, the exemption encompassed the entire business of baseball.

With the passage of the Curt Flood Act, baseball can now argue that Congress has acted. As discussed above, the Act is specifically designed to repeal baseball's antitrust exemption as it applies to Major League Baseball players. A reasonable interpretation of Congress' decision to only include Major League Baseball players, therefore would be that Congress did not want the entire business of baseball to be covered under a blanket antitrust exemption. Congress could have included minor league baseball, the amateur draft, the relationship between the major leagues and the minors, franchise relocation, intellectual property, the Sports Broadcasting Act, umpires or any other area it wanted in the Curt Flood Act, but it specifically excluded them. It only stands to reason, therefore, that Congress in its actions, by failing to include the entire business of baseball in the Curt Flood Act, wanted everything not having to do with player relations exempt from antitrust laws.

If you accept this interpretation of the Curt Flood Act, the arguments presented in *Piazza*...and *Postema* that baseball's antitrust exemption is just limited to the reserve system, no longer have any value. Therefore, the Act, instead of weakening baseball's antitrust exemption, actually makes it stronger.

## Notes & Questions

1. In the famous *Federal Baseball* decision, what was the court's basis for holding that Major League Baseball was not involved in interstate commerce?

2. Had the *Gardella* case been appealed to the U.S. Supreme Court rather than settled, do you think that the Supreme Court might have affirmed the Second Circuit's opinion? If so why? If not why not?

3. In *Toolson* and in *Flood* the Supreme Court held that Congress, not the judiciary, has the authority to determine whether baseball ought to be exempt from antitrust. What criteria should be considered in determining whether such issues ought to be resolved by the legislative or the judicial branch? In his dissent in *Flood*, Justice Douglas argued that the Supreme Court ought to have the authority to correct its own mistakes. What's wrong, if anything, with that logic?

4. Do you think that Wolohan is right? Has the Curt Flood Act actually strengthened Major League Baseball's position by preserving certain aspects of the antitrust exemption? Explain your answer.

## 15 United States Code § 2

### § 2. Monopolizing trade a felony; penalty

Every person who shall monopolize, or attempt to monopolize, or combine or conspire with any other person or persons, to monopolize any part of the trade or commerce among the several States, or with foreign nations, shall be deemed guilty of a felony, and, on conviction thereof, shall be punished by fine not exceeding $100,000,000 if a corporation, or, if any other person, $1,000,000, or by imprisonment not exceeding 10 years, or by both said punishments, in the discretion of the court.

## Notes & Questions

1. In the 1960's when the American Football League challenged the National Football League in terms of popularity, it also challenged the NFL in court, arguing that the NFL's monopoly had run afoul of Sherman section 2. *See* AFL v. NFL, 323 F. 2d 124 (4th Cir. 1963). In the 1980's the United States Football League made similar arguments against the NFL. *See* USFL v. NFL,

842 F.2d. 1335 (2d Cir. 1988). The USFL filed suit alleging violations of the Sherman Antitrust Act. The jury of the lower court awarded plaintiffs one dollar in damages after finding that defendants had willfully acquired or maintained monopoly power in a market consisting of major league professional football in the U.S. and that such monopolization had injured plaintiffs. On appeal, the lower court's verdict was affirmed. The anti-competitive activities on which the jury based its verdict did not justify a large damages verdict or sweeping injunctive relief. What types of conduct by the NFL might have been considered violative of the Sherman Act, section 2?

*Further Reading on Antitrust and Labor Law*

James R. Devine, *Baseball's Labor Wars in Historical Context*, 5 Marq. Sports L.J. 1 (1994).

Lee Goldman, *Sports, Antitrust, and the Single Entity Theory,* 63 TUL. L. REV. 751 (1989).

Daniel E. Lazaroff, *The Antitrust Implications of Franchise Relocation Restrictions in Professional Sports*, 53 FORDHAM L. REV. 157 (1984).

Robert A. McCormick, *Professional Football's Draft Eligibility Rule: The Labor Exemption and the Antitrust Laws*, 33 EMORY L.J. 375 (1984).

Matthew J. Mitten, *University Price Competition For Elite Students and Athletes: Illusions and Realities*, 36 S. TEXAS L. REV. 59 (1995).

Gary Roberts, *On the Scope and Effect of Baseball's Antitrust Exclusion*, 4 SETON HALL J. SPORT L. 321 (1994).

Stephen F. Ross, *Antitrust Options to Redress Anticompetitve Restraints and Monopolistic Practices by Professional Sports Leagues*, 52 CASE W. RES. L. REV. 133 (2001).

Stephen F. Ross, *Monopoly Sports Leagues*, 73 MINN. L. REV. 643 (1989).

Stephen F. Ross, *Open Competition in League Sports*, 2002 WIS. L. REV. 49 (2002).

Stephen F. Ross, *The Misunderstood Alliance Between Sports Fans, Players and the Antitrust Laws*, 1997 U. Ill. L. REV. 519 (1997).

John P. Sahl, *College Atheletes and Due Process Protection*, 21 ARIZ. St. L. J. 621 (1989).

John C. Weistart, *League Control of Market Opportunities: A Perspective on Competition and Cooperation in the Sports Industry*, 1984 DUKE L.J. 1013 (1984).

John C. Weistart & Cym H. Lowell, Law of Sports, Chapter 5 (Bobbs-Merrill Company, Inc., 1979).

# Chapter 7

## Some Constitutional Law Concerns

These cases illustrate a number of Constitutional issues that frequently arise in Sports Law. As a rule, the cases require application of fairly elementary Constitutional Law. Plaintiffs typically argue that a right guaranteed either by the federal or a state constitution has been violated. Two issues that often arise are whether a person's right to exercise speech or religion freely has been violated, and whether a person's liberty or property has been taken without due process of law. As such, courts must determine whether state action was involved.

Courts must also determine what level of scrutiny will be applied: rational basis; middle tier; or, strict scrutiny. There are three basic rules that one must keep in mind when analyzing cases such as these. First, as a rule, when a state law affects a fundamental right (such as freedom of religion or speech, protected by the first amendment), in order to be held constitutional, courts say that the rule must be designed to promote a **compelling governmental objective** and it must be **narrowly drafted** (by the **least restrictive means**) in a fashion to achieve that compelling governmental objective (**strict scrutiny**). Second, if a state law affects a "suspect class," courts say that, in order to be held constitutional, the rule must be designed to promote an **important governmental objective** and it must be **closely drafted** in a fashion to achieve that important governmental objective (**middle tier**). Third, in all cases where the state law at issue does not affect either a fundamental tight or a suspect class, courts say that, in order to held constitutional, the law must be designed merely to promote a **legitimate governmental objective** and it must be **rationally related** to achieving that legitimate governmental objective (**rational basis**).

*Brentwood Academy* analyzes the state action requirement as it applies to the 14th Amendment. *Spring Branch* is a case construing the

323

Texas State Constitution and its guarantees of equal protection and due process. *James*, like *Spring Branch*, considers the issue of whether a high school student's participation in extracurricular sports activities should be deemed a constitutionally protectable "property interest." *Jordan* also looks at this same issue, but does so in the emotionally-charged context of teenage alcohol consumption, school discipline, and the scholarship opportunities of a high school football player.

As you read these cases, you may find it helpful to consider the following two constitutional amendments.

## First Amendment

Congress shall make no law respecting an establishment of religion, or prohibiting the free exercise thereof; or abridging the freedom of speech, or of the press; or the right of the people peaceably to assemble, and to petition the government for a redress of grievances.

## Fourteenth Amendment (pertinent part)

No state shall make or enforce any law which shall abridge the privileges or immunities of citizens of the United States; nor shall any state deprive any person of life, liberty, or property, without due process of law; nor deny to any person within its jurisdiction the equal protection of the laws.

Justice SOUTER delivered the opinion of the Court.

The issue is whether a statewide association incorporated to regulate interscholastic athletic competition among public and private secondary schools may be regarded as engaging in state action when it enforces a rule against a member school. The association in question here includes most public schools located within the State, acts through their representatives, draws its officers from them, is largely funded by their dues and income received in their stead, and has historically been seen to regulate in lieu of the State Board of Education's exercise of its own authority. We hold that the association's regulatory activity may and should be treated as state action owing to the pervasive entwinement of state school officials in the structure of the association, there being no offsetting reason to see the association's acts in any other way.


I.

Respondent Tennessee Secondary School Athletic Association (Association) is a not-for-profit membership corporation organized to regulate interscholastic sport among the public and private high schools in Tennessee that belong to it. No school is forced to join, but without any other authority actually regulating interscholastic athletics, it enjoys the memberships of almost all the State's public high schools (some 290 of them or 84% of the Association's voting membership), far outnumbering the 55 private schools that belong. A member school's team may play or scrimmage only against the team of another member, absent a dispensation.

The Association's rulemaking arm is its legislative council, while its board of control tends to administration. The voting membership of each of these nine-person committees is limited under the Association's bylaws to high school principals, assistant principals, and superintendents elected by the member schools, and the public school administrators who so serve typically attend meetings during regular school hours. Although the Association's staff members are not paid by the State, they are eligible to join the State's public retirement system for its employees. Member schools pay dues to the Association, though the bulk of its revenue is gate receipts at member teams' football and basketball tournaments, many of them held in public arenas rented by the Association.

The constitution, bylaws, and rules of the Association set standards of school membership and the eligibility of students to play in interscholastic games. Each school, for example, is regulated in awarding financial aid, most coaches must have a Tennessee state teaching license, and players must meet minimum academic standards and hew to limits on student employment. Under the bylaws, "in all matters pertaining to the athletic relations of his school," the principal is responsible to the Association, which has the power "to suspend, to fine, or otherwise penalize any member school for the violation of any of the rules of the Association or for other just cause."

Ever since the Association was incorporated in 1925, Tennessee's State Board of Education (State Board) has (to use its own words) acknowledged the corporation's functions "in providing standards, rules and regulations for interscholastic competition in the public schools of Tennessee.". More recently, the State Board cited its statutory authority, Tenn.Code Ann. § 49-1-302 (1996), when it adopted language expressing the relationship between the Association and the State Board. Specifically, in 1972, it went so far as to adopt a rule expressly "designat [ing]" the Association as "the organization to supervise and regulate the athletic activities in which the public junior and senior high schools in Tennessee participate on an interscholastic basis." Tennessee State Board of Education, Administrative Rules and Regulations, Rule 0520-1-2-.26 (1972) (later moved to Rule 0520-1-2-.08).****

The action before us responds to a 1997 regulatory enforcement proceeding brought against petitioner, Brentwood Academy, a private parochial high school member of the Association. The Association's board of control found that Brentwood violated a rule prohibiting "undue influence" in recruiting athletes, when it wrote to incoming students and their parents about spring football practice. The Association accordingly placed Brentwood's athletic program on probation for four years, declared its football and boys' basketball teams ineligible to compete in playoffs for two years, and imposed a $3,000 fine. When these penalties were imposed, all the voting members of the board of control and legislative council were public school administrators.

Brentwood sued the Association and its executive director in federal court under Rev. Stat. § 1979, 42 U.S.C. § 1983, claiming that enforcement of the Rule was state action and a violation of the First and Fourteenth Amendments. The District Court entered summary judgment for Brentwood and enjoined the Association from enforcing the Rule. *Brentwood Academy v. Tennessee Secondary Schools Athletic Association,* 13 F.Supp.2d 670 (M.D.Tenn.1998). In holding the Association to be a state actor under § 1983 and the Fourteenth Amendment, the District Court found that the State had delegated authority over high school athletics to the Association, characterized the relationship between the Association and its public school members as symbiotic, and emphasized the predominantly public character of the Association's membership and leadership. The court relied on language in *National Collegiate Athletic Assn. v. Tarkanian,* 488 U.S. 179, 193, n. 13, 109 S.Ct. 454, 102 L.Ed.2d 469 (1988), suggesting that statewide interscholastic athletic associations are state actors, and on other federal cases in which such organizations had uniformly been held to be acting under color of state law.

The United States Court of Appeals for the Sixth Circuit reversed. 180 F.3d 758 (1999). It recognized that there is no single test to identify state actions and state actors but applied three criteria derived from *Blum v. Yaretsky,* 457 U.S. 991, 102 S.Ct. 2777, 73 L.Ed.2d 534 (1982), *Lugar v. Edmondson Oil Co.,* 457 U.S. 922, 102 S.Ct. 2744, 73 L.Ed.2d 482 (1982), and *Rendell--Baker v. Kohn,* 457 U.S. 830, 102 S.Ct. 2764, 73 L.Ed.2d 418 (1982), and found no state action under any of them. It said the District Court was mistaken in seeing a symbiotic relationship between the State and the Association, it emphasized that the Association was neither engaging in a traditional and exclusive public function nor responding to state compulsion, and it gave short shrift to the language from *Tarkanian* on which the District Court relied. Rehearing en banc was later denied over the dissent of two judges, who criticized the panel decision for creating a conflict among state and federal courts, for being inconsistent with *Tarkanian,* and for lacking support in the "functional" analysis of private activity required by *West v. Atkins,* 487 U.S. 42, 108 S.Ct. 2250, 101 L.Ed.2d 40 (1988), for assessing the significance of cooperation between public officials and a private actor. 190 F.3d 705 (C.A.6 1999) (Merritt, J., dissenting from denial of rehearing en banc).

We granted certiorari, 528 U.S. 1153, 120 S.Ct. 1156, 145 L.Ed.2d 1069 (2000), to resolve the conflict[1] and now reverse.

---

[1] A number of other courts have held statewide athletic associations to be state actors. *Griffin High School v. Illinois High School Assn.,* 822 F.2d 671, 674 (C.A.7 1987); *Clark v. Arizona Interscholastic Assn.,* 695 F.2d 1126, 1128 (C.A.9 1982), cert. denied, 464 U.S. 818, 104 S.Ct. 79, 78 L.Ed.2d 90 (1983); *In re United States ex rel. Missouri State High School Activities Assn.,* 682 F.2d 147, 151 (C.A.8 1982); *Louisiana High School Athletic Assn. v. St. Augustine High School,* 396 F.2d 224, 227-228 (C.A.5 1968); *Oklahoma High School Athletic Assn. v. Bray,* 321 F.2d 269,

II.

A.

[1][2] Our cases try to plot a line between state action subject to Fourteenth Amendment scrutiny and private conduct (however exceptionable) that is not. *Tarkanian, supra,* at 191, 109 S.Ct. 454; *Jackson v. Metropolitan Edison Co.,* 419 U.S. 345, 349, 95 S.Ct. 449, 42 L.Ed.2d 477 (1974). The judicial obligation is not only to " 'preserv[e] an area of individual freedom by limiting the reach of federal law' and avoi[d] the imposition of responsibility on a State for conduct it could not control," *Tarkanian, supra,* at 191, 109 S.Ct. 454 (quoting *Lugar, supra,* at 936- 937, 102 S.Ct. 2744), but also to assure that constitutional standards are invoked "when it can be said that the State is *responsible* for the specific conduct of which the plaintiff complains," *Blum, supra,* at 1004, 102 S.Ct. 2777 (emphasis in original). If the Fourteenth Amendment is not to be displaced, therefore, its ambit cannot be a simple line between States and people operating outside formally governmental organizations, and the deed of an ostensibly private organization or individual is to be treated sometimes as if a State had caused it to be performed. Thus, we say that state action may be found if, though only if, there is such a "close nexus between the State and the challenged action" that seemingly private behavior "may be fairly treated as that of the State itself." *Jackson, supra,* at 351, 95 S.Ct. 449.[2]

[3] What is fairly attributable is a matter of normative judgment, and the criteria lack rigid simplicity. From the range of circumstances that could point toward the State behind an individual face, no one fact can function as a necessary condition across the board for finding state action; nor is any set of circumstances absolutely sufficient, for there may be some countervailing reason against attributing activity to the government. See *Tarkanian,* 488 U.S., at 193, 196, 109 S.Ct. 454; *Polk County v. Dodson,* 454 U.S. 312, 102 S.Ct. 445, 70 L.Ed.2d 509 (1981).

---

272-273 (C.A.10 1963); *Indiana High School Athletic Assn. v. Carlberg,* 694 N.E.2d 222, 229 (Ind.1997); *Mississippi High School Activities Assn., Inc. v. Coleman,* 631 So.2d 768, 774-775 (Miss.1994); *Kleczek v. Rhode Island Interscholastic League, Inc.,* 612 A.2d 734, 736 (R.I.1992); see also *Moreland v. Western Penn. Interscholastic Athletic League,* 572 F.2d 121, 125 (C.A.3 1978) (state action conceded).

[2] If a defendant's conduct satisfies the state-action requirement of the Fourteenth Amendment, the conduct also constitutes action "under color of state law" for § 1983 purposes. *Lugar v. Edmondson Oil Co.,* 457 U.S. 922, 935, 102 S.Ct. 2744, 73 L.Ed.2d 482 (1982).

328

Our cases have identified a host of facts that can bear on the fairness of such an attribution. We have, for example, held that a challenged activity may be state action when it results from the State's exercise of "coercive power," *Blum,* 457 U.S., at 1004, 102 S.Ct. 2777, when the State provides "significant encouragement, either overt or covert," *ibid.,* or when a private actor operates as a "willful participant in joint activity with the State or its agents," *Lugar, supra,* at 941, 102 S.Ct. 2744 (internal quotation marks omitted). We have treated a nominally private entity as a state actor when it is controlled by an "agency of the State," *Pennsylvania v. Board of Directors of City Trusts of Philadelphia,* 353 U.S. 230, 231, 77 S.Ct. 806, 1 L.Ed.2d 792 (1957) *(per curiam),* when it has been delegated a public function by the State, cf., *e.g., West v. Atkins, supra,* at 56, 108 S.Ct. 2250; *Edmonson v. Leesville Concrete Co.,* 500 U.S. 614, 627-628, 111 S.Ct. 2077, 114 L.Ed.2d 660 (1991), when it is "entwined with governmental policies," or when government is "entwined in [its] management or control," *Evans v. Newton,* 382 U.S. 296, 299, 301, 86 S.Ct. 486, 15 L.Ed.2d 373 (1966).

[4] Amidst such variety, examples may be the best teachers, and examples from our cases are unequivocal in showing that the character of a legal entity is determined neither by its expressly private characterization in statutory law, nor by the failure of the law to acknowledge the entity's inseparability from recognized government officials or agencies. *Lebron v. National Railroad Passenger Corporation,* 513 U.S. 374, 115 S.Ct. 961, 130 L.Ed.2d 902 (1995), held that Amtrak was the Government for constitutional purposes, regardless of its congressional designation as private; it was organized under federal law to attain governmental objectives and was directed and controlled by federal appointees. *Pennsylvania v. Board of Directors of City Trusts of Philadelphia, supra,* held the privately endowed Girard College to be a state actor and enforcement of its private founder's limitation of admission to whites attributable to the State, because, consistent with the terms of the settlor's gift, the college's board of directors was a state agency established by state law. Ostensibly the converse situation occurred in *Evans v. Newton, supra,* which held that private trustees to whom a city had transferred a park were nonetheless state actors barred from enforcing racial segregation, since the park served the public purpose of providing community recreation, and "the municipality remain[ed] entwined in [its] management [and] control," *id.,* at 301, 86 S.Ct. 486.

These examples of public entwinement in the management and control of ostensibly separate trusts or corporations foreshadow this case, as this Court itself anticipated in *Tarkanian.* *Tarkanian* arose when an undoubtedly state actor, the University of Nevada, suspended its basketball coach, Tarkanian, in order to comply with rules and recommendations of the National Collegiate Athletic Association (NCAA). The coach charged the NCAA with state action, arguing that the state university had delegated its own functions to the NCAA, clothing the latter with authority to make and apply the university's rules, the result being joint action making the NCAA a state actor.

To be sure, it is not the strict holding in *Tarkanian* that points to our view of this case, for we found no state action on the part of the NCAA. We could see, on the one hand, that the university had some part in setting the NCAA's rules, and the Supreme Court of Nevada had gone so far as to hold that the NCAA had been delegated the university's traditionally exclusive public authority over personnel. 488 U.S., at 190, 109 S.Ct. 454. But on the other side, the NCAA's policies were shaped not by the University of Nevada alone, but by several hundred member institutions, most of them having no connection with Nevada, and exhibiting no color of Nevada law. *Id.,* at 193, 109 S.Ct. 454. Since it was difficult to see the NCAA, not as a collective membership, but as surrogate for the one State, we held the organization's connection with Nevada too insubstantial to ground a state-action claim. *Id.,* at 193, 196, 109 S.Ct. 454.

But dictum in *Tarkanian* pointed to a contrary result on facts like ours, with an organization whose member public schools are all within a single State. "The situation would, of course, be different if the [Association's] membership consisted entirely of institutions located within the same State, many of them public institutions created by the same sovereign." *Id.,* at 193, n. 13, 109 S.Ct. 454. To support our surmise, we approvingly cited two cases: *Clark v. Arizona Interscholastic Assn.,* 695 F.2d 1126 (C.A.9 1982), cert. denied, 464 U.S. 818, 104 S.Ct. 79, 78 L.Ed.2d 90 (1983), a challenge to a state high school athletic association that kept boys from playing on girls' interscholastic volleyball teams in Arizona; and *Louisiana High School Athletic Assn. v. St. Augustine High School,* 396 F.2d 224 (C.A.5 1968), a parochial school's attack on the racially segregated system of interscholastic high school athletics maintained by the athletic association. In each instance, the Court of Appeals treated the athletic association as a state actor.

B.

[5] Just as we foresaw in *Tarkanian,* the "necessarily fact-bound inquiry," *Lugar,* 457 U.S., at 939, 102 S.Ct. 2744, leads to the conclusion of state action here. The nominally private character of the Association is overborne by the pervasive entwinement of public institutions and public

officials in its composition and workings, and there is no substantial reason to claim unfairness in applying constitutional standards to it.

The Association is not an organization of natural persons acting on their own, but of schools, and of public schools to the extent of 84% of the total. Under the Association's bylaws, each member school is represented by its principal or a faculty member, who has a vote in selecting members of the governing legislative council and board of control from eligible principals, assistant principals, and superintendents.

Although the findings and prior opinions in this case include no express conclusion of law that public school officials act within the scope of their duties when they represent their institutions, no other view would be rational, the official nature of their involvement being shown in any number of ways. Interscholastic athletics obviously play an integral part in the public education of Tennessee, where nearly every public high school spends money on competitions among schools. Since a pickup system of interscholastic games would not do, these public teams need some mechanism to produce rules and regulate competition. The mechanism is an organization overwhelmingly composed of public school officials who select representatives (all of them public officials at the time in question here), who in turn adopt and enforce the rules that make the system work. Thus, by giving these jobs to the Association, the 290 public schools of Tennessee belonging to it can sensibly be seen as exercising their own authority to meet their own responsibilities. Unsurprisingly, then, the record indicates that half the council or board meetings documented here were held during official school hours, and that public schools have largely provided for the Association's financial support. A small portion of the Association's revenue comes from membership dues paid by the schools, and the principal part from gate receipts at tournaments among the member schools. *** The Association thus exercises the authority of the predominantly public schools to charge for admission to their games; the Association does not receive this money from the schools, but enjoys the schools' moneymaking capacity as its own.

In sum, to the extent of 84% of its membership, the Association is an organization of public schools represented by their officials acting in their official capacity to provide an integral element of secondary public schooling. There would be no recognizable Association, legal or tangible, without the public school officials, who do not merely control but overwhelmingly perform all but the purely ministerial acts by which the Association exists and functions in practical terms. Only the 16% minority of private school memberships prevents this entwinement of the Association and the public school system from being total and their identities totally indistinguishable.

To complement the entwinement of public school officials with the Association from the bottom up, the State of Tennessee has provided for entwinement from top down. State Board members are assigned ex officio to serve as members of the board of control and legislative council, and the Association's ministerial employees are treated as state employees to the extent of being eligible for membership in the state retirement system.

\*\*\*

[6] The entwinement down from the State Board is therefore unmistakable, just as the entwinement up from the member public schools is overwhelming. Entwinement will support a conclusion that an ostensibly private organization ought to be charged with a public character and judged by constitutional standards; entwinement to the degree shown here requires it.

[8] \*\*\*\* The Association suggests…that reversing the judgment here will somehow trigger an epidemic of unprecedented federal litigation. \*\*\* [T]he record raises no reason for alarm here. Save for the Sixth Circuit, every Court of Appeals to consider a statewide athletic association like the one here has found it a state actor. This majority view began taking shape even before *Tarkanian,* which cited two such decisions approvingly, see *supra,* at 931- 932 (and this was six years after *Blum, Rendell-Baker,* and *Lugar,* on which the Sixth Circuit relied here). No one, however, has pointed to any explosion of…cases against interscholastic athletic associations in the affected jurisdictions. Not to put too fine a point on it, two District Courts in Tennessee have previously held the Association itself to be a state actor [case citations omitted], but there is no evident wave of litigation working its way across the State. A reversal of the judgment here portends nothing more than the harmony of an outlying Circuit with precedent otherwise uniform.

\*\*\*

The judgment of the Court of Appeals for the Sixth Circuit is reversed, and the case is remanded for further proceedings consistent with this opinion.

*It is so ordered.*

Justice THOMAS, with whom THE CHIEF JUSTICE, Justice SCALIA, and Justice KENNEDY join, dissenting.

We have never found state action based upon mere "entwinement." Until today, we have found a private organization's acts to constitute state action only when the organization performed a public function; was created, coerced, or encouraged by the government; or acted in a symbiotic relationship with the government. The majority's holding--that the Tennessee Secondary School Athletic Association's (TSSAA) enforcement of its recruiting rule is state action--not only extends state-action doctrine beyond its permissible limits but also encroaches upon the realm of individual freedom that the doctrine was meant to protect. I respectfully dissent.

## Notes & Questions

1. There are multiple levels of analysis that must be considered when analyzing constitutional claims in a Sports Law context. As this case demonstrates, in order to prove a violation of the plaintiff's First or Fourteenth Amendment Rights, there must be "state action" present. For a moment, stop and reflect. What rights are guaranteed by the First and Fourteenth Amendments in the first place? How might rights such as these be violated in the context of sports? Give examples.

2. The Tennessee Secondary School Athletic Association, it seems, could be deemed to have been involved with "state action" pursuant to the "agency of the state" theory, "public function" doctrine, or the concept of "entwinement with government policies." On which of these theories did the Court rely, and why?

3. Explain the significance of the *Tarkanian* case on the outcome of the *Brentwood Academy* case.

# Spring Branch I.S.D. v. Chris Stamos
695 S.W.2d 556, (1985)
Supreme Court of Texas

RAY, Justice.

This is a direct appeal brought by the Attorney General, representing the Texas Education Agency, and others, seeking immediate appellate review of an order of the trial court which held unconstitutional, and enjoined enforcement of, a provision of the Texas Education Code. **** We hold that the statutory provision is not unconstitutional and reverse the judgment of the trial court.

Chris Stamos and others brought this suit on behalf of Nicky Stamos and others, seeking a permanent injunction against enforcement of the Texas "no pass, no play" rule by the Spring Branch and Alief Independent School Districts. The Texas Education Agency and the University Interscholastic League intervened. The district court issued a temporary restraining order and later, after a hearing, a temporary injunction enjoining all parties from enforcing the rule. This court issued an order staying the district court's order and setting the cause for expedited review.

THE "NO PASS, NO PLAY" RULE

The Second Called Session of the 68th Legislature adopted a package of educational reforms known as "H.B. 72." Act of July 13, 1984, Chapter 28, 1984 Tex.Gen. Laws, 2nd Called Session 269. A major provision of these educational reforms was the so-called "no pass, no play" rule, which generally requires that students maintain a "70" average in all classes to be eligible for participation in extracurricular activities. *See* Tex.Educ.Code Ann. § 21.920(b) (Vernon Supp.1985). The rule is incorporated in section 21.920 of the Texas Education Code and provides as follows:

> § 21.920. Extracurricular Activities
> (a) The State Board of Education by rule shall limit participation in and practice for extracurricular activities during the school day and the school week. The rules shall, to the extent possible, preserve the school day for academic activities without interruption for extracurricular activities. In scheduling those activities and practices, a district must comply with the rules of the board.

(b) A student, other than a mentally retarded student, enrolled in a school district in this state shall be suspended from participation in any extracurricular activity sponsored or sanctioned by the school district during the grade reporting period after a grade reporting period in which the student received a grade lower than the equivalent of 70 on a scale of 100 in any academic class. The campus principal may remove this suspension if the class is an identified honors or advanced class. A student may not be suspended under this subsection during the period in which school is recessed for the summer or during the initial grade reporting period of a regular school term on the basis of grades received in the final grade reporting period of the preceding regular school term.

(c) In this section, "mentally retarded" has the meaning assigned by Section 21.503(b)(5) of this code.

(d) Subsection (b) of this section applies beginning with the spring semester, 1985.

ISSUES RAISED

The sole issue before this court is the constitutionality of the no pass, no play rule. The district court held the rule unconstitutional on the grounds that it violated equal protection and due process guarantees. The burden is on the party attacking the constitutionality of an act of the legislature. *Texas Public Building Authority v. Mattox,* 686 S.W.2d 924, 927 (Tex.1985). There is a presumption in favor of the constitutionality of an act of the legislature. *See Sax v. Votteler,* 648 S.W.2d 661, 664 (Tex.1983).

This court has long recognized the important role education plays in the maintenance of our democratic society. Article VII of the Texas Constitution "discloses a well-considered purpose on the part of those who framed it to bring about the establishment and maintenance of a comprehensive system of public education, consisting of a general public free school system and a system of higher education." *Mumme v. Marrs,* 120 Tex. 383, 40 S.W.2d 31, 33 (1931). Section 1 of article VII of the Constitution establishes a mandatory duty upon the legislature to make suitable provision for the support and maintenance of public free schools. 40 S.W.2d at 36. The Constitution leaves to the legislature alone the determination of which methods, restrictions, and regulations are necessary and appropriate to carry out this duty, so long as that determination is not so arbitrary as to violate the constitutional rights of Texas' citizens. *Id.*

Equal Protection

Stamos challenges the constitutionality of the "no pass, no play" rule on the ground that it violates the equal protection clause of the Texas Constitution. The first determination this court must make in the context of equal protection analysis is the appropriate standard of review. When the classification created by a state regulatory scheme neither infringes upon fundamental rights or interests nor burdens an inherently suspect class, equal protection analysis requires that the classification be rationally related to a legitimate state interest. *Sullivan v. University Interscholastic League,* 616 S.W.2d 170, 172 (Tex.1981). Therefore, we must first determine whether the rule burdens an inherently suspect class or infringes upon fundamental rights or interests.

The no pass, no play rule classifies students based upon their achievement levels in their academic courses. We hold that those students who fail to maintain a minimum level of proficiency in all of their courses do not constitute the type of discrete, insular minority necessary to constitute a "suspect" class. *See United States v. Carolene Products Co.,* 304 U.S. 144, 152 n. 4, 58 S.Ct. 778, 783 n. 4, 82 L.Ed. 1234 (1938). Thus, the rule does not burden an inherently "suspect" class.

\*\*\*

Stamos also argues that the rule is subject to strict scrutiny under equal protection analysis because it impinges upon a fundamental right, *i.e.,* the right to participate in extracurricular activities. We note that the overwhelming majority of jurisdictions have held that a student's right to participation in extracurricular activities does *not* constitute a fundamental right. *See, e.g., Hardy v. University Interscholastic League,* 759 F.2d 1233, 1235 (5th Cir.1985); *Walsh v. Louisiana High School Athletic Ass'n,* 616 F.2d 152, 160-61 (5th Cir.1980); *Pennsylvania Interscholastic Athletic Ass'n, Inc. v. Greater Johnstown School District,* 76 Pa.Commw. 65, 463 A.2d 1198, 1202 (1983); and *Smith v. Crim,* 240 Ga. 390, 240 S.E.2d 884, 885 (1977).

Stamos cites the case of *Bell v. Lone Oak Independent School District,* 507 S.W.2d 636 (Tex.Civ.App.--Texarkana), *writ dism'd,* 515 S.W.2d 252 (Tex.1974) for the proposition that students have a fundamental right to participate in extracurricular activities. In *Bell,* a school regulation prohibited married students from participating in extracurricular activities. Because the regulation impinged upon the fundamental right of marriage, the court of appeals held the regulation subject to strict scrutiny and struck it down because the school district had shown no compelling interest to support its enforcement. 507 S.W.2d at 638-39. The presence of a fundamental right (marriage) distinguishes *Bell* from the present cause.

Fundamental rights have their genesis in the express and implied protections of personal liberty recognized in federal and state constitutions. A student's "right" to participate in extracurricular activities does not rise to the same level as the right to free speech or free exercise of religion, both of which have long been recognized as fundamental rights under our state and federal constitutions. We adopt the majority rule and hold that a student's right to participate in extracurricular activities *per se* does *not* rise to the level of a fundamental right under our constitution.

Because the no pass, no play rule neither infringes upon fundamental rights nor burdens an inherently suspect class, we hold that it is *not* subject to "strict" or heightened equal protection scrutiny. Rather, the rule must be judged by the standard set forth in *Sullivan v. UIL.* In *Sullivan,* this court struck down on equal protection grounds the U.I.L.'s non-transfer rule, which declared all non-seniors ineligible for varsity football and basketball competition for one year following their transfer to a new school. This court emphasized (1) the over-inclusiveness of the rule in light of its intended purpose of discouraging "recruitment" of student-athletes, and (2) the irrebuttable presumption created by the rule. *Sullivan,* 616 S.W.2d at 172-73. In view of these two factors, this court declared that the rule was *not* rationally related to its intended purpose. *Id.*

The no pass, no play rule distinguishes students based upon whether they maintain a satisfactory minimum level of performance in each of their classes. Students who fail to maintain a minimum proficiency in all of their classes are ineligible for participation in school-sponsored extracurricular activities for the following six-week period, with no carry over from one school year to the next. The rule provides a strong incentive for students wishing to participate in extracurricular activities to maintain minimum levels of performance in all of their classes. In view of the rule's objective to promote improved classroom performance by students, we find the rule rationally related to the legitimate state interest in providing a quality education to Texas' public school students. The rule does not suffer from either of the vices found determinative in *Sullivan v. UIL.*

The distinctions recognized in the rule for mentally retarded students and students enrolled in honors or advanced courses likewise do not render the rule violative of the equal protection guarantees of the Texas Constitution. While the statute itself does not deprive students of their right to equal protection of the law, we recognize that the discretion given to school principals in the rule's provision dealing with honors or advanced courses may well give rise to arbitrary or discriminatory application violative of equal protection principles. *See Yick Wo v. Hopkins,* 118 U.S. 356, 6 S.Ct. 1064, 30 L.Ed. 220 (1886). We are faced with no allegations of discriminatory application of the rule's honors exception in the present case.

Procedural Due Process

We begin our analysis of the due process arguments in this cause by recognizing that the strictures of due process apply only to the threatened deprivation of liberty and property interests deserving the protection of the federal and state constitutions. *Tarrant County v. Ashmore,* 635 S.W.2d 417, 422 (Tex.1982), *cert. denied,* 459 U.S. 1038, 103 S.Ct. 452, 74 L.Ed.2d 606 (1982); *Mathews v. Eldridge,* 424 U.S. 319, 332, 96 S.Ct. 893, 901, 47 L.Ed.2d 18 (1976); and *Board of Regents v. Roth,* 92 S.Ct. 2701, 2705, 33 L.Ed.2d 548 (1972). The federal courts have made it clear that the federal constitution's due process guarantees do not protect a student's interest in participating in extracurricular activities. *See Niles v. University Interscholastic League,* 715 F.2d 1027, 1031 (5th Cir.1983); *Mitchell v. Louisiana High School Athletic Ass'n,* 430 F.2d 1155, 1158 (5th Cir.1970); *see also, Hamilton v. Tennessee Secondary School Athletic Ass'n,* 552 F.2d 681, 682 (6th Cir.1976); and *Albach v. Odle,* 531 F.2d 983, 984-85 (10th Cir.1976). We must, then, examine our state constitution to determine whether its due process guarantees extend to a student's desire to participate in school-sponsored extracurricular activities.

A property or liberty interest must find its origin in some aspect of state law. *See Board of Regents v. Roth,* 408 U.S. at 577- 78, 92 S.Ct. 2709. Nothing in either our state constitution or statutes entitles students to an absolute right to participation in extracurricular activities. We are in agreement, therefore, with the overwhelming majority of jurisdictions that students do not possess a constitutionally protected interest in their participation in extracurricular activities. *See, e.g., Caso v. New York State Public High School Athletic Ass'n, Inc.,* 78 A.D.2d 41, 434 N.Y.S.2d 60, 64 (N.Y.App.Div.1980); *Menke v. Ohio High School Athletic Ass'n,* 2 Ohio App.3d 244, 441 N.E.2d 620, 624 (1981); *Whipple v. Oregon School Activities Ass'n,* 52 Or.App. 419, 629 P.2d 384, 386 (1981); *Adamek v. Pennsylvania Inter Scholastic Athletic Ass'n, Inc.,* 57 Pa.Commw. 261, 426 A.2d 1206, 1207 n. 1 (Pa.Commw.Ct.1981); and *Bailey v. Truby,* 321 S.E.2d 302, 314-15 (W.Va.1984). Therefore, the strictures of procedural due process do *not* apply to the determination by a campus principal, pursuant to section 21.920(b) of the Texas Education Code, as to whether a student who fails an identified honors or advanced course shall be permitted to participate in extracurricular activities.

[The Court's discussion of Substantive Due Process has been omitted]

Accordingly, we reverse the district court's judgment with regard to the constitutionality of section 21.920 of the Texas Education Code and dissolve the temporary injunction ordered by the district court.

## Notes & Questions

1. Explain the significance of the court's determination that the students affected by the no pass no play rule are not an inherently suspect class, and the significance of the court's determination that a student's right to participate in extracurricular activities is not a fundamental right.

### James v. Tallassee High School
907 F.Supp. 364 (1995)
United States District Court, M.D. Alabama, Northern Division

De MENT, District Judge.

STATEMENT OF FACTS

This is an action for declaratory and injunctive relief and damages on behalf of the plaintiff, Nancy James ("Ms. James"), who is, and was at all relevant times, a student at Tallassee High School. In 1993, the Tallassee City Board of Education adopted rules and regulations contained in a student handbook which established, among other things, guidelines for cheerleader selection, cheerleader eligibility, and the selection of a head and co-head cheerleader of the cheerleading squad for Tallassee High School. Specifically, these rules, printed in the 1994-95 Tallassee High School Student Handbook, provided that the head and co-head cheerleaders of the football and basketball cheerleading squads would be chosen by a majority of the cheerleaders on the respective squads.

In March, 1995, Carol Lowe ("Ms. Lowe"), in her capacity as the sponsor of the cheerleaders at Tallassee High School, adopted rules that differed from those in the handbook for selection of the head and co-head cheerleaders. Ms. Lowe's rules, given to each potential cheerleader, provided that Ms. Lowe would choose the head and co-head cheerleaders based on her discretion and the cheerleaders' scores in the try-outs.

After try-outs, Ms. James was selected to be a member of the Tallassee High School cheerleading squad. Once the cheerleading squad was named, Ms. James was chosen by Ms. Lowe to be the co-head cheerleader of the basketball squad; however, Ms. James was not chosen to be the head or co-head cheerleader of the football squad. James appealed the sponsor's decision because Ms. Lowe did not choose her as the head or co-head cheerleader of the football squad. Thereafter, a hearing was held on June 19, 1995, wherein the Tallassee Board of Education considered the selection process of the head and co-head cheerleading squads and rejected the plaintiff's appeal.

On August 15, 1995, Ms. James filed this action claiming that she deserves a remedy in federal court because Tallassee High School failed to follow the rules in the Tallassee High School student handbook. Specifically, Ms. James claims that the defendants violated her Fifth Amendment right to due process and her Fourteenth Amendment right to equal protection under the laws by denying her the opportunity to be head or co-head cheerleader of the football team. Ms. James further contends that she was "possibly denied" the opportunity to continue her education in college because she might have had a better chance of obtaining a college cheerleading scholarship. Therefore, Ms. James requests the court, among other things, to award her damages pursuant to 42 U.S.C. § 1983 for the violation of her constitutional rights, and to direct the defendants to hold an election of the head and co-head cheerleaders of the football and basketball squads by a majority of the cheerleading squad.

*** [The court discussed the appropriate standard of review for a motion to dismiss]

DISCUSSION

A. Due Process Clause Under the Fifth Amendment

Ms. James first alleges that she has been deprived of her due process rights under the Fifth Amendment. In order to prevail on this claim, Ms. James must show that the defendants have deprived her of either a liberty interest or a property interest. James raises her due process claim based on a denial of an alleged property interest in being selected as head or co-head cheerleader of the football cheerleading squad.

"To have a property interest in a benefit, a person clearly must have more than an abstract need or desire for it. He [or she] must have more than a unilateral expectation of it. He [or she] must, instead have a legitimate claim of entitlement to it." *Board of Regents v. Roth,* 408 U.S. 564, 577, 92 S.Ct. 2701, 2708, 33 L.Ed.2d 548 (1972). It is clear that a majority of the federal courts addressing the question have determined that a student does not have a cognizable property interest in participating in extracurricular activities at public institutions.

In *Mitchell v. Louisiana High School Athletic Association,* the former Fifth Circuit held that a high school student did not have a right to challenge his eligibility for high school athletics in federal court. 430 F.2d 1155, 1158 (5th Cir.1970).[1] In its holding, the *Mitchell* court noted that the privilege of participating in such an extracurricular activity did not rise to the level of a federal property interest that could be protected by the Constitution. *Id.* Similarly, the Tenth Circuit dismissed a student athlete's complaint challenging a rule that barred any athlete who transferred from his or her home district to a boarding school from participating in interscholastic athletics for a year, stating that "[p]articipation in interscholastic athletics is not a constitutionally protected civil right." *Albach v. Odle,* 531 F.2d 983, 984-85 (10th Cir.1976).

Moreover, at least one federal district court has specifically addressed the due process rights of a high school cheerleader. *See Haverkamp v. Unified School District Number 380,* 689 F.Supp. 1055 (D.C.Kan.1986). The *Haverkamp* court held that a high school cheerleader's position as head cheerleader, or even as a member of the cheerleading squad, did not constitute a property interest for the purposes of determining whether a plaintiff's due process rights had been violated. *Id.* at 1058. In fact, in

---

[1] Decisions of the former Fifth Circuit filed prior to October 1, 1981, constitute binding precedent in the Eleventh Circuit. *Bonner v. City of Prichard,* 661 F.2d 1206, 1209 (11th Cir.1981) (*en banc* ).

*Haverkamp,* the plaintiff had already been selected to the cheerleading squad and had been removed for disciplinary reasons.

In the present case, Ms. James has not lost a position as head or co-head cheerleader of the football cheerleading squad; rather, she was never selected to serve in that position. Thus, Ms. James has only a mere expectation of being chosen as the head or co-head of the football cheerleading squad. Furthermore, Ms. James was selected by Ms. Lowe to be the co-head basketball cheerleader. Thus, the court is not convinced that Ms. James' allegation that her opportunity to obtain a college cheerleading scholarship was substantially harmed. While the court does not wish to imply that it condones Ms. Lowe's unilateral action to change the rules governing the selection of head and co-head cheerleaders at Tallassee High School, the court believes that Ms. James does not have a federally-protected property interest in having the opportunity to be selected as the head or co-head cheerleader of the football cheerleading squad. Accordingly, the court finds that Ms. James' due process claim is due to be dismissed.

B. Equal Protection Clause Under the Fourteenth Amendment

Ms. James also alleges a violation of the Equal Protection Clause of the Fourteenth Amendment. To establish an equal protection claim, a plaintiff must initially show that he or she was treated differently from other individuals similarly situated. *Cleburne v. Cleburne Living Ctr.,* 473 U.S. 432, 439, 105 S.Ct. 3249, 3254, 87 L.Ed.2d 313 (1985) ("The Equal Protection Clause of the Fourteenth Amendment commands that no State shall 'deny to any person within its jurisdiction the equal protection of the laws,' which is essentially a direction that all persons similarly situated should be treated alike."). Thus, to survive a motion to dismiss on her equal protection claim, Ms. James must allege that she was treated differently than others who were similarly situated, *i.e.,* any other Tallassee High School students who were members of the cheerleading squad from which the head and co-head cheerleaders were chosen.

It is clear that Ms. James' complaint fails to state a claim upon which relief can be granted because it does not contain even a hint of an allegation that Ms. James was similarly situated to other Tallassee cheerleaders, yet treated more harshly or differently by the defendants than the other Tallassee cheerleaders. Therefore, even assuming the allegations in the complaint as true, it is abundantly clear to the court that Ms. James' equal protection claim must be dismissed pursuant to Rule 12(b)(6) because she has failed to allege sufficient facts to support an equal protection claim.

CONCLUSION

For the foregoing reasons, the court finds that defendants' motion to dismiss is due to be granted. A judgment in accordance with this memorandum opinion will be entered separately.

## Notes & Questions

1. In the field of Labor Law, employee handbooks are often treated as contracts. How might you articulate an argument on James's behalf, arguing that the Student Handbook which contained written procedures for cheerleader selection ought to have been treated as a contract? Develop the argument that James should win on a breach of contract theory.

2. Even if James didn't have a property interest in being appointed head cheerleader, isn't it true that she at the very least had a right to expect the school to follow its own written procedures? If so, why? If not, why not.

3. To what extent do you think that the court was concerned that other disgruntled cheerleaders and athletes who were cut from a team or demoted to JV might open the floodgates of litigation if it had ruled in James's favor?

### Jordan v. O'Fallon Township High School
706 NE 2d 137 (1999)
Appellate Court of Illinois, Fifth District

This case examines how O'Fallon Township High School (O'Fallon) officials withheld a student's participation in interscholastic athletics as punishment for his violation of the school's zero-tolerance conduct code. Before they are allowed to participate in any extracurricular activity, all O'Fallon students must agree in writing to abide by the code's ban on alcohol and drug use. Students who violate the code's ban are disciplined by school officials under procedures that do not necessarily comport with due process. School officials imposed discipline in this case without affording the student a formal hearing. The student was not allowed to confront witnesses who provided the evidence upon which the discipline was based. Nor was the student permitted to present witnesses to rebut that evidence.

The student sued to enjoin the disciplinary action. The trial court refused to grant an injunction, and the student appealed.

On appeal, the student claims that O'Fallon school officials violated the procedural due process component of the fourteenth amendment. U.S. Const., amend. XIV. He argues that school officials were constitutionally obliged to afford him a minimal due process hearing before discipline could be administered. ***

We now decide whether a talented high school football player with college athletic scholarship opportunities possesses an interest in playing high school football that due process protects. *** We conclude that O'Fallon school officials dispensed that process which was due and acted reasonably under the circumstances presented.

The 1997 O'Fallon High School football season highlighted the skills of a young man named Kevin Jordan. Jordan's ability to break tackles and find daylight brought several postseason honors, including his selection as team captain for the ensuing 1998 season. Jordan's ability also drew the attention of several universities. College coaches from across the country wrote to Jordan and expressed their interest in his future. Although the coaches did not extend scholarship offers, they clearly suggested that such offers would be forthcoming provided Jordan continued to excel as a high school football player in his senior season.

Thus, the 1998 season appeared to offer Jordan a legitimate chance to earn an athletic scholarship to a major university. The season's promise ended, however, when Jordan's playing privileges surrendered to enforcement of O'Fallon's zero-tolerance conduct code. School officials determined that Jordan violated the code's ban on alcohol use. As a result, the captain of O'Fallon's football team was suspended from play for the entire 1998 season. Kevin Jordan never played another down of high school football.

The suspension stemmed from an early morning encounter with O'Fallon police officers. The officers answered Jordan's 9-1-1 emergency call from a phone booth near an O'Fallon convenience store. When they arrived at the convenience store, they found a dishevelled and shoeless Jordan standing in the parking lot. It was 3 o'clock in the morning, and according to the officers, Jordan evidenced obvious signs of inebriation. His

344

eyes were glazed, his speech was slurred, and he smelled of alcohol. Jordan's condition was confirmed when, according to the officers, he admitted to alcohol consumption.

The officers, pursuant to a reciprocal reporting agreement with the school, reported the incident to O'Fallon school officials. An assistant principal reviewed their report, discussed it with them, and confronted Jordan. Jordan denied alcohol use. He also denied any admission to the contrary. He explained that his condition resulted from an attack by unknown assailants who threw beer bottles at him during the assault. He insisted that the smell of alcohol detected by the officers was misconstrued.

The assistant principal weighed what the officers and Jordan told him and decided that Jordan violated his commitment to remain alcohol- and drug-free. Jordan had a prior violation of the code's alcohol ban. Therefore, the assistant principal cited him for a second violation and informed him that he was suspended from participation in high school athletics for a period that encompassed the entire football season.

The assistant principal's action was reviewed by the O'Fallon Activity Council (Activity Council). The Activity Council is a body comprised of the principal, all assistant principals, the dean of students, the athletic director, the assistant athletic director, the band director, the head of speech activities, and the student council sponsor. The Activity Council reviews discipline only to determine whether the conduct code is interpreted consistently and applied uniformly. Its members agreed unanimously that the code was properly applied in Jordan's case.

Jordan's stepfather appealed to the school superintendent, who was empowered to review and override the disciplinary action. After agreeing to review the matter, the superintendent met with Jordan, his attorney, and his stepfather. Jordan, assisted by counsel, reiterated his version of the early morning encounter with O'Fallon police officers. Jordan was afforded the opportunity to present any information or make any comment he deemed important to the superintendent's review.

The superintendent listened to everything Jordan presented and reserved judgment until he could meet with the officers involved in the incident. Jordan's attorney was apprised of a planned meeting with the officers and was invited to attend. His schedule did not permit attendance, and the meeting was held without him.

The superintendent told the officers of Jordan's claims. The officers questioned the veracity of those claims, noting that Jordan's story had significantly changed from what he had earlier told them. They insisted that Jordan admitted to them that he had been drinking alcohol. They also expressed their opinion that Jordan's glassy eyes and slurred speech were the result of alcohol consumption. The possibility that the smell of alcohol resulted from an assault with beer bottles did not alter their opinion of Jordan's inebriated condition.

The superintendent told Jordan's attorney what the officers conveyed to him. He advised Jordan's attorney that he would not overrule the suspension and invited him to appeal to the O'Fallon Board of Education, the final arbiter of student discipline.

Throughout this process, Jordan's stepfather and attorney repeatedly requested a more formal proceeding. They wanted to confront the police officers and to call witnesses who could account for most of Jordan's activities on the night in question. Their call for a formal hearing went unheard.

Jordan did not appeal to the O'Fallon Board of Education. Instead, he commenced this action. He obtained a temporary restraining order that enjoined the suspension. The matter proceeded to a hearing on Jordan's request for a preliminary injunction pending a trial on the merits of the underlying lawsuit. Jordan argued that the disciplinary action was arbitrary and capricious and that the procedures employed were constitutionally infirm. The trial judge found that the evidence failed to establish a protected property or liberty interest. Therefore, the judge did not determine whether the process afforded met minimal constitutional procedural standards. He did hold, however, that the disciplinary action was neither arbitrary nor capricious. This appeal ensued.

Jordan challenges the school's power to sideline him in the manner employed. He argues that school officials cannot suspend him from participation in interscholastic athletics without first affording him a minimal due process hearing to contest the disciplinary action. At a minimum, he claims a right to confront his accusers and to present witnesses who could corroborate his denial of alcohol use.

[1][2] The fourteenth amendment forbids the State to deprive any person of life, liberty, or property without due process of law. U.S. Const., amend. XIV. Therefore, any person who raises a procedural due process claim must demonstrate that a protectable property or liberty interest is at

stake. *Hawkins v. National Collegiate Athletic Ass'n,* 652 F.Supp. 602, 610 (C.D.Ill.1987). Protected property interests are created " 'and their dimensions are defined' by an independent source such as State statutes or rules entitling * * * citizen[s] to certain benefits." *Goss v. Lopez,* 419 U.S. 565, 572-73, 95 S.Ct. 729, 735, 42 L.Ed.2d 725, 733 (1975), quoting *Board of Regents of State Colleges v. Roth,* 408 U.S. 564, 577, 92 S.Ct. 2701, 2709, 33 L.Ed.2d 548, 561 (1972). In *Board of Regents of State Colleges,* the Supreme Court addressed the parameters of a constitutionally protected property interest. In reviewing several cases that defined protected property interests in different contexts, the Supreme Court wrote:

> Certain attributes of "property" interests protected by procedural due process emerge from these decisions. To have a property interest in a benefit, a person clearly must have more than an abstract need or desire for it. He must have more than a unilateral expectation of it. He must, instead, have a legitimate claim of entitlement to it. *Board of Regents of State Colleges,* 408 U.S. at 577, 92 S.Ct. at 2709, 33 L.Ed.2d at 561.

Based upon this definition, courts have repeatedly held that there is no property or liberty interest in taking part in interscholastic athletics. *Clements v. Board of Education of Decatur Public School District No. 61,* 133 Ill.App.3d 531, 533, 88 Ill.Dec. 601, 478 N.E.2d 1209, 1210 (1985).

Students can need, want, and expect to participate in interscholastic athletics, but students are not *entitled* to participate in them. Football is neither an integral part of a quality education nor a requirement under any rule or regulation governing education in this State. Consequently, not every public high school in this State fields a football team. Those students who attend O'Fallon Township High School thus enjoy an opportunity that many other high school students are not permitted to enjoy. Simply put, playing high school football is a privilege rather than a right. *Todd v. Rush County Schools,* 133 F.3d 984, 986 (7th Cir.1998).

Jordan concedes that, standing alone, participation in interscholastic athletics does not rise to the level of a protected interest. Most students can be suspended from play without a constitutional right to a due process hearing. Notwithstanding, Jordan thinks that he should be treated differently. His reasoning follows.

Since he possesses athletic prowess, his participation in high school football can develop into something of substantial economic value. Unlike his less talented teammates, Jordan can turn participation in interscholastic athletics into a college scholarship. His participation thus rises to a protectable property interest that commands procedural due process. It follows that school officials could not ban him from a playing field where scholarship opportunities awaited, without first conducting a minimal due process hearing.

This argument is untenable. Since Jordan possessed no independent right to participate in high school football, the existence of a protected property interest depends upon whether he can legitimately claim the right to participate in order to earn college financial assistance. This in turn depends upon whether the hope of earning a college scholarship rises to the level of a protectable property interest. Under the circumstances presented, it does not.

Scholarship opportunities do not elevate participation in interscholastic athletics into an interest that due process protects because such opportunities are themselves mere expectancies. The acquisition of a scholarship remains contingent on far more than simply maintaining playing privileges.

Jordan's expectations of playing college football on an athletic scholarship were no doubt greater than those of other less talented players. Nevertheless, those expectations are no more constitutionally protected than less realistic expectations harbored by others. Jordan was not entitled to an athletic scholarship at the time when school officials considered disciplinary action. Nor did continued participation in high school football guarantee that his scholarship expectations would be fulfilled. Since Jordan's scholarship hopes could not meet the criteria for a protected property interest, those hopes could not impart due process protection to participation in high school football.

In holding that the opportunity to earn an athletic scholarship is too speculative to elevate participation in high school football to the level of a constitutionally protected interest, we note several contingencies that impact scholarship hopes. Here, Jordan would have had to again excel on the playing field. He would have had to meet academic and entrance exam requirements. He would have had to overcome the unreliable image that his disciplinary problems conveyed. And, most importantly, he would have had to stay healthy.

In this regard, it helps to consider the true nature of college football. It is a competitive business that exists in large part to produce the revenue that fuels college athletic programs. Its revenue-producing role operates upon a simple understanding of the relationship between winning and ticket sales. College coaches are strongly motivated to produce winning football teams. Therefore, they scour the country for good football players to fill their rosters.

College coaches possess a finite number of athletic scholarships to offer. Because they vie with each other for the best available talent, coaches must recruit more athletes than they have scholarships to offer. Their ultimate goal is to convince the best players to play for them. One thing is clear-- college coaches do not hand out athletic scholarships to players that are physically incapable of playing college football. The names of seriously injured players are not found on recruiting lists.

This look at college football's character tells us why even a player with obvious college-level skills can harbor no more than an expectation of college financial assistance so long as he is still playing high school football. Football can exact a swift and permanent toll on any player's scholarship hopes. The vagaries of the game do not spare talented players and have crushed the aspirations of some of the very best. An athletic scholarship offer can vanish from a running back's future as swiftly as a healthy knee. Therefore, athletic scholarships remain expectancies, regardless of a player's talent level, until that player completes high school football with his health firmly intact. A player's hopes, no matter how justified, cannot elevate his high school playing privileges to a protectable property interest at any stage where disciplinary action would be taken against those privileges.

Jordan did not possess the right to participate in interscholastic athletics. Nor did his scholarship opportunities confer such a right. Therefore, a protectable property interest was not at stake when the school imposed discipline, and a due process hearing was not required.

\*\*\*

We are consistently reluctant to intrude upon the disciplinary decisions of school districts. *Donaldson v. Board of Education for Danville School District No. 118,* 98 Ill.App.3d 438, 439, 53 Ill.Dec. 946, 424 N.E.2d 737, 738- 39 (1981). If the opportunity to earn college financial assistance were to elevate participation in interscholastic athletics into a protected property right, school districts would have to afford procedural due process in practically all disciplinary actions where student participation in outside activities was at stake. We cannot accept a notion that would invite a due process claim by every student engaged in interscholastic athletics and extracurricular activities. Judicial intervention in school discipline would become the rule rather than the exception unless school districts provided due process hearings in all such disciplinary actions.

For the reasons stated, we affirm the trial court's order denying a preliminary injunction.

Affirmed.

## Notes & Questions

1. As regards legal principles, discuss the similarities and differences between *James* and *Jordan*.

2. Suppose that the coach had decided not to allow Jordan to play because he had heard a rumor that Jordan had smoked cigarettes at a weekend party. Would that change the outcome of the case? Suppose instead that the coach had heard a rumor that Jordan had been drinking beer and smoking marijuana at a weekend party? The court states, "Of course, school officials cannot impose student punishment in a completely arbitrary and capricious manner." Give examples of the types of things that you believe would constitute "a completely arbitrary and capricious manner."

3. Kevin Jordan returned to school and played the following year, graduating with the class of 1999. He went on to play collegiate football at Millikin University in Decatur, Illinois.

### *Further reading on Constitutional Law*:

Walter T. Champion, *No Pass, No Play - Texas Style*, 5 ENT. & SPORTS LAW 5 (1986).

Lewis Kurlantzick, *John Rocker and Employee Discipline for Speech*, 11 MARQ. SPORTS L. REV. 185 (2001).

Matthew J. Mitten, *Amateur Athletes With Handicaps or Physical Abnormalities*, 71 NEB. L. REV. 987 (1992).

Matthew J. Mitten, *Sports Participation by Handicapped Athletes*, 10 ENT. & SPORTS LAW 15 (1982).

Robert E. Shepherd, Jr., *Why Can't Johnny Read or Play*, 1 SOVIET L. & BUS. NEWS 163 (1991).

# Chapter 8

## Title IX

---

This chapter examines one of the most important topics in Sports Law today, Title IX. Professor George's article summarizes the basic rules of Title IX and its application to athletics through formative case law. *Daniels* reviews the Title IX rules and expands upon them by interpreting the relevant Code of Federal Regulations provisions in light of the disparate treatment afforded a high school girls softball team. *Mercer* adds additional perspective in a case involving a collegiate contact sport, football. *Boucher* illustrates the types of struggles that colleges and universities have experienced in their efforts to comply with the proportionality requirements of Title IX, and *Boulhanis* takes that issue further, examining financial decisions and the potential for reverse discrimination that institutions face.

# TITLE IX AND THE SCHOLARSHIP DILEMMA

B. Glenn George
9 MARQ. SPORTS L. J. 273 (1999)

## I. A Brief History of Title IX

Although over [thirty]-five years old, Title IX...only developed as a driving force in intercollegiate athletics during the [1990's]. Title IX's prohibition, included in the Education Amendments of 1972, states in straight-forward terms that no one "shall, on the basis of sex, be excluded from participation in, be denied the benefits of, or be subjected to discrimination under any education program or activity receiving Federal financial assistance." Some schools responded immediately, and there were significant early gains in the participation rates of women in intercollegiate athletic programs. Prior to Title IX, women accounted for only fifteen percent of intercollegiate student athletes; the participation rate for women doubled by 1984.

The application of this prohibition to intercollegiate athletics, however, was not secured until 1988. Some early interpretations of the legislation had limited its application to the particular university programs actually receiving federal dollars. In 1984, the Supreme Court took the same position in the case of *Grove City College v. Bell*.[1] Congress acted four years later to overturn the result in Grove City College. The Civil Rights Restoration Act of 1987 (1988 Amendments)[2] amended Title IX to extend its prohibition against sex discrimination to the entire institution as long as a single program within the institution received federal funds. Thus, Title IX did not come into its own as a force in the world of intercollegiate athletics until [nearly two]...decade[s] ago.

In spite of Title IX's questionable application to intercollegiate athletics in its early days, the Secretary of the Department of Health, Education and Welfare moved ahead under statutory mandate to issue regulations governing college sports programs.[3] Those regulations were

---

[1] 465 U.S. 555 (1984).

[2] 20 U.S.C. § 1687 (1988).

[3] See Education Amendments of 1974, Pub. L. No. 93-380, § 844, 88 Stat. 612 (1974). The Javits Amendment, adopted by Congress in 1974, required the Department of Health, Education and Welfare to issue regulations under Title IX concerning intercollegiate athletic activities.

issued in 1975 and, interestingly enough, included a section on the allocation of financial aid:

(1) To the extent that a recipient awards athletic scholarship or grants-in-aid, it must provide reasonable opportunities for such award for members of each sex in proportion to the number of students of each sex participating in interscholastic or intercollegiate athletics.

(2) Separate athletic scholarships or grants-in-aid for members of each sex may be provided as part of separate athletic teams for members of each sex to the extent consistent with this paragraph and § 106.41.[4]

Another section of the 1975 regulations defined the concept of "equal opportunity" in college sports programs by listing ten factors for consideration. Four years later, the Secretary provided further enlightenment in the 1979 Policy Interpretation which focused exclusively on the application of Title IX to intercollegiate athletics. In 1980, enforcement authority was transferred to the newly created Department of Education and its Office for Civil Rights (OCR).

A. The First Wave: Proportionality in Participation Rates

Soon after the application of Title IX to intercollegiate athletics was secured in 1988, frustrated women athletes and their advocates turned to the judicial system for relief. A wave of litigation in the early 1990s focused primarily on the issue of participation rates, disputes which were often prompted by the institution's decisions to eliminate both men's and women's teams as part of general budget cuts. The question of participation opportunities understandably took precedent--issues like financial aid, equipment budgets, and practice facilities were irrelevant unless women's teams existed to enjoy those benefits.

OCR's definition of equity in participation rates, generally adopted by the courts, made most of these cases clear winners for the complaining women athletes. OCR's Policy Interpretation offered three avenues for demonstrating compliance in this area, yet only one option was available as a practical matter. In the 1975 regulations, the first factor in the consideration of equal opportunity was "[w]hether the selection of sports and levels of competition effectively accommodate the interests and abilities of members of both sexes." The 1979 Policy Interpretation elaborated on that requirement by establishing three possible measures:

---

[4] 34 C.F.R. § 106.37(c) (1997).

(1) Whether intercollegiate level participation opportunities for male and female students are provided in numbers substantially proportionate to their respective enrollments; or

(2) Where the members of one sex have been and are underrepresented among intercollegiate athletes, whether the institution can show a history and continuing practice of program expansion which is demonstrably responsive to the developing interest and abilities of the members of that sex; or

(3) Where the members of one sex are underrepresented among intercollegiate athletes, and the institution cannot show a continuing practice of program expansion such as that cited above, whether it can be demonstrated that the interests and abilities of the members of that sex have been fully and effectively accommodated by the present program.

As a practical matter, the first option under the Policy Interpretation--the proportionality standard--became the only relevant issue. The expansion of women's teams in the 1970s was followed by the elimination of both men's and women's teams in the 1990s as budgets tightened. Thus, few schools could point to any recent history of expanding opportunities for women, as required by the second option. The very uncertainty of defining and measuring what it means to "effectively accommodate the interests of both sexes" in option three apparently caused most courts to avoid that standard altogether. By default, the only safe harbor became the proportionality standard. Consequently, school after school lost on (or chose not to dispute) the simple calculation of comparing the percentage of women in the student body to the percentage of women in the intercollegiate athletic program.

*Cohen v. Brown University,*[5] perhaps one of the best known Title IX cases, is a good example. In 1991, Brown University decided to eliminate women's volleyball and gymnastics, as well as men's golf and water polo, in a belt-tightening move. The women sued and obtained a preliminary injunction to restore the women's teams. The plaintiff's proof was simple-- both before and after the cuts, the number of female intercollegiate athletes at Brown University continued to lag behind the percentage of women in the general student body. After two appeals to the First Circuit and a denial of certiorari by the Supreme Court, Brown University finally threw in the towel. Brown University's failure to convince the Supreme Court to reexamine the

---

[5] 809 F. Supp. 978 (D.R.I. 1992).

mechanical approach of the proportionality standard was understood by most as the loss of both the battle and the war.

Given the almost universal success of the proportionality standard, most institutions had a clear understanding of their participation obligations under Title IX and began moving toward compliance.

## Notes & Questions

1. Explain in your own words the significance of *Grove City College v. Bell*.

2. What role has the Office for Civil Rights played in the current status of Title IX?

3. Explain what the "proportionality standard" is.

### Daniels v. School Board of Brevard County
985 F. Supp. 1458 (1997)
United States District Court,
M.D. Florida, Orlando Division

CONWAY, District Judge.

## I. INTRODUCTION

The Plaintiffs in this action are Jessica and Jennifer Daniels, and their father, Daniel Daniels. Jessica and Jennifer are seniors at Merritt Island High School ("MIHS"). They both are members of the girls' varsity softball team.

Plaintiffs have sued the Defendant, School Board of Brevard County, based on disparities between the MIHS girls' softball and boys' baseball programs. They assert claims pursuant to 20 U.S.C. § 1681 ("Title IX") and the Florida Educational Equity Act, Fla.Stat. § 228.2001 ("the Florida Act").

Plaintiffs seek a preliminary injunction. On November 24, 1997, the Court heard oral argument on the motion. After considering the parties' evidentiary submissions, legal memoranda and arguments, the Court determines that the Plaintiffs are entitled to a preliminary injunction.

## II. PRELIMINARY INJUNCTION STANDARD

"A plaintiff moving for a preliminary injunction must show: (1) a substantial likelihood of success on the merits; (2) a substantial threat of irreparable injury; (3) that the threatened injury to the plaintiff outweighs the injury to the nonmovant; and (4) that the injunction would not disserve the public interest." *Statewide Detective Agency v. Miller,* 115 F.3d 904, 905 (11th Cir.1997).

## III. TITLE IX AND THE FLORIDA ACT

Subject to exceptions not pertinent here, Title IX provides:

No person in the United States shall, on the basis of sex, be excluded from participation in, be denied the benefits of, or be subjected to discrimination under any education program or activity receiving Federal financial assistance[.] 20 U.S.C. § 1681(a).

"Congress enacted Title IX in response to its finding--after extensive hearings held in 1970 by the House Special Subcommittee on Education--of pervasive discrimination against women with respect to educational opportunities." *Cohen v. Brown University,* 101 F.3d 155, 165 (1st Cir.1996), *cert. denied,* 520 U.S. 1186, 117 S.Ct. 1469, 137 L.Ed.2d 682 (1997). "Title IX was passed with two objectives in mind: 'to avoid the use of federal resources to support discriminatory practices,' and 'to provide individual citizens effective protection against those practices.' " *Id.* (quoting *Cannon v. University of Chicago,* 441 U.S. 677, 704, 99 S.Ct. 1946, 1961, 60 L.Ed.2d 560 (1979)).

Title IX is implemented with respect to athletic activities by 34 C.F.R. § 106.41. Section § 106.41(a) generally provides:

No person shall, on the basis of sex, be excluded from participation in, be denied the benefits of, be treated differently from another person or otherwise be discriminated against in any interscholastic, intercollegiate, club or intramural athletics offered by a recipient, and no recipient shall provide any such athletics separately on such basis.

Section 106.41(c) provides:

A recipient which operates or sponsors interscholastic, intercollegiate, club or intramural athletics shall provide equal athletic opportunity for members of both sexes. In determining whether equal opportunities are available the Director will consider, among other factors:

(1) Whether the selection of sports and levels of competition effectively accommodate the interests and abilities of members of both sexes;
(2) The provision of equipment and supplies;
(3) Scheduling of games and practice times;
(4) Travel and per diem allowance;
(5) Opportunity to receive coaching and academic tutoring;
(6) Assignment and compensation of coaches and tutors;
(7) Provision of locker rooms, practice and competitive facilities;
(8) Provision of medical and training facilities and services;
(9) Provision of housing and dining facilities and services;
(10) Publicity.

Unequal aggregate expenditures for members of each sex or unequal expenditures for male and female teams if a recipient operates or sponsors separate teams will not constitute noncompliance with this section, but the Assistant Secretary may consider the failure to provide necessary funds for teams for one sex in assessing equality of opportunity for members of each sex.

The Florida Act also prohibits, *inter alia,* gender discrimination in public education. It extends protection to those enrolled in public educational institutions which receive or benefit from either state or federal financial assistance. *See* Fla.Stat. § 228.2001(2)(a). The Florida Act lists the identical factors for assessing discrimination in athletics set forth in 34 C.F.R. § 106.41(c)(1)-(10). *See* Fla.Stat. § 228.2001(3)(d)(1)-(10).

UNIVERSITY OF WINCHESTER LIBRARY

## IV. ANALYSIS

### A. Substantial Likelihood of Success on the Merits

[1] Plaintiffs assert that the following inequalities exist at the MIHS softball and baseball facilities, and that these disparities violate Title IX and the Florida Act.

### Electronic Scoreboard

It is undisputed that the boys' baseball field has an electronic scoreboard, and that the girls' field has no scoreboard at all. At the preliminary injunction hearing, Defendant's counsel argued that a scoreboard is inessential to varsity softball play. The Court disagrees. A scoreboard is of obvious benefit to players who must keep track of the score, the innings, and the numbers of outs, balls and strikes at any given moment. The prestige factor of a scoreboard is also obvious. As with all the differences the Court addresses in this Order, the fact that the boys have a scoreboard and the girls do not sends a clear message to players, fellow students, teachers and the community at large, that girls' varsity softball is not as worthy as boys' varsity baseball.

### Batting Cage

It is also undisputed that the boys' baseball team has a batting cage and the girls' softball team does not. The use of a batting cage sharpens hitting skills. The girls' softball team is technically disadvantaged by the absence of such equipment. At the hearing, Plaintiffs' counsel represented that it would be difficult for the two teams to share one batting cage as a result of differences in the pitching machines each team uses. Accordingly, it appears that sharing the existing batting cage is not feasible.

### Bleachers

Photographs submitted by Plaintiffs starkly illustrate that the bleachers on the girls' softball field are in worse condition, and seat significantly fewer spectators, than the bleachers on the boys' field. In fact, at the preliminary injunction hearing, Defendant's counsel admitted that the girls' bleachers are actually "hand-me-downs" that the boys' team passed on to the girls' team after the boys' team received new bleachers. Again, the message this sends the players, spectators and community about the relative worth of the two teams is loud and clear.

## Signs

A sign reading "Merritt Island Baseball" is emblazoned in very large letters on the side of a portable structure adjacent to the boys' baseball field. The sign faces MIHS' student parking lot. This sign clearly publicizes only the boys' baseball team. Another sign is located just outside the left field fence of the boys' field. This billboard-type sign reads "Home of the Mustangs;" it faces toward the boys' field. Due to its location, the effect of this second sign is to advertise the boys' baseball team. There are no signs publicizing the girls' softball team.

## Bathroom Facilities

There are no restrooms located on the girls' softball field. Restrooms are located on the boys' baseball field. A fence separates the girls' field from the restrooms. There is a dispute concerning whether the coach of the girls' team has been provided with a key to a gate in the fence. Equal access to restroom facilities is such a clearly established right as to merit no further discussion.

## Concession Stand/Press Box/Announcer's Booth

A combination concession stand/press box/announcer's booth is located on the boys' baseball field. There is no such structure on the girls' softball field. These facilities affect player and spectator enjoyment of a sport, as well as attendance.

## Field Maintenance

The photographs submitted by Plaintiffs facially suggest that the girls' softball field is not as well-maintained as the boys' baseball field. However, at the preliminary injunction hearing, Defendant's counsel stated that the photographs were misleading because MIHS was in the process of reconditioning the girls' field at the time the photographs were taken. Defense counsel maintains that the reconditioning process continues. Accordingly, at this juncture, it is difficult for the Court to evaluate the comparative level of field maintenance.

## Lighting

The boys' baseball field is lighted for nighttime play; the girls' softball field is not. Apparently, this single factor was the impetus for this lawsuit.

Nighttime play affects spectator attendance, parental involvement, and player and spectator enjoyment. Nighttime games have a "big league" quality not associated with daytime play. Additionally, lighting affords more flexibility regarding practice scheduling. The absence of lighting on the girls' softball field detrimentally affects the girls' team in all these respects.

After Plaintiffs filed suit, the Brevard County School Board voted to install lighting at MIHS' girls softball field. Plaintiffs contend that they have not received assurance that the lighting will be in place by January 26, 1998, the beginning of the girls' season. Defendant's counsel stated at the preliminary injunction hearing that there is every reason to believe that lighting would be installed by that date. Unless the lighting is in place by January 26, 1998, MIHS will be enjoined from using the lights on the boys' baseball field.

The Court determines that the cumulative effect of the inequalities in the two athletic programs is so significant as to give Plaintiffs a substantial likelihood of success on the merits of the Title IX and Florida Act claims. The Defendant has chosen to favor the boys' baseball team with a lighted playing field, a scoreboard, a batting cage, superior bleachers, signs publicizing the team, bathroom facilities, and a concession stand/press box/announcer's booth, but has not seen fit to provide the girls softball team with any of these things. This disparity implicates several of the considerations listed in 34 C.F.R. § 106.41. *See* § 106.41(2) ("provision of equipment and supplies"), (3) ("[s]cheduling of games and practice times"), (7) ("[p]rovision of ... practice and competitive facilities"), (8) ( "[p]rovision of ... training facilities"), and (10) ("[p]ublicity"). A balance of the relevant factors favors the Plaintiffs.

[2] The Defendant seeks to avoid liability on the basis that it provides equal funding for the boys' and girls' programs. According to the Defendant, each team has a separate booster club which engages in separate fund-raising activities. The Defendant suggests that it cannot be held responsible if the fund-raising activities of one booster club are more successful than those of another. The Court rejects this argument. It is the Defendant's responsibility to ensure equal athletic opportunities, in accordance with Title IX. This funding system is one to which Defendant has acquiesced; Defendant is responsible for the consequences of that approach.

## B. Substantial Threat of Irreparable Injury

[3] Plaintiffs have also demonstrated a substantial threat of irreparable injury. Each day these inequalities go unredressed, the members of the girls' softball team, prospective members, students, faculty and the community at large, are sent a clear message that girls' high school varsity softball is not as worthy as boys' high school varsity baseball, *i.e.*, that girls are not as important as boys. In that regard, Plaintiffs have filed two expert affidavits detailing the effects of such unequal treatment on girls. Further, Jessica and Jennifer are seeking athletic scholarships, many of which, Plaintiffs maintain, are not decided until after the softball season is over. Accordingly, it is critical that the two girls do their best during their final season.

## C. Relative Harm/Public Interest

[4] Since these inequalities should have long ago been rectified, the Court is unsympathetic to Defendant's claims that it will be unduly harmed by the expenditure of funds necessary to level the playing field for girls' softball athletes. For too long, the girls' softball team has been denied athletic opportunity equal to the boys' baseball team. The harm associated with that treatment as second-class athletes is significant. In short, the balance of harms favors Plaintiffs. The players and all others associated with these programs, the school system as a whole, and the public at large, will benefit from a shift to equal treatment.

\*\*\*\*\*

## V. CONCLUSION

[6] After careful analysis, the Court determines that Plaintiffs are entitled to a preliminary injunction. At the preliminary injunction hearing, various possibilities of remedying the inequalities at issue were discussed. Since public funds are at stake, the Court will afford Defendant an opportunity to submit a plan addressing how Defendant proposes to remedy the inequalities identified in this Order, given the Court's determination that a preliminary injunction should issue. Such an approach has been recognized by other courts. *See Cohen v. Brown University,* 101 F.3d 155, 185-88 (1st Cir.1996), *cert. denied,* 520 U.S. 1186, 117 S.Ct. 1469, 137 L.Ed.2d 682 (1997).

In submitting its proposal, Defendant should be mindful of Title IX's salutary effects. As the Court of Appeals for the First Circuit recently observed in *Cohen:*

> There can be no doubt that Title IX has changed the face of women's sports as well as our society's interest in and attitude toward women athletes and women's sports. In addition, there is ample evidence that increased athletics participation opportunities for women and young girls, available as a result of Title IX enforcement, have had salutary effects in other areas of societal concern.
>
> One need look no further than the impressive performances of our country's women athletes in the 1996 Olympic Summer Games to see that Title IX has had a dramatic and positive impact on the capabilities of our women athletes, particularly in team sports. These Olympians represent the first full generation of women to grow up under the aegis of Title IX. The unprecedented success of these athletes is due, in no small measure, to Title IX's beneficent effects on women's sports, as the athletes themselves have acknowledged time and again. What stimulated this remarkable change in the quality of women's athletic competition was not a sudden, anomalous upsurge in women's interest in sports, but the enforcement of Title IX's mandate of gender equity in sports. 101 F.3d at 188 (citations omitted).

Based on the foregoing, it is ORDERED as follows:

1. Plaintiffs' Application for Preliminary Injunction and Request for Prompt Hearing (Dkt.3), filed October 9, 1997, is GRANTED.

2. Not later than December 15, 1997, Defendant shall serve and file a plan concerning how Defendant proposes to remedy the inequalities identified in this Order, given the Court's determination that a preliminary injunction should issue. ****

# Notes & Questions

1. The court compares the boys varsity baseball program to the girls varsity softball program. Are there other pairs of high school boys and girls sports to which the logic of the *Daniels* court might also be applied? Give examples, and discuss the pros and cons of requiring complete equality as regards facilities and equipment.

2. On an abstract level of principle, it is easy to understand the court's decision regarding equality in this case. Does the court satisfactorily explain why funds that come directly from the booster club are treated the way that they are? Parent booster clubs at high schools across America routinely hold fundraisers of various sorts (*e.g.,* bake sales, car washes, raffles, auctions) on behalf of bands, glee clubs, drama clubs, and sports teams. Does this case teach us that schools cannot allow those booster clubs to be entitled to use those funds for the their respective organizations? Explain.

## Mercer v. Duke University
190 F. 3d 643 (1999)
United States Court of Appeals, Fourth Circuit

LUTTIG, Circuit Judge:

[1] Appellant Heather Sue Mercer challenges the federal district court's holding that Title IX provides a blanket exemption for contact sports and the court's consequent dismissal of her claim that Duke University discriminated against her during her participation in Duke's intercollegiate football program. For the reasons that follow, we hold that where a university has allowed a member of the opposite sex to try out for a single-sex team in a contact sport, the university is, contrary to the holding of the district court, subject to Title IX and therefore prohibited from discriminating against that individual on the basis of his or her sex.

### I.

Appellee Duke University operates a Division I college football team. During the period relevant to this appeal (1994-98), appellee Fred Goldsmith was head coach of the Duke football team and appellant Heather Sue Mercer was a student at the school.

Before attending Duke, Mercer was an all-state kicker at Yorktown Heights High School in Yorktown Heights, New York. Upon enrolling at Duke in the fall of 1994, Mercer tried out for the Duke football team as a walk-on kicker. Mercer was the first--and to date, only--woman to try out for the team. Mercer did not initially make the team, and instead served as a manager during the 1994 season; however, she regularly attended practices in the fall of 1994 and participated in conditioning drills the following spring.

In April 1995, the seniors on the team selected Mercer to participate in the Blue-White Game, an intrasquad scrimmage played each spring. In that game, Mercer kicked the winning 28-yard field goal, giving the Blue team a 24-22 victory. The kick was subsequently shown on ESPN, the cable television sports network. Soon after the game, Goldsmith told the news media that Mercer was on the Duke football team, and Fred Chatham, the Duke kicking coach, told Mercer herself that she had made the team. Also, Mike Cragg, the Duke sports information director, asked Mercer to participate in a number of interviews with newspaper, radio, and television reporters, including one with representatives from "The Tonight Show."

Although Mercer did not play in any games during the 1995 season, she again regularly attended practices in the fall and participated in conditioning drills the following spring. Mercer was also officially listed by Duke as a member of the Duke football team on the team roster filed with the NCAA and was pictured in the Duke football yearbook.

During this latter period, Mercer alleges that she was the subject of discriminatory treatment by Duke. Specifically, she claims that Goldsmith did not permit her to attend summer camp, refused to allow her to dress for games or sit on the sidelines during games, and gave her fewer opportunities to participate in practices than other walk-on kickers. In addition, Mercer claims that Goldsmith made a number of offensive comments to her, including asking her why she was interested in football, wondering why she did not prefer to participate in beauty pageants rather than football, and suggesting that she sit in the stands with her boyfriend rather than on the sidelines.

At the beginning of the 1996 season, Goldsmith informed Mercer that he was dropping her from the team. Mercer alleges that Goldsmith's decision to exclude her from the team was on the basis of her sex because Goldsmith allowed other, less qualified walk-on kickers to remain on the team. Mercer attempted to participate in conditioning drills the following spring, but Goldsmith asked her to leave because the drills were only for members of the team. Goldsmith told Mercer, however, that she could try out for the team again in the fall.

On September 16, 1997, rather than try out for the team again, Mercer filed suit against Duke and Goldsmith, alleging sex discrimination in violation of Title IX of the Education Amendments of 1972, 20 U.S.C. § § 1681-1688, and negligent misrepresentation and breach of contract in violation of North Carolina law. Duke and Goldsmith filed a motion to dismiss for failure to state a claim under Title IX, and, after discovery was completed, Duke and Goldsmith filed additional motions for summary judgment and a motion to dismiss for lack of subject-matter jurisdiction. On November 9, 1998, the district court granted the motion to dismiss for failure to state a claim under Title IX, and dismissed the state-law claims without prejudice, refusing to exercise supplemental jurisdiction over those claims. The district court declined to rule on any of the other outstanding motions. The district court subsequently denied Mercer's motion to alter judgment.

From the district court's order dismissing her Title IX claim for failure to state a claim upon which relief can be granted and its order denying the motion to alter judgment, Mercer appeals.

## II.

Title IX prohibits discrimination on the basis of sex by educational institutions receiving federal funding. *See* 20 U.S.C. § 1681(a) ("No person in the United States shall, on the basis of sex, be excluded from participation in, be denied the benefits of, or be subjected to discrimination under any education program or activity receiving Federal financial assistance...."). Soon after enacting Title IX, Congress charged the Department of Health, Education, and Welfare (HEW) with responsibility for developing regulations regarding the applicability of Title IX to athletic programs. *See* Pub.L. No. 93-380, § 844, 88 Stat. 484 (1974). Acting upon that charge, HEW duly promulgated 34 C.F.R. § 106.41, which reads in relevant part as follows:

Athletics.

(a) General. No person shall, on the basis of sex, be excluded from participation in, be denied the benefits of, be treated differently from another person or otherwise be discriminated against in any interscholastic, intercollegiate, club or intramural athletics offered by a recipient, and no recipient shall provide any such athletics separately on such basis.

(b) Separate teams. Notwithstanding the requirements of paragraph (a) of this section, a recipient may operate or sponsor separate teams for members of each sex where selection for such teams is based upon competitive skill or the activity involved is a contact sport. However, where a recipient operates or sponsors a team in a particular sport for members of one sex but operates or sponsors no such team for members of the other sex, and athletic opportunities for members of that sex have previously been limited, members of the excluded sex must be allowed to try out for the team offered unless the sport involved is a contact sport. For the purposes of this part, contact sports include boxing, wrestling, rugby, ice hockey, football, basketball and other sports the purpose or major activity of which involves bodily contact. 34 C.F.R. § 106.41(a)-(b).

The district court held, and appellees contend on appeal, that, under this regulation, "contact sports, such as football, are specifically excluded from Title IX coverage." We disagree.

Subsections (a) and (b) of section 106.41 stand in a symbiotic relationship to one another. Subsection (a) establishes a baseline prohibition against sex discrimination in intercollegiate athletics, tracking almost identically the language in the parallel statutory provision prohibiting discrimination by federally funded educational institutions. In addition to generally barring discrimination on the basis of sex in intercollegiate athletics, subsection (a) specifically prohibits any covered institution from "provid[ing] any such athletics separately on such basis."

Standing alone, then, subsection (a) would require covered institutions to integrate all of their sports teams. In order to avoid such a result--which would have radically altered the face of intercollegiate athletics--HEW provided an explicit exception to the rule of subsection (a) in the first sentence of subsection (b), allowing covered institutions to "operate or sponsor separate teams for members of each sex where selection for such teams is based upon competitive skill or the activity involved is a contact sport." By its terms, this sentence permits covered institutions to operate separate teams for men and women in many sports, including contact sports such as football, rather than integrating those teams.

368

The first sentence of subsection (b), however, leaves unanswered the question of what, if any, restrictions apply to sports in which a covered institution operates a team for one sex, but operates no corresponding team for the other sex. HEW addressed this question in the second sentence of subsection (b).

This second sentence is applicable only when two predicate criteria are met: first, that the institution in question "operates or sponsors a team in a particular sport for members of one sex but operates or sponsors no such team for members of the other sex," and second, that "athletic opportunities for members of that sex have previously been limited." In this case, appellees do not dispute that athletic opportunities for women at Duke have previously been limited, and thus we assume that the second condition has been met. Further, we assume, without deciding, that Duke operated its football team "for members of one sex"--that is, for only men--but did not operate a separate team "for members of the other sex," and therefore that the first condition has also been satisfied.[1] Thus, insofar as the present appeal is concerned, we consider the predicate conditions to application of the sentence to have been met.

Provided that both of the conditions in the protasis of the second sentence of subsection (b) have been met, the apodosis of the sentence requires that "members of the excluded sex must be allowed to try out for the team offered unless the sport involved is a contact sport." The text of this clause, on its face, is incomplete: it affirmatively specifies that members of the excluded sex must be allowed to try out for single-sex teams where no team is provided for their sex except in the case of contact sports, but is silent regarding what requirements, if any, apply to single-sex teams in contact sports. As to contact sports, this clause is susceptible of two interpretations. First, it could be read to mean that "members of the excluded sex must be allowed to try out for the team offered unless the sport involved is a contact sport, *in which case the anti-discrimination provision of subsection (a) does*

---

[1] At various points in the record, Duke appears to concede that its football team was open to women during the relevant time period. *See, e.g.,* J.A. at 70-72, 91, 99-100. What is unclear, however, is whether the Duke football team was "for" only men, with women allowed to try out, or was "for" both men and women. If the football team was "for" both men and women, then subsection (b) is simply inapplicable, and Duke was subject to the general anti-discrimination rule in subsection (a). It may well be,on the facts as we understand them, that, at the summary-judgment or trial stage of the litigation, appellant can conclusively establish that Duke operated its football team "for" both men and women; however, appellant does not allege in her complaint that Duke operated such a team and therefore we proceed to address the possibility that Duke operated its football team "for" only men.

*not apply at all.*" Second, it could be interpreted to mean that "members of the excluded sex must be allowed to try out for the team offered unless the sport involved is a contact sport, *in which case members of the excluded sex need not be allowed to try out.*"

Appellees advocate the former reading, arguing that HEW intended through this clause to exempt contact sports entirely from the coverage of Title IX. We believe, however, that the latter reading is the more natural and intended meaning. The second sentence of subsection (b) does not purport in any way to state an exemption, whether for contact sports or for any other subcategory, from the general anti-discrimination rule stated in subsection (a). And HEW certainly knew how to provide for a complete exemption had it wished, Congress itself having provided a number of such exemptions in the very statute implemented by the regulation. Rather, the sentence says, and says only, that covered institutions must allow members of an excluded sex to try out for single-sex teams in non-contact sports. Therefore, the "unless" phrase at the end of the second clause of the sentence cannot (logically or grammatically) do anything more than except contact sports from the tryout requirement that the beginning of the second clause of the sentence imposes on all other sports.

Contrary to appellees' assertion, this reading of the regulation is perfectly consistent with the evident congressional intent not to require the sexual integration of intercollegiate contact sports. If a university chooses not to permit members of the opposite sex to tryout for a single-sex contact-sports team, this interpretation respects that choice. At the same time, however, the reading of the regulation we adopt today, unlike the one advanced by appellees, ensures that the likewise indisputable congressional intent to prohibit discrimination in all circumstances where such discrimination is unreasonable--for example, where the university itself has voluntarily opened the team in question to members of both sexes--is not frustrated.

We therefore construe the second sentence of subsection (b) as providing that in non-contact sports, but not in contact sports, covered institutions must allow members of an excluded sex to try out for single-sex teams. Once an institution has allowed a member of one sex to try out for a team operated by the institution for the other sex in a contact sport, subsection (b) is simply no longer applicable, and the institution is subject to the general anti-discrimination provision of subsection (a). To the extent that the Third Circuit intended to hold otherwise in *Williams v. School Dist. of Bethlehem, Pa.,* 998 F.2d 168, 174 (3d Cir.1993), with its lone unexplained statement that, "[i]f it is determined that [a particular sport] is a contact sport, no other inquiry is necessary because that will be dispositive of the title IX claim," we reject such a conclusion as inconsistent with the language of the regulation.

Accordingly, because appellant has alleged that Duke allowed her to try out for its football team (and actually made her a member of the team), then discriminated against her and ultimately excluded her from participation in the sport on the basis of her sex, we conclude that she has stated a claim under the applicable regulation, and therefore under Title IX. We take to heart appellees' cautionary observation that, in so holding, we thereby become "the first Court in United States history to recognize such a cause of action." Br. of Appellees at 20. Where, as here, however, the university invites women into what appellees characterize as the "traditionally all-male bastion of collegiate football," *id.* at 20 n. 10, we are convinced that this reading of the regulation is the only one permissible under law.

The district court's order granting appellees' motion to dismiss for failure to state a claim is hereby reversed, and the case remanded for further proceedings.

*REVERSED AND REMANDED*

*Heather Mercer, published courtesy Donnan*

# Notes & Questions

1. The court quotes C.F.R. sect. 106.41 (b), which states that a school "may operate or sponsor separate teams for members of each sex where selection for such teams is based upon competitive skill or the activity involved is a contact sport."  Can you think of varsity sports at the high school or college level where selection is *not* "based upon competitive skill"?  Just what is this "based upon competitive skill" language supposed to mean?

2. Suppose that, because a school does not field a male gymnastics team, a male gymnast wants to try out for his high school's girls gymnastics team. How does C.F.R. sect. 106.41 (b) apply to this situation?

3. Is the practical effect of the *Mercer* decision likely to be that institutions simply will be disinclined to permit females to try out for contact sports, in order to avoid allegations of discrimination?  Explain why or why not.

4. Suppose that a talented female high school athlete wants to try out for the boys baseball or wrestling team. How does C.F.R. sect. 106.41 (b) apply to this situation?  Suppose that the sport is golf?

## Boucher v. Syracuse University
164 F. 3d. 113 (1999)
United States Court of Appeals, Second Circuit

CALABRESI, Circuit Judge:

Former female club athletes at Syracuse University ("Syracuse" or "the University") appeal from an April 3, 1998 judgment of the United States District Court for the Northern District of New York (Frederick J. Scullin, Jr., *J.*) granting summary judgment to Syracuse on a Title IX accommodation claim.  Plaintiffs also appeal two orders of June 12, 1996.  The first such order dismissed their Title IX equal treatment claims, and the second conditionally certified a class.

We affirm in part, dismiss the appeal in part, and vacate and remand in part.

Plaintiff students "individually and on behalf of all others similarly situated" filed suit in May of 1995 against Syracuse University, alleging numerous violations of Title IX of the Education Amendments of 1972, 20 U.S.C. § § 1681-1688, and its governing regulations. Seven of the eight named plaintiffs were at that time members of Syracuse's club lacrosse team and the eighth was a member of the University's club softball team. All plaintiffs have since graduated from the University.

The plaintiffs argued that Syracuse discriminated against female athletes in its allocation of participation opportunities (which includes decisions regarding which varsity teams to field as well as how many opportunities for participation by female varsity athletes are thereby created as a result of those decisions).[1] Plaintiffs also alleged that Syracuse provided unequal benefits to varsity female athletes as compared to varsity male athletes, and provided unequal scholarship funding to varsity female athletes as compared to varsity male athletes.[2]

Plaintiffs sought class certification in view of the fact that college students are a fluid group and that without such certification, mootness issues would likely arise. *See, e.g., Cook v. Colgate Univ.,* 992 F.2d 17, 19-20 (2d Cir.1993) (holding a Title IX appeal moot, once plaintiffs, seeking injunctive relief, had graduated). In their equal treatment claims, plaintiffs asked for declaratory and injunctive relief ordering the University to provide equal benefits and scholarships to varsity male and female athletes. In their accommodation claim, plaintiffs sought the establishment of varsity lacrosse and softball teams for women.

---

[1] This kind of Title IX claim is commonly referred to as an "accommodation" claim because it derives from the Title IX implementing regulations, which provide that in determining whether equal athletic opportunities for members of both sexes are available, the Office of Civil Rights of the Department of Education (the office charged with enforcement of Title IX) will consider, among other factors, "[w]hether the selection of sports and levels of competition effectively accommodate the interests and abilities of members of both sexes." 34 C.F.R. § 106.41(c)(1); *see also Cohen v. Brown Univ.,* 991 F.2d 888, 897 (1st Cir.1993) ("*Cohen I* ") (noting three major areas of regulatory compliance under Title IX: athletic financial assistance (scholarships), equivalence in other athletic benefits and opportunities, and effective accommodation of student interests and abilities).

[2] These types of Title IX claims are generally referred to as "equal treatment" claims because they derive from the Title IX regulations found at 34 C.F.R. § 106.37(c) and 106.41(c)(2)-(10), which call for equal provision of athletic scholarships as well as equal provision of other athletic benefits and opportunities among the sexes.

373

Just over 50% of the Syracuse's student population is female, yet, when this complaint was filed, women made up only 32.4% of its athletes. In its 1993-94 National Collegiate Athletic Association submission, Syracuse stated that of its 681 varsity student-athletes, 217 were women, while 464 were men. These numbers reflected a 19% disparity between the percentage of varsity athletes who were female and the percentage of the University's students who were female.[3]

At the time that this suit was begun in May of 1995, the University funded eleven men's varsity teams and nine women's varsity teams. Just prior to the filing of the complaint, Syracuse announced a plan to add two new varsity women's teams to its athletic program--women's varsity soccer and women's varsity lacrosse. These teams began to play, respectively, in the 1996-97 and the 1997-98 academic years, thus bringing the number of varsity teams funded by the school to eleven men's and eleven women's.[4]

The University established five of its nine women's varsity teams in 1971[5]--when it first funded women's varsity sports. It dropped one of these sports (fencing) in 1972, and replaced it with field hockey. Crew was added as a women's varsity team in 1977. Three additional women's sports were added to the varsity roster in 1981.[6] After 1981, no new women's varsity team was created by the University until the addition of the varsity soccer team in 1997. Thus, until the filing of this complaint in 1995, fourteen years passed by without the University creating any new women's varsity teams. In the course of this litigation, Syracuse announced plans to institute a varsity women's softball team which, according to the University's representations at oral argument, will begin play in the 1999-2000 academic year.

* * * *

On June 12, 1996, the district court granted summary judgment to the University on plaintiffs' equal treatment claims--those that challenged the alleged unequal allocation of benefits and scholarships between varsity men's and women's teams (brought under 34 C.F.R. § 106.41(c)(2)-(8), (10) and 34 C.F.R. § 106.37). The court held that since none of the named plaintiffs were varsity athletes, they did not have standing to assert the equal treatment

---

[3] Between 1990 and the time of the filing of this suit, the disparity between the percentage of varsity athletes who are female as compared to the percentage of the University's students who are female ranged from 19 to 22%.

[4] It is the case, however, that for Title IX accommodation purposes, it is the aggregate number of opportunities provided for each sex, and not the number of teams funded for each sex, that matters. *Cf. Cohen I,* 991 F.2d at 897.

[5] These were basketball, fencing, swimming, tennis, and volleyball.

[6] These were indoor track, outdoor track, and cross country.

374

claims. Its ruling on this issue was proper and we affirm the dismissal of plaintiffs' equal treatment claims substantially for the reasons the district court gave. *See Boucher v. Syracuse Univ.*, No. 95-CV-620, 1996 WL 328444 (N.D.N.Y. June 12, 1996). At the same time, the court ruled that plaintiffs could go forward with their accommodation claim and additionally deemed that the plaintiffs could pursue an equal treatment claim challenging the allocation of funds between male and female *club* teams--an action that the plaintiffs had not brought and never litigated.

\*\*\*

After a period of limited discovery, the district court granted summary judgment to the University on plaintiffs' accommodation claim. It found that although opportunities to participate in varsity athletics at Syracuse were not allocated equally between the sexes, the University nevertheless fell within one of the safe harbors set forth in the governing regulations of Title IX. (citation omitted). Under the implementing regulations, there are three safe harbor defenses to a claim of unequal accommodation of student interest in varsity athletics. *See* 34 C.F.R. § 106.41(c)(1); 44 Fed.Reg. 71413 (1979). The district court held that Syracuse met the requirements of the second safe harbor because it had "continued a practice of program expansion which is responsive to the abilities and interests of its student body."[7]

Specifically, the district court found that (1) Syracuse had a "strong history of adding women's sports programs"; (2) although between 1982 and 1995, the University had added no new varsity women's teams, it did fund additional scholarships and provide enhanced facilities, coaching, and support services for its women varsity athletes; (3) between 1982 and 1995, the absolute number of female participants in varsity sports had increased

---

[7] The court observed:

> Where a university has a practice of expanding its athletic program, approaching proportionality and meeting the needs of the under-represented gender; and continues to expand in response to its student body's interest and abilities, as well as that of secondary feeder schools; symmetry in athletic programs is not required under Title IX, and liability may be avoided. Under this "safe harbor" of a continuing practice of program expansion, courts look to the institution's past and continuing remedial efforts to provide nondiscriminatory participation opportunities through program expansion. 1998 WL 167296, at \*3 (citing *Cohen I*, 991 F.2d at 898; *Bryant*, 1996 WL 328446, at \*10; 44 Fed.Reg. 71,413).

from 148 to 217; and (4) Syracuse had established two new varsity women's teams since 1995 and planned to add a third in 1999-2000. *Id.*

Finally, the district court noted that in conducting the safe harbor analysis, a court "may consider whether there are any formal policies in place which might indicate that the institution is monitoring the pulse of its students' interests in anticipation of expansion." *Id.* Despite recognizing that the school had not established that it had any formal policy to allow students to voice their interests, the court concluded that "the best evidence of continued expansion is expansion itself." *Id.* Accordingly, it granted summary judgment to the University.

## *DISCUSSION*

*A. Lacrosse.*

Syracuse argues that this appeal is moot because it has already implemented a varsity women's lacrosse team and that there is, therefore, nothing left for the certified class to pursue. The plaintiffs counter that the appeal is not moot for two reasons. First, they state that they sought to amend their complaint in the district court to add a claim for damages and that the court improperly denied their motion. Second, they argue that their suit did not merely seek class certification of current and future students interested in playing varsity lacrosse, but that they also sought class certification of current and numerous future students interested in playing varsity softball, itself not yet a varsity sport.

It may well be that mootness would have been avoided had plaintiffs originally requested damages in their complaint. *See Cook,* 992 F.2d at 19-20 (noting that "a viable claim for damages generally avoids mootness of the action," but finding a Title IX appeal moot where plaintiffs had graduated, had sought relief solely on their own behalf, and had not appealed the district court's denial of their request for damages); *see also id.* at 19 (holding that an interest in preserving an award of attorneys' fees "is insufficient, standing alone, to sustain jurisdiction"). A request for damages, however, will not avoid mootness if it was "inserted after the complaint was filed in an attempt to breathe life into a moribund dispute." *McCabe v. Nassau County Med. Ctr.,* 453 F.2d 698, 702 (2d Cir.1971).

In the case before us, plaintiffs did not seek to amend their complaint to add a damages claim until three months after the University filed its motion for summary judgment and six months after the district court granted the University leave to file that motion. Moreover, in their papers in opposition to the University's motion, plaintiffs' counsel represented that if

376

the district court were to enter an order binding the University to its promise to establish varsity women's lacrosse and softball teams, then "plaintiffs shall submit an application for attorney's fees as *there is no longer a controversy between the parties* " (emphasis added). And on appeal, plaintiffs' counsel, despite being asked numerous times at oral argument to specify precisely what relief plaintiffs sought, failed ever to mention damages.(citation omitted). Under the circumstances, we are satisfied that the district court did not err in denying plaintiffs leave to amend their complaint to add a damages claim.

We, therefore, hold that insofar as plaintiffs' complaint sought a varsity lacrosse team, the claim is now moot, given that the team has been created and is already participating in intercollegiate play. *See County of Los Angeles v. Davis,* 440 U.S. 625, 631-32, 99 S.Ct. 1379, 59 L.Ed.2d 642 (1979) (finding case moot where there was no reasonable expectation that the alleged violation would recur). Accordingly, we take no position on whether the safe harbor defense made by Syracuse and granted by the district court was valid.

*B. Softball.*

Plaintiffs also contest the district court's failure to certify a sub-class of current and future women interested in playing varsity softball. They argue that this issue is not moot because such a team has not yet begun play. We agree with both contentions.

District judges have broad discretion over class definition. But under Rule 23(c)(1), courts are "required to reassess their class rulings as the case develops." *Barnes v. The American Tobacco Co.,* 161 F.3d 127, 140 (3d Cir.1998) [citations omitted]. And we agree with the Fifth Circuit that "[o]rdinarily, if a court discerns a conflict ... the proper solution is to create subclasses of persons whose interests are in accord." *Payne v. Travenol Labs., Inc.,* 673 F.2d 798, 812 (5th Cir.1982). We conclude that although the district court correctly found potential conflicts between members of a class that included both women interested in playing varsity lacrosse and women who wished to play varsity softball, it should have certified two sub-classes--one for each sport--rather than certifying only one class and excluding from that class members of the second.

That being said, the University represented both to the district court and to this Court that a varsity women's softball team is in the process of being established, and that the team will begin play during the 1999-2000 academic year. Because full implementation of a varsity women's softball team would render the remaining live aspect of this case moot, we again choose not to reach the merits of the University's safe harbor defense, and prefer instead to remand the case to the district court with instructions to dismiss the case if the University completes its plan to institute a varsity women's softball team by the date indicated. Should the University not live up to its representations, the district court is ordered to certify a class of current and future women students interested in playing varsity softball and to revisit the merits of the case at that time.

\* \* \* \*

We affirm the district court's dismissal of the plaintiffs' equal treatment claims with respect to varsity athletes for lack of standing.\*\*\* We vacate the district court's class certification order .... We remand the case to the district court for further proceedings consistent with this opinion with respect to the plaintiffs' claim as to varsity softball.

**Notes & Questions**

1. Given the slow pace of federal litigation, isn't it true that mootness will always be a problem for plaintiffs in Title IX litigation?

2. From the Syracuse University Athletics website:

Softball: The fourth-seeded Orange (36-21) was eliminated in the quarterfinal round of the 2006 BIG EAST Championship by No. 5 seed DePaul, 8-0.

Lacrosse: The women's lacrosse program was started in 1997. Syracuse will be home to the inaugural 2007 Women's BIG EAST Lacrosse Championship. The team finished with a record of 9-7-0 in the 2006 season and ranked 18th in the IWLCA coaches poll and 19th in the *Inside Lacrosse* media poll.

## Boulahanis v. Board of Regents
### 198 F. 3d. 633 (1999)
United States Court of Appeals, Seventh Circuit

FLAUM, Circuit Judge.

The plaintiffs-appellants, a group of former and prospective athletes at Illinois State University (the "University"), appeal the district court's grant of summary judgment to the University, alleging that the actions of the University in eliminating its men's wrestling and men's soccer programs constitute a violation of Title IX of the Education Amendments of 1972, 20 U.S.C. § 1681. In addition, the plaintiffs-appellants appeal the district court's dismissal of various claims of sex discrimination and race discrimination under 42 U.S.C. § 1983 and 42 U.S.C. § 1985(3) arising out of the same University actions, arguing that the district court incorrectly deemed those claims to be preempted. For the reasons set out below, we agree with the judgment of the district court and affirm.

### I. Facts

In the fall of 1993, the Gender Equity Committee of Illinois State University undertook a year-long investigation of gender equity and Title IX compliance at the University. The results of this study indicated that enrollment at the University was 45% male and 55% female, while athletic participation was 66% male and 34% female. The study concluded that these numbers did not constitute equitable participation opportunities for women. In response to this conclusion, the University began to consider ways to bring itself into compliance with Title IX.

Under Title IX, Illinois State University is required to "provide equal athletic opportunity" for men and women. 34 C.F.R. § 106.41(c). Equal opportunities are to be evaluated according to the following ten factors:

(1) Whether the selection of sports and levels of competition effectively accommodate the interests and abilities of members of both sexes;
(2) The provision of equipment and supplies;
(3) Scheduling of games and practice time;
(4) Travel and per diem allowance;
(5) Opportunity to receive coaching and academic tutoring;
(6) Assignment and compensation of coaches and tutors;

(7) Provision of locker rooms, practice and competitive facilities;

(8) Provision of medical and training facilities and services;

9) Provision of housing and dining facilities and services; and

(10) Publicity. *Id.*

In addition to these considerations, an "institution may violate Title IX solely by failing to accommodate the interests and abilities of student athletes of both sexes." *Kelley v. Board of Trustees*, 35 F.3d 265, 268 (7th Cir.1994) (citing *Roberts v. Colorado St. Bd. of Agric.*, 998 F.2d 824, 828 (10th Cir.1993); *Cohen v. Brown Univ.*, 991 F.2d 888, 897-98 (1st Cir.1993)).

In order to effectively accommodate the athletic interests of both male and female students, the University had three options under the policy interpretations of Title IX promulgated by the Office of Civil Rights: (1) provide participation opportunities for men and women that are substantially proportionate to their respective rates of enrollment as full-time undergraduate students; or (2) demonstrate a history and continuing practice of program expansion for the under-represented sex; or (3) fully and effectively accommodate the interests and abilities of the under-represented sex. 44 Fed.Reg. 71,418 (1979). Because the University had not added a women's sports program in over ten years, and because it did not believe it could accommodate effectively the interests and abilities of its women students, the University focused on achieving the goal of substantial proportionality. The University's desire to bring itself into compliance with Title IX through a showing of substantial proportionality was intensified by a 1995 audit by the National Collegiate Athletic Association. The results of that audit showed that the University was not in conformity with the requirements of Title IX.

The University considered ten options to achieve compliance with Title IX. These options included: (1) dropping men's wrestling; (2) dropping men's wrestling and men's soccer; (3) dropping men's wrestling, men's soccer, and men's tennis; (4) dropping men's wrestling and adding women's soccer; (5) dropping men's wrestling and men's soccer and adding women's soccer; (6) dropping men's wrestling, men's soccer, and men's tennis and adding women's soccer; (7) adding women's soccer; (8) adding women's soccer and bringing women to full funding; (9) dropping men's wrestling and men's soccer, adding women's soccer, and adjusting men's rosters and women's grants in aid; and (10) dropping men's wrestling and men's soccer, adding women's soccer, and adjusting men's rosters and grants in aid for both men and women. After careful consideration of these options, the University ultimately chose and implemented option number ten. This resulted in the addition of women's soccer and the elimination of men's soccer and men's wrestling. The implementation of this plan increased the athletic participation of women to 51.72% and decreased the athletic participation of men to 48.29%, thereby bringing the disparity between enrollment and participation to within three percentage points.

The plaintiffs-appellants are former members of the men's soccer and men's wrestling teams at Illinois State University who, as a consequence of the University's elimination of those programs under its gender equity plan, were no longer able to participate in those sports at the University. They contend that the University's decision to eliminate the programs in which they participated was based on sex, and is therefore a violation of Title IX. They also allege various violations of their constitutional rights.... The district court granted the University summary judgment on the Title IX claim, and dismissed the constitutional claims as preempted by the availability of a Title IX claim. It is from these decisions that the plaintiffs-appellants now appeal.

## II. Analysis

\*\*\*

### A.

Title IX states that "No person in the United States shall, on the basis of sex, be excluded from participation in, be denied the benefits of, or be subjected to discrimination under any education program or activity receiving Federal financial assistance." 20 U.S.C. § 1681(a). The plaintiffs-appellants contend that the University's actions in eliminating the men's soccer and men's wrestling programs were based solely on the sex of the participants. According to the plaintiffs-appellants, because these discriminatory actions would not have been taken "but for" the sex of the participants, the actions violate Title IX on its face. *See International Union v. Johnson Controls, Inc.*, 499 U.S. 187, 200, 111 S.Ct. 1196, 113 L.Ed.2d 158 (1991) (quoting *Los Angeles Dep't of Water and Power v. Manhart*, 435 U.S. 702, 711, 98 S.Ct. 1370, 55 L.Ed.2d 657 (1978) (citation omitted) (stating that the simple test for discrimination is "whether the evidence shows 'treatment of a person in a manner which but for that person's sex would have been different' ")).

The plaintiffs-appellants' argument is similar to one this Court has already considered in *Kelley v. Board of Trustees*, 35 F.3d 265 (7th Cir.1994). The plaintiffs in *Kelley* were members of the men's swimming team at the University of Illinois. That program was eliminated in an attempt by that university to cut its athletic budget by getting rid of teams that were not competitive on a national level. Although the men's swimming team at the University of Illinois was eliminated on this basis, the women's swimming program was maintained because of concerns about compliance with Title IX. *Id.* at 269. Members of the University of Illinois's men's swimming team, like the plaintiffs-appellants in this case, challenged the university's cancellation of the athletic program in which they participated as a violation of Title IX. We rejected that challenge, holding that the elimination of men's swimming did not violate Title IX because "men's participation in athletics [continued] to be more than substantially proportionate to their presence in [the University of Illinois's] student body." *Id.* at 270.

The plaintiffs-appellants contend that our decision in *Kelley* is distinguishable from the facts of this case, and is therefore not controlling. In attempting to distinguish *Kelley*, the plaintiffs-appellants rely on the financial and budgetary considerations that motivated the University of Illinois's athletic department to eliminate men's swimming. *See id.* at 269. According to the plaintiffs-appellants, a decision that is motivated by financial concerns, even if it includes sex-based considerations, does not violate Title IX. In contrast, a decision like the one in this case, that is motivated by the sex of the participants, does violate Title IX. In short, the plaintiffs-appellants attempt to draw a distinction between decisions in which sex is a consideration (as in *Kelley*) and decisions in which sex serves as the motivating factor (as in the present case).

We are not persuaded by the plaintiffs-appellants' attempt to distinguish decisions to eliminate athletic programs motivated by financial concerns from those based on considerations of sex. That distinction ignores the fact that a university's decision as to which athletic programs to offer necessarily entails budgetary considerations. For universities, decisions about cutting or adding athletic programs are based on a consideration of many factors including: the total size of the athletic department, which is governed by budgetary considerations, and the distribution of programs among men and women, which is governed by Title IX concerns. To say that one decision is financial, while another is sex-based, assumes that these two aspects can be neatly separated. They cannot. Absent financial concerns, Illinois State University presumably would rather have added women's programs while keeping its men's programs intact. Similarly, in the absence of Title IX concerns, the University of Illinois in *Kelley* would have cut both its men's and women's swimming programs in order to save money.[1] Ultimately, both the decision of the University in this case and the decision of the University of Illinois at issue in *Kelley* were based on a combination of financial and sex-based concerns that are not easily distinguished.

\*\*\*

[A] holding that universities cannot achieve substantial proportionality by cutting men's programs is tantamount to a requirement that universities achieve substantial proportionality through additional spending to add women's sports programs. This result would ignore the financial and budgetary constraints that universities face. *See Roberts v. Colorado St. Bd. of Agric.*, 998 F.2d 824, 830 (10th Cir.1993) ("[I]n times of economic hardship, few schools will be able to satisfy Title IX's effective accommodation requirement by continuing to expand their women's athletic programs."). Unless we are willing to mandate such spending, the agency's substantial proportionality rule must be read to allow the elimination of men's athletic programs to achieve compliance with Title IX.

The plaintiffs-appellants do not see such potential spending mandates as a problem because they read *Kelley* to permit the elimination of men's programs in order to address budgetary concerns. At the same time, they assume that such financially-motivated decisions can be readily discerned by courts. Yet given the practical difficulty of distinguishing financial and sex-based concerns, the effect of accepting such a distinction would only force universities under serious budget constraints to cast decisions made under the shadow of Title IX as financial ones. To be safe, they might even go so far as to add women's programs in order to create the kind of budgetary constraints that would justify cutting men's programs. In either case, the plaintiffs-appellants would be no better off than they are under existing law. Because we conclude that the plaintiffs-appellants' distinction would place universities in an unmanageable position, we reject the plaintiffs-appellants' attempt to distinguish *Kelley*.

As we noted in *Kelley*, the elimination of men's athletic programs is not a violation of Title IX as long as men's participation in athletics continues to be "substantially proportionate" to their enrollment. *See Kelley*, 35 F.3d at

---

[1] This is clearly illustrated by the fact that the University of Illinois "did not eliminate the women's swimming program because the school's legal counsel advised that such action would put the [u]niversity at risk of violating Title IX." *Kelley*, 35 F.3d at 269.

270.    After the elimination of men's soccer and men's wrestling at the University, the athletic participation of men remained within three percentage points of enrollment.    The plaintiffs-appellants do not contend that this disparity is outside the requirements of substantial proportionality. Because the University has achieved substantial proportionality between men's enrollment and men's participation in athletics, it is presumed to have accommodated the athletic interests of that sex.    *See Kelley*, 35 F.3d at 271; *see also Roberts*, 998 F.2d at 829 (" '[S]ubstantial proportionality' between athletic participation and undergraduate enrollment provides a safe harbor for recipients under Title IX.");    *Cohen*, 991 F.2d at 897-98 ("[A] university which does not wish to engage in extensive compliance analysis may stay on the sunny side of Title IX simply by maintaining gender parity between its student body and its athletic lineup.").    Under such circumstances, Illinois State University's actions in eliminating the programs at issue do not constitute a violation of Title IX.

## B.

The plaintiffs-appellants next contend that if Title IX is construed to permit the elimination of men's programs for reasons of sex, then Title IX as interpreted would violate the Equal Protection Clause.    The plaintiffs-appellants' argument is based on the idea that discrimination based on sex is permissible only when it is substantially related to an important government objective.    *See Metro Broadcasting, Inc. v. FCC*, 497 U.S. 547, 564-65, 110 S.Ct. 2997, 111 L.Ed.2d 445 (1990) (establishing an intermediate standard of scrutiny for sex discrimination); *Mississippi Univ. for Women v. Hogan*, 458 U.S. 718, 728, 102 S.Ct. 3331, 73 L.Ed.2d 1090 (1982) (same).    The plaintiffs-appellants do not challenge the assertion that assisting an under-represented group to achieve additional opportunities would constitute an important government objective.    They do argue that when viewed in isolation, the elimination of men's wrestling and men's soccer only served to decrease opportunities for men without providing any additional opportunities for women.    As such, the plaintiffs-appellants contend that increased opportunities for women cannot be the important government objective justifying this sex-based discrimination by the University.

As was the case with plaintiffs-appellants' first claim, this Court addressed the equal protection issue in *Kelley* and rejected it. As we held in *Kelley*, "Title IX's stated objective is not to ensure that the athletic opportunities available to women increase.    Rather its avowed purpose is to prohibit educational institutions from discriminating on the basis of sex." *Kelley*, 35 F.3d at 272.    The elimination of sex-based discrimination in federally-funded educational institutions is an important government objective, and the actions of Illinois State University in eliminating the men's soccer and men's wrestling programs were substantially related to that objective. *See id.* (citing *Mississippi Univ. for Women*, 458 U.S. at 728, 102 S.Ct. 3331 ("[A] gender-based classification favoring one sex can be justified if it intentionally and directly assists members of the sex that is disproportionately burdened.")). In light of these conclusions, we repeat our holding in *Kelley* that "[w]hile the effect of Title IX and the relevant regulation and policy interpretation is that institutions will sometimes consider gender when decreasing their athletic offerings, this limited consideration of sex does not violate the Constitution." *Id.*

\*\*\*

### III. Conclusion

The district court correctly determined that the actions of Illinois State University in eliminating its men's soccer and men's wrestling programs did not violate Title IX or the Equal Protection Clause.\*\*\*

AFFIRMED.

### Notes & Questions

1. Instead of deciding to cut teams summarily, would it be preferable for schools to phase them out gradually over the course of several years, so that scholarship players and others who were recruited would not be left out in the cold when a team is abruptly discontinued? Clearly, if a school were to adopt a "phase-out" approach, walk-ons would become essential during any phase-out period.

2. According to the court in *Boulahanis,* "a holding that universities cannot achieve substantial proportionality by cutting men's programs is tantamount to a requirement that universities achieve substantial proportionality through additional spending to add women's sports programs. This result would ignore the financial and budgetary constraints that universities face." To what extent do you believe the court simply does not wish to second-guess and micromanage a university's decisions regarding how it will achieve substantial proportionality? Would a contrary holding open the proverbial floodgates of litigation? Explain why or why not.

3. In *Miami University Wresting Club v Miami University,* 302 F.3d 608 (6th Cir. 2002), the Sixth Circuit took on the issue of whether cutting men's sports to make room for more female teams was a violation of Title IX. In this case, the Office of Civil Rights, which enforces Title IX, reviewed the University of Miami in response to a complaint filed that alleged the school discriminated against women. The OCR did find that the "rates of participation in athletics [did] not correspond to the percentage of male and female students," but that the proposed addition of women's cross country would adequately address the problem. Since there was, according to the school, a lack of funds, to make way for another team, they eliminated athletic activities that were previously available to males, such as wrestling. The effects were that athletic opportunities for the members of men's soccer, tennis, and wrestling were lost. The court first decided, on the issue of an equal protection claim, that there was no constitutional right to participate in athletics. As for the Title IX claim, "[t]itle IX prohibits gender inequity in connection with, among other things, the opportunity to participate in athletics. The Statue forces on opportunities for the underrepresented gender, and does not bestow rights on the historically overrepresented gender." Is this a good policy? Is that indeed the purpose of Title IX, and does this kind of policy reach the overall goals of the statute?

### *Further Reading on Title IX:*

Nancy Hogshead-Makar, *Playing Unfair: Commission's Opposition to Title IX Shows Bias Against Women's Sports*, L.A. Daily J. 6, Col 3 (March 11, 2003).

Daniel R. Marburger, *Is Title IX Really to Blame for the Decline in Intercollegiate Men's Nonrevenue Sport*, 14 MARQ. SPORTS L. REV. 65 (2003).

Barbara Osborne, *Pay Equity for Coaches and Athletic Administrators: An Element of Title IX*, 34 Univ. MICH. J.L. REFORM 231 (2001).

Rodney K. Smith, *Solving the Title IX Conundrum With Women's Football*, 38 S. TEX. L. REV. 9 (1997).

Symposium, *Competing in the 21st Century: Title IX, Gender Equity and Athletics*, 31 UNIV. MICH. J.L. REFORM 1 (2001).

John C. Weistart & Cym H. Lowell, Law of Sports, §2.10 Sex Discrimination (Bobbs-Merrill Company, Inc., 1979).

Darryl C. Wilson, *Title IX's Collegiate Sports Application Raises Serious Questions Regarding the Role of the NCAA*, 31 J. MARSHALL L. REV. 1303 (1998).

Darryl C. Wilson, *Parity Bowl IX: Barrier Breakers v. Common Sense Makers; The Serpentine Struggle for Gender Diversity in Collegiate Athletics*, 27 CUMB. L. REV. 397 (1996-1997).

# Chapter 9

## NCAA

---

These three articles provide an overview of the history, organization, structure, and governance of the NCAA, and a number of the most important legal and non-legal issues facing the NCAA and intercollegiate athletics today. The excerpts from Smith's article introduce the background and governance. Mitten's article focuses on antitrust concerns. And Lynch's article takes a provocative look at the difficult balance between the educational goals and the athletic and financial aspects of modern college sports.

When reading these articles, it is best to read them actively, with specific goals in mind. First, you should read them with an eye to uncovering any pertinent laws and legal rules applicable to the NCAA. Similarly, you should be on the lookout for any administrative regulations also (*i.e.,* the NCAA's own regulations). You should also adjust your reading radar in an effort to discern policy. In particular try to think about what *values* are being promoted by the laws and regulations discussed. In addition, think about whose *interests* are being protected by laws and regulations (*e.g.,* coaches, alumni, student athletes, corporations). Lastly, try to decide whether you think that the author has a specific point of view. Is the author biased? Does the author have a particular axe to grind?

# A BRIEF HISTORY OF THE NATIONAL COLLEGIATE ATHLETIC ASSOCIATION'S ROLE IN REGULATING INTERCOLLEGIATE ATHLETICS

Rodney K. Smith

11 MARQ. SPORTS L. REV. 9 (2000)

## I. Introduction

As one whose scholarship focuses on religious liberty and sport, I am often asked why I write in such seemingly disparate areas. My typical response is that given my interest in the role of religion in society, I certainly should be interested in sport, the religion of the American people. This response invariably engenders a slight smile and chuckle. I fear that there is some truth to the statement. Although I do not have the statistics necessary to prove it, my impression is that as many adults are zealously devoted to "the game" on any given day as are devoted to a worship service at a religious institution. As a people, we seem almost fixated on sport and devote much space in newspapers and newscasts to sport, with little space being allocated to religion. Yet, the discourse regarding sport is generally just description of events occurring, and rarely peers more deeply into the ramifications of specific issues, or of the general issue of our virtually thoughtless zeal for sport in contemporary society. While I find this to be personally troubling, it is just such thoughtless zeal as to sport, and the desire to see one's team win at virtually any cost, that contributes to the increasing regulation of athletics at virtually all levels.

Devotees of a given team, including coaches and fans alike, often strive mightily to find clever ways to unbalance the playing field in their team's favor through questionable recruiting techniques or other devices. This propensity to seek undue advantages in sport has made regulation of intercollegiate athletics a necessity in order to maintain even a semblance of a balanced playing field. Each new, creative way of bending the rules to create an undue advantage has necessarily led to the development of new rules and regulations. In turn, the growth in the number of rules has required development of an extensive structure to ensure that the rules are enforced.

In this essay, I will briefly examine the historical development of the National Collegiate Athletic Association (hereinafter NCAA) and the regulation of intercollegiate athletics. I will also offer some general comments regarding the history and future of the regulation of intercollegiate athletics.

390

## II. A Brief History of the National Collegiate Athletic Association

### A. 1840-1910

The need for regulation of intercollegiate athletics in the United States has existed for at least a century and a half. One of the earliest interschool athletic events was a highbrow regatta between Harvard and Yale Universities, which was commercially sponsored by the then powerful Elkins Railroad Line. Harvard University sought to gain an undue advantage over its academic rival Yale by obtaining the services of a coxswain who was not a student. Thus, the commercialization and propensity to seek unfair advantages existed virtually from the beginning of organized intercollegiate athletics in the United States. The problem of cheating, which was no doubt compounded by the increasing commercialization of sport, was a matter of concern. Initially, these concerns led institutions to move the athletic teams from student control to faculty oversight. Nevertheless, by the latter part of the nineteenth century, two leading university presidents were voicing their fears that intercollegiate athletics were out of control. President Eliot at Harvard was very concerned about the impact that commercialization of intercollegiate athletics was having, and charged that "lofty gate receipts from college athletics had turned amateur contests into major commercial spectacles." In the same year, President Walker of the Massachusetts Institute of Technology bemoaned the fact that intercollegiate athletics had lost its academic moorings and opined that "[i]f the movement shall continue at the same rate, it will soon be fairly a question whether the letters B.A. stand more for Bachelor of Arts or Bachelor of Athletics." In turn, recognizing the difficulty of overseeing intercollegiate athletics at the institutional level, whether through the faculty or the student governance, conferences were being created both to facilitate the playing of a schedule of games and to provide a modicum of regulation at a broader level.

Despite the shift from student control to faculty oversight and some conference regulation, intercollegiate athletics remained under-regulated and a source of substantial concern. Rising concerns regarding the need to control the excesses of intercollegiate athletics were compounded by the fact that in 1905 alone, there were over eighteen deaths and one hundred major injuries in intercollegiate football. National attention was turned to intercollegiate athletics when President Roosevelt called for a White House conference to review football rules. President Roosevelt invited officials from the major football programs to participate. Deaths and injuries in football persisted, however, and Chancellor Henry MacCracken of New York University called for a national meeting of representatives of the nation's major intercollegiate football programs to determine whether football could be regulated or had to be abolished at the intercollegiate level. Representatives of many major intercollegiate football programs accepted Chancellor MacCracken's invitation and ultimately formed a Rules Committee. President Roosevelt then sought to have participants in the White House conference meet with the new Rules Committee. This combined effort on the part of educators and the White House eventually led to a concerted effort to reform intercollegiate football rules, resulting in the formation of the Intercollegiate Athletic Association (hereinafter IAA), with sixty-two original members. In 1910, the IAA was renamed the NCAA. Initially, the NCAA was formed to formulate rules that could be applied to the various intercollegiate sports.

In the years prior to the formation of the NCAA, schools wrestled with the same issues that we face today: the extreme pressure to win, which is compounded by the commercialization of sport, and the need for regulations and a regulatory body to ensure fairness and safety. In terms of regulation, between 1840 and 1910, there was a movement from loose student control of athletics to faculty oversight, from faculty oversight to the creation of conferences, and, ultimately, to the development of a national entity for governance purposes.

B. 1910-1970

In its early years, the NCAA did not play a major role in governing intercollegiate athletics. It did begin to stretch beyond merely making rules for football and other games played, to the creation of a national championship event in various sports. Indeed, students, with some faculty oversight, continued to be the major force in running intercollegiate athletics. By the 1920s, however, intercollegiate athletics were quickly becoming an integral part of higher education in the United States. Public interest in sport at the intercollegiate level, which had always been high, continued to increase in intensity, particularly as successful and entertaining programs developed, and also with increasing access to higher education on the part of students from all segments of society.

With this growing interest in intercollegiate sports and attendant increases in commercialization, outside attention again focused on governance and related issues. In 1929, the highly respected Carnegie Foundation for the Advancement of Education issued a significant report regarding intercollegiate athletics and made the following finding:

392

[A] change of values is needed in a field that is sodden with the commercial and the material and the vested interests that these forces have created. Commercialism in college athletics must be diminished and college sport must rise to a point where it is esteemed primarily and sincerely for the opportunities it affords to mature youth.

The Carnegie Report, echoing themes that appear ever so relevant in the year 2000, concluded that college presidents could reclaim the integrity of sport. College administrators "could change the policies permitting commercialized and professionalized athletics that boards of trustees had previously sanctioned."

While the NCAA made some minor attempts to restructure rules to increase integrity in the governance of intercollegiate athletics, those efforts were insufficient to keep pace with the growing commercialization of, and interest in, intercollegiate athletics. Recruitment of athletes was not new, but the rising desire to win, with all its commercial ramifications, contributed to recruitment being raised to new heights. Red Grange, for example, is often given credit for "starting the competition for football talent through . . . recruiting." Public interest in intercollegiate athletics continued to increase with support from the federal government during the 1930s. The capacity of the NCAA to regulate excesses was not equal to the daunting task presented by the growth of, interest in, and commercialization of sport.

After World War II, with a dramatic increase in access to higher education on the part of all segments of society, largely through government support for returning military personnel to attend college, public interest expanded even more dramatically than it had in the past. Increased interest, not surprisingly, led to even greater commercialization of intercollegiate athletics. With the advent of television, the presence of radios in the vast majority of homes in the United States, and the broadcasting of major sporting events, these pressures further intensified. More colleges and universities started athletic programs, while others expanded existing programs, in an effort to respond to increasing interest in intercollegiate athletics. These factors, coupled with a series of gambling scandals and recruiting excesses, caused the NCAA to promulgate additional rules, resulting in an expansion of its governance authority.

In 1948, the NCAA enacted the so-called "Sanity Code," which was designed to "alleviate the proliferation of exploitive practices in the recruitment of student-athletes." To enforce the rules in the Sanity Code, the NCAA created the Constitutional Compliance Committee to interpret rules and investigate possible violations. Neither the Sanity Code with its rules, nor the Constitutional Compliance Committee with its enforcement responsibility, were successful because their only sanction was expulsion, which was so severe that it rendered the Committee impotent and the rules ineffectual. Recognizing this, the NCAA repealed the Sanity Code in 1951, replacing the Constitutional Compliance Committee with the Committee on Infractions, which was given broader sanctioning authority. Thus, in 1951, the NCAA began to exercise more earnestly the authority which it had been given by its members.

Two other factors are worth noting in the 1950s: (1) Walter Byers became Executive Director of the NCAA, and contributed to strengthening the NCAA, and its enforcement division, over the coming years to televise intercollegiate football; and (2) the NCAA negotiated its first contract valued in excess of one million dollars, opening the door to increasingly lucrative television contracts in the future. The NCAA was entering a new era, in which its enforcement authority had been increased, a strong individual had been hired as executive director, and revenues from television were beginning to provide it with the wherewithal to strengthen its capacity in enforcing the rules that were being promulgated. Through the 1950s and 1960s, the NCAA's enforcement capacity increased annually.

C. 1971-1983

By 1971, as its enforcement capacity had grown yearly in response to new excesses arising from increased interest and commercialization, the NCAA was beginning to be criticized for alleged unfairness in the exercise of its enhanced enforcement authority. Responding to these criticisms, the NCAA formed a committee to study the enforcement process, and ultimately, in 1973, adopted recommendations developed by that committee designed to divide the prosecutorial and investigative roles of the Committee on Infractions. In the early 1970s, as well, the membership of the NCAA decided to create divisions, whereby schools would be placed in divisions that would better reflect their competitive capacity. Despite these efforts, however, by 1976, when the NCAA was given additional authority to enforce the rules by penalizing schools directly, and, as a result, athletes, coaches, and administrators indirectly, criticism of the NCAA's enforcement authority grew even more widespread. Indeed, in 1978, the United States House of Representatives Subcommittee on Oversight and Investigation held hearings to investigate the alleged unfairness of the NCAA's enforcement processes. Once again, the NCAA responded by adopting changes in its rules designed to address many of the criticisms made during the course of the hearings. While concerns were somewhat abated, the NCAA's enforcement processes continued to be the source of substantial criticism through the 1970s and 1980s.

The NCAA found itself caught between two critiques. On the one hand, it was criticized for responding inadequately to the increased commercialization of intercollegiate athletics, with all its attendant excesses; while on the other hand, it was criticized for unfairly exercising its regulatory authority. Another factor began to have a major impact as well. University and college presidents were becoming more directly concerned with the operation of the NCAA for two major reasons: (1) as enrollments were beginning to drop, and expenses were increasing in athletics and elsewhere, presidents began, with some ambivalence, to see athletics as an expense, and as a potential revenue and public relations source; and (2) they personally came to understand that their reputations as presidents were often tied to the success of the athletic program and they were, therefore, becoming even more fearful of the NCAA's enforcement authority.

D. 1984-1999

In difficult economic times for higher education in the 1980s, university presidents increasingly found themselves caught between the pressures applied by influential members of boards of trustees and alumni, who often demanded winning athletic programs, and faculty and educators, who feared the rising commercialization of athletics and its impact on academic values. Many presidents were determined to take an active, collective role in the governance of the NCAA, so they formed the influential Presidents Commission in response to these pressures. In 1984, the Presidents Commission began to assert its authority, and by 1985, it took dramatic action by exercising their authority to call a special convention to be held in June of 1985. This quick assertion of power led one sports writer to conclude that "There is no doubt who is running college sports. It's the college presidents."

The presidents initially were involved in a number of efforts to change the rules, particularly in the interest of cost containment. These efforts were not all successful. Over time, however, the presidents were gaining a better understanding of the workings of the NCAA, and they were beginning to take far more interest in the actual governance of intercollegiate athletics. A little over a decade later, the presidents' involvement grew to the extent that they had changed the very governance structure of the NCAA, with the addition of an Executive Committee and a Board of Directors for the various divisions, both of which are made up of presidents or chief executive officers.

In *NCAA v. Tarkanian*, in a 5-4 decision, the United States Supreme Court held that the NCAA was not a state actor, freeing the NCAA from defending against due process allegations brought by Coach Jerry Tarkanian. Despite this victory, concerns persisted regarding due process in the NCAA's enforcement processes. In time, the presidents decided to take action in reforming the enforcement process. The presidents were involved in forming a Special Committee to Review the NCAA Enforcement and Infractions Process, and supported the naming of one of their own, President Rex E. Lee of Brigham Young University, as Chairman. This distinguished committee, which included other luminaries such as former Chief Justice of the United States Supreme Court Warren E. Burger, issued a report in 1991. The Committee made the following basic recommendations: (1) "Enhance the adequacy of the initial notice of an impending investigation and assure a personal visit by the enforcement staff with the institution's chief executive officer;" (2) "Establish a 'summary disposition' procedure for treating major violations at a reasonably early stage in the investigation;" (3) "Liberalize the use of tape recordings and the availability of such recordings to involved parties;" (4) "Use former judges or other eminent legal authorities as hearing officers in cases involving major violations and not resolved in the 'summary disposition' process;" (5) "Hearings should be open to the greatest extent possible;" (6) "Provide transcripts of all infractions hearings to appropriate involved parties;" (7) "Refine and enhance the role of the Committee on Infractions and establish a limited appellate process beyond that committee;" (8) "Adopt a formal conflict-of-interest policy;" (9) "Expand the public reporting of infractions cases;" (10) "Make available a compilation of previous committee decisions;" and (11) "Study the structure and procedures of the enforcement staff." These recommendations have been taken seriously, and, as implemented, are helping to improve the enforcement processes.

During this time period, there were a number of additional developments that had an impact on the role of the NCAA in fulfilling its enforcement and governance of responsibilities. Even in a short history, like this one, a few of those developments are noteworthy.

As the role of television and the revenue it brings to intercollegiate athletics has grown in magnitude, the desire for an increasing share of those dollars has become intense. The first television event in the 1950s was a college football game, and the televising of college football games remained under the NCAA's control for a number of years. In time, however, a group of powerful intercollegiate football programs were determined to challenge the NCAA's handling of the televising of games involving their schools. In

*NCAA v. Board of Regents*, the United States Supreme Court held that the NCAA had violated antitrust laws. This provided an opening for those schools, and the bowls that would ultimately court them, to directly reap the revenues from the televising of their football games. This shift has effectively created a new division in football called the College Football Association, which is made up of the football powerhouses in Division I. Because these schools have been able to funnel more television revenues in their direction, which has led to increases in other forms of revenue, they have gained access to resources that have unbalanced the playing field in football and other sports.

Another matter that has dramatically impacted intercollegiate athletics during the past two decades is Title IX, with its call for gender equity in intercollegiate athletics. With some emphasis on proportionality in opportunities and equity in expenditures for coaches and other purposes in women's sports, new opportunities have been made available for women in intercollegiate athletics. The cost of these expanded opportunities have been high, however, particularly given that few institutions have women's teams that generate sufficient revenue to cover the cost of these added programs. This increase in net expenses has placed significant pressure on intercollegiate athletic programs, particularly given that the presidents are cost-containment conscious, desiring that athletic programs be self-sufficient. Revenue producing male sports, therefore, have to bear the weight of funding women's sports. This, in turn, raises racial equity concerns because most of the revenue producing male sports are made up predominantly of male student-athletes of color, who are expected to deliver a product that will not only produce sufficient revenue to cover its own expenses, but also a substantial portion of the costs of gender equity and male sports that are not revenue producing.

The gender equity and television issues have been largely economic in their impact, but they do indirectly impact the role of the NCAA in governance. Since football funding has been diverted from the NCAA to the football powerhouses, the NCAA for the most part has had to rely even more heavily on its revenue from the lucrative television contract for the Division I basketball championship. Heavy reliance on this funding source raises racial equity issues, since student-athletes of color, particularly African-American athletes, are the source of those revenues. Thus, the very governance costs of the NCAA are covered predominantly by the efforts of these student-athletes of color. This inequity is exacerbated by the fact that schools and conferences rely heavily on revenues from the basketball tournament to fund their own institutional and conference needs.

Generally, developments during the past two decades have focused on governance and economic issues. There have been some efforts, however, to enhance academic integrity and revitalize the role of faculty and students in overseeing intercollegiate athletics. Of particular note in this regard has been the implementation of the certification process for intercollegiate athletic programs. The certification process involves faculty, students (particularly student-athletes), and staff from an institution in preparing an in-depth self-study, including substantial institutional data in the form of required appendices. The study covers the following areas: Governance and Rules Compliance, Academic Integrity, Fiscal Integrity, and Commitment to Equity. This process helps institutions focus on academic values and related issues. These efforts also provide the chief executive officers with additional information and a potentially enhanced role in intercollegiate athletics at the campus level.

The past two decades have been active ones for the NCAA. With meteoric rises in television and related revenues, the commercialization of intercollegiate athletics has continued to grow at a pace that places significant strain on institutions and the NCAA. These commercial pressures, together with increasing costs related to non-revenue producing sports, costly gender equity requirements, and other resource demands (*e.g.*, new facilities), make it challenging to maintain a viable enforcement process and a balanced playing field.

### III. The Future

Over the past 150 years, the desire to win at virtually any cost, combined with the increases in public interest in intercollegiate athletics, in a consumer sense, have led inexorably to a highly commercialized world of intercollegiate athletics. These factors have created new incentives for universities and conferences to find new ways to obtain an advantage over their competitors. This desire to gain an unfair competitive advantage has necessarily led to an expansion in rules and regulations. This proliferation of rules and the development of increasingly sophisticated regulatory systems necessary to enforce those rules, together with the importance that attaches to enforcement decisions, both economically and in terms of an institution's reputation (and derivatively its chief executive officer's career), places great strain on the capacity of the NCAA to govern intercollegiate athletics. This strain is unlikely to dissipate in the future because the pressures that have created the strain do not appear to be susceptible, in a practical sense, to amelioration. Indeed, the one certainty in the future of the NCAA is the likelihood that big-time intercollegiate athletics will be engaged in the same point-counterpoint that has characterized its history; increased commercialization and public pressure leading to more sophisticated rules and regulatory systems.

As rules and regulatory systems continue along the road of increased sophistication, the NCAA will more closely resemble its industry counterparts. It will develop an enforcement system that is more legalistic in its nature, as regulatory proliferation leads to increasing demands for fairness. In such a milieu, chief executive officers will have to take their responsibilities for intercollegiate athletics even more seriously. It can be hoped, as well, that their involvement, and the increased involvement on the part of faculty and staff, through the certification process and otherwise, will lead to a more responsible system in terms of the maintenance of academic values. If the NCAA and those who lead at the institutional and conference levels are unable to maintain academic values in the face of economics and related pressures, the government may be less than a proverbial step away.

## Notes & Questions

1. Explain the relationship between money and the pressure that college athletic directors, coaches, and players feel to win.

2. What are the pros and cons of the increased commercialism of intercollegiate sports?

3. To what extent does it matter that the so-called revenue producing sports "foot the bill" for all of the other sports at the intercollegiate level? Should that affect legal relationships or regulations? If so why, if not why not?

# APPLYING ANTITRUST LAW TO NCAA REGULATION OF "BIG TIME" COLLEGE ATHLETICS: THE NEED TO SHIFT FROM NOSTALGIC 19TH AND 20TH CENTURY IDEALS OF AMATEURISM TO THE ECONOMIC REALITIES OF THE 21ST CENTURY

Matthew J. Mitten
11 MARQ. SPORTS L. REV. 1 (2000)

The original purpose of intercollegiate athletics was to provide an extracurricular activity for talented students who attended college primarily to earn an academic degree that would enable them to pursue a career outside of professional athletics. According to the National Collegiate Athletic Association ("NCAA"), "[s]tudent-athletes shall be amateurs in an intercollegiate sport, and their participation should be motivated primarily by education and by the physical, mental and social benefits to be derived. Student participation in intercollegiate athletics is an avocation, and student-athletes should be protected from exploitation by professional and commercial enterprises." Today, this concept of an "amateur" athlete and the student-athlete model still applies for most sports and most students, especially women's sports and men's non-revenue sports.

Not all NCAA sponsored sports fit neatly within this amateur model. Athletes participating in NCAA Division I football and basketball often are more interested in developing their skills in hope of a future professional playing career than in earning a college degree. In fact, universities sponsoring "big-time" football and basketball programs effectively serve as a farm system for the National Football League and National Basketball Association by providing the training environment and playing field for talented football and basketball players to hone their physical talents.

The tremendous public popularity of men's college football and basketball creates a substantial revenue-generating capacity and the prospect of increased visibility for universities. The significant economic rewards of winning have generated fierce off-field competition among universities for inputs necessary to produce winning teams (e.g., coaches and players) as well as efforts to fully exploit the economic value of their athletic products by maximizing fan and booster support, television revenues, and commercial sponsorships. The economic realities of this environment contrast sharply with the nostalgic ideal of the college amateur athlete whose participation in a sport is merely incidental to a university's provision of higher education in an academic environment.

The NCAA's basic regulatory objective is "to maintain intercollegiate athletics as an integral part of the educational program and the athlete as an integral part of the student body and, by so doing, retain a clear line of demarcation between intercollegiate athletics and professional sports." In other words, the NCAA seeks to: 1) preserve the amateur nature of college sports; 2) as a component part of higher education; and 3) to ensure competitive balance on the playing field. Although these are laudable objectives, they are quite difficult to achieve given the economic reality of "big-time" college athletics, namely an existing "athletics arms race" fueled by the multi-million dollar economic rewards of winning teams fielded by members operating "big time" programs.

The NCAA effectively determines the permissible nature and scope of virtually all aspects of both on-field and off-field competition among its members. It appears to function as an economic cartel in its regulation of Division I football and basketball programs. The NCAA's member schools are economic competitors that collectively possess monopsony power over the demand for college football and basketball players and monopoly power over the supply of college football and basketball games. They frequently agree to limit (or prohibit) free market forces from determining input prices for players, output of games, and other aspects of economic competition among themselves. The NCAA polices and enforces its rules and agreements by disciplining violators. Although individual NCAA members have an incentive to gain a competitive advantage by not complying with the association's rules, there is an economic necessity to remain a part of this national organization to reap the economic rewards of "big-time" college sports.

Given the economic realities of "big-time" college athletics, many NCAA rules limiting economic competition among universities appear to violate the federal antitrust laws. However, although there have been several antitrust suits challenging the legality of NCAA imposed restraints affecting Division I football and basketball, most litigation has been unsuccessful. In analyzing judicial treatment of the NCAA and its rules for antitrust purposes, it is important to look at the historical evolution of antitrust jurisprudence concerning intercollegiate athletics. Courts initially held that NCAA rule-making, regulatory, or enforcement activities do not sufficiently impact interstate trade or commerce to establish Sherman Act jurisdiction. NCAA rules designed to promote amateurism and protect academic integrity were deemed to constitute regulation of noncommercial activity that does not trigger antitrust scrutiny. Beginning in the mid-1970s, courts began recognizing that the provision and regulation of "big-time" intercollegiate athletics is business activity subject to the Sherman Act, but were reluctant to find that NCAA regulations violated the antitrust laws.

In 1984, in *NCAA v. Board of Regents*,[1] the Supreme Court held that the NCAA does not have a blanket exemption from the antitrust laws, although it is a nonprofit entity with educational objectives, because the "NCAA and its member institutions are in fact organized to maximize revenues." The Court invalidated NCAA restrictions on its members' sale of television rights to football games that prevented economic competition among them. However, the Court acknowledged the NCAA's role "as the guardian of an important American tradition" and its "historic role in the preservation and encouragement of intercollegiate amateur athletics." The Court's majority strongly suggested that primarily noncommercial NCAA rules to preserve amateurism, academic integrity, and competitive balance do not violate the antitrust laws.

After *Board of Regents*, courts generally have rejected antitrust challenges to NCAA rules by providing great deference and discretion to the NCAA. These courts have assumed that NCAA rules are ancillary noncommercial restraints necessary to produce intercollegiate athletics and/or to further legitimate higher education objectives. Courts appear eager to find that NCAA regulation that does not directly fix prices for inputs (*e.g.,* coaches' salaries) or the sale of output (*e.g.,* television rights) is either: 1) characterized as noncommercial and not subject to antitrust challenge; 2) not found to have significant anticompetitive effects; or 3) assumed to be procompetitive by being the least restrictive means of furthering the NCAA's stated objectives (which are usually judicially deemed to be legitimate).

On the one hand, courts have held that agreements among NCAA member schools that directly fix prices in input or output markets for college sports are illegal. The *Board of Regents* Court ruled that the NCAA's exclusive football television rights plan violates the antitrust laws because it effectively establishes a set price for televised football games without any offsetting procompetitive justification, such as preserving competitive balance or the integrity of intercollegiate athletics. Consistent with *Board of Regents*, in *Law v. NCAA*, the Tenth Circuit recently held that an NCAA imposed cap of $16,000.00 on Division I entry-level basketball coaches' salaries is an unreasonable restraint of trade as a matter of law.[2] Applying the

---

[1] NCAA v. Board of Regents, 468 U.S. 85 (1984).
[2] Law v. NCAA, 134 F.3d 1010 (10th Cir. 1998).

truncated or "quick look" rule of reason, the court found this salary cap has the naked anticompetitive effect of fixing one of the costs of producing Division I basketball games without furthering product availability or competitive balance among NCAA members in the least restrictive manner.

At the other end of the spectrum, courts have uniformly upheld NCAA eligibility standards that athletes must satisfy to participate in intercollegiate athletics. Athlete eligibility requirements promulgated by the NCAA appear to be virtually per se legal under the antitrust laws. Courts have rejected antitrust challenges to NCAA regulations designed to preserve the amateur nature of college sports, such as the "no draft" and "no agent" rules and the imposition of disciplinary sanctions on institutions for violation of the NCAA's amateurism rules.

In *Smith v. NCAA*,[3] the Third Circuit ruled that an NCAA eligibility rule prohibiting a student from participating in intercollegiate sports while enrolled in a graduate program at an institution other than where she earned her undergraduate degree does not violate the antitrust laws. The court distinguished Law because the challenged rule is not "a restriction on [any] business activities of [NCAA] institutions." Moreover, *Law* observed that "courts should afford the NCAA plenty of room under the antitrust laws to preserve the amateur character of intercollegiate athletics."

Adidas's recent antitrust challenge to NCAA restrictions on its members' sale of promotional rights to sponsors illustrates judicial unwillingness to acknowledge that universities engage in economic competition among themselves off the playing field and that some NCAA rules may restrain trade. In *Adidas America, Inc. v. NCAA*, Adidas alleged that NCAA limits on the size of manufacturer logos on uniforms and playing equipment unreasonably restrained competition among NCAA member institutions for the sale of advertising rights. The court initially denied Adidas's motion for a preliminary injunction against enforcement of this rule. Observing that *Law* provides no guidance regarding the line between commercial and noncommercial activities, the court characterized the subject NCAA regulation as noncommercial because it does not have the purpose or effect of giving NCAA members a direct economic benefit. Rather, it found the rule furthered the NCAA's legitimate objective of preventing the commercialization of college sports, notwithstanding that patches identifying football bowl game sponsors on player uniforms are not subject to the size limits of this rule (not to mention that athletes may be required to wear a

---

[3] 139 F. 3d 180 (3rd Cir. 1998).

particular manufacturer's shoes as part of a sponsorship agreement with an NCAA university).

Subsequently, the court granted the NCAA's motion to dismiss Adidas's complaint. **** [T]he court concluded that the NCAA's rule restricting the size of manufacturer logos on uniforms has no significant anticompetitive effect as a matter of law.

The Adidas trial court's disposition of the case is another example of unwarranted judicial deference to NCAA regulation of economic competition among its member institutions. The Adidas holding is inconsistent with the *Board of Regents* and *Law* precedent establishing a framework of antitrust analysis for NCAA regulatory activity with a commercial impact. Adidas's allegations, at the very least, raise a factual issue for discovery regarding the anticompetitive effects of this NCAA rule. If the limitation on logo size has the effect of reducing economic competition among NCAA members, the NCAA must prove that it furthers a valid procompetitive objective that cannot be accomplished by a substantially less restrictive means.

There is no valid justification for permitting the NCAA to determine arbitrarily the permissible degree of economic competition among its members or, in light of these universities significant economic self-interest, for courts to defer to the NCAA's judgment. Courts should abandon anachronistic precedent based on unrealistic ideals of the "amateur" nature of "big-time" college athletics and develop a principled antitrust jurisprudence more consistent with the economic realities of college sports in the 21st century.

I am not advocating that all NCAA regulation of competition violates the antitrust laws. However, courts should not continue to make unrealistic or unwarranted assumptions about the economic effects of NCAA rules reducing or eliminating competition among its approximately 1,100 member schools. NCAA regulation that has anticompetitive, intrabrand effects should be proven to be the least restrictive means of promoting interbrand competition as a matter of fact, rather than being presumed to do so as a matter of law.

**Notes & Questions**

1. The International Olympic Committee used to treat amateurism as something sacrosanct, like the NCAA currently does. The IOC, however,

has sharply curtailed its position on this matter, now permitting professionals to compete in the Olympic Games. If the NCAA were to change its rules to permit athletes to earn money from their sport during their period of eligibility, what might be the pros and cons?

2. Are there plausible legal remedies for the "arms race" that currently exists in big time college athletics? If so, articulate what they might be and how they might alleviate the problem.


## QUID PRO QUO: RESTORING EDUCATIONAL PRIMACY TO COLLEGE BASKETBALL

Tanyon T. Lynch
12 MARQ. SPORTS L. REV. 595 (2002)

### I. INTRODUCTION

Together, Division I-A football and Division I men's basketball make up what is commonly referred to as "big-time college sports." Unfortunately, the intensely commercial nature of big-time college sports presents a constant threat to the National Collegiate Athletic Association's (NCAA) most sacred principle: amateurism. The NCAA's strict amateurism regulations have long been criticized as exploitive, hypocritical, and unenforceable. To address these issues, Division I legislators are currently debating amateurism deregulation proposals that would allow student-athletes to accept certain forms of compensation and to engage in brief professional careers without forfeiting NCAA eligibility.

This article examines the synergy between NCAA amateurism deregulation and the National Basketball Association's (NBA) fledgling National Basketball Development League (NBDL). It posits that amateurism deregulation coupled with the NBDL will provide a much-needed catalyst for restoring educational primacy to college basketball. Although the forthcoming analysis may be applied to a variety of college sports, this article's scope will be limited to Division I men's basketball.

Part II of this article introduces the organizational structure of intercollegiate athletics. Part III discusses the primary threats to educational primacy in college athletics programs. This section explains how competitive pressure, commercialism, and professionalism have caused many elite college athletics programs to lose sight of the primary purpose of colleges and universities.

Part IV introduces the potential guardians of educational primacy in college athletics programs. Included among this group are colleges and universities, conferences, the NCAA, legislatures, and the judicial system. This section describes the role undertaken by each of these institutions in ensuring that student-athletes receive a meaningful education.

Part V evaluates the practicality and potential impact of two Division I amateurism deregulation proposals: (1) pay-for-play and (2) former professional eligibility. It argues that Division I should adopt the latter proposal, which would allow athletes with brief professional sports careers to retain NCAA eligibility. Under this proposal, former professionals would lose one season of eligibility and would be required to satisfy one academic year in residence before they could participate in intercollegiate competition. In effect, this requirement would compel both the athlete and the university to make a substantial and immediate investment in the athlete's educational development. Hence the former professional eligibility proposal would enhance educational primacy to a greater extent than the pay-for-play proposal, which merely addresses athletes' financial needs.

Part VI demonstrates how Division I amateurism deregulation and the NBDL will interact to bolster the principle of educational primacy. It argues that the NBDL would be the better choice for those college-aged athletes intending to pursue a professional basketball career. As a result, the NBDL and college teams will inevitably become competitors for the limited pool of elite college-aged basketball players. When given the choice between college and NBDL basketball, those players that choose college would be implicitly demonstrating their commitment to education. Moreover, former professional eligibility would allow similarly committed athletes with short-lived NBDL careers to retain the opportunity to attend college on an athletic scholarship.

The NBDL will signal the end of Division I's privileged status as the de facto minor league of the NBA. As the preferred route to the NBA, the NBDL could substantially decrease the quality of the talent pool from which colleges choose their athletes. To curb the loss of revenue that could occur as the quality of the college game deteriorates, college basketball programs will need to devise ways to compete with the NBDL for elite young athletes. Yet the financial limitations of college athletics programs will prevent them from offering student-athletes the equivalent of a NBDL salary. Therefore, this article concludes that the most viable response to competition from the NBDL involves allowing college basketball players to obtain more value from the collegiate experience.

## II. OVERVIEW OF THE ORGANIZATIONAL STRUCTURE OF COLLEGE ATHLETICS

Colleges and universities providing athletics programs typically belong to regional and national governing bodies that provide administrative, legislative, and promotional support for their members. Conferences provide this support at the regional level. At the national level, this support is provided by either the NCAA or the National Association of Intercollegiate Athletics. This article's analysis will be limited to the NCAA, the most influential regulator of college athletics.

Although the NCAA's principle of institutional control requires university presidents to assume ultimate responsibility for athletics programs, this authority is usually delegated to the institution's athletics director, who reports to either the university president or a vice president. Coaches and administrative staff in the athletics department report to the athletics director whose daily responsibilities may include generating revenue in addition to managing facilities, media relations, and academic affairs. Therefore, in reality, the athletics director bears most of the burden for assuring that the athletics department's goals remain consistent with the overall purpose of the university.

University presidents also delegate responsibilities for their athletics programs to collegiate conferences. In most major conferences, university presidents serve as the board of directors, which ultimately retains authority over conference operations. Historically, conferences existed primarily to provide schools with a reliable source of competitors. The modern conference's operations include monitoring compliance with conference and NCAA policies, managing conference championships, structuring broadcasting contracts, and redistributing revenues. The conference's commissioner either oversees or performs these functions.

Despite its voluntary nature, the NCAA is the leading regulatory body for intercollegiate athletics. Formed in 1906 with only 39 charter members, the NCAA now consists of over 1200 institutions, conferences, and organizations. The association is divided into three major membership categories: Division I, II, and III. Schools with football programs are further subdivided into Divisions I-A and I-AA. In 1997, the NCAA restructured its organizational scheme to provide for greater divisional autonomy. As a result, each division now has its own governing body.

# III. THREATS TO EDUCATIONAL PRIMACY

The United States stands alone in combining higher education with athletic development. College athletics programs offer countless benefits to sponsoring institutions and participating students. At the institutional level, college athletics can play a role in increasing the institution's visibility and unifying the university community. Furthermore, these programs generate revenues from a variety of sources, including gate receipts, corporate sponsorships, and television rights fees. At the student level, athletics programs can provide educational opportunities for students who otherwise could not afford to attend college. Participation in college athletics can also facilitate the development of valuable attributes such as, leadership, competitiveness, discipline, and teamwork. To reap these and other substantial benefits, colleges and universities pour millions of dollars into their athletics programs. Ideally, all college athletics programs would place student-athletes' educational priorities first. Yet in practice, this does not occur. Under the current regime, competitive pressure to win games, commercialism, and professionalism often lead to the subordination of educational primacy. To understand how amateurism deregulation and the NBDL will interact to bolster educational primacy, one must first understand the problems of the current regime. To this end, the earlier sections of this article provide an in-depth description of these problems.

## A. Competitive Pressure

Successful basketball teams generate millions of dollars in revenue from ticket sales, guarantees, payouts from tournaments, television rights fees, licensed merchandise, and corporate sponsorships. Additional benefits thought to accrue to athletically successful schools include additional tuition and fees from increased enrollments and an increase in alumni donations. However, when costs enter the equation, the vast majority of universities lose money on athletics programs. Still, many programs subscribe to the philosophy that "the team that spends the most wins the most."

When the team wins consistently, coaches reap substantial benefits from the team's success. This occurs because, increasingly, coaches' job security and base salaries are tied to their competitive records. In addition to high base salaries, successful coaches might also receive home loans, automobiles, deferred compensation, and bonuses for winning. Winning coaches can further supplement their university income with income from shoe contracts, sports camps, and appearances on radio and television talk shows.

Competitive pressure constitutes the first major threat to educational primacy. Competitive pressure may be generated either internally by inherently competitive coaches or externally by the financial incentives to win games. But regardless of its origin, this pressure eventually trickles down to student-athletes. As such, the pressure to win, if left unchecked, usually manifests itself in ways that seriously conflict with the principle of educational primacy. That is, perverse incentives at either the institutional or coach level can result in the intentional subordination of educational primacy. This section addresses coaches' ability to effectuate this subordination.

Many basketball players enter college academically deficient. Add to this deficiency, forty to sixty hours per week of athletic activities, and missed classes, and the result is an athlete unlikely to graduate. In fact, only forty-three percent of all NCAA basketball players graduate within six years and, of those athletes who do graduate, many do not receive a meaningful degree. As a result, some critics condemn Division I basketball programs for exploiting athletes until the end of their eligibility and then summarily discarding them. This exploitation is often facilitated by coaches, who exert considerable influence over the administrative processes governing student-athlete affairs. The areas in which coaches may exert the most influence are admissions, financial aid, and academic services.

To build and sustain successful programs, coaches frequently recruit student-athletes that fall decisively below their schools' regular admissions standards. Athletes who fail to meet a school's regular admissions standards may still be admitted through "special" or "wild-card" admissions processes. The "wild card" admissions process gives a coach a limited number of "no questions asked" admits. Therefore, the wild card process places the admit decision completely within the coach's discretion, limited only by NCAA eligibility standards. "Special admissions" is the process by which the admissions office admits athletes who, although they do not meet the school's regular admissions standards, enrich the student body nonetheless. Although this process is also available to legacies, musicians, and other students with desirable characteristics, a study conducted in 1991 shows that football and men's basketball players in elite sports programs are six times more likely than other students to have been special admits.

To successfully recruit a blue-chip athlete, a coach might find it necessary to exaggerate the athlete's educational prospects. For example, in

*Ross v. Creighton University*, the coaching staff recruited Kevin Ross to play basketball at "an academically superior university," despite his severely deficient academic background. To obtain his commitment, Ross was assured that he "would receive a meaningful education." Yet after four years as a student-athlete, Ross dropped out of the university with the language skills of a fourth grader. Under the NCAA's current rules, Ross would not have met the initial eligibility standards and, therefore, he probably would not have been admitted to Creighton.

After an athlete enrolls in school, coaches can exert substantial influence over the athlete's academic future. The key source of this influence resides in a coach's ability to cancel an athlete's scholarship. Before the one-year renewable athletic scholarship came into existence in 1973, athletes received four-year scholarships that continued even after they withdrew from their sports. Today, NCAA rules permit expedited cancellation for athletes who voluntarily withdraw from their sports. Thus, cancellation power gives coaches a powerful tool that can be used to alter a student-athlete's academic priorities.

NCAA rules limit an athlete's participation in "countable athletically related activities" to four hours per day and twenty hours per week. However, many student-athletes complain that the "voluntary workout" exception swallows this rule. That is, to the extent that coaches use time spent on voluntary workouts to determine an athlete's status on the team, the workouts are not truly voluntary. Consequently, some athletes still spend forty to sixty hours per week on their sports, which invariably limits the amount of time that the athletes spend studying and attending classes.

Given athletes' rigorous game and workout schedules, similarly demanding academic programs would present a constant threat to NCAA eligibility. This threat would be even more pronounced for marginal students. To protect against the risk of an athlete becoming ineligible for competition, coaches often steer athletes into less demanding majors or courses. At some schools, these less demanding majors might include general studies, physical education, or sports management. Although most athletics departments provide extensive academic support services for student-athletes, in the absence of sufficient time to indulge these services, even a hollow major can threaten an athlete's eligibility.

When legitimate attempts to keep athletes on the court prove futile, competitive pressure and perverse incentives can combine to produce academic scandals, as was the case at the University of Minnesota from 1994 through 1999. During this time period, the head men's basketball coach, an academic counselor, and a secretary engaged in the most egregious academic fraud that the NCAA Committee on Infractions had seen since the early 1980s. Specifically, with the head coach's knowledge, a secretary completed four hundred assignments for student-athletes and the secretary's sister, a tutor, authored forty-eight papers for student-athletes. The NCAA's institutional sanctions for these and other violations included placing the university on probation for four years, vacating team and individual records, and decreasing grants-in-aid, official visits, and evaluation opportunities in men's basketball. As for the wrongdoers, the head coach was forced to resign and the contracts of his two accomplices were never renewed.

Often times, student-athletes must choose between athletic success and academic success. Coaches substantially influence this choice through their power to withdraw financial aid and playing time. To the extent that coaches feel pressured to use their influence to push athletes to the borderline of academic failure or fraud, the principle of educational primacy suffers along with the university's academic reputation.

B. Commercialism

The commercial model of college athletics gives priority to the spectators' entertainment needs, rather than to the student-athletes' educational needs. Corporate sponsorships, broadcasting contracts, product value, and market share dominate this model, where student-athletes and coaches are viewed as entertainment products. The Final Four exemplifies the commercial model of college athletics.

Commercialism constitutes the second major threat to educational primacy. In addition to subordinating educational primacy, commercialism increases the pressure to win. That is, dependence on revenues from gate receipts, corporate sponsorships, and television contracts intensifies external pressures to win. Furthermore, for "celebrity" teams, commercialism intensifies the pressure to win by creating an expectation by fans that these teams will continue their winning streaks indefinitely. As previously stated, the pressure to win, regardless of its source, poses its own threat to educational primacy. Critics of the commercial model of college athletics argue that, besides increasing the pressure to win, commercialism encourages academically intrusive scheduling and financially exploits student-athletes.

Media-driven schedules for athletic contests can assist in the subordination of educational primacy. That is, mid-week and late-night games scheduled to accommodate media demands often conflict with student-athletes' academic obligations. For instance, bowl game scheduling

411

UNIVERSITY OF WINCHESTER
LIBRARY

forces athletes to practice during final exam periods. Moreover, the "Final Four" teams of the NCAA tournament will miss at least three weeks of classes during March. Although such academically intrusive schedules can maximize television revenues and media exposure, these gains often come at the expense of the athletes' academic success.

Commercialism also raises concerns of financial exploitation for student-athletes. At most college games, corporate logos can be seen on uniforms, hats, and scoreboards among other places. In 1995, sponsorship and signage income for the average Division I-A school exceeded $450,000. The prototypical sponsorship deal is the shoe contract, which provides athletes with free sneakers and apparel, and might also provide significant outside income for college coaches. In return, shoe companies receive millions of dollars in television exposure for the logos displayed on players' shoes and uniforms. Although these arrangements enrich athletics departments, coaches, and sponsors, many student-athletes, whose incomes are restricted by NCAA amateurism rules, feel that they are being exploited by such arrangements.

Few athletics departments generate sufficient revenue to cover the full cost of their programs. Although booster club donations, corporate sponsorships and the like provide additional revenues for athletics departments, most college athletics programs still require financial support from general university funds. Sympathizers of commercialized college sports cite the precarious financial condition of college athletics programs as support for the present and continued commercialization of college athletics.

C. Professionalism

As early as the late-nineteenth century, the desire to produce winning athletic teams led universities to seek out highly skilled athletes, many of whom had little interest in academics. In fact, some of these early college athletes were not even students. In return for their athletic services, early student-athletes received "scholarships, sinecure jobs, gifts from alumni and citizens, and a hundred other types of financial compensation." Current NCAA amateurism rules forbid all but the first category of compensation for student-athletes.

Modern universities attract athletes with promises of free tuition, room and board, and academic support services. All of which are sanctioned by NCAA regulations. As an additional incentive, a few universities have resorted to the use of prohibited "extra benefits" to lure the best athletes. The use of financial incentives in recruiting, whether NCAA-sanctioned or

412

prohibited, allows college teams to attract higher quality athletes, thereby improving the teams' revenue potential. Yet recruiting such highly qualified athletes also requires a corresponding commitment to provide the academic services, coaching staffs, and facilities necessary to support these athletes. The ability to provide the requisite support services helps to explain why well-funded athletics programs generally field the most competitive teams.

Professionalism poses the third threat to educational primacy. As an inherent form of pay-for-play, the athletic scholarship can be viewed as a manifestation of the professionalism that characterizes "amateur" college athletics. Accordingly, educational primacy is subverted because student-athletes cannot withdraw from their sports, even for academic reasons, without suffering the detrimental economic consequences of such a decision.

Further evidence of the professionalization of college sports lies in the fact that college athletics programs have become training grounds for professional sports careers. Indeed some athletes attend college for the sole purpose of advancing their professional sports careers. Professionalized college athletics demand that its participants train and perform at the highest possible level. These demands subvert educational primacy by requiring time commitments that are often inconsistent with a student-athlete's student status. In addition to weakening the principle of educational primacy, the commercialized, professionalized model of college athletics can also be self-defeating. That is, professionalized athletes usually abandon the team when they reach a level of play sufficiently high to attract opportunities from major professional leagues.

Competitive pressure, commercialism, and professionalism constitute the three main threats to educational primacy. If left unchecked, these threats can combine to overshadow the academic purpose of institutions of higher education. The threats are interrelated in that commercialism intensifies competitive pressure and competitive pressure encourages professionalism. Hence, any attempt to safeguard the principle of educational primacy must address all three of its major threats.

## IV. GOVERNANCE OF THE PRINCIPLE EDUCATIONAL PRIMACY

The principle of educational primacy requires that a student-athlete's status as a student take precedence over his or her status as an athlete. In the world of college athletics, this principle competes with the demands of competitive pressure, commercialism, and professionalism. Various governance structures exist to safeguard the principle of educational primacy

413

against these competing interests. These structures may be divided into two broad categories: (1) internal and (2) external. The internal governance structure consists of universities, conferences, and the NCAA, whereas the legislature and courts comprise the external governance structure. External involvement in the regulation of college athletics is very limited. Consequently, college athletics is dominated by internal governance structures, which are plagued by self-interest and conflicting goals.

## A. Internal Governance

Internal governance of the principle of educational primacy has two main benefits. First, internal governance saves the government the cost of regulation. Second, internal governance structures can detect and remedy problems more quickly than external governance structures. To the extent that internal governance structures fail to adequately safeguard the principle of educational primacy, external governance structures can provide a meaningful oversight function.

The primary purpose of the university is education and, therefore, it is the university's responsibility to provide an environment conducive to that purpose. Ideally, athletics programs would peacefully coexist with the university's primary purpose and would place educational priorities over those of athletics. Yet, historically, university athletics programs have exhibited a tendency to operate in opposition to the university's primary purpose.

Self-interest and perverse incentives can prevent individual universities from effectively policing the principle of educational primacy. College admissions standards vary and, as previously noted, schools lower these standards for elite athletes to build successful teams. Furthermore, universities alone determine what constitutes good academic standing once a student enrolls. Thus, a school may relax both its admissions standards and its standards for good academic standing to accommodate an athlete's eligibility. Lenient academic policies for student-athletes clearly conflict with the goals of higher education. As a result, faculty members at some institutions have banded together in an attempt to expose and reform these policies. However, institutional athletic interests have very little incentive to implement the reforms since doing so could place the schools at a recruiting and competitive disadvantage.

Conferences share common eligibility standards, which might be higher than those required by the NCAA. To this extent, conferences can regulate their members' academic standards to ensure that they do not fall to unacceptable levels. However a conference that sets its academic standards too high might find itself at a competitive disadvantage in inter-conference competition.

In addition to the regulation of academic policies, conferences promote their respective athletic contests and redistribute revenues among their members. Historically, conference members aligned themselves because of shared geography and competitive and academic philosophies. More recently, members' revenue potential has become the most important common denominator. To maximize revenues, conferences become parties to broadcasting contracts, which often require academically intrusive schedules. Absent external pressure to do so, a single conference has very little incentive to oppose its own policies regarding the scheduling of televised athletic contests. To do so would decrease its revenue potential and hence its attractiveness to present and future members.

****

The NCAA also acts as a promoter and economic regulator of collegiate athletics. Indeed, the promotion and economic regulation of college athletics are the NCAA's dominant functions. In this capacity, the NCAA experiences role conflict similar to that experienced by universities and conferences. The Division I governance structure reinforces this conflict because it is dominated by the major conferences and their concerns. As previously stated, a major concern of many conferences is the generation of revenues.

Although the NCAA manual contains hundreds of pages of rules, the small size of the NCAA's enforcement staff impairs its ability to detect violations of those rules. As a result, the NCAA relies mainly on informants and institutional self-reporting to apprise it of alleged violations. Once the NCAA becomes aware of potential violations, lack of judicially enforceable discovery power limits its ability to gather and verify pertinent information. To lessen the impact of these limitations, the NCAA encourages schools to cooperate with NCAA investigators in return for reduced penalties. NCAA penalties for the most flagrant violations usually result only in the loss of scholarships and recruiting visits and perhaps probation for the offending university. Commentators use the NCAA's inadequate detection methods and light penalties as evidence of its lack of commitment to the enforcement of its rules, academic or otherwise.

The NCAA's national character makes it the ideal institution to promulgate and enforce uniform rules that encourage educational primacy.

However, as an entity, the NCAA profits from activities that threaten educational primacy. In fact, the NCAA is financially dependent upon its basketball tournament, which capitalizes upon all three threats to educational primacy. Strict enforcement of the principle of educational primacy by the NCAA would force the organization into financial ruin.

Since a university's primary purpose is to educate its students, the university is the ideal entity to police the principle of educational primacy. However, historically and even today universities have not adequately done this, absent outside intervention. Since conferences and the NCAA are financially dependent on activities that compete with the principle of educational primacy, they do not and cannot be expected to vigorously police or enforce the principle of educational primacy. To summarize, self-interest and conflicting goals have prevented all three internal governance structures from adequately policing the principle. The next section discusses how external governance structures have dealt with these problems.

B. External Governance

Internal governance structures regulate both the economic and educational aspects of intercollegiate athletics. This conflicting role, in which economic concerns often take precedence over student-athletes' educational concerns, supports an increased role for external regulation. Yet, courts and legislatures have largely declined invitations to intervene in university/student-athlete relations.

With the exception of Title IX, Congress does not interfere with the NCAA's regulation of the university/student-athlete relationship. To further insure this relationship against congressional intervention, the NCAA maintains an office in Washington, D.C., which employs full-time lobbyists. At the state level, legislative intervention is generally limited to the regulation of student-athlete relationships with sports agents and funding restrictions for college athletics programs.

Although the threat of litigation might enhance the status of educational primacy in college athletics programs, courts have been reluctant to hold universities liable for the failure to educate individual student-athletes. To this end, courts uniformly deny negligent admissions and educational malpractice claims. Difficulties in establishing educational standards, injury, causation, and remedies are cited as reasons for courts' hostility towards these claims. In addition, courts fear that allowing such claims would induce floods of litigation by disgruntled students.

Contract claims can provide an alternative to educational malpractice and negligent admissions claims. In Ross, the court noted that if Ross could establish that the university failed to honor a specific contractual promise, a breach of contract action might exist. Commentators further suggest that claims based on contract law's implied obligation of good faith might be available to plaintiffs harmed by a university's failure to educate. Courts, however, warn against attempts to recast educational malpractice claims as contract claims.

Courts and legislatures have, for the most part, chosen to play a passive role in the regulation of college athletics. This passiveness has, in effect, given the NCAA virtually unlimited power over the future of college athletics. Therefore, any serious attempts to reform college athletics must focus on the NCAA.

As the most powerful regulator of college athletics programs, the NCAA is in a unique position to strengthen the principle of educational primacy. Yet any attempt to strengthen educational primacy must also minimize its major threats, *i.e.* competitive pressures, commercialism, and professionalism. Even if institutional interests militate against the NCAA implementing legislation that directly strengthens educational primacy, the NCAA should, at the very least, take steps to ensure that future legislative amendments do not further weaken the principle. Amateurism deregulation is an area in which the NCAA can implement this laudable goal.

## V. AMATEURISM DEREGULATION

The NCAA's definition of "amateur" cries out for reform. Under present rules, athletes lose their amateur status when they sign a contract to play for a professional team, even if they never in fact play for the team. Ironically, a U.S. athlete that plays on a professional team in one sport remains eligible to play a different sport. Similarly, many international athletes with previous participation on international "professional teams" remain eligible. Growing dissatisfaction with the inequities and inconsistencies in the current NCAA amateurism rules recently propelled amateurism deregulation to the forefront of Division I's legislative agenda.

Division I amateurism reform suggestions boil down to essentially two proposals. The first proposal would allow enrolled student-athletes to receive payments in addition to a full grant-in-aid without forfeiting eligibility. The second proposal would allow prospective student-athletes to retain eligibility even if they have briefly participated on a professional team.

This section evaluates the merits of both proposals and concludes that the second proposal is more consistent with the principle of educational primacy.

A. Pay-for-Play

To be eligible for a collegiate sports team, an athlete must be considered an "amateur." Under current NCAA bylaws, athletes lose eligibility in a given sport once they accept compensation for participating in that sport. These bylaws seek to ensure that institutions maintain "a clear line of demarcation between college athletics and professional sports."

U.S. colleges have long compensated student-athletes for their athletic abilities. In the late-1800s teams regularly paid participating athletes, some of whom were not even students. In response to these and other abuses, NCAA members adopted the Sanity Code in 1948, which prohibited financial aid based solely on athletic ability. A mere three years later, the membership abandoned the code as unworkable. Today, student-athletes may receive athletic scholarships covering an institution's "cost of attendance." In essence, athletic scholarships constitute a form of compensation based on athletic skill. Hence, under the plain meaning of the NCAA's rules, athletic scholarship recipients are not, and never have been, true amateurs.

The proposed changes to the current compensatory scheme would allow student-athletes to accept compensation in excess of the cost of attendance. These proposals stem primarily from an attempt by the NCAA to provide incentives for elite athletes to delay their professional sports careers until graduation. By sanctioning supplemental income, these proposals also respond to the argument that big-time college athletics financially exploit student-athletes, many of whom come from low-income families.

The immediate financial rewards of playing professionally prompt many elite basketball players to begin professional careers prior to graduation. The early exit of these players guts college basketball rosters and injures the quality of the college game. Pay-for-play supporters believe that providing athletes with additional financial incentives will encourage them to delay their professional careers until after graduation.

Elite college basketball players generate revenues for their schools that far exceed the value of a full grant-in-aid. While the typical grant-in-aid is worth only $30,000, a top player might generate as much as $1 million in revenue annually. Although reformers would like student-athletes to reap more of the fruits of their labor, current NCAA amateurism regulations

418

would prevent this from occurring. Currently, the only way to provide athletes with compensation more closely related to their market value is through covert payments.

Reformers propose several methods by which the NCAA might allow student-athletes to legitimately receive additional athletically-related compensation ("pay-for-play"). These methods include part-time employment, stipends, loans, and prize money. Although athletes could theoretically undertake part-time employment to supplement their athletic scholarships, team and academic activities would prevent many of them from working the hours needed to earn significant additional income. In fact, current NCAA rules limit student-athletes' earnings from employment to a mere $2000.00 during the academic year. Although stipends would not present the scheduling difficulties of part-time employment, most athletics programs lack the funding to provide stipends. Loans based on an athlete's anticipated earnings would present similar funding concerns. ****

Pay-for-play would clearly benefit student-athletes financially. However, there are several reasons why pay-for-play falls short as an approach to amateurism deregulation. First, pay-for-play weakens the principle of educational primacy by strengthening its threats. Second, the proposals will not deter athletes from leaving college early to compete on professional teams. Third, the financial implications of pay-for-play make its implementation impractical for the vast majority of institutions.

Pay-for-play will strengthen all of the major threats to educational primacy: competitive pressures, commercialism, and professionalism. Pay-for-play will intensify competitive pressures on student-athletes to the extent that performance expectations increase along with the athletes' compensation. That is, coaches might expect a higher level of performance and student-athletes might feel obligated to provide a higher level of performance if they are being paid to play. Furthermore, any attempts to raise the funds necessary to finance stipends or loans might result in a corresponding increase in commercialism. As previously stated, commercialism compounds the pressure to win and intrudes upon the athletes' academic lives. Intense competitive pressures can increase the recruitment of academically-underprepared, professionalized athletes. In light of these facts, it is unlikely that pay-for-play will enhance student-athletes' overall educational experience in accordance with the principle of student-athlete welfare.

Furthermore, pay-for-play will not encourage student-athletes with professional potential to delay their professional careers. First, colleges will never be able to compete with professional teams in terms of players' salaries. Second, offering athletes additional compensation as an incentive to remain in college assumes that the athletes enrolled in college to receive an education. Such an assumption ignores the fact that many elite athletes attend college for exposure and athletic training, rather than for educational purposes. If a player's main goal in attending college is to obtain sufficient exposure and training to launch a professional career, then it is unlikely that the player will remain in college once the opportunity for a professional career presents itself.

Moreover, practical considerations would prevent the widespread implementation of pay-for-play. That is, inadequate funding would prevent most universities from offering athletes modest stipends, let alone amounts sufficient to cause them to defer potentially lucrative professional careers. Many schools lack sufficient funding for basic athletic scholarships. Add to the cost of scholarships, the cost of student-athlete salaries and the cost of complying with the tax and labor laws implicated by an employer-employee relationship, and many schools would be forced to drop their athletics programs altogether. Even schools that currently profit from their athletics programs would be unlikely to break even in a pay-for-play regime.

**** Given the destructive effects that pay-for-play will wreak on student-athlete education and athletics departments' finances, this sort of approach to amateurism deregulation should not even be seriously considered.

B. Former Professional Eligibility

NCAA regulations do not allow an athlete to correct a mistaken decision to pursue a professional sports career. NCAA amateurism regulations state that an athlete who signs a contract to play on a professional team or who knowingly competes on a professional team forfeits his or her eligibility. In effect, participation on a professional team is used as a proxy for athletes with skills too advanced for intercollegiate competition. The amateurism regulations attempt to foster competitive equity among college athletics teams by eliminating this class of athletes from the college recruiting pool.

The NCAA's Division I Management Council recently reviewed an amateurism deregulation package which included a proposal that would give high school graduates the option to compete on professional teams for a limited time without forfeiting NCAA eligibility ("the proposal"). The proposal is based on the "Tennis Rule," which allows tennis players to compete in "organized competition" for up to one year after graduating from high school. Under the proposal, athletes who compete in "organized competition" for more than one year would forfeit all Division I eligibility. When the proposal was first introduced, it extended the Tennis Rule to all sports. However, the Academics/Eligibility/Compliance Cabinet (AEC Cabinet) recently recommended the exclusion of basketball from the proposal, citing the sport's unique susceptibility to third party influences, *e.g.* agents, boosters, and non-scholastic coaches.

Men's basketball boasts the NCAA's lowest graduation rates. As such, men's basketball players stand to gain immensely from any proposal that bolsters educational primacy. As this section will soon demonstrate, allowing former professionals to retain eligibility will bolster educational primacy. Therefore, basketball should not be excluded from the proposal.

The current amateurism rules regarding professional athletes were intended to prevent schools from recruiting "ringers" whose sole purpose for matriculation was to play sports. Historically, athletes were allowed to matriculate one day and play the next, regardless of their academic standing. Today, NCAA eligibility and transfer regulations place limitations on such practices.

Allowing athletes to experiment briefly with professional sports careers prior to enrolling in college will advance student-athlete welfare in several ways. First, granting former professionals eligibility will promote educational primacy. Second, it will expand the number of athletic opportunities available to athletes immediately after high school. Lastly, former professional eligibility will provide athletes with a valuable bargaining tool.

The proposal will promote educational primacy since, like redshirting, it requires an institution to make a considerable investment in an athlete's education before the institution can benefit from the athlete's athletic skills. The proposal's year in residence requirement will require former professionals to immediately forfeit one full year of exposure. This waiting period would dissuade all but the most academically-inclined former professionals from joining college teams.

Former professional eligibility will also advance student-athlete welfare by increasing the number of athletics options available to recent high school graduates. Under current NCAA regulations, participation on a college team is no longer an option for an athlete who is considered to be a professional. Hence most high school graduates must choose between college teams and professional teams, without having experienced either. Permitting athletes to compete professionally for a brief period would improve their ability to evaluate their potential for and interest in a professional sports career. Perhaps after having actually experienced the rigors of a professional sports career, some athletes might decide that pursuing a college education is more consistent with their long-term goals.

Additionally, former professional eligibility will improve athletes' bargaining power with professional leagues. Currently, an athlete forfeits eligibility by entering a professional draft prior to enrolling in college. If professional athletes could retain eligibility, they could use it to obtain negotiation leverage with professional teams. That is, a drafted athlete could more confidently reject an inadequate offer from a professional team in favor of a college team since, under the proposal, being drafted would no longer render the athlete ineligible. If a professional team was sufficiently interested in retaining the athlete's services, it might improve its offer to prevent the athlete from joining a college team. The proposal also minimizes the effect that former professional eligibility will have on the competitive equity of intercollegiate athletics. The one-year waiting period will curtail schools' recruitment of ringers. Moreover, by limiting the experimental professional period to one year, the proposal will have a minimal effect on competitive equity. That is, an athlete engaging in such a brief professional sports career is not likely to have gained a substantial competitive advantage.

\*\*\*\*

The NCAA's amateurism regulations are ripe for reform. Given the present financial state of college athletics, pay-for-play is not a viable reform. Former professional eligibility, on the other hand, is a viable reform that... promotes educational primacy.... If implemented, the proposal coupled with the opportunities provided by the NBA's fledgling developmental league, could restore educational primacy to college basketball.

## VI. THE NATIONAL BASKETBALL DEVELOPMENT LEAGUE

College basketball teams have long served as the NBA's de facto minor league. The most recent trend in college basketball is that an increasing number of players are abandoning college teams for the NBA prior to completing their degrees and prior to attaining NBA caliber basketball skills. NBA officials blame the proliferation of underdeveloped talent for the league's declining quality of play and waning popularity. With no end in sight, the present trend among elite college players promises to further saturate the ranks of the NBA with underdeveloped talent.

To better accommodate its developmental needs, the NBA plans to launch the National Basketball Development League (NBDL) in eight southeastern cities beginning in November 2001. The NBDL will serve as the NBA's official minor league. Unlike college teams, the NBDL will give the NBA more control over player development and, unlike existing basketball minor leagues, the NBDL will have the full financial and marketing support of the NBA behind it.

NBDL officials maintain that the new league will not compete with college teams. However, because the NBDL will be recruiting college-aged players displaying a level of talent just below that of NBA players, it will inevitably skim talent from college teams. The NBDL's minimum age requirement is the only factor that will prevent its recruiting efforts from completely overlapping those of college teams. At minimum, a NBDL player must be either twenty years old or at least eighteen if the player was previously drafted by a NBA team and subsequently cut. The NBDL will not impose an upper age limit.

The NBDL will offer those players seeking professional basketball careers a viable alternative to college basketball teams. Recognizing the potential threat that the NBDL poses to the future of college basketball, some coaches openly question the league's professed desire not to compete with college basketball. These coaches' sentiments were expressed by Duke University's famed basketball coach Mike Krzyzewski who commented that "[t]here's no question [that] the league will compete with college [basketball]." Krzyzewski further commented that he wasn't "sure how much it will hurt [college basketball]."

A. The Benefits of the NBDL

The NBA recruits heavily from college teams. Consequently, many elite basketball players see college, not as an educational opportunity, but as the gateway to a professional basketball career. So it is not surprising that the vast majority of these players either leave college early or forgo college altogether.

From an educational primacy standpoint, the NBDL will help college basketball more than it will hurt it. That is, the league will siphon off those players with little or no desire to receive a college education. Contrastingly, those players choosing to attend college will be more likely to be there because they want to earn a degree, and not because college is the only viable route to the NBA. Furthermore, the inclusion of basketball in the former professional eligibility proposal will allow players with short-lived NBDL careers to remain eligible for college teams. As previously stated, these players will possess a similar commitment to education.

Lacking the drawbacks of college basketball teams, the NBDL promises to become the route of choice for athletes with NBA aspirations. Unlike college players, NBDL players will be able to receive compensation for their athletic skill without risking their status on the team. The average NBDL salary will be approximately $30,000.00, the value of a typical financial aid package. However, NBDL players will not be burdened with the daily responsibilities of dual athlete and student status. Some of the NBDL's critics argue that the league will leave many players without a future and without a degree. Yet this type of criticism ignores the reality that, under the status quo, many basketball players never graduate and that many of those who do graduate lack the basic skills that a college degree is supposed to represent.

In addition to salaries, the NBDL will also rival college teams in exposure opportunities. Each of the NDBL's teams will play a fifty-six game regular season followed by a playoff. Current NCAA regulations prevent college teams from playing more than twenty-eight regular season games. The NBDL's partnerships with SFX Entertainment, a worldwide concert promoter, and ESPN, a major sports network, will ensure that the teams receive adequate media exposure. In fact, some games will be broadcast via television, radio, and the Internet. Hence, the NBDL is well-positioned to offer athletes the same opportunities for exposure that they now seek from college teams.

The NBDL's success could wreak havoc on the finances of the NCAA and its members. That is, as NBDL games begin to displace college games, the NCAA's members can expect to see a corresponding decrease in their television rights fees. To mitigate this loss of revenue, schools might be forced to either increase fees and fund-raising or implement cost-savings measures, such as reducing athletic scholarships or postponing capital and personnel expenditures.

The rights fees from the men's basketball tournament are the NCAA's main source of income. The NCAA's contract with CBS is supposed to provide it with $6 billion in rights fees over the next eleven years. However, if ratings for the tournament continue to decline with the level of play, the NCAA might be forced to renegotiate the contract prior to its expiration date.

424

## B. Potential University Responses: The Benefits of College

The NBDL could be a double-edged sword for college basketball. On the one hand, it could help to restore educational primacy to college basketball by siphoning off those players with no interest in a college education. On the other hand, the league could also siphon off the potential revenue that could have been generated by those players. However, there are several ways in which the NCAA and its members can attempt to minimize the NBDL's impact on college teams.

First, schools must reemphasize the importance of a college education to high school recruits. They could do this by providing prospective student-athletes with information on the likelihood and duration of typical professional basketball careers. Furthermore, instead of misleading players with respect to their prospects for a professional basketball career, schools could stress the need for players to have marketable skills besides athletic prowess. In so doing, schools could emphasize the ways in which their institutions could provide these skills.

Second, athletes must be given a meaningful opportunity to take advantage of their schools' academic programs. At the national level, this could be accomplished by shortening playing seasons and placing scheduling restrictions on weekday games requiring travel. At the institutional level, schools could increase support services for academically risky student-athletes and make voluntary workouts truly voluntary.

Lastly, the NCAA should implement the former professional eligibility proposal for all sports, including basketball. College teams will inevitably lose some players to the NBDL. Current NCAA regulations bar all former professionals from college teams, regardless of the duration of their professional careers. Implementing the proposal would allow players with short-lived NBDL careers to remain eligible for college teams. Former NBDL players would be more likely to enroll in college to receive an education, rather than to rehabilitate their professional sports careers. Moreover, colleges would be able to select from an additional class of highly-skilled athletes that would be more likely to remain with the program until graduation.

## VII. CONCLUSION

This article illustrates how amateurism deregulation and the NBDL could interact to bolster the principle of educational primacy. For basketball players with NBA ambitions, the NBDL would be a viable, and perhaps superior, alternative to college teams. Consequently, the presence of the NBDL could help to ensure that players choosing to attend college will do so because they value education, and not because college is the only viable route to the NBA. The implementation of former professional eligibility would allow basketball players with brief NBDL careers and renewed academic aspirations to retain the opportunity to attend college on an athletic scholarship. Hence, former professional eligibility and the NBDL could interact to bolster educational primacy by making it more likely that both pre- and post-professional basketball players would enroll in universities for academic, rather than athletic reasons.

The NBDL will end Division I's privileged status as the NBA's minor league. As the preferred gateway to the NBA, the NBDL could substantially decrease the quality of the college game. To curb the corresponding loss of revenue, elite college basketball programs will need to devise ways to compete with the NBDL for quality basketball players. Because the financial realities of college athletics programs will prevent them from offering pay-for-play, the programs should focus on ways to allow basketball players to obtain more educational value from the collegiate experience. By increasing the educational value of the collegiate experience for basketball players, schools would be more likely to attract skillful high school prospects whose interests are consistent with the academic missions of colleges and universities. And even if some prospects still choose to go to the NBDL immediately after high school, the proposal, if implemented, would give them a chance to change their minds.

## Notes & Questions

1. Summarize Lynch's views regarding the relationship between amateurism, the pressure to win, and commercialism in collegiate athletics. Pay particular attention to the relationship between those things and academics.

2. What are the pros and cons of internal (schools, conferences, NCAA) versus external (courts, Congress) governance of intercollegiate athletics?

4. The NBA Development League currently boasts 12 teams, and appears to be flourishing. *See* http://www.nba.com/dleague/.

5. In his book, *The Carolina Way*, former University of North Carolina basketball coach Dean Smith made a number of suggestions for improving college athletics. Among his suggestions are the following:

1) Give each Division I men's and women's basketball player on scholarship and each Division I-A football scholarship athlete a $2,000 stipend.

2) Require all Division I basketball players to spend a year in residence at the college prior to becoming eligible. According to Coach Smith, "It would give the freshmen time to adjust to the academic demands of college life without the pressures, travel, and practice time involved in varsity basketball or football. Fewer classes would be missed."

3) "The NCAA should tell Division I schools that the lowest 1 percent of freshman admissions can't be recruited athletes. We would then help a small group of students who couldn't help us in athletics. That would also take care of the lame excuse presented by some coaches that just being on a college campus helps a young athlete, even if he or she has no chance to graduate. We all know that current NCAA admission standards requiring a certain SAT score, a certain grade average in certain core courses, and other requirements are not working."

Discuss each of these three suggestions, and explain what you consider to be the strengths and weaknesses of each.

6. For a critical view regarding these and similar issues, *see* Murray Sperber, BEER AND CIRCUS: HOW BIG-TIME COLLEGE SPORTS IS CRIPPLING UNDERGRADUATE EDUCATION (2000).

### *Further Reading on NCAA:*

Burlette W. Carter, *Responding to the Perversion of in Loco Parentis: Using a Nonprofit Organization to Support Student Athletes*, 35 IND. L. REV. 851 (2001/2002).

Burlette W. Carter, *Student-Athlete Welfare in a Restructured NCAA*, 2 VA. J. SPORTS & L. 1 (2000).

Robert N. Davis, *Athletic Reform: Missing the Bases in University Athletics*, 20 CAP. U.L. REV. 597 (1991).

Timothy Davis, *A Model of Institutional Governance for Intercollegiate Athletics*, 1995 WIS. L. REV 599 (1995).

Timothy Davis, *African American Student Athletes: Marginalizing the NCAA Regulatory Structure*, 6 MARQ. SPORTS L.J. 199 (1996).

Timothy Davis, *An Absence of Good Faith: Defining A University's Educational Obligation to Student-Athletes*, 28 HOUS. L. REV. 743 (1991).

Timothy Davis, *Intercollegiate Athletics: Competing Models and Conflicting Realities*, 25 RUTGERS L.J. 269 (1994).

Timothy Davis, *Intercollegiate Athletics in the Next Millennium*, 9 MARQ. SPORTS L.J. 253 (1999).

C. Peter Goplerud III, *Pay for Play for College Athletes: Now, More than Ever,* 38 S. TEX. L. REV. 1081 (1997).

Alfred Dennis Mathewson, *Intercollegiate Athletics and the Assignment of Legal Rights*, 35 St. LOUIS U. L.J. 39 (1990).

Rodney K. Smith, *A Brief History of the NCAA Role in Regulating Intercollegiate Athletics*, 11 MARQ. SPORTS L. REV. 9 (2000).

Rodney K. Smith, *Little Ado About Something: Playing Games with the Reform of Big Time Intercollegiate Athletics*, 20 CAP. U. L. REV. 567 (1991).

John C. Weistart & Cym H. Lowell, Law of Sports, §§1.02-1.06 Regulation of Amateur Athletics (Bobbs-Merrill Company, Inc., 1979).

John C. Weistart & Cym H. Lowell, Law of Sports, §1.10 Regulation of Amateur Athletics (Bobbs-Merrill Company, Inc., 1979).

Stanton Wheeler, *Rethinking Amateurism and the NCAA*, 15 STAN. L. & POLY. REV. 213 (2004).

Ray Yasser, *A Comprehensive Blueprint for the Reform of Intercollegiate Athletics*, 3 MARQ. SPORTS L.J. 123 (1993).

Ray Yasser*, Are Scholarship Athletes at Big-Time Programs Really University Employees*, 9 BLACK L.J. 65 (1984).

428

Ray Yasser, *The Black Athletes Equal Protection Case Against the NCAA's New Academic Standard*, 19 GONZ. L. REV. 83 (1983).

Sherry Young, *The NCAA Enforcement Program and Due Process, the Case for Internal Reform*, 43 SYRACUSE L. REV. 747 (1992).

# Chapter 10

## Agency

---

This chapter outlines a number of issues that relate to sports agency, and the unique fiduciary and confidentiality concerns that an agency relationship entails. Many students enter a Sports Law class thinking that they would like to become sports agents. The actor Tom Cruise certainly made the life of a sports agent look appealing in the movie *Jerry McGuire*. And the HBO series (now in reruns on ESPN Classic) *ARLI$$* may have enough truth in it to add to its humor. The materials in this chapter should raise your consciousness about many of the major issues associated with sports agency. *Argovitz, Brown,* and *Walters* illustrate the kinds of conduct about which agents must be vigilant. In addition to the glamour and prestige, there is potential for immoral and illegal activity that could lead to conflicts of interest and conflicts with a variety of authorities. The Sports Agent Responsibility & Trust Act (SPARTA), signed into law in September 2004, provides federal law and guidelines for sports agents and their dealings with amateur athletes. As the first major federal statute on this topic, you will benefit from becoming familiar with its provisions. The Keller-Smith & Affrunti article provides excellent practical advice for agents, and also offers a sensible perspective on the unique nature of representing Olympic athletes.

## Detroit Lions and Billy Sims v. Argovitz
### 580 F.Supp.542 (1984)
United States District Court, E.D. Michigan, Southern Division

DeMASCIO, District Judge.

The plot for this Saturday afternoon serial began when Billy Sims, having signed a contract with the Houston Gamblers on July 1, 1983, signed a second contract with the Detroit Lions on December 16, 1983. On December 18, 1983, the Detroit Lions, Inc. (Lions) and Billy R. Sims filed a complaint…seeking a judicial determination that the July 1, 1983, contract between Sims and the Houston Gamblers, Inc. (Gamblers) is invalid because the defendant Jerry Argovitz (Argovitz) breached his fiduciary duty when negotiating the Gamblers' contract and because the contract was otherwise tainted by fraud and misrepresentation. ****

For the reasons that follow, we have concluded that Argovitz's breach of his fiduciary duty during negotiations for the Gamblers' contract was so pronounced, so egregious, that to deny recision would be unconscionable.

Sometime in February or March 1983, Argovitz told Sims that he had applied for a Houston franchise in the newly formed United States Football League (USFL). In May 1983, Sims attended a press conference in Houston at which Argovitz announced that his application for a franchise had been approved. The evidence persuades us that Sims did not know the extent of Argovitz's interest in the Gamblers. He did not know the amount of Argovitz's original investment, or that Argovitz was obligated for 29 percent of a $1.5 million letter of credit, or that Argovitz was the president of the Gamblers' Corporation at an annual salary of $275,000 and 5 percent the yearly cash flow. The defendants could not justifiably expect Sims to comprehend the ramifications of Argovitz's interest in the Gamblers or the manner in which that interest would create an untenable conflict of interest, a conflict that would inevitably breach Argovitz's fiduciary duty to Sims. Argovitz knew, or should have known, that he could not act as Sims' agent under any circumstances when dealing with the Gamblers. Even the USFL Constitution itself prohibits a holder of any interest in a member club from acting "as the contracting agent or representative for any player."

Pending the approval of his application for a USFL franchise in Houston, Argovitz continued his negotiations with the Lions on behalf of Sims. On April 5, 1983, Argovitz offered Sims's services to the Lions for $6 million over a four-year period. The offer included a demand for a $1 million interest-free loan to be repaid over 10 years, and for skill and injury guarantees for three years. The Lions quickly responded with a counter offer on April 7, 1983, in the face amount of $1.5 million over a five-year period with additional incentives not relevant here. The negotiating process was working. The Lions were trying to determine what Argovitz really believed the market value for Sims really was. On May 3, 1983, with his Gamblers franchise assured, Argovitz significantly reduced his offer to the Lions. He now offered Sims to the Lions for $3 million over a four-year period, one-half of the amount of his April 5, 1983, offer. Argovitz's May 3rd offer included a demand for $50,000 to permit Sims to purchase an annuity. Argovitz also dropped his previous demand for skill guarantees. The May 10, 1983 offer submitted by the Lions brought the parties much closer.

On May 30, 1983, Argovitz asked for $3.5 million over a five-year period. This offer included an interest-free loan and injury protection insurance but made no demand for skill guarantees. The May 30 offer now requested $400,000 to allow Sims to purchase an annuity. On June 1, 1983, Argovitz and the Lions were only $500,000 apart. We find that the negotiations between the Lions and Argovitz were progressing normally, not laterally as Argovitz represented to Sims. The Lions were not "dragging their feet." Throughout the entire month of June 1983, Mr. Frederick Nash, the Lions' skilled negotiator and a fastidious lawyer, was involved in investigating the possibility of providing an attractive annuity for Sims and at the same time doing his best to avoid the granting of either skill or injury guarantees. The evidence establishes that on June 22, 1983, the Lions and Argovitz were very close to reaching an agreement on the value of Sims's services.

Apparently, in the midst of his negotiations with the Lions and with his Gamblers franchise in hand, Argovitz decided that he would seek an offer from the Gamblers. Mr. Bernard Lerner, one of Argovitz's partners in the Gamblers agreed to negotiate a contract with Sims. Since Lerner admitted that he had no knowledge whatsoever about football, we must infer that Argovitz at the very least told Lerner the amount of money required to sign Sims and further pressed upon Lerner the Gamblers' absolute need to obtain Sims' services. In the Gamblers' organization, only Argovitz knew the value of Sims' services and how critical it was for the Gamblers to obtain Sims. In Argovitz's words, Sims would make the Gamblers' franchise.

On June 29, 1983, at Lerner's behest, Sims and his wife went to Houston to negotiate with a team that was partially owned by his own agent.

When Sims arrived in Houston, he believed that the Lions organization was not negotiating in good faith; that it was not really interested in his services. His ego was bruised and his emotional outlook toward the Lions was visible to Burrough and Argovitz. Clearly, virtually all the information that Sims had up to that date came from Argovitz. Sims and the Gamblers did not discuss a future contract on the night of June 29th. The negotiations began on the morning of June 30, 1983, and ended that afternoon. At the morning meeting, Lerner offered Sims a $3.5 million five-year contract, which included three years of skill and injury guarantees. The offer included a $500,000 loan at an interest rate of 1 percent over prime. It was from this loan that Argovitz planned to receive the $100,000 balance of his fee for acting as an agent in negotiating a contract with his own team. Burrough testified that Sims would have accepted that offer on the spot because he was finally receiving the guarantee that he had been requesting from the Lions, guarantees that Argovitz dropped without too much quarrel. Argovitz and Burrough took Sims and his wife into another room to discuss the offer. Argovitz did tell Sims that he thought the Lions would match the Gamblers financial package and asked Sims whether he (Argovitz) should telephone the Lions. But, it is clear from the evidence that neither Sims nor Burrough believed that the Lions would match the offer. We find that Sims told Argovitz not to call the Lions for purely emotional reasons. As we have noted, Sims believed that the Lions' organization was not that interested in him and his pride was wounded. Burrough clearly admitted that he was aware of the emotional basis for Sims' decision not to have Argovitz phone the Lions, and we must conclude from the extremely close relationship between Argovitz and Sims that Argovitz knew it as well. When Sims went back to Lerner's office, he agreed to become a Gambler on the terms offered. At that moment, Argovitz irreparably breached his fiduciary duty. As agent for Sims he had the duty to telephone the Lions, receive its final offer, and present the terms of both offers to Sims. Then and only then could it be said that Sims made an intelligent and knowing decision to accept the Gamblers' offer.

During these negotiations at the Gamblers' office, Mr. Nash of the Lions telephoned Argovitz, but even though Argovitz was at his office, he declined to accept the telephone call. Argovitz tried to return Nash's call after Sims had accepted the Gamblers' offer, but it was after 5, p.m. and Nash had left for the July 4th weekend. When he declined to accept Mr. Nash's call, Argovitz's breach of his fiduciary duty became even more pronounced. Following Nash's example, Argovitz left for his weekend trip, leaving his principal to sign the contracts with the Gamblers the next day, July 1, 1983. The defendants, in their supplemental trial brief, assert that neither Argovitz nor Burrough can be held responsible for following Sims's instruction not to contact the Lions on June 30, 1983. Although it is generally true that an agent is not liable for losses occurring as a result of following his principal's instructions, the rule of law is not applicable when the agent has placed himself in a position adverse to that of his principal.

During the evening of June 30, 1983, Burrough struggled with the fact that they had not presented the Gamblers' offer to the Lions. He knew, as does the court, that Argovitz now had the wedge that he needed to bring finality to the Lions' negotiations. Burrough was acutely aware of the fact that Sims' actions were emotionally motivated and realized that the responsibility for Sims' future rested with him. We view with some disdain the fact that Argovitz had, in effect, delegated his entire fiduciary responsibility on the eve of his principal's most important career decision. On July 1, 1983, it was Lerner who gave lip service to Argovitz's conspicuous conflict of interest. It was Lerner, not Argovitz, who advised Sims that Argovitz's position with the Gamblers presented a conflict of interest and that Sims could, if he wished, obtain an attorney or another agent. Argovitz, upon whom Sims had relied for the past four years, was not even there. Burrough, conscious of Sims' emotional responses, never advised Sims to wait until he had talked with the Lions before making a final decision. Argovitz's conflict of interest and self dealing put him in the position where he would not even use the wedge he now had to negotiate with the Lions, a wedge that is the dream of every agent. Two expert witnesses testified that an agent should telephone a team that he has been negotiating with once he has an offer in hand. Mr. Woolf, plaintiff's expert, testified that an offer from another team is probably the most important factor in negotiations. Mr. Lustig, defendant's expert, believed that it was prudent for him to telephone the Buffalo Bills and inform that organization of the Gamblers' offer to Jim Kelly, despite the fact that he believed the Bills had already made its best offer to his principal. The evidence here convinces us that Argovitz's negotiations with the Lions were ongoing and it had not made its final offer. Argovitz did not follow the common practice described by both expert witnesses. He did not do this because he knew that the Lions would not leave Sims without a contract and he further knew that if he made that type of call Sims would be lost to the Gamblers, a team he owned.

On November 12, 1983, when Sims was in Houston for the Lions game with the Houston Oilers, Argovitz asked Sims to come to his home and sign certain papers. He represented to Sims that certain papers of his contract had been mistakenly overlooked and now needed to be signed. Included among those papers he asked Sims to sign was a waiver of any claim that Sims might have against Argovitz for his blatant breach of his fiduciary duty brought on by his glaring conflict of interest. Sims did not receive independent advice with regard to the wisdom of signing such a waiver. Despite having sold his agency business in September, Argovitz did not even tell Sims' new agent of his intention to have Sims sign a waiver. Nevertheless, Sims, an unsophisticated young man, signed the waiver. This is another example of the questionable conduct on the part of Argovitz who still had business management obligations to Sims. In spite of his fiduciary relationship he had Sims sign a waiver without advising him to obtain independent counseling.

Argovitz's negotiations with Lustig, Jim Kelly's agent, illustrates the difficulties that develop when an agent negotiates a contract where his personal interests conflict with those of his principal. Lustig, an independent agent, ignored Argovitz's admonishment not to "shop" the Gamblers' offer to Kelly. Lustig called the NFL team that he had been negotiating with because it was the "prudent" thing to do. The Gamblers agreed to pay Kelly, an untested rookie quarterback $3.2 million for five years. His compensation was $60,000 less than Sims's, a former Heisman Trophy winner and a proven star in the NFL. Lustig also obtained a number of favorable clauses from Argovitz; the most impressive one being that Kelly was assured of being one of the three top paid quarterbacks in the USFL if he performed as well as expected. If Argovitz had been free from conflicting interests he would have demanded similar benefits for Sims. Argovitz claimed that the nondisclosure clause in Kelly's contract prevented him from mentioning the Kelly contract to Sims. We view this contention as frivolous. Requesting these benefits for Sims did not require disclosure of Kelly's contract. Moreover, Argovitz's failure to obtain personal guarantees for Sims without adequately warning Sims about the risks and uncertainties of a new league constituted a clear breach of his fiduciary duty.

The parties submitted a great deal of evidence and argued a number of peripheral issues. Although most of the issues were not determinative factors in our decision, they do demonstrate that Argovitz had a history of fulfilling his fiduciary duties in an irresponsible manner. One cannot help but wonder whether Argovitz took his fiduciary duty seriously. For example, after investing approximately $76,000 of Sims' money, Argovitz, with or without the prior knowledge of his principal, received a finder's fee. Despite the fact that Sims paid Argovitz a 2 percent fee, Argovitz accepted $3800 from a person with whom he invested Sims' money. In March 1983, Argovitz had all of his veteran players, including Sims, sign a new agency contract with less favorable payment terms for the players even though they already had an ongoing agency agreement with him. He did this after he sold his entire agency business to Career Sports. Finally, Argovitz was prepared to take the remainder of his 5 percent agency fee for negotiating

Sims's contract with the Gamblers from monies the Gamblers loaned to Sims at an interest rate of 1 percent over prime. It mattered little to Argovitz that Sims would have to pay interest on the $100,000 that Argovitz was ready to accept. While these practices by Argovitz are troublesome, we do not find them decisive in examining Argovitz's conduct while negotiating the Gamblers' contract on June 30 and July 1, 1983. We find this circumstantial evidence useful only insofar as it has aided the court in understanding the manner in which these parties conducted business.

We are mindful that Sims was less than forthright when testifying before the court. However, we agree with plaintiff's counsel that the facts as presented through the testimony of other witnesses are so unappealing that we can disregard Sims' testimony entirely. We remain persuaded that on balance, Argovitz's breach of his fiduciary duty was so egregious that a court of equity cannot permit him to benefit by his own wrongful breach. We conclude that Argovitz's conduct in negotiating Sims' contract with the Gamblers rendered it invalid.

## CONCLUSIONS OF LAW

****

3. The relationship between a principal and agent is fiduciary in nature, and as such imposes a duty of loyalty, good faith, and fair and honest dealing on the agent. *Anderson v. Griffith,* 501 S.W.2d 695, 700 (Tex.Civ.App.1973).

4. A fiduciary relationship arises not only from a formal principal-agent relationship, but also from informal relationships of trust and confidence. *Thigpen v. Locke,* 363 S.W.2d 247, 253 (Tex.1962); *Adickes v. Andreoli,* 600 S.W.2d 939, 945-46 (Tex.Civ.App.1980).

5. In light of the express agency agreement, and the relationship between Sims and Argovitz, Argovitz clearly owed Sims the fiduciary duties of an agent at all times relevant to this lawsuit.

6. An agent's duty of loyalty requires that he not have a personal stake that conflicts with the principal's interest in a transaction in which he represents his principal. As stated in *Burleson v. Earnest,* 153 S.W.2d 869 (Tex.Civ.App.1941):

(T)he principal is entitled to the best efforts and unbiased judgment of his agent.... (T)he law denies the right of an agent to assume any relationship that is antagonistic to his duty to his principal, and it has many times been held that the agent cannot be both buyer and seller at the same time nor connect his own interests with property involved in his dealings as an agent for another. *Id.* at 874.

7. A fiduciary violates the prohibition against self-dealing not only by dealing with himself on his principal's behalf, but also by dealing on his principal's behalf with a third party in which he has an interest, such as a partnership in which he is a member. ****

8. Where an agent has an interest adverse to that of his principal in a transaction in which he purports to act on behalf of his principal, the transaction is voidable by the principal unless the agent disclosed all material facts within the agent's knowledge that might affect the principal's judgment. *Burleson v. Earnest,* 153 S.W.2d at 874-75.

9. The mere fact that the contract is fair to the principal does not deny the principal the right to rescind the contract when it was negotiated by an agent in violation of the prohibition against self-dealing. ****

10. Once it has been shown that an agent had an interest in a transaction involving his principal antagonistic to the principal's interest, fraud on the part of the agent is presumed. The burden of proof then rests upon the agent to show that his principal had full knowledge, not only of the fact that the agent was interested, but also of every material fact known to the agent which might affect the principal and that having such knowledge, the principal freely consented to the transaction.

11. It is not sufficient for the agent merely to inform the principal that he has an interest that conflicts with the principal's interest. Rather, he must inform the principal "of all facts that come to his knowledge that are or may be material or which might affect his principal's rights or interests or influence the action he takes." *Anderson v. Griffith,* 501 S.W.2d 695, 700 (Tex.Civ.App.1973).

12. Argovitz clearly had a personal interest in signing Sims with the Gamblers that was adverse to Sims' interest--he had an ownership interest in the Gamblers and thus would profit if the Gamblers were profitable, and would incur substantial personal liabilities should the Gamblers not be financially successful. Since this showing has been made, fraud on Argovitz's part is presumed, and the Gamblers' contract must be rescinded

438

unless Argovitz has shown by a preponderance of the evidence that he informed Sims of every material fact that might have influenced Sims' decision whether or not to sign the Gamblers' contract.

\*\*\*\*

17. As a court sitting in equity, we conclude that recision is the appropriate remedy. We are dismayed by Argovitz's egregious conduct. The careless fashion in which Argovitz went about ascertaining the highest price for Sims' service convinces us of the wisdom of the maxim: no man can faithfully serve two masters whose interests are in conflict.

Judgment will be entered for the plaintiffs rescinding the Gamblers' contract with Sims.

## Notes & Questions

1. Is the court saying categorically that someone with an ownership interest in a professional team cannot legally also act as a player agent? Or is the court saying that someone with an ownership interest in a professional team may legally also act as a player agent, but if s/he does so, s/he has an obligation to make disclosures to his/her principal that are more open than those that Argovitz made to Sims?

2. Can you pinpoint a time at which Argovitz crossed the line and breached his fiduciary duty to Sims?

3. There probably are things that Sims should have done differently in an effort to avoid this type of situation with his agent. Give examples.

4. If you had been Argovitz's lawyer, what would you have advised him to do during his negotiations with the Lions?

5. The court cites numerous instances of Argovitz's wrongdoing. Make a list of them.

**Brown v. Woolf**

554 F.Supp. 1206 (1983)

United States District Court, S.D. Indiana, Indianapolis Division

STECKLER, District Judge.

This matter comes before the Court on the motions of defendant, Robert G. Woolf, for partial summary judgment and for summary judgment. Fed.R.Civ.P. 56.

The complaint in this diversity action seeks compensatory and punitive damages and the imposition of a trust on a fee Woolf allegedly received, all stemming from Woolf's alleged constructive fraud and breach of fiduciary duty in the negotiation of a contract for the 1974-75 hockey season for Brown who was a professional hockey player. Brown alleges that prior to the 1973-74 season he had engaged the services of Woolf, a well known sports attorney and agent, who represents many professional athletes, has authored a book, and has appeared in the media in connection with such representation, to negotiate a contract for him with the Pittsburgh Penguins of the National Hockey League. Brown had a professionally successful season that year under the contract Woolf negotiated for him and accordingly again engaged Woolf's services prior to the 1974-75 season. During the negotiations in July 1974, the Penguins offered Brown a two-year contract at $80,000.00 per year but Brown rejected the offer allegedly because Woolf asserted that he could obtain a better, long-term, no-cut contract with a deferred compensation feature with the Indianapolis Racers, which at the time was a new team in a new league. On July 31, 1974, Brown signed a five-year contract with the Racers. Thereafter, it is alleged the Racers began having financial difficulties. Brown avers that Woolf continued to represent [him] and negotiated two reductions in his compensation including the loss of a retirement fund at the same time Woolf was attempting to get his own fee payment from the Racers. Ultimately the Racers' assets were seized and the organizers defaulted on their obligations to Brown. He avers that he received only $185,000.00 of the total $800,000.00 compensation under the Racer contract but that Woolf received his full $40,000.00 fee (5% of the contract) from the Racers.

Brown alleges that Woolf made numerous material mis-representations upon which he relied both during the negotiation of the Racer contract and at the time of the subsequent modifications. Brown further avers that Woolf breached his fiduciary duty to [him] by failing to conduct any investigation into the financial stability of the Racers, failing to

440

investigate possible consequences of the deferred compensation package in the Racers' contract, failing to obtain guarantees or collateral, and by negotiating reductions in [his] compensation from the Racers while insisting on receiving all of his own. Brown theorizes that such conduct amounts to a prima facie case of constructive fraud for which he should receive compensatory and punitive damages and have a trust impressed on the $40,000.00 fee Woolf received from the Racers.

Woolf's motion for partial summary judgment attacks Brown's claim for punitive damages, contending that plaintiff has no evidence to support such an award and should not be allowed to rest on the allegations of his complaint. Further, he claims that punitive damages are unavailable as a matter of law in a constructive fraud case because no proof of fraudulent intent is required. By his motion for summary judgment, Woolf attacks several aspects of Brown's claims against him. He argues (1) that Brown cannot recover on a breach of contract theory because Robert G. Woolf, the individual, was acting merely as the agent and employee of Robert Woolf Associates, Inc. (RWA), (2) that Woolf's conduct could not amount to constructive fraud because (a) Brown alleges only negligent acts, (b) there is no evidence Woolf deceived Brown or violated a position of trust, (c) there is no showing of harm to the public interest, and (d) there is no evidence that Woolf obtained an unconscionable advantage at Brown's expense.

Turning first to the questions raised in the motion for partial summary judgment, the Court could find no Indiana case specifically discussing the availability of punitive damages in an action based upon the theory of constructive fraud. Cases from other jurisdictions reflect a division of authority. The Court concludes that Indiana courts would not adopt a per se rule prohibiting such damages in a constructive fraud action, but would rather consider the facts and circumstances of each case. If elements of recklessness, or oppressive conduct are demonstrated, punitive damages could be awarded. [citations omitted].

Indiana cases contain several formulizations of the tort of constructive fraud. Generally it is characterized as acts or a course of conduct from which an unconscionable advantage is or may be derived, or a breach of confidence coupled with an unjust enrichment which shocks the conscience, or a breach of duty, including mistake, duress or undue influence, which the law declares fraudulent because of a tendency to deceive, injure the public interest or violate the public or private confidence [citations omitted]. Another formulization found in the cases involves the making of a false statement, by the dominant party in a confidential or fiduciary relationship or by one who holds himself out as an expert, upon which the plaintiff reasonably relies to his detriment. The defendant need not know the statement is false nor make the false statement with fraudulent intent. *Coffey v. Wininger,* 156 Ind.App. 233, 296 N.E.2d 154 (1973); *Smart & Perry Ford Sales, Inc. v. Weaver,* 149 Ind.App. 693, 274 N.E.2d 718 (1971).

The Court believes that both formulizations are rife with questions of fact, *inter alia,* the existence or nonexistence of a confidential or fiduciary relationship, and the question of reliance on false representations, as well as questions of credibility.

Woolf argues that despite the customary existence of such fact questions in a constructive fraud case, judgment is appropriate in this instance because Brown has produced nothing to demonstrate the existence of fact questions. He makes a similar argument in the motion for partial summary judgment on the punitive damages issue.

Rule 56(e), Fed.R.Civ. states in pertinent part:

When a motion for summary judgment is made and supported as provided in this rule, an adverse party may not rest upon the mere allegations or denials of his pleading, but his response, by affidavits or as otherwise provided in this rule, must set forth specific facts showing that there is a genuine issue for trial. If he does not so respond, summary judgment, *if appropriate,* shall be entered against him. [Emphasis supplied.]

In this case, Woolf has offered affidavits, excerpts of depositions, and photocopies of various documents to support his motions. He contends that such materials demonstrate that reasonable minds could not conclude that [he] did the acts with which the complaint charges him. In response, Brown rather belatedly offered portions of [his] depositions as well as arguing that issues such as those raised by a complaint based on constructive fraud are inherently unsuited to resolution on a motion for summary judgment.

Having carefully considered the motions and briefs and having examined the evidentiary materials submitted, the Court concludes that summary judgment would not be appropriate in this action. The Court is not persuaded that there are no fact questions remaining unresolved in this controversy such that Woolf is entitled to judgment as a matter of law. As movant for summary judgment, defendant bears the "heavy burden" of clearly demonstrating the absence of any genuine issue of a material fact. [citations omitted].

By reason of the foregoing, defendant's motions for partial summary judgment and for summary judgment are hereby DENIED.

## Notes & Questions

1. Explain what the court means by the term "constructive fraud." What facts does Brown allege that arguably constitute constructive fraud?

### United States v. Walters and Bloom
913 F.2d. 388 (1990)
United States Court of Appeals, Seventh Circuit

BAUER, Chief Judge.

Norby Walters and Lloyd Bloom were sports agents who specialized in representing college football players. Walters and Bloom would recruit young players still in college and secretly sign them to exclusive representation contracts. The players would then lie about the existence of their contracts on the amateur athletic eligibility forms they submitted to their universities. The athletes would then continue to receive scholarships from these universities and play football on the schools' teams. Walters and Bloom were convicted on charges of mail fraud, RICO violations and conspiracy for their participation in this scheme. They now appeal to this court, contending that several errors were committed during their trial that should render their convictions invalid. We believe that fundamental errors occurred at trial which prejudiced the defendants' ability to receive a fair trial. We, therefore, reverse and remand with instructions for a new trial.

### I. BACKGROUND

Norby Walters, a former nightclub owner, and Lloyd Bloom, a 25-year-old, self-described salesman, together formed World Sports & Entertainment ("WS & E") in August 1984. In the past, Walters had represented entertainers such as the Jackson Five, Dionne Warwick and The New Edition. With their new enterprise, Bloom and Walters hoped to make

443

the transition from managing musical entertainers to representing professional athletes.

Walters and Bloom would entice talented college football players to sign exclusive representation contracts with WS & E by providing signing bonuses in cash, no-interest loans, sports cars and other incentives. As it was in the interest of both the agents and their clients for the players to retain their college eligibility, the contracts were post-dated and the agreements were kept secret by both sides.

The National Collegiate Athletic Association ("NCAA") forbids players from signing with an agent or receiving compensation for athletics before the expiration of collegiate athletic eligibility. An athlete who violates these rules is considered to have waived his eligibility in return for payment, and can no longer compete in college athletics. Schools who are members of the NCAA require their players to submit forms testifying to the lack of such restrictions on their eligibility. The forms are then filed with the NCAA. Thus, the players who had signed agreements with Walters and Bloom would lie to their colleges on these eligibility forms in order to continue to receive scholarships and to play for their school teams.

Prior to beginning their enterprise, in January 1985, Walters and Bloom consulted with attorneys at the law firm of Shea & Gould in New York concerning the possible legal ramifications of these agreements. Lonn Trost, the head of the sports law department at Shea & Gould, informed the agents that while they were violating NCAA rules by signing athletes who then continued to play for their college teams, they were not violating any laws. Trost and other attorneys at Shea & Gould admit that they were aware that athletes would probably have to conceal this arrangement from their universities. They contend, however, that they were not aware that the athletes would lie openly on their NCAA eligibility forms.

Walters and Bloom were much more successful recruiters than agents or negotiators. In all, 58 college football players entered into representation agreements with WS & E. Only two players, however, continued the relationship after graduation from college. The vast majority felt cheated by Walters' and Bloom's clandestine tactics and signed with other agents prior to the NFL draft. Walters and Bloom again consulted with Shea & Gould to consider enforcement of the contracts. The agents were out not only their anticipated representation fees, but the loans they had made to the players up front. Their attorneys believed that the contracts were enforceable, but recommended against litigation. The government alleges, and several former clients testified, that Walters and Bloom personally threatened them in an attempt to enforce these contracts.   One player, Maurice Douglas, was told his legs would be broken before the NFL draft if he did not repay his loan to WS & E.

On August 24, 1988, Walters and Bloom were charged in a seven-count indictment with mail fraud, RICO violations, and conspiracy in the Northern District of Illinois.   Count I alleged conspiracy to engage in a pattern of racketeering activity, and Count VII alleged substantive violations of the Racketeer Influenced and Corrupt Organizations Act ("RICO"), specifically 18 U.S.C. § 1962(c) & (d).   The predicate acts for these RICO charges included extortion, attempted extortion, mail fraud, wire fraud, collection of credit by extortionate means, and the use of interstate facilities in the furtherances of unlawful activity.   Counts II-V separately charged the defendants with substantive mail fraud counts against the University of Michigan, Michigan State University, the University of Iowa and Purdue University, respectively, in violation of 18 U.S.C. § 1341.   Count VI alleged conspiracy to commit mail fraud in violation of 18 U.S.C. § 371.

A jury trial was held before Judge George M. Marovich from March 6, 1989 through April 6, 1989.   After a week of deliberation, the jury found Walters and Bloom guilty on five of the seven counts.   The defendants were found not guilty of mail fraud against two of the universities under Counts III and IV.   In a special verdict, the jury indicated that it did not find that Walters or Bloom had committed the extortion-related charges.   On June 19, 1989, Judge Marovich sentenced Walters to five years in custody to be followed by five years probation.   Bloom received a three-year sentence to be followed by five years probation.   Both defendants moved for a new trial and upon the denial of this motion filed a timely notice of appeal.

## II. DISCUSSION

\*\*\*\*

The linchpin of Walters' defense was that his actions were taken in good faith based upon the advice of his attorneys.   If the jury accepted this characterization of the events, Walters could not have been considered to have formed the specific intent necessary to commit fraud upon the universities.   *See United States v. Martin-Trigona,* 684 F.2d 485, 492 (7th Cir.1984) ("good faith, or the absence of an intent to defraud, is a complete defense to a charge of mail fraud.")   This court has often stated, "[t]he defendant in a criminal case is entitled to have the jury consider any theory of the defense which is supported by the law and which has some foundation in the evidence, however tenuous." *United States v. Briscoe,* 896 F.2d 1476,

1512 (7th Cir.1990). *See also United States v. Boucher,* 796 F.2d 972, 975 (7th Cir.1986); *United States v. Grimes,* 413 F.2d 1376, 1378 (7th Cir.1969). On appeal, therefore, we must determine whether the evidence supports Walters' theory of good faith reliance on the advice of his counsel. *See United States v. Kelley,* 864 F.2d 569, 572 (7th Cir.1989).

In January of 1985, Walters met with attorneys at Shea & Gould. In March of that year, he began signing his first clients. Walters' discussions with counsel, therefore, predated the actions taken in violation of the NCAA rules. The government vigorously contends that Walters did not reveal to his attorneys that his clients would lie on eligibility forms. By not revealing this material fact, the prosecution argues, Walters cannot now raise the advice-of-counsel defense. Walters, however, stresses that he was not aware of these forms.

Both sides admit that Walters' counsel informed him that although he would be violating NCAA rules by concealing the early recruiting of these athletes, he would not break the law by signing these concealed arrangements. It is not unreasonable to assume that the sports law experts at Shea & Gould would be aware of the eligibility forms required of athletes by universities and the NCAA. Nor would it have been unreasonable for those attorneys to have considered how these forms might be addressed by Walters's technically ineligible clients. The lack of discussion could signal that Walters was unaware of the forms or that the Shea & Gould attorneys tacitly considered these forms in issuing their legal opinion.

The one possibility accepted by the court--that Walters simply chose to lie to his attorneys about his plans--seems patently unreasonable. Walters, by all accounts, was a rather unethical and unsavory businessman. He frequently operated outside the boundaries of truth and honesty. Yet, this does not persuade us that he would conceal material information from his attorney. Walters apparently sought out Shea & Gould *because* he feared that his actions might be illegal. Such a client is more likely to reveal all relevant information than one unconcerned by the consequences of his acts.

The trial court, however, is the place to make these determinations; it is not for us to determine whether Walters actually concealed material information from his attorneys. Whether Walters did conceal such information or not, however, the fact remains that there is substantial doubt about the circumstances of his legal advice. Such questions must be resolved by the jury--not the court. If Walters demonstrated evidence that he had provided to his attorneys all material information known to him, then the court must at least tender an instruction on the advice-of-counsel defense.

446

We believe Walters presented sufficient evidence on which to support his theory of defense. He deserved an instruction explaining this theory. Nor can "arguments of counsel ... substitute for instructions by the court [.]" *Taylor v. Kentucky,* 436 U.S. 478, 488-89, 98 S.Ct. 1930, 1936-37, 56 L.Ed.2d 468 (1978). Amid a sea of facts and inferences, instructions are the jury's only compass. Here, they were cast adrift. The court's failure to provide an instruction on Walters' theory of defense infected the fairness of his trial. Walters established the basis for such a defense and deserved such an instruction. The refusal to provide an advice-of-counsel instruction was therefore reversible error.

## III. CONCLUSION

The court erred by not providing an advice-of-counsel instruction to the jury as requested by Walters. Walters reasonably developed this defense and he deserved to have the jury, not the court, determine its validity. He was substantially prejudiced by the omission.

**Notes & Questions**

1. What civil actions do you suppose that the college athletes who were their clients could bring against Walters and Bloom based upon these facts? Explain how those legal theories might play out at trial.

2. What civil actions do you suppose that the colleges where Walters's and Blooms's clients attended could bring against them based on these facts? Explain how those legal theories might play out at trial.

3. What civil actions do you suppose that the NCAA could bring against Walters and Bloom based upon these facts? Explain how those legal theories might play out at trial.

# UNITED STATES PUBLIC LAWS
## SPORTS AGENT RESPONSIBILITY AND TRUST ACT

An Act To designate certain conduct by sports agents relating to the signing of contracts with student athletes as unfair and deceptive acts or practices to be regulated by the Federal Trade Commission.

Be it enacted by the Senate and House of Representatives of the United States
of America in Congress assembled,

## 15 USCA § 7801 NOTE

### SECTION 1. SHORT TITLE.

This Act may be cited as the "Sports Agent Responsibility and Trust Act".

## 15 USCA § 7801

### SEC. 2. DEFINITIONS.

As used in this Act, the following definitions apply:
(1) AGENCY CONTRACT.--The term "agency contract" means an oral or written agreement in which a student athlete authorizes a person to negotiate or solicit on behalf of the student athlete a professional sports contract or an endorsement contract.
(2) ATHLETE AGENT.--The term "athlete agent" means an individual who enters into an agency contract with a student athlete, or directly or indirectly recruits or solicits a student athlete to enter into an agency contract, and does not include a spouse, parent, sibling, grandparent, or guardian of such student athlete, any legal counsel for purposes other than that of representative agency, or an individual acting solely on behalf of a professional sports team or professional sports organization.
(3) ATHLETIC DIRECTOR.--The term "athletic director" means an individual responsible for administering the athletic program of an educational institution or, in the case that such program is administered separately, the athletic program for male students or the athletic program for female students, as appropriate.
(4) COMMISSION.--The term "Commission" means the Federal Trade Commission.

(5) ENDORSEMENT CONTRACT.--The term "endorsement contract" means an agreement under which a student athlete is employed or receives consideration for the use by the other party of that individual's person, name, image, or likeness in the promotion of any product, service, or event.

(6) INTERCOLLEGIATE SPORT.--The term "intercollegiate sport" means a sport played at the collegiate level for which eligibility requirements for participation by a student athlete are established by a national association for the promotion or regulation of college athletics.

(7) PROFESSIONAL SPORTS CONTRACT.--The term "professional sports contract" means an agreement under which an individual is employed, or agrees to render services, as a player on a professional sports team, with a professional sports organization, or as a professional athlete.

(8) STATE.--The term "State" includes a State of the United States, the District of Columbia, Puerto Rico, the United States Virgin Islands, or any territory or insular possession subject to the jurisdiction of the United States.

(9) STUDENT ATHLETE.--The term "student athlete" means an individual who engages in, is eligible to engage in, or may be eligible in the future to engage in, any intercollegiate sport. An individual who is permanently ineligible to participate in a particular intercollegiate sport is not a student athlete for purposes of that sport.

## 15 USCA § 7802

## SEC. 3. REGULATION OF UNFAIR AND DECEPTIVE ACTS AND PRACTICES IN CONNECTION WITH THE CONTACT BETWEEN AN ATHLETE AGENT AND A STUDENT ATHLETE.

(a) CONDUCT PROHIBITED.--It is unlawful for an athlete agent to--

(1) directly or indirectly recruit or solicit a student athlete to enter into an agency contract, by--

(A) giving any false or misleading information or making a false promise or representation; or

(B) providing anything of value to a student athlete or anyone associated with the student athlete before the student athlete enters into an agency contract, including any consideration in the form of a loan, or acting in the capacity of a guarantor or co-guarantor for any debt;

(2) enter into an agency contract with a student athlete without providing the student athlete with the disclosure document described in subsection (b); or

(3) predate or postdate an agency contract.

(b) REQUIRED DISCLOSURE BY ATHLETE AGENTS TO STUDENT ATHLETES.--

(1) IN GENERAL.--In conjunction with the entering into of an agency contract, an athlete agent shall provide to the student athlete, or, if the student

athlete is under the age of 18, to such student athlete's parent or legal guardian, a disclosure document that meets the requirements of this subsection. Such disclosure document is separate from and in addition to any disclosure which may be required under State law.

(2) SIGNATURE OF STUDENT ATHLETE.--The disclosure document must be signed by the student athlete, or, if the student athlete is under the age of 18, by such student athlete's parent or legal guardian, prior to entering into the agency contract.

(3) REQUIRED LANGUAGE.--The disclosure document must contain, in close proximity to the signature of the student athlete, or, if the student athlete is under the age of 18, the signature of such student athlete's parent or legal guardian, a conspicuous notice in boldface type stating: "Warning to Student Athlete: If you agree orally or in writing to be represented by an agent now or in the future you may lose your eligibility to compete as a student athlete in your sport. Within 72 hours after entering into this contract or before the next athletic event in which you are eligible to participate, whichever occurs first, both you and the agent by whom you are agreeing to be represented must notify the athletic director of the educational institution at which you are enrolled, or other individual responsible for athletic programs at such educational institution, that you have entered into an agency contract.".

15 USCA § 7803

SEC. 4. ENFORCEMENT.

(a) UNFAIR OR DECEPTIVE ACT OR PRACTICE.--A violation of this Act shall be treated as a violation of a rule defining an unfair or deceptive act or practice prescribed under section 18(a)(1)(B) of the Federal Trade Commission Act (15 U.S.C. 57a(a)(1)(B)).

(b) ACTIONS BY THE COMMISSION.--The Commission shall enforce this Act in the same manner, by the same means, and with the same jurisdiction, powers, and duties as though all applicable terms and provisions of the Federal Trade Commission Act (15 U.S.C. 41 et seq.) were incorporated into and made a part of this Act.

## SEC. 5. ACTIONS BY STATES.

(a) IN GENERAL.--
(1) CIVIL ACTIONS.--In any case in which the attorney general of a State has reason to believe that an interest of the residents of that State has been or is threatened or adversely affected by the engagement of any athlete agent in a practice that violates section 3 of this Act, the State may bring a civil action on behalf of the residents of the State in a district court of the United States of appropriate jurisdiction to--
(A) enjoin that practice;
(B) enforce compliance with this Act; or
(C) obtain damage, restitution, or other compensation on behalf of residents of the State.
(2) NOTICE.--
(A) IN GENERAL.--Before filing an action under paragraph (1), the attorney general of the State involved shall provide to the Commission--
(i) written notice of that action; and
(ii) a copy of the complaint for that action.
(B) EXEMPTION.--Subparagraph (A) shall not apply with respect to the filing of an action by an attorney general of a State under this subsection, if the attorney general determines that it is not feasible to provide the notice described in that subparagraph before filing of the action. In such case, the attorney general of a State shall provide notice and a copy of the complaint to the Commission at the same time as the attorney general files the action.
(b) INTERVENTION.--
(1) IN GENERAL.--On receiving notice under subsection (a)(2), the Commission shall have the right to intervene in the action that is the subject of the notice.
(2) EFFECT OF INTERVENTION.--If the Commission intervenes in an action under subsection (a), it shall have the right--
(A) to be heard with respect to any matter that arises in that action; and
(B) to file a petition for appeal.
(c) CONSTRUCTION.--For purposes of bringing any civil action under subsection (a), nothing in this title shall be construed to prevent an attorney general of a State from exercising the powers conferred on the attorney general by the laws of that State to--
(1) conduct investigations;
(2) administer oaths or affirmations; or
(3) compel the attendance of witnesses or the production of documentary and other evidence.
(d) ACTIONS BY THE COMMISSION.--In any case in which an action is

instituted by or on behalf of the Commission for a violation of section 3, no State may, during the pendency of that action, institute an action under subsection (a) against any defendant named in the complaint in that action.

(e) VENUE.--Any action brought under subsection (a) may be brought in the district court of the United States that meets applicable requirements relating to venue under section 1391 of title 28, United States Code.

(f) SERVICE OF PROCESS.--In an action brought under subsection (a), process may be served in any district in which the defendant--

(1) is an inhabitant; or

(2) may be found.

## 15 USCA § 7805

### SEC. 6. PROTECTION OF EDUCATIONAL INSTITUTION.

(a) NOTICE REQUIRED.--Within 72 hours after entering into an agency contract or before the next athletic event in which the student athlete may participate, whichever occurs first, the athlete agent and the student athlete shall each inform the athletic director of the educational institution at which the student athlete is enrolled, or other individual responsible for athletic programs at such educational institution, that the student athlete has entered into an agency contract, and the athlete agent shall provide the athletic director with notice in writing of such a contract.

(b) CIVIL REMEDY.--

(1) IN GENERAL.--An educational institution has a right of action against an athlete agent for damages caused by a violation of this Act.

(2) DAMAGES.--Damages of an educational institution may include and are limited to actual losses and expenses incurred because, as a result of the conduct of the athlete agent, the educational institution was injured by a violation of this Act or was penalized, disqualified, or suspended from participation in athletics by a national association for the promotion and regulation of athletics, by an athletic conference, or by reasonable self-imposed disciplinary action taken to mitigate actions likely to be imposed by such an association or conference.

(3) COSTS AND ATTORNEYS FEES.--In an action taken under this section, the court may award to the prevailing party costs and reasonable attorneys fees.

(4) EFFECT ON OTHER RIGHTS, REMEDIES AND DEFENSES.--This section does not restrict the rights, remedies, or defenses of any person under law or equity.

SEC. 7. LIMITATION.

Nothing in this Act shall be construed to prohibit an individual from seeking any remedies available under existing Federal or State law or equity.

15 USCA § 7807

SEC. 8. SENSE OF CONGRESS.

It is the sense of Congress that States should enact the Uniform Athlete Agents Act of 2000 drafted by the National Conference of Commissioners on Uniform State Laws, to protect student athletes and the integrity of amateur sports from unscrupulous sports agents. In particular, it is the sense of Congress that States should enact the provisions relating to the registration of sports agents, the required form of contract, the right of the student athlete to cancel an agency contract, the disclosure requirements relating to record maintenance, reporting, renewal, notice, warning, and security, and the provisions for reciprocity among the States.

**Notes & Questions**

1. What acts does SPARTA prohibit?

2. Identify the actions that SPARTA requires from agents.

3. What is the role of the State Attorneys General in the enforcement of SPARTA? What is the role of the FTC?

4. Explain the import of the warning required in the agency contract.

5. How would SPARTA's prohibitions apply to the conduct of Walters and Bloom?

# GOING FOR THE GOLD: THE REPRESENTATION OF OLYMPIC ATHLETES

Sara Lee Keller-Smith and Sherri A. Affrunti
3 Villanova Sports & Ent. L.J. 443 (1996).

## I. Introduction

The International Olympic Committee (IOC) recently amended its rules regarding "amateur" status, thereby allowing "professional" athletes to compete in Olympic competition. The IOC rule change allows each International Federation (IF) and National Governing Body (NGB) to establish its own rules regarding "professional" athlete participation in national and international competitions, provided that the IF and NGB rules are not more expansive than those of the IOC. The amended IOC rule has resulted in the elimination of the strict "amateur" competition that many individuals have come to associate with the Olympic Games and has opened the door for increased attorney-agent representation of Olympic competitors, as unique opportunities in product endorsement, performance and appearance income become available for these athletes.

This Article presents an overview of the issues which will confront an attorney who undertakes the representation of an Olympic athlete. Part II defines "amateur" athlete, discussing the concept in both its historical and modern sense. Part II also analyzes the recent IOC rule change which now allows professional athletes to compete as "eligible athletes" in the Olympics. Part III examines the unique attorney-client relationship which is formed when an attorney undertakes to represent an Olympic athlete and explores the ethical obligations and dilemmas which arise from that relationship. Part IV provides practical suggestions for a representation agreement for an Olympic athlete. Part V concludes that only the well-informed and conscientious attorney should undertake the representation of an Olympic athlete.

## II. Background: What is an Amateur?

### A. Greece: The Original Olympics

Mention the ancient Olympics and you might find that many individuals are awed by the "Olympic ideal," believing that in ancient

Athens, if nowhere else, money and prizes did not motivate the athletes.[1] Indeed, many people tend to think that the notion "[it] is not to win, but to take part" is rooted in antiquity-that such a viewpoint was established by the Greeks in the creation of the very first Olympic Games. However, this is a misconception. For the Greek Olympic athletes, the converse was true. "Taking part and winning were the ancient goal." Even to get second place, therefore, was a disgrace for the Greeks. True "amateurs," as we define the term today, did not exist.

Although many people believe that the concept of the "amateur athlete" originated in ancient Greece, the term had no place in Greek life. In ancient Greece, Olympic victors could expect to be substantially rewarded for their victory. Although the only prize awarded to an athlete at the ancient Olympics was a crown made from the branches of wild olive, Olympic victors were substantially rewarded by their city-states upon their return home from the Games. The Greeks believed that an Olympic victory was owed to the favor and approval of the gods of both the athlete and his city. The victory ensured honor, glory, fame and rewards. In the world of ancient Greece, therefore, "'athlete' literally meant, and always meant, 'competitor for a prize.'"

B. The Modern Olympic Movement: The Seeds of "Amateurism" Planted

In 1892, a Frenchman named Baron de Coubertin began a campaign to revise the Olympic Games. The spirit of the international competition which Coubertin established ideologically followed the ancient Greek practice--allowing men of all countries to temporarily set aside their differences in an effort to recognize, and perhaps promote, man's physical and mental prowess, democratic equality and human brotherhood. In actuality, the modern movement conformed more to the ideals of earlier British competitions, rather than to the ideals of the ancient Olympics. Like the British, Coubertin, and several of his followers, sought to establish an elitist system of athletic competition by prohibiting Olympic athletes from receiving remuneration of any kind. These rules limited the economic opportunities available to modern Olympians and, for many years, prevented potential Olympic athletes who did not have funding and support from competing.

---

[1] This belief is far from correct, for the idea that an athlete could not earn money from competitions was foreign to the Greeks, particularly as Olympic victories became more important to the city-states as a way of bringing prestige to their city. See Waldo E. Sweet, Sport and Recreation in Ancient Greece 121 (1987).

## C. The Olympics Today

Today, the IOC and several of its associated organizations have abandoned Coubertin's original definition of amateurism and have returned to the true ancient practice which permitted Olympic athletes to be rewarded in their athletic endeavors. As a result of this rule change enacted by the IOC and adopted by most of the IFs and NGBs, Olympic contenders may now receive remuneration while training and competing as "eligible" Olympic athletes. This modification of the century old ban on the receipt of money by "eligible" athletes has resulted in tremendous economic opportunities for Olympic athletes. Today, unlike the past, Olympic athletes successfully compete with professional athletes for endorsements and sponsorship opportunities. Further, Olympic athletes now have the chance to capitalize on their athletic ability through participation in recently developed, NGB sanctioned, pay-for-participation events which compensate the athlete for his or her appearance in sports such as skating, gymnastics, soccer and track. Furthermore, unlike the original IOC definition for eligibility, today's eligibility code allows professional athletes, who were formerly banned from the Olympic Games, to enter Olympic competition, thereby increasing the demands on these athletes and furthering the commercialization surrounding the Games.

Past prohibitions on the ability of Olympic athletes to receive any money other than limited approved funds for living expenses or training costs have been removed in many Olympic sports, thereby allowing Olympic athletes to legitimately earn money while competing. Some Olympic athletes now enjoy economic opportunities and lifestyle changes which they were previously forced to avoid. Unlike prior years, many Olympic athletes may now openly endorse products and services, serve as coaches for other organizations, or compete in non-Olympic events for cash rewards. Because of this ability, as well as the growing commercialism surrounding the Olympic Games due to the popularity of athletics with the public, Olympic athletes today, like professional athletes, need advisors for tax planning, estate planning, investment advice and contract negotiations.

The advent of money promotions and the availability of Olympic athletes as product and service spokespersons, coaches and non-Olympic competitors, therefore, has caused the representation of Olympic athletes to become big business for attorneys and non-attorneys alike. Competent attorneys may now choose to represent these Olympic athletes, due to the expanse of sports law and the trend toward attorney-agents rather than non-attorney agents in the sports arena.

### III. Ethical Considerations

Notwithstanding the lack of regulation by the IOC, IFs, NGBs and other Olympic organizations,[2] an attorney representing an Olympic athlete, unlike an agent,[3] is subject to the applicable rules of professional conduct enacted by his or her licensing state. Ethical considerations apply to the representation of an athlete whether the representing attorney acts as the athlete's attorney or agent. Different from an agent, an attorney must always zealously represent the interests of the client-athlete and heed the utmost ethical standards in his or her actions.

#### A. The Model Rules of Professional Conduct Background

On August 2, 1983 the American Bar Association House of Delegates adopted the Model Rules of Professional Conduct (Model Rules). These Model Rules, as enacted, in whole or part, by most state bar associations or disciplinary boards set forth the rules of reason under which an attorney should practice. An attorney failing to abide by these Model Rules may be subject to state disciplinary action and loss of licensure. "Some of the Rules are imperatives, cast in terms of 'shall' or 'shall not' . . . others, generally cast in the term of 'may' or 'should,' are permissive and define areas under the Rules in which the lawyer has professional discretion."

---

[2] Unlike the National Football League Players Association (NFLPA), National Basketball Players Association (NBPA), Major League Baseball Players Association (MLBPA) and National Hockey League Players Association (NHLPA), neither the IOC, the IFs, nor the NGBs regulate or register agents representing Olympic athletes. The NFLPA, NBPA, NLBPA and NHLPA require player agents to execute standard representation agreements. See NFLPA Standard Representation Agreement between Contract Advisor and Player and NBPA Standard Player Agent Contract, reprinted in 2 Law of Professional and Amateur Sports (Gary A. Uberstine ed., 1994). The regulations of these Player Associations impose strict limitations on fees, regulate who can become player agents, and provide arbitration mechanisms for resolution of conflicts. See generally NBPA Regs, reprinted in 2 Law of Professional and Amateur Sports (Gary A. Uberstine ed., 1994).

[3] The Restatement of Agency defines an agent as "one who acts for or in the place of another by authority from him" or "a person who represents another in contractual negotiations," or "a business representative whose function is to bring about, modify, effect ... contractual obligations between the principal and third persons." Restatement (Second) of Agency s 1 (1958).

B. The Specific Rules of Professional Conduct to Consider in the Attorney/Agent-Client Relationship

The following discussion is a sampling of the Model Rules as they may apply to the attorney as agent (attorney-agent) scenario. Any attorney-agent representing an Olympic athlete should consult the applicable rules of conduct adopted by his or her state of licensure. Other than existing state statutes regulating "agents," these rules of conduct provide the only guide for the attorney-agent in determining his or her course of conduct in the representation of the Olympic athlete.

### 1. Scope of Representation

The Olympic athlete, with the assistance of the attorney-agent, should set the scope of the attorney's representation at the time the attorney is initially retained. It is essential for both the attorney-agent and the Olympic athlete to clearly understand the terms of the engagement. These terms should be reduced to a written agreement setting forth the specific services to be provided by the attorney-agent and the fees for such services. Thereafter, the attorney-agent is obligated not to exceed the boundaries of the engagement without the Olympic athlete's consent. If another professional is retained to assist in the Olympic athlete's representation, it is imperative that the agreement spell out who is responsible for their expenses and how they will be paid.

### 2. Competence

An attorney is obligated to provide his or her client with competent representation. For an attorney representing an Olympic athlete, competent representation includes knowledge and understanding of the rules and regulations governing the Olympic athlete's sport, especially the rules dealing with the athlete's eligibility. Hence, this representation will include a working knowledge of the rules and regulations of the Olympic athlete's NGB and IF, the IOC and possibly, the NCAA. Moreover, an attorney-agent representing an Olympic athlete who wishes to capitalize on his or her athletic ability through commercial endorsements and media contracts owes the Olympic athlete the skill and knowledge necessary to competently handle these negotiations. Such endorsements and contracts involve complex areas of knowledge, and the complexity may increase when an Olympic athlete is involved. Competence in the areas of endorsements and media contracts may depend on knowledge of other deals, knowledge of general industry standards and possibly an awareness of other regulations binding the Olympic athlete's conduct. Because the attorney-agent may not possess the requisite familiarity with these types of commercial transactions, it may be necessary for the attorney to seek the assistance of an expert to insure that competent counsel is given.

### 3. Diligence

Upon undertaking to represent an Olympic athlete, the attorney-agent should proceed with commitment and dedication to the Olympic athlete. The attorney-agent must, therefore, render his or her professional services diligently and promptly. Since most Olympic athletes have a small window of opportunity in which to benefit from their athletic prowess, it is important not to delay the pursuit of commercial opportunities for that athlete. Any delay may result in the loss of thousands of dollars for the Olympic athlete and a malpractice claim against the attorney-agent.

### 4. Communication

The representation of an Olympic athlete is a personal relationship, in which the attorney-agent's most important role is as a communicator. Most Olympic athletes will consume themselves with training and preparation for the Olympic Games and will not spend the necessary time and energy to keep informed of daily developments in commercial and endorsement opportunities or other financial matters. The attorney-agent must routinely advise an Olympic athlete of the status of all affairs in which the attorney represents the athlete. Such advice is particularly important when the Olympic athlete is seeking commercial opportunities. Even when the Olympic athlete delegates authority to the attorney-agent to negotiate endorsement or other contracts, the attorney-agent must inform the Olympic athlete of any and all offers, inquiries and developments as they arise. In conveying the information, the attorney-agent should explain the opportunity or development to the Olympic athlete in as much detail as necessary to fully inform the athlete of his or her options. The attorney-agent must advise the Olympic athlete of all considerations which will help the athlete make a reasonable decision whether to accept or reject the offer. An attorney-agent may not withhold information which serves his or her own interest or convenience.

### 5. Effective Advising

The attorney-agent relationship defies normal legal boundaries. An attorney-agent's role when representing an Olympic athlete may include giving advice to the Olympic athlete in areas ranging from contract pricing to costume design.[4] The advice needed may not require legal research or interpretation. The attorney-agent is required to draw upon personal knowledge and experience and to exercise independent professional judgment in counseling the client, even if these consultations do not require expert legal opinion. In all circumstances, the attorney-agent's advice should be direct and honest.

## 6. Confidentiality of Information

Any non-public information revealed to an attorney-agent representing an Olympic athlete shall not be revealed to any other person without the consent of the athlete. Any business relationship involves a great probability of receiving information that may be of interest to another client, or to other individuals. Confidentiality of the information is crucial to the success and longevity of the relationship between the attorney-agent and the Olympic athlete.

## 7. Safekeeping Property

If the attorney-agent is to handle the Olympic athlete's finances, the authorized use of the Olympic athlete's funds should be specifically described to the Olympic athlete before the services are rendered. Further, records of any and all transactions on behalf of the Olympic athlete should be accurately kept. If an attorney-agent holds or receives property from an Olympic athlete whom he or she represents, such property must be segregated and appropriately safeguarded. In an athlete-agent context, for example, the attorney-agent often receives payments on behalf of his or her client, particularly from the Olympic athlete's endorsement contracts; such

---

[4] Surprisingly, an Olympic contender's costume may spurn controversy if other individuals, whether involved in the Games or not, find the costume shocking. See, e.g., Mike Downey, Winter Olympics: Notebook, L.A. Times, Feb. 10, 1994, at 7 (noting that Katarina Witt's costumes were criticized as "unduly provocative"); David Dykstra, For a Short Program, a Short Costume, L.A. Times, Mar. 5, 1988, at 3 (commenting that "[a]fter viewing Katarina Witt's short program and her even shorter costume, I can state that brevity is the soul of Witt"); Mike Kupper, Winter Olympics Notes Decision to Give Gault Yet Another Chance Renews Controversy, L.A. Times, Feb. 25, 1988, at 8 (declaring that "Katarina Witt may attract less attention for her performance in ... figure skating short program for what she is wearing-or what she isn't wearing. Her costume leaves little to the imagination" and discussing Witt's reaction to costume controversy); see also Randy Harvey, For Trenary, It Figures to Be a Skater's Waltz, L.A. Times, Feb. 8, 1989, at 1 (noting ISU passed edict eliminating unitards, like that worn by Debbie Thomas; plunging necklines, like those composing Katarina Witt's costumes and non-covering bottoms, like those pageanted by Jill Trenary).

funds must not be commingled with funds of the attorney-agent and shall be kept separate until distribution and an accounting is provided. Upon receipt of funds the attorney-agent must notify the Olympic athlete immediately and promptly deliver to the athlete those funds which the athlete is entitled to receive. The failure to safeguard an Olympic athlete's property is a clear violation of the attorney-agent's fiduciary duty.

## 8. Conflict of Interest-General Rule

An attorney-agent must not represent an Olympic athlete if that representation is directly adverse to the representation of any other client, or if that representation will constrain the attorney's duties to another client, unless the attorney-agent reasonably believes the representation will not adversely affect the representation of the other client. Even if the attorney-agent believes that the dual representation will not adversely affect the Olympic athlete and the other client, both the athlete and the other party must be informed of the potential for conflicted interests and both must consent to the dual representation after consultation despite this knowledge.

The potential for conflict in the representation of an Olympic athlete exists in several instances. For example, an attorney-agent may be requested to represent the athlete, the coach and the athlete's parents. Similarly, a conflict may arise if the attorney-agent chooses to represent more than one Olympic athlete who performs in the same sport.[5] The attorney-agent may also have an opportunity to represent the Olympic athlete's gym or club. Despite any initial appearances that these aforementioned parties may have similar interests, conflicts may still arise after representation has begun. The attorney-agent must make an initial evaluation of the feasibility of any such dual representation, based upon his or her personal knowledge at the moment that the dual-representation is requested and what he or she reasonably

---

[5] Representing more than one Olympic athlete who compete in one sport may lead to conflicts, for example, when the attorney-agent is negotiating endorsement contracts. If a particular corporation is not seeking a specific Olympic athlete, but rather is simply looking for any athlete from a particular sport to endorse its product, an attorney-agent who represents more than one athlete in that sport will have difficulty zealously representing each athlete's interests. In such a case, the attorney-agent may be forced to withdraw from the representation of both athletes. See Model Rules, supra note 63, Rule 1.7. Further, if questions arise concerning the scoring of an event when one client-athlete loses the gold medal but the other client-athlete wins, the attorney-agent may be forced to withdraw from representing either athlete. Id. Even if real conflicts of interest do not arise, the attorney-agent may experience difficulty in representing more than one Olympic athlete if an athlete perceives that another athlete is being favored. Id.

believes will happen in the future. If the attorney-agent is disqualified from representing the Olympic athlete due to a conflict of interest, the attorney-agent's firm may also be disqualified.

### 9. Conflict of Interest-Prohibited Transactions

An attorney-agent may "not enter into a business transaction with [an Olympic athlete] or knowingly acquire an ownership, possessory, security or other pecuniary interest adverse to [that athlete] unless" the transaction is fair and reasonable; the athlete is fully advised of the ramifications of the transaction; the athlete has been given the opportunity to obtain independent counsel; and the athlete has consented in writing. Often the representation of Olympic athletes includes the negotiation of business transactions in which the attorney-agent may participate either in lieu of fees or otherwise. These business transactions include promoting events, selling book rights or lining up sponsors. In any of these circumstances, it is imperative that the attorney-agent fully disclose to the Olympic athlete any and all remuneration the attorney-agent will receive from any source, together with other terms and conditions of the proposed transaction.

### 10. Representation of Minor Athletes

An attorney-agent's obligation to properly advise and consult with his or her Olympic client-athlete is not altered by the Olympic athlete's disability, including his or her minority status. Many successful Olympic athletes are minors, in particular female gymnasts and figure skaters. Representing these Olympic athletes may present special problems not faced when representing Olympic athletes who are of majority. At all times, the attorney-agent must insure that the Olympic athlete's wishes, and not those of the parents or coaches, are followed-even if that Olympic athlete is a minor.

When undertaking the representation of a minor athlete, the attorney-agent must be cognizant that the law provides special protection for a minor athlete. For instance, a minor, upon coming of the age of majority, may disaffirm a contract possibly without any requirement of restitution.[6] The attorney-agent must beware of this possibility when negotiating endorsements and appearances for the athlete. The attorney-agent must also

---

[6] Restatement (Second) of Contracts s 14 cmt. C (1981); see also Restatement (Second) of Agency s 20 (1958) ("The contract of an infant to employ an agent is voidable by him, as is any contract made for him by such agent ...."). Some states have altered this by statute. See, e.g., Cal. Family Code s 6712 (West 1994); Fla. Stat. Ann. s 743.08.3(a) (West 1986 & Supp. 1996); N.Y. Arts & Cult. Aff. Law s 35.03.1 (McKinney 1996).

beware of state statutes which may nullify contracts signed by parents or guardians on behalf of the minor without court approval. Moreover, the attorney-agent must take preventive measures to ensure that capital earned by the minor Olympic athlete is preserved for his or her future use.

## 11. Fees

A prominent distinction between attorney-agents and non-attorney-agents in the representation of Olympic athletes is the manner in which their fees are determined. Agents' fees are usually charged based on a percentage of the income generated for the athlete, unless statutory restrictions prohibit such fee schedules.[7] Attorney-agents, on the other hand, generally bill on an hourly or flat fee basis. Unlike agents who often have no restraints prohibiting methods of billing and fees unless a state statute exists specifically imposing such restraints or a regulatory body for the sport imposes an internal regulation prohibiting certain billing methods, attorney-agents are constrained by the Model Rules to ensure their fees are reasonable. Whether a fee charged to an Olympic client-athlete is reasonable will vary with the circumstances and is generally determined by examining several factors, including the time and effort involved, the novelty of the issue, the experience and knowledge of the attorney, and the results obtained. An attorney-agent may negotiate a contingent fee arrangement with the Olympic athlete, provided the fee is reasonable by the aforementioned standards. No matter what method of billing the Olympic athlete selects, the attorney-agent must communicate the basis for the fees to the Olympic athlete "before or within a reasonable time after commencing representation."

## 12. Solicitation and Advertising

Unlike a non-attorney agent who may actively approach an athlete seeking to be retained to negotiate the athlete's commercial enterprises and maintain the athlete's finances, an attorney-agent may not actively solicit representation of or contractual arrangements with Olympic athletes. An attorney-agent desiring to market his or her abilities as an attorney-agent has only a limited ability to advertise his or her services through the public

---

[7] Most agents regularly charge between six and ten percent of athlete's earnings but...some agents have been successful in charging up to twenty-five percent of athlete's negotiated contract). Some states regulate the amount of percentage which an agent or an attorney acting as agent may legally receive from a client. See, e.g., Cal. Lab. Code s 1531(b) (West 1994) ("no athlete agent shall collect a fee in any calendar year which exceeds 10 percent of the total compensation"). Further, the NFL, NBA, NHL and MLB regulate rates agents can receive from professional athletes. See, e.g., NBPA Regulations (1995).

media.  The attorney-agent is therefore forced to rely on his or her ability and competence in the field, with the garnishing hope that the competent and successful representation of one Olympic athlete will lead to the representation of other Olympic athletes.  Despite the limited ability to advertise and the need to depend on his or her own reputation in order to expand the number of Olympic athlete-clients one individual represents, an attorney-agent should never pay any fees or remuneration to someone who recommends the attorney to an Olympic athlete.  Although it may be tempting for the attorney-agent to offer an inducement to a coach or parent in order to obtain an Olympic athlete as a client, particularly when those coaches or parents have personal contact with other competing athletes, doing so is clearly prohibited by the Model Rules.

## IV. The Representation Agreement

In any circumstance, an attorney-agent initiating a relationship with a new client would be foolish to do so without a written representation agreement. The representation agreement between an Olympic athlete and an attorney-agent-whether the attorney is acting also as agent or simply as legal counsel-requires special consideration.  Unlike the typical fee letter published by most law firms, an agreement with an Olympic athlete must anticipate situations not usually encountered in other attorney-client relationships.  The nuances peculiar to an attorney-agent's representation of an Olympic athlete should be given special consideration when drafting the representation agreement.

### A. Identifying the Parties

Agreements characteristically begin with a brief recital describing the parties to the agreement.  The drafting of such a recital presumes that the drafter knows the identity of the parties. This may not be the case. While the identity of the athlete is known, that person may not have the legal capacity to contract.[8] In certain jurisdictions, a guardianship proceeding may be required to designate the proper and lawful contracting party.  The penalties for failing to consider the ramifications of improper execution are severe.

---

[8] If the Olympic athlete is a minor, he or she cannot lawfully be bound to a contract signed by them prior to their age of majority. The Restatement of Contracts Section 12, Capacity to Contract, provides that, "[n]o one can be bound by contract who has not legal capacity...." Restatement (Second) of Contracts s 12 (1981).  The Restatement of Contracts also states, in Section 14, Infants, that, "[u]nless statute provides otherwise, a natural person has the capacity to incur only voidable contractual duties until the beginning of the day before the person's eighteenth birthday." Id. at s 14.

464

Having identified the proper contracting party for the athlete is only half of the answer. Who contracts for the attorney-agent? If an attorney is a solo practitioner, this question is easily resolved. However, many attorneys practice in firms with fees for legal representation being paid to the firm. Since the firm receives the fees and probably establishes the parameter for fees and expenses charged to the Olympic athlete, the firm should be a party to the agreement.

As a practical matter, the Olympic athlete should insist that the attorney-agent(s) actually providing the representation also be a party to the agreement. The attorney-athlete relationship is a personal one and the agreement should recognize the reliance and confidence being placed by the Olympic athlete on those selected to actually perform the services.

B. Identifying the Scope of the Representation

The representation agreement should clearly define the services to be provided by the attorney to the athlete. These services may range from the negotiation and documentation of a specific contract to the procurement of income producing opportunities. The description of the services to be provided should not be general in nature. It could be disastrous for an attorney to agree to generally represent an athlete in all matters related to their Olympic career. For example, most attorneys are ill-equipped to handle the public relations aspects of an Olympic athlete. The economics of a law firm do not favorably align with the time-consuming task of soliciting offers for an athlete and most athletes do not have the economic resources to pay for these services on an hourly basis.

The services provided by an attorney-agent are best limited to the following:

i. providing advice regarding (but not actively soliciting) income producing opportunities offered to the athlete;
ii. negotiating, documenting and closing contracts relating to such offers;
iii. representing the athlete in disputes before the applicable NGB, the IOC or other regulatory bodies having jurisdiction over the athlete; and
iv. assisting in the collection and enforcement of the athlete's contracts.

Firms with diverse expertise may also provide the athlete with tax planning advice including counseling in the areas of pension and profit sharing plans and estate planning. Any attorney lacking specific expertise in these areas should avoid agreeing to provide such services, unless such advice is limited to assisting the athlete in selecting other professionals to provide these services.

## C. Providing for Special Circumstances

The representation agreement should clearly define the rights and responsibilities of each party thereto. It should describe the services to be performed and the method and timing for payments thereunder. The agreement should include a termination provision and restrict assignability by both parties. Its most important characteristics should be clarity and completeness.

### 1. Decision Making; Ability to Bind

The representation agreement should clearly acknowledge that the attorney-agent is not authorized to make decisions for the Olympic athlete. The representation agreement should declare that the attorney-agent's lack of authority to make decisions for the Olympic athlete encompasses a lack of authority for the attorney-agent to bind the Olympic athlete to any contract. This provision protects both parties from and against any misunderstanding, by requiring the Olympic athlete to make all final decisions and to sign all agreements. To the extent an Olympic athlete intends to protect his or her eligibility under the rules of the NCAA, the attorney-agent should take care to advise the athlete about any possible violation of those rules. Any decision regarding such eligibility must be made by the Olympic athlete.

### 2. Handling the Athlete's Personal Finances

The attorney-agent may agree to handle the personal finances of the Olympic athlete. The cost to the Olympic athlete for an attorney-agent to handle his or her personal finances may outweigh the benefit. Unless this task can be assigned to a loyal and trustworthy assistant, it is doubtful that an Olympic athlete can afford to pay an attorney for these services on an hourly rate. This is one area that an attorney-agent may choose to recommend another professional to provide the service. If the attorney-agent is not responsible for the day to day finances of the athlete, the representation agreement should include instructions for the delivery of funds received by the attorney-agent on behalf of the Olympic athlete.

### 3. Exclusivity

An Olympic athlete may request that the attorney-agent refrain from the representation of any other Olympic athlete competing in the same sport.

Similarly, the attorney-agent may desire that he or she act as the exclusive representative of the Olympic athlete. These types of exclusivity clauses should be included in the representation agreement.

## 4. Assignability

Rights and obligations existing under a contract may be assigned unless precluded by contract. The representation agreement should clearly preclude the right of either party to assign their respective rights and obligations thereunder.

## 5. Arbitration

The representation agreement may provide a mechanism for handling disputes between the attorney-agent and the Olympic athlete. The most common form of dispute resolution provision is an arbitration clause. Whether to include an arbitration provision is a difficult decision. Arbitration is generally a quicker and less costly method of dispute resolution. It is also a proceeding more likely to be swayed by the personal feelings and views of the arbitrators.

## 6. Choice of Law

The selection of the state law governing the interpretation of the agreement is important. A court is not bound by a choice of governing law if the facts involved require the application of another state's laws. Choice of law rules may require application of state laws which are not favorable to the terms of the agreement.

## 7. Compensation

The method of compensating the attorney-agent may vary depending upon the types of services the attorney has agreed to perform. Typically, attorney-agents are compensated at an hourly rate for the time spent on completing the task. Alternative forms of compensation may be considered. Contingent fee arrangements have long been the method of compensating agents. The Olympic athlete only pays in these arrangements if income is produced. A contingent arrangement is permitted by the Rules, but is only appropriate if the attorney-agent has agreed to procure income producing opportunities for the Olympic athlete.

An attorney-agent may also agree to a combination fee arrangement by utilizing an hourly rate mechanism with an ultimate fee cap for a particular task. Fixed fees are slowly becoming a common denominator in the marketing of legal services. By fixing a cap the Olympic athlete has the assurance of knowing that the legal fees incurred will not exceed the agreed-upon amount.

Compensation may also include reimbursement of expenses. Many law firms charge their clients for telephone calls, facsimiles, copying and other ancillary services. The representation agreement must state whether the expenses incurred by the attorney-agent are included or excluded from his or her fee. If specific expenses are to be charged separately, they should be specifically recited in the agreement. Regardless of the method chosen for compensation, the attorney-agent's fee must be reasonable.

### 8. Terminating the Representation Agreement

The circumstances under which either party may terminate the representation agreement must be set forth in the agreement. The window of opportunity available to an Olympic athlete is usually short, and therefore a failed agency relationship may impact the ability of both parties to maximize their earnings realized from their relationship.

The agreement should be terminable by the Olympic athlete if the attorney-agent (a) breaches his or her duties under the agreement and fails to remedy that breach upon reasonable notice, (b) commits fraud, (c) dies, or (d) is no longer employed by the firm that is the party to the agreement. It is important that the agreement not immediately terminate on the occurrence of any of these events. The Olympic athlete should have the right to survey the situation and determine whether or not the agreement should terminate. Due to the innate conflict of interest, this decision should be made by the Olympic athlete with the assistance of independent counsel.

The attorney-agent may desire to terminate the agreement if the Olympic athlete is no longer able to compete, whether due to injury or ineligibility. This is especially appropriate if the attorney-agent has agreed to procure opportunities for the Olympic athlete which no longer exist or if the agreement contains a provision preventing the attorney from representing other Olympic athletes in the same sport.

Due to the personal nature of this relationship, both parties should also have the right to end their relationship upon giving reasonable notice to the other party. A failed attorney-athlete relationship is an invitation to litigation and should be avoided at all cost. Upon termination, the attorney-agent should be compensated for work completed and expenses incurred, if they are the responsibility of the Olympic athlete. If the attorney-agent is compensated on a percentage of income produced, he or she should be entitled to receive a post-termination percentage of any income contracted for by the Olympic athlete prior to the date of termination.

## V. Conclusion

The representation of an Olympic athlete is an exciting yet danger filled exploit. To provide effective representation to an Olympic athlete, the attorney-agent must be cognizant of the laws of the applicable states, including the laws governing minors and agents, and the rules and regulations of the IOC, the USOC, the applicable NGB and its international affiliate, and the NCAA. Moreover, a general understanding of commercial endorsements, television contracts and media relations is crucial to the representation.

The inexperienced and ignorant attorney-agent may subject himself to a plethora of problems if he or she fails to understand the ramifications of his or her relationship with the Olympic athlete. Unlike representing a professional football or baseball player, there is no players' association with a strict set of rules and regulations to guide the attorney-agent in the representation of an Olympic athlete. Until the IOC, the USOC or the NGBs enact regulations legislating the representation of the Olympic athlete by third parties, the attorney-agent is left to fend for himself. Failure to heed the Rules and to identify, research and understand the myriad...issues endemic to such representation will almost certainly lead to a failed attorney-client relationship, possible disciplinary action and, at worst, disbarment.

## Notes & Questions

1. What are the special or unique considerations that an agent for an Olympic athlete must take into account? In other words, explain how representation of an Olympic athlete might differ from representation of a professional football, basketball, or baseball player.

2. In addition to the special considerations regarding the capacity to contract, there are other legal problems associated with representing minor athletes (typically figure skaters and gymnasts). For example what problems do you think that you might encounter in arranging production of a television commercial? Do you suppose, for example, that there are state child labor laws that affect the hours that a minor can work on the set? Do you suppose

that there are state laws regarding providing tutoring in the event that the minor has to miss school for training or taping commercial advertisements?

***Further Reading on Agency:***

Walter T. Champion, *Attorneys Qua Sports Agents: An Ethical Conundrum*, 7 MARQ. SPORTS L.J. 349 (1997).

Phillip Closius, *Hell Hath No Fury Like a Fan Scorned: State Regulation of Sports Agents*, 30 U. TOL. L. REV. 511 (1999).

Robert N. Davis, *Exploring the Contours of Agent Regulation: The Uniform Athlete Agents Act*, 8 VILL. SPORTS & ENT. L.J. 1 (2001).

W. Jack Grosse, *The Regulation, Control, and Protection of Athlete Agents*, 19 N. KY. L. REV. 49 (1991).

Jan Stiglitz, *NCAA Based Agent Regulation, Who are We Protecting*, 67 N.D. L. REV. 215 (1991).

John C. Weistart & Cym H. Lowell, Law of Sports, §3.17-3.19 (Bobbs-Merrill Company, Inc., 1979.

# Chapter 11

## Intellectual Property

A significant number of legal concerns in today's sports marketplace relate to intellectual property. Broadcast rights and copyrights for sporting events form the bases for multimillion dollar industries. The growth of sports-exclusive television such as ESPN has been phenomenal (*i.e.,* ESPN 2, ESPN-News, ESPNU, CSTV, etc.). The cases in this chapter introduce several key concepts and questions about copyright, misappropriation, trademark law, and the right of publicity. *Pittsburgh Athletic* and *Motorola* introduce the fundamental rules regarding Copyright and Misappropriation. *Monster Communications* expands our understanding of Copyright Law and sheds light on one of the most intriguing aspects of copyright, fair use.

The *Wizards* case presents a Trademark primer against a background of facts which are far from uncommon in the modern world of sports where franchises relocate and change their names with increasing regularity (the most recent example being the transformation of the Montreal Expos to the Washington Nationals). *O'Brien* offers an historical perspective on the important right of publicity. And *Abdul-Jabbar* exemplifies a more mature application of the principles first developed in the *O'Brien* dissent, and presents a fairly matter-of-fact summary of the current status of the law.

## Pittsburgh Athletic Co. v. KQV Broadcasting
24 F.Supp. 490 (1938)
District Court, W.D. Pennsylvania

SCHOONMAKER, District Judge.

This is an action in equity in which plaintiffs ask for a preliminary injunction to restrain defendant from broadcasting play-by-play reports and descriptions of baseball games played by the "'Pirates," a professional baseball team owned by Pittsburgh Athletic Company, both at its home baseball park in Pittsburgh, known as "Forbes Field," and at baseball parks in other cities.

\*\*\*

Defendant disclaimed any intention to broadcast the news of any games played by the "Pirates" in cities other than Pittsburgh during the current season; and by affidavit filed in this case stated that no news had been broadcast by it of such "away" games since May 26, 1938.  For that reason there appears to be no such danger of imminent injury to the rights of the plaintiffs as to justify a preliminary injunction, so far as concern any games played by the "Pirates" in cities other than Pittsburgh.

As to the games played, and to be played at Forbes Field in Pittsburgh, defendant admits it has broadcast play-by-play news of the Pittsburgh games, and asserts its intention to continue so to do, averring it secures the news thus broadcast and to be broadcast by it in the future from observers whom it has stationed at vantage points outside Forbes Field who can see over the enclosure of that field and observe the plays as they are made.  It asserts it has a legal right to continue this practice.

The essential facts are not in dispute.  The question at issue is primarily a question of law.  Is the defendant within its legal rights in the practices thus pursued by it? The essential facts of the case may be briefly summarized as follows:

The plaintiff Pittsburgh Athletic Company owns a professional baseball team known as the "Pirates," and is a member of an association known as the "National League."  With the several teams of the members of the League, the "Pirates" play baseball both at its home field and at the home fields of the other members of the League in various cities. The home games are played at a baseball park known as "Forbes Field" which is enclosed by high fences and structures so that the public are admitted only to the Park to witness the games at Forbes Field by the payment of an admission ticket, which provides that the holder of the admission ticket agrees not to give out any news of the game while it is in progress.

The Pittsburgh Athletic Company has granted by written contract, for a valuable consideration, to General Mills, Inc., the exclusive right to broadcast, play-by-play, descriptions or accounts of the games played by the "Pirates" at this and other fields. The National Broadcasting Company, also for a valuable consideration, has contracted with General Mills, Inc., to broadcast by radio over stations KDKA and WWSW, play-by-play descriptions of these games. The Socony-Vacuum Oil Company has purchased for a valuable consideration a half interest in the contract of the General Mills, Inc.

The defendant operates at Pittsburgh a radio broadcasting station known as KQV, from which it has in the past broadcast by radio play-by-play descriptions of the games played by the "Pirates" at Pittsburgh, and asserts its intention to continue in so doing. The defendant secures the information which it broadcasts from its own paid observers whom it stations at vantage points outside Forbes Field on premises leased by defendant. These vantage points are so located that the defendant's observers can see over the enclosures the games as they are played in Forbes Field.

On this state of facts, we are of the opinion that the plaintiffs have presented a case which entitles them under the law to a preliminary injunction.

It is perfectly clear that the exclusive right to broadcast play-by-play descriptions of the games played by the "Pirates" at their home field rests in the plaintiffs, General Mills, Inc., and the Socony-Vacuum Oil Company under the contract with the Pittsburgh Athletic Company. That is a property right of the plaintiffs with which defendant is interfering when it broadcasts the play-by-play description of the ball games obtained by the observers on the outside of the enclosure.

The plaintiffs and the defendant are using baseball news as material for profit. The Athletic Company has, at great expense, acquired and maintains a baseball park, pays the players who participate in the game, and have, as we view it, a legitimate right to capitalize on the news value of their games by selling exclusive broadcasting rights to companies which value them as affording advertising mediums for their merchandise. This right the defendant interferes with when it uses its broadcasting facilities for giving out the identical news obtained by its paid observers stationed at points outside Forbes Field for the purpose of securing information which it cannot otherwise acquire. This, in our judgment, amounts to unfair competition, and is a violation of the property rights of the plaintiffs. For it is our opinion that the Pittsburgh Athletic Company, by reason of its creation of the game, its control of the park, and its restriction of the dissemination of news therefrom, has a property right in such news, and the right to control the use thereof for a reasonable time following the games.

The communication of news of the ball games by the Pittsburgh Athletic Company, or by its licensed news agencies, is not a general publication and does not destroy that right. This view is supported by the so-called "ticker cases"; *Board of Trade v. Christie Grain & Stock Co.*, 198 U.S. 236, 25 S.Ct. 637, 49 L.Ed. 1031....

On the unfair competition feature of the case, we rest our opinion on the case of *International News Service v. Associated Press*, 248 U.S. 215, 39 S.Ct. 68, 63 L.Ed. 211, 2 A.L.R. 293. In that case the court enjoined the International News Service from copying news from bulletin boards and early editions of Associated Press newspapers, and selling such news so long as it had commercial value to the Associated Press. The Supreme Court said:

> * * * Regarding the news, therefore, as but the material out of which both parties are seeking to make profits at the same time and in the same field, we hardly can fail to recognize that for this purpose, and as between them, it must be regarded as quasi property, irrespective of the rights of either as against the public.

> In order to sustain the jurisdiction of equity over the controversy, we need not affirm any general and absolute property in the news as such. The rule that a court of equity concerns itself only in the protection of property rights treats any civil right of a pecuniary nature as a property right...and the right to acquire property by honest labor or the conduct of a lawful business is as much entitled to protection as the right to guard property already acquired. * * *

And again at pages 239, 240, 39 S.Ct.at page 72:

> * * * The right of the purchaser of a single newspaper to spread knowledge of its contents gratuitously, for any legitimate purpose not unreasonably interfering with the complainant's right to make merchandise of it, may be admitted; but to transmit that news for commercial use, in competition with complainant-- which is what defendant has done and seeks to justify-- is a very different matter. * * *

***

Defendant contends it is not unfairly competing... because it obtains no compensation from a sponsor or otherwise from its baseball broadcasts. It concedes, however, that KQV seeks by its broadcast of news of baseball games to cultivate the good will of the public for its radio station. The fact that no revenue is obtained directly from the broadcast is not controlling, as these broadcasts are undoubtedly designed to aid in obtaining advertising business. [citations omitted].

Defendant seeks to justify its action on the ground that the information it receives from its observers stationed on its own property without trespassing on plaintiffs' property, may be lawfully broadcast by it. We cannot follow defendant's counsel in this contention for the reasons above stated. The cases cited by them we have carefully studied and are unable to accept as authority. In the Australian case, *Victoria Park Racing, etc., v. Taylor,* 37 New South Wales 322, where the information broadcast was obtained from a tower adjoining a race track, the court refused an injunction, because there was neither a trespass on plaintiff's race track, or a nuisance created by defendant.

The doctrine of unfair competition is not recognized under the English Common Law. Therefore this decision is not an authority.

In the case of *Sports and General Press Agency v. Our Dogs Publishing Company,* (1916) 2 K.B. 880, which involved the taking of photographs from a point outside the dog-shows grounds, is likewise a case for the application of English law. The question of unfair competition was not considered at all, and could not be recognized under the English law.

***

UNIVERSITY OF WINCHESTER LIBRARY

Conclusions of Law.

1. This Court has jurisdiction of this cause by reason of diversity of citizenship and the amount in controversy.

2. The right, title and interest in and to the baseball games played within the parks of members of the National League, including Pittsburgh, including the property right in, and the sole right of, disseminating or publishing or selling, or licensing the right to disseminate, news, reports, descriptions, or accounts of games played in such parks, during the playing thereof, is vested exclusively in such members.

3. The actions and threatened actions of the defendant constitute a direct and irreparable interference with, and an appropriation of, the plaintiffs' normal and legitimate business; and said action is calculated to, and does, result in the unjust enrichment of the defendant at the expense of the plaintiffs and each of them.

4. The defendant's unauthorized broadcasts of information concerning games played by the Pittsburgh team constitute unfair competition with the plaintiffs and each of them.

5. The defendant wrongfully deprives the plaintiffs and each of them of the just benefits of their labors and expenditures in respect of the baseball games and the public dissemination of news thereof as alleged in the complaint....

****

8. The plaintiffs have no adequate remedy at law.

9. The plaintiffs are entitled to and are hereby granted a preliminary injunction.

## Notes & Questions

1. According to the court, "It is perfectly clear that the exclusive right to broadcast play-by-play descriptions of the games played by the `Pirates' at their home field rests in the plaintiffs, General Mills, Inc., and the Socony-Vacuum Oil Company under the contract with the Pittsburgh Athletic Company." Why is that so perfectly clear? A play-by-play account is essentially a description of raw data - merely facts, *ie.,* who's on first, how many out, balls, strikes, etc. Facts are news, and news is generally deemed to be in the public domain.

2. The *NBA v. Motorola* case that follows explains the *International News Service* case in greater detail and depth.

### The National Basketball Association v. Motorola, Inc.
105 F.3d. 841 (1997)
United States Court of Appeals, Second Circuit

WINTER, Circuit Judge:

Motorola, Inc. and Sports Team Analysis and Tracking Systems ("STATS") appeal from a permanent injunction entered by Judge Preska. The injunction concerns a handheld pager sold by Motorola and marketed under the name "SportsTrax," which displays updated information of professional basketball games in progress. The injunction prohibits appellants, absent authorization from the National Basketball Association and NBA Properties, Inc. (collectively the "NBA"), from transmitting scores or other data about NBA games in progress via the pagers, STATS's site on America On-Line's computer dial-up service, or "any equivalent means."

The crux of the dispute concerns the extent to which a state law "hot-news" misappropriation claim based on *International News Service v. Associated Press,* 248 U.S. 215, 39 S.Ct. 68, 63 L.Ed. 211 (1918) ("INS "), survives preemption by the federal Copyright Act and whether the NBA's claim fits within the surviving INS-type claims. We hold that a narrow "hot-news" exception does survive preemption. However, we also hold that appellants' transmission of "real-time" NBA game scores and information tabulated from television and radio broadcasts of games in progress does not constitute a misappropriation of "hot news" that is the property of the NBA.

\*\*\*

## I. BACKGROUND

The facts are largely undisputed. Motorola manufactures and markets the SportsTrax paging device while STATS supplies the game information that is transmitted to the pagers. The product became available to the public in January 1996, at a retail price of about $200. SportsTrax's pager has an inch-and-a-half by inch-and-a-half screen and operates in four basic modes: "current," "statistics," "final scores" and "demonstration." It is the "current" mode that gives rise to the present dispute.[1] In that mode, SportsTrax displays the following information on NBA games in progress: (i) the teams playing; (ii) score changes; (iii) the team in possession of the ball; (iv) whether the team is in the free throw bonus;(v) the quarter of the game; and (vi) time remaining in the quarter. The information is updated every two to three minutes, with more frequent updates near the end of the first half and the end of the game. There is a lag of approximately two or three minutes between events in the game itself and when the information appears on the pager screen.

SportsTrax operation relies on a "data feed" supplied by STATS reporters who watch the games on television or listen to them on the radio. The reporters key into a personal computer changes in the score and other information such as successful and missed shots, fouls, and clock updates. The information is relayed by modem to STATS's host computer, which compiles, analyzes, and formats the data for retransmission. The information is then sent to a common carrier, which then sends it via satellite

---

[1] The other three SportsTrax modes involve information that is far less contemporaneous than that provided in the "current" mode. In the "statistics" mode, the SportsTrax pager displays a variety of player and team statistics, such as field goal shooting percentages and top scorers. However, these are calculated only at half-time and when the game is over. In the "final scores" mode, the unit displays final scores from the previous day's games. In the "demonstration" mode, the unit merely simulates information shown during a hypothetical NBA game. The core issue in the instant matter is the dissemination of continuously-updated real-time NBA information in the "current" mode. Because we conclude that the dissemination of such real-time information is lawful, the other modes need no further description or discussion.

478

to various local FM radio networks that in turn emit the signal received by the individual SportsTrax pagers.

Although the NBA's complaint concerned only the SportsTrax device, the NBA offered evidence at trial concerning STATS's America On-Line ("AOL") site. Starting in January, 1996, users who accessed STATS's AOL site, typically via a modem attached to a home computer, were provided with slightly more comprehensive and detailed real-time game information than is displayed on a SportsTrax pager. On the AOL site, game scores are updated every 15 seconds to a minute, and the player and team statistics are updated each minute. The district court's original decision and judgment...did not address the AOL site, because "NBA's complaint and the evidence proffered at trial were devoted largely to SportsTrax." [citation omitted]. Upon motion by the NBA, however, the district court amended its decision and judgment and enjoined use of the real-time game information on STATS's AOL site.... Because the record on appeal, the briefs of the parties, and oral argument primarily addressed the SportsTrax device, we similarly focus on that product. However, we regard the legal issues as identical with respect to both products, and our holding applies equally to SportsTrax and STATS's AOL site.

The NBA's complaint asserted six claims for relief: (i) state law unfair competition by misappropriation; (ii) false advertising under Section 43(a) of the Lanham Act, 15 U.S.C. § 1125(a); (iii) false representation of origin under Section 43(a) of the Lanham Act; (iv) state and common law unfair competition by false advertising and false designation of origin; (v) federal copyright infringement; and (vi) unlawful interception of communications under the Communications Act of 1934, 47 U.S.C. § 605. Motorola counterclaimed, alleging that the NBA unlawfully interfered with Motorola's contractual relations with four individual NBA teams that had agreed to sponsor and advertise SportsTrax.

The district court dismissed all of the NBA's claims except the first-- misappropriation under New York law. The court also dismissed Motorola's counterclaim. Finding Motorola and STATS liable for misappropriation, Judge Preska entered the permanent injunction, reserved the calculation of damages for subsequent proceedings, and stayed execution of the injunction pending appeal. Motorola and STATS appeal from the injunction, while NBA cross-appeals from the district court's dismissal of its Lanham Act false-advertising claim. The issues before us, therefore, are the state law misappropriation and Lanham Act claims.

## II. THE STATE LAW MISAPPROPRIATION CLAIM

### A. Summary of Ruling

Because our disposition of the state law misappropriation claim rests in large part on preemption by the Copyright Act, our discussion necessarily goes beyond the elements of a misappropriation claim under New York law, and a summary of our ruling here will perhaps render that discussion--or at least the need for it--more understandable.

The issues before us are ones that have arisen in various forms over the course of this century as technology has steadily increased the speed and quantity of information transmission. Today, individuals at home, at work, or elsewhere, can use a computer, pager, or other device to obtain highly selective kinds of information virtually at will. *International News Service v. Associated Press,* 248 U.S. 215, 39 S.Ct. 68, 63 L.Ed. 211 (1918) ( "INS ") was one of the first cases to address the issues raised by these technological advances, although the technology involved in that case was primitive by contemporary standards. INS involved two wire services, the Associated Press ("AP") and International News Service ("INS"), that transmitted newsstories by wire to member newspapers. Id. INS would lift factual stories from AP bulletins and send them by wire to INS papers. Id. at 231, 39 S.Ct. at 69-70. INS would also take factual stories from east coast AP papers and wire them to INS papers on the west coast that had yet to publish because of time differentials. Id. at 238, 39 S.Ct. at 72. The Supreme Court held that INS's conduct was a common-law misappropriation of AP's property. Id. at 242, 39 S.Ct. at 73-74.

With the advance of technology, radio stations began "live" broadcasts of events such as baseball games and operas, and various entrepreneurs began to use the transmissions of others in one way or another for their own profit. In response, New York courts created a body of misappropriation law, loosely based on INS, that sought to apply ethical standards to the use by one party of another's transmissions of events.

Federal copyright law played little active role in this area until 1976. Before then, it appears to have been the general understanding--there being no caselaw of consequence--that live events such as baseball games were not copyrightable. Moreover, doubt existed even as to whether a recorded broadcast or videotape of such an event was copyrightable. In 1976,

480

however, Congress passed legislation expressly affording copyright protection to simultaneously-recorded broadcasts of live performances such as sports events. See 17 U.S.C. § 101. Such protection was not extended to the underlying events.

The 1976 amendments also contained provisions preempting state law claims that enforced rights "equivalent" to exclusive copyright protections when the work to which the state claim was being applied fell within the area of copyright protection. See 17 U.S.C. § 301. Based on legislative history of the 1976 amendments, it is generally agreed that a "hot-news" INS-like claim survives preemption. H.R. No. 94-1476 at 132 (1976), reprinted in 1976 U.S.C.C.A.N. 5659, 5748. However, much of New York misappropriation law after INS goes well beyond "hot-news" claims and is preempted.

We hold that the surviving "hot-news" INS-like claim is limited to cases where: (i) a plaintiff generates or gathers information at a cost; (ii) the information is time-sensitive; (iii) a defendant's use of the information constitutes free riding on the plaintiff's efforts; (iv) the defendant is in direct competition with a product or service offered by the plaintiffs; and (v) the ability of other parties to free-ride on the efforts of the plaintiff or others would so reduce the incentive to produce the product or service that its existence or quality would be substantially threatened. We conclude that SportsTrax does not meet that test.

B. Copyrights in Events or Broadcasts of Events

The NBA asserted copyright infringement claims with regard both to the underlying games and to their broadcasts. The district court dismissed these claims, and the NBA does not appeal from their dismissal. Nevertheless, discussion of the infringement claims is necessary to provide the framework for analyzing the viability of the NBA's state law misappropriation claim in light of the Copyright Act's preemptive effect.

1. Infringement of a Copyright in the Underlying Games

In our view, the underlying basketball games do not fall within the subject matter of federal copyright protection because they do not constitute "original works of authorship" under 17 U.S.C. § 102(a). Section 102(a) lists eight categories of "works of authorship" covered by the act, including such categories as "literary works," "musical works," and "dramatic works." The list does not include athletic events, and, although the list is concededly non-exclusive, such events are neither similar nor analogous to any of the listed categories.

The text of Section 102(a) reads:

> § 102. Subject matter of copyright: In general
>
> (a) Copyright protection subsists, in accordance with this title, in original works of authorship fixed in any tangible medium of expression, now known or later developed, from which they can be perceived, reproduced, or otherwise communicated, either directly or with the aid of a machine or device. Works of authorship include the following categories:
>
> (1) literary works;
> (2) musical works, including any accompanying words;
> (3) dramatic works, including any accompanying music;
> (4) pantomimes and choreographic works;
> (6) motion pictures and other audiovisual works;
> (7) sound recordings; and
> (8) architectural works.

Sports events are not "authored" in any common sense of the word. There is, of course, at least at the professional level, considerable preparation for a game. However, the preparation is as much an expression of hope or faith as a determination of what will actually happen. Unlike movies, plays, television programs, or operas, athletic events are competitive and have no underlying script. Preparation may even cause mistakes to succeed, like the broken play in football that gains yardage because the opposition could not expect it. Athletic events may also result in wholly unanticipated occurrences, the most notable recent event being in a championship baseball game in which interference with a fly ball caused an umpire to signal erroneously a home run.

What "authorship" there is in a sports event, moreover, must be open to copying by competitors if fans are to be attracted. If the inventor of the T-formation in football had been able to copyright it, the sport might have come to an end instead of prospering. Even where athletic preparation most resembles authorship--figure skating, gymnastics, and, some would uncharitably say, professional wrestling--a performer who conceives and executes a particularly graceful and difficult--or, in the case of wrestling, seemingly painful--acrobatic feat cannot copyright it without impairing the underlying competition in the future. A claim of being the only athlete to perform a feat doesn't mean much if no one else is allowed to try.

For many of these reasons, *Nimmer on Copyright* concludes that the "[f]ar more reasonable" position is that athletic events are not copyrightable. 1 M. Nimmer & D. Nimmer, Nimmer on Copyright § 2.09[F] at 2-170.1 (1996). Nimmer notes that, among other problems, the number of joint copyright owners would arguably include the league, the teams, the athletes, umpires, stadium workers and even fans, who all contribute to the "work."

Concededly, caselaw is scarce on the issue of whether organized events themselves are copyrightable, but what there is indicates that they are not. See *Production Contractors, Inc. v. WGN Continental Broadcasting Co.*, 622 F.Supp. 1500 (N.D.Ill.1985) (Christmas parade is not a work of authorship entitled to copyright protection). In claiming a copyright in the underlying games, the NBA relied in part on a footnote in *Baltimore Orioles, Inc. v. Major League Baseball Players Assn.*, 805 F.2d 663, 669 n. 7 (7th Cir.1986), cert. denied, 480 U.S. 941, 107 S.Ct. 1593, 94 L.Ed.2d 782 (1987), which stated that the "[p]layers' performances" contain the "modest creativity required for copyright ability." However, the court went on to state, "Moreover, even if the [p]layers' performances were not sufficiently creative, the [p]layers agree that the cameramen and director contribute creative labor to the telecasts." Id. This last sentence indicates that the court was considering the copyright ability of telecasts--not the underlying games, which obviously can be played without cameras.

We believe that the lack of caselaw is attributable to a general understanding that athletic events were, and are, uncopyrightable. Indeed, prior to 1976, there was even doubt that broadcasts describing or depicting such events, which have a far stronger case for copyrightability than the events themselves, were entitled to copyright protection. Indeed, as described in the next subsection of this opinion, Congress found it necessary to extend such protection to recorded broadcasts of live events. The fact that Congress did not extend such protection to the events themselves confirms our view that the district court correctly held that appellants were not infringing a copyright in the NBA games.

*2. Infringement of a Copyright in the Broadcasts of NBA Games*

As noted, recorded broadcasts of NBA games--as opposed to the games themselves--are now entitled to copyright protection. The Copyright Act was amended in 1976 specifically to insure that simultaneously-recorded transmissions of live performances and sporting events would meet the Act's requirement that the original work of authorship be "fixed in any tangible medium of expression." 17 U.S.C. § 102(a). Accordingly, Section 101 of the Act, containing definitions, was amended to read:

> A work consisting of sounds, images, or both, that are being transmitted, is "fixed" for purposes of this title if a fixation of the work is being made simultaneously with its transmission. 17 U.S.C. § 101.

Congress specifically had sporting events in mind:

> [T]he bill seeks to resolve, through the definition of "fixation" in section 101, the status of live broadcasts--sports, news coverage, live performances of music, etc.--that are reaching the public in unfixed form but that are simultaneously being recorded.
> H.R. No. 94-1476 at 52, *reprinted in* 1976 U.S.C.C.A.N. at 5665.

The House Report also makes clear that it is the broadcast, not the underlying game, that is the subject of copyright protection. In explaining how game broadcasts meet the Act's requirement that the subject matter be an "original work[ ] of authorship," 17 U.S.C. § 102(a), the House Report stated:

> When a football game is being covered by four television cameras, with a director guiding the activities of the four cameramen and choosing which of their electronic images are sent out to the public and in what order, there is little doubt that what the cameramen and the director are doing constitutes "authorship." H.R. No. 94-1476 at 52, *reprinted in* 1976 U.S.C.C.A.N. at 5665.

Although the broadcasts are protected under copyright law, the district court correctly held that Motorola and STATS did not infringe NBA's copyright because they reproduced only facts from the broadcasts, not the expression or description of the game that constitutes the broadcast. The "fact/expression dichotomy" is a bedrock principle of copyright law that "limits severely the scope of protection in fact-based works." *Feist Publications, Inc. v. Rural Tel. Service Co.,* 499 U.S. 340, 350, 111 S.Ct. 1282, 1290, 113 L.Ed.2d 358 (1991). " 'No author may copyright facts or ideas. The copyright is limited to those aspects of the work--termed 'expression'--that display the stamp of the author's originality.' " *Id.* (quoting

*Harper & Row, Publishers, Inc. v. Nation Enter.*, 471 U.S. 539, 547, 105 S.Ct. 2218, 2224, 85 L.Ed.2d 588 (1985)).

We agree with the district court that the "[d]efendants provide purely factual information which any patron of an NBA game could acquire from the arena without any involvement from the director, cameramen, or others who contribute to the originality of a broadcast." 939 F.Supp. at 1094. Because the SportsTrax device and AOL site reproduce only factual information culled from the broadcasts and none of the copyrightable expression of the games, appellants did not infringe the copyright of the broadcasts.

## C. *The State-Law Misappropriation Claim*

The district court's injunction was based on its conclusion that, under New York law, defendants had unlawfully misappropriated the NBA's property rights in its games. The district court reached this conclusion by holding: (i) that the NBA's misappropriation claim relating to the underlying games was not preempted by Section 301 of the Copyright Act; and (ii) that, under New York common law, defendants had engaged in unlawful misappropriation. *Id.* at 1094-1107. We disagree.

### 1. *Preemption Under the Copyright Act*

a) Summary

When Congress amended the Copyright Act in 1976, it provided for the preemption of state law claims that are interrelated with copyright claims in certain ways. Under 17 U.S.C. § 301, a state law claim is preempted when: (i) the state law claim seeks to vindicate "legal or equitable rights that are equivalent" to one of the bundle of exclusive rights already protected by copyright law under 17 U.S.C. § 106--styled the "general scope requirement"; and (ii) the particular work to which the state law claim is being applied falls within the type of works protected by the Copyright Act under Sections 102 and 103--styled the "subject matter requirement."

The district court concluded that the NBA's misappropriation claim was not preempted because, with respect to the underlying games, as opposed to the broadcasts, the subject matter requirement was not met. 939 F.Supp. at 1097. *** The district court then relied on a series of older New York misappropriation cases involving radio broadcasts that considerably broadened *INS*. We hold that where the challenged copying or misappropriation relates in part to the copyrighted broadcasts of the games, the subject matter requirement is met as to both the broadcasts and the games. *** We do find that a properly-narrowed *INS* "hot-news" misappropriation claim survives preemption because it fails the general scope requirement, but that the broader theory of the radio broadcast cases relied upon by the district court were preempted when Congress extended copyright protection to simultaneously-recorded broadcasts.

*** [The Court's extensive discussion of "Partial Preemption" has been omitted].

Our conclusion, therefore, is that only a narrow "hot-news" misappropriation claim survives preemption for actions concerning material within the realm of copyright. See also 1 McCarthy on Trademarks and Unfair Competition (4th ed. 1996), § 10:69, at 10-134 (discussing National Exhibition Co. v. Fass, 133 N.Y.S.2d 379 (Sup.Ct.1954), Muzak, 30 N.Y.S.2d 419, and other cases relied upon by NBA that pre-date the 1976 amendment to the Copyright Act and concluding that after the amendment, "state misappropriation law would be unnecessary and would be preempted: protection is solely under federal copyright").

In our view, the elements central to an INS claim are: (i) the plaintiff generates or collects information at some cost or expense, see FII, 808 F.2d at 206; INS, 248 U.S. at 240, 39 S.Ct. at 72-73; (ii) the value of the information is highly time-sensitive, see FII, 808 F.2d at 209; INS, 248 U.S. at 231, 39 S.Ct. at 69-70; Restatement (Third) Unfair Competition, § 38 cmt. c.; (iii) the defendant's use of the information constitutes free-riding on the plaintiff's costly efforts to generate or collect it, see FII, 808 F.2d at 207; INS, 248 U.S. at 239-40, 39 S.Ct. at 72-73; Restatement § 38 at cmt. c.; McCarthy, § 10:73 at 10-139; (iv) the defendant's use of the information is in direct competition with a product or service offered by the plaintiff, FII, 808 F.2d at 209, INS, 248 U.S. at 240, 39 S.Ct. at 72-73; (v) the ability of other parties to free-ride on the efforts of the plaintiff would so reduce the incentive to produce the product or service that its existence or quality would be substantially threatened, FII, 808 F.2d at 209; Restatement, § 38 at cmt. c.; INS, 248 U.S. at 241, 39 S.Ct. at 73 ("[INS's conduct] would render [AP's] publication profitless, or so little profitable as in effect to cut off the service by rendering the cost prohibitive in comparison with the return.").

INS is not about ethics; it is about the protection of property rights in time-sensitive information so that the information will be made available to the public by profit seeking entrepreneurs. If services like AP were not assured of property rights in the news they pay to collect, they would cease to collect it. The ability of their competitors to appropriate their product at only nominal cost and thereby to disseminate a competing product at a lower price would destroy the incentive to collect news in the first place. The newspaper-reading public would suffer because no one would have an incentive to collect "hot news."

We therefore find the extra elements--those in addition to the elements of copyright infringement--that allow a "hotnews" claim to survive preemption are: (i) the time-sensitive value of factual information, (ii) the free-riding by a defendant, and (iii) the threat to the very existence of the product or service provided by the plaintiff.

2. The Legality of SportsTrax

We conclude that Motorola and STATS have not engaged in unlawful misappropriation under the "hot-news" test set out above. To be sure, some of the elements of a "hot-news" INS claim are met. The information transmitted to SportsTrax is not precisely contemporaneous, but it is nevertheless time-sensitive. Also, the NBA does provide, or will shortly do so, information like that available through SportsTrax. It now offers a service called "Gamestats" that provides official play-by-play game sheets and half-time and final box scores within each arena. It also provides such information to the media in each arena. In the future, the NBA plans to enhance Gamestats so that it will be networked between the various arenas and will support a pager product analogous to SportsTrax. SportsTrax will of course directly compete with an enhanced Gamestats.

However, there are critical elements missing in the NBA's attempt to assert a "hot-news" INS-type claim. As framed by the NBA, their claim compresses and confuses three different informational products. The first product is generating the information by playing the games; the second product is transmitting live, full descriptions of those games; and the third product is collecting and retransmitting strictly factual information about the games. The first and second products are the NBA's primary business: producing basketball games for live attendance and licensing copyrighted broadcasts of those games. The collection and retransmission of strictly factual material about the games is a different product: *e.g.*, box-scores in newspapers, summaries of statistics on television sports news, and real-time facts to be transmitted to pagers. In our view, the NBA has failed to show any competitive effect whatsoever from SportsTrax on the first and second products and a lack of any free-riding by SportsTrax on the third.

With regard to the NBA's primary products--producing basketball games with live attendance and licensing copyrighted broadcasts of those games--there is no evidence that anyone regards SportsTrax or the AOL site as a substitute for attending NBA games or watching them on television. In fact, Motorola markets SportsTrax as being designed "for those times when you cannot be at the arena, watch the game on TV, or listen to the radio ..."

The NBA argues that the pager market is also relevant to a "hot-news" INS-type claim and that SportsTrax's future competition with Gamestats satisfies any missing element. We agree that there is a separate market for the real-time transmission of factual information to pagers or similar devices, such as STATS's AOL site. However, we disagree that SportsTrax is in any sense free-riding off Gamestats.

An indispensable element of an INS "hot-news" claim is free riding by a defendant on a plaintiff's product, enabling the defendant to produce a directly competitive product for less money because it has lower costs. SportsTrax is not such a product. The use of pagers to transmit real-time information about NBA games requires: (i) the collecting of facts about the games; (ii) the transmission of these facts on a network; (iii) the assembling of them by the particular service; and (iv) the transmission of them to pagers or an on-line computer site. Appellants are in no way free-riding on Gamestats. Motorola and STATS expend their own resources to collect purely factual information generated in NBA games to transmit to SportsTrax pagers. They have their own network and assemble and transmit data themselves.

To be sure, if appellants in the future were to collect facts from an enhanced Gamestats pager to retransmit them to SportsTrax pagers, that would constitute free-riding and might well cause Gamestats to be unprofitable because it had to bear costs to collect facts that SportsTrax did not. If the appropriation of facts from one pager to another pager service were allowed, transmission of current information on NBA games to pagers or similar devices would be substantially deterred because any potential transmitter would know that the first entrant would quickly encounter a lower cost competitor free-riding on the originator's transmissions.

However, that is not the case in the instant matter. SportsTrax and Gamestats are each bearing their own costs of collecting factual information on NBA games, and, if one produces a product that is cheaper or otherwise superior to the other, that producer will prevail in the marketplace. This is obviously not the situation against which INS was intended to prevent: the potential lack of any such product or service because of the anticipation of free-riding.

For the foregoing reasons, the NBA has not shown any damage to any of its products based on free-riding by Motorola and STATS, and the NBA's misappropriation claim based on New York law is preempted.

\*\*\*

## IV. CONCLUSION

We vacate the injunction entered by the district court and order that the NBA's claim for misappropriation be dismissed.\*\*\*

### Notes & Questions

1. Isn't this case merely a modern version of *Pittsburgh Athletic*? Observers relay factual information about the course of an athletic contest to the public. Does the holding of this case conflict with *Pittburgh Athletic*? Or is there a rational way to distinguish these cases? Explain.

2. Explain what the court means when it says that "athletic events are not copyrightable." If that is true, then why do broadcasts of all sporting events claim to be copyrighted?

3. If the facts of sports broadcasts are not copyrightable, then what is the subject of copyright protection about sporting events?

4. The court denies that SportsTrax is free-riding. Do you think that KQV was free-riding in *Pittsburgh Athletic*? Explain.

# MONSTER COMMUNICATIONS, INC., v. TURNER BROADCASTING SYSTEM, INC.

935 F.Supp. 490 (1996)

United States District Court, S.D. New York

KAPLAN, District Judge.

For two decades, Muhammed Ali, born Cassius Clay, was the dominant public figure in the world of boxing as an Olympic gold medalist, professional contender, and heavyweight champion of the world three times. He was also an arresting personality and a controversial figure whose flamboyance, adherence to the Nation of Islam, conviction for draft evasion despite a claim of conscientious objector status, and ultimate vindication on the draft charge by a unanimous Supreme Court[1] frequently made him a focus of public attention. It therefore is far from surprising that his life has become a subject of intense interest to film makers, the circumstances that gives rise to this case.

Plaintiff Monster Communications, Inc. ("Monster") made and owns an 84 minute motion picture called "When We Were Kings" ("Kings") which is scheduled for world theatrical release in October 1996. The film is an account of the 1974 heavyweight title fight between Ali and George Foreman that was held in Zaire and referred to by Ali and others as the "rumble in the jungle." It is a serious film, and it recently won a grand jury award at the Sundance Film Festival. Monster believes that "Kings" has a substantial chance of achieving great commercial and critical success.

The cloud on the horizon, from Monster's point of view, is a documentary called "Ali--The Whole Story" ("Story"), which is scheduled to premiere on Turner Network Television on Tuesday, September 3, 1996. Monster claims that Story infringes its copyright in film footage contained in Kings because Story contains a number of film clips, aggregating approximately between 41 seconds and two minutes, that appear in Kings and allegedly are owned by Monster.

On Friday, August 30, 1996, Monster brought this action against Turner and MA Projects ("MA"), said to be the licensor to Turner of certain

---

[1] *Clay v. United States,* 403 U.S. 698, 91 S.Ct. 2068, 29 L.Ed.2d 810 (1971).

footage used in Story, for copyright infringement. It sought a temporary restraining order and preliminary injunction restraining Turner from exhibiting or distributing any of the Zaire footage allegedly owned by plaintiff, relief which would preclude the broadcast of Story in its present form. The Court heard argument on the afternoon of August 30, 1996, at which time the parties agreed that the application for a temporary restraining order would be treated by the Court as the motion for a preliminary injunction. An evidentiary hearing was held on September 1, 1996 at which time the Court rendered a bench decision denying the motion but reserved the right to amplify and edit its remarks. This memorandum contains the Court's findings of fact and conclusions of law on the motion for a preliminary injunction thus edited and amended.

## Discussion

In order to obtain a preliminary injunction, the movant must show "(a) irreparable harm and (b) either (1) likelihood of success on the merits or (2) sufficiently serious questions going to the merits to make them a fair ground for litigation and a balance of hardships tipping decidedly toward the party requesting the preliminary relief." *Jackson Dairy, Inc. v. H.P. Hood & Sons, Inc.,* 596 F.2d 70, 72 (2d Cir.1979).

*Irreparable Injury*

The requirement of threatened irreparable harm is readily satisfied in this case. Infringement of a copyright is presumed to give rise to such harm. *Fisher-Price, Inc. v. Well-Made Toy Mfg. Corp.,* 25 F.3d 119, 124 (2d Cir.1994). Moreover, if defendants are threatening to infringe copyrighted material owned by the plaintiff, the extent of the harm to the plaintiff could not readily be measured, a factor that traditionally constitutes irreparable harm.

\*\*\*\*

*Likelihood of Success*

Once Monster obtained a copy of Story last week, the dispute became more focused. At the commencement of this action, plaintiff claimed that there were twenty film clips in Story totaling two to three minutes in length that appear also in Kings. During the hearing on September 1, plaintiff indicated that it would not press this motion, although reserving its rights to seek other relief, with respect to three of the twenty clips.[2] Turner edited three of the allegedly infringing clips out of Story before the hearing. It contends that four of the remaining fourteen allegedly infringing clips, which aggregate 16 seconds in Story, are not the same as plaintiff's footage in Kings and must have been taken by another photographer.[3] It concedes that nine of the clips appear both in Kings and Story and that their aggregate duration in Story is 41 seconds. In consequence, it is clear for purposes of this motion that the Turner film contains between nine and fourteen clips that appear also in Kings and which aggregate a minimum of 41 seconds and perhaps as much as two minutes, although it seems likely that the aggregate duration is more like one minute.

\*\*\*

Section 107 of the Copyright Act, 17 U.S.C. § 107, codifies the defense of fair use. One may use and reproduce a copyrighted work "for purposes such as criticism, comment, news reporting, teaching ..., scholarship, or research" provided the use is a fair one. The factors to be considered in determining the fairness of the use include "(1) the purpose and character of the use, including whether such use is of a commercial nature or is for nonprofit educational purposes; (2) the nature of the copyrighted work; (3) the amount and substantiality of the portion used in relation to the copyrighted work as a whole; and (4) the effect of the use upon the potential market for or value of the copyrighted work." *Id.*

The allegedly infringing work, Story, is a biography. While it is commercial in nature, it "undeniably constitutes a combination of comment, criticism, scholarship and research, all of which enjoy favored status under § 107." *Arica Institute, Inc. v. Palmer,* 761 F.Supp. 1056, 1067 (S.D.N.Y.1991), *aff'd,* 970 F.2d 1067 (2d Cir.1992). As Turner argues,

---

[2] The three clips in question do not appear in Kings, but appear in other footage in which plaintiff claims copyright. Plaintiff did not press the motion as to these clips because it was unable to produce, on the expedited schedule on which the motion was heard, a certificate of registration of copyright covering those clips.

[3] The Court viewed the four disputed clips at the hearing. The limitations of the format in and the equipment by which they were presented did not permit, in the available time, a determination as to whether these four clips are identical to footage that appears in Kings. Turner contends also that one of the clips plaintiff says appears in Story in fact is not there. As the clip is extremely short, a determination would have required a more detailed examination of Story than time permitted. As will appear, the uncertainties as to the disputed clips are not material to disposition of the motion.

492

there can be little doubt that Ali is a figure of legitimate public concern and that his television biography is a subject of public interest. Hence, the first of the fair use factors cuts in favor of Turner although, as the Nimmers point out, it does not "necessitate a finding of fair use." 3 MELVILLE B. NIMMER & DAVID NIMMER, NIMMER ON COPYRIGHT ("NIMMER") § 13.05[A][1][*a*], at 13- 161 to 162 (1995); *see also New Era Publications International, ApS v. Henry Holt & Co., Inc.*, 873 F.2d 576, 583 (2d Cir.1989), *cert. denied*, 493 U.S. 1094, 110 S.Ct. 1168, 107 L.Ed.2d 1071 (1990); *Rosemont Enterprises, Inc. v. Random House, Inc.*, 366 F.2d 303, 307 (2d Cir.1966), *cert. denied*, 385 U.S. 1009, 87 S.Ct. 714, 17 L.Ed.2d 546 (1967).

The second of the factors, the nature of the copyrighted work, focuses on the degree of creativity of the copyrighted work. "[T]he more creative the primary work, the more protection it should be accorded from copying." *Amsinck v. Columbia Pictures Industries, Inc.*, 862 F.Supp. 1044, 1050 (S.D.N.Y.1994). *Accord,* 3 NIMMER § 13.05[A][2][*a*], at 13-174 to 175. Here there is no doubt in the Court's mind that plaintiff's film, Kings, is a creative and notable work. But defendants are not alleged to be infringing Kings. Rather, the claim is that Story uses certain film clips--photographic images--of actual historical events that appear also in Kings.[4]

Anyone who has seen any of the great pieces of photojournalism--for example, Alfred Eisenstadt's classic image of a thrilled sailor exuberantly kissing a woman in Times Square on V-J Day and the stirring photograph of U.S. Marines raising the American flag atop Mount Surabachi on Iwo Jima-- or, perhaps in some eyes, more artistic, but nevertheless representational, photography--such as Ansel Adams' work and the portraits of Yousuf Karsh --must acknowledge that photographic images of actual people, places and events may be as creative and deserving of protection as purely fanciful creations. Nevertheless, history has its demands. There is a public interest in receiving information concerning the world in which we live. The more newsworthy the person or event depicted, the greater the concern that too narrow a view of the fair use defense will deprive the public of significant information. Moreover, only a finite number of photographers capture images of a given historical event. Hence, without denying for a moment the creativity inherent in the film clips of actual events relating to the Zaire fight, the degree of protection that properly may be afforded to them must take into account that too narrow a view of the fair use defense could materially

---

[4] The footage is not of the fight itself. It includes shots of Ali and Foreman training, arriving in Zaire, of Ali walking with his wife, and other such events.

undermine the ability of other Ali biographers to tell, in motion picture or perhaps still photographic form, an important part of his story. *See, e.g., Rosemont Enterprises, Inc.,* 366 F.2d at 307. This of course is not to say that historical film footage loses all copyright protection,[5] only that its character as historical film footage may strengthen somewhat the hand of a fair use defendant as compared with an alleged infringer of a fanciful work or a work presented in a medium that offers a greater variety of forms of expression.

Here, the footage in question, although historical, does not remotely approach the Second Circuit's paradigmatic example of an image the informational content of which would weigh heaviest in favor of an alleged infringer, the Zapruder film of the Kennedy assassination. *See Roy Export Company,* 672 F.2d at 1099. Moreover, having viewed both films, the Court finds that Story would not have been diminished in any material way had it not included the allegedly infringing footage. On the other hand, the level of creativity inherent in this footage, as distinguished from the use made of the footage in Kings, appears not to be especially substantial. All things considered, the second of the fair use factors is essentially neutral.

The third of the fair use factors is the amount and substantiality of the portion used, a factor that cuts very heavily in favor of Turner for several reasons.

The first is that Kings is 84 minutes in length; Story is 94. The allegedly infringing portions of Story consist of nine to fourteen film clips aggregating a minimum of 41 seconds and a maximum of one to two minutes, which is 0.7 to 2.1 percent of the film. A number of the allegedly

---

[5] While the Second Circuit has "acknowledged in passing the conceivable occurrence of some 'rare,' 'almost unique' circumstance, such as those surrounding the Zapruder film [of President Kennedy's assassination], in which 'it is at least arguable that the informational value of [the] film cannot be separated from the photographer's expression, ... thereby indicating that both should be in the public domain,' *Iowa State University Research Foundation, Inc. v. American Broadcasting Cos., Inc.,* 621 F.2d 57, 61 n. 6 (2d Cir.1980), [it has] also stated the general rule that '[c]onflicts between interests protected by the first amendment and the copyright laws thus far have been resolved by application of the fair use doctrine,' *Wainwright Securities, Inc. v. Wall Street Transcript Corp.,* [558 F.2d 91,] 95 [2d Cir.1977]." *Roy Export Co. Establishment of Vaduz, Liechtenstein v. Columbia Broadcasting System, Inc.,* 672 F.2d 1095, 1100 (2d Cir.), *cert. denied,* 459 U.S. 826, 103 S.Ct. 60, 74 L.Ed.2d 63 (1982).

494

infringing clips are less than three seconds long.    From any quantitative standpoint, the allegedly infringing use is small.

Second, the allegedly infringing footage is by no means the focus of Story. Indeed, the two movies are quite different.   Kings is devoted almost entirely to the Zaire fight.   It touches only fleetingly on the rest of Ali's life and career.    It focuses heavily on the fact that the Zaire fight involved two African-American fighters traveling to fight in Africa, the continent of their ancestors' origin, and the impact of that experience on them and on Zaire. Story, on the other hand, is a biography of Ali from childhood to the present. It is, as its title promises, "Muhammed Ali--The Whole Story."    The segment concerning the Zaire fight occupies approximately nine of its 94 minutes.   It is a very different work.

Third, the Court viewed both movies within a short span of hours, Kings first and then Story, for the purpose of attempting to detect in Story, without prompting, whether and to what extent it employed footage used in Kings. Although there were a couple of occasions on which such uses were apparent, they were far fewer than the seventeen that plaintiff claims exist. That of course is not to say that the parties are mistaken.    Rather, the conclusion that flows is that the allegedly infringing uses are not particularly noticeable even if one is looking for them.

For all of these reasons, the Court finds that the "amount and substantiality" factor strongly favors the defendants.  *Harper & Row Publishers, Inc. v. Nation Enterprises,* 471 U.S. 539, 105 S.Ct. 2218, 85 L.Ed.2d 588 (1985), is not to the contrary.   While the Supreme Court there concluded that the use of only 300 of 200,000 words of the memoirs of former President Ford was a substantial appropriation, it did so on the basis of the trial court's finding that the alleged infringer "took what was essentially the heart of the book." *Id.* at 564-65, 105 S.Ct. at 2233 (quoting 557 F.Supp. 1067, 1072 (S.D.N.Y.1983)).   The material at issue here has no remotely comparable significance in Kings.

The final fair use factor, the effect of the infringing use on the market for the original copyrighted work, is the most important.  *Harper & Row Publishers, Inc.,* 471 U.S. at 566, 105 S.Ct. at 2233.   In considering it, however, it is critical to bear in mind that the only effect of which plaintiff properly may complain is that caused by the alleged infringement. [citations omitted] In other words, the issue here is not whether the wide dissemination of Turner's television biography of Ali only weeks before the theatrical release of Monster's film will undercut the market for Kings.   It is whether the use in Turner's film of up to fourteen clips of historical footage, aggregating between 41 seconds and two minutes, will undercut the market for Kings. Having viewed both movies, the Court concludes that the segments in Story are unlikely to have any such effect. The uses in Story are too few, too short, and too small in relation to the whole. If the broadcast of Story impacts Kings' reception, it almost surely will be as a result of their common subject, not their minute or so of common footage. As the *New Era* court wrote in a case involving two written biographies of L. Ron Hubbard:

> "[T]here may be purchasers who are sufficiently interested in Hubbard to purchase one book about him but not two. [Defendant's book] may have an adverse impact on the marketability of Hubbard's [autobiography] with those purchasers simply by exhausting their interest. *That is not within the concern of the copyright statute.*" *Id.* at 1523 (emphasis supplied).

\*\*\*\*

*Iowa State University Research Foundation, Inc. v. American Broadcasting Companies, Inc.*, 621 F.2d 57 (2d Cir.1980), which has not been cited by the parties, warrants brief mention because it bears some resemblance to this case, although it does not support a different result. In that case, ABC used approximately eight percent of the footage from a copyrighted film biography of an Olympic wrestler as part of a vignette on the life of the athlete in its coverage of the Olympics. The Second Circuit held that the fair use defense was properly rejected. In doing so, however, it relied heavily upon the facts that ABC had exclusive television rights to broadcast the Olympic games, obtained plaintiff's film to assess its value for possible purchase, and then simply took what it desired without plaintiff's consent. In view of the exclusivity of ABC's broadcast rights, its actions deprived the plaintiff of "an extremely significant market" for its work. *Id.* at 62. Moreover, the unfairness of its conduct was found relevant to the availability of the equitable defense of fair use. The circumstances of this case are quite different.

Thus, although the record is not as complete as it might be, given the very expedited character of these proceedings, the balance of the statutory fair use factors appear to cut heavily in favor of the defendants. Accordingly, the Court concludes that plaintiff is unlikely to prevail on the merits, even assuming that it has protectible rights in the footage in question, because the defendants are likely to establish that their use is a fair one within the meaning of the Copyright Act.

\*\*\*\*

## Conclusion

For the foregoing reasons, the motion for a preliminary injunction is denied.


**NOTES & QUESTIONS**

1. According to the court, "Infringement of a copyright is presumed to give rise to" irreparable harm. Why do you think that such a presumption exists? Most courts take the position that a plaintiff must show both a "likelihood of success on the merits" and "irreparable harm" in order to be entitled to a preliminary injunction. It is common for courts also to state that for an injunction to issue "the balance of hardships must tip decidedly in favor of the party seeking the injunction."

2. Explain how each § 107 fair use factor either favors or disfavors a finding of fair use. What is the relevance of each factor to the issue of whether a use should be considered "fair"?

## B. TRADEMARKS

## HARLEM WIZARDS ENTERTAINMENT BASKETBALL v. NBA PROPERTIES, INC.
952 F.Supp. 1084 (1997).
United States District Court, D. New Jersey

WALLS, District Judge.

Plaintiff, Harlem Wizards Entertainment Basketball, Inc. ("Harlem Wizards") is a theatrical basketball organization that performs "show basketball" in the tradition established by the world famous Harlem Globetrotters. Defendant, the Capital Bullets Basketball Club, commonly known as the "Washington Bullets," is a member team of the National Basketball Association ("NBA"), the world's preeminent professional basketball league, also a named defendant in this action. The third defendant is NBA Properties, Inc. ("NBA Properties"), the entity which holds the licensing rights of the names of NBA member teams.

On February 22, 1996, the Washington Bullets publicly announced that beginning the 1997-1998 NBA season, the team would formally change its name to the "Washington Wizards." Soon after, Harlem Wizards filed this lawsuit against the Washington Bullets and the other mentioned defendants, alleging that the proposed name change infringed its trademark in violation of Section 43 of the Lanham Act, The New Jersey Trademark Act, N.J.S.A. 56:4-1 and common law. Plaintiff seeks a permanent injunction enjoining these defendants from using the trademark WIZARDS and various damage awards.

\*\*\*

## THE RECORD

\*\*\*

The following are the relevant facts of this controversy. In this case, because such evidence is uncontroverted, its credibility and that of the witnesses from whom it was adduced is absent. However, the parties

498

vigorously challenge the legal significance of this evidence, which the Court reviews together with its findings in the *Discussion* section of this opinion.

From its founding in 1962, Harlem Wizards has promoted itself as a show basketball team. In its advertisements and promotional materials, Harlem Wizards frequently compares itself to the better known Harlem Globetrotters, which developed and popularized the show basketball genre. For example, Harlem Wizards bills itself as the "Avis of comedy basketball," the Harlem Globetrotters clearly being Hertz, and also as the "grassroots version of the Harlem Globetrotters." Although Harlem Wizards' biggest market is in the Northeast, the team has traveled throughout the United States and, to some extent, internationally. For the past three years, Harlem Wizards has actually consisted of two teams: one team which actively tours the country and a local team which performs mostly in the New York City metropolitan area.

Harlem Wizards generally performs at high schools, colleges, summer camps, and charitable events. Plaintiff has no home arena where it regularly plays before fans who can regularly attend its games nor does it participate in any formalized basketball league competitions. Unlike a traditional professional competitive sports team, plaintiff does not advertise its services directly to consumers through the media, but instead promotes itself through direct mail solicitation to its typical customers--schools, camps and charities, at trade shows for performance acts, and in "amusement business" trade magazines such as the "Cavalcade of Acts and Attractions." Schools and other organizations can purchase plaintiff's services for a flat fee of $3,500.00 and travel expenses, although plaintiff will sometimes accept a smaller fee in exchange for a portion of game proceeds.

In a typical Harlem Wizards "game," plaintiff plays against a "team" selected by the organization which purchased the team's services. Opposing team members are not professional athletes but ordinary citizens such as plumbers, teachers, police officers, coaches, politicians and students. A resulting game combines competitive basketball, trick basketball and comedic basketball entertainment. During the first and third quarters of the game, the Harlem Wizards mostly play competitive basketball against their opponents, moderating its level of competitiveness to the opposing team's athletic prowess. During the second and fourth quarters, the team players engage in comedic antics such as passing the ball between their legs, throwing water at their opponents, rolling down their opponents' socks and befuddling the other team's members by handing them the ball and then quickly snatching it away. In addition to these game performances, Harlem Wizards makes frequent paid appearances at fairs, festivals, parties, school assembly programs, pep rallies, and bar mitzvahs. Over the years, the Harlem Wizards team has on at least two occasions played during the half-time intermissions of NBA basketball games.

In connection with its games and appearances, plaintiff sells a variety of merchandise bearing the team's name. There, spectators can purchase t-shirts, sweatshirts, caps, basketballs, posters, banners, and pictures as souvenirs but none of the merchandise is available in retail stores. Plaintiff has used both the marks HARLEM WIZARDS and WIZARDS as its logo on merchandise and team uniforms. During the mid-1980s, the team used WIZARDS on its uniforms and it plans to use WIZARDS as its mark during its 1996-1997 season. Plaintiff does not have specific color scheme or a design that it uses continuously as part of its logo.

At trial, plaintiff sought to emphasize that show basketball is only part of Harlem Wizards' repertoire. The record, however, clearly demonstrates that over the last thirty-five years, the team has played few competitive basketball games without any comedic entertainment, and almost always during international tours. According to Todd Davis, the team has not played a competitive game on American soil since the late 1970s or early 1980s. Plaintiff's witness Claude Henderson, who first joined the Harlem Wizards in 1967, testified that the team played its last fully competitive game in 1979.

Washington Bullets is a NBA member team owned and operated by Capital Bullets Basketball Club. Founded in 1961, the franchise originated in Chicago, where it was first known as the Chicago Packers and later, the Chicago Zephyrs. It then moved to Baltimore, Maryland in 1963 and became known as the Baltimore Bullets. In 1973, the team moved to Washington, D.C. and changed its name to the Capital Bullets. The following year, the team adopted the name the Washington Bullets.

The NBA, which celebrates its fiftieth anniversary this year, is made up of twenty-nine member teams that play annually against each other from November until June. The league is divided into two conferences, Eastern and Western, and four divisions, Atlantic, Midwest, Central and Pacific. The NBA has strict rules governing the games as well as player conduct on and off the court. As an NBA franchise, the Bullets play eighty-two games--forty-one at "home" and forty-one "away"--against other NBA member teams from November until mid-April. Games are divided into four twelve minute quarters. Following regular season play, sixteen teams compete in the NBA championship playoffs.

500

Fans can regularly attend Washington Bullets games or watch them on television. NBA basketball is promoted directly to its fans through television advertisements, regular television programming such as "Inside Stuff" and "Inside NBA," and other media sports coverage. The NBA also has a series of grants, licenses to manufacturers to produce various products bearing the NBA logo and those of its twenty-nine member teams. Specific labeling and tagging is used to identify all NBA and NBA team products; the NBA logo of a ball-dribbling player appears on all of its products. NBA merchandise is widely available for sale in retail outlets throughout the United States.

For the past few years, Abe Pollin, owner of the Washington Bullets, had been considering changing the name of the franchise out of concern that the term "Bullets" had a negative connotation. In January 1995, the Washington Bullets first informed the NBA that it was considering changing the team name, logo and uniform beginning the 1997-1998 season. In August 1995, Susan O'Malley, president of the Washington Bullets, sent the NBA's Paula Hanson a letter which listed eight possible new names for the team, including the name WIZARDS. Hanson forwarded the letter to Kathryn Barrett, the NBA's in-house trademark counsel, and requested that she arrange for a preliminary trademark search to determine if for any reason any of the names listed were not be available for use. A few days later Hanson forwarded the preliminary search results to O'Malley. The use of WIZARDS was not interdicted.

Along with its name change, the Washington Bullets unveiled a new anti-violence initiative that concentrated on Washington, D.C. junior high and middle schools. To publicize the name change and anti-violence initiative, the Washington Bullets staged a contest in conjunction with Boston Market Restaurants, "The Washington Post," NBC4, the local NBC affiliate and other media sponsors, inviting fans to take part in the name-change process. The contest, called "Boston Market Renames the Bullets," occurred in two phases. From November 1, 1995 until December 15, 1995, fans could suggest new names for the team by completing entry ballots at Boston Market restaurants. Then, from early February until February 22, 1996, fans could vote on one of five names selected from the earlier submissions selected by a "Blue Ribbon Panel" by calling a 900 telephone number. The contest culminated with a live network announcement of the winning name by Abe Pollin on February 22, 1996.

By January 1996, the Blue Ribbon Panel had selected five names out of approximately 3,000 to be included during the second phase of the contest: Washington Dragons, Washington Express, Washington Sea Dogs,

Washington Stallions, and Washington Wizards. O'Malley forwarded these five names to Hanson. Hanson then sent these names to Barrett who arranged for full trademark searches to be conducted on every name except the Washington Dragons, a mark for which the NBA had previously filed a trademark application in anticipation that another NBA team might want to adopt it. Full trademark applications were filed for Washington Sea Dogs, Washington Stallions, Washington Express, and Washington Wizards. The firm of Thomson and Thomson conducted the trademark searches on January 29, 1996 and mailed them to the NBA on February 2, 1996. The trademark search for the mark WIZARDS retrieved 575 potential references and sixty-three were included for the NBA's review. Harlem Wizards was among those entities listed and plaintiff's services were described as professional sports. None of the names submitted by defendants was discarded as the result of the trademark searches.

After the Washington Bullets announced that its new name would be the Washington Wizards on February 22, 1996, the NBA in-house creative services designed several different potential logos for the team. As of yet, no final decision has been made regarding a final logo but defendants claim that the final logo will be unique, and like all other NBA logos, have a distinct color scheme. On February 8 and February 29, 1996, Plaintiff filed trademark applications first for HARLEM WIZARDS and then WIZARDS.

\*\*\*\*

*Evidence of Actual Confusion and Likelihood of Confusion*

1. *Individual Testimony*

At trial, plaintiff offered testimony by two current Harlem Wizards' players regarding incidents that purportedly showed the existence of actual consumer confusion between the Harlem Wizards and Washington Wizards. \*\*\*

2. *Survey Evidence*

Both parties commissioned consumer surveys and presented their results at trial. Plaintiff offered results from two related surveys conducted by Dr. Michael Rappeport of RL Associates in May 1996 to support its assertion that the Washington Bullets' name change would result in the likelihood of confusion between the Harlem Wizards and the Washington Wizards. Dr. Rappeport conducted one survey in Northern New Jersey and the other in the Washington, D.C. area. Combined, the 309 respondents who participated in both studies were aged eighteen or older and had either attended a basketball event or watched a televised basketball event at least twice in the past year. ***

Defendants commissioned their own survey by Dr. Jacob Jacoby to prove that no likelihood of confusion exists between the two teams and that none is likely in the future. Defendants' survey interviewed 365 respondents in sixteen cities across the country. All of the respondents were aged fourteen or older and had watched an NBA, college, high school or some other type of organized basketball game or exhibition during the last twelve months. ***

## DISCUSSION

***

### I

*Trademark Infringement*

Plaintiff claims trademark infringement under Section 43(a) of the Lanham Act, The New Jersey Trademark Act (N.J.S.A. 56:4-1) and common law. N.J.S.A. 56:4-1 is the statutory equivalent of Section 43(a)(1) of the Lanham Act and the analysis for trademark infringement under New Jersey common law is the same as under Section 43(a)(1). [citation omitted] Thus, the Court's discussion with respect to plaintiff's Section 43(a) claim addresses its state law claims as well.

Plaintiff relies on the reverse confusion theory of trademark infringement first recognized by the Third Circuit Court of Appeals in *Fisons Horticulture, Inc. v. Vigoro Industries, Inc.,* 30 F.3d 466, 474-75, 31 U.S.P.Q.2d 1592, 1598 (3d Cir.1994). In an ordinary trademark infringement case, the alleged trademark infringer takes advantage of the reputation and good will of a senior trademark owner by adopting a similar or identical mark. *Id.* at 473-74, 31 U.S.P.Q.2d at 1597-1598. In contrast, reverse confusion arises when a larger, more powerful entity adopts the trademark of a smaller, less powerful trademark user and thereby causes confusion as to the origin of the senior trademark user's goods or services. *See, e.g., Sands, Taylor & Wood Co. v. Quaker Oats Co.,* 978 F.2d 947 (7th Cir.1992), *cert. denied,* 507 U.S. 1042, 113 S.Ct. 1879, 123 L.Ed.2d 497 (1993) (finding that Quaker Oats Co.'s use of "Thirst Aid" for its product Gatorade infringed on the registered "Thirst-Aid" trademark owned and formerly used by small Vermont beverage company)... Because the junior user is a larger company with greater financial ability and trademark recognition in the marketplace, it can easily overwhelm the senior user by flooding the market with promotion of its similar trademark. *Fisons,* 30 F.3d at 474-75, 31 U.S.P.Q.2d at 1598. The strength of the junior user's promotional campaigns leads consumers to believe that the senior user's products derive from that of the junior user or that the senior user is actually the trademark infringer. *Id.* As a result, the senior user "loses the value of the trademark--its product identity, corporate identity, control over its goodwill and reputation, and ability to move into new markets." *Id.* (quoting *Ameritech, Inc. v. American Information Technologies Corp.,* 811 F.2d 960, 964 (6th Cir.1987)). The federal courts and legal commentators have observed that failure to recognize reverse confusion would essentially immunize from unfair competition liability companies that have well established trade names and the financial ability to advertise a senior mark taken from smaller, less powerful competitors. *See id; Big O Tire Dealers, Inc. v. Goodyear Tire & Rubber Co.,* 561 F.2d 1365, 1372 (10th Cir.1977).

The Lanham Act protects "an owner's interest in its trademark by keeping the public free from confusion as to the source of goods and ensuring fair competition," and extends to protect trademark owners against reverse confusion trademark infringement. *Fisons,* 30 F.3d at 474-75, 31 U.S.P.Q.2d at 1598 (internal quotations omitted). Section 43(a) of the Lanham Act, 15 U.S.C. § 1125(a) provides that:

> Any person who, on or in connection with any goods or services ... uses in commerce any word, term, name, symbol or device, or any combination thereof, or any false designation of origin, false or misleading description of fact, or false or misleading representation of fact, which--(A) is likely to cause confusion, or to cause mistake, or to deceive as to the affiliation, connection, or association of such person with another person, or as to the origin, sponsorship, or approval of his or her goods, services, or commercial activities by another person, or (B) in commercial advertising or promotion, misrepresents the nature, characteristics, qualities, or geographic origin of his or her or another person's goods, services or commercial activities-- shall be liable in a civil action by any person who believes that he or she is or is likely to be damaged by such act. 15 U.S.C. § 1125(a)(1).

Federal Courts have long recognized that Section 43(a)(1) "protects unregistered service marks in the same manner and to the same extent as registered marks" out of acknowledgement that trademark rights emanate from use and not only registration. *FM 103.1, Inc.,* 929 F.Supp. at 194. *See Two Pesos, Inc. v. Taco Cabana, Inc.,* 505 U.S. 763, 768, 112 S.Ct. 2753, 2757, 120 L.Ed.2d 615, *reh'g denied,* 505 U.S. 1244, 113 S.Ct. 20, 120 L.Ed.2d 947 (1992)... To prevail on a trademark infringement claim under Section 43(a) of the Lanham Act, a plaintiff must establish that: (1) the mark is valid and legally protectable; (2) the plaintiff owns the mark; and (3) the defendant's use of the mark to identify goods or services is likely to create confusion concerning the origin of such goods and services. *Fisons,* 30 F.3d at 472-73 [other citations omitted].

\*\*\*

Trademark law evaluates marks along a continuum of distinctiveness, from the nondistinctive to the inherently distinctive: Marks are (1) generic, (2) descriptive, (3) suggestive or (4) arbitrary, or fanciful. A generic term functions as the common descriptive name of a class of products and are generally not legally protectable. *See, e.g., A.J. Canfield,* 808 F.2d at 292 ("chocolate fudge" is generic when used in connection with chocolate fudge flavored soda); *Kellogg Co. v. National Biscuit Co.,* 305 U.S. 111, 59 S.Ct. 109, 83 L.Ed. 73, 29 U.S.P.Q.2d 296 (1938) ("shredded wheat" is generic term when used for a breakfast cereal). A descriptive mark immediately conveys a characteristic, ingredient or quality of the article or service it identifies and acquires protected status only if the plaintiff can demonstrate that the goods or services have achieved secondary meaning. *See, e.g., Transfer Print Foils, Inc. v. Transfer Print America, Inc.,* 720 F.Supp. 425, 12 U.S.P.Q.2d 1753 (D.N.J.1989) ("Transfer Print" is descriptive for surface decorating machines, related technical machines, material and related technical services to distributors and manufacturers who require designs or words placed on their products). Suggestive, arbitrary and fanciful marks are afforded the highest level of trademark protection. *See AMF Inc. v. Sleekcraft Boats,* 599 F.2d 341, 349 (9th Cir.1979). A suggestive mark requires the consumer to use imagination, thought, or perception to determine the character of the goods or service. *A.J. Canfield,* 808 F.2d at 297. *See, e.g., Taj Mahal Enterprises, Ltd. v. Trump,* 745 F.Supp. 240 (D.N.J.1990) ("Taj Mahal" suggestive of an Indian restaurant). An arbitrary mark employs terms that do not describe or suggest any attribute of goods or services sold and a fanciful mark uses unfamiliar language coined expressly for the purpose of trademark protection. *See Sunenblick v. Harrell,* 895 F.Supp. 616, 624 (S.D.N.Y.1995), *aff'd,* 101 F.3d 684 (2d Cir.1996), *cert. denied,* 519 U.S. 964, 117 S.Ct. 386, 136 L.Ed.2d 303 (1996).

As a threshold matter, this Court must determine whether the mark WIZARDS is inherently distinctive, that is, whether it can be defined as suggestive, arbitrary or fanciful. At the outset, the Court acknowledges that assessing a mark's distinctiveness is not an "exact science" and that the subtle distinctions between these categories can be slippery and elusive. Nonetheless, a mark elicits a particular and quantifiable consumer reaction. Plaintiff asserts that the mark WIZARDS is an arbitrary or fanciful term and thus subject to the highest level of trademark protection. According to plaintiff, the term WIZARDS has no specific meaning when used in connection with basketball services, apparel, or related merchandise. In opposition, defendants advance several arguments. First, defendants argue that plaintiff's mark, to the extent that it has acquired one, consists only of the term HARLEM WIZARDS in its entirety. Defendants stress that the term "Harlem" is an essential element of plaintiff's mark and identity as a show basketball team. In support of this argument, they note that several show basketball teams have sought to capitalize on the genre established by the Harlem Globetrotters by adopting "Harlem" as part of their appellation. Defendants also argue that plaintiff, since its inception, has only sporadically used the term WIZARDS alone as a mark and then only in contexts where the consumer already knows that such materials pertain to the Harlem Wizards. Second, defendants claim that the mark WIZARDS is not inherently distinctive because it describes the nature of plaintiff's services, the "trickery," "wizardry" and "magic" of its basketball performances. As a descriptive mark, plaintiff would have to demonstrate that it has achieved secondary meaning, an unlikely proposition because its consumer recognition level is virtually nonexistent as evidenced by the survey results presented by both parties.

This Court finds that although plaintiff has used the mark HARLEM WIZARDS more consistently than the mark WIZARDS over the years, its use of the mark WIZARDS has nevertheless been sufficient to establish trademark rights. The Court, however, finds that plaintiff's mark is suggestive rather than, as plaintiff asserts, arbitrary or fanciful. The term WIZARDS does not describe accurately plaintiff's services because regardless how talented plaintiff's team members may be, they do not perform magic or even magically. Rather, the mark WIZARDS is accurately defined as suggestive because it asks the consumer to fantasize, to use his or her imagination to connect the idea of magic and the supernatural with show basketball. Because the Court finds that the mark WIZARDS is inherently distinctive, it now turns to the question of whether a likelihood of confusion exists between both parties' use of the mark.

## II

Plaintiff bears the burden of establishing that defendants' concurrent use of the mark WIZARDS will create a likelihood of confusion among basketball fans between the Harlem Wizards and the Washington Wizards. The showing of proof necessary for a plaintiff to prevail depends upon whether the goods or services offered by the trademark owner and alleged infringer are competitive or noncompetitive. If the action involves competing goods, "the court need rarely look beyond the mark itself." *Interpace Corp. v. Lapp, Inc.,* 721 F.2d 460, 462 (3d Cir.1983). In such cases, the court simply analyzes whether the similarity of the marks engenders confusion. In actions where the goods are non-competing, "the similarity of the marks is only one of a number of factors the court must examine to determine the likelihood of confusion." *Fisons,* 30 F.3d at 473, 31 U.S.P.Q.2d at 1596. If the goods or services are noncompeting,

> the court must look beyond the trademark to the nature of the products themselves, and to the context in which they are marketed and sold. The closer the relationship between the products, and the more similar their sale contexts, the greater the likelihood of confusion. Once a trademark owner demonstrates the likelihood of confusion, it is entitled to injunctive relief. *Id.* (quoting *Lapp,* 721 F.2d at 462 (citations omitted)).

Likelihood of confusion exists if the consuming public assumes upon viewing a mark that the products or service represented by the mark is associated with a different product or service represented by a similar mark. *See* 3 J. Thomas McCarthy, McCarthy on Trademarks and Unfair Competition § 2301[1] (1992). To measure the likelihood of confusion in a reverse confusion case, a court applies the same test developed to assess the likelihood of confusion in direct confusion cases. The Court of Appeals for the Third Circuit has identified ten factors to be considered in determining whether a likelihood of confusion exists in the marketplace regarding the source of a product or service. *Fisons,* 30 F.3d at 473-74, 31 U.S.P.Q.2d at 1597 [other case citations omitted]. These factors are:

(1) the degree of similarity between the owner's mark and the alleged infringing mark;
(2) the strength of owner's mark;
(3) the price of the goods and others factors indicative of the care and attention expected of consumers when making a purchase;

(4) the length of time the defendant has used the mark without evidence of actual confusion arising;

(5) the intent of the defendant in adopting the mark;

(6) the evidence of actual confusion;

(7) whether the goods [or services], though not competing, are marketed through the same channels of trade and advertised through the same media;

(8) the extent to which the targets of the parties sales efforts are the same;

(9) the relationship of the goods [or services] in the minds of consumers because of similarity of function; and

(10) other facts suggesting that the consuming public might expect the defendant's market, or that he is likely to expand into that market.

In determining whether a likelihood of confusion exists, courts must weigh each factor separately. *Fisons,* 30 F.3d at 481-82, 31 U.S.P.Q.2d at 1604.

*1. Similarity of Services*

The Court first addresses whether the services offered by the parties are similar because in its view, this factor is the most dispositive regarding the existence of any likelihood of confusion. Courts have held that where the goods and services offered by the plaintiff and defendant are dissimilar or non-competitive, consumer confusion is less likely to occur. *See, e.g., Taj Mahal,* 745 F.Supp. at 250; *Sunenblick,* 895 F.Supp. at 629. In *Taj Mahal,* the court held that the differences in services offered by plaintiff, a restaurant serving Indian cuisine, and those of defendant, a hotel and casino, were sufficiently different as to contribute significantly to a finding that no trademark infringement had occurred or would occur. *Id.* at 250. ***

This case presents dissimilarity between services comparable to those presented in *Taj Mahal.* Plaintiff would have this Court simply lump the services of plaintiff and defendants under the heading of basketball or entertainment and, on that basis alone, find that the parties engage in confusingly similar services. Numerous cases, however, illustrate that even when two products or services fall within the same general field, it does not mean that the two products or services are sufficiently similar to create a likelihood of confusion. Meaningful differences between the products and services are often cited as a factor tending to negate reverse confusion, even when the products are superficially within the same category. For example, in *Sunenblick,* the court found no reverse confusion between jazz records and hip-hop records sold under the identical mark UPTOWN RECORDS because although the recordings were both musical products, they were marketed to different consumers and sold in separate sections of record stores. *Id.* at 629.***

The show basketball performed by plaintiff is markedly distinct from NBA competitive basketball in myriad ways. As a show basketball team, plaintiff simply does not play NBA level competitive basketball. Even accepting plaintiff's contention that it has on many occasions played genuinely competitive basketball during the first and third quarters of its games, it is undisputed that the remaining quarters are reserved for comedy routines and fancy tricks. It is inconceivable that the NBA would adopt such a "show" format. Plaintiff also plays against any team put together by the organization that purchases its services. Consequently, its competition is ordinary citizens and not serious NBA level athletes. Furthermore, as a show basketball team, plaintiff does not play in a league, whereas in the NBA, league competition is an intrinsic element of the sport. Also in contrast to the NBA, a large proportion of plaintiff's performances are non-game appearances such as school assembly programs. And with respect to plaintiff, there is no proof that the athletic quality of its average player is similar to that of an NBA team member. These are but a few examples of the dissimilarity between the parties' services. Therefore, the court finds that when every aspect of the two teams is compared, there is glaring dissimilarity. Any similarity between the two teams is superficial and the result of creating overinclusive categories that are irrelevant to the likelihood of confusion.

## 2. Channels of Trade and Target Audience

The similarities between the channels of trade and target audiences of the two teams are closely related and therefore, the Court considers these two factors together. The channels of trade that plaintiff uses are not similar to those used by defendants. Plaintiff established that it targets event organizers at high schools, colleges, and charitable organizations and advertises through direct mail solicitation, participation at trade shows, and trade magazines. Plaintiff does not advertise on television, radio or in the popular print media. Plaintiff's merchandise is only available as souvenirs at its games and appearances. In contrast, the Washington Bullets, as a NBA member team, advertises its services directly to sports fans through television and print media and its merchandise is widely available in retail stores. Moreover, as a show basketball team, plaintiff competes with other show and comedy basketball teams for customers and not with the NBA. For example, plaintiff frequently refers to the Harlem Globetrotters in its advertisements and promotional material because it is seeking to reach that more famous team's audience. Therefore, the Court finds that plaintiff has failed to establish that it shares the same channels of trade and target audience as defendants.

## 3. *Similarities Between the Marks*

In considering the similarity between two marks, the court "must compare the appearance, sound and meaning of the marks, as well as the manner in which they are used." *Taj Mahal,* 745 F.Supp. at 247 (citing *Caesars World, Inc. v. Caesar's Palace,* 490 F.Supp. 818, 824 (D.N.J.1980)). When "making such a comparison, the relevant factor is 'the overall impression created by the mark as a whole rather than simply comparing the individual features of the marks.' " *Id.* (quoting *John H. Harland Co. v. Clarke Checks, Inc.,* 711 F.2d 966, 975 (11th Cir.1983)). Marks "are confusingly similar if ordinary consumers would likely conclude that ... [the products or services] share a common source, affiliation, connection or sponsorship." *Fisons,* 30 F.3d at 477, 31 U.S.P.Q.2d at 1600. In trademark actions that involve picture or design marks, similarity of appearance is controlling. 3 J. McCarthy, McCarthy on Trademarks and Unfair Competition § 23.07. However, "[s]imilarity is not limited to the eye or ear. The mental impact of a similarity of meaning may be so pervasive as to outweigh any visual or phonetic differences." *Id.* at § 23.08. If two marks create essentially the same overall impression, it is highly probable that the two marks are confusingly similar. *See id* at 477-79, 31 U.S.P.Q.2d at 1601; *Ford Motor Co.,* 930 F.2d at 293; *Opticians Ass'n of America,* 920 F.2d at 195. Nevertheless, "[s]imilarity of the marks is merely one of the relevant factors, and it is not dispositive on the issue of likelihood of confusion." *Taj Mahal,* 745 F.Supp. at 247.

The Court finds that the evidence presented establishes that plaintiff uses the mark HARLEM WIZARDS with great frequency and uses the mark WIZARDS with sufficient regularity on its uniforms and merchandise. Defendants have used and plan to continue using the marks WASHINGTON WIZARDS and WIZARDS. The Court finds that when compared in their entirety, the marks HARLEM WIZARDS and WASHINGTON WIZARDS are similar and use by the parties of the mark WIZARDS alone is obviously identical.

The use of a design as part of a mark minimizes any likelihood of confusion. 3 J. McCarthy, McCarthy on Trademarks and Unfair Competition § 23.15[5]. Because defendants have not yet selected a logo, it is impossible to consider the similarities in logo design and merchandise. Nonetheless, the Court notes that the Washington Bullets' logo when selected will presumably have a unique logo and color scheme and will contain the NBA's distinctive tagging and logo of a ball-dribbling player. In contrast, plaintiff lacks a consistent logo and distinctive colors. Therefore, it is highly unlikely that merchandise offered by the parties will result in the likelihood of confusion among consumers. The Court also concludes that the linguistic similarity between the contested marks will not result in the likelihood of confusion because the services offered are markedly dissimilar and the parties do not target the same audience.

### 4. *Strength of Plaintiff's Mark*

Traditionally, "the term strength as it applies to trademarks refers to the distinctiveness of the mark, or more precisely, its tendency to identify the goods sold under the mark as emanating from a particular, although a possible anonymous source." *Taj Mahal,* 745 F.Supp. at 248. The degree of distinctiveness attributed to a mark is, in part, determined by its placement on the continuum of distinctiveness discussed in Part II. (citations omitted). Classification of a mark as suggestive, however, "is not necessarily dispositive on the issue of its strength, which must finally be determined in reference to its commercial context." *Sunenblick,* 895 F.Supp. at 626. It is possible that a mark "may be conceptually strong and yet commercially weak if it lacks the requisite 'origin-indicating' quality in the eyes of the consumer." *Id.*

\*\*\*

This Court has already determined that the mark WIZARDS is suggestive and therefore, inherently distinctive. Nonetheless, this categorization of plaintiff's mark does not in and of itself establish that plaintiff's mark is strong and that the likelihood of confusion exists. Although plaintiff's mark is distinctive, it is undeniably commercially weak. Plaintiff's own survey results reveal the weakness of its mark: in Northern New Jersey, plaintiff's strongest market, only six out of fifty-nine people associated the mark WIZARDS with plaintiff. In defendants' survey, only four percent of people across the nation associated the mark with plaintiff. This weakness is of course understandable because plaintiff admittedly does not advertise its mark directly to consumers. In evaluating this likelihood-of-confusion factor, the Court does not hold plaintiff to the same standard as defendants who have the financial ability to expend large sums of money on promotion and advertising. Nonetheless, the Court finds that the inherent distinctiveness of plaintiff's mark does not override its marked commercial weakness, even when this factor is weighed more heavily. Because the mark is weak it fails to identify plaintiff's services with a particular source. Therefore, the Court finds that this factor favors the defendants.

*5. Factors Indicative of the Care and Attention Expected of Consumers When Making a Purchase*

It is widely accepted as true that consumers are less likely to be confused about the origin of specific goods or services if such goods are expensive because the amount of care and attention expended by consumers increases proportionately as the price of the desired goods or services increases. *Taj Mahal,* 745 F.Supp. at 248-249; *Restaurant Lutece, Inc. v. Houbigant, Inc.,* 593 F.Supp. 588, 595 (D.N.J.1984). Plaintiff's goods and services include games, appearances and merchandise. Harlem Wizards' tickets typically sell for between five and eight dollars while NBA tickets are significantly more expensive, requiring somewhat of an inheritance as a paying source. It is not surprising therefore, that the average NBA fan earns about $60,000 a year. Given the disparity between ticket prices of the plaintiff and the NBA alone, it is unlikely that likelihood of confusion exists between the parties' services. Moreover, NBA fans are generally sophisticated and knowledgeable of their sport; they read about their favorite teams in the sports pages or listen to sports reporting and commentary on television and radio. Therefore, the Court finds it unlikely that consumers will attend a Harlem Wizards' game expecting to see NBA basketball or purchase NBA tickets expecting to see the Harlem Wizards perform show basketball.

\*\*\*

*6. Evidence of Actual Confusion*

It is well established that in a trademark infringement action, a plaintiff need not present evidence of actual confusion and need only show that a likelihood of confusion exists. *Ford Motor Co.,* 930 F.2d at 292. However, "evidence of actual confusion, where shown, is highly probative of the likelihood of confusion." *Sunenblick,* 895 F.Supp. at 629. As evidence of actual confusion, plaintiff relies on individual testimony regarding actual incidents of confusion between the marks, consumer survey results and expert testimony. First, plaintiff offered testimony by current Harlem Wizards' players who recounted incidents when they wore Harlem Wizards' shirts or jackets and strangers misidentified the garments as belonging to the Washington Wizards or asked the players if they played for the Washington Wizards. The Court finds that these examples are too weak and few to establish actual confusion. Actual confusion is not the same as clear mistake or misidentification on the part of consumers, many of whom it turns out

512

were children. Moreover, there is no evidence that these purported instances of actual confusion could have any effect on consumer purchasing decisions.

Survey evidence can sometimes demonstrate evidence of actual confusion but only to the extent "that the survey mirrors the real world setting which can create an instance of actual confusion." 3 J. McCarthy, McCarthy on Trademarks and Unfair Competition § 23.01[3][a].***

This Court is wary to draw conclusions from the survey results introduced by both parties, because of the small samples used. Nonetheless, the survey results introduced by both parties clearly demonstrate that consumer recognition of plaintiff is almost nonexistent. Consequently, the Court finds that plaintiff has failed to prove the occurrence of actual confusion.

## 7. Defendants' Intent in Adopting the Mark

Ordinarily, the relevant intent inquiry in a trademark infringement case involves determining "whether the defendant adopted a mark with the intent of promoting confusion and appropriating the prior user's good will." *Fisons*, 30 F.3d at 479, 31 U.S.P.Q.2d at 1602 (internal quotations omitted). In *Fisons*, the Court of Appeals held that although this relevant intent inquiry is both important and appropriate in traditional cases of direct confusion, such an inquiry serves no purpose in a reverse confusion case. *Id.* In reverse confusion cases, the junior user simply does not attempt to take advantage of the senior user's good will and reputation; instead the junior user seeks to overwhelm it. *Id.* The Court of Appeals then identified as a more appropriate inquiry whether the defendant was careless in conducting its trademark name search and in considering the likelihood of confusion with other companies that used similar marks. *Id.*

Defendants produced testimony and exhibits indicating that they had arranged for trademark searches to be done before and during the name-change contest. It appears that defendants did not engage in additional investigation after it learned that plaintiff used the federally unregistered mark HARLEM WIZARDS and provided sports entertainment services. Nonetheless, there is no evidence that defendants adopted the mark WIZARDS in bad faith. None of the employees involved in narrowing the names to a final selection of five names had previously heard of plaintiff. Although two Washington Bullets employees were familiar with plaintiff before the "name contest", neither of them was involved in the preparation, promotion or name selection before or during the event. Moreover, defendants had sought the advice of counsel before adopting the new name.

Therefore, the Court finds that there is no proof that defendants were careless in the selection of WIZARDS as the new mark for the Washington Bullets and in considering the likelihood of confusion with similar marks of other companies.

8. *Likelihood of Expansion*

Whether there is a likelihood that plaintiff will expand into a market where a defendant already actively participates is a crucial factor in cases involving non-competitive goods and services because one of the "chief reasons for granting a trademark owner protection in a market not his own is to protect his right someday to enter that market." *Lapp,* 721 F.2d at 464 (citation omitted). Therefore, when it appears likely that a trademark owner will soon enter the defendant's field, this factor weighs in favor of injunctive relief. *Fisons,* 30 F.3d at 473-74, 31 U.S.P.Q.2d at 1597. It is very unlikely that the Harlem Wizards will expand its services to include purely competitive basketball. Plaintiff has offered no evidence that it entertains any expansion plans to begin playing NBA-level basketball. Rather, the expansion plans alluded to in its five-year business plans center around emerging as the second greatest show basketball team in the country. Hence, because there is no likelihood that plaintiff plans to play professional competitive basketball, this factor weighs against injunctive relief.

9. *Other Factors that Suggest that the Public Would Expect the Plaintiff Offer a Similar Service*

Based on the evidence presented, the Court finds that there are no other factors that would lead consumers to believe that plaintiff offers services similar to the NBA. For nearly thirty-five years, plaintiff has limited its services to show basketball, a service that is separate and distinct from NBA basketball. Plaintiff has not shown that it plans to chart a new course by entering the world of professional competitive basketball. The evidence presented inevitably leads to the conclusion that under these circumstances, a wizard is not a wizard. Therefore, for the reasons stated, the Court finds that the Washington Bullets' adoption of the Washington Wizards as its new name poses no likelihood of injury to the Harlem Wizards in the marketplace and dismisses plaintiff's federal and state law claims.

## CONCLUSION

For the reasons stated in this Court's Opinion; It is on this 27th day of January 1997; ORDERED that the complaint is hereby dismissed.

The two logos discussed in this case

## Notes & Questions

1. Explain what the court means when it says that "trademark rights emanate from use and not only registration."

2. Explain what the court means when it says that "Trademark law evaluates marks along a continuum of distinctiveness, from the nondistinctive to the inherently distinctive: Marks are (1) generic, (2) descriptive, (3) suggestive or (4) arbitrary, or fanciful."

3. Why does the court conclude that the mark Wizards is "suggestive"?

4. Why does a court need to analyze 10 factors in order to assess "likelihood of confusion"? Why can't the court simply compare the plaintiff's mark with the defendant's and assess whether the two marks are substantially similar?

# C. RIGHT OF PUBLICITY

## O'Brien v. Pabst Sales Co.
124 F. 2d. 167 (1942)
Circuit Court of Appeals, Fifth Circuit

HUTCHESON, Circuit Judge.

Plaintiff, in physique as in prowess as a hurler, a modern David, is a famous football player. Defendant, in bulk, if not in brass and vulnerability, a modern Goliath, is a distributor of Pabst beer. Plaintiff, among other honors received during the year 1938, was picked by Grantland Rice on his Collier's All American Football Team. Defendant, as a part of its advertising publicity for 1939, following its custom of getting out football schedule calendars, placed an order with the Inland Lithographing Company, to prepare for and furnish to it, 35,000 Pabst 1939 football calendars. The calendars were to carry complete schedules of all major college games; professional schedules; and pictures of Grantland Rice's 1938 All American Football Team, the Inland Company to furnish photographs and necessary releases.

At the top of the calendar, as thus printed and circulated, were the words 'Pabst Blue Ribbon.' Directly underneath were the words 'Football Calendar, 1939'; to the left of these words was a photograph of O'Brien in football uniform characteristically poised for the throw; to the right of them was a glass having on it the words 'Pabst Breweries, Blue Ribbon Export Beer'; and to the right of the glass still, a bottle of beer, having on it 'Pabst Blue Ribbon Beer.' Directly below these was the intercollegiate football schedule for 1939, and in the center of the calendar were pictures, including that of O'Brien, of Grantland Rice's All American Football Team for 1938. Near the bottom was the schedule of the national football league and on the very bottom margin, were the words 'Pabst Famous Blue Ribbon Beer.'

Claiming that this use of his photograph as part of defendant's advertising was an invasion of his right of privacy and that he had been damaged thereby, plaintiff brought this suit.

The defenses were three. The first was that if the mere use of one's picture in truthful and respectable advertising would be an actionable invasion of privacy in the case of a private person, the use here was not, as to plaintiff, such an invasion, for as a result of his activities and prowess in football, his chosen field, and their nationwide and deliberate publicizing with his consent and in his interest, he was no longer, as to them, a private but a public person, and as to their additional publication he had no right of privacy. The second defense was that plaintiff, in his own interest and that of Texas Christian University, had posed for and had authorized the publicity department of T.C.U. to distribute his picture and biographical data to newspapers, magazines, sports journals and the public generally, and that the particular picture whose use is complained of had been in due course obtained from and payment for it had been made to the T.C.U. publicity department. Third, no injury to appellant's person, property or reputation had been or could be shown and there was therefore no basis for a recovery. The testimony fully supported these defenses. It showed that plaintiff, then 23 years old, had been playing football for 14 years, four years of that time with Texas Christian University, and two with the Philadelphia Eagles, a professional football team. During that period he had received many and distinguished trophies and honors as an outstanding player of the game. He had in fact been the recipient of practically every worthwhile football trophy and recognition, being picked by Grantland Rice on his Collier's All American Football Team, and by Liberty on their All Players All American Team, and many other so-called All American Football Teams. Plaintiff testified that he had not given permission to use his picture, indeed had not known of the calendar until some time after its publication and circulation; that he was a member of the Allied Youth of America, the main theme of which was the doing away with alcohol among young people; that he had had opportunities to sell his endorsement for beer and alcoholic beverages and had refused it; and that he was greatly embarrassed and humiliated when he saw the calendar and realized that his face and name was associated with publicity for the sale of beer. But he did not, nor did anyone for him, testify to a single fact which would show that he had suffered pecuniary damage in any amount. In addition, on cross-examination he testified; that he had repeatedly posed for photographs for use in publicizing himself and the T.C.U. football team; that Mr. Ridings, director of publicity and news service of T.C.U. without obtaining particular, but with his general, approval and consent, had furnished numberless photographs to various people, periodicals and magazines; and that the pictures of those composing Grantland Rice's All American Football Team which appeared on the calendar including his own picture, were first publicized in Collier's magazine, a magazine of widest circulation.

On defendants' part, it was shown that following the instructions given by the defendant, the calendar company had written to the T.C.U.

Director[1] of publicity for, and obtained from him, the photograph for use in the calendar, paying him $1 therefor, and that the photograph had been used in the belief that the necessary consent to do so had been obtained. The proof that plaintiff had posed for many football pictures for the publicity department of T.C.U. for the purpose of having them widely circulated over the United States was overwhelming and uncontradicted. Mr. Riding, director of publicity, testified that Davey O'Brien was perhaps the most publicized football player of the year 1938-39; that it was the function of his office to permit and increase the publicity of football players; that his office had furnished some 800 photographs of plaintiff to sports editors, magazines, etc.; that if anybody made a request for a picture of O'Brien he would ordinarily grant the request without asking what they were going to do with it; that the picture in the upper left hand corner of the calendar is a very popular picture of O'Brien and perhaps his most famous pose, and that the publicity department had general authority to furnish plaintiff's pictures for publicity purposes but had never knowingly furnished any for use in commercial advertising except with O'Brien's consent and approval.

At the conclusion of this evidence, it being apparent that the picture had been obtained from one having real or apparent authority to furnish it, that no right of privacy of O'Brien's had been violated by the mere publishing of his picture and that if any actionable wrong had been done him, it must be found in the fact that the publication impliedly declared that O'Brien was endorsing or recommending the use of Pabst beer, plaintiff's contention centered around this point.

The District Judge agreed with defendant that no case had been made out. He was of the opinion: that considered from the standpoint merely of an invasion of plaintiff's right of privacy, no case was made out, because plaintiff was an outstanding national football figure and had completely publicized his name and his pictures. He was of the opinion too, that considered from the point of view that the calendar damaged him because it falsely, though only impliedly, represented that plaintiff was a user of or was commending the use of, Pabst beer, no case was made out because nothing in the calendar or football schedule could be reasonably so construed; every fact in it was truthfully stated and there was no representation or suggestion of

---

[1] 'Director of Publicity, Texas Christian University, Fort Worth, Texas.
'Dear Sir: We would like to secure an 8 x 10 action picture of David O'Brien one showing him throwing a football similar to the one enclosed of Sammy Baugh. This is to be used on our 1939 schedule of football games.
'Send invoice with picture and we will remit by return mail. 'Thanking you for your cooperation, we remain,
'Very truly yours, 'B. E. Callahan, 'Publisher.'

any kind that O'Brien or any of the other football celebrities whose pictures it showed were beer drinkers or were recommending its drinking to others; the business of making and selling beer is a legitimate and eminently respectable business and people of all walks and views in life, without injury to or reflection upon themselves, drink it, and that any association of O'Brien's picture with a glass of beer could not possibly disgrace or reflect upon or cause him damage. He directed a verdict for defendant.

Plaintiff is here urging that the judgment be reversed and the cause remanded for a new trial, first because as a matter of law plaintiff showed damage in that his name was used for the commercial purpose of advertising beer, and second, because there was an issue of fact as to whether the calendar reasonably conveyed to the public the false impression that plaintiff was a user of and was endorsing or recommending the use of beer. We cannot agree with appellant. We think it perfectly plain that the District Judge was right both in the view he took that nothing in the publication violated plaintiff's right of privacy and that nothing in it could be legitimately or reasonably construed as falsely stating that he used, endorsed, or recommended the use of Pabst's beer.

Assuming then, what is by no means clear, that an action for right of privacy would lie in Texas at the suit of a private person we think it clear that the action fails; because plaintiff is not such a person and the publicity he got was only that which he had been constantly seeking and receiving; and because the use of the photograph was by permission, and there were no statements or representations made in connection with it, which were or could be either false, erroneous or damaging to plaintiff. Nothing in the majority opinion purports to deal with or express an opinion on the matter dealt with in the dissenting opinion, the right of a person to recover on quantum meruit, for the use of his name for advertising purposes. That was not the case pleaded and attempted to be brought. The case was not for the value of plaintiff's name in advertising a product but for damages by way of injury to him in using his name in advertising beer. Throughout the pleadings, the record and the brief, plaintiff has uniformly taken the position that he is not suing for the reasonable value of his endorsement of beer, on the contrary, the whole burden of his pleading and brief is the repeated asseveration, that he would not and did not endorse beer, and the complaint is that he was damaged by the invasion of his privacy in so using his picture as to create the impression that he was endorsing beer.

The judgment was right. It is affirmed.

On Petition for Rehearing.

PER CURIAM.

As neither of the judges who concurred in the judgment of the court in the above numbered and entitled cause is of the opinion that the petition for rehearing should be granted, it is ordered that said petition be and the same is hereby denied.

HOLMES, Circuit Judge (dissenting).

There is no Texas statute or decision directly in point, but I think, under the Texas common law, the appellant is entitled to recover the reasonable value of the use in trade and commerce of his picture for advertisement purposes, to the extent that such use was appropriated by appellee.

The State of Texas, early in its history, adopted the common law of England, so far as it was not inconsistent with its constitution and laws, and provided that such common law, together with such constitution and laws, should be the rule of decision and continue in force until altered or repealed by the legislature.

The right of privacy is distinct from the right to use one's name or picture for purposes of commercial advertisement. The latter is a property right that belongs to every one; it may have much or little, or only a nominal, value; but it is a personal right, which may not be violated with impunity.

The great property rights created by the demands of modern methods of advertising are of comparatively recent origin, and may not have been in existence in January, 1840, but the common law of Texas is subject to growth and adaptation in the land of its adoption, as well as it was in the country of its origin. The capacity of the common law of Texas 'to draw inspiration from every fountain of justice' has not been diminished by time, though a century has passed since its adoption by the legislature of that state.

No one can doubt that commercial advertisers customarily pay for the right to use the name and likeness of a person who has become famous. The evidence in this case shows that appellant refused an offer by a New York beer company of $400 for an endorsement of its beer, and the appellee apparently recognized that it was necessary to obtain the consent of the